Alleghany County Virginia

MARRIAGES

1822–1872

Compiled by

Carletta Lanear Nelson

HERITAGE BOOKS
2015

HERITAGE BOOKS

AN IMPRINT OF HERITAGE BOOKS, INC.

Books, CDs, and more—Worldwide

For our listing of thousands of titles see our website
at
www.HeritageBooks.com

Published 2015 by
HERITAGE BOOKS, INC.
Publishing Division
5810 Ruatan Street
Berwyn Heights, Md. 20740

International Standard Book Numbers
Paperbound: 978-0-7884-0038-4
Clothbound: 978-0-7884-6210-8

TABLE OF CONTENTS

III

ABBREVIATIONS

Alleg. - Alleghany
Auth.   - Authorization to Marry Parties
B. (b.) - Born
Cath. - Catholic
Cert. - Certificate
Clk. - Clerk Of Court
Co. - County
Cov. - Covington
CTOL - Certificate To Obtain A Marriage License,
       also contains Authorization to Marry
       Parties [Marriage License]
CTOLMR - Certificate To Obtain A Marriage License
       with Authorization To Marry Parties, and
       Minister's Return -- All on one form
       [Marriage License]
D.C. - Deputy Clerk Of Court
J.P. - Justice Of Peace
dau./o - Daughter of
Esq. - Esquire
L. - Lived
Lic. - License
Mar. - Married, Marriage
Meth. E. Church (M. E. Church) - Methodist
       Episcopal Church
Min., Mins. - Minister, Minister's
Mins. Ret. - Minister's Return
mos. - Months
Occup. - Occupation
PA, Penn. - Pennsylvania
PL. - Place of Marriage
res. - Residence
S. Meth. - Southern Methodist Church
s/o. - Son of
Teste (Wit.) - Testified to seeing or witnessing
       document written or signed or giving or
       hearing an oral oath
VA - Virginia
W. VA. - West Virginia
yrs. - years
C.A.C. - Clerk of Alleghany County
bk. - book
[See Index for Index Abbreviations]

Alleghany County, Virginia was formed in 1822 from Botetourt County, Bath County, and Monroe County, Virginia.

Many of its earliest settlers to this section of the state were said to be Scottish, Irish, and English with some Germans.

Monroe County was formed in 1799 from Mercer County, Morgan County, and Greenbrier County, Virginia.

In 1863 the state of West Virginia came into existence and Monroe County became a part of that state.

I mention this because there were many who came to Alleghany County from Monroe County to get their licenses to marry.

File records at the Clerk's office at the Alleghany County Courthouse in Covington, Virginia, have recently been organized by the Alleghany Highlands Genealogical Society after many years of neglect in doing so nor in filing them in cabinets.

The Society also gave me some help in deciphering a few of the names in the records of the Minister's Return Lists. I have listed the names as I found them concerning their spelling. In some cases the names were listed several ways in the documents, and I have listed these also. Many names were difficult to make out and I have spelled them as best I could and in some cases, listed several interpretations.

I have combined what was on the Minister's Marriage Return List Book and the Marriage Register Book (1) and what was on the actual (original) documents in the files. Some records have been lost and the only documentation is on the books. In such cases there is no way to verify what is on the books. Some book listings only have written marriage consents to back them up. Others have written notes from ministers giving either one or several marriages at a time. Some of those notes gave other information about the couple or the families involved. Sometimes the minister reported a marriage more than once.

Some records have no marriage dates. A license was gotten, but it is not known for sure if the marriage took place; but since they are written in the books, it is assumed they did. There are also several documents in the files that are not on the books. I have listed the contents of these as they were written.

Many licenses were never returned to the courthouse. It is not until 1850 that the date of obtaining the license was mentioned in the books in addition to the marriage date. Around 1854, licenses began to be found more frequently in the files; and shortly after 1854, 99% seem to be in the files.

In 1854 with the beginning of Book (1), more information was gotten than previously thus giving the genealogist more information on ancestors. I have endeavored to list ALL the information that was available in the records and on the books --as well as the many discrepancies between the books and the original documents.

You will find mention of a "5 ¢ Inter. Revenue Certificate" stamp and a "2 ¢ Bankshare" stamp. No one knows what these were for. It is assumed by the present Clerk of Court, Mike Wolfe, that they represent some fee that was collected and the stamps were placed on the license to show this.

A Marriage License form was used first when forms began to be used that had a minister's return on it. This was followed around 1858 by a Certificate to Obtain a Marriage License [hereafter called "CTOL"] with a Clerk's Marriage Authorization used as a Marriage License. Then around 1861 a form was used that had a Clerk's Marriage Authorization, a Certificate to Obtain a Marriage License and a Minister's Return [hereafter called "CTOLMR"] on it. Any one or more of the three forms could be found for a record after 1861.

Many records do not state whether the parties were black or white. Starting around the Civil War and thereafter, marriages of some

FOREWORD (Continued)

"Freedmen" and "Freedwomen" and later other Negro marriages were recorded which should be of help to those researching black genealogy. I might mention that I know of one instance at a date later than this book will go when a black couple was listed as "white;" so if you think you have the name correct, you may want to further check out the listing if the person's color does not match what you expected.

The microfilm records were apparently made from the book records. I hope this book will clear up many of the problems researchers have had. Many marriage dates on the books turned out not to be the actual marriage dates. There were also many discrepancies in the names as well as other information on the book with the actual documents. Many records have deteriorated with some in bits and pieces and others well preserved.

I hope that my research for this book will be of help to many who have sought information on their families and have not been able to find them since every name listed in the documents is listed here.

My thanks to the many who have helped with my research, especially my father, Carl Hubert Nelson, whose 51 years of work on the Cheaspeake and Ohio Railway and who has lived in this area all his life have given me much information concerning where to look for information and his knowledge of the railway tracks in the area.

The index has been alphabetized by both a widow's married name and her maiden name when known. A child's name may have a related name in () if the mother has another last name. I hope this will help to find remarriages and children who may otherwise be missed in regular searches.

Carletta Lanear Nelson
August 30, 1993

General Delivery
Selma, Virginia 24474

GEOGRAPHIC LOCATIONS

Alleghany, VA (Alleghany Station) - Take I64 West
from Covington, VA, to exit Rt. 159 and Rt.
60 East, turn left following Rt. 159 to
Crows and Rt. 311 North, turn right follow
Rt. 311 North just past the highway culbert
tunnel, turn left on County Rt. 602. A
railway station or depot was located on the
left about a mile up the road on 602.

Alleghany Valley - unable to determine, but may
have referred to land in a valley going to
Alleghany Station mentioned above.

Bend of the Jackson River - Covington, VA, area,
river runs from north thru town and makes a
big bend around the southern part of the
town and returns to run east along I64.

Blue Spring Run - Place on Rt. 18 South shortly
before come to County Rt. 615. The "Run" or
creek follows Rt. 615 and County Rt. 616 off
Rt. 18 South of Covington, VA.

Boiling Springs, VA - on Rt. 18 South of Covington, VA

Callaghan - Take I64 West from Covington, VA, to
exit Rt. 159 and Rt. 60 East, turn left
following road to County Rt. 600, turn right
on Rt. 600, follow Rt. 600 until it runs into County Rt. 661 (Rt. 600 will turn right).
You are in Callaghan. Follow Rt. 661 until
it turns right under the I64 bridge to go
up Ogley's Creek.

Callaghan's - Most likely refers to Callaghan's
Tavern that was located in the Callaghan
area. (See directions above.)

Cast Steel Run - Take Rt. 18 South of Covington,
VA, follow it until you come to County Rt.
614. Turn right and follow Rt. 614 until

X

GEOGRAPHIC LOCATIONS (Continued)

until you come to County Rt. 600. Turn
right and follow Rt. 600 to Humpback Bridge
and Rt. 60 East. Turn right on Rt. 60 East
and return to Covington, VA.

Castle Run - unable to locate, but apparently in
Alleghany County, VA

Cedar Run - (? Cedar Creek) Take Rt. 220 North.
Turn left on County Rt. 687. Follow Rt.
687 to Lower Cascades Golf Course and turn
left on County Rt. 605. It is between the
areas of Callison and Kincaid and south of
Bacova. (Directions from Covington, VA)

City of Clifton Forge, VA - I64 East from Covington, VA, exit at Rt. 60 East and Rt. 220
South at Dabney S. Lancaster Community
College. (There are two exits - before and
on the other side of town.)

City of Covington, VA - County seat of Alleghany
County, VA. I64 West exit Rt. 220 North.
(There are two exits - before and on the
other side of town.)

City of Staunton, VA - In Augusta County, VA,
near Junction I81 North and I 64 East at
Rt. 250 West (?North) exit.

County of Alleghany, VA - borders West Virginia
state line, Covington is the county seat,
I64 West runs thru it.

County of Bath, VA - north of Alleghany County.
Warm Springs, VA, is the county seat, Rt.
220 North runs thru it.

County of Botetourt, VA - south of Alleghany
County. Fincastle is county seat, Rt. 220
South runs thru it. It begins at the south-
ern end of Iron Gate, VA.

XI

GEOGRAPHIC LOCATIONS (Continued)

County of Craig, VA - south of Alleghany County. New Castle is the county seat. Rt. 311 at Junction Rt. 42 South and County Rt. 615 is middle of New Castle.

County of Greebrier, W. VA - borders VA state line. Lewisburg is county seat. I64 West exit Rt. 219 South to Junction Rt. 60 West in Lewisburg.

County of Monroe, W. VA - borders VA state line. Union is county seat. Rt. 3 Junction with Rt. 219 South in Union.

Cove Creek - In Monroe County, W. VA., Rt. 3 area between Gap Mills, Moncove Lake, Glace, and Sweet Springs, W. VA. Runs into Alleg. Co.

Cowpasture Bridge - Rt. 269 East from Clifton Forge, VA, just past County Rt. 633 at Sharon. Peter's Bridge,Rt.42 past Rt.630 Griffith's.

Cowpasture River - Runs South down Rt. 42 from close to Millboro Springs to right on County Rt. 635 thru "Nicely Town" to right on County Rt. 269 to County Rt. 633 at Sharon Gables, follow Rt. 633 to Rt. 220 South at southern end of Iron Gate, VA, where it joins Jackson River and both rivers form to make the James River.

Craigs Creek - in Botetourt County, VA, and in Craig County, VA, County Rt. 615 from New Castle, VA (starts near Rt. 311) to Eagle Rock, VA (Rt. 220 South) where it joins the James River.

Deisher's Schoolhouse - on Craigs Creek in Craig County, VA.

Dunlap Creek - Rt. 60 West of Covington, VA and along Rt. 159 to Rt. 311 at Crow's and along Rt. 311 South to approximately "Earlhurst" near Sweet Chalybeate Springs.

XII

GEOGRAPHIC LOCATIONS (Continued)

"Edge Hill" - Covington, VA, area

Falling Springs Valley - (From Covington, VA)
Rt. 220 North from Falls to Bath County
line. The springs runs from the junction
of County Rt. 687 with County Rt. 640, along
Rt. 640 to Rt. 220 North. Falling Springs
Falls Overlook is about 1/4 mile to the
right of County Rt. 640 on Rt. 220 South.
The town of Falling Springs is found on
County Rt. 687 shortly before you come to
County Rt. 640.

Fletcher's Chapel - at Callaghan, County Rt. 661
off Rt. 159. This is the next right after
passing the turnoff to County Rt. 600 at
Callaghan. (West of Covington, VA)

Fork Run Church - unable to locate

Griffith's Turnout - Rt. 42 North from Clifton
Forge, VA,, turn right on County Rt. 630 to
bend of road at the river's edge. This is
Griffith's.

Healing Springs, VA - Rt. 220 North of Covington,
VA, near Hot Springs, VA

High Bridge (High Fill) (Big Fill) - unable to
locate, may refer to a section of railway
track where dirt was used to form a bridge
rather than build a structure to cross the
area. This could have been many places on
the railroad.

Holloway Farm - unable to locate, but in Alleghany County, VA

Hotel, Cogbill's - Covington, VA.

Hotel, J. J. Stack's - unable to locate , but
could be in Sweet Springs, W.VA. area since
his daughter was born in Monroe Co., W.VA.,

and they lived in Alleghany County, VA.
Stack Mines was located near Crows, VA.

Hotel, McCurdy's - It was first opened in 1855
    on Main St. in Covington, VA. In July 1869
    it was opened on Dickey St. which is now
    Hawthorne St. near the railroad tracks.
    McCurdy House was sold in 1891 and burned
    in 1892.

Hotel, Robt. Skeen's - Covington, VA.

Jackson River - It is formed in Highland County,
    VA, following Rt. 220 South then leads off
    flowing into Lake Moomaw north of Covington,
    VA. It flows out of the lake following
    County Rt. 687 to Rt. 220 South and by this
    route to Covington and I64 where it leaves
    I64 and makes a big bend around the southern
    part of the city and then returns to follow
    I64 East to Clifton Forge, VA, where it
    follows Rt. 220 South to the southern end
    of Iron Gate where it merges with the Cow-
    pasture River and the two form the James
    River.

Jackson River Depot - Virginia Railway began at
    this depot and ran to Millboro, VA and
    beyond around the time of the Civil War.
    The depot was located somewhere between
    Covington, VA and Iron Gate, VA. It was
    most likely located at what is now Selma or
    Clifton Forge, VA, although there were iron
    furnaces at Low Moor, VA.

Jerry's Run - I64 West of Covington, VA, on
    Brushy Mountain to the left of I64 between
    Callaghan and where Rt. 311 North meets I64.

Jordan's Forge - believed to be near Rt. 42 North
    and the old Red Hill Tunnel and Griffith's
    Knob near or on the Cowpasture River during
    the Civil War.

GEOGRAPHIC LOCATIONS (Continued)

Jordan's Furnace - possibly Rt. 269 off I64 East
    of Clifton Forge, VA, at Longdale near the
    Lucy Selina Inn (now Firmstone Manor). The
    furnace is referred to locally as the Lucy
    Selina Furnace or Longdale Furnace but is
    believed to have been called "Jordan's Fur-
    nace" at one time. [There is also Jordan
    Mines at the Junction of Rt. 18 South from
    Covington, VA, and County Rt. 616 where iron
    ore was dug. I was unable to find out
    whether there was a furnace in this area.]

Kellỳ's work (? mrk) - unable to determine

Kimberlin's Mill - unable to determine, but in
    Rich Patch area of Alleghany Co., VA.

Laurel Fork - Highland County, VA, northwest of
    Monterey, VA, close to the W. VA. state line

Laurel Run - close to the W. VA. state line, and
    west-southwest of Crows off Rt. 311 North
    and Tuckahoe Creek in W. VA. close to White
    Sulphur Springs, W. VA. Tuckahoe Road runs
    from White Sulphur Springs toward Glace.
    [There is also a Laurel Branch near Rt. 18
    South on its west side before you get to
    County Rt. 619 or come to Blue Spring Run.

Lick Run Bridge - Bridge over James River on Rt.
    220 South at southern end of Iron Gate, VA.

Lucy Selina Furnace - on Rt. 269 in Longdale sec-
    tion of Alleghany Co., VA, believed called
    "Jordan's Furnace" at one time and locally
    Longdale Furnace. Take I64 East of Clifton
    Forge, VA, at exit Rt. 269, Longdale Furnace
    and Rt. 850, turn right on Rt. 269. Furnace
    stacks are on right across the creek and the
    old "Lucy Selina Inn" (now called "Firmstone
    Manor") is on the left.

McClintic's Mill - in Bath Co., VA, near Warm

Springs, VA.

Morris Hill - County Rt. 600 and County Rt. 666 near Lake Moomaw north of Covington, VA. Rt. 220 North then left on County Rt. 687 then left on County Rt. 641 then right on County Rt. 666 will take you there and left on County Rt. 600 at Fortney Branch will bring you the full circle to County Rt. 641.

Ogley's Creek (Ogle Creek) - on County Rt. 661 from Callaghan, VA, west of Covington, VA. Take I64 West at exit Rt. 159 West, Rt. 60 East and Humpback Bridge, turn left following Rt. 159, turn right on County Rt. 600 which runs straight into County Rt. 661 before Rt. 600 turns right. Follow Rt. 661 to where road goes under I64 West. From there you will be on Ogley's Creek. Follow Rt. 661 to where Rt. 781 turns left. From this point on, on Rt. 661 you will be on Johnson's Creek. Rt. 661 eventually returns to Rt. 600 where a right will bring you to where you started up Rt. 661.

Peter's Mountain - Rt. 60 West from Covington, VA, turn left on County Rt. 600 at Humpback Bridge, Rt. 600 follows the mountain, County Rt. 613 which turns left after crossing Peter's Mountain brings you to Boiling Springs, VA, on Rt. 18 South of Covington, VA.

Potts Creek - runs along Rt. 18 South from Covington, VA

R. S. Spring - unable to determine meaning, may refer to Red Sulphur Springs, W.VA., or Red Sweet Springs, VA (now called Sweet Chalybeate Springs, VA)

Red Sulphur Springs, VA (now W.VA.) - North of Peterstown, W.VA., on Rt. 12 in Monroe Co., W. VA.

GEOGRAPHIC LOCATIONS (Continued)

Red Sweet Springs, VA - Rt. 311 South near Sweet
    Springs, W. VA. It is now called Sweet
    Chalybeate Springs, VA. It was an ante-
    bellum resort.

Rich Patch - County Rt. 616 from Low Moor, VA.
    Take I64 West of Clifton Forge, VA, at exit
    County Rt. 696 at Low Moor, VA, turn left,
    go under the railway underpass and turn
    right on County Rt. 616. Follow Rt. 616 to
    where County Rt. 621 turns left to Roaring
    Run Furnace. Rich Patch was so named be-
    cause of a very high grade of iron ore that
    was mined in the area.

Salt Sulphur Springs, VA (now W. VA) - on Rt. 219
    between Union, W. VA. and Peterstown, W. VA.
    There was a resort in the area.

Simpson's Creek - County Rts. 269 and 850 East
    from Sharon Gables to top of North Mountain
    at Rich Hole Wilderness Area. Take I64 East
    of Clifton Forge, VA, to exit Rt. 42, turn
    right,then left on County Rts. 269 and 850
    and follow Rts. 269 then 850 as Simpson's
    Creek runs beside them.

Snake Run - County Rt. 604 off Rt. 311 to left on
    County Rt. 600 to Junction with County Rt.
    613. To reach take from Covington, VA, I64
    West to exit County Rt. 159 and Rt. 60 East
    Humpback Bridge at Callaghan, turn left fol-
    low County Rt. 159 to Crows. Turn left on
    Rt. 311 South at road forks, follow Rt. 311
    South to County Rt. 604, turn left and fol-
    low to County Rt. 600, turn left and follow
    to County Rt. 613. You have passed through
    Snake Run. Continue on County Rt. 600 to
    Humpback Bridge and Rt. 60 East. Turn right
    on Rt. 60 East and return to Covington.

Stephen's Hook - unable to determine, Rich Patch
    area in Alleghany Co., VA.

XVII

Sweet Sulphur Springs - unable to determine,
    (? maybe near Union, W.VA. or ? another name
    for Sweet Springs, W.VA.)

Sweet Springs, VA (now W.VA.) - on Rt. 311 South
    at Junction of Rt. 3.   Take I64 West to
    exit Rt. 159 and Rt. 60 East Humpback Bri-
    dge, turn left and follow Rt. 159 to Crows
    and turn left on Rt. 311 South and follow
    it to Sweet Springs, W.VA.

Tavern, George Masters' - unable to determine,
    (possibly Alleghany County, VA.   There was
    a George W. Masters who lived in the county
    in July 1872)

Tavern, Robert Skeener - Covington, VA.

Tavern, Wm. B. Sprowl's - unable to determine

Tunnel, Alleghany - Cheaspeake and Ohio Railway
    Tunnel off Rt. 311 North near W. VA. state
    line at Alleghany, VA. (Alleghany Station)
    left on County Rt. 602.   From Covington, VA
    take I64 West exit at County Rt. 159 and
    Rt. 60 East, turn left following Rt. 159 to
    Crows, VA, turn right on Rt. 311 North
    following it thru highway culbert tunnel,
    turn left on Rt. 602.   The tunnel is not
    far to the right down the tracks past the
    old Alleghany Railway Station.

Tunnel, Lewis - Cheaspeake and Ohio Railway Tun-
    nel off Rt. 311 North near W. Va. state
    line at Alleghany, VA, (Alleghany Station)
    left on County Rt. 602.   From Covington, VA,
    take I64 West exit at County Rt. 159 and Rt.
    60 East, turn left following Rt. 159 to
    Crows, VA, turn right on Rt. 311 North
    following it thru highway culbert tunnel,
    turn left on Rt. 602, go to Alleghany Rail-
    way Station.   The tunnel is down the railway
    tracks to the left of the station a mile or

two.

Tunnel, Mud - Cheaspeake and Ohio Railway Tunnel just beyond Humpback Bridge (Rt. 600) over Dunlap Creek near Callaghan. Can be seen from I64 West near exit County Rt. 159 and Rt. 60 East. You can find the tunnel by taking this exit, turn right on Rt. 60 East, follow it, turn right on County Rt. 600 at Humpback Bridge, follow Rt. 600 to highway bridge over the creek, turn right at bridge, follow road to tunnel.

Tunnel, Red Hill - was a Cheaspeake and Ohio Railway Tunnel on Rt. 42 North of Clifton Forge, VA, on Cowpasture River just beyond the "Nicely Town" section (County Rt. 635) of Alleghany County. The tunnel no longer exists, having been replaced by the state highway bridge.

White Rock Gap - County Rt. 623 off County Rt. 616 from Low Moor, VA. Can be reached from Clifton Forge, VA, by I64 West exit at Low Moor, VA, County Rt. 696, turn left, follow road thru railway underpass, turn right on Rt. 616, follow it to Rt. 623, turn left. The road is a deadend.

Wilson Creek - From Clifton Forge, VA, take I64 East to exit Rt. 220 South, County Rt. 629, and Rt. 220 South at Cliftondale Park, turn left on Rt. 629. The creek follows the road beyound Douthat State Park where it turns left and follows a U. S. Forest Service road which comes out on Rt. 188 North where you can turn left following Smith Creek and return to Rose St. in Clifton Forge, VA.

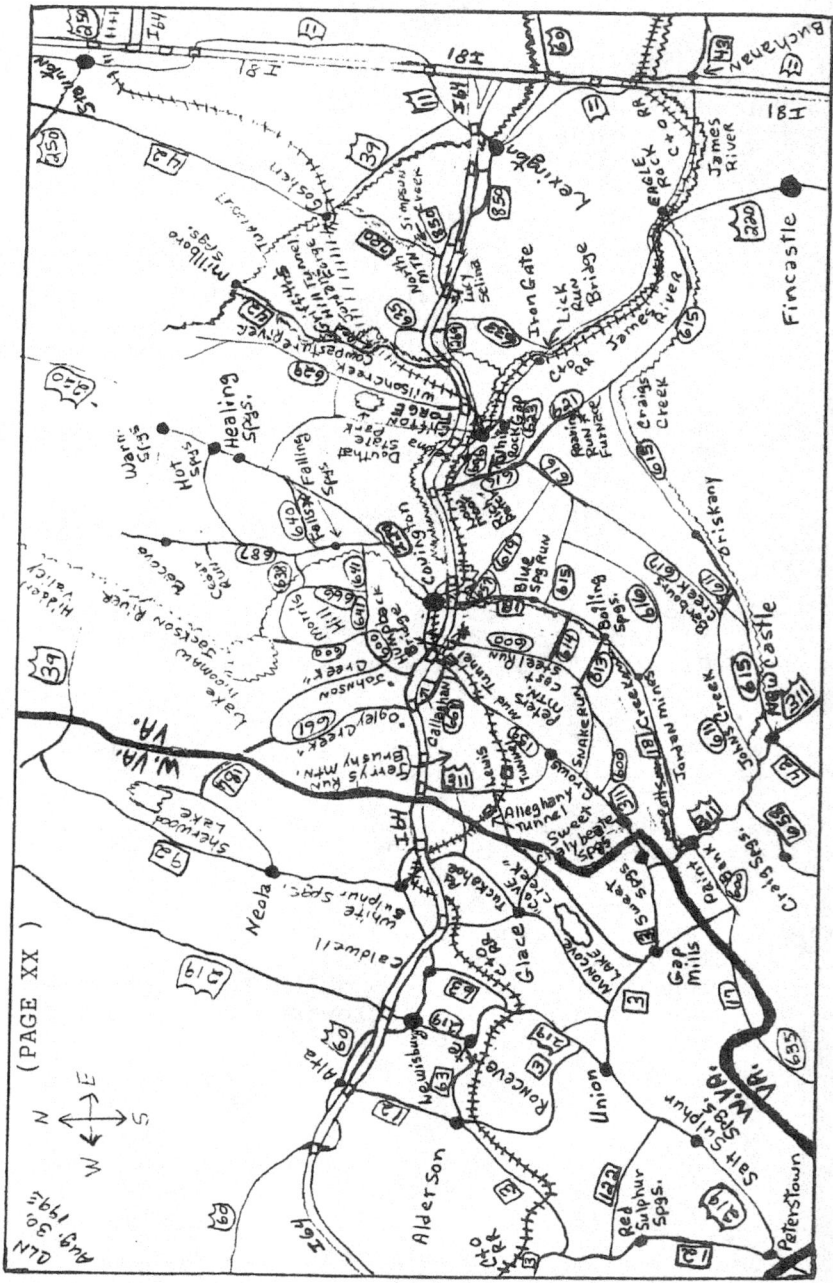

(PAGE XX)

N
W — E
S

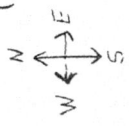

GLN
Aug. 30, 1992

W. Va. / Va.

Sherwood Lake

Neola

Caldwell
White Sulphur Spgs.

Alderson

Lewisburg
Ronceverte
Union
Gap Mills

Salt Sulphur Spgs.
Red Sulphur Spgs.
Peterstown

Monroce Lake
Glace Creek
Tuckahoe
Sweet Spgs.
"Sweet Creek Cove"
Sycamore Spgs.
Paint Bank
Craigs Creek

Alleghany Tunnel
Lewis Tunnel
Ogley Creek
Callaghan
Peters Mtn.
Tunnel
Johns Creek
Newcastle
Craig Creek

Jerry's Run
Brushy Mtn.
Johnson Creek
Kanawha
Covington
Dunlap Creek
Morris Hill
Snake Run
Steel Run
Blue Spg Run
Boiling Spgs.
Barbours Creek
Oriskany

Hidden Valley
Jackson River Valley
Lake Moomaw
Bolar

Hot Spgs.
Healing Spgs.
Warm Spgs.
Cedar Creek
Back Creek
Douthat State Park
Clifton Forge
Rich Patch
Rainy Run
Iron Furnace
Craigs Creek

Millboro
Millboro Springs
Windy Cove
Fort Lewis Mtn.
Cowpasture River
Wilson Creek
Selma
Iron Gate
Lick Run Bridge
James River
C & O RR
Pump Gap
Buck Gap

Goshen
Rockbridge Alum Springs
North Mtn.
Simpson Creek
Craigsville
Augusta Spgs.
Lexington
Jug Branch
Eagle Rock
James River
Fincastle
Buchanan

Marriage Date	Page 1

03-28-1822   George Duke and Mary C. Brunnemer.
Mar. by Joseph Pennell.

10-10-1822   Fielding Wills and Margaret P. Crider.
Mar. by Joseph Pennell.

10-17-1822   Vincent Wright and Matilda Humphries.
Mar. by Joseph Pennell.

10-24-1822   Jacob Armontrout and Catharine Aritt.
Mar. by Joseph Pennell.

12-10-1822   Thomas Byrd and Diannah Kimberlin.
Mar. by Joseph Pennell.

01-28-1823   Hamilton Bess and Rebecca King.
Mar. by Joseph Pennell.

05-10-1822   Joseph Crow and Rebecca Sawyers.
Mar. by Elisha Knox.

08-23-1822   Thomas Smith and Elizabeth Damron.
Mar. by Elisha Knox.

08-30-1822   William Gillaspie and Mary Minnick.
Mar. by Elisha Knox.

09-13-1822   Hugh Bryan and Nancy Sawyers.
Mar. by Elisha Knox.

09-13-1822   Lewis Acre and Polly Cleek.
Mar. by Elisha Knox.

12-13-1822   Francis Edgar and Sarah Lockhart.
Mar. by Elisha Knox.

02-21-1823 Elias Hook and Nancy Hansbarger.
Mar. by Elisha Knox.

03-13-1823 Lambert Rosendale and Sarah Kincaid.
Mar. by Elisha Knox.

10-23-1823 George F. Dudly and Jane T. Mann.
Mar. by Amos Smith.

07-03-1823 John Bennett and Catharine Quickle.
Mar. by Joseph Pennell.

02-17-1824 Charles Allen and Polly Withors
(? Withey). Mar. by Joseph Pennell.

03-25-1824 Sampson Persinger and Rebecca Stull.
Mar. by Joseph Pennell.

08-15-1824 Isaac Steele and Julia Callaghan.
Mar. by Elisha Knox.

04-22-1825 William Shawver and Kesiah Ross.
Mar. by Elisha Knox.

06-02-1825 John Mallow and Martha Carpenter.
Mar. by Elisha Knox.

Page 2

01-20-1825 Henry Frazier and Elizabeth Wright.
Mar. by John A. Vanlear.

02-23-1825 William Brunnemer and Sally Carpenter.
Mar. by John A. Vanlear.

01-10-1826 Peter Dressler and Patsy Fleet.
Mar. by Elisha Knox.

11-10-1825 William F. Morton and Catharine Mallow.
Mar. by Elisha Knox.

03-23-1826 John Williams and Abigale Sivey
(? Sively). Mar. by Elisha Knox.

(Minister Returns - Continued)

06-23-1825   Peter Helmintollor (? Holmintoller)
              and Polly Johnson. Mar. by Joseph
              Pennell.

08-25-1825   Richard A. Claughton and Susan Printz.
              Mar. by Joseph Pennell.

10-06-1825   Jacob Stull and Margaret Bennett.
              Mar. by Joseph Pennell.

01-17-1826   Moses Anders and Catharine Wolf.
              Mar. by Joseph Pennell.

02-14-1826   Sampson Wolf and Elizabeth Quickle.
              Mar. by Joseph Pennell.

05-26-1826   George Shirky (? Shirkey) and Ellen
              Callaghan. Mar. by Elisha Knox.

05-04-1826   Isaac Knox and Catharine Brunnemer.
              Mar. by Elisha Knox.

10-10-1826   William Kyle and Agness Shawver.
              Mar. by Elisha Knox.

12-01-1825   William Lemon and Harriett Pitzer.
              Mar. by John A. Vanlear.

12-01-1825   John Armontrout and Rachael Pitzer.
              Mar. by Jno. A. Vanlear.

12-15-1825   William Brown and Elizabeth Lemmon.
              Mar. by Jno. A. Vanlear.

12-22-1825   Alexander Gillaspie and Patsy (?Polly)
              Wright. Mar. by Jno. A. Vanlear.

12-22-1825   Moses Hart and Margaret Nicely.
              Mar. by Jno. A. Vanlear.

02-01-1827   Alexander Broyhill (?Rayhill) and
              Elizabeth Johnson. Mar. by Joseph
              Pennell. (Name was ink smeared.)

(Minister Returns - Continued)

03-15-1827 Jacob Bishop and Margaret Moyers.
            Mar. by Joseph Pennell.

04-12-1827 Jacob Kimberlin and Nancy Blair.
            Mar. by Joseph Pennell.

Page 3

11-20-1827 George Wolf and Sarah Paxton by
            publication. Mar. by Joseph Pennell.

08-13-1827 George Dressler and Malinda Dressler.
            Mar. by Elisha Knox.

07-20-1827 Hugh B. Rusk and Julia McCallister.
            Mar. by Elisha Knox.

11-27-1827 James Ruble (? Keeble) and Agness
            Oliver. Mar. by Elisha Knox.

10-18-1827 Francis Standly and Mary C. Massie.
            Mar. by Elisha Knox.

03-12-1827 John Gray (? Gross) and Julia Ann
            Taylor. Mar. by Elisha Knox.

04-17-1827 David Lange and Garethe (? Ganthe)
            Ann Walton. Mar. by Elisha Knox.

10-12-1828 Abraham Bishop and Mary Brunnemer.
            Mar. by Elixha Knox.

12-03- [no year listed (? 1828 or 1827)]
            Joseph B. Clark and Christena Dressler.
            Mar. by Elisha Knox.

10-30-1828 Jacob L. Bromwell and Charlott
            Brennemer. Mar. by Elisha Knox.

03-12-1829 William Duke and Nancy Glasburn.
            Mar. by Elisha Knox.

02-16-1829 William Clark and Elizabeth Morris.
            Mar. by James Watts.

(Minister Returns - Continued)

02-05-1829   Hugh Duke and Paulina L. White.
             Mar. by Elisha Knox.

06- [no rest of date (? 1829)]
             Divquid (? David) Pitzer and Sally
             Moyers. Mar. by Elisha Knox.

06-19-1828   Alexander Sawyers and Sarah Stone.
             Mar. by Joseph Pennell.

03-26-1829   John Duke and Judith Humphries.
             Mar. by Joseph Pennell.

09-03-1829   John Wright and Jane Anders.
             Mar. by Joseph Pennell.

09-24-1829   John Knox and Synthia McCallister.
             Mar. by Jgnalius (? Jonatin) H.
             Tackitt.

12-15-1829   John H. Pleasants and Mary L. Massie.
             Mar. by James Watts.

02-16-1829   Lewis T. Mann and Sally Cotton.
             Mar. by James Watts.

03-18-1830   Andrew Surber and Caroline Hansbarger.
             Mar. by Jno. A. Vanlear.

06-17-1830   Hamilton C. Grady and Nancy Fudge.
             Mar. by Jno. A. Vanlear.

07-08-1830   Benjamin Douglas and Harriet
             Morrison. Mar. by Jno. A. Vanlear.

Page 4

12-01-1829   Henry Gillaspy and Mildred Heivley
             (? Hevrley) by publication.
             Mar. by Joseph Pennell.

12-08-1829   Peter Landers and Rachel Carson.
             Mar. by Joseph Pennell.

- 5 -

(Minister Returns - Continued)

01-28-1830   John Arritt and Elizabeth Bowyer.
Mar. by Joseph Pennell.

02-13-1830   Nimrode Bush and Sarah Spencer by
publication. Mar. by Joseph Pennell.

05-20-1830   James Terry and Leah Pinkey by
publication. Mar. by Joseph Pennell.

08-05-1830   Allen Persinger and Paulina Peters
by license. Mar. by Joseph Pennell.

08-19-1830   Roling Simmons and Mary Bush.
Mar. by Joseph Pennell.

08-24-1830   Samuel Bush and Mary Meyers (?Myers).
Mar. by Joseph Pennell.

09-05-1830   Isacc Fridley and Elizabeth Stull.
Mar. by Joseph Pennell.

10-31-1830   Porterfield Boyod (? Boyed) and
Rachel Nichol (? Nickol) by public-
cation. Mar. by Joseph Pennell.

12-07-1830   Franklin Allen and Nancy Persinger
by license. Mar. by Joseph Pennell.

02-01-1831   Joseph Skeen and Sabina Davis.
Mar. by Hezekiah Best.

11-22-1830   Samuel Gordan (? Gordon) and Mary
Caldwell. Mar. by William Shumaker.

[no date listed but 1831]
Charles King and Jane Bennet.
Mar. by William Shumaker.

[no date listed but 1831]
Thomas Dorolly and Elizabeth Huet
(? Hurt) by publication. Mar. by
William Shumaker.

(Minister Returns - Continued)

[no date listed but 1831]
        Joseph Terry and Mahala Wolf.
        Mar. by William Shumaker.

[no date listed but 1831]
        Samuel Robison and Rachael Campbell
        by license. Mar. by William Shumaker.
        (Robison may be Robinson ?).

[no date listed but 1831]
        Sampson Bennet and Febe Fridley by
        license. Mar. by William Shumaker.

[no date listed but 1831]
        Robert Goodwin and Lililian Reynolds
        by license. Mar. by William Shumaker.

[no date listed but 1831]
        George Forbes (? Forbess) and
        Elizabeth Dobey by license. Mar.
        by William Shumaker.

10-20-1831 Israel James and Mary Callaghan by
        license. Mar. by William H. Enos.

01-18-1831 George Armontrout and Rebeccah
        Maggard. Mar. by Joseph Pennell.

02-15-1831 Fielding Jarvis and Sarah Ervin.
        Mar. by Joseph Pennell.

(? February) Do the 24th, 1831
        Lee Persinger and Kisiah Hook.
        Mar. by Joseph Pennell.

06-16-1831 Julius Dew and Jane Stull.
        Mar. by Joseph Pennell.

07-12-1831 John C. Flint and Margaret Shields.
        Mar. by Joseph Pennell.

10-06-1831 Charles Bush and Sarah Carson.
        Mar. by Joseph Pennell.

(Minister Returns - Continued)

12-15-1831 Abraham Armontrout and Bethsaida
           Wolf. Mar. by Joseph Pennell.

Page 5

02-03-1831 Samuel Brown and Sarah Mann by
           license. Mar. by James Watts.

03-03-1831 Benjamine Cotton and Charlotte Knox
           by license. Mar. by James Watts.

05-19-1831 Wm. Goheen and Frances Nicely.
           Mar. by John A. Vanlear.

09-09-1830 Joseph Sevely (? Sively) and
           Elizabeth Brunnemer. Mar. by John
           A. Vanlear.

08-19-1830 Robert Payne and Hannah Milhollin.
           Mar. by John A. Vanlear.

08-05-1830 Thos. Tate and Rachael Blair.
           Mar. by John A. Vanlear.

05-19-1831 James Carson and Caroline Wolf.
           Mar. by Jacob Douss.

06-22-1831 John Byers and Caroline Lemmon.
           Mar. by Davis Kinninson.

07-01-1832 Christopher Damron and Julia Ann
           Catharine Mann. Mar. by Charles
           B. Leffel.

02-28-1832 Andrew Damron and Mary Watts.
           Mar. by Wm. H. Enos.

02-12-1833 Benjamin P. Jamison and Margaret
           Siveley (? Sively). Mar. by William
           Shumaker.

09-01-1832 Moses Smith and Agnes Fleet.
           Mar. by Alfred A. Eskridge.

(Minister Returns - Continued)

11-05-1832   Gilson Douglas and Ankey Ross.
                Mar. by Alfred A. Eskridge.

11-03-1832   Nelson Clarkston and Margaret Keyser.
                Mar. by Alfred A. Eskridge.

01-10-1832   John Morris and Mary Ann Clarkston.
                Mar. by Alexander Freeman.

04-12-1832   Archer Sawyers and Susannah Lark.
                Mar. by Joseph Pennell.

04-26-1832   Henry Armstrong and Julia Hinton.
                Mar. by Joseph Pennell.

07-03-1832   Adam Persinger and Rebecca Carpenter.
                Mar. by Joseph Pennell.

11-29-1832   William Carson and Sally Hepler.
                Mar. by Joseph Pennell.

12-27-1832   John Brown and Betsy Dew.
                Mar. by Joseph Pennell.

01-24-1832   Abrahrum J. Huddleston and Leah
                Bowen. Mar. by Joseph Pennell.

08-18-1833   John Oiler and Rebecca Bess.
                Mar. by Wm. Shumaker.

10-09-1832   George Moyer and Julia A. Dressler.
                Mar. by James Watts.

11-15-1832   Eli Hook and Mary Ann Cox.
                Mar. by John A. Vanlear.

12-27-1832   William Thomas and Mariah Wright.
                Mar. by John A. Vanlear.

06-18-1832   Daniel G. White and Mary I. Holloway.
                Mar. by John A. Vanlear.

07-18-1833   Lewis Nicely and Anna Nicely.
                Mar. by John A. Vanlear.

(Minister Returns - Continued)

06-11-1833   Preston Simpson and Rachel Keeble.
           Mar. by James Paine.

Page 6

08-01-1833   Archibald M. Kincaid and Catherine
           Fudge. Mar. by Joseph Meniken.

07-07-1833   Thomas Reynolds and Margaret Taylor.
           Mar. by Joseph Meniken.

08-15-1833   John Pinkney and Mary Magdaline Wolf.
           Mar. by Joseph Pennell.

09-01-1833   Madison Hook and Mary Kimberlin.
           Mar. by Joseph Pennell.

(? September) Do the 19th, 1833
           William Evans and Kisiah Harmon.
           Mar. by Joseph Pennell.

10-17-1833   John Armontrout and Barbara Bush.
           Mar. by Jospeh Pennell.

11-05-1833   James Stull and Hanna King.
           Mar. by Joseph Pennell.

01-15-1834   William Bennet and Catharine Stull.
           Mar. by Joseph Pennell.

03-25-1834   Henry Myers and Elizabeth Aritt.
           Mar. by Joseph Pennell.

(? March) Do the 27th, 1834
           Samuel Stull and Elizabeth Ann Deeds.
           Mar. by Joseph Pennell.

04-08-1834   Henry Quickel and Peggy Simmons.
           Mar. by Joseph Pennell.

05-18-1834   John Craft and Elizabeth Matheney
           (? Matheny). Mar. by Joseph Pennell.

(Minister Returns - Continued)

07-17-1834 John Hepler and Sarah Johnston.
            Mar. by Joseph Pennell.

10-26-1834 Griffith (? Griffeth) Ross and Harriet
            Cox. Mar. by James Watts.

01-14-1834 Dennison Rose and Eliza A. Kimberlin.
            Mar. by James Watts.

10-31-1833 Joseph Kimberlin and Hannah Griffith.
            Mar. by John A. Vanlear.

01-23-1834 John K. E. Shumaker and Eliza M.
            Matthews. Mar. by John A. Vanlear.

02-18-1834 William G. Peter and Louisa Sively.
            Mar. by John A. Vanlear.

03-11-1834 Isaac W. Tackitt and Amanga (? Amanda)
            Jane Brunnemer. Mar. by John A.
            Vanlear.

03-25-1834 William Deeds and Rachael Haynes.
            Mar. by John A. Vanlear.

04-08-1834 Campbell Karnes and Martha Blair.
            Mar. by John A. Vanlear.

04-26-1834 William Haynes, Jr. and Elizabeth
            Morrison. Mar. by John A. Vanlear.

02-15-1834 William Byer and Maria Semmon
            (? Simmon). Mar. by Joseph Meniken.

06-01-1834 James Tate and Martha Dressler.
            Mar. by Joseph Meniken.

11-21-1834 Samuel Dickson and Margarett Callaghan.
            Mar. by Joseph Meniken.

12-18-1834 William F. Morton and Maria Louisa
            Fudge. Mar. by Joseph Meniken.

(Minister Returns - Continued)

01-29-1835   Francis Gardner and Liza Kincaid.
             Mar. by Joseph Meniken.

02-12-1835   William Clarkston and Harriet Karnes.
             Mar. by Joseph Meniken.

10-07-1834   Samuel Nicely and Elizabeth Robinson.
             Mar. by John A. Vanlear.

11-27-1834   Andrew Hickman and Delila Armontrout.
             Mar. by John A. Vanlear.

11-27-1834   Addison Hoilman and Malinda
             Armontrout. Mar. by John A. Vanlear.

12-30-1834   John Armstrong and Nancy McDaniel.
             Mar. by John A. Vanlear.

04-16-1835   Joby Ownsby and Mary Jane Matthews.
             Mar. by John A. Vanlear.

04-16-1835   Samuel Gillaspie and Mary Sively.
             Mar. by John A. Vanlear.

06-04-1835   Noraden D. Early and Mary Sanders
             (alias) Narcissa Douglas. Mar. by
             John A. Vanlear.

06-25-1835   John Hook and Eliza Holms (? Helms).
             Mar. by John A. Vanlear.

Page 7

12-04-1834   John Landers and Sarah Sumpter.
             Mar. by Joseph Pennell.

02-05-1834   Thomas Harmon and Polly Bowyer.
             Mar. by Joseph Pennell.

02-19-1834   Jefferson Griffey and Margaret Bush.
             Mar. by Joseph Pennell.

(Minister Returns - Continued)

04-30-1834   Joseph Armontrout and Mary Wolf.
Mar. by Joseph Pennell.

05-07-1834   John Carson and Eujama N. Linton.
Mar. by Joseph Pennell.

06-04-1834   Benjamin Clement and Malinda
Armstrong. Mar. by Joseph Pennell.

06-09-1834   Andrew Wilson and Mahaley Pinkley.
Mar. by Joseph Pennell.

10-20-1834   Hugh Humphries and Rachel B. Pinkley.
Mar. by Joseph Pennell.

11-12-1834   Henry Clarkson and Granville
Persinger. Mar. by Joseph Pennell.

10-29-1835   Henry Bennet and Polly Fridley.
Mar. by William Shumaker.

05-28-1835   Jesse Bright and Frances Thompson.
Mar. by Jno. W. Richardson.

06-04-1835   James Rodgers and Nancy Harmon.
Mar. by Jno. W. Richardson.

06-18-1835   William P. Kierne (? Kieme) and
Mary Burk. Mar. by Jno. W. Richardson.

08-13-1835   Isaac Moon and Elizabeth Wiford.
Mar. by Jno. W. Richardson.

01-26-1836   James H. Boswell and Maria Callaghan.
Mar. by Jno. W. Richardson.

(? January) Do the 27th, 1836
James O. Hobbs and Elizabeth Y.
Boswell. Mar. by Jno. W. Richardson.

(? January) Do the 28th, 1836
Samuel Gross and Mary Hoover.
Mar. by Jno. W. Richardson.

(Minister Returns - Continued)

12-02-1835   Elisha Erwin (?Ervin) and Elizabeth
             Griffith. Mar. by John A. Vanlear.

01-21-1836   Thomas Mozingo (? Mazingo) and
             Rebecca Hoileman. Mar. by John A.
             Vanlear.

12-10-1835   George Harmon and Parnelia Dew.
             Mar. by Joseph Pennell.

03-10-1836   George W. Trussler and Savenia Dew.
             Mar. by Joseph Pennell.

07-28-1836   Joseph Deeds and Elizabeth Mary Hook.
             Mar. by Joseph Pennell.

09-29-1836   Wm. Edgar and Phoebe Deeds.
             Mar. by Joseph Pennell.

12-08-1836   Samuel Byer and Harriet Simmons.
             Mar. by Joseph Pennell.

11-24-1836   Nathaniel McKenney and Sarah Pitzer.
             Mar. by John W. Richardson.

02-09-1837   Ephraine Simmons, Jr. and Susan Bush.
             Mar. by William Shumaker.

06-09-1836   Henry Kimberlin and Charlotte Stull.
             Mar. by Joseph Pennell.

07-04-1836   Oliver Jones and Sanis Semter.
             (Note: This spelling may have been
             by sound and may have meant Janice
             Sumpter.) Mar. by Joseph Pennell.

02-09-1837   Jackson Rose and Ruth Wolf.
             Mar. by Joseph Pennell.

02-09-1837   Absolem Dew and Sarah Stull.
             Mar. by Joseph Pennell.

(Minister Returns - Continued)

05-11-1837   George Wright and Elizabeth Bennet.
              Mar. by Joseph Pennell.

05-18-1837   Jabez Johnson and Mariah Persinger.
              Mar. by Joseph Pennell.

Page 8

11-09-1837   William H. Quickel and Elizabeth
              Persinger. Mar. by Joseph Pennell.

11-09-1837   George P. King and Nancy Bennet.
              Mar. by Joseph Pennell.

12-13-1837   Gideon Fridley and Ruth R. King.
              Mar. by Joseph Pennell.

12-14-1837   Michael Tingler and Polly Fridley.
              Mar. by Joseph Pennell.

06-14-1838   John G. McKenney and Lucy Dew.
              Mar. by Joseph Pennell.

01-14-1839   Martin Persinger and Catharine Dew.
              Mar. by Joseph Pennell.

01-24-1839   Thomas Fridley and Delila Wolf.
              Mar. by Joseph Pennell.

02-14-1839   Jacob Wolf and Sarah Armontrout.
              Mar. by Joseph Pennell.

02-17-1839   Zebidee Persinger and Mary Quickel.
              Mar. by Joseph Pennell.

08-15-1839   Lewis Fridley and Harriet P. Hepler.
              Mar. by Joseph Pennell.

12-18-1839   John Bowyer and Nancy Craft.
              Mar. by Joseph Pennell.

01-09-1840   Andrew Bush and Elizabeth Stull.
              Mar. by Joseph Pennell.

(Minister Returns - Continued)

07-25-1839   Caleb Griffith and Elizabeth Mann. Mar. by Zach^h Jordan.

09-05-1839   William Henduson (? Henderson) and Lucinda Morris. Mar. by Zach^h Jordan.

12-19-1839   William R. Martin and Margaret Silvers. Mar. by Zach^h Jordan.

12-25-1839   Michael G. Cotton and Elizabeth Hardy. Mar. by Zach^h Jordan.

02-12-1840   Harry Karnes and Rebecca Fleet. Mar. by Zach^h Jordan.

03-01-1840   Jonathan Belcher and Jane Wright. Mar. by Joseph Pennell.

07-16-1840   Adam Bush and Margaret Wolf. Mar. by Joseph Pennell.

07-23-1840   Felander (? Frelander) Counts and Sarah Ann Thomas. Mar. by Joseph Pennell.

11-12-1840   Eli Persinger and Lydia Fridly. Mar. by Joseph Pennell.

11-19-1840   Hays F. Whitesides and Martha Jane Ragland. Mar. by Joseph Pennell.

12-24-1840   James Flarherty and Eliza Ann D. Gilbert. Mar. by Joseph Pennell.

04-16-1840   William Short and Jane Matheney. Mar. by William P. Bishop.

11-11-1841   Cornelius Tyree and Sophina H. Pullium. Mar. by James Remley.

09-20-1835   John McD. (? M. D.) Mann and Julia Morris. Mar. by Dion C. Pharr.

(Minister Returns - Continued)

12-02-1835   Francis Goode and Malinda Bush.   Mar.
              by Dion C. Pharr.

12-03-1835   Thomas L. Perry and Joanna Brunnemer.
              Mar. by Dion C. Pharr.

03-16-1836   William Stone and Jane Brown.   Mar.
              by Dion C. Pharr.

04-26-1836   John Brown and Patsey E. Littlepage.
              Mar. by Dion C. Pharr.

06-15-1837   Galbraith Kyle and Elizabeth G. Mann.
              Mar. by Dion C. Pharr.

04-(04 or 11 ?)-1838
              Augustus Moyers and Elizabeth M.
              Kendel.   Mar. by Dion C. Pharr.

07-12-1838   Anderson Brown and Barbara Dressler.
              Mar. by Dion C. Pharr.

02-14-1839   John Deacon and Mary Ann Hammer.
              Mar. by Dion C. Pharr.

02-19-1839   Jacob Nicely and Margaret Downey.
              Mar. by Dion C. Pharr.

07-23-1839   John A. Black and Rachael Hansbarger.
              Mar. by Dion C. Pharr.

03-07-1839   Daniel Leighton and Louisa Reynolds.
              Mar. by Dion C. Pharr.

05-20-1839   _____hn E. Hamner (Part of name
              missing--suspect may have been John)
              and Avelinah Paris.   Mar. by Dion C.
              Pharr.

Page 9

03-26-1840   Austin Gilbert and Susan Oiler.
              Mar. by Rev. Dion C. Pharr.

05-05-1840   Ira F. Jordan and Polly Skeen.
Mar. by Rev. Dion C. Pharr.

08-01-1840   William Moss and Lydia Myers.
Mar. by Rev. Dion C. Pharr.

08-05-1840   Joseph H. Lantz and Catharine Anders.
Mar. by Rev. Dion C. Pharr.

08-13-1840   George W. Goodwin and Maria Karnes.
Mar. by Rev. Dion C. Pharr.

09-24-1840   William Ross and Lucy Cox.
Mar. by Rev. Dion C. Pharr.

10-01-1840   Harry Hoover and Barbara McCallister.
Mar. by Rev. Dion C. Pharr.

10-08-1840   Quincy Forbass (? Forbess) and
Elizabeth Lynxwiler. Mar. by Rev.
Dion C. Pharr.

11-05-1840   James M. Monroe and Sarah Ann May.
Mar. by Rev. Dion C. Pharr.

11-12-1840   Thomas Hardy and Miss Sophia M.
Brown. Mar. by Rev. Dion C. Pharr.

11-13-1840   John C. Taylor and Margaret V.
Maston. Mar. by Rev. Dion C. Pharr.

11-25-1840   Stephen Wright and Catharine Alexander. Mar. by Rev. Dion C. Pharr.

12-24-1840   Henry B. Harmon and Mary Ann Fudge.
Mar. by Rev. Dion C. Pharr.

01-21-1841   James Lemon and Rebecca Persinger.
Mar. by Rev. Dion C. Pharr.

12-29-1840   David B. Lockheart and Nancy Kimberlin. Mar. by Rev. Dion C. Pharr.

(Minister Returns - Continued)

06-02-1841 William Leighton and Emily Morrison.
Mar. by Rev. Dion C. Pharr.

07-08-1841 George W. Lemon and Diannah Kesler.
Mar. by Rev. Dion C. Pharr.

08-11-1841 Wm. H. Quickel and Margaret L.
Jamison. Mar. by Rev. Dion C. Pharr.

09-02-1841 Charles Fridly and Barbara Harmon.
Mar. by Rev. Dion C. Pharr.

09-23-1841 William Damron and Benjamina Mann.
Mar. by Rev. Dion C. Pharr.

10-24-1841 Francis M. Jones and Evaline Bratton.
Mar. by Rev. Dion C. Pharr.

11-04-1841 John Brown and Louisa Rigney.
Mar. by Rev. Dion C. Pharr.

09-02-1841 Roderick M. Tinsley and Mary Ann
Karnes. Mar. by David Trout.

10-26-1841 Nelson Fridley and Elizabeth
Armontrout. Mar. by David Trout.

02-15-1838 Charles C. Payne and Frances Pitzer.
Mar. by Dion C. Pharr.

05-30-1841 Ephraim Simmons and Judith Reynolds.
Mar. by Joseph Pennell.

08-25-1841 Wm. T. Moses and Mary Adaline
Persinger. Mar. by Joseph Pennell.

11-17-1841 Joseph Hall and Sarah P. Dew.
Mar. by Joseph Pennell.

01-13-1842 John Deeds and Patsey Armontrout.
Mar. by Joseph Pennell.

02-17-1842 Wm. Holley and Malinda Dew.
Mar. by Joseph Pennell.

(Minister Returns - Continued)

03-01-1842   Jacob Wolf and Maria Elvira (? Elvina)
                E. Stull. Mar. by Joseph Pennell.

03-01-1842   Wm. Linton and Rebecca Dew.
                Mar. by Joseph Pennell.

05-19-1842   Thomas W. Pleasants and Nancy
                Matheny. Mar. by William Shumaker.

07-31-1842   John Cleak (? Clark) and Sarah Hinton.
                Mar. by William Shumaker.

11-30-1842   William W. Taylor and Mary G. Boswell.
                Mar. by Philip B. Reese.

12-28-1843   Samuel Matheney and Jane Monroe.
                Mar. by William Shumaker.

02-23-1843   Wm. Dickson and July Ann Monroe.
                Mar. by William Shumaker.

10-25-1843   Jesse Fridly and July Ann Persinger.
                Mar. by.William Shumaker.

09-07-1843   Milton Armontrout and Rebecca Stull.
                Mar. by Joseph Pennell.

03-05-1844   Hugh Wolf and Lydia Fridley.
                Mar. by Joseph Pennell.

07-04-1844   George Stull and Charlotte Persinger.
                Mar. by Joseph Pennell.

08-15-1844   George Byer (Byers on actual list)
                and Ann Dew. Mar. by Joseph Pennell.

Page 10

07-04-1844   David Byer and Elizabeth B. Neel by
                license. Mar. by William H. Renick.

11-24-1844   James Karnes and Ann Eliza Hayse.
                Mar. by W. G. Murgrave.

(Minister Returns - Continued)

03-24-1845   John Bennet and Nancy Persinger.
             Mar. by William Shumaker.

06-26-1844   Samuel Kittinger and Ruthy Simmons.
             Mar. by Jacob Carper.

07-04-1844   George Stull and Charlotte Persinger.
             Mar. by Joseph Pennell.(Listed Twice)

08-15-1844   George Byers and Ann Dew. Mar.
             by Joseph Pennell. (Listed Twice)

02-03-1845   (on book) 02-13-1845 (on Mins. List)
             James Wilson and Elizabeth Hepler.
             Mar. by Joseph Pennell.

06-10-1845   Anderson Humphries and Mary Ann
             Bennet. Mar. by J. Scott.

04-28-1841   James Morrison [Jas. Morrison (on
             Mins. List)] and Mary Jane Haynes.
             Mar. by Henry H. Paine.

05-17-1842   William P. Tate [Wm. Tate (on Mins.
             List)] and Margaret E. Kayser [Mar-
             garet Kayser (on Mins. List)]. Mar.
             by Henry H. Paine.

11-30-1843   Circle Nicely and Harriet Ross.
             Mar. by Henry H. Paine.

02-15-1845   (on book) 01-15-1846 (on Mins. List)
             William W. Smith and Mary Ann Hardy
             by license. Mar. by John L. Gilbert.

09-09-1845   Robert M. Wiley and Mary A. E. Scott
             by license. Mar. by John L. Gilbert.

08-27-1845   William McCallister and Amanda Snead
             [Amanda M. Snead (on Mins. List)] by
             license. Mar. by John L. Gilbert.
             (Married 08-27-1846 on Mins. List)

(Minister Returns - Continued)

02-03-1846   William H. Medley and Emely Almira
Jane Burk by license. Mar. by John
L. Gilbert.

10-04-1845   Caleb Sites and Catharine Kindle by
license. Mar. by John L. Gilbert.

12-30-1845   William Weekline (Wm. Weekline on
Mins. List) and Virginia Blakee by
license. Mar. by William Taylor,
Member of Balt. Conf.   Andrew
Fudge, Clerk of Court.

06-26-1845   Michael Hann and Magdaline Nicely.
Mar. by W. G. Murgrave.

05-17-1842   William Tate (Wm. Tate on Mins.List)
and Margaret Keyser (Margaret Kayser
on Mins. List). Mar. by Henry H.
Paine. (Listed Twice)

04-28-1841   James Morrison (Jas. Morrison on Mins.
List) and Mary Jane Haynes. Mar. by
Henry H. Paine. (Listed Twice)

11-30-1843   Circle Nicely and Harriet Ross.
Mar. by Henry H. Paine. (Listed Twice)

02-13-1846   John H. Smith and Louisa Harmon by
license. Mar. by A. J. Elmore.

11-17-1846   Alexander Persinger and Purthina
Roberts. Mar. by A. J. Elmore.

06-04-1846   William W. Rose and Jane Persinger by
license. Mar. by John L. Gilbert.

04-02-1846   John Doss and Nancy Paxton by license.
Mar. by Dexter A. Snow.

03-05-1846   John Stone and Elizabeth Landers.
Mar. by Joseph Pennell.

(Minister Returns - Continued)

08-04-1846   Jacob Wolf and Gilla Wolf.
              Mar. by Joseph Pennell.

10-15-1846   Alfred Walker and Betty L. Dew.
              Mar. by Joseph Pennell.

10-20-1846   William Dunsmore (Wm. Dunsmore on
              Mins. List) and Sarah Aritt.
              Mar. by Joseph Pennell.

03-22-1847   Andrew Persinger and Mary Terry.
              Mar. by Joseph Pennell.

03-17-1847   (11-17-1846 on Mins. List)
              Alexander Persinger and Purthina
              Roberts by license. Mar. by A. J.
              Elmore. (Listed Twice)

07-28-1847   James G. Plymale and Amanda J.
              Persinger. Mar. by Tillotson A.
              Morgan, Methodist Episcopal Minister.

09-22-1847   Samuel Wilson and Sarah C. Arrington.
              Mar. by Tillotson A. Morgan.

10-28-1847   Robert Dickson and Sarah Jane
              Callaghan. Mar. by Tillotson A.
              Morgan.

09-08-1847   George Matheny (Geo. Matheny on Mins.
              List) and Martha Printz (Prinz on
              Mins. List) by license. Mar. by
              Wm. H. Wilson.

12-22-1847   Andrew J. Smith and Virginia M. Jones
              (could be ? James on list) by license.
              Mar. by Wm. H. Wilson.

Page 11

09-22-1847   William Booth and Martha Rowen.
              Mar. by Joseph Pennell.

- 23 -

(Minister Returns - Continued)

10-21-1847 John Pinkley and Mary A. E. Byers.
Mar. by Joseph Pennell.

02-17-1848 Abraham Wolf and Hetty Terry.
Mar. by Joseph Pennell.

10-12-1848 Fielding P. Sizer and Mary P. Wolf.
Mar. by Joseph Pennell.

10-17-1848 John A. Andrews and Eliza N. Wolf.
Mar. by Joseph Pennell.

12-30-1847 James Y. Lemon and Margaret Kessler
by license. Mar. by J. P. Corron.

10-31-1848 John A. Beckner (Becknor on Mins.
List) and Martha J. Lantz. Mar. by
Tillotson A. Morgan, Minister of the
Gospel, Methodist E. Church, Balt.
Conference.

10-31-1848 John P. Callaghan and Sarah E. Bishop.
Mar. by Tillotson A. Morgan, Meth.
Episc. Church, Balt. Conference.

09-07-1849 Augustus McReynolds (McRinolds on
Mins. List) and Ruth Anders by license.
Mar. by J. Hank.

08-11-1849 James Cook and Mary C. Thacker.
Mar. by James T. Phelps.

09-27-1849 William H. Kiney and Sarah J. Vaughan.
Mar. by James T. Phelps.

10-05-1849 Austin Snead and Jane E. Bratten.
Mar. by James T. Phelps.

10-17-1849 William Cunningham and Lucinda Kindle.
Mar. by James T. Phelps.

11-08-1849 William J. Givens and Sarah J. Kindle.
Mar. by James T. Phelps.

(Minister Returns - Continued)

12-27-1849   Moses Walton and Sarah Smith.
Mar. by James T. Phelps.

02-14-1850   Samuel T. Martin and Julia G.
Gilliland. Mar. by James T. Phelps.

07-02-1850   John C. Wood and Maria S. Gillaspie
(Book) (Maria S. Gilliland on Mins.
List). Mar. by James T. Phelps.

11-29-1849   J. P. Kefauver and Sarah A. Sively
by license. Mar. by J. P. Corron.
Andrew Fudge, Clerk of Court.

04-18-1850   Jonathan Jones and Elizabeth Anders
by license. Mar. by A. J. Elmore.

Page 12

08-08-1850   Henry Myers and Charlotte Persinger.
Mar. by J. Scott. Date of License:
07-24-1850.

08-08-1850   Jno. B. Davis (John B. Davies on Mins.
List) and Joannah (Joanna on Mins.
List) Armontrout. Mar. by Dion C.
Pharr. Date of Lic:08-07-1850.

08-07-1850   Oliver P. Gray and Rebecca R. Scott.
Mar. by Dion C. Pharr. Date of Lic.:
08-07-1850.

09-18-1850   William H. Gillaspie and Elizabeth A.
Gillaspie. Mar. by Dion C. Pharr.
Date of Lic.: 09-02-1850.

08-29-1850   Joseph Terry and Elizabeth Aritt.
Mar. by A. J. Elmore. Date of Lic.:
08-27-1850

09-05-1850   Charles P. Shumaker and Ellen Lantz
(Ellonor H. Lantz on Mins. List). Mar.
by A. J. Elmore. Date of Lic.:
09-05-1850

(Minister Returns - Continued)

10-17-1850   Allen Johnson and Julia A. Armentrout.
Mar. by Dion C. Pharr. Date of Lic.:
10-08-1850.

10-16-1850   Wm. Helmantoller and Rebecca B.
Plymale. Mar. by Dion C. Pharr.
Date of Lic.: 10-08-1850.

10-31-1850   Matthews D. Brown and Mary Smith.
Mar. by J. T. Phelps. Date of Lic.:
10-25-1850.

11-19-1850   William W. Gillaspie (No middle
initial on Mins. List) and Mary M.
Nicely. Mar. by Jno. M. Cochran.
Date of Lic.: 11-11-1850.

11-26-1850   David J. Wise and Julia E. Callaghan.
Mar. by J. T. Phelps. Date of Lic.:
11-26-1850.

(No Mar. Date)
   John O. Bennet and Sarah J.
(? Persinger). Mar. by (no minister
name). Date of Lic.: 11-26-1850.

12-05-1850   Jacob Wolf and Mary Wolf (Mary E.
Wolf on Mins. List). Mar. by A. J.
Elmore. Date of Lic.: 11-30-1850.

01-16-1851   Erasmus (Eruzmus on Mins. List) T.
Williams and Leah C. Jones. Mar. by
J. P. Corron. Date of Lic.:01-15-1851.

01-23-1850   Malcijah Hancock and Synthia A.
Bradford. Mar. by J. Scott. Date of
Lic.: 01-20-1851.

02-02-1851   Jesse J. Jackson and Rachel Stinesheet
(? Stonestreet on Mins. List). Mar.by
J. T. Corron. Date of Lic: 01-23-1851.

02-19-1851   George W. Wolf and Palina (Polina on
Mins.List) Wolf. Mar. by A. J. Elmore.
Date of Lic.: 02-13-1851.

(Minister Returns - Continued)

03-06-1851   George Persinger and Mary J. Tingler.
             Mar. by J. Scott.   Date of Lic.:
             03-04-1851.

03-20-1851   William Smith and Cornelia A. Boley.
             Mar. by Dion C. Pharr.   Date of Lic.:
             03-17-1851.

04-10-1851   Jacob Rayhill and Rebecca A. King.
             Mar. by Dion C. Pharr.   Date of Lic.:
             03-24-1851.

04-02-1851   James O. Persinger and Miriah T.
             Bennet.   Mar. by Dion C. Pharr.
             Date of Lic.:   03-31-1851.

04-24-1851   Henry Gilliland and Mary J. Hook.
             Mar. by Dion C. Pharr.   Date of Lic.:
             04-16-1851.

07-07-1851   Peter Hinton and Marietta Crawford.
             Mar. by Dion C. Pharr.   Date of Lic.:
             07-07-1851.

08-21-1851   William Dickson and Elizabeth J.
             Hayse.   Mar. by J. P. Corren [J. T.
             Corron (on Mins. List)].   Date of
             Lic.:   08-18-1851.   Andrew Fudge,
             Clerk of Court.

08-02-1851   (on book) 08-28-1851 (on Mins. List)
             Joseph Dickson and Martha M. Monroe.
             Mar. by J. P. Corron [J. T. Corron on
             Mins.List).   Date of Lic: 08-25-1851.

09-04-1851   Nicholas Shumaker and Phobe [Phebe on
             Mins. List] Hoover.   Mar. by Dion C.
             Pharr.   Date of Lic.:   08-29-1851.

09-12-1851   Nimrod Bush and Sarah Persinger.
             Mar. by Dion C. Pharr.   Date of Lic.:
             09-06-1851.

(Minister Returns - Continued)

09-11-1851   Shelton R. Harmon and Elizabeth
Fuory. Mar. by Dion C. Pharr. Date
of Lic.: 09-10-1851.

10-01-1851   John S. Aritt [Arritt on Mins. List]
and Phobe [Phebe (on Mins. List)]
Terry. Mar. by A. J. Elmore. Date
of Lic.: 09-15-1851.

09-25-1851   Joseph C. Whiten and Martha A. Sizer.
Mar. by Dion C. Pharr. Date of Lic.:
09-21-1851

11-17-1851   Martin [Morton (on Mins. List)] Lemon
and Frances [Francis (on Mins. List)]
Reynolds. Mar. by Dion C. Pharr.
Date of Lic.: 11-13-1851.

12-04-1851   Charles E. Farmer and Mary E. [C.
(on Mins. List)] Bishop. Mar. by D.
Shoaff. Date of Lic.: 12-04-1851.

12-04-1851   Jordan Helmantoller [Hellmantoller
(on Mins. List)] and Rebecca Hook
[Rebecca L. Hook (on Mins. List)].
Mar. by D. Shoaff, Methodist Episco-
pal Church. Date of Lic: 11-26-1851.

Page 13

12-18-1851   Henry Fry and Mary E. Anderson. Mar.
by D. Shraff [Shoaff (on Mins. List)].
Date of Lic.: 12-16-1851.

12-16-1851   Robert Childs and Sarah E. Harmon.
Mar. by Dion C. Pharr. Date of Lic.:
12-15-1852 (? 1851).

(No Mar. Date)
    John T. Deaton and Grandvill D.
Haynes. Mar. by [No Minister Name].
Date of Lic.: 01-03-1852.

(Minister Returns - Continued)

01-29-1852   Henry Hoilman and Salina Davidson.
             Mar. by D. Shoaff. Date of Lic.:
             01-28-1852.

(No Mar. Date)
             Geo. F. (? Harras) and Ann J. Snead.
             Mar. by (No Minister Name). Date of
             Lic.: 02-03-1852

04-25-1852   Richard Woody and Frances J. A.
             McDaniel. Mar. by A. S. Hogshead.
             Date of Lic.: 02-11-1852.

03-04-1852   Thomas Shumaker [Thomas T. Shumaker
             on Mins. List] and Mary J. Sawyers.
             Mar. by J. P. Corron. Date of Lic.:
             02-21-1852.

(No Mar. Date)
             Alexander Welcher and Sarah Oiler.
             Mar. by (No Minister Name). Date of
             Lic.: 03-03-1852.

(No Mar. Date)
             George Freeland and Delila Oiler.
             Mar. by (No Minister Name). Date of
             Lic.: 04-21-1852.

05-12-1852   Henry Jones and Mary Jane Root.
             Mar. by A. S. Hogshead. Date of
             Lic.: 05-07-1852.

(No Mar. Date)
             John (? Saulavait) and Harriet
             Griffith. Mar. by (No Minister
             Name). Date of Lic.: 07-29-1852.

06-22-1852   John J. Paxton and Eliza J. Layne.
             Mar. by A. S. Hogshead. Date of
             Lic.: 06-21-1852.

07-27-1852   Charles L. Humphries and Rebecca B.

Stull. Mar. by J. W. Kelley. Date of Lic.: 07-26-1852.

(No Mar. Date)

William Persinger and Mary E. Wolf. Mar. by (No Minister Name). Date of Lic.: 08-16-1852.

08-24-1852 George McNabb and Margaret C. Gillaspie. Mar. by J. W. Kelley. Date of Lic.: 08-24-1852.

10-14-1852 Henry Dressler and Elizabeth Fry. Mar. by A. S. Hogshead. Date of Lic.: 10-13-1852.

09-01-1852 John W. Wyatt [John W. Wyat (on Mins. List)] and Mary A. Kendall [Mary A. Kindell (on Mins. List)]. Mar. by J. P. Corron. Date of Lic.: 09-01-1852.

10-19-1852 Charles H. Dressler and Eliza H. Robinson. Mar. by J. W. Kelley. Date of Lic.: 10-18-1852.

11-04-1852 Jonathan Armontrout and Susan E. Rayhill. Mar. by A. S. Hogshead. Date of Lic.: 10-30-1852.

11-10-1852 John F. Richardson and Margaret J. B. Johnson [Margaret J. P. Johnson (on Mins. List)]. Mar. by A. S. Hogshead. Date of Lic.: 11-02-1852.

11-04-1852 Samuel Brown and Sarah Jane Myers. Mar. by J. W. Kelley. Date of Lic.: 11-04-1852.

11-04-1852 Daniel [Danl. (on Mins. List)] K. Rader and Frances Ann Brown. Mar. by J. W. Kelley. Date of Lic:11-04-1852.

(Minister Returns - Continued)

11-18-1852   William Craft and Sarah Ann Plymale.
             Mar. by A. S. Hogshead. Date of
             Lic.: 11-10-1852.

11-17-1852   John A. Jones and Juda B. Carter.
             Mar. by H. J. Bland. Date of Lic.:
             11-13-1852.

11-25-1852   W. H. Dean [Wm. H. Dean (on Mins.
             List)] and Malinda Kilingsworth.
             Mar. by J. W. Kelley. Date of Lic.:
             11-25-1852.

11-30-1852   Edwin Kyle and E. M. Mallow [Eliza-
             beth E. Mallow (on Mins. List)].
             Mar. by A. S. Hogshead. Date of
             Lic.: 11-29-1852.

01-27-1853   W. M. Faudree [William A. Faudree
             (on Mins. List)] and Lucy Blaker.
             Mar. by Dion C. Pharr. Date of Lic.:
             01-11-1853.

02-15-1853   James [Jarvis (on Mins. List)] A.
             Simmons and Mary A. Bowyers. Mar.
             by A. S. Hogshead. Date of Lic.:
             02-09-1853.

02-17-1853   Frederick A. Taylor and Elizabeth
             Guy. Mar. by J. W. Kelley, Minister
             of M. E. Church. Date of Lic.:
             02-15-1853. Both lived in Alleg. Co.

03-08-1853   George W. Eddy and Eliza [Elisa (on
             Mins. List)] C. Jones. Mar. by J.
             P. Corron [J. T. Corron on Mins.
             List] who lived at White Sulphur
             Springs, VA (now W.VA.). Date of
             Lic.: 02-22-1853.

03-17-1853   Simon Hoylman and Frances Kendell
             [Kindell (on Mins. List)]. Mar. by

J. W. Kelley. Date of Lic.:
03-14-1853. Married on Ogles Creek,
VA.

03-23-1853   William M. Scott and Mary Jane Scott.
Mar. by A. S. Hogshead. Date of Lic:
03-23-1853.

04-05-1853   John N. Haynes and Malinda N. [T.
(on Mins. List)] Leighton. Mar. by
Dion C. Pharr. Date of Lic.:
03-30-1853.

Page 14

04-07-1853   John A. Bush and Jane K. Clark. Mar.
by John W. Kelly. Date of Lic.:
04-07-1853. Mar. in Covington, VA.

04-12-1853   George W. Hammond [Dr. George W.
Hammond on bride's father's consent]
and Emiline Scott. Mar. by A. S.
Hogshead. Date of Lic: 04-12-1853.
Consent of father, William Scott,
Wit. Robert M. Wiley and G. W. Hines
and Clk. acknowledged on 04-12-1853.

04-21-1853   William J. Lewis and Nancy E. Carson.
Mar. by A. S. Hogshead. Date of Lic:
04-20-1853.

05-05-1853   James Low and Sarah A. [Ann (on Mins.
List)] Black. Mar. by John W.
Kelley. Date of Lic: 04-20-1853.
Mar. at Skeen's Forge.

05-21-1853 (on book) 05-24-1853 (on Mins. List)
Wm. H. Dressler [William H. Dressler
(on Mins. List)] and Mary A. K. Hart
[Mary E. K. Hart (on Mins. List)].
Mar. by A. S. Hogshead. Date of Lic:
05-21-1853.

(Minister Returns - Continued)

07-12-1853   Martin E. Cosby and Alice [Allice (on Mins. List)] H. Jackson. Mar. by John W. Kelley, Mins. of M. E. Church, Cov., VA. Date of Lic.: 06-29-1853.

08-04-1853   Jacob A. Aritt and Diannah J. Sizer. Mar. by A. J. Elmore. Date of Lic.: 07-22-1853. Jacob was age 19 on his birthday on 06-09-1853 and a farmer. s/o: George and Elizabeth Aritt. His father was dead and his mother had mar. Moses G. Wright. He was born in Alleg. Co. A request for a Mar. Lic. to be issued was made by John Aritt, guardian of Jacob A. Aritt and Wit. by Mary M. Arritt and Michael Aritt on 07-22-1853. Diannah was age 17 on her birthday on 01-27-1853. dau/o: Fielding Sizer whose consent on 07-18-1853 was signed Fielding P. Sizer and Wit. by John S. Aritt and Michael Aritt. On the consent the groom was listed as Jacob Anderson Aritt and the bride as Diannah Jane Sizer. Fielding Sizer lived in Alleg. Co. Andrew Fudge, Clk.

09-08-1853   Cornelius B. Deeds and Sarah G.[Green (on Mins. List)] Carson. Mar. by J. W. Boteler who lived at Sweet Springs VA (now W.VA.). Date of Lic.: 09-05-1853. Cornelius was single and age 27. Sarah was single and age 19. Father's consent was signed James Carson and Wit. by Lee Persinger and H. D. Gilliland.

(No Mar. Date)
  Lemuel Brown and Margaret J. Wilcher. Mar. by (No Minister Name). Date of Lic.: 10-03-1853.

10-11-1853   Chapman J. Nida and Mary C. Myers.
Mar. by John W. Kelley. Date of Lic:
10-06-1853. Chapman was a farmer,
age 24 and single. Mary was single,
age 18, proven by oath of David Nida.
Both parties lived in Alleg. Co.
Consent of father, Henry Myers, Wit.
by David J. Nida and George W.
Tingler.

10-15-1853   Patrick Birn and Aurena [Arveney (on
father's consent)] Griffith. Mar. by
J. W. Boteler who lived on Dunlap
Creek. Date of Lic.: 10-07-1853.
Patrick was single, age 22, a labor-
er, and from Monroe Co., VA (now W.
VA). Aurena was single, age 21, and
lived in Alleg. Co., VA. Consent of
father, Wesley Griffith, Wit. by John
Sullivan.

10-13-1853   Harvey Humphries and Mary J. Quickel.
Mar. by Davis M. Wood who lived at
Pleasant Hill in Botetourt Co., VA.
Date of Lic: 10-09-1853. Harvey was
age 23 and Mary was age 19, proven
by oath of Joseph Ervin 10-09-1853.
Both parties were in moderate circum-
stances. Mar. at res. of Widow
Quickel in Rich Patch near Nichols
Knob. Consent of mother, J. Peggy
Quickel, on 10-08-1853 Wit. by John
Humphries, Joseph Ervin, and Mandy C.
Quickel. Rev. Wood was of the M. E.
Church.

11-10-1853   Thomas Gilbert and Sarah Griffith.
Mar. by J. W. Boteler. Date of Lic:
11-10-1853. Consent of father,
Wesley Griffith on 11-09-1853. Proven oath Wit. by Benjamin Griffith.

(Minister Returns - Continued)

(No Mar. Date)
        James A. Crowder and Amanda C.
        Armontrout. Mar. by (No Minister
        Name). Date of Lic: 12-15-1853.
        (See Mar. date 12-16-1853. Listed
        Twice.)

01-09-1854 (on book) 01-03-1854 (on Mins. List)
        John D. Sadler and Manda Jane
        Karnes [Amanda J. Karnes (on Mins.
        List)]. Mar. by A. S. Hogshead.
        Date of Lic.: 12-29-1853.

01-06-1854 Samuel W. Childs and Elizabeth N.
        Ellis. Mar. by Dion C. Pharr. Date
        of Lic.: 12-31-1853. [Mins. List
        Mar.: 01-04-1854]

01-06-1854 Richard G. Ellis and Mary Ann Childs.
        Mar. by Dion C. Pharr. Date of Lic:
        12-31-1853. [Mins. List Mar.:
        01-04-1854)

12-28-1853 John W. Terry and Louisa Griffith.
        Both of Alleg. Co. Mar. by J. W.
        Boteler. Date of Lic.: 12-24-1853.

12-21-1853 Wm. S. Gilliland [William S. Gilla-
        land (on Mins. List)] and Mary Jane
        Deeds. Mar. by Dion C. Pharr. Date
        of Lic.: 12-19-1853. Father's consent
        signed Wm. Deeds, Wit. Wm. H. Haynes,
        Jr., Anthony Harmon, and C. L. Haynes
        was dated 12-19-1853.

12-16-1853 James A. Crowder and Amanda C. Armon-
        trout. Mar. by Dion C. Pharr. Date
        of Lic: 12-15-1853. (Listed Twice-
        first without date) Father's consent
        has Mandy Catharine Armontrout as
        bride's name and signed by Abraham
        Armontrout, Wit. Joseph Armontrout,

(Minister Returns - Continued)

        Michael Aritt was dated 12-12-1853.

01-18-1854   Richard Fridley and Elizabeth Bennet.
        Mar. by Dion C. Pharr. Date of Lic.:
        01-16-1854.

02-14-1854   J. W. Boteler and Susan H. Printz.
        Mar. by Edward W. Waring. Date of
        Lic: 01-28-1854. Father's consent
        lists groom's name as Rev. J. Wesley
        Boteler and was signed by Susan's
        father, Cornelius Printz, on 01-18-
        1854. William Sawyers, D.C.'s state-
        ment of 01-28-1854 says George W.
        Matheney appeared before him and said
        that Susan H. Printz was 21 yrs. old.
        The following is taken from a note to
        Andrew Fudge, Esq., C.A.C. and states
        the license was dated 01-28-1854:
        "....Rev. John W. Boteler, aged 25,
        single, native of Washington, D. C.,
        son of John D. and Eliza Boteler, at
        present traveling Sweet Springs Cir-
        cuit of the Methodist E. Church, and
        by occupation a minister of said
        church, and Susan H. Printz, aged 23,
        single, a native of Bottetourt Co.,
        Va., and a resident of Alleghany Co.,
        daughter of Cornelius and Hester A.
        Printz, were united in the Holy State
        of Matrimony, at the home of Cornel-
        ius Printz, Alleghany Co., Va., on
        the 14th day of February 1854.
            Edwin H. Waring
            Minister of the Methodist E.
            Church
        Dunlap's Creek, Va., Feb. 14, 1854"

(No Mar. Date)

        Eli Putnam and Nancy Griffith. Mar.
        by (No Minister Name). Date of Lic.:
        02-(? 11)-1854. Father's consent

(Minister Returns - Continued)

dated 02-09-1854 was signed Orlando
Griffith, Wit. Joshua Griffith and
William H. Gilliland.

03-09-1854   George W. Tingler and Caroline Humphries. Mar. by A. S. Hogshead. Date
of Lic.: 03-06-1854.

03-23-1854   William Ballard and Parmelia Ellis.
Mar. by Dion C. Pharr. Date of Lic.:
03-18-1854.

(No Mar. Date)

Richard Kiefe and Margaret Carr.
Mar. by (No Minister Name). Date of
Lic.: 03-21-1854.
The following is the father's consent
statement:
"To the Clerk of the Covington Court
March the 20th, 1854
Sir Please let the bearer Richard
Reefe [?Keefe] and my daughter
Hannarah Carr have a marriage license
                    John Carr
Witness George Brown
         Richard Ruffe"
Andrew Fudge,Clk., statement follows:
"Proven by the oath of George Brown
as to the....unknown age of said John
Carr.   21 March 1854"
[Part of the above statement cannot
be made out to show it's true mean-
ing.]

(No Mar. Date)

Henry Myers and Sarah A. Nicely.
Mar. by (No Minister Name). Date of
Lic.: 04-17-1854.

04-26-1854   James Paxton and Nancy Oiler. Mar.
by Dion C. Pharr. Date of Lic.:
04-25-1854.

(Minister Returns - Continued)

05-04-1854   John Hepler [John Hepler, Jr., (on
              Mins. List)] and Margaret Wolf. Mar.
              by A. S. Hogshead. Date of Lic.:
              05-01-1854.

05-11-1854   George Jameson and Mary E. Wolf.
              Mar. by Dion C. Pharr. Date of Lic:
              05-06-1854. On the consent, groom's
              name George Jamison and was signed
              William H. Quickel, Teste by John
              Humphries. On 05-01-1854 consent of
              guardian of Mary E. Wolf given by
              John Aritt, Teste John Humphries.
              On 05-06-1854 proven oath of John
              Humphries given to Andrew Fudge, Clk.

05-23-1854   Francis Tyree and Martha M. Surber.
              Mar. by Dion C. Pharr. Date of Lic:
              05-17-1854. Father's consent given
              on 05-19-1854 was signed Levi Surber.

05-23-1854   Ferdinand H. Paul and Jane M. Hughes.
              Mar. by Dion C. Pharr. Date of Lic:
              05- ?3 - 1854 (page tore). [Jane R.
              Hughes (on Mins. List)]

(No Mar. Date)
              William Sorrel and Frances Ann
              Sorrel. Mar. by (No Minister Name).
              Date of Lic: 05-29-1854. [Listed
              Twice--See Part II, Mar. Date: 06-01-
              1854]

(No Mar. Date)
              Charles F. Hoy and Nancy W. Reynolds.
              Mar. by (No Minister Name). Date of
              Lic.: 05-29-1854. [Listed Twice -
              See Part II, Mar. Date: 05-30-1854]

05-31-1854   Manson L. Boley [Manson D. Boley (on
              Mins. List)] and Rebecca Boley. Mar.
              by D. C. Pharr. Date of Lic.: 05-30-
              1854.

(Minister Returns - Continued)

06-29-1854   Jacob M. Nicely and Margaret
              Leighton. Mar. by A. S. Hogshead.
              Date of Lic.: 06- ?9 - 1854 (Page
              tore - Lic. date not mentioned on
              Ret. List.)

(No Mar. Date)
              Andrew J. Keyser and Catharine Kean.
              Mar. by (No Minister Name). Date of
              Lic.:   07-17-1854. [? date error]
              [Listed Twice - See Part II, Mar.
              Date: None listed, but Mar. Lic.
              signed by minister on 02-26-1854]

(No Mar. Date)
              John A. Dickson and Margaret Keyser.
              Mar. by (No Minister Name). Date of
              Lic.:   07- (?) -1854 (page tore).
              [Listed Twice - See Part II, Mar.
              Date: 08-16-1854]

(No Mar. Date)
              Philip Johnson and Catharine E. Ray-
              hill. Mar. by (No Minister Name).
              Date of Lic.:   10- (?) -1854. [List-
              ed Twice - See Part II, Mar. Date:
              father acknowledged return certifi-
              cate on 10-18-1854 and consent on
              10-07-1854] [Page tore on Lic. date]

(No Mar. Date)
              John Crowly and Edney (? T.) Davis
              [Edna J. Davis (on Lic.)]. Mar. by
              (No Minister Name). Date of Lic.:
              12- (?) -1854 (page tore). [Listed
              Twice - See Part II, Mar. Date:
              12-30-1854]

(No Mar. Date)
              Christian Roadcap and Elizabeth
              Williamson. Mar. by (No Minister
              Name). Date of Lic: 08-08-1855.
              [Listed Twice - See Part II, 01-19-

(Minister Returns - Continued)

1855]

09-30-1854   George Sively [George L. Sively (on
             Mins. List)] and Mary C. Sively.
             Mar. by A. S. Hogshead. Date of Lic:
             08- (?) -1854 (page tore). [Mar.
             Date on Mins. List: 08-30-1854.]

             Page 15

(No Mar. Date)
             Richard H. Wilcher and Mary A. Oiler.
             Mar. by (No Minister Name). Date of
             Lic.: 01-09-1855. [Listed Twice -
             See Part II, Mar. Date: 01-09-1855]

The following are additions to Part I:

Page 5
11-09-1831   Alexander Simpson and Sarah Foster.
             Mar. by Davis Kinninson.

[Minister's Note to Clk. of Court - Could not
find on Marriage Return Book]
"This is to certify that on the 15th day of April
1847. I celebrated the rites of matrimony between Mr. Moses Smith & Miss Sarah M. Dew by authority of a license from the hand of Mr. A. Fudge,
Clerk of Alleghany County, Va.
                         John L. Gilbert"

[The following father's consent was also found,
but I could not find any other records on it.]
                    "Alleghany Co., Va.
             Dec. 19th 1849 [? 1847]
I hereby signify my willingness for Bob Watson to
marry my daughter Sophia Wright & request that
license be given him.
                         John Wright
Teste
    J. F. Hughes"

- 40 -

Marriage
Date
                          Page 1

05-30-1854 Charles F. Hoy, 55, widower, B: New
  # 1   Market, Shenandoah Co., VA, Occup:
            Tending a ferry and farming, s/o:
            Zachariah Hoy (on book) [Zachariah
            and Elizabeth Hoy (on Lic.)]; and
            Nancy W. Reynolds, 25, single, B:
            Rich Patch, Alleg. Co., VA, dau/o:
            Dioclesian Reynolds (on book) [Dio-
            clesian and Polly Reynolds (on Lic)].
            Both parties lived in Alleg. Co. PL:
            Dioclesian Reynold's res., Alleg. Co.
            (on Lic.). Mar. by Davis M. Wood,
            Deacon of M. E. Church with Lic. to
            marry. Oath was made by James Reyn-
            olds that Nancy was over 21 yrs. of
            age, Teste William Sawyers, D.C. on
            05-29-1854.

12-15-1854 James Sulivan (on book) [James Sulli-
  # 2   van (on Lic.), 30 (on book) [about
            30 (on Lic.)], widower, B: Ireland,
            s/o: Patrick Sulivan (on bk) [Pat-
            rick Sulivan and Mary Shea (on Lic)],
            Occup: Public Mails (on bk) [Public
            Works (on Lic.)]; and Mary Sulivan
            (on bk) [Mary Shea (on Lic.)], 40 (on
            bk) [about 40 (on Lic.)], widow, B:
            Ireland, dau/o: Cornelius Sulivan (on
            bk) [Cornelius Sulivan and Margaret
            Shea (on Lic.)]. It was not listed
            where either party lived. PL: Monroe
            Co., VA (now W. VA.). Mar. by J. W.
            (? or H) Walters, Catholic Priest,
            signed Lic. on 12-15-1854.

12-24-1854   (on bk)   12-26-1854 (on Lic.)
   # 3   Lewis Baker, 23, single, B: Monroe
             Co., VA (now W. VA.), Occup: farmer,
             s/o: Jacob and Mary Baker; and Cath.
             M. Worsham (on bk) [Cathrine matilda
             Worsham (on Lic.)], 18 yrs. 12 days,
             single, B: Monroe Co., VA (now W.VA),
             dau/o: Daniel and E. Worsham (on bk)
             [Daniel and Emmaline Worsham (on
             Lic.)]. Both parties lived in Alleg.
             Co. Mar. by J. Wesley Boteler, M. E.
             Church, signed Lic. on 01-05-1855.
             PL: Alleg. Co., VA, Daniel Worsham's
             res. (on Lic.). Consent dated 12-15-
             1854 and signed by father, Daniel
             Worsham, has daughter's name spelled
             Catharine, and was Wit. by C. Alan
             M. Peters. Proven oath that Daniel
             Worsham signed the consent was made
             by Allen M. Peters on 12-15-1854,
             Teste A. Fudge, Clk.

10-12-1854   Philip Johnson (on bk) [Phillip
   # 4   Johnson (on consent)], 21, single,
             B: Alleg. Co., VA, Occup: farmer,
             s/o: Bernard and Ann Johnson; and
             Catharine E. Rayhill, 17, single, B:
             Alleg. Co., VA, dau/o: Alexander and
             E. Rayhill. Both parties lived in
             Alleg. Co. Mar. by A. S. Hogshead.
             PL: Alleg. Co., VA. Consent dated
             10-07-1854 and signed by father, A.
             Rayhill, Teste Thomas T. Plymale and
             Cherpman J. Nida. "Alleghany County
             Court Clerk's Office, 10-18-1854:
             Thomas J. Plymale made oath that
             Alexander Rayhill acknowledged the
             return certificate to be an act and
             deed. Teste William Sawyers, D.C."

10-31-1854   George C. Brown, 26, single, B: Cum-
   # 5   berland Co., VA, Occup: carpenter,

s/o: Charles and Mary Brown (on bk)
[Chesley and Mary Brown (on Lic.)];
and <u>Mary A. Byrd</u>, 18, single, B.:
Botetourt Co., VA, dau/o: Allen M.
and Margaret B. Byrd. Both parties
lived in Alleg. Co. Mar. by A. S.
Hogshead, signed Lic. on 10-31-1854.
PL: Allen M. Byrd's res., McClintic's
Mill, Bath Co., VA. (on Lic.).

11-16-1854   <u>John Tyree</u>, 27, single, B: Bath Co.,
  # 6   VA, Occup: blacksmith, s/o: John R.
and Nancy Tyree: and <u>Eliza J. Surber</u>
(on bk) [<u>Eliza Jane Surber</u> (on Lic)],
22, single, B: Bath Co., VA, dau/o:
Levi and Sally Surber. Both lived in
Alleg. Co. Mar. by A. S. Hogshead,
signed Lic. on 11-16-1854. PL:
Alleg. Co., VA, George Master's Tavern (on Lic.).

06-01-1854   <u>William Sorrel</u>, 24, single, B: Bote-
  # 7   tourt Co., VA, Occup: colier, (on
parents listed on bk) [Thomas and
Mary Sorrel (on Lic.)]; and <u>Frances
A. Sorrel</u> (on bk) [<u>Frances Ann Sor-
rel</u> (on Lic.)], 19, single, B: Botetourt Co., VA, (no parents listed).
Both lived in Alleg. Co. Mar. by T.
F. McClure, M. E. Church, signed Lic.
on 02-26-1855. PL: Jordan's Furnace,
Alleg. Co., VA (on Lic.).

08-16-1854   <u>Jno. A. Dickson</u> (on bk) [<u>John A.
Dickson</u> (on Lic.)], 29 [born on 02-
09-1826 (on Lic.)], single, B: Rockbridge Co., VA, Occup: carpenter,
s/o: Thos. and Sally Dickson (on bk)
[Thomas and Sally Dixon (on Lic.)];
and <u>Margaret Keyser</u>, 25, single, B:
Alleg. Co., VA, dau/o: Fleming and
N. Keyser (on bk) [Fleming and Nancy

(Mar. Register Book (1) - Continued)

Keyser (on Lic.)]. Both lived in
Alleg. Co. Mar. by T. F. McClure,
M. E. Church, signed Lic. on 08-17-
1854. PL: Fleming Keyser's res. on
Jackson River, Alleg. Co. (on Lic.).

(No Mar. Date)
9   Andr. J. Keyser (on bk) [Andrew T.
Keyser (on Lic.)], 21, single, B:
Alleg. Co., VA, s/o: Fleming and
Nancy Keyser, Occup: carpenter; and
Cath. A. Kean (on bk) [Catharine A.
Kean (on Lic.)], 17 (on bk) [age 14
(on Lic.)], single, B: Alleg. Co.,
VA, dau/o: Saml. and Rebecca Kean
(on bk) [Samuel and Rebecca Kean (on
Lic.)]. Both lived in Alleg. Co.
Mar. by T. F. McClure, M. E. Church,
signed Lic. on 02-26-1854. PL: Sam-
uel Kean's res. on Dunlap Creek,
Alleg. Co., VA. (on Lic.).

02-01-1855 [date on bk is date listed where
10   groom and minister signed Lic.; ? BK
date could be date Lic. obtained or
date of planned mar. may have been
moved up]
02-26-1855 (date of mar. on Lic.)
Logan S. Humphries, 24, single, B:
Alleg. Co., VA, Occup: farmer, s/o:
Jesse and Eunice Humphries; and
Sarah E. Matheney, 16, single, B:
Botetourt Co., VA, dau/o:_____
and Ann Matheney. Both lived in
Alleg. Co. Mar. by T. F. McClure,
M. E. Church. PL: Rich Patch, Alleg.
Co., VA (on Lic.). Consent dated on
01-29-1855 signed by father, Samuel
Matheney, Teste Madison Hook.

02-08-1855 Saml. Anderson, 21, single, B: Augus-
11   ta Co., VA, Occup: farmer, s/o: ____

- 44 -

and Arabella Anderson; and <u>Mary F. Handley</u>, 21 (on bk) [nearly 21 (on Lic.)], single, B: Bath Co., VA, dau/o: Mary Mason. Both lived in Alleg. Co. Mar. by T. F. McClure, M. E. Church. PL: Jackson River, Alleg. Co., VA (on Lic.).

03-13-1855
12

<u>Daniel Griffin</u>, 25, single, B: Ireland, Occup: farmer, s/o: Andrew Griffin and Margaret O'Conner; and (<u>no name listed</u>), 19, single, B: Ireland, dau/o: Morris Relihan and Margaret O'Conner. Both lived in Alleg. Co. Mar. by J. H. Walters, Catholic Priest. PL: Sweet Springs, Alleg. Co., VA [Note: Sweet Springs is now in Monroe Co., W.VA. just over the VA state line.]

03-22-1855
13

<u>Charles S. Karnes</u>, 21, single, B: Alleg. Co., VA, Occup: farmer, s/o: Jacob and Sarah (on bk) [Jacob (deceased) and Sarah Karnes (on Lic.)]; and <u>Nancy B. Andress</u>, 19, single, B: Alleg. Co., VA, dau/o: William and Elizabeth (on bk) [William and Elizabeth Andress (on Lic.)]. Mar. by S. P. Huff, Baptist. Both lived in Alleg. Co. PL: Wm. Andrey's res., Alleg. Co., VA (on Lic.).

04-19-1855
14

<u>Isaac P. Damron</u>, 39 yrs. 10 mos. 4 days, single, B: Dunlap Creek, Alleg. Co., VA, s/o: Joseph Damron and Rebecca Neel, Occup: Mechanic and Cabinet V.C.; and <u>Margaret Bennet</u>, 18 yrs. 5 mos., single, B: Rich Patch, Alleg. Co., VA, dau/o: Sampson Bennet and Phebe King (on bk) [Sampson Bennet and Phebe Fridley (on Lic.)]. Both lived in Alleg. Co. Mar. by C.

C. Cronin, M. E. Church. PL: David
Byers res. on Potts Creek, Alleg. Co.
Consent dated 04-14-1855 signed by
father, Sampson Bennet, Wit. Michael
Aritt and Nelson Fridley.

04-25-1855   Harrison Hanoly (on bk) [Harrison
  # 15   Handly (on Lic.)], 30, single, B:
             Greenbrier Co., VA (now W.VA), Occup:
             farmer, s/o: John and Elizabeth Han-
             oly (on bk) [John Handly and Eliza-
             beth Shanklin (on Lic.)]; and Susan
             M. Mann, 25, single, B: Alleg. Co.,
             VA, dau/o: Moses H. and Alice Mann
             (on bk) [Moses H. Mann and Alice Mc-
             Clintic (on Lic.)]. Mar. by C. C.
             Cronin, M. E. Church. PL: Moses H.
             Mann's res., Alleg. Co. Both lived
             in Alleg. Co. Consent dated 04-25-
             1855, signed by Moses H. Mann, no
             witnesses listed, was sent to Andrew
             Fudge, Clk.

06-14-1855   George Carson, 52, widower, B: Snake
  # 16   Run, Alleg. Co., VA, Occup: farmer,
             s/o: Jno. [John and Nancy Carson (on
             Lic.)]; and Margaret Hunter, 23,
             single, B: Greenbrier Co., VA (now W.
             VA), dau/o: Matthew and E. Hunter (on
             bk) [Matthew and Elizabeth Hunter (on
             Lic.)]. Mar. by C. C. Cronin, M. E.
             Church. PL: Snake Run, Alleg. Co.,
             VA (on Lic.). "Greenbrier County to
             wit Virginia: This day George White
             of the aforesaid county personally
             appeared before me a justice of the
             peace in said county and made oath
             that Margaret Hunter of Alleghany
             County is twenty-one years of age.
             Given under my hand this 10th Day of
             April 1855. David Surber, J.P."
             Both lived in Alleg. Co.

(Mar. Register Book (1) - Continued)

08-23-1855   Andrew J. Bennet (on bk) [Andrew J.
17   Bennit (on Lic.)], 19, single, B:
              Rich Patch near Stephen's Hook, Alleg.
              Co., VA (on Lic.), Occup: farmer,
              s/O: William and Sarah Bennet (on
              bk) [William and Sarah C. Bennit (on
              Lic.)]; and Margaret Fridley (on bk)
              [Margaret Fridly (on Lic.)], 14 (on
              bk) [14 last January (on Lic.)],
              single, B: Rich Patch near Kimberlin's
              Mill, Alleg. Co., VA, dau/o: Gideon
              and Ruth Fridley (on bk) [Gideon and
              Ruth Fridly (on Lic.)]. Both lived
              in Alleg. Co. Mar. by Davis M. Wood,
              Local Deacon of M. E. Church with Lic.
              to marry. PL: John King's farm near
              Kimberlin's Mill, Alleg. Co., VA (on
              Lic.).

10-17-1855   Madison Kelley (on bk) [Madison Kelly
18   (on Lic.)], 31, single, B: Botetourt
              Co., VA, Occup: common laborer, s/o:
              John and Catharine Kelly; and Hanna-
              bell C. King (on bk) [Hannah M. Cath-
              arine King (on Lic.)], 19, single, B:
              Alleg. Co., VA, dau/o: Ruth King (on
              bk) [Rutha King (on Lic.)]. Both
              lived in Alleg. Co. Mar. by Abraham
              Buhrman, mins. of gospel. PL: John
              King res., Alleg. Co., VA. "To the
              Clerk of Alleghany County Court, Dear
              Sir: You are hereby authorized to
              issue a marriage License to Madison
              Kelly of Botetourt County to marry my
              Daughter, Hannah M. Katharine King
              and by so doing this shall be your
              sufficient authority. Given under my
              hand this 2nd day of October 1855.
                      Ruthy (her X mark) King
              Wit. Gideon (his X mark) Fridly"
              "Proven by the oath of Gideon Fridly
              15 Oct. 1855. A. Fudge, Clk."

10-04-1855   James A. Keyser, 26, single, Occup:
19   farmer, B: Alleg. Co., VA, s/o: James
             and Lucinda Keyser; and Lucy Thomp-
             son, 19, single, B: Bath Co., VA,
             dau/o: Abner and Sarah Thompson.
             Both lived in Alleg. Co. Mar. by C.
             C. Cronin, M. E. Church. PL: Alleg.
             Co., VA.

02-26-1855   Robert A. Pleasants, 23, single, B:
20   Rockbridge Co., VA, Occup: black-
             smith, s/o: Thomas and Susan Pleas-
             ants: and Martha Matheney, 21,
             single, B: Alleg. Co., VA, dau/o:
             Saml. and Nancy Matheney (on bk)
             [Samuel and Nancy Matheney (on Lic.)].
             Both lived in Alleg. Co. Mar. by A.
             S. Hogshead, mins. of gospel. PL:
             Cowpasture Bridge, Alleg. Co., VA (on
             Lic.). Consent has Martha Matheny
             and was signed by Thomas (? T. or M.)
             Pleasants, Teste Thomas J. Pleasants
             and Lorenzo D. Matheney.

09-20-1855   Nelson J. Gilbert (on bk) [Andrew J.
21   Gilbert (on Lic.)], 24, single, B:
             Botetourt Co., VA, Occup: farmer,
             s/o: David and Alice Gilbert; and
             Mary A. Helmantoller (on bk) [Mary
             Ann Helmantoller (on Lic.)], 16,
             single, B: Alleg. Co., VA, dau/o:
             Peter and Mary Helmantoller. Both
             lived in Alleg. Co. Mar. by A. S.
             Hogshead. PL: Peter Helmantoller's
             res., Alleg. Co., VA (on Lic.).
             "THE COMMONWEALTH OF VIRGINIA
             To any minister of the gospel, or
             other person, legally authorized to
             celebrate the rites of matrimony in
             this county.
                 Alleghany County Clerk's
                 Office, 19 Septr. 1855.

These are to Authorize you to Celebrate the Rites of Matrimony, according to the Forms and Ceremonies of
your Church, between
    [Andrew J. Gilbert & Mary Ann
    Helmantoller]
        OF ALLEGHANY COUNTY:
And for your so doing this shall be
your Authority. Given under my hand
the Day and Year aforesaid.
        [Andr. Fudge   ] Clk."
[Note: This was an unusual document
and the only one that was found like
it in the files. Form was printed by
Crane and Wheeler, Lewisburg, VA (now
W.VA.).]

09-02-1855 (on bk) 08-02-1855 (on Lic.)
22   Matthew L. Purdell (on bk) [Mathew L.
            Pendell (on Lic.)], 28 (on bk) [29
            (on Lic.)], widower, B: Rockbridge
            Co., VA, Occup: Miller, s/o: Mary A.
            Purdell (on bk) [Mary A. Pendell (on
            Lic.)]; and Millerd R. Lemon (on bk)
            [Mildred R. Lemon (on Lic.)], 28
            widow, B: Alleg. Co., VA, dau/o: Wm.
            H. Haynes. Both lived in Alleg. Co.
            Mar. by A. S. Hogshead. PL: Alleg.
            Co., VA, Wm. B. Sprowl's Tavern (on
            Lic.).

01-09-1855 Richard H. Wilcher, 23, single, B:
23   Rockbridge Co., VA, Occup: laborer,
            s/o: Richard and Jane Wilcher; and
            Mary A. Oiler, 23, single, B: Bote-
            tourt Co., VA, dau/o: Wm. and Eliza-
            beth Oiler (on bk) [William and Eliz-
            abeth Oiler (on Lic.)]. Both lived
            in Alleg. Co. Mar. by A. S. Hogshead.
            PL: Covington, VA.

01-19-1855 (on bk) 01-18-1855 (on Lic.)
24   Christian Roadcap, 27, single, Occup:

(Mar. Register Book (1) - Continued)

farmer, B: Rockbridge Co., VA, s/o:
Christian and Elizabeth Roadcap; and
Elizabeth Williamson, 23, single, B:
Scotland, dau/o: Andr. and Jane Will-
iamson (on bk) [Andrew and Jane Will-
iamson (on Lic.)]. Both lived in
Alleg. Co. Mar. by A. S. Hogshead.
PL: Alleg. Co., VA, Andrew Williamson
res. (on Lic.).

01-25-1855   Michael Downey, 21, single, Occup:
 # 25   colier, B: Alleg. Co., VA, s/o: Arch-
             ibald and Eliz. Downey (on bk) [Arch-
             obold and Elizabeth Downey (on Lic)];
             and Martha Craft, 20, single, B: Al-
             leg. Co., VA, dau/o: James and Sofa
             Craft. Both lived in Alleg. Co.
             Mar. by A. S. Hogshead. PL: Alleg.
             Co., VA, near Cowpasture Bridge (on
             Lic.). Consent dated 01-23-1855 was
             signed James (his X mark) Craft, Wit.
             Thomas M. Pleasants and Robert (his X
             mark) Downey. Proven oath of Robert
             Downey as to acknowledgement of the
             written named James Craft, Teste
             Andr. Fudge, Clk. on 01-24-1855.

02-21-1855   Wm. McCalfin (on bk) [William McCal-
 # 26   pin (on Lic.)], 26, single, B: Rock-
             bridge Co., VA, Occup: Farmer, s/o:
             Jos. and Catharine McCalfin (on bk)
             [Joseph and Catharine McCalpin (on
             Lic.)]; and Agness G. Ogdon, 19,
             single, B: Amherst Co., VA, dau/o:
             Allen and Lucinda Ogdon. Both lived
             in Alleg. Co. Mar. by A. S. Hogshead.
             PL: Alleg. Co., VA, Mr. McDaniel's in
             White Rock Gap (on Lic.).

03-22-1855   David Huddleston, 21, single, Occup:
 # 27   farmer, B: Alleg. Co., VA, s/o: Abra-
             ham J. and Leah Huddleston (on bk)

(Mar. Register Book (1) - Continued)

[Abraham and Leah Huddleston (on
Lic.)]; and <u>Agness Hook</u>, 21, single,
B: Alleg. Co., VA, dau/o: Elias and
Nancy Hook. Mar. by A. S. Hogshead.
PL: Alleg. Co., VA, Gordon Helmantol-
er's res. (on Lic.). Both lived in
Alleg. Co.

04-05-1855 <u>James A. Honnon</u>, 28, single, Occup:
  # 28   farmer, B: Alleg. Co., VA, s/o: Elizabeth Hannon; and <u>Elizabeth Lewis</u>,
22, single, B: Alleg. Co., VA, dau/o:
John and Elizabeth Lewis. Both lived
in Alleg. Co. Mar. by A. S. Hogshead.
PL: Covington, VA.

07-12-1855 <u>Thomas Carter</u>, 23, single, Occup:
  # 29   farmer, B: Monroe Co., VA (now W.VA),
s/o: Lemuel and _____ Carter; and
<u>Grandville E. Aritt</u> (on bk) [<u>Gran-
ville E. Aritt</u> (on Lic.), 20, B:
Alleg. Co., VA, single, dau/o: Jno.
and Elizabeth Aritt (on bk) [John and
Elizabeth Aritt (on Lic.)]. PL: Alleg. Co., VA, John Aritt's at Boiling
Springs, VA, (on Lic.). Mar. by A.
S. Hogshead. Both lived in Alleg.
Co. Consent dated 07-11-1855 was
signed by John Aritt, Teste Gerard
Carter and Hary H. Arritt. Proven
oath of Gerard Carter as witness to
acknowledgement of John Aritt, 07-11-
1855, Andr. Fudge, Clk.

11-15-1855 <u>Lenford Bachlet</u> (on bk) [<u>Linford
  # 30   Bachtel</u> (on Lic.)], 32, single, B:
Chester Po Co., VA (on bk) [Chester
Co., Penn. (on Lic.)], Occup: Dealer
in copperware, s/o: Saml. and Eliz.
Bachtel; and <u>Martha J. Armontrout</u>,
37, single, B: Alleg. Co., VA, dau/o:
Geo. and Cath. Armontrout (on bk)

[Geo. and Catharane Armontrout (on Lic.)]. Both lived in Alleg. Co. PL: Smith Armontrout's res., Alleg. Co., VA. Mar. by A. S. Hogshead.

12-20-1855   John Carter (on bk) [Jarred Carter
31   (on Lic.)], 31, single, Occup: farm-
              er, B: Halifax Co., VA, s/o: Lemuel
              and Martha Carter; and Mary M. Aritt,
              24, single, B: Alleg. Co., VA, dau/o:
              John and Eliz. Aritt (on bk) [John
              and Elizabeth Aritt (on Lic.)]. PL:
              John Aritt res., Alleg. Co., VA. (on
              Lic.). Mar. by A. S. Hogshead. Both
              lived in Alleg. Co. Consent dated
              12-17-1855 signed by John Aritt,
              Teste Thomas Carter and Grandville
              Carter. Proven oath of Thomas Carter
              as to acknowledgement of John Aritt,
              12-17-1855, A. Fudge, Clk.

12-20-1855   Paul Gleason, 23, single, B: Nelson
32   Co., VA, Occup: stone mason, s/o:
              Michael and Nancy Gleason; and Selina
              Gilliland (on bk) [Selena E. Gilli-
              land (on Lic.)], 23 single, B: Alleg.
              Co., VA, dau/o: Agness Gilliland (on
              bk) [Egness Gilliland (on Lic.)].
              Both lived in Alleg. Co. Mar. by A.
              S. Hogshead. PL: Haynes res., Alleg.
              Co., VA. "Clerk's Office of Alleghany
              Co., 12-18-1855: Charles Haynes made
              oath that Selena E. Gilliland's over
              age 21 & wants lic. to marry Paul
              Gleason. Isaac Green, Deputy Clk."

12-30-1855   (on bk) 12-30-1854 (on Lic.)
33   John Crowley (on bk) [John Crowly (on
              Lic.)], 24, single, B: Ireland, Oc-
              cup: laborer, s/o: Wm. and Ellen Crow-
              ley (on bk) [William and Ellen Crowly
              (on Lic.)]; and Edney Davis (on bk)

(Mar. Register Book (1) - Continued)

[Edna J. Davis (on Lic.)], 36, single, B: Halifax Co., VA, dau/o: Jas. and Nancy Davis (on bk) [James and Nancy Davis (on Lic.)]. Mar. by A.S. Hogshead. PL: Covington, VA. Both lived in Alleg. Co. Lic. was signed by minister on 12-30-1854.

12-19-1855 William A. Carter, 27, single, B:
34   Botetourt Co., VA, Occup: farmer, s/o: Jno. and Lucy Carter (on bk) [John L. and Lucy Carter (on Lic.)]; and Ann E. Bridget (on bk) [Ann E. Bridget (on Lic.)], 23, single, B: Bath Co., VA, dau/o: Geo. and Phebe Bridgeet (on bk) [George and Phebe Bridgeet (on Lic.)]. Mar. by C. C. Cronin, M. E. Church. PL: Alleg. Co. Both lived in Alleg. Co., VA.

01-08-1856 Henry J. Carter and Elizabeth R.
35   Jones married in Alleg. Co., VA. She is the dau/o. Josiah C. Jones. Consent dated 01-08-1856 was signed by Josiah C. Jones, Wit. Henry Jones. There was no other information on this.

Page 2

01-03-1856 (on Lic.) [Book date is smudged like
1   it was changed from 01-06 or 26-1856 and looks like 01-36-1856] Jacob Grose, 33, single, Occup: farmer, B: Bath Co., VA, s/o: Jacob and Chris Grose (on bk) [Jacob and Christeana Grose (on Lic.)]; and Sidney Fry, 23, single, B: Augusta Co., VA, dau/o: Jno. and Mary Fry (on bk) [John and Mary Fry (on Lic.)]. Mar. by C. C. Cronin, M. E. Church. PL: Jacob Grose, Jr., res., Alleg. Co., VA (on Lic.). Both lived in Alleg. Co.

- 53 -

01-26-1856 Wm. B. Black (on bk) [William B.
2   Black (on Lic.)], 50, widower, Occup:
            farmer, B: Brunswick Co., VA, s/o:
            Jno. and Rebecca Black (on bk) [John
            and Rebecca Black (on Lic.)]; and
            Nancy Porter, 28, single, B: Botet-
            tourt Co., VA, dau/o: Wm. and Mary
            Porter (on bk) [William and Mary
            Porter (on Lic.)]. Both lived in
            Rockbridge Co., VA. Mar. by C. C.
            Cronin. PL: Alleg. Co., VA. Oath
            given on 01-27-1856 by Ezekial Porter
            that Nancy was over 21 yrs. old,
            Isaac Skeen, D.C.

02-02-1856 (on bk) 02-21-1856 (on Lic.)
3   Archibald H. Smith, 22, single, Oc-
            cup: farmer, B: Alleg. Co., VA, s/o:
            Thos. and Elizabeth Smith (on bk)
            [Thomas E. and Elizabeth Smith (on
            Lic.)]; and Rebecca A. Hepler (on bk)
            [Rebecca Ann Hepler (on Lic.)], 26,
            single, B: Alleg. Co., VA, dau/o:
            David and Betshe Hepler (on bk)
            [David and Bathsheba Hepler (on Lic)].
            PL: Alleg. Co., VA. Both lived in
            Alleg. Co. Mar. by C. C. Cronin, M.
            E. Church, signed Lic. 02-21-1856.

02-14-1856 James S. Bush, 21, single, Occup:
4   farmer, B: Greenbrier Co., VA (now
            W. VA.), s/o: Nimrod and Sarah Bush;
            and Susan Hepler, 22, single, B:
            Alleg. Co., VA, dau/o: David and
            Absha Hepler (on bk) [David and
            Abasha Hepler (on Lic.)]. Both lived
            in Alleg. Co. Mar. by C. C. Cronin.
            PL: Alleg. Co., VA. Oath given by
            John A. Hepler that Susan over 21 and
            wants Lic. to marry, 02-07-1856,
            Isaac Skeen, D.C.

(Mar. Register Book (1) - Continued)

07-03-1856 James Brooks, 30, single, Occup:
5   Doctor, B: Mason Co., VA. (now W.VA),
            Lived: Mason Co., VA. (now W.VA.),
            s/o: Lawson and Cath. Brooks (on bk)
            [Lawson and Catharine Brooks (on
            Lic.)]; and Emma Stuart (on bk) [Emma
            Stewart (on Lic.)], 26, single, B:
            Shenandoah Co., VA, Lived: Alleg. Co,
            VA, dau/o: Fielding and Leah Stuart
            (on bk) [Fielding and Leah Stewart
            (on Lic.)]. Mar. by C. C. Cronin.
            PL: Covington, VA.

06-19-1856 Joseph Terry (on bk) [Joseph Tery (on
6   Lic.)], 33, widower, Occup: farmer,
            B: Alleg. Co., VA, s/o: Wm. and Eliza
            Terry (on bk) [William and Eliza Tery
            (on Lic.)]; and Harriet S. Hepler,
            18, single, B: Alleg. Co., VA, dau/o:
            Jno. and Sarah Hepler (on bk) [John
            and Sarah Hepler (on Lic.)]. Both
            lived in Alleg. Co. Mar. by C. C.
            Cronin. PL: Alleg. Co., VA.

07-02-1856 Michael Armentrout, 20, single, B:
7   Alleg. Co., VA, Occup: farmer, s/o:
            Jacob and Cath. Armontrout (on bk)
            [Jacob and Catharine Armontrout (on
            Lic.)]; and Elizabeth Wolf, 23, sing-
            le, B: Alleg. Co., VA, dau/o: Isaac
            and Martha Wolf. Both lived in Alleg.
            Co. Mar. by C. C. Cronin, M. E.
            Church. PL: Rich Patch, Alleg. Co.,
            VA. (on Lic.). Consent dated 07-01-
            1856 signed by Jacob Armontrout,
            Teste David Byer and Michael Aritt.
            Proven oath of Michael Aritt as to
            acknowledgement of Jacob Armontrout
            to consent, Andr. Fudge, Clk.

04-01-1856 Wm. P. Bowyer (on bk) [William Patton
8   Bowyer (on Lic.)], 24 yrs. 2 mos. 26

days, single, Occup: carpenter, B:
Botetourt Co., VA, Lived: Monroe Co.,
VA (now W.VA.), s/o: Jno. and Eliza-
beth Bowyer (on bk) [John and Eliza-
beth Bowyer (on Lic.)]; and Mary J.
Blaker (on bk) [Mary Jane Blaker (on
Lic.)], 19 yrs. 10 mos. 23 days,
single, B: Monroe Co., VA (now W.VA),
Lived: Alleg. Co., VA, dau/o: James
and Ailcy Blaker. Mar. by J. Wesley
Boteler, M. E. Church. PL: James
Blaker res., Alleg. Co., VA (on Lic).

09-06-1855   James Law, 23, single, Occup: farmer,
 # 9   B: England, Lived: __, s/o: Aaron and
             Elizabeth Law: and Mary Sprouse (on
             bk) [Mary Spouce (on Lic.)], 18,
             single, B: Albermarle Co., VA, dau/o:
             Jefferson and Susan Sprouse (on bk)
             [Jefferson and Susan Spouce (on Lic)].
             Mar. by C. C. Cronin, M. E. Church.
             PL: Alleg. Co., VA. It was not
             listed where Mary lived.

08-22-1855   Albert Pitzer (on bk) [Albert B.
 # 10   Pitzer (on Lic.)], 32, widower, B:
             Alleg. Co., VA, Occup: farmer, Lived:
             __, S/o: Bernard and Jane Pitzer;
             and Catharine Boswell, 34, single, B:
             Covington, Alleg. Co., VA, Lived: __,
             dau/o: John L. and Martha Boswell (on
             bk) [John Lee and Martha H. Boswell
             (on Lic.)]. Mar. by C. C. Cronin, M.
             E. Church. PL: Covington, VA.

08-07-1856   Aron Clark (on bk) [Aaron Clarke (on
 # 11   Lic.)], 27, single, B: Alleg. Co.,VA,
             Occup: blacksmith, s/o: Joseph and
             Christeana Clark (on bk) [Joseph and
             Christeana Clarke (on Lic.)]; and
             Clementine Kemper, 21, single, B:
             Botetourt Co., VA, dau/o: Geo. and

Eliza Kemper. Mar. by C. C. Cronin, M. E. Church. Both lived in Covington, Alleg. Co., VA. PL: Covington, VA.

08-19-1856   Marshal B. Brown, 26, single, Occup:
12   farmer, B: Stafford Co., VA, s/o:
             Wm. and Lucinda Brown: and Elizabeth
             C. Lowman, 21, single, B: Augusta
             Co., VA, dau/o: Sam'l. and Lydia
             Lowman. Mar. by C. C. Cronin. Both
             lived in Covington, VA. PL: Coving-
             ton, Alleg. Co., VA.

07-31-1856   Thos. J. Plymale (on bk) [Thomas J.
13   Plymale (on Lic.)], 22, single, B:
             Botetourt Co., VA, Occup: farmer,
             s/o: Wm. B. and Elizabeth Plymale;
             and Sarah Huddleston (on bk) [Sarah
             Huddleson (on Lic.)], 20, single, B:
             Alleg. Co., VA, dau/o: Abraham and
             Leah Huddleston (on bk) [Abraham and
             Leah Huddleson (on Lic.)]. Both
             lived in Alleg. Co. Mar. by C. C.
             Cronin. PL: Alleg. Co., VA.

09-12-1856   Jacob Amick, 28, single, B: Nicholas
14   Co., VA (now W.VA.), Occup: farmer,
             Lived: Nicholas Co., VA (now W.VA.),
             s/o: Jacob and Rachael Amick; and
             Henrietta Boley, 18, single, B: Mon-
             roe Co., VA (now W.VA.), Lived: Al-
             leg. Co., VA, dau/o: Bluford and Mary
             Boley. Mar. by C. C. Cronin. PL:
             Alleg. Co., VA.

09-02-1856   Joseph Boswell, 24, single, Occup:
15   farmer, B: Alleg. Co., VA, Lived:__,
             s/o: Jno. and Martha Boswell (on bk)
             [John and Martha Boswell (on Lic.)];
             and Jennette Stuart (on bk) [Jenett
             Stewart (on Lic.)], 18, single, B:

(Mar. Register Book (1) - Continued)

Roanoke, VA, Lived: ___, dau/o:
Fielding and Leah Stuart (on bk)
[Fielding and Leah Stewart (on Lic)].
Mar. by C. C. Cronin. PL: Covington,
Alleg. Co., VA.

09-23-1856   Wm. F. Gray, 25, single, B; Bote-
 # 16   tourt Co., VA, Occup: Boatman, Lived:
             Botetourt Co., VA, s/o: Geo. and
             Eliz. Gray (on bk) [George and Eliza-
             beth Gray (on Lic.)]; and Sarah A. V.
             Bacon, 21, single, B: Richmond, VA,
             Lived: Covington, Alleg. Co., VA,
             dau/o: Sam'l. and Cath. Bacon (on bk)
             [Sam'l. and Catharine Bacon (on
             Lic.)]. Mar. by C. C. Cronin, M. E.
             Church. PL: Covington, Alleg. Co.,
             VA.

08-21-1856   Jos. A. Thomas (on bk) [Joseph Arthur
 # 17   Thomas (on Lic.)], 26 yrs. 3 mos. 28
             days, single, B: Fluvanna Co., VA,
             Occup: Carpenter, s/o: Valentine and
             Thusar A. Thomas (on bk) [Valentine
             and Thursa Ann Thomas (on Lic.)]; and
             Ann Burden, 26 yrs. 11 mos. 27 days,
             widow, B: County Armagh, Ireland,
             dau/o: Thos. and Mary Crow (on bk)
             [Thomas and Mary Crow (on Lic.)].
             Both lived in Alleg. Co. PL: Alleg.
             Co., VA, Col. John Crow's res.   Mar.
             by J. Wesley Boteler, M. E. Church.
             "Sir: Mr. Thomas will aply to you
             for licns today. Mrs. Anne Burden is
             a widdow from New York. She is a re-
             lation of mine at lest 25 years old;
             you will therefore be so good as to
             give him the warrant.
                  Yours with respect,
                  John Crow 18 August 1856"
             "Alleghany County Court Clerk's Off-
             ice 18 August 1856:
                  This day Joseph A. Thomas appeared

(Mar. Register Book (1) - Continued)

before me and made oath that <u>Ann
Burden</u> is over the age of Twenty-one
years. Given under my hand the day
and date aforesaid.
                    Andr. Fudge, Clk."

08-26-1856   <u>Oliver Metheney</u>, 28, single, B: Al-
  # 18   leg. Co., VA, Occup: blacksmith, s/o:
             Sam'l. and Nancy Metheney (on bk)
             [Samuel and Nancy Metheney (on Lic)];
             and <u>Catharine J. Brown</u>, 21, single,
             B: Alleg. Co., VA, dau/o: Wm. B. and
             Elizabeth Brown. Both lived in Al-
             leg. Co. Mar. by Abraham Buhrman.
             PL: Alleg. Co., VA, on Simpson's
             Creek at Wm. Brown's res. (on Lic.).
             "Mr. Andrew Fudge:
             Sir, please to issue license to Mr.
             <u>Oliver Matheney</u> for marriage to my
             daughter, <u>Catharine Brown</u>. August
             25, 1856.
                          William B. Brown
             Wit. Madison Brown"
             "Proven by the oath Madison Brown as
             to the acknowledgement of W. B. Brown
             25 Augt. 1856.
                          Teste A. Fudge, Clk."

12-31-1855   <u>Sam'l. Willard</u> (on bk) [<u>Samuel Will-
  # 19   ard</u> (on Lic.)], 24, single, B: Hali-
             fax Co., VA, Lived: ___, Occup: ___,
             s/o: ___; and <u>Almyra V. Humphries</u>,
             21, single, B: Alleg. Co., VA, Lived:
             ___, dau/o: Jessee and Unice Humph-
             ries. Mar. by A. S. Hogshead. PL:
             Covington, Alleg. Co., VA. Clerk's
             Office Alleg. Co. 12-31-1855:
             "This day James A. Simmons and Thomas
             M. Arrington came before me in my
             office and made oath that <u>A. V. Hum-
             phries</u> is over the age of 21 years.
             Given under my hand this 31st Dec.
             1855. Isaac Skeen, D.C."

(Mar. Register Book (1) - Continued)

02-14-1856   Geo. Nagle (on bk) [George Fogel (on
20   Lic.)], 34 (on bk) [36 (on Lic.)],
             single, B: Germany, Occup: __, s/o:
             __; and Barbara Quickel, 47, single,
             B: Alleg. Co., VA, dau/o: Adam and
             Mary Quickel. Both lived in Alleg.
             Co., VA, (on Lic.). Mar. by A. S.
             Hogshead. PL: Alleg. Co., VA, at
             Harrison Quickel's res. (on Lic.).
             (Nagle is what spelling looks like on
             book.)

02-20-1856   Duncan B. McDonel (on bk) [Duncan B.
21   McDonnell (on Lic.)], 28, single, B:
             Canada West, Occup: Railroad Super-
             intendent, Lived: VA. Central Rail-
             road, s/o: Donald and Flora McDonnell
             (on bk) [Donald and Flora McDonell
             (on Lic.)]; and Christiana William-
             son (on bk) [Christina Williamson
             (on Lic.)], 22, single, B: Fife Shine,
             Scotland, Lived: Alleg. Co., VA, dau/
             o: Andr. and Jane Williamson (on bk)
             [Andrew and Jane Williamson (on Lic)].
             Mar. by A. S. Hogshead. PL: Alleg.
             Co., VA.

03-06-1856   Lewallen Bess (on bk) [Luallen Bess
22   (on Lic.)], 22, single, B: Alleg. Co.,
             VA. Occup: Laborer, s/o: Rebecca Bess;
             and Mary Bess, 18, single, B: Alleg.
             Co., VA, dau/o: Henry Bess. Both
             lived in Alleg. Co. Mar. by A. S.
             Hogshead. PL: Covington, VA. Consent
             for Mary Bess dated 03-06-1856 has
             Lewallen H. Bess and signed Henry
             (his X mark) Bess, Teste Jos. H. Per-
             singer and John F. Bess.

01-03-1856   Archer Sawyers, 50, widow, B: Alleg.
23   Co., VA, Occup: farmer, s/o: Sampson
             and Nancy Sawyers (on bk) [Sampson

and Mary Sawyers (on Lic.)]; and
Susan Lewis, 29 (on bk) [27 (on Lic)],
single, B: Alleg. Co., VA, dau/o:
Jno. and Elizabeth Lewis (on bk)
[John and Elizabeth Lewis (on Lic.)].
Both lived in Alleg. Co., VA. Mar.
by A. S. Hogshead. PL: Alleg. Co.,
VA, at John Lewis res. (on Lic.).
"Alleghany County Court Clerk's Office, 2 Jany. 1856:
    This day John W. Lewis personally
appeared before the undersigned &
made oath that Susan Lewis to whom I
have this day issued a marriage license to Archer Sawyers is over the
age of 21 years.
            Teste Andr. Fudge, Clk."

10-29-1856 John J. Jordan, 28, single, B: Alleg.
24   Co., VA, Occup: Engineer, s/o: Edwin
            and Mary J. Jordan (on bk) [Edwin and
            Jane Jordan (on Lic.)]; and Agness M.
            Steele, 19, single, B: Alleg. Co.,
            VA, dau/o: Isaac and Julia Steele.
            Both lived in Alleg. Co. Mar. by A.
            S. Hogshead. PL: Callaghan, Alleg.
            Co., VA. (on Lic.).

12-04-1856 Sam'l. Chewing (on bk) [Samuel Chewn-
25   ing (on Lic.)], 22, single, B: Nelson
            Co., VA, Occup: brickmaker (on bk)
            [Brickmason (on Lic.)], Lived: Salem,
            Roanoke Co., VA, (on Lic.), Jos. and
            Lucinda Chewing; and Betsada Boley
            (on bk) [Rosoltha Boley (on Lic.)],
            16, single, B: Monroe Co., VA (now W.
            VA), Lived: Alleg. Co., VA, dau/o:
            Bluford and R. Boley (on bk) [Bluford
            and Rosoltha Boley (on Lic.)]. Mar.
            by James M. Rice. PL: Alleg. Co., VA,
            at Mrs. Boley's res. near R. S.Spring
            (on Lic.).

(Mar. Register Book (1) - Continued)

10-23-1856 James H. Dickson, 35, single, B:
26   Rockbridge Co., VA, Occup: Carpenter,
            s/o: Jos. and Nancy Dickson (on bk)
            [?Jones (?James) and Nancy Dickson
            (on Lic.)]; and Lucinda Stiles, 21,
            single, B: Alleg. Co., VA, dau/o:
            Geo. W. and Mary Stiles (on bk) [Geo-
            rge W. and Mary M. Stiles (on Lic)].
            Both lived in Alleg. Co. Mar. by C.
            C. Cronin. PL: Alleg. Co., VA. Con-
            sent dated 10-22-1856 has Loncinda
            Stiles and signed by George W. (his
            X mark) Steiles, Wit. William C.East.
            Proven oath 10-22-1856 of W. C. East
            to George W. Steiles acknowledgement
            of consent, Andr. Fudge, Clk.

11-20-1856 James H. Karnes (on bk) [John H.
27   Karnes (on Lic.)], 24, single, B:
            Alleg. Co., VA, Occup: farmer, Lived:
            Bath Co., VA, s/o: Jacob and Sarah
            Karnes; and Elizabeth P. Thompson,
            23, single, B: Bath Co., VA, Lived:
            Alleg. Co., VA, dau/o: Abner and
            Sarah Thompson. Mar. by C. C. Cro-
            nin. PL: Bath Co., VA.

11-14-1856 Geo. Huffman, 24, single, Occup: far-
28   mer, B: Alleg. Co., VA, s/o: Soloman
            and Susan Huffman; and Catharine
            Lewis, 19, single, B: Alleg. Co., VA,
            dau/o: Jno. and Elizabeth Lewis (on
            bk) [John and Elizabeth Lewis (on
            Lic.)]. Both lived in Alleg. Co.
            Mar. by C. C. Cronin, M. E. Church.
            PL: Alleg. Co., VA.

11-06-1856 James Huffman, 21, single, Occup:
29   farmer, B: Greenbrier Co., VA (now
            W.VA), s/o: Soloman and Susan Huff-
            man; and Sarah A. Herbert, 19, sing-
            le, B: Monroe Co., VA (now W.VA),

dau/o: Wm. and Levina Herbert (on bk)
[William and Lavenia Herbert (on
Lic.)]. Both lived in Alleg. Co.
Mar. by C. C. Cronin, M. E. Church.
PL: Alleg. Co., VA. Consent dated
10-23-1856 signed by Wm. Herbert,
Wit. James (his X mark) Huffman.
Proven oath of James Huffman 10-25-
1856 of Wm. Herbert acknowledgement
of consent, Andr. Fudge, Clk.

12-18-1856   Joshua Kelly (on bk) [Joshua Kelley
30   (on Lic.)], 27, single, B: Bedford
             Co., PA., Occup: Hammerman, s/o:
             James and Rebecca Kelly (on bk)
             [James and Rebecca Kelley (on Lic)];
             and Patsey Moyers, 37, widow, B: Bath
             Co., VA, dau/o: Wm. and Nancy Oliver
             (on bk) [William and Lucy Oliver (on
             Lic.)]. Both lived in Alleg. Co.
             Mar. by C. C. Cronin. PL: Alleg.
             Co., VA.

12-17-1856   John L. Porter, 23, single, Occup:
31   Wheelwright, B: Botetourt Co., VA,
             s/o: Ezekiel and Matilda Porter; and
             Manama Callaghan (on bk) [Manamme
             Callighan (on Lic.)], 21, single, B:
             Alleg. Co., VA, dau/o: Chas. and
             Nancy Callaghan (on bk) [Charles and
             and Nancy Callighan (on Lic.)]. Both
             lived in Alleg. Co. PL: Alleg. Co.,
             VA. Mar. by C. C. Cronin, M. E.
             Church.
             "Alleghany County to wit: This day
             Nancy Callaghan, wife of Charles Cal-
             laghan, came before me a Justice of
             the Peace for the county aforesaid &
             made oath that Mariamne Callaghan
             daughter of Charles Callaghan of this
             county is over the age of twenty-one
             years. Given under my hand this 16th

Dec. 1856.
    John S. Boswell, Junr., J.P."
"To the Clerk of Alleghany,
    You are authorized to issue lic-
ense to celebrate the rites of matrimony between <u>John L. Porter</u> & myself.
              <u>Mariamne Callaghan</u>
Witness: Robt. Dickson."

04-02-1857   <u>Tilford J. Bratton</u>, 26 yrs. 36 mos.
32   (on bk) [26 yrs. 9 mos. 23 days (on
            Lic.)], single, B: Covington, Alleg.
            Co., VA, Occup: blacksmith, s/o:
            Robert and Hannah Bratton (on bk)
            [Robert Bratton and Hannah Otey (on
            Lic.)]; and <u>Martha Leighton</u>, 23 yrs.
            3 mos. 3 days, single, B: Botetourt
            Co., VA, dau/o: Isaac and Sarah
            Leighton (on bk) [Isaac Leighton and
            Sarah Adams (on Lic.)]. Both lived
            in Alleg. Co. Mar. by J. Wesley
            Boteler, M. E. Church. PL: Alleg.
            Co., VA.

Page 3

02-16-1857   <u>James Fridley</u>, 31, single, Occup:
1   farmer, B: Rockingham Co., VA, s/o:
            Jno. and Hanna L. Fridley (on bk)
            [John and Hannah Fridley (on Lic.)];
            and <u>Martha Bess</u>, 21, single, B: Al-
            leg. Co., VA, dau/o: Henry and Nelly
            Bess (on bk) [Henry and Nellie Bess
            (on Lic.)]. Both lived in Alleg. Co.
            Mar. by C. C. Cronin, M. E. Church.
            PL: Dunlap Creek, Alleg. Co., VA (on
            Lic.)

02-27-1857   <u>Jabes M. Hepler</u> and <u>Rebecca Jane</u>
1 ½   <u>Sively</u>, dau/o: Andrew Sively (on bk).
            Mar. by ___. PL: Alleg. Co., VA.
            Consent dated 07-27-1857 (? 02-27-

1857) has <u>Iabes M. Hepler</u> and <u>Rebecca Jane Seively</u> was signed by Andrew J. Sively, Wit. James M. Carson and A. M. Reynolds. [Note: There was no other information on this.]

02-01-1857
2

<u>James Oliver</u>, 41, widower, B: Bath Co., VA, Occup: farmer, s/o: Wm. and Lucy Oliver; and <u>Sidney A. Keyser</u> (on bk) [<u>Sidney A. Keeser</u> (on Lic.)], 24, B: Alleg. Co., VA, single, dau/o: Jas. and Lucinda Keyser (on bk) [James and Lucinda Keeser (on LIc.)]. Both lived in Alleg. Co. Mar. by C. C. Cronin, M. E. Church. PL: Covington, Alleg. Co., VA.

02-05-1857
3

<u>Stephen A. Pritchard</u> (on bk) [<u>Stephen C. Pritchard</u> (on Lic.)], 30, single, B: Frederick Co., VA, Occup: farmer, Lived: Shenandoah Co., VA, s/o: Stephen and Mary Pritchard; and <u>Mary F. McCallister</u> (on bk) [<u>Mary F. McAloster</u> (on Lic.)], 19, single, B: Greenbrier Co., VA (now W.VA.), Lived: Alleg. Co., VA, dau/o: Arch'. and M. McCallister (on bk) [Archabald and M. McAloster (on Lic.)]. Mar. by C. C. Cronin, M. E. Church. PL: Alleg. Co., VA.

02-10-1857
4

<u>Charles Thomas</u> (on bk) [<u>Charles William Thomas</u> (on Lic.)], 22, single, B: Alleg. Co., VA, Occup: farmer, s/o: W. B. and Mary Thomas (on bk) [Wright B. and Mary Thomas (on Lic.)]; and <u>Sarah M. Wolf</u> (on bk)[<u>Margaret Wolfe</u> (on Lic.)], 25, single, B: Alleg. Co, VA, dau/o: John and Sarah Wolf (on bk) [John Wolfe and Sarah Rayhill (on Lic.)]. Both lived in Alleg. Co. Mar. by Lorenzo D. Nixon. PL: At widow

Sarah Wolfe's res., Potts Creek,
Alleg. Co., VA (on Lic.).

01-29-1857   John C. Howard, 23, single, B: Prince
5   Edward Co., VA, Occup: farmer, s/o:
              John and Eliz. Howard (on bk) [John
              and Elizabeth Howard (on Lic.)]; and
              Harriet A. Leighton, 18, single, B:
              Alleg. Co., VA, dau/o: Jno. and Eliza
              Leighton. Both lived in Alleg. Co.
              Mar. by C. C. Cronin, M. E. Church.
              PL: Covington, Alleg. Co., VA.

09-10-1856   Wm. Adams (on bk) [William Adams (on
6   Lic.)], 27, single, B: Kentucky,
              Occup: common laborer, s/o: unknown
              [Note on Lic.: "not known having died
              when he was young"]; and Cath. S.
              Rose (on bk) [Catharine S. Rose (on
              Lic.)], 28, widow, B: Alleg. Co., VA,
              dau/o: C. and Nancy Lemon (on bk)
              [(? Koonror or ? Koonrod) and Nancy
              Lemon (on Lic.)]. Both lived in Al-
              leg. Co. Mar. by Abraham Buhrman.
              PL: Mr. Thomas J. Peters res. near
              Clifton Forge, VA (on Lic.). Proven
              oath of Morton Lemon that Catharine
              was over 21 yrs. old, dated 09-08-
              1856, Wit. Andr. Fudge, Clk.

04-30-1857   Alchany Bush (on bk) [Alchany W. Bush
7   (on Lic.)], 24, single, Occup: far-
              mer, B: Alleg. Co., VA, s/o: Sam'l.
              and Mary Bush; and Julia a. H. Hepler
              (on bk) [Julia A. R. Hepler (on Lic)],
              19, single, B: Alleg. Co., VA, dau/o:
              Jno. and Sarah Hepler (on book) [John
              and Sarah Hepler (on Lic.)]. Both
              lived in Alleg. Co. Mar. by H. S.
              Williams, M. E. Church. PL: Alleg.
              Co., VA. Proven oath of John Johnson
              to John Hepler's acknowledgement of

consent, 04-27-1857, Teste A. Fudge,
Clk. Consent: "<u>Julia Anna Rebecca
Hepler</u> is not 21 but has obtained my
consent, 04-24-1857, signed John (his
X mark) Hepler, Attest: John Johnson,
Edward Eavans."

07-06-1857 <u>Michael Courtney</u>, 28, single, B: Ire-
8   land, Occup: laborer on Railroad,
           Lived: C & O Railroad, s/o: Tim and
           Nancy Courtney (on bk) [Tim and Ann
           Courtney (on Lic.)]; and <u>Lucy M. Har-
           low</u>, 16, single, B: Louisa Co., VA,
           Lived: near Covington, Alleg. Co.,
           VA, dau/o: Thos. and Lucy Harlow (on
           bk) [Thomas and Lucy Harlow (on Lic)].
           Mar. by Alfred Buhrman. PL: near
           Covington, Alleg. Co., VA. [Lic.
           information notes: "<u>Michael</u> - 28 yrs.
           old as near as can be ascertained;
           <u>Lucy</u> will be 16 yrs. old in next Aug-
           ust; <u>Michael</u> lives on Covington and
           Ohio Railroad"] [Author Note: The
           Covington and Ohio Railroad ran from
           Covington westward to Ohio. It is
           now known as the Chesapeake and Ohio
           Railway or Chessie System.]

06-10-1857 <u>James H. Steveson</u> (on bk) [<u>James H.
8 ½   Stevenson</u> (on Lic.)], s/o: _____
           Stevenson; and <u>Sarah Ann Mann</u>, dau/o:
           Moses M. Mann. Mar. by _____. PL:
           Alleg. Co., VA.
           "Jackson River, Alleghany, VA.
                   June the 10th, 1857
           Andrew C. Fudge, Esqr., C. A. Co.
           Dear Sir:
                   Being quite indisposed and not
           well able to come--I authorize Robert
           W. Handley, my brother-in-law, to act
           for me in obtaining license to marry
           <u>Miss Sarah A. Man</u>, daughter of Moses

Man, Esqr.
<u>James H. Stevenson</u>"
"June 10, 1857
Mr. Fudge this is to author you to
grant a licen to <u>James Stevenson</u> to
marry my daughter, <u>Sarah Ann</u>.
Yours with Respect
                    Moses M. Mann
Teste James Mann"
[Note: There was no other information
on this in the files.]

06-04-1857 <u>Jno. Johnson</u> (on bk) [<u>John Johnson</u>
10   (on Lic.)], 28, single, B: Alleg.
            Co., VA, Occup: farmer, Lived: _____,
            Date of Birth on Lic: 08-31-1829,
            s/o: Bernard and Ann Johnson; and
            <u>Sarah J. Bush</u> (on bk) [<u>Sarah J. S.
            Bush</u> (on Lic.)], 26, single, B: Alleg.
            Co., VA, Lived: _____, Date of Birth
            on Lic: 07-28-1831, dau/o: Sam'l.
            and Polly Bush (on bk) [Samuel and
            Poly Bush (on Lic.)]. Mar. by Jacob
            Brillhart, M. E. Church, South. PL:
            Alleg. Co., VA.

07-05-1857 <u>Wm. A. Tyree</u> (on bk) [<u>William A.
11   Tyree</u> (on Lic.)], 45, single, B: Bath
            Co., VA, Occup: farmer, s/o: Jno. and
            Eliz. Tyree (on bk) [Jno. and Elisa-
            beth Tyree (on Lic.)]; and <u>Ann E.
            Anderson</u>, 21, single, B: Augusta Co.,
            VA, dau/o: Hy and Esabel Tyree (on
            bk) [Henry and Isabella Tyree (on
            Lic.)]. Mar. by S. P. (or ? T.) Huff,
            Minister of Gospel. PL: Healing
            Springs, VA.
            "To the Clerk of the County Court of
            Alleghany County, Virginia
                You will please issue a marriage
            license to <u>William A. Tyree</u> to marry
            my daughter <u>Ann E. Anderson</u> she being

under age and I here by giving my
conset to her marriage. Given under
my hand in the said county this 2d
day of July 1857.
Henry (his X mark) Anderson
Witness Wm. H. Anderson"
Both lived in Alleg. Co., VA.

07-22-1857   Henry C. Vaughan, 23 yrs. 6 mos.,
 # 12   single, B: Bedford Co., VA, Occup:
              various (on Lic.), s/o: Wm. and Eliza
              Vaughan (on bk) [William and Elisa
              Vaughan (on Lic.)]; and Evaline J.
              Kindle, 16 yrs. 6 mos., single, B:
              Alleg. Co., VA, dau/o: Joel and
              Delela Kindle (on bk) [Joel and
              Delia Kindle (on Lic.)]. Both lived
              in Alleg. Co. Mar. by Alfred Buhrman
              Minister of the Gospel. PL: Alleg.
              Co., VA. Consent has Eveline J.
              Kindell and was signed by Joel Kin-
              dell, Teste J. W. Wyatt. Proven oath
              of Kindell acknowledgement given by
              Jno. W. Wyatt on 07-22-1857 to Andr.
              Fudge, Clk.

09(08)-28-1857 (on bk) 08-28-1857 (on Lic.)
 # 13   Wm. R. Armstrong (on bk) William R.
              Armstrong (on Lic.), 29, single, B:
              Alleg. Co., VA, Occup: farmer, s/o:
              I. and Elizabeth Armstrong (on bk)
              [Israel and Elisabeth Armstrong (on
              Lic.)]; and Mary A. Bennet, 23, sing-
              le, B: Alleg. Co., VA, dau/o: Eliza-
              beth Bennet (on bk) [Phebe Bennet (on
              Lic.) (Sampson Bennet - ink blotted
              on Lic. -?as through trying to mark
              through)]. Both lived in Alleg. Co.
              Mar. by Alfred Buhrman. PL: Rich
              Patch, Alleg. Co., VA (on Lic.).
              Proven oath of John H. Stone that
              Sampson Bennet, father of Mary Ann

Bennet, made oath that she was over
21 from his own knowledge, 08-24-1857,
Andr. Fudge, Clk.

09-04-1857   (on bk)   09-03-2857 (on Lic.)
14   Geo. W. Craft (on bk) [George W. Craft
             (on Lic.)], 22 yrs. and about 9 mos.,
             single, B: Alleg. Co., VA, Occup: far-
             mer, s/o: Jno. and Elizabeth Craft
             (on bk) [John and Elisabeth Craft (on
             Lic.)]; and M. R. E. McDaniel (on bk)
             Mary R. E. McDaniel (on Lic), 15, B:
             Alleg. Co., VA, single, dau/o: Jno. S.
             and Phebe McDaniel (on bk) [John and
             Rebecca N. McDaniel (on Lic.)].   Both
             lived in Alleg. Co. Mar. by Alfred
             Buhrman. PL: Alleg. Co., VA. Consent
             signed by John S. McDaniel states
             Mary R. E. McDaniel to marry 08-28-
             185_, Wit. John M. Williams. Proven
             oath of John M. Williams to McDaniel
             acknowledgement of consent on 09-01-
             1857, Andr. Fudge, Clk.

08-13-1857   Jno. Connel (on bk) [John Connel (on
15   Lic.)], 28, single, B: Ireland, Occup:
             Miner, s/o: Jno. and Mary Connel (on
             bk) [John O'Connel and May Foley (on
             Lic.)]; and Ellen O'Sulivan, 21, sin-
             gle, B: Ireland, dau/o: Jno. and Cath.
             Sulivan (on bk) [John O'Sullivan and
             Catherine Dnycol (on Lic.)].   Both
             lived O.R.R. (on bk) [C & O R.R. (on
             Lic.)]. Mar. by J. W. Waters, Mins.
             of Gospel. PL: Alleg., VA [Note:
             Don't know if this refers to Alleg.
             Co. or the place called "Alleghany"
             that lies west of Covington on Rt.311
             near the W. Va. state line.]

09-29-1857   Jos. M. Mays (on bk) [Joseph M. Mays
16   (on Lic.)], 22, single, B: Bath Co.,
             VA. Occup: farmer, s/o: Nancy Mays;

and <u>Sarah E. Nicely</u>, 16, single, B:
Alleg. Co., VA, dau/o: Jacob and Mar-
garet Nicely. Both lived in Alleg.
Co. Mar. by Abraham Buhrman. PL:
Alleg. Co., VA, on Simpson Creek (on
Lic.).

10-19-1857 <u>Jas. A. Harmon</u> (on bk) [<u>James A. Har-</u>
17   <u>mon</u> (on Lic.)], 31, widower, B: Alleg.
Co., VA, Occup: farmer, s/o: Peter
and Mary Harmon; and <u>Rebecca Bess</u>,
19, single, B: Alleg. Co., VA, dau/o:
Joseph and Jane Bess. Both lived in
Alleg. Co. Mar. by S. T. Mallory, M.
E. Church, South. PL: Covington,
Alleg. Co., VA.

10-29-1857 <u>Geo W. Dickson</u> (on bk) [<u>George W.</u>
18   <u>Dickson</u> (on Lic.)], 26, single, B:
Gap Mills, Monroe Co., VA (now W.VA),
Occup: farmer, Lived: Gap Mills, Monroe Co., VA (now W.VA.) (on Lic.),
s/o: Jno. and Nancy Dickson (on bk)
[John and Nancy Dickson (on Lic.)];
and <u>Eliz. Jones</u> (on bk) [<u>Elisabeth</u>
<u>Jones</u> (on Lic.)], 22, single, B: Al-
leg. Co., VA, Lived: near Gap Mills,
Monroe Co., VA (now W.VA.) (on Lic.),
dau/o: Josiah and Nancy Jones (on bk)
[Josiah and Martha Jones (on Lic.)].
Lic. says <u>George</u> was "26 the 15th of
last June", and listed under this,
<u>Elisabeth</u> was "22 yrs old same time
this month". Mar. by Alfred Buhrman.
PL: Covington, Alleg. Co., VA (on
Lic.).

10-13-1857 <u>Jno. M. Carter</u> (on bk) [<u>John M. Carter</u>
19   (on Lic.)], 30, single, B: Bedford
Co., VA, Occup: farmer, s/o: Jno. L.
and Lucy Carter (on bk) [John Carter
and Lucy Eubank (on Lic.)]; and <u>Susan</u>

Smales (on bk) Susan Snales (on Lic)],
21, single, B: Greenbrier Co., VA,
(now W.VA.), dau/o: Matthias and Mary
A. Smales (on bk) [Matthias and Mary
Ann Snales (on Lic.)]. [Note: last
name is difficult to read because of
way it was written where the "m"--
"n" is.]. Both lived in Alleg. Co.
Mar. by Staunton Field, M. E. Church,
South. PL: Alleg. Co., VA, at Callahan's (on Lic.).

11-17-1857   Matthew O Conner (on bk) [Matthew
20   O'Conner (on Lic.)], 28, single, B:
             Ireland, Occup: farmer, s/o: M. and
             Honora King (on bk) [Mathew O'Connor
             and Honora King (on Lic.)]; and Jonna
             Conway (on bk) [Joanna Conway (on
             Lic.)], 19, single, B: Ireland, dau/o:
             James Conway and C. Farton (on bk)
             [John Conway and Catherine Fenton (on
             Lic.)]. Both lived in Alleg. Co.
             Mar. by J. H. Waters, Mins. of gospel.
             PL: Alleghany [Note: Don't know if
             this refers to Alleg. Co. or the
             place called "Alleghany" that lies
             above Covington on Rt. 311 near the
             W. VA. state line.] Consent dated
             11-17-1857 was signed John (his X
             mark) Conway, Wit. Pat Kenedy. Proven
             oath of Robert Kenady of Conway's con-
             sent dated 11-17-1857, Andr. Fudge,
             Clk.

12-31-1857   Dingud Riddlesbarger (on bk) [Dingud
21   Ridlesbarger (on Lic.)], 23, single,
             B: Botetourt Co., VA, Occup: carpen-
             ter, Lived: Botetourt Co., VA, s/o:
             Sam'l. and Susan Riddlesbarger (on bk)
             [Samuel and Suasan Ridlesbarger (on
             Lic.)]; and Rebecca Stull, 23, single,
             B: Alleg. Co., VA, Lived: Alleg. Co.,

VA, dau/o: Sam'l. and E. Stull (on bk) [Samuel and Elisabeth Stull (on Lic)]. Mar. by S. T. Mallory, Mins. PL: Alleg. Co., VA.

12-21-1857   Isaiah S. Cumings (on bk) [Isaiah
22   Stanley Cumnings (on Lic.)], 25, B:
              Alleg. Co., VA, single, Occup: farmer,
              s/o: A. and Rebeca Cumings (on bk)
              [Abraham and Rebeca Cumnings (on
              Lic.)]; and Ruth Ann Unger, 17, B:
              Pevel Co., Ohio (way looks on Lic.),
              single, dau/o: Aron and Julia Unger
              (on bk) [Aaron and Julia Ann Unger
              (on Lic.)]. Both lived in Alleg. Co.
              Mar. by S. T. Mallory, Mins. PL:
              Covington, Alleg. Co., VA (on Lic.).

12-24-1857   Jno. M. Crutchfield (on bk) [John M.
23   Crutchfield (on Lic.), 25, single, B:
              Richmond, VA, Occup: stone cutter,
              s/o: Jno. M. and Cath. Crutchfield
              (on bk) [John M. and Catharine Crutch-
              field (on Lic.)]; and Alcinda Douglas,
              23, single, B: Alleg. Co., VA, dau/o:
              B. and Harriet Douglas (on bk) [Ben-
              jamin and Harriet Douglas (on Lic.)].
              Both lived in Alleg. Co. Mar. by S.
              T. Mallory. PL: Alleg. Co., VA.
              "Alleghany County to wit:
                   This day James Shanklin made
              oath before me a Justice of said Coun-
              ty that he is well acquainted with
              Alcinda Douglas and that she is over
              the age of 21 years.
                   Given under my hand this 22nd
              Dec. 1857.
                        John S. Boswell, J.P."
              "Alleghany County to wit:
                   This day David Williamson made
              oath that he knows that Alcinda Doug-
              las desires license to issue to cel-
              ebrate the rites of matrimony between

John M. Crutchfield and herself.
Given under my hand this 22nd
Dec. 1857.
James Shanklin, J.P."

12-17-1857   Wm. A. Grose (on bk) [William A.
24   Grose (on Lic.)], 33, widower, B:
Bath Co., VA, Occup: Millrite, Lived:
Bath Co., VA, s/o: Hy and Elizabeth
Grose (on bk) [Henry and Elisabeth
Grose (on Lic.)]; and Eliz. J. Mann
(on bk) [Elisabeth J. Mann (on Lic)],
19, single, B: Alleg. Co., VA, Lived:
Alleg. Co., VA, dau/o: Ar. G. and
Clementine Mann (on bk) [Archabald G.
and Clementine C. Mann (on Lic.)].
Lic. states William "was 33 years old
25th of last October." Mar. by
Alfred Buhrman, Mins. PL: Alleg. Co,
VA, at Archabald Mann's res. (on Lic).

12-17-1857   Andr. J. Surber (on bk) [Andrew Jack-
25   son Surber (on Lic.)], 27, single, B:
Botetourt Co., VA, Occup: farmer, s/o:
Andr. and Larissa Surber (on bk)
[Adrew and (? Lurana -smeared-) Sur-
ber (on Lic.)]; and Maria L. Hubbard
(on bk) [Maria Luemily Hubbard (on
Lic.)], 17, single, B: Botetourt Co.,
VA (Lic. has "17 yrs. in January 1858),
dau/o: Sam'l. and Eliz. Hubbard (on
bk) [Samuel W. Hubbard and Elizabeth
Patterson Gillham (on Lic.)]. Both
lived in Alleg. Co. Mar. by Lorenzo
D. Nixon, Mins. PL: Alleg. Co., VA.,
at Sam'l. W. Hubbard res. (on Lic.).
Consent has name as LuEmily Hubbard
and was dated 12-12-1857 and signed
S. W. Hubbard, Teste Henry Walker and
Joseph H. Hall.
"Alleghany County Court Clks Office
14 Dec 1857
This day, Samuel E. Hubbard, son

of the within named Samuel W. Hubbard
made oath before me that the within
certificate together with the signature thereto attached is in the proper handwriting of his father, S. W.
Hubbard. given under my hand this
day and date aforesaid.
Andr. Fudge, Clk."

04-04-1857 (on bk)   04-09-1857 (on Lic.)
 # 26   Patrick Nolin, 26, single, B: Ireland,
Occup: merchant, s/o: Patrick and
Mary Nolin (on bk) [Patrick Nolin and
Mary Feannelly (on Lic.)]; and Frances
Baldwin, 17, single, B: Rockbridge
Co., VA, dau/o: Peter Baldwin and
Eveaeen Ann Kellen (on bk) [Peter
Baldwin and Ann Keller (on Lic.)].
Both lived in Alleghany [Note: Don't
know if refers to Alleg. Co. or place
on Rt. 311 called "Alleghany" near
W. VA. state line.]   Mar. by J. H.
Waters. PL: Sweet Springs, VA (now
W.VA.) (on Lic.). Mins. signed Lic.
on April 9, 1857. Consent of mother
dated on 04-01-1857 and signed
     Eveaeen Baldwin   / Francisco
      Eveaun (X mark) / Baldwin
(apparently written for mother by
daughter). Clerk of Court 04-04-1857,
Michael Murfey made oath that Evance
Baldwin the mother of Franciso Baldwin gave him her written consent for
Patrick Nalin to marry her daughter.

06-23-1857   Sam'l. Coleman, 36, single, B: Caro-
 # 9   line Co., VA, Occup: Railroad Conduct-
or, s/o: Sam'l. and Mary Coleman (on
bk) [Samuel Coleman and Mary D. his
wife (on Lic.)]; and Margaret E. Jordan, 23, single, B: Alleg. Co., VA,
dau/o: Ed. and Mary Jordan (on bk)

[Edwin Jordan and Mary I. his wife
(on Lic.)]. Both lived in Alleg. Co.
(on Lic.). Mar. by J. P. Corron,
Baptist. PL: Cowpasture Bridge, Alleg. Co., VA (on Lic.). Edwin Jordan, Jr., made oath Margaret, daughter of Edwin Jordan, is over 21 yrs.
old. Affidavit was made so Samuel
Coleman could obtain a marriage Lic.
from Andrew Fudge, Clk., 06-20-1857.

Page 3

02-01-1858   Michael Barrett (on bk) [Michael Bar-
1   ritt (on Lic.)], 21, single, B: Ire-
             land, Occup: laborer, s/o: Jno. Bar-
             rett and Mary Hogan (on bk) [John
             Barritt and Mary Hargan (on Lic.)],
             [Lic. has Occup. as "Public Work");
             and Honora Kennelly, 18, single, B:
             Ireland, dau/o: Jno. Kennelly and M.
             Conner (on bk) [John Kennelly and
             Mary Connor (on Lic.)]. Mar. by J.H.
             Waters. PL: Alleg. Co., VA.   Both
             lived in Alleg. Co.

02-16-1858   Jno. Fitzgerald (on bk) [John Fitz-
2   gerald (on Lic.)], 23 single, B: Ire-
             land, Occup: laborer, s/o: Thos. Fitz-
             gerald and E. Francis (on bk) [Thos.
             Fitzgerald and Ellen Francis (on
             Lic.)], [Lic. has Occup. as "Public
             Works"]; and Mary Fitzgerald, 16,
             single, B: State of New York, dau/o:
             T. Fitzgerald and C. Stack (on bk)
             [Thos. Fitzgerald and Catherine Stack
             (on Lic.)]. Mar. by J. H. Waters.
             PL: Alleg. Co., VA.   Both lived in
             Alleg. Co.

02-18-1858   William Cassada (on bk) [William Cas-
3   sedy (on Lic.)], 35, single, B: Essex

Co., New Jersey, Occup: School Teacher, s/o: C. Cassada and Jane Cassada (on bk) [Conn Cassedy and Jane Cassedy (on Lic.)], Lived: Alleg. Co., VA, Falling Springs Valley (on Lic.); and Mary Jones, 40, widow, B: Alleg. Co., VA, dau/o: D (page tore) and Mary Calaghan (on bk) [Dennis and Margaret Callahan (on Lic.)], Lived: Alleg. Co., VA, Ogle's Creek (on Lic). Mar. by Alfred Buhrman. PL; Alleg. Co., VA, Mr. Lockheart's on Ogle's Creek (on Lic.).

02-22-1858 (on bk)   02-25-1858 (on Lic.)
4   Isaac Sorrell (on bk) [Isaack Sourel (on Lic.)], 22, single, B: Botetourt Co., VA, Occup: Common Laborer (on Lic.), Lived: Botetourt Co., VA, s/o: Thos. and Mary Sorrell (on bk) [Thomas and Mary Sourel (on Lic.)]; and Eliza A. Leighton (on bk) [Elizan A. Leyton (on Lic.)], 24, single, B: Nelson Co., VA, Lived: Alleg. Co., VA, dau/o: Wm. and Nancy Leighton (on bk) [Wm. and Nancy Leyton (on Lic.)]. Mar. by Abraham Buhrman. PL: Alleg. Co., VA, Simpson's Creek (on Lic.). Oath of age over 21 of Eliza A. Leighton was made by Matthias Nicely, Andr. Fudge, Clk.

02-25-1858 David L. Roadcap, 33, single, B:Rockbridge Co., VA, Occup: farmer, Lived: Rockbridge Co., VA, s/o: Christian and E. Roadcap (on bk) [Christian and Elizabeth Roadcap (on Lic.)];   and Nancy Williamson, 21, single, B: Scotland, Lived: Alleg. Co., VA, dau/o: Andr. and Jane Williamson (on bk) [Andrew and Jane Williamson (on Lic)]. Mar. by S. T. Huff. PL: Alleg. Co.,

VA, at Andrew Williamson's res. (on
Lic.).

03-04-1858   Benj. C. Carlisle (on bk) [Benjamin
6   Christopher Carlisle (on Lic.)], 23
              yrs. 10 mos. 10 days, single, B: Mon-
              roe Co., VA (now W.VA.), Occup: far-
              mer, s/o: Sam'l. and Jane Carlisle
              (on bk) [Samuel and Jane Carlisle (on
              Lic.)]; and Margaret E. Pittser (on
              bk) [Margaret E. Billey (on Lic.)],
              31 yrs. 11 mos. 18 days, widow B:
              Botetourt Co., VA, dau/o: Cary and
              Lucinda Pittser (on bk)   [Cary A.
              Pillser (? difficult to make out) and
              Lucinda Pittser (on Lic.)]. Both
              lived in Monroe Co., VA (now W.VA.).
              Mar. by S. Hargiss. PL: Alleg. Co.,
              VA, J. J. Stacks Hotel (on Lic.).

03-17-1858   Francis B. (? or R.) Wright, 24, sin-
7   gle, B: Alleg. Co., VA (on bk) [Mon-
              roe Co., VA (now W.VA.) (on Lic.)],
              Occup: farmer, s/o: Jno. and Cath-
              arine Wright (on bk) [John and Cath-
              arine Wright (on Lic.)]; and Charlot-
              te Rayhill (on bk) [Charlotte M. Ray-
              hill (on Lic.)], 23, single, B: Alleg.
              Co., VA, dau/o: Alexander and Eliza-
              beth Rayhill (on bk) [Alexandre and
              Elisabeth (no last name listed) (on
              Lic.)]. Both lived in Alleg. Co.,
              VA. PL: Alleg. Co., VA. Mar. by S.
              T. Mallory, M. E. Church, South.

03-24-1858   Dewitt C. Steele, 24, single, B: Al-
8   leg. Co., VA, Covington (on Lic.),
              Occup: farmer, s/o: Isaac and Julia
              Steele; and Mary C. Mallow, 22, sing-
              le, B: Alleg. Co., VA,   dau/o: Jno.
              and Martha Mallow (on bk) [John and
              Martha Mallow (on Lic.)]. Both lived

in Alleg. Co., VA. Mar. by S. T.
Mallory, M. E. Church, South. PL:
Alleg. Co., VA.

04-01-1858   Chas. L. Rowan (on bk) [Charles L.
  # 9   Rowan (on Lic.)] [Note: Genealogy
              Society wrote "Bowan" on document
              storage envelope, but looks like
              "Rowan" to me on book and Lic.], 25,
              single, B: Monroe Co., VA (now W.VA),
              Occup: farmer, s/o: Boston and Fran-
              ces Rowan; and Nancy Sarver (on bk)
              Nancy H. Sarver (on Lic.), 21, sing-
              le, B: Craig Co., VA, dau/o: Jno. and
              Martha Sarver (on bk) [John and Mar-
              tha Sarver (on Lic.)]. Mar. by S. T.
              Mallory. PL: Alleg. Co., VA. Both
              lived in Craig Co., VA. Oath made by
              Nancy H. Sarver that she was "21 to
              the best of her knowledge and belief
              and from the family record kept by
              her parents", 03-31-1858, Wm. Herbert,
              J. P. Alleg. Co., VA.

02-25-1858   Oliver Thompson, 28 [Lic. states age
  # 10   "28 the 19th Dec. next"], B: Alleg.
              Co., VA, Occup: farmer [Lic. states
              "labourer-farmer"], s/o: Abner and
              Sarah Thompson; and Mary F. Surber
              (on bk) [Mary Frances Surber (on
              Lic.)], 21 [Lic. states "21 the 22nd
              July last"], single, B: Bath Co., VA,
              dau/o: Levi and Sally Surber (on bk)
              [Levi Surber and Sally Hanger (on
              Lic.)]. Mar. by John T. Tabler,Mins.
              of gospel. PL: Alleg. at Levi Surber
              res. [Note: Don't know if refers to
              Alleg. Co. or place on Rt. 311 call-
              ed "Alleghany" near W.VA. state line.]
              Both lived in Alleg. Co. Consent
              dated 02-23-1858 has name Olliver
              Tompson and was signed by Levi Surber,

Teste L. F. Tyree and L. M. Huff.
Proven oath of Wm. anders that Levi
Surber wrote consent, Teste Andr.
Fudge, Clk. 24 Feb 1858.

03-18-1858   John J. Bennet (on bk) [John J. Ben-
11   nett (on Lic.)], 22, single, B: Alleg.
             Co., VA, Occup: farmer, s/o: Solomon
             and Susan Bennet (on bk) [Soloman and
             Susan Bennett (on Lic.)]; and Mary A.
             Bennet (on bk) [Mary A. Bennett (on
             Lic.)], 16, single, B: Alleg. Co., VA,
             dau/o: Jacob and Peggy Tingler. Both
             lived in Alleg. Co. Mar. by William
             R. Stringer. PL: Alleg. [Note: Don't
             know if refers to Alleg. Co. or place
             on Rt. 311 called "Alleghany" near W.
             VA. state line.]

04-25-1858   Patrick Sullivan, 23, single, B: Ire-
12   land, Occup: farmer [Lic. says labour-
             er], s/o: Mary Sulivan (on bk) [Daniel
             Sullivan and Mary McCarthey (on Lic)];
             and Mary Sullivan, 17, single, B: Ire-
             land, dau/o: Mich'l.and Betsy Sulli-
             van (on bk) [Micheal Sullivan and
             Betsey Harris (on Lic.)]. Both lived
             in Alleg. Co. Mar. by J. H. Waters.
             PL: Alleg. Co., VA.

05-13-1858   E. P. Tinsley (on bk) [E. O. Tinsley
13   (on Lic.)], 31, single, Occup: farmer,
             B: Alleg. Co., VA (on bk) [Amherst Co.
             VA (on Lic.)], s/o: Bennet and Perme-
             lia Tinsley; and Maria F. Fridley (on
             bk) [Mariah F. Fridley (on Lic.)], 23,
             single, B: Alleg. Co., VA,   dau/o:
             Isaac and E. Fridley (on bk) [Isaac
             and Elizabeth Fridley (on Lic.)].
             Both lived in Alleg. Co., VA. Mar. by
             Abraham Buhrman. PL: Rich Patch, Al-
             leg. Co., VA (on Lic.).

04-22-1858   (on bk)   04-21-1858 Wednesday 8:00 P.M.
  # 14   (on Lic.)
             Dennis Callaghan, 42, widower, Occup:
             farmer-carpenter, B: Rich Patch, Al-
             leg. Co., VA (on Lic), s/o: John and
             Sarah Callaghan; and Rebecca S. Mann,
             28, single, B: Alleg. Co., VA, at L.
             T. Mann's, dau/o: Lewis T. and Sarah
             Mann. He lived near White Rock Gap
             in Rich Patch, and she lived at L. T.
             Mann's--both in Alleg. Co. Mar. by
             Davis M. Woods, Local Deacon of M. E.
             Church who signed Lic. on 04-22-1858.
             PL: Alleg. Co., VA, Jackson River,
             Lewis T. Mann's res. [Note on Lic.
             to Clerk: Davis Woods wrote that he
             had made a mistake on a name and had
             written Lewis C. Mann on the Lic. when
             it should have been Lewis T. Mann.]

05-18-1858   Sampson Humphries, 21 yrs. 7 mos.
  # 15   [Note on Lic.: "would be 22 next Oct-
             ober"], single, B: Alleg. Co., VA, at
             head of Blue Spring Run, Rich Patch
             (on Lic.), Occup: farmer, s/o: Wm.
             and Ruthy Humphries (on bk) [William
             and Ruthy Humphries (on Lic.)]; and
             Ruthy M. Quickle (on bk) [Ruthy M.
             Quicle (on Lic.)], 18 yrs. 4 mos. ["18
             last January" (on Lic.)], single, B:
             Alleg. Co., VA, Rich Patch near Blue
             Spring (on Lic.), dau/o: Henry and
             Peggy Quickle (on bk) [Henry and Peggy
             Quicle (on Lic.)]. Both lived in Al-
             leg. Co., VA. He lived at his fa-
             ther's, William Humphries, house (on
             Lic.). She lived with her mother,
             Peggy Quicle (on Lic.). Mar. by Davis
             M. Woods, Local Deacon of M. E. Church.
             PL: Alleg. Co., VA, at widow Peggy
             Quickle's res. (on Lic.). Consent
             signed 05-11-1858 and signed by Mar-

garet Quickel has name <u>Ruthy M. Quick-</u>
<u>el</u>, Wit. Jacob H. Wolf and Anderson
Persinger. Proven oath of Jacob H.
Wolf on 11th May 1858 as to consent.

05-24-1858 (on bk)   05-23-1858 (on Lic.)
 # 16   <u>Thomas Smales</u>, 40, widower, Occup:
           farmer, B: Augusta Co., VA, s/o: Mat-
           hew and Mary Smales; and <u>Mary Carter</u>,
           23, single, B: Bedford Co., VA, dau/o:
           John and Nancy Carter (on bk) [John
           Carter and Nancy (on Lic.)].   Both
           lived in Alleg. Co., VA--he at Callag-
           han's and she at Covington. Mar. by
           S. T. Mallory, M. E. Church, South,
           who signed the Lic. on 05-24-1858.
           PL: Alleg. Co., VA, at Callaghan's.

06-08-1858 <u>Wm. H. Fridley</u>, 19, single, Occup:
 # 17   farmer, B: Alleg. Co., VA, s/o: James
           Armontrout and Delila Fridley;   and
           <u>Martha Hamler</u> (on bk) [<u>Marthay Hamlet</u>
           (on Lic.)], 26, single, B: Charlotte
           Co., VA, dau/o: Henry and Mary Hamler
           (on bk) [Henry and Mary Hamlet (on
           Lic.)].   Both lived in Alleg. Co., VA.
           Mar. by S. T. Mallory, M. E. Church.
           PL: Alleg. Co., VA, Covington (on
           Lic.).

07-16-1858 (on bk))7-07-1858 (on Lic.)
 # 18   <u>Wm. L. Damron</u> (on bk) [<u>William L. Dam-</u>
           <u>ron</u> (on Lic.)], 30 yrs. 6 mos. 4 days
           [Note on Lic.: "was 30 the 12th of
           January 1858"], single, B: Alleg. Co.,
           VA, Occup: Physician, s/o: Joseph and
           Lucy Damron; and <u>Annie C. Noel</u>, 20
           yrs. 11 mos. 19 days [Note on Lic.:
           "will be 21 the 27th of July 1858"],
           single, B: Charlottesville, VA [Note:
           This is in Albemarle Co., VA], dau/o:
           Robt. C. and Louisa Noel (on bk) [Rob-

ert C. and Lewisa Noel (on Lic.)].
Both lived in Alleg. Co., VA. Mar. by
Alfred Buhrman, who signed the Lic. on
07-16-1858. PL: Alleg. Co., VA, Morris Hill (on Lic.). Consent was signed by R. C. Noel, Teste W. J. Cosby,
sworn to cert. of R. C. Noel before
W. J. Cosby 6 July 1858 acknowledged
by Lewis P. Holloway, Clk.

07-16-1858   (on bk)   06-15-1858 (on Lic.)
  # 19   Wm. E. Lewis (on bk) [William E. Lewis
            (on Lic.)], 24 yrs. 8 mos. 10 days
            [Note on Lic.: "will be 25 yrs. old
            26th Nov. 1858"], single, B: Monroe
            Co., VA (now W.VA.), Occup: farmer,
            Lived: Dewitt Co., Illinois, s/o:
            Zebada B. and Elizabeth Lewis (on bk)
            [Zebadee B. and Elisabeth Lewis (on
            Lic.)]; and Minerva A. Groff (on bk)
            [Manerva A. Goff (on Lic.)], 21 yrs.
            1 mo. 4 days [Note on Lic.: "was 21
            the 12th of June 1858"], single, B:
            Monroe Co., VA (now W.VA.), Lived:
            Alleg. Co., VA, dau/o: John and Har-
            riet Groff (on bk) [John and Harriet
            Goff (on Lic.)]. Mar. by Alfred Buhr-
            man who signed the Lic. 07-16-1858.
            PL: Alleg. Co., VA, Mr. Goff's res.

07-29-1858 (on bk)   08-03-1858 (on Lic.)
  # 20   [Author Note: A "Certificate To Obtain
           A Marriage License" began to be used
           with this marriage. The following is
           what was printed on it.
           "CERTIFICATE TO OBTAIN A MARRIAGE
           LICENSE
           Having applied to the Clerk of the
           County Court of Alleghany for a Mar-
           riage License, and being requested I
           make the following Certificate, as
           required by the Act of the General

Assembly, passed April 7th, 1858."
[Note: Marriage Lic. date and other
information is asked for and is signed by the person applying for the
license and the date that person
signed the certificate. There is no
place designated for the minister who
performs the ceremony to sign their
name or to put a date of signing the
license.]
"Within two months after the Marriage
shall have taken place, the Minister
solemnizing the same, must certify
the fact to the Clerk of Court."]
Andr. J. Turner (on bk) [Andrew J.
Turner (on Lic.)], 27, single, B:
Page Co., VA, Occup: House Carpenter,
s/o: Litha Turner; and Lucy J. Gilliland, 20 yrs. 4 mos. 28 days [Note on
Lic.: "21--1st March 1859"], single,
B: Alleg. Co., VA, dau/o: Jos. and
Mahaletts Gilliland (on bk) [Joseph
and Mahala Gilliland (on Lic.)]. Both
lived in Alleg. Co., VA. Mar. by
_____.   PL: Alleg. Co., VA. An-
drew J. Turner signed CTOL on 07-29-
1858. Consent was signed [(?Ma/o/de
-- hard to read, could be Matalda)
Gilliland (Seal)]on 07-26-1858, Wit.
James Shanklin and Henry D. Shanklin.
James Shanklin made oath as to consent, Teste L. P. Holloway, Clk.

Page 4

08-03-1858   Thomas W. Richardson (on bk) [Thos.
  # 1   W. Richardson (on Lic.)], 26, single,
              B: Alleg. Co., VA, Occup: farmer, s/o:
              Thos. and Margaret Richardson; and
              Eliza S. Johnson, 26 [Lic. says "about
              26"], single, B: Alleg. Co., VA, dau/
              o: Dave and Elizabeth Johnston (on
              bk) [David and Elizabeth Johnson (on

(Mar. Register Book (1) - Continued)

Lic.)]. Both lived in Alleg. Co.,VA.
CTOL was signed by Thomas W. Richardson on 08-02-1858. Note from S. T.
Mallory, Mins. M. E. Church, South:
08-03-1858 married Thomas W. Richardson and Elisa S. Johnson at residence
of David Johnson, Alleg. Co. signed
on 08-04-1858.

08-15-1858   Jno. Hollerin, 30, widower, B: Ire-
2   land, Occup: laborer (on bk) [Public
               Works (on Lic.)], s/o: Jno. and Mary
               Hollerin (on bk) [Jno. Hollorin and
               Mary-Feant-(as is on Lic.)]; and Mar-
               garet Driscol, 17, single, B: Ireland,
               dau/o: Patrick and Mary Discel (on
               bk) [Patrick Driscol and Mary Crow-
               ley (on Lic.)]. Both lived in Alleg.
               Co. Mar. by J. H. Walters, Mins. of
               Gospel, Catholic. PL: Alleg. Co., VA.
               "I do hereby certify that Mary Disch-
               el this day gave her consent for her
               daughter Margaret to marry John Harlan.
               Given under my hand this 13th day of
               August 1858.
                     Timothy (his X mark) Haventon"
               [Author Note: This was a Lic. and not
               a CTOL.]

08-24-1858   Lorenzo D. Lowther, 32, single, B:
3   Harrison Co., VA (now W.VA.), Occup:
               R. Road Conductor, s/o: Wm. W. and
               Melipa [? Melissa] Lowther (on bk)
               [William and Mellipi (? Mellissi)
               Lowther (on Lic.)]; and Elizabeth A.
               Cotton, 17 yrs. 11 mos., B: Green-
               brier Co., VA (now W.VA), single, dau/
               o: Michael Cotton and _____. Both
               lived in Alleg. Co., VA. Mar. by S.
               T. Mallory, M. E. Church. PL: Alleg.
               Co., VA. CTOL signed by L. D. Lowther

- 85 -

Railroad Contractor on 08-20-1858.
Consent of grandfather, Jno. Hardy,
for E. A. Cotton to marry L. D. Lowther dated on 08-20-1858 to L. Holo-
way, Clk. Mins. note of S. T. Mallory, M. E. Church, South: On 08-24-
1858 at the residence of John Hardy,
Alleg. Co., VA, married Lorenzo D.
Lowther and Elisabeth Cotton and was
signed 08-31-1858.[Lorenzo's mother's
name was very difficult to read.]

09-14-1858   Daniel Circle (on bk) [Danl. Circle
  # 4   (on Lic.)], 34, widower, Occup: far-
               mer, B: Botetourt Co., VA, Lived:
               Nicholas Co., VA (now W.VA.), s/o:
               John and Martha L. Circle (on bk)
               [John L. and Martha Lee Circle (on
               Lic.)]; and Ellen Williamson (on bk)
               [Elen Williamson (on Lic.)], 30, sin-
               gle, B: Fife Co., Scotland, Lived:
               Alleg. Co., VA, dau/o: Andr. and Jane
               Williamson. Mar. by J. M. Rice, Pre-
               sbyterian. PL: Alleg. Co.,VA. [Lic.
               apparently altered to be CTOL and was
               signed by Daniel Circle on 09-13-1858]

09-16-1858   Henry Humphries, 24 ["24 next January"
  # 5   (on Lic.)], single, B: Alleg. Co., VA,
               Occup: farmer, s/o: Wm. and Ruth Hump-
               hries (on bk) [William and Ruthy Hump-
               hries (on Lic.)]; and Mary Ann Sim-
               mons, 40 -supposed to be (on bk) (age
               not listed on Lic.), single, B: Alleg.
               Co., VA, dau/o: Ephraim and Ruth Sim-
               mons (on bk) [Epraim and Ruth Simmons
               (on Lic.)]. Mar. by A. Behrman. PL:
               Alleg. Co., VA. CTOL signed on 09-
               13-1858 by Henry Humphries.

09-28-1858   John F. Graham, 26, single, Occup:
  # 6   Minister of Gospel, B: Mifflaw Co.,

(Mar. Register Book (1) - Continued)

PA (on bk) [Mifflan Co., PA (on Lic.)], Lived: Bath Co., VA, s/o: David and Catharine Graham; and <u>Louisa Damron</u>, 16, single, B: Alleg. Co. VA, Lived: Covington, Alleg. Co., VA, dau/o: Wm. and Bev. E. Damron. Mar. by A. Behrman. PL: Covington, VA. CTOL signed 09-28-1858 by <u>J. F. Graham</u>. Consent signed by Wm. Damron on 09-28-1858 listed daughter's name as <u>Louisa Allen Damron</u>.

10-07-1858   <u>Wm. Matheny</u> (on bk) [<u>William Matheny</u>
7   (on Lic.)], 27 yrs. 6 mos. [Lic. says "28 last April"], single, Occup: farmer, B: Rockingham Co., VA, Lived: Alleg. [Note: Don't know if refers to Alleg. Co. or place on Rt. 311 called "Alleghany" near W.VA. state line.], s/o: Sam'l. and Mary Matheny; and <u>Lucinda L. Clark</u>, Age: __, single, B: Covington, Alleg. Co., VA, Lived: Covington, VA, dau/o: Jos. B. and Christina Clark (on bk) [Joseph B. and Christena Clark (on Lic.)]. Mar. by A. Behrman. PL: Covington, VA. CTOL signed 10-06-1858 by <u>William Matheny</u>.

10-17-1858   <u>Solomon Johnston</u> (on bk) [<u>Solomon Johnson</u>
8   <u>Johnson</u> (on Lic.)], 22, single, B: Harrison Co., VA (now W.VA.), Occup: merchant, s/o: Jno. S. and Eliza Johnston (on bk) [John S. and Eliza Johnson (on Lic.)]; and <u>Isabela W. Warren</u> (on bk) [<u>Isabell W. Warren</u> (on Lic)], 18, single, B: Alleg. Co., VA, dau/o: James and ____ Warren (on bk) [Jas. and _____ Warren (on Lic.)]. Both lived in Alleg. Co., VA. He lived at Sweet Springs, VA (now W.VA.). Mar. by S. T. Mallory, M. E. Church, South.

(Mar. Register Book (1) - Continued)

PL: Alleg. Co., VA. [This was a Lic. form not CTOL.]

10-21-1858
9

Charles M. Stull (on bk) [Charles S. Stull (on Lic.)], 21 yrs. 4 mos. 5 days [Note on Lic.: "21-- 16 June 1859"], single, B: Alleg. Co., VA, Occup: farmer, s/o: James and Hannah Stull; and Virginia M. Davis, 18 yrs. 6 mos. 21 days [Note on Lic.: "18 -- 26 March 1859"], single, B: Bedford Co., VA, dau/o: _____. Both lived in Alleg. Co., VA. Mar. by S. T. Mallory, M. E. Church, South; and his note to Clk. dated on 11-03-1858 says he married Charles M. Stull and Virginia M. Davis on 10-__-1858 [no day listed]. CTOL was signed on 10-18-1858 by Charles S. M. Stull. Consent signed by Hannah (her X mark) Stull for Charles S. M. Stull to marry Virginia Davis was dated 10-18-1858,Wit. J. J. Stull. PL: Alleg. Co., VA. [Note: Birth year listed as on Lic.]

11-11-1858
10

Arthur L. Caldwell, 35, widower, B: Botetourt Co., VA, Occup: Stock Raiser and Dealer, Lived: California, s/o: Bartlet and Margaret Caldwell (on bk) [Bartlett and Margaret Caldwell (on Lic.)]; and Sarah Gibbon (on bk) [Sarah Gibbons (on Lic.)], 28,widower, B: Alleg. Co., VA, Lived: Alleg. Co., VA, dau/o: James and ____ Kendall (on bk) [James and ____ Kindle (on Lic)]. Mar. by A. Behrman. PL: Alleghany [Note: Don't know if refers to Alleg. Co. or place on Rt. 311 called "Alleghany" near W.VA. state line.] No marriage date or place or signature on CTOL which was dated 10th Nov. 1858.

(Mar. Register Book (1) - Continued)

11-17-1858   (on bk)   11-17-____ (on CTOL)
  # 11   Bradley Carter, 25, single, Occup:
             farmer, B: Monroe Co., VA (now W.VA.),
             Lived: Monroe Co., VA (now W.VA.),
             s/o: Lemuel and Patsy Carter, [CTOL
             has that both Bradley Carter and ____
             (his bride) lived in Alleg. Co., VA];
             and Rosanna (?Hanna) (on bk) [no name
             listed on CTOL], 17, single, B: Alleg.
             Co., VA, Lived: Alleg. Co., VA, dau/o:
             Thos. and Mary (?Hamer) (on bk) [Thos.
             and Mary (?Hamun) (on Lic.)]. CTOL
             has no signature or date Lic. was
             obtained. Mar. by S. T. Mallory, M.E.
             Church, South, who sent a note to Clk.
             on 11-22-1858 that he married Bradley
             Carter and Rosanna Harmon on 11-17-
             1858. PL: Alleg. Co., VA.

12-24-1858   (on bk)   12-23-1858 (on CTOL)
  # 12   Mason D. Helms (on bk) [Mason V. Hel-
             lums (on Lic.)], 24, single, B: Indi-
             ana, Occup: farmer, Lived: Craig Co.,
             VA, s/o: John and Rebecca Helms (on
             bk) [John and Rebecca Hellums (on
             Lic.)]; and Margaret A. Bennet (on bk)
             [Margaret Ann Bennett (on Lic.)], 19,
             single, B: Alleg. Co., VA, Lived: Al-
             leg. Co., VA, dau/o: Solomon and Susan
             Bennet (on bk) [Solomon and Susan
             Bennett (on Lic.)]. PL: Alleg. Co.,VA.
             Mar. by S. T. Mallory. CTOL dated on
             12-21-1858 and under obtainee's place
             of signature S. T. Mallory signed Cert.
             Consent was dated 12-13-1858 and sign-
             ed by Susan (her X mark) Bennett, Teste
             John J. Bennett. Proven oath of John
             J. Bennett that consent was made by
             Susan Bennett, J. Carpenter, D.C.

12-05-1858   Thomas Malory, 22, single, Occup: Lab-
  # 13   orer, B: Ireland, s/o: not ascertained

(Mar. Register Book (1) - Continued)

[not listed on Lic.]; and <u>Martha Reed</u>,
22, single, B: Alleg. Co., VA, dau/o:
Robert and Rebecca Reed. Mar. by A.
Behrman. Both lived in Alleg. Co.,VA.
PL: Alleghany [Don't know if refers to
Alleg. Co. or to place on Rt. 311
called "Alleghany".]
"Alleghany County Court Clerk's Office
5th December 1858:
    This day Hezekiah Patterson came
before me in my office and made oath
that <u>Martha Reed</u> is over the age of
21 years and that she desires license
to issue to celebrate the rites of
matrimony between herself and <u>Thomas
Molonay</u>.
    Given under my hand this the 5th
December 1858.
            Jos. Carpenter, D. C."

12-23-1858   (on bk)   12-29-1858 (on CTOL)
  # 14   <u>John R. Thomas</u>, 26, single, Occup:
carpenter, B: Rockbridge Co., VA,
Lived: Bath Co., VA, s/o: Elizabeth
and Peter Thomas; and <u>Susan E. Walton</u>
(on bk) [<u>Susan Elizabeth Walton</u> (on
Lic.)], 19, single, B: Pocahontas Co.,
VA (now W.VA.), Lived: Alleg. Co., VA,
dau/o: Jas. M. and Maria Walton (on
bk) [James M. and Maria Walton (on
Lic.)]. PL: Alleg. Co., VA.   Mar. by
S. T. Mallory, M. E. Church, whose
note to the Clk. signed 12-31-1858
says they were married on 12-29-1858.
CTOL was dated 12-23-1858 and signed
<u>John R. Thomas</u>. Consent was dated
12-23-1858, signed by Maria Walton,
and delivered in the presence of William Walton who is the brother of <u>Eliza-
beth Walton</u>, Teste Lewis P. Holloway,
Clk.

(Mar. Register Book (1) - Continued)

12-27-1858   (on bk)   12-30-____   (on CTOL)
  # 15   <u>John M. Kesterson</u> (on bk) [<u>Jno. M.</u>
             <u>Kesterson</u> (on Lic.)], 22, single, B:
             Augusta Co., VA, Occup: Carpenter,
             s/o: Wm. and Mary Kesterson (on bk)
             [William and Mary Kesterson (on Lic)];
             and <u>Mary A. Fry</u>, (on bk) [<u>Nancy A.</u>
             <u>Fry</u> (on Lic.)], 22, single, B: Alleg.
             Co., VA, dau/o: John and Mary Fry.
             Both lived in Alleg. Co., VA. Mar.
             by S. T. Mallory. PL: Alleg. Co., VA.
             CTOL signed on 12-27-1858 by <u>John M.</u>
             <u>Kesterson</u>. Consent has <u>Nancy A. Fry</u>
             and was signed on 12-27-1858 by John
             Fry, Teste F. M. Kesterson and Samuel
             Fry. Oath in office to consent given
             was signed on 12-27-1858, L. P. Hol-
             loway, Clk.

01-03-1859   (on bk) (No marriage date on CTOL)
  # 1   <u>James Flaherty</u>, 24, single, B: Ire-
             land, Occup: laborer, s/o: James and
             Joanna Flaherty; and <u>Catharine Fouly</u>,
             20, single, B: Ireland, dau/o: Pat-
             rick and Ellen Fouly. Both lived in
             Alleg. Co., VA. Mar. by J. H. Walt-
             ers, Catholic Priest who signed the
             CTOL on 01-03-1859. PL: Alleghany
             [Don't know if refers to Alleg. Co.
             or to place on Rt. 311 called "Alleg-
             hany".] Consent was dated 12-18-1858
             and signed by brother and guardian,
             Martin (his X mark) Fouly, Wit. J.
             Carpenter who made oath that above
             writing was done in his presence.

01-05-1859   <u>Chas. M. McElwee</u>, 32, single, B: Bath,
  # 2   VA [Note: believe this refers to Bath
             Co. but County reference was left off
             on bk--no documents were found in the
             files for this Mar.], Occup: Railroad
             Agent, s/o: John and _____ McElwee;

and <u>Rebeca J. Allen</u>, 33, single, B:
Alleg. Co., Va, dau/o: John and Jane
Allen. Both lived in Alleghany
[Don't know if refers to Alleg. Co.
or place called "Alleghany" on Rt.
311 near W.VA. state line]. Mar. by
J. M. Rice, Presbyterian Mins. PL:
Alleghany Co., VA.

01-11-1859   <u>Allen Beckner</u>, 24, single, B: Botet-
  # 3   ourt Co., VA, Occup: farmer, Lived:
              Botetourt Co., VA, Salt Peter Cave
              (on Lic.), s/o: David and Elizabeth
              Beckner (on bk) [David and Bitcy Beck-
              ner (on Lic.)]; and <u>Martha J. Holmes</u>
              (on bk) [<u>Martha</u> (? Jane --ink blotted)
              <u>Holmes</u> (on Lic.)], 17, single, B:
              Botetourt Co., VA, Lived: Alleg. Co.,
              VA, dau/o: James and Martha A. Holmes
              (on bk) [James and Martha Ann Holmes
              (on Lic.)]. Mar. by A. Behrman, M.
              E. Church, North. PL: Alleghany at
              Mr. Myers res. [Don't know if refers
              to Alleg. Co. or place on Rt. 311
              called "Alleghany" near W.VA. state
              line] CTOL was signed on 01-10-1859
              by <u>Allen Beckner</u>. James Holmes gave
              consent in person on 01-10-1859, Jos.
              Carpenter, D. C.

01-25-1859   (on bk)   (No Mar. date on CTOL)
  # 4   <u>John Boley</u>, 24, single, B: Monroe Co.,
              VA (now W.VA.), Occup: farmer, s/o:
              Pitman and Ellen Boley; and <u>Sarah</u>
              <u>Boley</u>, 22, single, B: Campbell Co.,
              VA, dau/o: Presley and Nancy Boley.
              Both lived in Alleg. Co. PL: Alleg-
              hany [Don't know if refers to Alleg.
              Co. or to place called "Alleghany"
              on Rt. 311 near W.VA. state line].
              CTOL was signed on 01-25-1859 by <u>John</u>
              <u>W. Boley</u>. Age oath for <u>Sarah Boley</u>

was made by J. Newton Boley that she was 22 yrs. old, Teste Lewis P. Holloway, Clk. Mar. by A. Behrman, M. E. Church, North.

02-04-1859   (on bk) 02-08-1859 (on Mins. Note)
5   Thomas Shumaker (on bk) [Thos. Shumaker (on Lic.)], 24, single, Occup: Day laborer (on Lic.), B: Alleg. Co., VA, s/o: Jno. K. E. and Elizabeth Shumaker (on bk) [John A. and Rebecca Smith (on Lic.)]; and Mary A. Smith, 22 [Note on Lic: "last August"], single, B: Franklin Co., VA, dau/o: Jno. A. and Rebeca J. Smith (on bk) [John K. E. and Eliza Shumaker (on Lic.)]. [Note: Parents names listed backwards on Lic.] Both lived in Alleg. Co., VA. Mar. by S. T. Mallory, M. E. Church, South. PL: Alleghany [Don't know if refers to Alleg. Co. or to place on Rt. 311 called "Alleghany" near W.VA. state line] CTOL signed on 02-04-1859 by Thomas (his X mark) Shumaker. Age oath sworn by Mary A. Smith that she was 21, Teste Lewis P. Holloway, Clk. Note to Clk. from S. T. Mallory said he married Thomas Shumaker and Mary A. Smith on 02-08-1859 and was dated 14th March 1859.

***** S. T. Mallory, Mins. M. E. Church, South included in a note to the Clerk of Court of Alleghany Co. which was dated 14th March 1859 (see above marriage) that he had married Mr. A. A. Perkins and Miss Elisabitt J. C. Kincaid on 03-03-1859. There is no mention on the Mar. Book nor other documents or records about this to be found in the files.*******************************

(Mar. Register Book (1) - Continued)

02-17-1859
6

Thomas Crogham (on bk) [Thomas Crog-han (on Lic.)], 25, single, B; Ireland, Occup: laborer, s/o: Michael and Hannera Cragham (on bk) [Michael and Hanora Croghan (on Lic.)]; and Mary Flanagan, 16, single, B: Ireland, dau/o: Mike and Barbara Flanagan (on bk) [Michael and Barbara Flanagan (on Lic.)]. Both lived in Alleg. Co. He lived in Clifton Forge, VA. Mar. by J. H. Walters, Catholic Church, sent note to Clk. that he married ~~Joanna~~ Mary Flanagan [shown as on note] on 02-17-1859. PL: Alleg. Co., VA, Covington (on Lic.). CTOL was signed on 02-17-1859 by Thomas Crog-han.

03-31-1859
7

John Patterson, 45, widower, Occup: R. Road Supt., B: Scotland, s/o: Francis and Helen Patterson; and Martha A. Simpson, 33, widow, B: Alleg. Co., VA, dau/o: Fleming and Nancy Keyser (on bk) [Fleming Keyser and Nancy ____ (on Lic.)]. Both lived in Alleg. Co. PL: Alleg. at Fleming Kiser res. (on Mins. Note). Mar. by P. B. Smith of Warms Springs, VA, M. E. Church, whose note to Clk. signed on 04-16-1859 said he married the couple on 03-31-1859 at Fleming Kiser res. CTOL was signed on 03-31-1859. Consent gave authorization to John Patterson to get Lic. and was signed by M. A. Simpson on 03-30-1859, Wit. Fleming Keyser and lists name as Martha Ann Simpson.

04-28-1859
8

John Rhine, 25, single, B: Ireland, Karry Co. (on Lic.) [Note: probably means Kerry Co.], Occup: Day laborer, s/o: Dennis and Catharine Rhine; and

- 94 -

(Mar. Register Book (1) - Continued)

Mary Neligham (on bk) [Mary Nelligan
(on Lic.)], 25, single, B: Ireland,
Karry Co. (on Lic.) [Note: Probably
means Kerry Co.], dau/o: James Neligham (on bk) [James Nelligan and ____
(on Lic.)]. Both lived in Alleg. Co.
PL: Sweet Springs, VA (now W.VA.).
Mar. by J. H. Walters, Catholic Church, whose note to the Clk. said he
had married the couple on 04-28-1859.
Clk's. Note: Cert. was returned to
Mins. to fill in blanks on CTOL for
Mar. information and he did so and
returned it to the Clk. CTOL was
signed on 04-25-1859 by John (his X
mark) Rhine.

03-31-1859   Henry Bliss, 25, single, B: Germany,
9   Occup: Stone Cutter, s/o: Nicholas
             and Catharine Bliss; and Mary S.
             Night, 21, single, B: Virginia, dau/o:
             unknown (on bk) [not listed on Lic.--
             Mins. asked to obtain but could not
             find where it was ever gotten]. Both
             lived in Alleg. Co., VA. PL: Alleg-
             hany [Don't know if refers to Alleg.
             Co. or place on Rt. 311 called "Alleg-
             hany" near W.VA. state lien]. Mar.
             by S. T. Mallory, M. E. Church, South,
             whose note to Clk. signed 04-13-1859
             has Mary S. Knight who was married on
             03-31-1859. CTOL was signed by Henry
             Bliss on 03-29-1859. Consent says
             Mary Susan Knight and was signed on
             03-29-1859 by Lovast (his X mark)
             Knight.

03-31-1859   John A. Hepler, 24, single, Occup:
9 ½   farmer, B: Alleg. Co., VA, s/o: David
             and Bersheba Hepler; and Mary C.
             Cahoon (on bk) [Mary C. Carson (on
             Lic.)], 20 [Lic. has 20 yrs. 8 mos.],

single, B: Alleg. Co., VA, dau/o:
James and Caroline Carson. Both lived in Alleg. Co. CTOL was signed by
<u>John A. Hepler</u> and Rev. Johnzey Leef
on 03-30-1859. PL: Alleghany [Don't
know if refers to Alleg. Co. or place
called "Alleghany" on Rt. 311 near W.
VA state line]. Mar. by Johnzey Leef.
Consent dated 03-29-1859 says <u>Mary C.
Carson</u>, 20 yrs. 8 mos. 26 days old
and was signed by father, James Carson, Wit. James M. Carson.

04-13-1859   <u>Wm. Hoylman</u> (on bk) [<u>Wm. T. Hoylman</u>
10   (on CTOL); <u>Wm. F. Hoylman</u> (on Lic.)],
              33, single, B: Botetourt Co., VA,
              Occup: farmer, Lived: Alleg. Co., VA,
              s/o: Simon and Mary Hoylman (on bk
              and Lic.) [Limon and Mary Hoylman (on
              CTOL)]; and <u>Minerva G. Porter</u> (on bk)
              [<u>Minerva G. J. Porter</u> (on Lic.)], 27,
              single, B: Rockbridge Co., VA [Lic.
              says Botetourt Co., VA], Lived: Alleg.
              Co., VA, dau/o: E. G. and Matilda
              Porter (on bk) [Ezekial G. and Matil-
              da Porter (on Lic.)]. CTOL signed on
              04-11-1859 by <u>William T. Hoylman.</u>
              Mar. by H. A. Gaver, M. E. Church, N.
              who signed Lic. on 04-13-1859. PL:
              Covington, VA (on bk and Lic.) [Alleg.
              Co. (on CTOL)].

02-10-1859   (on bk)   02-20-1859 (on CTOL)
11   <u>Dan'l. Dobbin</u> (on bk) [<u>Daniel Dolbins</u>
              (on CTOL)], 21, single, B: Ireland,
              Occup: laborer, s/o: Michael and Cath-
              arine Dobbins (on bk) [Michael Dolbin
              and Catharine Dolbin (on CTOL)]; and
              <u>Mary Connel</u>, 21, single, B: Ireland,
              dau/o: Patrick and ___ Connel. CTOL
              signed on 02-19-1859 by <u>Daniel (his X
              mark) Dobbins</u>. Consent and oath of

(Mar. Register Book (1) - Continued)

age given by witness Jeffrey (his X
mark) Connel on 02-19-1859. Mar. by
J. H. Walters, Catholic Church. PL:
Kelly's Work (? Mrk--can't read),
Alleg. Co., VA (on Lic.). Both lived
in Alleg. Co., VA.

02-___-1859   Jeffery Connel, B: Ireland; and Joanna
11 ½   Connel, 19, B: Ireland, dau/o: Peter
              Harrigan and ____. Mar. by _____.
              Both Lived in Alleg. Co. PL: Alleg.
              Co., VA. [NO COPY OF A LICENSE OR
              CTOL IN FILES. No other information
              was found.]
              Consent:
              "To the Clerk of the County Court of
              Alleghany   Feb. 1859
                   This is to authorize you to issue
              license to celebrate the rights of
              matrimony between my Daughter, Joanna
              Connel & Jeffrey Connel.
                   Given under my hand this the __
              day of February 1859.
                   Peter (his X mark) Horrigan
              the girl's father gives Consent and
              she is 19 years of age.
              Wit. Dan'l. Dobbins"
              "Proven by the oath of Daniel Dolbin
              the Subscribing witness. J. Carpenter,
              Clk."

04-24-1859   Patrick Coody (on bk) [Patrick Coady
12   (on CTOL)], 22 [Age was penciled over
              to 25 on CTOL], single, B: Ireland,
              Co. of Haterford [Note: possibly means
              Waterford Co.], Occup: Laborer (on bk)
              [Boss (on CTOL)], s/o: Edward and Mary
              Coady; and Catharine Rowan (on bk)
              [Catherine Ronaw (on CTOL)], 17, sing-
              le, B: Co. of Cork, Ireland, dau/o:
              Jas. and Bridgett Rowan (on bk) [James
              and Bridgett Ronaw (on CTOL)]. Mar.

by J. H. Waters (on bk) J. H. Walters
(on Mins. note to clerk that he had
Mar. the parties on 04-24-1859),
Catholic Church. PL: Alleg. Co., VA.
CTOL signed by <u>Patrick Coady</u> on 04-
24-1859. Both lived in Alleg. Co.

05-09-1859 (on bk) 05-14-1859 (on CTOL)
  # 13   <u>Richard Murry</u> (on bk) [<u>Richard Murray</u>
            (on CTOL)], 30, widower, B: Farmoy,
            Ireland [Note: I find no county on
            Irish map with this spelling or pro-
            nounciation. The closest spelling
            seems to be "Mayo County" or "Ferma-
            nagh County"] Occup; mechanic, s/o:
            Jeremiah and Cate Murry (on bk) [Jere-
            miah and Catharine Murry (on CTOL)];
            and <u>Bridgett Roradin</u> (on bk-page tore)
            [<u>Bridget Rusradan</u> (on CTOL)], 30,
            widower, B: Farmoy, Ireland [See note
            above], dau/o: John and Elizabeth
            Roradin (on bk) [John Riordan and
            Eliza Keef (on CTOL)]. PL: Alleg. Co,
            VA. Both lived in Alleg. Co. Mar. by
            J. H. Waters (on bk) [J. H. Walters
            (on Mins. note to clerk says married
            on 05-14-1859)], Catholic Church.
            CTOL signed on 05-09-1859 by <u>Richard
            Murray</u>. "License granted upon eviden-
            ce of John Duran who Testified Mrs.
            Roradon was of age.
                    Teste L. P. Holloway, Clk."

06-23-1859 <u>Dennis Harrington</u>, 22, single, B: Ire-
  # 14   land, Occup: laborer, s/o: Jeremiah
           and Margarit Harrington (on bk) [Jere-
           miah and Margaret Harrington (on
           Lic.)]; and <u>Joana Harrington</u>, 18,
           single, B: Ireland, dau/o: unknown.
           PL: Alleg. Co., VA. Mar. by J. H.
           Waters (on bk) [J. H. Walters (on
           Mins. note to clerk says Mar. 06-23-

1859 "according to customs of my church"], Catholic Church. Both lived in Alleg. Co., VA. CTOL signed on 06-22-1859 by Dennis (his X mark) Harrington. On Lic. "Issued upon the oath of Daniel Sullivan."

06-17-1859
15

(on bk)   06-19-1859 (on CTOL)
Martin Quinlan, 26, single, Occup: laborer, B: Ireland, s/o: Darby and Margaret Quinlan (on bk) [Darby and Margaret Quinlin (on CTOL)]; and Ellen Dugan, 25, single, B: Ireland, dau/o: unknown (on bk) [none listed on CTOL]. Both lived in Alleg. Co., VA. PL: Alleg. Co., VA. Mar. by J. H. Waters (on bk) [J. H. Walters, Catholic Church (on note to clerk says married 06-19-1859)]. CTOL signed 06-11-1859 by Martin Quinlen. "Delivered to Martin Quinlen upon the oath of Partrick Quinlen a cousin of the within named Ellen Quinlen.
          Teste Jos. Carpenter, D. C."

06-20-1859
16

William M. Brown (on bk) [Wm. M. Brown (on CTOL)], 32, single, B: Alleg. Co., VA, Occup: farmer, s/o: Samuel and Francis Brown (on bk) [Sam'l. and Frances Brown (on CTOL)]; and Emma V. Brown, 22, single, B: Alleg. Co., VA, dau/o: Samuel and Sarah Brown (on bk) [Sam'l. and Sarah Brown (on CTOL)]. Both lived in Alleg. Co. PL: Covington, Alleg. Co., VA. Mar. by S. T. Mallory, M. E. Church, South. CTOL signed on 06-20-1859 by Wm. M. Brown. [Author's Note: Suspect this may have been a double wedding with the following couple in # 17. This CTOL and their CTOL were joined together side by side.]

06-20-1859   Isaac N. Linkenhoger (on bk) [Isaac
17   W. Linkenhoger (on CTOL)], 23, sing-
             le, B: Botetourt Co., VA, Occup: far-
             mer, s/o: Adam and Mary Linkenhoger
             (on bk) [Adam and May Linkenhoger
             (on CTOL)]; and Sarah Brown, 21, sin-
             gle, B: Tennessee, dau/o: James M.
             and Nancy Brown. PL: Alleg. Co., VA,
             Covington (on CTOL).   Both lived in
             Alleg. Co.   Mar. by S. T. Mallory,
             M. E. Church, South. CTOL signed on
             06-20-1859 by Isaac Wistley Linken-
             hoker. [Author's Note: Suspect this
             may have been a double wedding with
             the couple above in # 16. This CTOL
             and their CTOL were joined together
             side by side.]

06-20-1859   (on bk)   07-14-1859 (on CTOL)
18   John D. D. Ragland, 35, widower, B:
             Alleg. Co., VA, Occup: School Teacher,
             s/o: James T. and Polly Ragland (on
             bk) [James P. and Polly Ragland (on
             CTOL)]; and Sophia E. Beckner, 27,
             single, B; Monroe Co., VA (now W.VA),
             dau/o: Daniel and Margaret Beckner
             (on bk) [Daniel and Margaret R. Bec-
             kner (on CTOL)]. PL: Alleg. Co., VA.
             Both lived in Alleg. Co. (on bk) [he
             lived in Monroe Co., VA (now W. VA.)
             and she lived in Alleg. Co., VA. (on
             CTOL)]. Mar. by H. B. Rose, Presby-
             terian Church.   CTOL signed 07-06-
             1859 by John D. D. Ragland.
             "Red Sweet Springs, VA, July 14, 1859
             To Clerk of Alleghany County Court
                 Dear Sir
                 This will certify that I Offici-
             ated at John D. D. Ragland & Sophia
             E. Beckner's marriage July 14, 1859
                              Truly yours

H. B. Rose
N. B. I understand Mr. Ragland that
you had filled up the certificate of
his marriage, & that that was the
reason you did not send one with the
license.   H. B. R."
[Note: Believe the above refers to
the Cert. of Mar. that the Mins. gives
the couple to show they are married.]

08-02-1859   Chas K. Humphries (on bk) [Charles K.
19   Humphries (on CTOL)], 20, single, B:
             Alleg. Co., VA, Occup: farmer, s/o:
             Wm. and Ruth Humphries (on bk) [Will-
             iam and Ruthy Humphries (on CTOL)];
             and Nancy M. Simmons, 24, single, B:
             Alleg. Co., VA, dau/o: Ephraim and
             Ruth Simmons (on bk) [Ephraim and
             Ruthy Simmons (on CTOL)]. Both lived
             in Alleg. Co. PL: Alleg. Co., VA.
             Mar. by H. A. Gaver, M. E. Church, N.
             sent note to clk. saying mar. on 08-
             02-1859 and signed on 09-04-1859.
             CTOL signed on 08-01-1859 by Charles
             K. (his X mark) Humphries. Author-
             ization to issue Lic. given 08-01-
             1859 by William Humphries. Age oath
             given by Harvey Humphries, J. Carpen-
             ter, D. C.

08-02-1859   Chas. Fridley (on bk) [Charles Fridly
20   (on CTOL)], 21 (on bk) [21 yrs. 6 mos.
             (on CTOL)], single, B: Alleg. Co., VA,
             Occup: farmer, s/o: Isaac and E. Frid-
             ley (on bk) [Isaac and Elizabeth Frid-
             ly (on CTOL)]; and Granville Humphries,
             28, single, B: Alleg. Co., VA, dau/o:
             Wm. and Ruth Humphries (on bk) [Will-
             iam and Rutha Humphries (on CTOL)].
             Both lived in Alleg. Co. PL: Alleg.
             Co., VA. Mar. by H. A. Gaver, M. E.
             Church, N., note to clk. says mar. on
             08-02-1859 was signed 09-04-1859.
             CTOL signed by Charles Fridly on 08-01-
             1859.

07-07-1859   Francis Bostic (on bk) [Francis Cos-
  # 21   tic (on CTOL)], 20, single, Occup:
              farmer, B: Chesterfield Co., VA.,
              s/o: Josiah and Martha Ann Bostic (on
              bk) [Josiah and Marthan Ann Crostic
              (on CTOL)]; and Nancy Owen, 17, sin-
              gle, B: Monroe Co., VA (now W.VA.),
              dau/o: John and Rhoda Owen (on bk)
              [John Owen and Rhoda Owens (on CTOL)].
              Both lived in Alleg. Co. PL: Alleg.
              Co., VA. Mar. by S. T. Mallory.
              CTOL signed 07-06-1859 by Francis
              Crostic.

08-02-1859   Jos. W. Persinger (on bk) [Joseph W.
  # 22   H. Persinger (on CTOL)], 23, single,
              B: Alleg. Co., VA, Occup: farmer, s/o:
              none listed on bk [Joseph and Char-
              lotte Persinger (on CTOL)]; and Sarah
              M. Terry, 23, single, B: Alleg. Co.,
              VA, dau/o: Joseph Persinger and Char-
              lotte Persinger (on bk--error on bk)
              [Joseph and Elizabeth Terry (on CTOL)].
              Both lived in Alleg. Co., VA. PL:
              Alleg. Co., VA. Mar. by H. A. Gaver,
              M. E. Church, note to clk. says mar.
              on 08-02-1859 was signed 09-04-1859.
              Age oath given by William H. Quickell,
              Jr., Teste Lewis P. Holloway, Clk.
              CTOL signed on 08-01-1859 by Jos. W.
              H. (his X mark) Persinger.

08-04-1859   Frederic Riddlebarger (on bk) [Fred-
  # 23   erick Riddlesbarger (on CTOL)], 23,
              single, B: Alleg. Co., VA (on bk)
              [Botetourt Co., VA (on CTOL)], Occup:
              farmer, s/o: Sam'l. and Elizabeth
              Riddlebarger (on bk) [Sam'l. and Eliz-
              abeth Riddlesbarger (on CTOL)]; and
              Frances E. Morrison, 18, single, B:
              Alleg. Co., VA, dau/o: James and Jane
              Morrison (on bk) [James D. and Jane
              Morrison (on CTOL)]. Both lived in

Alleg. Co. (on bk) [He lived in Botetourt Co., VA, and she lived in Alleg.
Co. (on CTOL)]. CTOL signed on 08-
01-1859 by Frederick Riddlesbarger.
Mar. by H. A. Gaver, M. E. Church, S.,
note to clk. has name as Frederick
Riddlesbarger and says mar. on 08-04-
1859 was signed on 09-04-1859. PL:
Alleg. Co., VA.

06-30-1859   Wm. Hix (on bk) [William Hix (on
24   CTOL)], 30, single, B: Alleg. Co., VA
             (on bk) [Buckingham Co., VA (on CTOL)],
             Occup: blacksmith, s/o: Arch and Jane
             Hix (on bk) [Archibald and Jane Hix
             (on CTOL)]; and Margaret Crawford (on
             bk) [Margaret M. Crawford (on CTOL)],
             23, single, B: Alleg. Co., VA, dau/o:
             Owen Crawford (on bk) [Owen & _____
             Crawford (on CTOL)]. Both lived in
             Alleg. Co. PL: Alleg. Co., VA. Mar.
             by H. A. Gaver, M. E. Church, S. CTOL
             signed on 06-30-1859 by Wm. Hix. Con-
             sent: Jackson River 06-30-1859 signed
             Oen (his X mark) Crofford, Wit. Peter
             Hinton.

10-13-1859   Frances Leighton (on bk) [Francis M.
25   Leighton (on CTOL)], 26 (on bk) [26
             yrs. 11 mos. (on CTOL)], single, B:
             Alleg. Co., VA (on bk) [Botetourt Co.,
             VA (on CTOL)], Occup: farmer, s/o:
             Isaac and Sarah Leighton (on bk)
             [Isaac N. and Sarah Leighton (on
             CTOL)]; and Elizabeth F. Persinger,
             18, single, B: Alleg. Co., VA, dau/o:
             Jos. H. and Mary Persinger. Both liv-
             ed in Alleg. Co. PL: Alleg. Co., VA.
             Mar. by H. A. Gaver, M. E. Church, S.,
             note to clk. says mar. but did not
             list date. CTOL signed on 10-12-1859
             by Francis M. Leighton.

10-11-1859   Jacob B. Long, 26, single, Occup:
26   carpenter, B: Rockingham Co., VA, s/o:
              Geo. and Martha Long (on bk) [George
              and Martha Long (on CTOL)]; and Annie
              E. Simpson, 19, single, B: Alleg. Co.,
              VA, dau/o: Alex. and Sarah Simpson
              (on bk) [Alexander and Sarah Simpson
              (on CTOL)]. Both lived in Alleg. Co.
              PL: Covington, Alleg. Co., VA (on
              Lic). Mar. by H. A. Gaver, M. E.
              Church, S., note to clk. no mar. date
              given. Lic. changed to CTOL was sign-
              ed 10-11-1859 by Jacob B. Long.

10-16-1859   John Fitzgerald, 24, single, Occup:
27   laborer; B: Ireland, s/o: John and
              Margaret Fitzgerald; and Margaret
              Murphy, 19, single, B: Ireland, dau/o:
              Jas. and _____ Murphy (on bk) [James
              and _____ Murphy (on CTOL)]. Both
              lived in Alleg. Co. PL: Alleg. Co.,
              VA. Mar. by J. H. Walters, Catholic,
              note to clerk says mar. parties on
              10-16-1859. CTOL signed on 10-14-1859
              by John (his X mark) Fitzgerald.

08-04-1859   Fred. A. Hickman (on bk) [Frederick
28   A. Hickman (on CTOL)], 28, single, B:
              Botetourt Co., VA, Occup: laborer,
              s/o: Pleasant and R. Hickman (on bk)
              [Pleasant and Rebecca Hickman (on
              CTOL)]; and Elizabeth Duncan, 21,
              single, B: Amherst Co., VA, dau/o:
              Geo. and Frances Duncan (on bk) [Geo-
              rge and Frances Duncan (on CTOL)].
              Both lived in Alleg. Co. PL: Alleg.
              Co., VA. Mar. by C. P. Murrill, M. E.
              Church, S., note to clerk says mar.
              08-04-1859. CTOL signed 08-04-1859 by
              F. A. Hickman. Age oath given by
              Ambrose B. Hayden, Teste J. Carpenter,
              D. C.

09-29-1859   Dr. G. McDonald (on bk) [Dr. Gabriel
  # 29   McDonald (on CTOL)], 32, single, B:
             Campbell Co., VA, Occup: Physician,
             s/o: Jas. and M. E. McDonald (on bk)
             [Thompson and Lydia M. McAllister (on
             CTOL)--believe error in putting names
             in correct places]; and Clara McAllis-
             ter (on bk) [Clara McCallister (on
             CTOL)], 19, single, B: Franklin Co.,
             Tenn., dau/o: Thompson and Lydia Mc-
             Callister (on bk) [James McDonald and
             Mary G. McDonald (on CTOL)--believe
             error in putting names in correct
             places]. Both lived in Alleg. Co. (on
             bk) [both lived in Covington, VA (on
             CTOL)]. CTOL signed on 09-29-1859 by
             G. McDonald. PL: Covington, Alleg.
             Co., VA. Mar. by James M. Rice, Pres-
             byterian, note to clk. says mar. on
             09-29-1859.

                        Page 5

10-27-1859   Benjn. S. Cook (on bk) [Benjamin S.
  # 30   Cook (on CTOL)], 26, single, B: Monroe
             Co., VA (now W.VA.), Occup: laborer,
             s/o: Thos. N. and Cath. Cook (on bk)
             [Thomas N. and Catharine Cook (on
             CTOL)]; and Sarah E. Hoke, 19 (on bk)
             [? 14 (on CTOL)], single, B: Monroe
             Co., VA (now W.VA.), dau/o: Josiah
             and Marg. Hoke (on bk) [Josiah and
             Margaret Hoke (on CTOL)]. Both lived
             in Alleg. Co. PL: Covington (on bk)
             [Alleg. Co., VA (on CTOL)]. CTOL
             signed on 10-25-1859 by B. S. Cook.
             Mar. by H. A. Gaver, Northern Meth. or
             B.R., note to clk. says mar. on 10-27-
             1859 and signed Hamilton A. Gaver.
             "Delivered to B. S. Cook in the pres-
             ence of Josiah Hoke the Father of the
             young lady. Teste J. Carpenter, D.C."
             [Note: This apparently refers to Lic.]

09-23-1859   Alfred Huffman, 27, widower, B: Craig
31   Co., VA, Occup: farmer, s/o: Andr.
              and Betsy Huffman (on bk) [Andrew and
              Betsey Huffman (on Lic.)]; and Har-
              riet Terry, 25, single, B: Alleg. Co,
              VA, dau/o: William and Eliz. Terry
              (on bk) [William and Elizabeth Terry
              (on Lic.)]. Both lived in Alleg. Co.
              PL: Sweet Springs, VA (on bk) [Red
              Sweet Springs, Alleg. Co., VA (on
              Lic.)]. Mar. by Johnzey Leef, mins.
              of gospel, who signed the Lic. on
              09-23-1859.

11-08-1859   Aaron D. Clark, 30, single (on bk)
32   [widower (on CTOL)], B: Alleg. Co.,
              VA, Occup: smith (refers to black-
              smith), s/o: Jos. and Christ. Clark
              (on bk) [Jos. and Christina Clark (on
              CTOL)]; and Harriet Farmer, 22, sing-
              le, B: Bedford Co., VA, dau/o: M. B.
              and Martha Farmer. Both lived in
              Covington, Alleg. Co., VA. PL: Cov-
              ington, VA. Mar. by Hamilton A.
              Gaver, Northern Meth. E. Church, note
              to clk. has no mar. date but says mar.
              parties. CTOL signed on 11-08-1859
              by Aaron D. Clark. Issued on M. B.
              Farmer's request, Teste J. Carpenter,
              D. C.

10-21-1859   Michael Flinn, 25, single, B: Ireland,
33   Occup: laborer, s/o: Michael and Mary
              Flinn; and Ellen Ervine (on bk) [Ellen
              Irvine (on CTOL)], age blotted out
              with ink (on bk) [22 (on CTOL)], sin-
              gle, B: Ireland, dau/o: Maurice and
              Ann Ervine (on bk) [Maurice Irvin and
              Ann Wall (on CTOL)]. Both lived in
              Alleg. Co. PL: Alleg. Co., VA. Mar.
              by J. H. Walters, Catholic, note to
              clk. says mar. on 10-21-1859. CTOL
              signed on 10-21-1859 by Michael Flinn.

(Mar. Register Book (1) - Continued)

Age oath given by Daniel Croghan,
Teste J. Carpenter.

12-17-1859   John Dunnahoo, 33, single, B: Ire-
34   land, Occup: laborer, s/o: John Dunn-
              ahoo and Ellen (on bk) [John Dunnahoo
              and Ellen Forely (on CTOL)]; and Ann
              Rochford, 30, widow, B: Ireland,
              dau/o: Thos. O'Donnel and Mary (on
              bk) [Thos. O'Donnel and Mary White
              (on CTOL)]. Both lived in Covington,
              Alleg. Co., VA. PL: Covington, VA.
              Mar. by J. H. Walters, Catholic, note
              to clk. says mar. on 12-17-1859.
              CTOL signed on 12-17-1859 by John
              (his X mark) Dunnahoo. Age oath of
              Mrs. Rochford given by Thos. Gofney,
              Teste J. Carpenter, D. C.

10-30-1859   Thomas Taverin (on bk) [Thomas Tover-
35   in (on CTOL)], 40, widower, B: Ire-
              land, Occup: laborer, s/o: Wm. and
              Bridgett Taverin (on bk) [Wm. and
              Bridgett Toverin (on CTOL)]; and Mary
              Murry, 26, single, B: Ireland, dau/o:
              Murtaugh and Mary Murry (on bk) [Mur-
              laugh Murry and Mary Roach (on CTOL)].
              Both lived in Alleg. Co. PL: High
              Bridge, Alleg. Co., VA. Mar. by J.
              H. Walters, Catholic, note to clk.
              says mar. on 10-29-1859. CTOL signed
              on 10-28-1859 by Thomas (his X mark)
              Taverin. Age oath of Mary Murphy
              given by James Kennedy, Teste J. Car-
              penter, D. C.

12-29-1859   John E. Orndorf (on bk) [John C. Orn-
36   dorff (on Lic.)], 21, single, B:
              Shenandoah Co., VA, Occup: laborer
              (on bk) [Stage Driver (on Lic.)],
              [Age: "Twenty-one years and upwards"
              (on Lic.)], s/o: Israel and Rebecca

- 107 -

Orn. (on bk) [Israel and Rebecca
Orndorff (on Lic.)]; and <u>Mary F.
Smails</u>, 17, single, B: Greenbrier Co.,
VA (now W.VA.), dau/o: Thos. and Mary
Smails (on bk) [Thomas and Mary F.
Smails (on Lic.)]. Both lived in
Alleg. Co. (on bk) [He lived in Shen-
andoah Co., VA and she lived in Alleg.
Co., VA (on Lic.)]. PL: Alleg. Co.,
VA, at Callaghan's. Mar. by H. A.
Gaver who signed Lic. 12-29-1859.

10-07-1859   <u>John J. Hayse</u>, 30, single, B: Amherst
37   Co., VA, Occup: Carpenter, s/o: James
and Dephia Hayse (on bk) [James and
Delphia Hayse (on CTOL)]; and <u>Maria
F. McAllister</u> (on bk) [<u>Maria F. McCal-
lister</u> (on CTOL)], 21 ["1st Sept. day
not recollected" (on CTOL)], single,
B: Alleg. Co., VA, dau/o: Rufus and
Nancy McAllister (on bk) [Rufus and
Nancy McCallister (on CTOL)]. Both
lived in Alleg. Co., VA. PL: Alleg.
Co., VA. Mar. by H. A. Gaver, Mins.
Meth., note to clk. says mar. on Oct.
1859. CTOL signed on 10-07-1859 by
<u>John J. Hayse.</u> "License granted upon
evidence of Hugh B. Rusk sworn to
give evidence before me in my office
& who testifited that <u>Maria F. McCal-
lister</u> is 21 years of age. Teste
Lewis P. Holloway, Clk."

*******[CTOL found in files but No record on bk]
[On back of CTOL has written January
25, 1860]
Certificate To Obtain License:
Date of Mar.: 02-28-____
Place of Mar.: Alleghany
Names of Parties: <u>Josiah Smith</u> and
                  <u>Mary J. Andrews</u>
Husband's Age: 22

Wife's Age: 21
Husband's Marital Status: Single
Wife's Marital Status: Single
Husband's Birthplace: Alleghany Co.,
          VA
Wife's Birthplace: Bath Co., VA.
Husband's Place of Residence:
          Alleghany Co., VA.
Wife's Place of Residence:
          Alleghany Co., VA.
Husband's Parents: Peter and Susanah
          Smith
Wife's Parents: William and Eliza-
          beth Andrews
Husband's Occupation: farmer
CTOL signed 25th of February 1860 or
          1862 [ink blot in 0 and looks
          like 2 was written in, blot
          makes date unsure] by Josh Smith
****

01-12-1860   John Daily (on bk) [John Dailey (on
  # 1   CTOL)], 25, single, B: Ireland, Occup:
             laborer, s/o: Thos. and Nora Daily
             (on bk) [Thomas and Nora Daily (on
             CTOL)]; and Elizabeth Harris (on bk)
             [Elizabeth Harriss (on CTOL)], 28,
             widow, B: Ireland, dau/o: James and
             Cath. Harris (on bk) [James and Cath-
             arine Harriss (on CTOL)]. Both lived
             in Alleg. Co. PL: Alleghany. Mar.
             by J. H. Walters, Catholic, note to
             clk. says mar. on 01-12-1860. CTOL
             signed on 01-03-1860 by John (his X
             mark) Daily. "Authorized to issue by
             lady who made oath that she was over
             21 years of age, J. Carpenter, D.C."

01-17-1860   Perry Bennet (on bk) [Perry Bennett
  # 2   (on CTOL)], 34, widower, B: Boone Co.,
             VA (now W.VA.), Occup: carpenter, s/o:
             Thos. and Tenpy Bennet (on bk) [Thomas

and Tempy (?Temssy) Bennett (on CTOL)]; and <u>Eliza F. Gillespie</u> (on bk) [<u>Eliza Francis Gillaspie</u> (Note: Martha overwritten by Eliza) (on CTOL)], 19, single, B: Bath Co., VA, dau/o: Samuel and Polly Gillaspie. Both lived in Alleg. Co., VA. PL: Alleg. Co., VA. Mar. by Hamilton A. Gaver, N. Meth. E. Church. CTOL signed on 01-09-1860 by <u>Perry Bennett</u>. "Permission given by H. Quickle, guardian of the lady. Teste Jos. Carpenter, D.C."

02-16-1860 <u>Wm. H. Terrill</u> (on bk) [<u>Wm. H. Terril</u>
3   (on CTOL)], 59, widower, B: Orange Co., VA, Lived: Warm Springs, VA, Occup: lawyer, s/o: Wm. and Jane Terrill (on bk) [William and Jane Terrill (on CTOL)]; and <u>Rachel C. Scott</u>, 49, widow, B: Bath Co., VA, Lived: Covington, VA, dau/o: James Hamilton and R. Ham (on bk) [James Hamilton and Rachel Hamilton (on CTOL)]. PL: Covington, VA. Mar. by James M. Rice, Presbyterian, note to clk. says mar. on 02-16-1860 and has name <u>William H. Terril</u> and signed James M. Rice on 03-14-1860. CTOL signed on 02-16-1860 by <u>William H. Terrill</u>.

02-20-1860 <u>William A. Walton</u>, age unknown and
4   CTOL is blank, single, B: Botetourt Co., VA, Occup: carpenter, Lived: Mercer Co., VA (now W.VA.), s/o: unknown on bk. and blank on CTOL; and <u>Margaretta Nicely</u>, 18, single, B: Bath Co., VA, Lived: Alleg. Co., VA, dau/o: Jacob and Margaretta Nicely (on bk) [Jacob and Margaret Niceley (on CTOL)]. PL: Covington, VA, Robert Skeener Tavern. Mar. by J. C. Tinsley, S. Meth. CTOL dated and signed by J. C.

Tinsley, mins. on 02-22-1860. "I certify that I solomised the above dated marriage."

02-28-1860   John J. Strickler, 25, single, Occup:
5   farmer, B: Rockbridge Co., VA, s/o:
              Dan'l. and Mary J. Strickler (on bk)
              [Daniel M. and Mary Jane Strickler
              (on CTOL)]; and Margaret L. Robinson,
              27, single, B: Alleg. Co., VA, dau/o:
              Wm. and E. Robinson. Both lived in
              Alleg. Co. PL: Alleg. Co., VA. Mar.
              by Joshua C. Tinsley, S. Meth., note
              says mar. 02-28-1860. CTOL signed
              02-27-1860 by Jno. J. Strickler.
              Cert. issued upon authority of Mr. Wm.
              Robinson, the father, Teste J. Car-
              penter, D. C.

01-16-1860   James Fitzgerald, 35, single, Occup:
6   laborer, B: Ireland, s/o: Phil and
              Grace Fitzgerald (on bk) [Phil Fitz-
              gerald and Grace Connel (on CTOL)];
              and Mary Crowly (on ck) [Mary Crouly
              (on CTOL)], 30, single (on bk) [widow
              (on CTOL)], B: Ireland, dau/o: Dan'l.
              and Mary Crowly (on bk) [Daniel ____
              and Mary Canten (on CTOL)]. Both
              lived in Alleg. Co. PL: Alleg. Co.,
              VA. Mar. by J. H. Walters, Catholic
              Church, note says mar. on 01-16-1860.
              CTOL signed 01-16-1860 by James (his
              X mark) Fitzgerald. Auth. issued upon
              cert. of J. H. Walters, Teste J. Car-
              penter, D. C.

04-11-1860   Benton Wiley, 25, single, B: Craig Co.
7   VA, Occup: farmer, Lived: Craig Co.,
              VA, s/o: Robert and Lucy Wiley; and
              Miss Sallie C. Scott, 19, single, B:
              Alleg. Co., VA, Lived: Alleg. Co., VA,
              dau/o: William and Catharine Scott.

Mar. by Joshua C. Tinsley, S. Meth.,
note says mar. 04-11-1860 at house of
bride's father, Wm. Scott. CTOL signed on 04-11-1860 by Benton Wiley. PL:
Covington, Alleg. Co., VA.

03-12-1860 (on bk)   03-28-1860 (on CTOL)
  # 8   Daniel L. Hornbarger, 22, single, B:
            Montgomery Co., VA, Lived: Montgomery
            Co., VA, s/o: Daniel and Nancy Horn-
            barger; and Maria L. C. S. Harman (on
            bk) [Maria Louisa Catharine Sarah Har-
            man (on CTOL)], 21, single, B: Alleg.
            Co., VA, Lived: Alleg. Co., VA, dau/o:
            Andr. and Sarah Harman (on bk) [Andrew
            and Sarah Harman (on CTOL)]. PL: Al-
            leg. , VA. Mar. by H. A. Gaver (Ham-
            ilton A. Gaver), N. Meth. E. Church,
            note says mar. but doesn't give date.
            Cert. issued upon authority of Andr.
            Harmon, "father of the young lady,"
            Teste J. Carpenter, D. C. CTOL sign-
            ed on 03-12-1860 by Daniel L. Horn-
            barger.

03-29-1860 Chas. A. Persinger (on bk) [Charles A.
  # 9   Persinger (on CTOL)], 23, single, B:
            Alleg. Co., VA, Occup: farmer, s/o:
            Henry and Annie Persinger; and Sophi-
            mia M. Myers (on bk) [Sophronia M.
            Myers (on CTOL)], age unknown (on bk)
            [____ (on CTOL)], single, B: Alleg. Co.
            VA, dau/o: Henry and Elizabeth Myers.
            PL: "The res. of girl's parents",
            Alleg. Co., VA (on CTOL). Both lived
            in Alleg. Co. Mar. by Joshua C. Tins-
            ley, S. Meth. CTOL signed on 03-29-
            1860 by Joshua C. Tinsley.
            "This certificate of marriage issued
            upon certificate of Henry Myers,
            Father of the Girl and proved by Ander-
            son Persinger a subscribing witness
            thereto, Teste J. Carpenter, D. C."

Consent has her name as <u>Sophronia M. Myers</u> and signed on 03-16-1860 by Henry Myers, Wit. Anderson Persinger and William (his X mark) Persinger.

05-03-1860
10

<u>Caleb Stone</u> (on bk) [<u>Caleb Slone</u> (on Lic.)], 30, widower, B: Greenbrier Co. VA (now W.VA.) (on bk) [Franklin Co., VA (on Lic.)], Occup: laborer, s/o: John and Sally Stone (on bk) [John and Sally Slone (on Lic.)]; and <u>Mary Newcomb</u> (on bk) [<u>Nancy Newcomb</u> (on Lic.)], 20, single, B: Botetourt Co., VA, dau/o: John and Betsy Newcomb. Both lived in Alleg. Co. PL: Alleg. Co., VA. Mar. by Joshua C. Tinsley, S. Meth., note says mar. on 05-03-1860.

04-24-1860
11

<u>James S. Nida</u>, 21, single, B: Giles Co., VA, Occup: farmer, s/o: David and Mary Nida; and <u>Louisa D. Myers</u>, 17, single, B: Alleg. Co., VA, dau/o: Henry and Elizabeth Myers. Both lived in Alleg. Co. PL: Alleg. Co., VA. Mar. by Joshua C. Tinsley, S. Meth. Consent for <u>Louisy D. Myers</u> and <u>James S. (? or T) Nida</u> to mar. dated 04-23-1860 signed by Henry Myers, Wit. Chapman I. Nida, A. McReynolds (? A. M. Reynolds). NO LIC. OR CTOL IN FILES.

04-24-1860
12

(on bk) _____ (on CTOL for Mar. Date)
<u>Peter Shipner</u>, 27, single, B: Germany, Occup: Stone mason, s/o: Henry and Elizabeth Shipner; and <u>Mary A. Redinger</u> (on bk) [<u>Mary Ann Redinger</u> (on CTOL)], 18 or 19, single, B: Bedford Co., VA, dau/o: Nicholas and Louisa Redinger. Both lived in Alleg. Co. Mar. by J. H. Walters, Catholic Priest,

(Mar. Register Book (1) - Continued)

note says mar. on 04-24-1860 (as on
note--believe is 14th). PL: Alleg.,
VA. CTOL signed on 04-14-1860 by
Peter Shepner.

04-22-1860   James C. Winebrenner, 23, single, B:
13   Monroe Co., VA (now W.VA.), Occup:
             brick mason, s/o: Peter and Mary A.
             Winebrenner (on bk) [Peter and Mary
             Ann Winebrenner (on CTOL)]; and Mary
             F. Stone, 23, single, B: Alleg. Co.,
             VA, dau/o: William and Jane Stone.
             Both lived in Alleg. Co. PL: Alleg.
             Co., VA. Mar. by Joshua C. Tinsley,
             S. Meth., note says mar. at house of
             bride's father on 04-22-1860 signed
             on 04-23-1860. CTOL signed on 04-19-
             1860 by James C. Winebrenner. Con-
             sent dated 04-18-1860 signed William
             Stone. Cert. of age over 21 on 04-
             19-1860 by William Stone.

05-27-1860   (on bk) 06-05-____ (on CTOL)
14   Virgil S. Plymale (on bk) [Virgil S.
             Plymal (on CTOL)], 20 yrs. 7 mos. 15
             days, single, B: Alleg. Co., VA,
             Occup: farmer, s/o: Wm. B. and Eliza-
             beth Plymale; and Sarah Craft, 22,
             single, B: Botetourt Co.,VA, dau/o:
             _____ and Elizabeth Craft. Both lived
             in Alleg. Co. PL: Alleg. Co., VA.
             Mar. by _____. CTOL signed on 05-27-
             1859, by Virgile A. (? Sotougre or
             Sotougro) Plymale.

06-17-1860   John McGrath, 27, single, B: Ireland,
15   County of Claire (on CTOL) [Note:
             possibly means Clare Co.), Occup:
             laborer (on bk) [Laborer on Railroad
             (on CTOL)], s/o: John and Margarett
             McGath (on bk) [John and Margaret Mc-
             Grath (on CTOL)]; and Catharine Han-

- 114 -

nassy, 20, single, B: Limrick Co.,
Ireland (on CTOL), dau/o: Patrick and
Mary Hannassy. Both lived in Alleg.
Co. PL: Alleg. Co., VA. Mar. by J.
H. Walters, Catholic Priest, note says
mar. 06-17-1860. CTOL signed by John
McGrath on 06-07-1860.

06-14-1860   George A. Poor, 20, single, Occup:
  # 16   laborer, B: Botetourt Co., VA, s/o:
              Solomon and Elizabeth Poor (on bk)
              [Solomon and Elizabeth A. Poor (on
              Lic.)]; and Mary F. Wood, 28, widow,
              B: Alleg. Co., VA (on bk) [Buckingham
              Co., VA (on Lic.)], dau/o: David and
              Jane Wood. Both lived in Alleg. Co.,
              VA. Mar. by H. A. Gaver, N. Meth. who
              signed Lic. on 06-14-1860. PL: Alleg.
              Co., VA. Lic. granted on oath of Mary
              F. Woods on 06-12-1860, Lewis P. Holl-
              oway, Clk.
              "June the 9th 1860
                  This certifies that I the (page
              tore) gawideain of Geo. A. Poe do this
              (page tore) declare myself willing
              that the said G. A. Poe do lawfully
              marry Mrs. Mary Woods on the 14th day
              of June 1860
                      Given under my hand and /seal/
                          Elizbeth A. (her X mark) Poe
              Wit. James Isiah Isaiah (his X mark)
                  Poor"
              [Note: There is a seal in a circle with
              a crown inside it at the top of the
              paper consent is on thus indicating it
              was probably written on stationery.]

07-24-1860   (on bk)   07-25-1860 (on CTOL)
  # 17   Jacob O. Terry, 23 ["8th day of Octo-
              ber 1860" (on CTOL)], Occup: farmer
              and tanner, single, B: Alleg. Co., VA,
              s/o: Joseph and Mahala Terry; and

Sophia W. Dew, 20, single, B: Alleg. Co., VA, dau/o: Absalom and Sarah Dew. Both lived in Alleg. Co. PL: Alleg. Co., VA. Mar. by James L. Smyth, O. M. CTOL [which was Lic. altered to CTOL] was signed by Jacob O. Terry on 07-20-1860. Consent dated 07-19-1860 by Absalom Dew, Wit. John S. Persinger.

07-26-1860   John A. Fleshman, 30 ["on the 14 July
18   1860" (on CTOL)], single, B: Greenbrier Co., VA (now W. VA.), Occup: Constable, Lived: Greenbrier Co., VA, (now W.VA.), s/o: Simon and Sarah Fleshman; and Mary Given (on bk) [Mary Ann Given (on Lic.)], 25, single, B: Monroe Co., VA (now W.VA.), Lived: Alleg. Co., VA, dau/o: David G. and Catharine Given (on bk) [David G. and Catharine Bowyer Given (on Lic.)]. PL: Alleg. Co., VA. Mar. by J. C. Tinsley, S. Meth., signed Lic. 08-01-1860 as Joshua C. Tinsley. Consent to marry and that she is of age signed 06-12-1860 by D. G. Given, Teste J. B. Scott.

08-07-1860   (on bk) _____ (on CTOL)
19   James Gaugh, 26 or 27, single, B: County Limrick, Ireland (on Lic.), Occup: laborer, s/o: John and Catharine Gaugh; and Nancy Ham, 29, single, B: Augusta, VA [Note: I assume it is Augusta Co. but have no way of knowing for sure. I cannot find a town named Augusta on present day maps.], dau/o: Martin and Hester Ham. Mar. by _____. PL: Alleg. Co., VA. CTOL signed 08-07-1860 by James Gaugh.

(Mar. Register Book (1) - Continued)

08-16-1860
20

John W. Armontrout, 23 (on bk) [23 yrs. 2 mos. 21 days (on CTOL)], single, B: Rockbridge Co., VA, Occup: farmer, Lived: Rockbridge Co., VA, s/o: Jacob and Nancy Armintrout (on bk) [Jacob and Nancy Armontrout (on CTOL)]; and Mary J. Nicely (on bk) [Mary Jane Nicely (on CTOL)], 23 (on bk) [23 yrs. 5 " October (believe may mean age 23 on Oct. 5, but (") was under word "mos." where John's age was listed) (on CTOL)], single, B: Alleg. Co., VA, Lived: Alleg. Co., VA, dau/o: Lewis and Ann Nicely (on bk) [Lewis and Anna Nicely (on CTOL)]. PL: Alleg. Co., VA. Mar. by _____. CTOL [Lic. altered to CTOL] signed 08-06-1860 by John W. Armontrout.

08-20-1860
21

Jeremiah Conner (on bk) [Jeremiah Conners (on CTOL)], 23, single, B: Ireland, Occup: laborer, s/o: Jeremiah and Hanorah Conner (on bk) [Jeremiah and Hanorah Conners (on CTOL)]; and Margarett Dunford (on bk) [Margaret Dunford (on CTOL)], 23, single, B: Ireland, dau/o: James and Hannah Dunnivant. Both lived in Alleg. Co., VA. Mar. by J. H. Walters, C. Priest, note to clk. says mar. 08-20-1860. PL: Alleg. Co., VA. CTOL signed on 08-20-1860 by Jeremah (his X mark) Conners.

09-21-1860
22

(on bk)   09-20-1860 (on CTOL)
Wm. L. Evans, 29, single, B: Halifax Co., VA, Occup: farmer, s/o: Elisha and Mary Evans (on bk) [Elisha and May (?Mary) Evans (on CTOL)]; and Sarah M. McCoy, 22, single, B: Rockbridge Co., VA, dau/o: James and Nancy McCoy. Both lived in Alleg. Co. PL: Alleg. Co., VA. Mar. by

- 117 -

(Mar. Register Book (1) - Continued)

Staunton Field, S. Meth., note to clk.
says mar. 09-20-1860 and signed 10-29-
1860. CTOL signed 09-18-1860 by Wm.
L. Evans.

11-15-1860 (on bk) 11-15-____ (on CTOL)
 # 23   Absolom F. Ross (on bk) [Absalom F.
           Ross (on Lic.)], 24, single, Occup:
           varied, B: Augusta Co., VA, s/o: Jos.
           D. and Winney Ross (on bk) [Jos. D.
           and Wincy Ross (on CTOL)]; and Margar-
           ette A. Terrill (on bk) [Margarett An
           Terrill (on CTOL)], 18, single, B:
           Augusta Co., VA, dau/o: James and
           Julia Terrill (on bk) [James and Julia
           An Terrill (on CTOL)]. Both lived in
           Alleg. Co., VA. PL: Alleg. Co., VA.
           Mar. by ____. CTOL [Lic. altered to
           CTOL] signed 11-15-1860 by Absalom F.
           Ross.

12-11-1860 (on bk) 12-11-____ (on CTOL)
 # 24   Mathew P. Surber (on bk) [Mathew T.
           Surber (on CTOL)], 26, single, B:
           Bath Co., VA, Occup: farmer, Lived:
           Bath Co., VA, s/o: Adam and Jane Sur-
           ber; and Lucy J. King (on bk) [L. J.
           King (on CTOL)], 19, single, B: Alleg.
           Co., VA, Lived: Alleg. Co., VA, dau/o:
           Wm. and Eliza King (on bk) [Eliza King
           (only--on CTOL)]. PL: Mrs. King's
           res., Alleg. Co., VA (on Lic.). Mar.
           by ____. CTOL signed 12-03-1860 by
           M. P. (? T) Surber.

12-20-1860 (on bk) -20-____ (on CTOL)
 # 25   Patterson Evans, 22, single, B: Bot-
           etourt Co., VA, Occup: Waggoneer, s/o:
           Abraham and S. A. Evans (on bk) [Abra-
           ham and Sarah A. Evans (on CTOL)]; and
           Mary A. Bratton, 21, single, B: Alleg.
           Co., VA, dau/o: Robt. and Hannah Brat-

(Mar. Register Book (1) - Continued)

ton (on bk) [Robert and Hannah Bratton (on CTOL)]. Both lived in Alleg. Co., Va. PL: Covington, VA. Mar. by H. A. Gaver, N. Meth. CTOL signed on 12-20-1860 by Patterson Evans.

12-29-1860
26

(on bk) 12-29-____ (on CTOL)
William Rearidan, 30, single, B: Ireland, Occup: laborer, s/o: Daniel and Joanna Murphy (on bk) [Daniel and Johanan Murphy (on CTOL)]; and Joana Conner (on bk) [Johana Harington Conner (as on CTOL)], 26, widow, B: Ireland, dau/o: David and Johana Harrington (on bk) [David and Johana Harington (on CTOL)]. Both lived in Alleg. Co. PL: Alleg. Co., VA. Mar. by J. H. Walters, C. Priest, note to clk. says mar. on 12-29-1860. CTOL (Lic. altered to CTOL) signed by William Rearidan with no date of signature.

11-15-1860
27

(on bk) 11-15-____ (on CTOL)
Lorenzo Kimberlin, 26, single, B: Alleg. Co., VA (on bk) [Tennessee (only --on CTOL)], Occup: farmer, s/o: Wm. and Elizabeth Kimberlin (on bk) [Wm. and Elizabeth Kimberlin (on CTOL)]; and M. E. M. Wolf (on bk) [Mary E. M. Wolfe (on CTOL)], 19, single, B: Alleg. Co., VA, dau/o: G. W. and Paulin Wolf (on bk) [George W. and Paulina Wolfe (on CTOL)]. Both lived in Alleg. Co. PL: Alleg. Co., VA. Mar. by S. Fields, S. Meth., note to clk. says mar. 11-15-1860. CTOL (Lic. altered to CTOL) signed on 11-14-1860 by Lorenzo Kimberlin.

12-24-1860
28

(on bk) 01-08-1861 (on CTOL)
Hugh L. Siders, 52, widower, Occup: farmer, B: Frederick Co., Maryland,

(Mar. Register Book (1) - Continued)

Lived: Rockbridge Co., VA, s/o: Conrad and Margaret Siders; and Sarah Ann Nicely, 35, single, B: Alleg. Co., VA, Lived: Alleg. Co., VA, dau/o: George and Sarah Nicely. PL: Alleg. Co., VA. Mar. by ____ . CTOL signed on 12-24-1860 by Hugh r Siders (as signed and deciphered).

01-28-1860   (on bk)   01-28-____ (on CTOL)
29   John Wright, 30, single, B: Ireland, Occup: Stone cutter, s/o: John and Julia Wright; and Margarett Irvine, 18, single, B: Ireland, dau/o: James and Ann Irvine. Both lived in Alleg. Co., VA. PL: Alleg. Co., VA. Mar. by ____ . CTOL signed on 01-27-1860 by John Wright. [On back of certificate clk. wrote "Jany. 27, 1861".]

Page 6

02-27-1861   Jacob H. Bridgett, 24, single, B: Alleg. Co., VA, Occup: miller, s/o: Geo. W. and Phebe Bridgett (on bk) [George W. and Phebe Bridgett (on CTOL)]; and Charlotte A. Mallow, 22, single, B: Alleg. Co., VA, dau/o: Jno. and Martha Mallow (on bk) [John and Martha Mallow (on CTOL)]. Both lived in Alleg. Co., VA. PL: Alleghany, VA. Mar. by James M. Rice, note to clk. says mar. 02-27-1861 and signed 03-14-1861 by mins. CTOL signed on 02-27-1861 by J. H. Bridgett.

*****Beginning with the following entry, a new form is seen in the files. It contains at the top the Marriage License which is an authorization to marry the parties named. In the middle is the Certificate To Obtain A Marriage

License which contains all the information pertinent concerning both parties. The bottom part is the Minister's Return where the date he per-
formed the marriage is listed and the
place where the marriage took place
with the minister's signature. This
new form was set up because of an ACT
passed March 15, 1861. The minister
was supposed to return the form within
10 days of the marriage, but in some
cases this did not happen. In some
cases the old form CTOL with the Marriage Lic. Authorization is used and
the new form is also used. Hereafter
I will refer to the old form as CTOL
as done previously and the new form
as CTOLMR to denote the difference.***

* * * * * * * * * *

04-18-1861   William A. Bennet, 24, single, Occup:
  # 2   farmer, B: Alleg. Co., VA, s/o: Solo-
              mon and Susan Bennet; and Jane Persin-
              ger, 20, single, B: Alleg. Co., VA,
              dau/o: Charlotte Persinger [Note: says
              "Illegatimate"]. Both lived in Alleg.
              Co., VA. PL: Alleghany, VA. CTOLMR
              signed 04-15-1861 by Lewis P. Holloway,
              Clk. Return says mar. 04-18-1861 at
              Moses Wright's res. by H. A. Gaver.

08-15-1861   John A. Beard, 36, single, Occup: car-
  # 3   penter, B: Fred. Co., Maryland (on bk)
              [Frederick Co., Maryland (on CTOLMR)],
              s/o: John and Amelia Beard; and Har-
              riet A. T. Kyle (on bk) [Harret A. T.
              Kyle (on CTOLMR)], 26, single, B: Cov-
              ington, Alleg. Co., VA, dau/o: Wm. and
              Eliza Kyle. Both lived in Covington,
              Alleg. Co., VA. PL: Covington, VA.
              CTOLMR signed on 08-15-1861 by Wm. G.
              Holloway, D. Clk. Return says mar.

08-15-1861 at res. of Mrs. Kyle by J. W. Ewan.

10-03-1861   William F. Blaker (on bk) [Wm. F.
4   Blaker (on CTOL)], 28, widower, Occup:
            farmer, B: Alleg. Co., VA, s/o: James
            and Eley Blaker: and Sarah R. Jones,
            24, single, B: Covington, Alleg. Co.,
            VA, dau/o: Josiah C. and Martha Jones.
            Both lived in Alleg. Co. PL: Alleg.
            Co., VA. CTOL signed on 09-30-1861
            by Wm. F. Blaker. CTOLMR signed 09-
            30-1861 Wm. G. Holloway, D. Clk. Re-
            turn says mar. 10-03-1861 at Josiah C.
            Jones in Alleg. Co., VA. by H. B.
            Rose. Consent signed by J. C. Jones
            and dated 09-29-1861, Wit. John A.
            Jones.

02-06-1861   Wm. T. Crawford, 21, single, B: Alleg.
5   Co., VA, Occup: farmer, s/o: Owen and
            Coatney Crawford; and Mary Jane Shu-
            maker, 23, single, B: Covington, Al-
            leg. Co., VA (on bk) [Alleg. Co., VA
            --only--on CTOL)], dau/o: Jno. K. E.
            and Eliza Shumaker (on bk) [John K.
            and Eliza Shumaker (on CTOL)]. Both
            lived in Alleg. Co., VA. PL: Alleg.
            Co., VA. Mar. by ____. CTOL signed
            on 02-06-1861 by William (his X mark)
            Crawford. [Note on Book: Wm. Hollo-
            way, D. C.: "I find no return of the
            minister. I have the date of marriage
            as it is set forth in certificate of
            the applied court."]

07-17-1861   Thomas Charry, 35, single, B: County
            Clary, Ireland [Note: possibly means
            Clare Co.], Occup: Boss on Railroad,
            s/o: Mathias and Bridgett Charry (on
            bk) [Matthias and Bridgett Chary (on
            CTOLMR)]; and Bridgett Coleman, 40,

(Mar. Register Book (1) - Continued)

widow, B: Covington, Alleg. Co., VA
(on bk) [County Clary, Ireland (on
CTOLMR) (Note: possibly means Clare
Co.)], dau/o: Pat. and Bridgett Coleman (on bk) [Patrick and Bridgett
Coleman (on CTOLMR)]. Both lived in
Alleg. Co. PL: Alleg. Co., VA.
CTOLMR signed on 07-03-1861 by Wm. G.
Holloway, D. C. Return says mar. on
07-17-1861 in Alleg. Co., VA, by J.
H. Walters. [Note on Book: Wm. Holloway, D.C.: "I find no return of
the minister. I have the date of marriage as it is set forth in certificate of the applied court."]

01-08-1861 Robert Dore, 28, single, Occup: lab-
7   orer, B: Limerick Co., Ireland, s/o:
          Robt. and Catharine Dore; and Ellen
          Hederman, 22, single, B: Covington,
          Alleg. Co., VA (on bk) [Limerick Co.,
          Ireland (on CTOL)], dau/o: Thomas and
          Nancy Hederman. Both lived in Alleg.
          Co. PL: Alleg. Co., VA. Mar. by J.
          H. Walters, whose note to clerk says
          mar. 01-08-1861 and has names as
          Robert Doore and Ellen Hedeman. CTOL
          signed by Robt. Dore on 01-07-1861.
          [Note on book by Wm. Holloway, D. P.:
          "I find no return of the minister. I
          have the date of marriage as it is set
          forth in certificate of the applied
          court."] [Author's Note: This seems
          odd since the minister's note is on
          the CTOL. The note is the minister's
          return I would think.]

03-19-1861 William Eggars, 27, single, B: New
8   York City, N. Y., Occup: Stone cutter,
          s/o: Daniel and Caroline Eggars (on
          bk) [Dan'l. and Caroline Eggars (on
          CTOL)]; and Lucy Ann Kelley (on bk)

- 123 -

[Lucy Ann Kelly (on CTOL)], 20, single, B: Botetourt Co., VA, dau/o: Henry and Catharine Kelley (on bk) [Henry and Cinthia Kelly (on CTOL)]. Both lived in Alleg. Co. PL: Covington, Alleg. Co., VA. Mar. by ____. CTOL signed on 03-19-1861 by William Egger. [Note on book by Wm. Holloway, D. C.: "I find no return of the minister. I have the date of marriage as it is set forth in certificate of the applied court."]

05-24-1861 Robert R. Fury, 21, single, b: Monroe
9   Co., VA (now W.VA.), Occup: farmer, s/o: Robert and Ellen Fury; and Barbara Lewis, 21, single, B: Alleg. Co, VA, dau/o: John and Elizabeth Lewis. Both lived in Alleg. Co. PL: ~~Peter E.-Lewis-res.~~ Covington, Alleg. Co., VA (as on CTOLMR). Mar. by J. W. Ewan. CTOLMR signed 05-20-1861 by Lewis P. Holloway, Clk. Return says mar. 05-24-1861 at Covington, Alleg. Co., VA, by J. W. Evan. Age and consent sworn to by Shelton Harmon, Teste Wm. G. Holloway, D. Clk.

01-31-1861 Robert Hepler, 19, single, B: Alleg.
10   Co., VA, Occup: farmer, s/o: John and Sallie Hepler; and Mary Jane Hepler, 23, single, B: Monroe Co., VA (now W. VA.), dau/o: David and Basha Hepler. Both lived in Alleg. Co. PL: Alleg. Co., VA. Mar. by ____. [Note on bk. by Wm. Holloway, D.C.: "I find no return of the minister. I have the date of marriage as it is set forth in certificate of the applied court."] CTOL signed 01-25-1861 by Robert Hepler.

(Mar. Register Book (1) - Continued)

03-11-1861
 # 11
William P. Hornberger (on bk) [William P. Hornbarger (on CTOL)], 25, single, B: Montgomery Co., VA, Lived: Montgomery Co., VA, Occup: farmer, s/o: Daniel and Nancy Hornberger (on bk) [Daniel and Nancy Hornbarger (on CTOL)]; and Mary Evans, 21, single, B: Alleg. Co.,VA, Lived: Alleg. Co., VA, dau/o: William and Deliah Evans. PL: Alleg. Co., VA. Mar. by James M. Rice whose note to clk. has names as William P. Hernberger and Mary Evans and says mar. 03-11-1861 signed on 03-14-1861 by James M. Rice. CTOL signed on 03-11-1861 by William P. (his X mark) Hornbarger.

08-08-1861
 # 12
Sampson Humphries, 24, widower, B: Alleg. Co., VA, Occup: farmer, s/o: Wm. and Ruth Humphries; and Ruthy Ann Byer, 17, single, B: Alleg. Co., VA, dau/o: Sam'l. and Harriet Byer (on bk) [Samuel and Harriet Byer (on CTOLMR)]. Both lived in Alleg. Co., VA. PL: Samuel Byer's res. in Alleg. Co., VA (on CTOLMR). Mar. by J. W. Ewan whose return says mar. 08-08-1861 at Samuel Byer's res. Cert. of Samuel Byer sworn to by Wm. E. Byer, his son, Wm. G. Holloway, D. C. CTOLMR signed on 08-05-1861 by Wm. G. Holloway, D.C. [Cert. referred to above was Byer's acknowledgement of the marriage.]

02-07-1861
 # 13
(on bk)   January __, ____ (on CTOL) Maurice Irwine (on bk) [Morris Irwin (on CTOL)], 21, single, B: Ireland, Occup: laborer, s/o: Jas. and Anne Irwine (on bk) [Jammes and Ane Irwine (on CTOL)]; and Mary McCarthy, age:__, single, B: Alleg. Co., VA (on bk) [Ireland (on CTOL)], dau/o: Jno. and

(Mar. Register Book (1) - Continued)

Mary McCarthy (on bk) [John and Mary
McCarthy (on CTOL)]. Both lived in
Alleg. Co. PL: Alleg. Co., VA. Mar.
by J. H. Walters whose note to clk.
says mar. 02-07-1861 and has names
Maurice Irwine and Mary McCarthy.
CTOL signed Maurice Irwin on __ -03-
1861.

05-22-1861   (on bk)   05-23-1861 (on CTOLMR)
14   Lewis Johnson, 23, single, B: Alleg.
Co., VA, Occup: farmer, s/o: Jabes
and Maria W. Johnson; and Milissa
Phelps Rose or Milipa Phelps Rose
(on bk) [Melissa Phelps Rose or Melipa
Phelps Rose (on CTOLMR)], 22, single,
B: Alleg. Co., VA, dau/o: Denison and
Eliza Rose. Both lived in Alleg. Co.,
VA. PL: Robt. Skeens Hotel in Coving-
ton, VA (on CTOLMR). CTOLMR signed
05-22-1861, Wm. G. Holloway, D. C.
Mins. Ret. mar. on 05-22-1861 at Cov-
ington, Alleg. Co., VA by J. W. Ewan.
[Author's Note: Believe clk. made
error in mar. date on CTOLMR because
wrote "23" and changed to "22" on Mar.
Authorization and on CTOL part of
form.]

09-10-1861   Abraham Jones [only name listed of
15   marrying parties (on bk and CTOL);
both parties listed (on CTOLMR)], 28
single, B: Bath Co., VA, Lived: Greenbrier Co., VA (now W.VA.), Occup: farmer, s/o: Abel and Mary Jones; and
Catharine Moyers, 23, single, B: Alleg. Co., VA, Lived: Alleg. Co., VA,
dau/o: Geo. and Julia Ann Moyers (on
bk) [Geo. and July Ann Moyers (on
CTOL); George and Julia Ann Moyers
(on CTOLMR)]. PL: George Moyer's res.
Alleg. Co., VA (on CTOLMR). CTOL

signed on 09-10-1861 by <u>Abraham Jones</u>,
Wit. George (his X mark) Moyers.
CTOLMR signed 09-10-1861 by Wm. G.
Holloway, D. C. Mins. Ret. says mar.
on 09-10-1861 at house of bride's
father in Alleg. Co., VA, by James M.
Rice. [Two forms used--CTOL and
CTOLMR]

03-11-1861   <u>James D. Myers</u>, 24, single, B: Giles
   # 16   Co., VA, Lived: Monroe Co., VA (now
              W.VA.), Occup: farmer, s/o: Adam and
              Margarett Myers (on bk) [Adam and
              Margaret Myers (on one CTOL and
              "Margaritt" on the other CTOL); and
              <u>Deliah Nida</u>, 32, single, B: Alleg.
              Co., VA (on bk) [Both CTOL forms have
              Giles Co., VA], Lived: Alleg. Co.,
              VA, dau/o: David and Mary Nida. Mar.
              by Johnzey Leef. PL: Potts Creek,
              Alleg. Co., VA (on CTOL). There were
              two CTOL forms for this marriage.
              CTOL signed on 03-11-1861 by Johnzey
              Leef, the minister. CTOL signed on
              03-11-1861 by <u>James D. Myers</u>. [One
              form seems to be used to obtain the
              lic. and the other seems to be used
              for the minister's return.]

03-12-1861   (on bk)   03-12-____ (on CTOL)
   # 17   <u>Thomas K. Menfee</u>, 27, single, B: Jef-
              ferson Co., VA (now W.VA), Occup:
              Railroading, s/o: Benjamin K. and
              Emily Menefee (on bk) [Benjamin K.
              and Emily Menifee (on CTOL)]; and
              <u>Jennetta F. Persinger</u>, 22, single, B:
              Alleg. Co., VA, dau/o: Andr. and Eliz-
              abeth Persinger (on bk) [Andrew and
              Elizabeth Persinger (on CTOL)]. CTOL
              signed on 03-11-1861 by <u>T. K. Menefee</u>.
              Mar. by James M. Rice, whose note to
              the clk. on 03-14-1861 says mar. on

03-12-1861. Both lived in Alleg. Co., VA. PL: Alleg. Co., VA.

03-14-1861 Jubel W. McCormack (or ? McOrmack)
18   (on bk) [Jubel W. McOrmack (on CTOL)],
            28, single, B: Franklin Co., VA,
            Occup: farmer, s/o: John and Susan
            McCormack (or ? McOrmack) (on bk)
            [John and Susan McOrmack (on CTOL)];
            and Sarah J. Weaver (on bk) [Sarah J.
            Waren (on CTOL)], 21, single, B: Al-
            leg. Co., VA, dau/o: James and ____
            Weaver (on bk) [James and ___ Warren
            (on CTOL)]. Both lived in Alleg. Co.
            PL: Alleg. Co., VA. Mar. by _____.
            CTOL signed on 03-13-1861 by J. W.
            McOrmack. [Note on bk: Wm. Holloway,
            D. C.: "I find no return of the
            minister. I have the date of marriage
            as it is set forth in certificate of
            the applied court."]

01-18-1861 (on bk)   01-18-____   (on CTOL)
19   Patrick Manahan (on bk) [Patrick Min-
            ahan (on CTOL)], 22, single, B: Ire-
            land, Occup: laborer, s/o: Thos. and
            Mary L. Minahan; and Catharine Michael,
            22, single, B: Alleg. Co., VA (on bk)
            [Ireland (on CTOL)], dau/o: Patrick
            and Johanna Michael (on bk) [Patrick
            and Johanna Milchael (on CTOL)]. Both
            lived in Alleg. Co., VA. PL: Alleg.
            Co., VA. Mar. by ____. CTOL signed on
            01-16-1861 by Patrick Moynahan.

06-18-1861 James Mayse, 19, single, B: Bath Co.,
20   VA, Lived: Botetourt Co., VA, Occup:
            farmer, s/o: Nancy Mayse (no other
            name listed); and Mary Nicely, 18,
            single, B: Alleg. Co., VA, Lived: Al-
            leg. Co., VA, dau/o: Jacob and Margar-
            ett Nicely. Mar. by Abraham Buhrman.
            PL: Jacob Nicely's res Alleg. Co., VA,

(on CTOLMR). CTOLMR signed on 06-18-1861 by Wm. G. Holloway, D. C. Mins. Ret. says mar. 06-18-1861 at Jacob Nicely's "near Jourdens Forge" [Note: believe means Jordan's Forge] by Abraham Buhrman. Consent dated on 06-17-1861 has names James Mayse and daughter, Mary Nicely, and was signed by Jacob (his X mark) Nicely, Wit. Joseph (his X mark) Mayse and William H. Lemon. On back of consent a note says Joseph Mayse made oath to the father's consent, Wm. G. Holloway, D. C. "This is to certify that Nancy Mayse is willing for James Mayse to marry Mary Nicely, June 18, 1861. Witness my hand day and date. Simon Hoilman, Witness, Joseph (his X mark) Mayse, Witness." On back of this consent a note says "Joseph Mayse made oath that Nancy Mayse give the within certificate and requested him & the other subscribing witness to attest the same. Wm. G. Holloway, D. Clk."

08-15-1861
21

Sam'l. B. McCoy (on bk0 [Samuel B. McCoy (on CTOL & CTOLMR)], 36, widower, B: Rockbridge Co., VA, Occup: farmer, s/o: James and Nancy McCoy; and Elizabeth Moyers, 21 (on bk) ["about 21" (on CTOL & CTOLMR)], single, B: Alleg. Co., VA, dau/o: Augustus and Margarett Moyers (on bk) [Augusta and Margarett Moyers (on CTOL & CTOLMR)]. PL: Alleg. Co., VA, Mrs. Elizabeth Lockhart's res. (on CTOLMR). Both lived in Alleg. Co., VA. Mar. by J. W. Ewan. CTOL signed 08-12-1861 by Samuel B. McCoy, Teste Joel Kindell. Age oath for Elizabeth made by Joel Kindell, Uncle. CTOLMR signed on 08-

12-1861 by Wm. G. Holloway, D. C.
Mins. Ret. says mar. on 08-15-1861
at Mrs. Lockhart's res. by J. W.
Ewan. "Elizabeth Moyer lives with
Mrs. Elizabeth Lockhart, has no father, mother, nor guardian as far as I
know, has very little or no estate.
She is my niece and there is no objection on my part to her marriage
with Mr. Samuel B. McCoy nor do I believe there is any objection to said
marriage by any of her relations.
She is about twenty-one years old. I
cannot say her precise age.
                    Joel Kindell
Answered & signed upon oaths
                    Wm. G. Holloway, D. Clk."

09-12-1861   Sam'l. McCary (on bk) [Samuel McCary
22   (on CTOL & CTOLMR)], 28, single, Born
             and Lived: Greenbrier Co., VA (now W.
             VA.), Occup: Painter, s/o: Philip and
             Maria McCary (on bk) [Phillip and
             Maria Cary (on CTOL & CTOLMR)]; and
             Harriet S. Wood (on bk) [Harriett S.
             Wood (on CTOL & CTOLMR)], 26, single,
             Born and Lived: Randolph Co., VA (now
             W.VA.), dau/o: Augustus and Mary Wood.
             Mar. by M. A. Davidson. PL: Coving-
             ton, Alleg. Co., VA. CTOL signed on
             09-12-1861 by Sam'l. M. Cary. CTOLMR
             signed on 09-12-1861 by Wm. G. Hollo-
             way, D. C. Mins. Ret. says mar. on
             09-12-1861 at Covington, Alleg. Co.,
             VA, by M. A. Davidson, P. Note to
             Clerk says Harriet S. Wood authorizes
             marriage between herself and Samuel
             McCary on 09-12-1861 and was signed
             Harriet S. Wood, Wit. F. Davidson,
             Martha A. Davidson.
             "Bath County to wit.
                 This day personally appeared be-

fore me the undersigned: Mr. Elvira
E. Armentrout of the County of Bath
and state of VA., and Miss Sarah I.
C. Wood of Randolph County, Va., and
made oath that they know of their
own knowledge that Miss Harriet S.
Wood of the county of Randolph and
state aforesaid is over and above
twenty-one years of age. Given under
my hand this 12th day of September
1861.
Thomas Sittington, J. P."

10-07-1861   John Nealson (on bk) [John Nealon
23   (on CTOL & CTOLMR)], 23, single, B:
Clare Co., Ireland (on bk) [County
of Clair, Ireland (on CTOLMR)], Liv-
ed: Greenbrier Co., VA (now W.VA.),
Occup: Mason, s/o: Martin and Mary
Nealson (on bk) [Martin and Mary
Nealon (on CTOL & CTOLMR)]; and Mary
Hynes, 19, single, B: Randolph Co.,
VA (now W.VA.) (on bk) [County of
Clair, Ireland (on CTOL & CTOLMR)],
Lived: Alleg. Co., VA, dau/o: Michael
and Bridgett Hynes (on bk) [Michael
and Bridget Hynes (on CTOL & CTOLMR)].
Mar. by J. H. Walters. PL: High
Fill, Alleg. Co., VA (on CTOLMR).
CTOL signed 10-04-1861 by John Nelon,
Wit. Patrick Hynes. CTOLMR signed
10-04-1861 by Wm. G. Holloway, D. Clk.
Mins. Ret. says married on 10-07-1861
at High Bridge, Alleg. Co., VA. Fa-
ther's consent dated 10-04-1861 has
name as John Nealon and was signed
Michael Hynes, Wit. Patrick Hynes.

03-14-1861   Alexd. A. Perkins (on bk) [Alexander
24   A. Perkins (on CTOL)], 33, widower,
B: Pocahontas Co., VA (now W.VA.),
Occup: farmer, s/o: Tyree and Jane

V. Perkins (on bk) [Tynis H. (?A.
?G.) and Jane V. Perkins (on CTOL)];
and Sarah E. Mann, 23, single, B: Alleg. Co., VA, dau/o: Jno. M. D. and
Julia Mann (on bk) [John McD. and
Julia Mann (on CTOL)]. Both lived in
Alleg. Co. PL: Alleg. Co., VA. Mar.
by _____. CTOL signed on 03-07-1861
by A A. Perkins. [Note on Bk: Wm.
G. Holloway, D. C.:   "I find no return of the minister. I have the
date of marriage as it is set forth
in certificate of the applied court."]

10-10-1861   James M. Rice, 41, widower, B: Bed-
25   ford Co., VA, Lived: Alleg. Co., VA,
              Occup: Minister of Presbyterian Chur-
              ch, s/o: Sam'l. D. and Sarah D. Rice;
              and Mary J. Damron, 29, single, B:
              Alleg. Co., VA, Lived: Covington, Al-
              leg. Co., VA, dau/o: Andr. and Mary
              W. Damron (on bk) [Andrew and Mary W.
              Damron (on CTOL & CTOLMR)]. Mar. by
              Genham Goble. PL: Andrew Damron's
              res. Covington, VA (on CTOLMR). CTOL
              signed by James M. Rice, Attest And-
              rew Damron. CTOLMR signed by Wm. G.
              Holloway, D. C. on 10-10-1861. Mins.
              Ret. says mar. 10-10-1861 at Andrew
              Damron's res. Covington, VA, by
              Genham Goble.

05-26-1861   (on bk)   05-25-1861 (on CTOLMR)
26   Castlereigh Summers, 38, widower, B:
              Bedford Co., VA, Lived: Alleg. Co.,
              VA, Occup: Cattle Dealer, s/o: Sam'l.
              and Ann Summers (on bk) [Samuel and
              Ann Summers (on CTOLMR)]; and Jane
              Bacon (on bk) [Mary Jane Bacon (on
              CTOLMR)], 24, single, B: Richmond
              City, VA, Lived: Covington, Alleg.
              Co., VA, dau/o: Sam'l. and Mary Jane
              Bacon (on bk) [Samuel and Mary Jane

Bacon (on CTOLMR)]. On CTOLMR says both lived in Alleg. Co., VA. PL: Robert Skeen's Hotel, Covington, VA (on CTOLMR). Mar. by Stuart S. Rider. CTOLMR signed 05-25-1861 Wm. G. Holloway, D. C. Mins. Ret. says mar. on 05-26-1861 at Robert Skeen's Hotel, Covington, VA. Consent dated 05-24-1861 was signed Samuel (his X mark) Bacon, Wit. H. W. Cole has groom's name as Castlereigh Summers.

09-15-1861
27

Timothy Sullivan, 26, single, B: County Cork, Ireland, Lived: Alleg. Co., VA, Occup: laborer, s/o: John and Catharine Sullivan; and Hennora Driscol, 26, widow, B: County Cork, Ireland, Lived: Covington, Alleg. Co. VA, dau/o: Patrick and Mary Driscol. Mar. by J. H. Walters. PL: Big Fill, Alleg. Co., VA (on CTOLMR). CTOL and CTOLMR says both lived in Alleg. Co., VA. CTOL signed on 09-13-1861 by Timothy (his X mark) Sullivan, Wit. Cornelius (his X mark) Shea, Wm. G. Holloway, D. C. CTOLMR signed 09-13-1861 by Wm. G. Holloway, D. C. Mins. Ret. says mar. 09-15-1861 in Alleg. Co., VA by J. H. Walters.

07-11-1861
28

William Vance, 23, single, B: Monroe Co., VA (now W.VA.), Lived: Alleg. Co., VA, Occup: farmer, s/o: Wm. and Virginia Vance (on bk) [William and Virginia Vance (on CTOLMR)]; and Caroline Bostick, 24, single, B: Monroe Co., VA (now W.VA.), Lived: Covington, Alleg. Co., VA, dau/o: Wm. and Polly Bostick (on bk) [William and Polly Bostick (on CTOLMR)]. CTOLMR says both lived in Alleg. Co., VA. PL: Alleg. Co., VA. Mar. by

James M. Rice. J. D. Vance swore to
consent of parties to obtain the Lic.,
Wm. G. Holloway, D. C. CTOLMR signed 07-06-1861 by Wm. G. Holloway, D.
C. Mins. Ret. says mar. 07-11-1861
at house of Wm. Hoke, Alleg. Co., VA
by James M. Rice.

___-___-_____
29

(on bk)   03-12-1861 (on CTOL)
Joseph Zeigler, 23, single, B: Fred-
ericksburg, VA, Lived: Alleg. Co.,
VA, Occup: Clerk, s/o: Abraham and
Mary Zeigler (on bk) [Abraham and
Marth Zeigler (on CTOL)]; and Mary E.
Haynes, 21, single, B: Alleg. Co., VA,
Lived: Covington, VA (on bk) [Alleg.
Co., VA (on CTOL)], dau/o: Wm. H. and
Elizabeth Haynes (on bk) [William
and Elizabeth Haynes (on CTOL)]. PL:
Alleg. Co., VA. Mar. by ___. CTOL
signed on 03-11-1861 by J. Zeigler.
[Note on Book: Wm. G. Holloway, D.C.:
"I find no return of the minister.
I have the date of marriage as it is
set forth in certificate of the appl-
ied court."]   [See # 8 page 8 for 12-
09-1863 for 2nd Mar.]

___-___-_____
30

(on bk and CTOL)
King A. Wolf, 20, single, B: Alleg.
Co., VA, Lived: Alleg. Co., VA, Occup:
farmer, s/o: Abraham and Harriet Wolf;
and Arminda Kimberlin, 21, single, B:
Smith Co., Tennessee (on bk) [Smith
Co., West Tennessee (on CTOL)], Liv-
ed: Covington, VA (on bk) [Alleg. Co.
VA (on CTOL)], dau/o: Wm. and Eliza-
beth Kimberlin (on bk) [William and
Elizabeth Kimberlin (on CTOL)]. PL:
Alleg. Co., VA. Mar. by ___. CTOL
signed on 01-21-1861 by King A. Wolf.
[Note on Bk: Wm. G. Holloway, D.C.:
"I find no return of the minister. I

have the date of marriage as it is
set forth in certificate of the applied court."]

01-02-1862   Edward R. Evans, 26, single, B: Char-
1   lotte Co., VA, Occup: farmer, s/o:
             Elisha and Mary Evans; and Rebecca
             B. McCoy (on bk) [Rebecca V. McCoy
             (on CTOL & CTOLMR)], 21, single, B:
             Rockbridge Co., VA, dau/o: James and
             Nancy McCoy. PL: Alleg. Co., VA,
             James McCoy's res. (on CTOLMR). Mar.
             by S. S. Ryder. Both lived in Alleg.
             Co., VA. CTOL signed 12-31-1861 by
             Edward (his X mark) R. Evans, Teste
             William E. McCoy. CTOLMR signed 12-
             31-1861 by Wm. G. Holloway, D. C.
             Mins. Ret. signed S. S. Rider says
             mar. 01-02-1862 at James McCoy's res.
             in Alleg. Co., VA. Note on back
             CTOLMR says   " Georgia ....Manufact-
             urers & Machanists, Farmers Bank of
             Chattahoochn." [Author's Note: I
             have no idea what this could mean,
             and it may have nothing to do with
             the couple.]

01-09-1862   Peter McArdle, 26, single, B: County
2   Covan, Ireland (on bk) [County Cavan,
             Ireland (on CTOLMR)], Occup: Wagoneer
             and Railroader, s/o: Henry McArdle
             and Ellen (on bk) [Henry and Ellen
             McArdle (on CTOLMR)]; and Ann Gorman
             (on bk & Mar. Auth.) [Ame Gorman (on
             CTOL part of CTOLMR)], 22 (on bk)
             ["about 22 yrs" (on CTOLMR)], single,
             B: Alleg. Co., Maryland, dau/o: Ber-
             nard and Catherine Gorman (on bk)
             [Bernard and Cathrine Gorman (on CTOL
             MR)]. Both Lived in Alleg. Co., VA
             (on bk) [Alleg. Co. near Covington,
             VA (on CTOLMR)]. PL: Alleg. co., VA.

Mar. by J. H. Walters. CTOLMR signed Wm. G. Holloway, D. C. Mins. Ret.
says mar. 01-09-1862 near Covington
in Alleg. Co., VA by J. H. Walters.

02-06-1862 Joseph P. (? T.) Stull, 31, single,
3   B: Alleg. Co., VA, Occup: farmer, s/o:
           Jacob and Margaret Stull; and Mary E.
           Stull (on bk) [Mary Ellen Stull (as
           on CTOL)], 21, single, B: Alleg. Co.,
           VA, dau/o: John and Ann Stull. PL:
           Alleg. Co., VA "Rich Patch" (on CTOL
           MR). Mar. by Jas. M. Rice. CTOL
           signed 02-04-1862 by Joseph T. Stull.
           Age oath on CTOL that Mary is 21 was
           signed by George L. Stull. CTOLMR
           signed on 02-04-1862 by Wm. G. Hollo-
           way, D. C. Mins. Ret. says mar. on
           02-06-1862 at Mrs. Ann Stull's res.
           in Alleg. Co., VA and signed by James
           M. Rice. Both lived in Alleg. Co.,VA.

02-12-1862 John Wall, 26, single, B: Ireland,
4   Occup: laborer, s/o: John and Hannah
           Wall; and Jane Sullivan, 18, single,
           B: State of Rhode Island, dau/o: Dan-
           iel and Mary Sullivan. Both lived in
           Alleg. Co., VA. PL: Alleg. Co., VA.
           Mar. by J. H. Walters. CTOLMR signed
           on 02-10-1862 by Wm. G. Holloway, D.
           C. Mins. Ret. signed by J. H. Walters
           says mar. on 02-12-1862 in Alleg. Co.,
           VA at Dunlap Creek.

02-20-1862 Benjamin F. Griffith, 23, single, B:
5   Monroe Co., VA (now W.VA.), Occup:
           farmer, s/o: Wesley and Nicy Griffith;
           and Margaret S. Herbert, 21, single,
           B: Alleg. Co., VA, dau/o: Wm. and Lur-
           eua Herbert (on bk) [Wm. and Luvena
           Herbert (on CTOLMR)]. Both lived in
           Alleg. Co. PL: Alleg. Co., VA. Mar.

by Henry B. Rose. CTOLMR signed 02-11-1862 by Wm. G. Holloway, D. C. Mins. Ret. says mar. 02-20-1862 at Wm. Herbert's res. in Alleg. Co., VA. Consent signed on 02-11-1862 by Wm. Herbert says "This is to certify that I authorize Benjamin Griffith to set my signature to the Clerk's gurantee bond. Given under my hand this 11 day February 1862. Wm. Herbert" CTOLMR says place of mar. was to be Cove Creek [Note: which is in Monroe Co., W.VA. and runs into VA near Sweet Springs, W.VA.]

04-01-1862 Archilles Dew, 60, widower, Occup:
6   farmer, s/o: Wm. and Mary Dew; and
            Sarah Persinger, 27, single, dau/o:
            ____ and Charlotte Myers ["Now" (as
            on CTOL)]. Both were born and lived
            in Alleg. Co., VA. PL: Alleg. Co.,
            VA. Mar. by ____. CTOL signed on
            03-27-1862 by Archilles Dew, Teste
            Henry Myers.

05-10-1862 James R. Cave, 24, single, B: Page
7   Co., VA, Occup: laborer, s/o: Thomas
            and Elizabeth Cave; and Sarah E.
            Brown, 23, single, B: Rockbridge Co.,
            VA, dau/o: Lemuel and Sarah Brown.
            PL: Alleg. Co., VA, "Bend of Jackson
            River" (on CTOLMR). Both lived in
            Alleg. Co., VA. Mar. by G. G. Brooke.
            CTOLMR signed 05-09-1862 by Wm.
            G. Holloway, D. C. Mins. Ret. says
            mar. on 05-10-1862 at house of ____
            Alleg. Co., VA. [See # 32 Mar. Register Page 7, 05-09-1862, listed
            twice]

08-14-1862 Jacob Bowyer, 64 (on bk) ["64 past"
8   (on CTOL)], widower, B: Monroe Co.,

VA (now W. VA.), Lived: Monroe Co.,
VA (now W.VA.) ["about 7 miles above
Sweet Springs" (on CTOL)], Occup:
farmer, s/o: Adam and Christina Bowyer (on bk) [Adam and Christianna
Bowyer (on CTOL)]; and Margaret Damron, 26, (on bk) ["about 26 yrs" (on
CTOL)], widow, B: Alleg. Co., VA,
Lived: Alleg. Co., VA, "Snake Run"
(on CTOL), dau/o: Sampson and _____
Bennett (on bk) [Sampson and Mary
Bennet (as on CTOL)]. Mar. by H. B.
Rose. PL: Alleg. Co., VA "at res.
of Mrs. Margaret Damron on Snake Run"
(on CTOL). CTOL signed by Jacob Bowyer. CTOLMR: Marriage Authorization
filled in with Jacob Bowyer and Margaret Damron and signed on 08-13-1862
by W. M. Scott, Pro Tem. and CTOL
part not filled in. Mins. Ret. says
mar. 08-14-1862 at Mrs. Margaret Damron's in Alleg. Co., VA and signed by
H. B. Rose.

09-10-1862   Wednesday
  # 9   James H. Tyree, 30, single, B: Bath
              Co., VA, Occup: Gunsmith, s/o: John
              R. and Nancy Tyree; and Eliza Guy,
              22, single, B: England, dau/o: Will-
              iam and Mary Guy (on bk) [Wm. and
              Mary Guy (on CTOL)]. PL: Alleg. Co.,
              VA. Both lived in Alleg. Co., VA.
              Mar. by S. S. Ryder. CTOL signed on
              09-09-1862 by James H. Tyree. Mar.
              Auth. written by clk. on back of CTOL
              by W. M. Scott, Clk. Pro Tem. Mins.
              note on back says mar. on 09-10-1862
              at hosue of William Guy by S. S.
              Ryder.

09-11-1862   John Garibaldia, 31, single, B: Italy,
  # 10   Occup: farmer, s/o: Domineck and The-

rissa Garibaldia; and <u>Sarah A. V. Poor</u>, 26, single, B: Alleg. Co., VA, dau/o: Soloman and Mary Poor. PL: Alleg. Co., VA (on bk) ["Potts Creek" (on CTOL)]. Both lived in Alleg. Co, VA "Potts Creek" (on CTOL). Mar. by S. S. Ryder. CTOL signed on 09-05-1862 by W. M. Scott, Clk. Pro Tem. and <u>John Garibaldi</u>. Mar. Auth. of clk. on back of CTOL. Mins. Ret. on back says mar. 09-11-1862 at house of Mary Poor on Potts Creek by S. S. Ryder.

11-13-1862
11

Thursday
<u>Christopher Fry</u>, 35, single, B: Rockingham Co., VA, Occup: farmer, s/o: John and Mary Fry; and <u>Dianna Strong</u>, 22, single, B: Alleg. Co., VA (on bk) ["born at William Strong's" (only thing listed on CTOLMR)], dau/o: William and Dianna Strong (on bk) [Dianah Strong (only name listed on CTOLMR)]. Both lived in Alleg. Co., VA. PL: Alleg. Co., VA "Jackson River" (on CTOL). Mar. by Stuart S. Ryder. CTOLMR signed on 10-05-1862 by W. M. Scott, Clk. Pro Tem. Mins. Ret. says mar. 10-13-1862 at Mathias Brown's.

12-04-1862
12

<u>James Morrison</u>, 46, widower, Occup: laborer, B: Culpepper, VA, s/o: ___ & ___ Morrison (on bk) ["unknown" (on CTOLMR)]; and <u>Margarette Lawson</u>, 37, single, B: Alleg. Co., VA, dau/o: ___ & ___ Lawson (on bk) ["unknown" (on CTOLMR)]. Both lived in Alleg. Co., VA. Mar. by G. G. Brooke. PL: Alleg. Co., VA "Campbell Karnes's res." (on CTOLMR). CTOLMR signed on 12-01-1862 by W. M. Scott, Clk. Pro. Tem.

(Mar. Register Book (1) - Continued)

Mins. Ret. says mar. on 12-04-1862 at house of C. Carnes. [See # 33 Mar. Register page 7, 12-01-1862, listed twice]

Page 7

09-18-1862 Jos. P. Stone, 45, widower, B: Alleg.
1   Co., VA, Occup: farmer, s/o: John and
            Mary Stone; and Lucinda C. Sizer, 29,
            single, B: Botetourt Co., VA, dau/o:
            F. P. and ___ Sizer (on bk) [Fielding
            P. and ___ Sizer (on CTOL)]. Both
            lived in Alleg. Co., VA. Mar. by H.
            B. Rose. PL: Alleg. Co., VA "Potts
            Creek" (on CTOL). Handwritten CTOL
            on legal size note paper signed on
            09-11-1862 by Jos. P. Stone. Mar.
            Auth. says Joseph P. Stone and was
            signed by W. M. Scott, Clk. Pro Tem.
            Mins. note on back says mar. 09-18-
            1862.

09-31-1862 (on bk)   09-30-1862 (on Mins. Ret.)
2   Caleb Griffith, 22, single, Occup:
            farmer, s/o: Orlando and Lucy Griff-
            ith; and Elizabeth Deeds, 26, single,
            dau/o: Wm. and Eliz. Deeds (on bk)
            [William and Elizabeth Deeds (on
            CTOLMR)]. Both were born and lived
            in Alleg. Co., VA. Mar. by Jas. M.
            Rice. PL: Alleg. Co., VA "Cowpasture
            River" (on CTOLMR). CTOLMR signed on
            09-28-1862 by W. M. Scott, Clk. Pro
            Tem. Mins. Ret. says mar. 09-30-1862
            on Cowpasture River "alias Griffith's
            Turnout" was signed by James M. Rice.

05-13-1863 James Crookshanks, 36, widower, B:
3   Greenbrier Co., VA (now W.VA.), Occup:
            blacksmith, s/o: Alexander and Marga-
            ritta Crookshanks (on bk) [Alexander

- 140 -

and Margarette Crookshanks (on CTOL
MR)]; and <u>Mrs. Mary Ford</u>, 25, widow,
B: Greenbrier Co., VA (now W.VA.),
dau/o: Peter and ___ Levisay. Both
lived in Greenbrier Co., VA (now W.
VA). Mar. by Jas. M. Rice. PL: Cov-
ington, VA. CTOLMR signed on 05-13-
1863 by W. M. Scott, Clk. Pro Tem.
Mins. Ret. says mar. 05-13-1863 at
Covington, Alleg. Co. signed by
James M. Rice.

05-19-1863   <u>Anthony B. Barrett</u>, 21, single, B:
4   Fayette Co., VA (now W.VA.), Lived:
             Kanawha Co., VA (now W.VA.), Occup:
             farmer, s/o: Emanuel and Clara Bar-
             rett (on bk) [Amanuel and Clara Bar-
             rett (on CTOLMR)]; and <u>Lucy Ann Glad-</u>
             <u>well</u>, 15, single, B: Augusta Co.,
             VA, Lived: Alleg. Co., VA, dau/o:
             Valentine and Sarah Gladwell. Mar.
             by W. Kennedy. PL: Alleg. Co., VA.
             CTOLMR signed on 05-19-1863 by W. M.
             Scott, Clk. Pro. Tem. Mins. Ret.
             says mar. on 05-19-1863 at Mrs.
             Reece's res. in Alleg. Co., VA.

06-21-1864   (on bk) 06-23-1864 Thursday (on
5   CTOLMR)
             <u>William Bowen</u>, 21, single, B: Giles
             Co., VA, Occup: farmer, s/o: Johner
             and Nancy Bowen (on bk) [Johnson and
             Nancy Bowen (on CTOLMR)]; and <u>Mary</u>
             <u>J. Fridley</u> (on bk) [<u>Mary Jane Frid-</u>
             <u>ley</u> (on CTOLMR)], 25, single, B: Al-
             leg. Co., VA, dau/o: John and Ruth
             Fridley (on bk) [John and Rutha Frid-
             ley (on CTOLMR)]. Both lived in Al-
             leg. Co., VA, Blue Spring Run (on
             CTOLMR). PL: Alleg. Co., VA "Blue
             Spring Run" (on CTOLMR). Mar. by J.
             M. Rice. CTOLMR signed on 06-21-1864

by W. M. Scott, Clk. Pro Tem. Mins.
Ret. says mar. 06-23-1864 at house
of Mrs. Fridley, the bride's mother
signed by James M. Rice.

10-01-1864   (on bk)   10-11-1864 (on CTOLMR)
6   M. A. Smith (on bk) [Mark A. Smith
              (on CTOLMR)], 31, single, Occup: far-
              mer, B: Alleg. Co., VA (on bk) [Meck-
              linburg Co., VA (on CTOLMR)], s/o:
              J. J. and Lucy Smith (on bk) [John
              J. and Lucy Smith (on CTOLMR)]; and
              M. E. Rogers (on bk) [Margaret E.
              Rogers (on CTOLMR)], 27, widow, B:
              Alleg. Co., VA, dau/o: (? S). and M.
              Walker (on bk) [Henry and Maria Wal-
              ker (on CTOLMR)]. Both lived in Al-
              leg. Co., VA. PL: Alleg. Co., VA
              "Potts Creek". Mar. by H. B. Rose.
              CTOLMR signed on 10-01-1864 by Jos-
              eph T. Fudge, Clk. Mins. Ret. says
              mar. on 10-11-1864 on Potts Creek.

10-07-1864   (on bk)   10-11-1864 Tuesday (on
7   CTOLMR)
              G. W. Wilkson (on bk) [George W.
              Wilkerson (on CTOLMR)], 27, single,
              Occup: carpenter, s/o: E. and M.
              Wilkson (on bk) [Elijah and Mary
              Wilkerson (on CTOLMR)]; and E. W.
              Carter (on bk) [Elvira W. Carter (on
              CTOLMR)], 23, single, dau/o: L. and
              M. Carter (on bk) [Lemuel and Martha
              Carter (on CTOLMR)]. Both were born
              and lived in Alleg. Co., VA (on bk),
              but CTOLMR says George was born in
              Henrico Co., VA and that Elvira was
              born in Alleg. Co., VA. Both lived
              in Alleg. Co., VA. PL: Alleg. Co.,
              VA "Snake Run". Mar. by H. B. Rose.
              CTOLMR signed on 10-07-1864 by W. M.
              Scott, D. C. Mins. Ret. says mar.

(Mar. Register Book (1) - Continued)

on 10-11-1864 in Alleg. Co.

11-28-1864   (on bk)   12-01-1864 (on CTOLMR)
  # 8   S. S. Nicely (on bk) [Samuel S. Nice-
                ly (on CTOLMR)], 20, single, Occup:
                farmer, s/o: A. J. and N. Nicely (on
                bk) [A. S. And Nellie Nicely (on
                CTOLMR)]; and S. M. Nicely (on bk)
                [Sarah M. Nicely (on CTOLMR)], 23,
                single, dau/o: L. and A. Nicely (on
                bk) [Lewis and Annie Nicely (on CTOL
                MR)].   Both were born and lived in
                Alleg. Co., VA. PL: Alleg. Co., VA
                "Cowpasture River". Mar. by D. M.
                Wood. CTOLMR signed on 11-28-1864 by
                W. M. Scott, D. C. Mins. Ret. says
                mar. on 12-01-1864 at res. of Annie
                Nicely (widow) signed by Davis M.
                Wood, L. D.

05-24-1864   Tuesday
  # 9   Patrick Sullivan, 46, single, B: Co.
                of Cork, Ireland, Occup: laborer, s/o:
                John and Lelia Sullivan (on bk) [John
                and Julia Sullivan (on CTOLMR)]; and
                Mary O'Conner, 35, widow, B: Co. of
                Kerry, Ireland, dau/o: Eugene and
                Catherine Daley. Both lived in Alleg.
                Co., VA. PL: Alleg. Co., VA "Red
                Sweet Springs". Mar. by J. H. Walt-
                ers. CTOLMR signed on 05-18-1864 by
                W. M. Scott, Clk. Pro Tem. Mins. Ret.
                says mar. 05-24-1864 at Sweet Springs,
                Monroe Co., VA (now W.VA.).

01-29-1864   Saturday
  # 10   John Leary, 57, widower, B: Ireland,
                Occup: laborer, s/o: Sylva and Mary
                Leary; and Margarette Burke, 36,
                widow, B: Ireland, dau/o: Jeremiah
                and Julia Burke (on bk) [Jeremiah and
                Julia Burk (on CTOLMR) written in

- 143 -

pencil)]. Both lived in Alleg. Co.
PL: Alleg. Co., VA, "Red-Sweet-Spr-
ings" (as on CTOLMR--may have been
changed by minister since handwriting
is similar). Mar. by J. H. Walters.
CTOLMR signed on 01-27-1864 by W. M.
Scott, Clk. Pro Tem. Mins. Ret. says
mar. on 01-29-1864 in Alleg. Co.,VA.

12-29-1864   John L. Bennett, 23, single, Occup:
11   farmer, s/o: William and Catharine
             Bennett; and Susan M. Persinger, 30,
             single, dau/o: ___ and Betsey Persin-
             ger. Both born and lived in Alleg.
             Co., VA. PL: Alleg. Co., VA "Rich
             Patch". Mar. by S. S. Ryder. CTOLMR
             signed 12-27-1864 by W. M. Scott, D.
             C. Mar. Auth. signed 12-27-1864 by
             W. M. Scott, Clk. Pro Tem. Mins. Ret.
             says mar. 12-29-1865 in Rich Patch in
             Alleg. Co., VA signed S. S. Ryder.
             [Author's Note: The minister may
             have made a mistake on the year be-
             cause he probably didn't return the
             Lic. to the court until after 01-01-
             1865.]

03-01-1864   Tuesday
12   Thomas P. Bowles, 28, single, B: Bed-
             ford Co., VA, Lived: Bedford Co., VA,
             Occup: merchant, s/o: John H. and
             Nancy C. Bowles; and Lillian William-
             son (on bk) [Lilly Williamson (on
             CTOLMR)], 22, single, B: Scotland,
             Lived: Alleg. Co., VA, dau/o: Andrew
             and Jean Williamson. Mar. by James
             M. Rice. PL: Alleg. Co., VA "Jackson
             River". CTOLMR signed on 02-29-1864
             by W. M. Scott, Clk. Pro Tem. Lilly
             Williamson on Mar. Auth. dated 02-29-
             1864. Mins. Ret. says mar. on 03-01-
             1864 at the hosue of the bride's

father was signed by James M. Rice.

04-19-1864   Tuesday
  # 13   <u>Davis M. Humphries</u> (on bk) [<u>David M.
             Humphries</u> (on CTOLMR)], 21, single,
             Occup: farmer, s/o: William and Rutha
             Humphries; and <u>Martha S. Byer</u>, 21 (on
             bk) [20 (on CTOLMR)], single, dau/o:
             Samuel and Henrietta Byer (on bk)
             [Samuel and Harriette Byer (on CTOL
             MR)]. Both lived in Alleg. Co., VA
             "Rich Patch". Both were born in Al-
             leg. Co., VA. PL: Alleg. Co., VA
             "Rich Patch". Mar. by S. S. Ryder.
             <u>Davis M. Humphries</u> is name on Mar.
             Auth. dated 04-18-1864 and signed W.
             M. Scott, Clk. Pro Tem. CTOLMR sign-
             ed on 04-18-1864 by W. M. Scott, Clk.
             Pro Tem. Mins. Ret. says mar. on
             04-19-1864 at Samuel Byer's was sign-
             ed by S. S. Ryder.

09-30-1865   (on bk and in CTOL part of CTOLMR)
  # 1   08-30-1865 (on Mins. Ret.)
             <u>Geo. W. Wright</u> (on bk) [<u>G. L. Wright</u>
             (on Mar. Auth.) <u>George Lee Wright</u> (on
             CTOLMR)], 22, single, Occup: farmer,
             s/o: Geo. W. and Eliz. Wright (on bk)
             [George W. and Elizabeth Wright (on
             CTOLMR)]; and <u>Charlotte Johnston</u> (on
             bk) [<u>Charlott Johnston</u> (on CTOLMR)],
             21, single, dau/o: Jabez and Maria
             Johnston (on bk) [Jabz and Maria John-
             ston (on CTOLMR)]. Both were born and
             lived in Alleg. Co., VA. PL: Alleg.
             Co., VA "Jabz Johnston's res." Mar.
             by J. M. Rice. CTOLMR signed on 08-
             28-1865 by Jos. T. Fudge, Clk. Mins.
             Ret. says mar. 08-30-1865 ar res. of
             bride's father was signed by James M.
             Rice. [Note: The minister was re-
             quired to return the Lic. within 10

(Mar. Register Book (1) - Continued)

days per ACT passed on 03-15-1861.]

09-06-1865
2

W. A. McCray (on bk) [Wm. Alexander
McCray (on CTOLMR)], 24, single,
Occup: carpenter, B: Bath Co., VA,
s/o: A. and M. J. McCray (on bk) [Al-
exander and Mary Jane McCray (on
CTOLMR)]; and Martha A. Mallow (on
bk) [Mattie Arabella Mallow (on CTOL
MR)], 24, single, B: Alleg. Co., VA,
dau/o: John and Martha Mallow (on bk)
[John and Mattie Mallow (on CTOLMR)].
Both lived in Alleg. Co., VA. PL:
Alleg. Co., VA "res. of Wm. M. Mal-
low". Mar. by J. M. Rice. Wm. A.
McCray and Mattie A. Mallow on Mar.
Auth. signed on 09-05-1865 by Jos. T.
Fudge, Clk. CTOLMR signed 09-05-1865
by Joseph T. Fudge, Clk. Mins. Ret.
says mar. 09-06-1865 at res. of
bride's father was signed James M.
Rice.

09-26-1865
3

H. L. Hall (on bk) [Henry Lewis Hall
(on CTOLMR)], 23, single, B: Alleg.
Co., VA, Occup: farmer, s/o: J. H.
and S. P. Hall (on bk) [Joseph H. and
Sarah P. Hall (on CTOLMR)]; and Rebec-
ca B. Bess (on bk) [Rebecca Beviline
Bess (on CTOLMR)], 21, single, B: Al-
leg. Co., VA, dau/o: Hamilton and
Rebecca Bess. Both lived in Alleg.
Co., VA. PL: Alleg. Co., VA "Potts
Creek". Mar. by J. B. Davis. CTOLMR
signed on 09-19-1865 by Joseph T.
Fudge, Clk. Mins. Ret. says mar. on
09-26-1865 at Hamilton Bess's res.
was signed John B. Davis.
"Alleghany County Court Clerk's Office
     This day John L. Bess personally
appeared before me Joseph T. Fudge,
Clerk of the County Court of said

County and made oath that <u>Rebecca B.</u>
<u>Bess</u> the daughter of Hamilton Bess
and affianced bride of <u>Henry L. Hall</u>
is over the age of twenty years of
age.
 Given under my hand as Clerk
aforesaid this 19th day of September
1865.
     Jos. T. Fudge, Clk."

09-26-1865 <u>Jacob Nicely</u>, 20, single, Occup: far-
 # 4 mer, s/o: A. J. and Hester Nicely;
and <u>Nannie E. Nicely</u>, 18, single,
dau/o: John and E. Nicely (on bk)
[John and Elizabeth Nicely (on CTOL
MR)]. Both were born and lived in
Alleg. Co., VA. PL: Alleg. Co., VA
"J. A. Nicely res." Mar. by Abraham
Buhrman. CTOLMR signed by Joseph T.
Fudge, Clk. on 09-25-1865. Mins. Ret.
says mar. on 09-26-1865 at John A.
Nicely's in Alleg. Co.
"Alleghany County Court Clerk's Office
 This day personally appeared before me, Joseph T. Fudge, Clerk of
the said court, A. J. Nicely the Subscribing witness to the within certificate and made oath that the said
certificate was the geniune handwriting of John and Elizabeth Nicely and
that they acknowledged the same to
be their act and deed--
 Given under my hand this 25th
day of September 1865.
    Joseph T. Fudge, Clerk"

09-26-1865 <u>G. W. Wright</u> (on bk) [<u>Gitanio W. Wri-</u>
 # 5 <u>ght</u> (on CTOLMR)], 19, single, Occup:
farmer, s/o: G. W. and E. Wright (on
bk) [Geo. W. and Elizabeth Wright
(on CTOLMR)]; and <u>E. A. Bush</u> (on bk)
[<u>Elizabeth A. Bush</u> (on CTOLMR)], 23,

(Mar. Register Book (1) - Continued)

single, dau/o: Adam and P. Bush (on
bk) [Adam and Peggy Bush (on CTOLMR)].
Both were born and lived in Alleg. Co,
VA. PL: Alleg. Co., VA "G. W. Wright's res. Potts Creek". Mar. by John
B. Davis. CTOLMR signed on 09-25-1865
by Jos. T. Fudge, Clk. Mins. Ret.
says mar. on 09-26-1865 at George W.
Wright's res. Consent dated 09-24-
1865 and signed G. W. Wright stated
Gitanio's age was "rising nineteen
years" and Elizabeth's age was "rising
twenty three". Oath of Gitanio W.
Wright dated 09-25-1865 stated that
certificate and signature were geniune
handwriting of his father and that
Elizabeth was over 21 and was signed
by Joseph T. Fudge, Clk.

09-26-1865   (on bk)   __-__-____ (on CTOLMR)
   # 6   08-27-1865 (on Mins. Ret.)
            Lee Persinger, 54, widower, Occup:
            farmer, s/o: Moses and Choltt Persing-
            er (on bk) [Moses and Charlotte Per-
            singer (on CTOLMR)]; and D. M. Helman-
            toller (on bk) [Delolah M. Helmentoll-
            er (on CTOLMR)], 33, single, dau/o:
            P. and M. Helmantoller (on bk) [Peter
            and Mary Helmentoller (on CTOLMR)].
            Both born and lived in Alleg. Co., VA.
            PL: Alleg. Co., VA "Peter's Mountain".
            Mar. by S. S. Rider. Delolah M. Hel-
            mentoller on Mar. Auth. dated 08-21-
            1865 signed Joseph T. Fudge, Clk.
            CTOLMR signed on 08-21-1865 by Joseph
            T. Fudge, Clk. Mins. Ret. says mar.
            08-27-1865 on Peter's Mountain in Al-
            leg. Co., VA, was signed by S. S.
            Ryder.

09-13-1865   Wm. C. Mann (on bk) [William Clark
   # 7   Mann (on CTOLMR)], 20, single, Occup:

farmer, s/o: A. G. and Clementine
Mann (on bk) [Archibald G. and Clementine Mann (on CTOLMR)]; and P. A. Mc-
Callister (on bk) [Phebe Agnes McCallister (on CTOLMR)], 18, single, dau/
o: A. and M. S. McCallister (on bk)
[Archibald and Margaret Susan McCallister (on CTOLMR)]. Both born and
lived in Alleg. Co., VA. PL: Alleg.
Co., VA "res. of bride's father".
Mar. by S. S. Rider. CTOLMR signed
09-12-1865 by Jos. T. Fudge, Clk.
Mins. Ret. says mar. 09-13-1865 at
Archabald McCalister's in Alleg. Co.,
VA, was signed S. S. Ryder.

09-05-1865
8

J. M. Boswell (on bk) [Joseph Merriken
Boswell (on CTOLMR)], 32, widower,
Occup: farmer, s/o: J. L. and M. A.
Boswell (on bk) [John Lee and Martha
Ann Boswell (on CTOLMR)]; and V. C.
Persinger (on bk) [Virginia Catherine
Persinger (on CTOLMR)], 24, single,
dau/o: A. and E. Persinger (on bk)
[Andrew and Elizabeth Persinger (on
CTOLMR)]. Both born and lived in Alleg. Co., VA, but Joseph was born in
Covington, and both lived in Covington, VA. PL: Alleg. Co., VA "near
Covington". Mar. by S. S. Rider.
CTOLMR signed 08-26-1865 by Joseph T.
Fudge, Clk. Mar. Auth. has names
Joseph M. Boswell and Jennie C. Persinger. Mins. Ret. says mar. 09-05-
1865 near Covington, VA, was signed by
S. S. Ryder.

09-21-1865
9

Thursday
J. C. Bess (on bk) [John C. Bess (on
CTOLMR)], 25, single, Occup: farmer,
s/o: H. and N. Bess (on bk) [Henry and
Nellie Bess (on CTOLMR)]; and E. Oiler

(on bk) [Elizabeth Oiler (on CTOLMR)],
21, single, dau/o: J. and B. Oiler
(on bk) [John and Beckie Oiler (on
CTOLMR)]. Both born and lived in Alleg. Co., VA. PL: Alleg. Co., VA
"Henry Bess's res. Potts Creek". Mar.
by S. S. Rider. CTOLMR signed on 09-
21-1865 by Jos. T. Fudge, Clk. Mins.
Ret. says mar. 09-21-1865 at house of
Henry Bess was signed by S. S. Ryder.

01-09-1865 (on bk)   01-10-1864 Tuesday (on
10   CTOLMR)   01-10-1865 (on Mins. Ret.)
            J. P. Payne (on bk) [James P. Payne
            (on CTOLMR)], 24, single, Occup: far-
            mer, s/o: L. and L. Payne (on bk)
            [Lewis and Louisa Payne (on CTOLMR)];
            and M. C. Carpenter (on bk) [Mary C.
            Carpenter (on Mar. Auth.; no bride's
            name on CTOL part of CTOLMR)],   20,
            single, dau/o: S. and M. A. Carpenter
            (on bk) [Samuel and Marsha A. Carpen-
            ter (on CTOLMR)]. Both born and liv-
            ed in Alleg. Co., VA on bk., but CTOL
            MR says James was born in Bath Co.,
            VA. PL: Alleg. Co., VA "Bend of Jack-
            son River". Mar. by S. S. Rice (on
            bk). CTOLMR signed 01-09-1865 by W.
            M. Scott, D. C. Mins. Ret. says 01-
            10-1865 at Sam'l. Carpenter's res. was
            signed by S. S. Ryder.

02-09-1865 Tuesday
11   M. L. Harwood (on bk) [Marion Leon
            Howard (on CTOLMR)], 23, single, Oc-
            cup: Shoemaker, s/o: R. A. and E. Har-
            wood (on bk) [Richard A. and Eliza
            Howard (on CTOLMR)]; and R. J. Evans
            (on bk) [Rebecca Jane Evans (on CTOL
            MR)], 21, single, dau/o: W. and K.
            Evans (on bk) [William and Kessiah
            Evans (on CTOLMR)]. Both born and

(Mar. Register Book (1) - Continued)

lived in Alleg. Co., VA (on bk), but Marion was born in Charles County, Maryland (on CTOLMR). PL: Alleg. Co, VA "Rich Patch". Mar. by J. M. Rice. Mar. Auth. has Marion L. Horwood. CTOLMR signed on 02-09-1865 by W. M. Scott, D. C. Mins. Ret. says mar. on 02-09-1865 at house of A. Harman was signed by James M. Rice.

02-19-1865
12

(on bk) 02-22-1865 Wednesday (on CTOLMR and Mins. Ret.) W. H. McPherson (on bk) [William Harrison McPherson (on CTOLMR)], 24, single, Occup: blacksmith, s/o: J. and M. McPherson (on bk) [John and Mary McPherson (on CTOLMR)]; and C. A. Sullender (on bk) [Charlotte Ann Sullinder (on CTOLMR)], 21, single, dau/o: W. and S. Sullender (on bk) [William and (? Savlrona ?Saperona ? Sasserona --can't read) Sullinder (on CTOLMR)]. Both born and lived in Alleg. Co., VA (on bk), but William was born in Roanoke Co., VA (on CTOLMR). PL: Alleg. Co., VA "Potts Creek". Mar. by S. S. Ryder. CTOLMR signed on 02-18-1865 by W. M. Scott, D. C. Mins. Ret. says mar. 02-22-1865 at William Sulinders in Alleg. Co.

02-06-1865
13

(on bk) 02-09-1865 Thursday (on CTOLMR and Mins. Ret.) G. P. Persinger (on bk) [George Payne Persinger (on CTOLMR)], 25, single, Occup: farmer, s/o: J. H. and M. Persinger (on bk) [Joseph H. and Mary Persinger (on CTOLMR)]; and C. I. King (on bk) [Charlotte Isabella King (on CTOLMR)], 18, single, dau/o: G. P. and Nancy King (on bk) [George P. and Nancy King (on CTOLMR)]. Both born

and lived in Alleg. Co., VA. PL:
Alleg. Co., VA "Rich Patch". Mar.
by S. S. Ryder. CTOLMR signed on
02-06-1865 by W. M. Scott, D. C.
Mins. Ret. says mar. 02-09-1865 in
Rich Patch in Alleg. Co., VA.

03-20-1865   (on bk) 03-30-1865 Thursday (on
14   CTOLMR and Mins. Ret.)
               S. S. Carpenter (on bk) [Samuel S.
               Carpenter (on CTOLMR)], 23, single,
               Occup: farmer, s/o: S. and M. A. Car-
               penter (on bk) [Samuel and Mareh A.
               Carpenter (on CTOLMR)]; and Mary A.
               Griffith, 23, single, dau/o: C. and
               E. J. Griffith (on bk) [Caleb and
               Elizabeth J. Griffith (on CTOLMR)].
               Both born and lived in Alleg. Co., VA.
               PL: Alleg. Co., VA "Jackson's River".
               Mar. by S. S. Ryder. CTOLMR signed
               on 03-20-1865 by W. M. Scott, D. C.
               Mins. Ret. says mar. on 03-30-1865 at
               Caleb Griffith's in Alleg. Co., VA.

03-30-1865   (on bk) 03-31-1865 Friday (on CTOLMR
15   and Mins. Ret.)
               J. S. Nida (on bk) [James S. Nida (on
               CTOLMR)], 26, single (on bk) [widower
               (on CTOLMR)], Occup: farmer, s/o: D.
               and M. Nida (on bk) [David and Mary
               Nida (on CTOLMR)]; and E. F. Persing-
               er (on bk) [Eliza F. Persinger (on
               CTOLMR)], 21, single, dau/o:___ and
               Christ Persinger (on bk) [___ and
               Charlotte Persinger (on CTOLMR)].
               Both born and lived in Alleg. Co.,
               VA (on bk), but James was born in
               Giles Co. VA (on CTOLMR). PL: Alleg.
               Co., VA "Potts Creek". Mar. by John
               B. Davis. CTOLMR signed on 03-30-1865
               by W. M. Scott, D. C. Mins. Ret. says
               mar. 03-31-1865 at Henry Myers's res.

(Mar. Register Book (1) - Continued)

Potts Creek in Alleg. Co., VA.

05-09-1865   (on bk) 05-10-1865 Wednesday (on
  # 16   CTOLMR and Mins. Ret.)
             A. A. McAllister (on bk) [Abram Adam
             McAllister (on CTOLMR)], 24, single,
             Occup: farmer, s/o: T. and L. McAl-
             lister (on bk) [Thompson and Lydia
             McAllister (on CTOLMR)]; and J. E.
             Stratton (on bk) [Julia Ellen Strat-
             ton (on CTOLMR)], 25, single, dau/o:
             J. D. and M. A. Stratton (on bk)
             [Joseph D. and Mary A. Stratton (on
             CTOLMR)]. Both born and lived in Al-
             leg. Co., VA (on bk), but Abram was
             born in Franklin Co., VA; and Julia
             was born in Kanawha Co., VA (now W.
             VA) (on CTOLMR); and Julia lived in
             Covington in Alleg. Co. (on CTOLMR).
             PL: Alleg. Co., VA "Covington". Mar.
             by James M. Rice. Mar. Auth. has A.
             Adam McAllister and J. Ellen Stratton.
             CTOLMR signed on 05-09-1865 by W. M.
             Scott, D. C. Mins. Ret. says mar. on
             05-10-1865 at Mrs. Rock's in Coving-
             ton, VA.

05-10-1865   (on bk) 05-17-1865 Wednesday (on
  # 17   CTOLMR and Mins. Ret.)
             John Griffith, 43, single (on bk)
             [widower (on CTOLMR)], Occup: farmer,
             s/o: R. and S. Griffith (on bk) [Rob-
             ert and Sarah Griffith (on CTOLMR)];
             and M. Mann (on bk) [Margarette Mann
             (on CTOLMR)], 22, single, dau/o: J. M.
             D. and J. Mann (on bk) [John McDowell
             and Julia Mann (on CTOLMR)]. Both
             born and lived in Alleg. Co., VA. PL:
             Alleg. Co., VA "Jackson's River." Mar.
             by S. S. Rider. CTOLMR signed on 05-
             10-1865 by W. M. Scott, D. C. Mins.
             Ret. says mar. on 05-17-1865 at John

- 153 -

McD. Mann's in Alleg. Co., VA, was
signed S. S. Ryder.

05-18-1865   Thursday
18   E. Hennessey (on bk) [Edward Hennes-
             sey (on CTOLMR)], 25, single, Occup:
             farmer, s/o: P. and M. Hennessey (on
             bk) [Patrick and Mary Hennessey (on
             CTOLMR)]; and M. Steers (on bk) [Mar-
             garette Steers (on CTOLMR)], 20,
             single, dau/o: Erwin and E. Steers
             (on bk) [Evans and Elizabeth Steers
             (on CTOLMR)]. Both born and lived in
             Alleg. Co., VA, but Edward was born
             in County Limerick, Ireland and lived
             in Greenbrier Co., VA (now W.VA.) (on
             CTOLMR) and Margarette was born in
             the State of Pennsylvania and lived
             in Alleg. Co., VA (on CTOLMR). PL:
             Alleg. Co., VA "Jackson's River."
             Mar. by J. H. Walters. CTOLMR signed
             on 05-18-1865 by W. M. Scott, D. C.
             Mins. Ret. says mar. 05-18-1865 in
             Alleg. Co., VA.

05-22-1865   (on bk)   05-25-1865 Thursday (on
19   CTOLMR and Mins. Ret.)
             D. C. Stull (on bk) [Daniel R. Stull
             (on CTOL part of CTOLMR); Daniel C.
             Stull (on Mar. Auth.)], 22, single,
             Occup: farmer, s/o: J. and H. Stull
             (on bk) [James and Hannah Stull (on
             CTOLMR)]; and S. J. Persinger (on bk)
             [Salina J. Persinger (on CTOLMR)],
             21, single, dau/o: J. H. and M. Per-
             singer (on bk) [Joseph H. and Mary P.
             Persinger (on CTOLMR)]. Both lived
             and born in Alleg. Co., VA. PL: Al-
             leg. Co., VA "Potts Creek." Mar. by
             J. M. Rice. CTOLMR signed on 05-22-
             1865 at Mr. Jos. Persinger's on Potts
             Creek was signed James M. Rice.

(Mar. Register Book (1) - Continued)

05-31-1865   (on bk) 06-01-1865 (on CTOLMR and
   # 20   Mins. Ret.)
               J. D. Vance (on bk) [John D. Vance
               (on CTOLMR)], 35, single, Occup: far-
               mer, s/o: J. and C. Vance (on bk)
               [Jacob and Catharine Vance (on CTOL
               MR)]; and Lucinda Vance, 23, single,
               dau/o: W. and V. Vance (on bk) [Will-
               iam and Virginia Vance (on CTOLMR)].
               Both born and lived in Alleg. Co., VA
               (on bk), but both were born in Monroe
               Co., VA (now W.VA.) (on CTOLMR). PL:
               Alleg. Co., VA "William Vance's res.
               on Ogley's Creek." Mar. by T. S.
               Wade. CTOLMR signed on 05-31-1865 by
               W. M. Scott, D. C. Mins. Ret. says
               mar. 06-01-1865 at Wm. Vance's res.
               in Alleg. Co., VA.

06-04-1865   (on bk) 06-07-1865 Wednesday (on
   # 21   CTOLMR and Mins. Ret.)
               G. H. Gilbert (on bk) [George H. Gil-
               bert (on CTOLMR)], 24, single, Occup:
               farmer, s/o: D. and A. Gilbert (on bk)
               [David and Alcy Gilbert (on CTOLMR)];
               and G. L. Lockhart (on bk) [George-
               anna L. Lockhart (on CTOLMR)], 21,
               single, dau/o: D. B. and N. Lockhart
               (on bk) [David B. and Nancy Lockhart
               (on CTOLMR)]. Both lived and born in
               Alleg. Co., VA. PL: Alleg. Co., VA
               "Potts Creek". Mar. by S. S. Ryder.
               CTOLMR signed on 06-04-1865 by W. M.
               Scott, D. C. Mins. Ret. says mar. on
               06-07-1865 at Potts Creek in Alleg.
               Co., VA. Age oath signed by James C.
               Gilbert on 06-04-1865, Teste W. M.
               Scott, D. C.

06-10-1865   (on bk) 06-13-1865 Tuesday (on CTOLMR
   # 22   and Mins. Ret.)
               B. W. Green (on bk) [Benjamin Ward

Green (on CTOLMR)], 27, single, B:
Monroe Co., VA (now W.VA), Lived:
Monroe Co., VA (now W.VA.), Occup:
farmer, s/o: B. and M. Green (on bk)
[Benjamin and Margarette Green (on
CTOLMR)]; and M. A. Deeds (on bk)
[Martha A. Deeds (on CTOLMR)], 22,
single, Born and Lived: Alleg. Co.,
VA, dau/o: W. and R. Deeds (on bk)
[William and Rachel Deeds (on CTOLMR)]
PL: Alleg. Co., VA "Wm. Gilliland's
res." Mar. by S. S. Ryder. CTOLMR
signed 06-10-1865 by W. M. Scott, D.
C. Mins. Ret. says mar. on 06-13-
1865 at Wm. Gilliland's Alleg. Co.,
VA. Consent of father signed 06-09-
1865 by Wm. Deeds from Wilson Creek,
Wit. Joseph R. P. Deeds.

08-26-1865   (on bk) 09-07-1865 (on CTOLMR and
  # 23   Mins. Ret.)
              W. H. Walker (on bk) [Wade Hampton
              Walker (on CTOLMR)], 27, single, Oc-
              cup: farmer, s/o: H. and M. Walker
              (on bk) [Henry and Maria Walker (on
              CTOLMR)]; and V. C. Carson (on bk)
              [Virginia Catherine Carson (on CTOL
              MR)], 25, single, dau/o: J. and C.
              Carson (on bk) [James and Caroline
              Carson (on CTOLMR)]. Both were born
              and lived in Alleg. Co., VA (on bk),
              but Wade was born in Craig Co., VA
              (on CTOLMR). PL: Alleg. Co., VA
              "Caroline Carson's res." Mar. by J.
              B. Davis. CTOLMR signed on 08-26-
              1865 by Joseph T. Fudge, Clk. Mins.
              Ret. says mar. on 09-07-1865 at Caro-
              line Carson's was signed by John B.
              Davis.

08-29-1865   (on bk) 08-31-1865 (on CTOLMR and
  # 24   Mins. Ret.)
              J. H. Arritt (on bk) [John Marion

- 156 -

Arritt (on CTOLMR)], 25, single, Occup: farmer, s/o: J. and E. Arritt
(on bk) [John and Elizabeth Arritt
(on CTOLMR)]; and M. E. Persinger (on
bk) [Margaret Elizabeth Persinger (on
CTOLMR)], 24, single, dau/o: H. and
A. Persinger (on bk) [Henry and Ann
Persinger (on CTOLMR)]. Both were
born and lived in Alleg. Co., VA. PL:
Alleg. Co., VA "res. of the late
Henry Persinger." Mar. by J. B. Davis.
CTOLMR signed on 08-29-1865 by Jos.
T. Fudge, Clk. Mins. Ret. says mar.
08-31-1865 at Anna Persinger's signed
by John B. Davis.

09-04-1865   (on bk) 09-07-1865 (on CTOLMR and
25   Mins. Ret.)
D. Boyer (on bk) [David Boyer (on
CTOLMR)], 23, single, Occup: farmer,
s/o: J. and Nancy Boyer (on bk) [John
and Nancy Boyer (on CTOLMR)]; and S.
A. Haynes (on bk) [Sarah Ann Haynes
(on CTOLMR)], 22, single, dau/o: L.
and M. Haynes (on bk) [Lemuel and Mary
Haynes (on CTOLMR)]. Both were born
and lived in Alleg. Co., VA. PL: Alleg. Co., VA "Lemuel Haynes's res."
Mar. by J. B. Davis. CTOLMR signed
on 09-04-1865 by Joseph T. Fudge, Clk.
Mins. Ret. says mar. on 09-07-1865 at
Lemuel Haynes signed by John B. Davis.

09-04-1865   (on bk) 09-07-1865 (on CTOLMR and
26   Mins. Ret.)
W. T. Venessen (on bk) [Wm. Thomas
Vanessan (on CTOLMR)], 22, single, B:
Botetourt Co., VA, Lived: Botetourt
Co., VA (on bk) [Alleg. Co., VA (on
CTOLMR)], Occup: farmer, s/o: W. and
L. Venessen (on bk) [William and Luc-
inda Vanesson (on CTOLMR)]; and Mary

Brown, 22, single, B: Alleg. Co., VA,
Lived: Alleg. Co., VA, dau/o: W. B.
and E. Brown (on bk) [William B. and
Elizabeth Brown (on CTOLMR)]. PL:
Alleg. Co., VA "Wm. B. Brown's res."
Mar. by Abraham Buhrman. Oath of
James Nicely that consent was hand-
writing of Wm. and Elizabeth Brown.
CTOLMR signed 09-04-1865 by Joseph
T. Fudge, Clk. Mins. Ret. says mar.
09-07-1865 at Mr. Wm. Brown's in Al-
leg. Co., VA. Consent dated 09-04-
1865 signed by William B. Brown and
Elizabeth Brown, Wit. James Nicely,
has groom's name Wm. T. (?Vannson
? Vamesson ? Vamepon --can't read).
[Author's Note: The last name of
the groom was difficult to read in
all places it was listed and I deciphered it as best I could.)

09-04-1865   (on bk)   09-07-1865 (on CTOLMR and
  # 27   Mins. Ret.)
              J. Persinger (on bk) [John Persinger
              (on CTOLMR)], 22, single, Occup; far-
              mer, s/o: Henry and A. Persinger (on
              bk) [Henry and Ann Persinger (on CTOL
              MR)]; and H. E. Haynes (on bk) [Har-
              riet Elizabeth Haynes (on CTOLMR)],
              20, single, dau/o: L. and M. Haynes
              (on bk) [Lemuel and Mary Haynes (on
              CTOLMR)]. Both were born and lived
              in Alleg. Co., VA. PL: Alleg. Co.,
              VA "Lemuel Haynes's res." Mar. by
              J. B. Davis. CTOLMR signed 09-04-
              1865 by Joseph T. Fudge, Clk. Mins.
              Ret. says mar. on 09-07-1865 at Lem-
              uel Haynes signed by John B. Davis.

09-05-1865   (on bk)   09-06-1865 (on CTOLMR and
  # 28   Mins. Ret.)
              J. A. King (on bk) [James Alfred King

(on CTOLMR)], 23, single, Occup: farmer, s/o: G. and Nancy King (on bk)
[George and Nancy King (on CTOLMR)];
and E. J. Smith (on bk) [Eliza Jane
Smith (on CTOLMR)], 23, single, dau/
o: J. C. and S. Smith [John Crocket
and Susan Smith (on CTOLMR)]. Both
born and lived in Alleg. Co., VA. PL:
Alleg. Co., VA "J. C. Smith's res."
Mar. by J. B. Davis. CTOLMR signed
on 09-05-1865 by Joseph T. Fudge, Clk.
Mins. Ret. says mar. 09-06-1865 at
John C. Smith's was signed John B.
Davis. Age oath of Franklin P. Tins-
ley for Eliza on 09-05-1865, Teste
Jos. T. Fudge, Clk.

09-06-1865   James Nicely, 40, single (on bk) [wid-
  # 29   ower (on CTOLMR)], Occup: farmer, s/o:
              J. and N. Nicely (on bk) [John and
              Nancy Nicely (on CTOLMR)]; and E.
              Broughman (on bk) [Elizabeth Broughman
              (on CTOLMR)], 25, single, dau/o: J.
              and M. E. Broughman (on bk) [James and
              Mary E. Broughman (on CTOLMR)]. Both
              born and lived in Alleg. Co., VA (on
              bk), but James was born in Rockbridge
              Co., VA and lived in Botetourt Co., VA
              and Elizabeth was born in Botetourt
              Co., VA, and lived in Alleg. Co., VA
              (on CTOLMR). PL: Alleg. Co., VA. Mar.
              by A. Buhrman. CTOLMR signed 09-06-
              8165 by Jos. T. Fudge, Clk. Mins. Ret.
              says mar. 09-06-1865 at C. H. Karnes's
              in Alleg. Co., VA, was signed Abraham
              Buhrman. Age oath by Andrew J. Brough-
              man 09-06-1865, Teste Joseph Fudge,
              Clk.

09-11-1865   (on bk. and Mins. Ret.) 09-12-1865
  # 30   (on CTOLMR)
              A. Given (on bk) [Adam Given (on CTOL-

MR)], 26, single, B: Monroe Co., VA
(now W.VA.), Lived: Monroe Co., VA
(now W.VA.) (on bk) [Alleg. Co., VA
(on CTOLMR)], Occup: farmer, s/o: D.
G. and C. Given (on bk) [David G. and
Catherine Given (on CTOLMR)]; and E.
A. Kyle (on bk) [Elizabeth Ann Kyle
(on CTOLMR)], 24, single, B: Alleg.
Co., VA, Lived: Alleg. Co., VA, dau/o:
G. and Julia Kyle (on bk) [Galbraith
and Julia Kyle (on CTOLMR)]. Mar.
by James M. Rice. PL: Alleg. Co.,
VA "John Mann's res." CTOLMR signed
09-11-1865 by Jos. T. Fudge, Clk.
Mins. Ret. says mar. 09-11-1865 at
res. of John Mann. Age oath by Augus-
tus A. Mann on 09-11-1865, Teste Jos.
T. Fudge, Clk.

09-28-1865 S. Wolf (on bk) [(? Seevi ?Seeri ?
31   Suvi) Woolf (on CTOLMR) --name hard
           to make out], 21, single, Born and
           Lived: Alleg. Co., VA, Occup: farmer,
           s/o: H. and L. Wolf (on bk) [Hugh and
           Lidia Woolf (on CTOLMR)]; and A. M.
           Paxton (on bk) [Ann Maria Paxton (on
           CTOLMR)], 21, single, Born and Lived:
           Botetourt Co., VA (on bk) [Alleg. Co.
           VA (on CTOLMR)], dau/o: W. B. and S.
           A. Paxton (on bk) [William B. and
           Sarah Ann Paxton (on CTOLMR)]. PL:
           Alleg. Co., VA "Mr. Paxton's res."
           (on CTOL). Mar. by J. B. Davis.
           CTOL signed on 09-28-1865 by William
           B. (his X mark) Paxton, Wit. Hugh
           Wolf. CTOLMR signed on 09-28-1865 by
           Joseph T. Fudge, Clk. Mins. Ret. says
           mar. on 09-28-1865 at Wm. Paxton's
           was signed John B. Davis.

05-09-1862 J. R. Cave, 24, single, B: Page Co.,
32   VA, s/o: T. and E. Cave, Occup: far-

(Mar. Register Book (1) - Continued)

mer; and S. E. Brown, 23, single, B: Rockbridge Co., VA, dau/o: Lemuel and S. Brown. Mar. by G. G. Brooke. PL: Alleg. Co., VA. Both lived in Alleg. Co., VA. [See # 7 Mar. Register page 6, 05-10-1862, listed twice. More information on # 7.]

12-01-1862 James Morrison, 46, widower, B: Cul-
33 pepper Co., VA, s/o: _____; and M. Lawson, 37, single, B: Rockbridge Co, VA, dau/o: ____. His occup. -farmer. Mar. by G. G. Brooke. Both lived in Alleg. Co., VA. PL: Alleg. Co., VA. [See # 12 Mar. Register page 6, 12-04-1862, listed twice. More information on # 12.]

02-16-1863 T. W. Nixon (on bk) [Theopholus Walk-
34 er Nixon (on CTOLMR)], 39, widower, B: Ireland, Occup: farmer (on bk) [Shoemaker (on CTOLMR)], s/o: F. R. and C. Nixon (on bk) [Frederick R. and Charlotte Nixon (on CTOLMR)]; and V. Boley (on bk) [Virginia Boley (on CTOLMR)], 19, single, B: Alleg. Co., VA (on bk) [Monroe Co., VA (now W.VA) (on CTOLMR)], dau/o: Pitman and M. Boly (on bk) [Pittman and Mary Boley (on CTOLMR)]. Both lived in Alleg. Co., VA. PL: Alleg. Co., VA. Mar. by G. G. Brooke. CTOLMR signed on 02-16-1863 by W. M. Scott, Clk. Mins. Ret. mar. date has line drawn where day goes and where month goes in 1863 at house of bride's father and was signed Geo. G. Brooke. The line drawn may indicate that date was the same as on the CTOLMR.

04-22-1863 (on bk) 04-23-1863 Thursday (on
35 CTOLMR and Mins. Ret.) J. W. Matheny (on bk) [John W. Mathe-

- 161 -

ney (on CTOLMR)], 23, single, Occup:
farmer, s/o: A. and M. Matheny (on
bk) [Asberry and Malinda Matheney (on
CTOLMR)]; and J. G. Morrison (on bk)
[Juliet Granville Morrison (on CTOL
MR)], 17, single, dau/o: J. and J.
Morrison (on bk) [James and Jane Morrison (on CTOLMR)]. Both born and
lived in Alleg. Co., VA (on bk), but
John was born in Botetourt Co., VA
(on CTOLMR). PL: Alleg. Co., VA,
"White Rock Gap." Mar. by G. G. Brooke. CTOLMR signed on 04-22-1863 by
W. M. Scott, Clk. Pro Tem. Mins. Ret.
says mar. "23 of _____ 1863 at home of
bride" was signed Geo. G. Brooke.

Page 8

09-10-1863   (on bk) 09-15-1863 Tuesday (on CTOL
36   and CTOLMR and Mins. Ret.)
              Lewis Sprouse, 22, single, B: Albemar-
le Co., VA, Charlottesville (on CTOL
MR), Occup: farmer, s/o: Jeff Sprouse
(on bk) [Jefferson Sprouse and _____
(on CTOLMR)]; and P. A. Moyers (on bk)
[Polly Anne Myers (on CTOL)], 17,
single, B: Alleg. Co., VA, dau/o: _____
(on bk) [Augustus Myers and Patsey
Oliver (on CTOL)]. Both lived in Alleg. Co., VA near Callaghan's. PL:
Alleg. Co., VA "at Callaghan's." Mar.
by G. G. Brooke. CTOL signed on 09-
11-1863 by Lewis Sprouse. CTOLMR
signed on 09-10-1863 by W. M. Scott,
Clk. Pro Tem. Mins. Ret. says mar.
"15th day of _____ 1863 at home of
bride" was signed Geo. G. Brooke.
Consent: "I authorize the Clerk of
the County Court of Alleghany to issue
license to celebrate the rites of matrimony between Lewis Sprouse and my
daughter Polly Ann Myers---

Septr. 10, 1863
Patsey (her X mark) Kelly"

05-05-1865   (on bk) 05-09-1865 Tuesday   (on
  # 37   CTOLMR and Mins. Ret.)
              S. L. Damron (on bk) [Stanard Little-
              ton Damron (on CTOLMR)], 28, single,
              Born and Lived: Alleg. co., VA, Occup:
              farmer, s/o: C. and J. A. C. Damron
              (on bk) [Christopher and Julia Ann C.
              Damron (on CTOLMR)]; and M. J. Woods
              (on bk) [Mary Jane Woods (on CTOLMR)],
              19, single, B: Lancaster Co., Pennsyl-
              vania, dau/o: M. and ___ Woods (on bk)
              [Moses and ___ Woods (on CTOLMR)],
              Lived: Alleg. Co., VA. PL: Alleg. Co.
              VA "Dunlap's Creek." Mar. by G. G.
              Brooke. CTOLMR signed on 05-05-1865
              by W. M. Scott, D. C. Mins. Ret. says
              mar. on 05-09-1865 at Mr. Woods was
              signed Geo. G. Brooke.

05-29-1865   (on bk) 06-01-1865 (on CTOLMR and
  # 38   Mins. Ret.)
              J. Wolf (on bk) [Jonathan Wolf (on
              CTOLMR)], 30, single, B: Preston Co.,
              VA (now W.VA.), Occup: farmer (on bk)
              [Teamster (only--on CTOLMR)], s/o:
              M. and E. Wolf (on bk) [Martin and
              Elizabeth Wolf (on CTOLMR)]; and H.
              Sawyers (on bk) [Henryetta Sawyers
              (on CTOLMR)], 26, single, B: Alleg.
              Co., VA, dau/o: A. and S. Sawyers (on
              bk) [Arch and Susan Sawyers (on CTOL
              MR)].   Both lived in Alleg. Co., VA.
              PL: Alleg. Co., VA "Arch. Sawyers
              res." Mar. by G. G. Brooke. CTOLMR
              signed on 05-29-1865 by Jos. T. Fudge,
              Clk. Mins. Ret. says mar. on 06-01-
              1865 by Geo. G. Brooke.

05-30-1865   Tuesday
  # 39   C. S. Anderson (on bk) [Charles Snyder

(Mar. Register Book (1) - Continued)

Anderson (on CTOLMR), 27, single, B:
Greenbrier Co., VA (now W.VA.) (on bk)
[Salem, Roanoke Co., VA (on CTOLMR)],
Lived: Salem, VA, Occup: farmer, s/o:
H. and M. Anderson (on bk) [Harry and
Mary Anderson (on CTOLMR)]; and P. J.
Feamster (on bk) [Patsey Jane Feamster
(on CTOLMR)], 23, single, B: Salem, VA
(on bk) [Greenbrier Co., VA (now W.VA)
(on CTOLMR)], Lived: Lewisburg, VA
(now W.VA.), dau/o: W. and P. J. Feam-
ster (on bk) [William and Patsey Jane
Feamster (on CTOLMR)]. Mar. by G. G.
Brooke. PL: Alleg. Co., VA, Coving-
ton. CTOLMR signed on 05-30-1865 by
W. M. Scott, D. C. Mins. Ret. says
mar. on 05-30-1865 at M. E. Parsonage
Covington, VA, by Geo. G. Brooke. Age
oath of Amanda Handley mentions that
William Feamster is deceased and was
signed 05-30-1865, Teste W. M. Scott,
D. C.

05-31-1865 (on bk) 06-01-1865 (on CTOLMR and
40   Mins. Ret.)
F. Bradshaw (on bk) [Franklin Bradshaw
(on CTOLMR)], 36, single, B: Bath Co.,
VA, Lived: Highland Co., VA, Occup:
farmer, s/o: J. and I. Bradshaw (on bk
[James and Isabella Bradshaw (on CTOL
MR)]; and E. V. Keyser (on bk) [Estal-
ine V. Keyser (on CTOLMR)], 28, single,
Born and Lived: Alleg. Co., VA, dau/o:
F. and N. Keyser (on bk) [Fleming and
Nancy Keyser (on CTOLMR)]. Mar. by G.
G. Brooke. PL: Alleg. Co., VA "Jack-
son's River at Mrs. Keyser's res."
CTOLMR signed on 05-31-1865 by W. M.
Scott, D. C. Mins. Ret. says mar. on
06-01-1865 at bride's res. by Geo. G.
Brooke.

(Mar. Register Book (1) - Continued)

08-23-1865 (on bk)   08-24-1865 (on CTOLMR and
41   Mins. Ret.)
            L. Lenz (on bk) [Leopold Lenz (on
            CTOLMR)], 30, single, B: Germany,
            Lived: Page Co., VA, Occup: farmer
            (on bk) [Minister of Gospel (only--
            on CTOLMR)], s/o: A. and R. Lenz (on
            bk) [Abraham and Rose Lenz (on CTOL
            MR)]; and S. C. Keyser (on bk) [Sarah
            Catherine Keyser (on CTOLMR)], 26,
            single, Born and Lived: Alleg. Co.,
            VA, dau/o: F. and N. Keyser (on bk)
            [Fleming and Nancy Keyser (on CTOLMR)].
            PL: Alleg. Co., VA "Morris Hill."
            Mar. by G. G. Brooke. CTOLMR signed
            08-23-1865 by Joseph T. Fudge, Clk.
            Mins. Ret. says mar. 08-24-1865 at
            bride's res. in Alleg. Co., VA, by
            Geo. G. Brooke, Minister.

09-12-1865 A. B. Pitzer (on bk) [Albert Bacon
42   Pitzer (on CTOLMR)], 43, widower, B:
            Alleg. Co., VA, Lived: Botetourt Co.,
            VA, Occup: farmer, s/o: B. and J.
            Pitzer (on bk) [Bernard and Jane Pit-
            zer (on CTOLMR)]; and J. M. Morton
            (on bk) [Jane Maria Morton (on CTOL
            MR)], 30, single, Born and Lived: Al-
            leg. Co., VA, dau/o: W. F. and M. L.
            Morton (on bk) [Wm. F. and Maria L.
            Morton (on CTOLMR)]. Mar. by G. G.
            Brooke. PL: Alleg. Co., VA "Coving-
            ton." CTOLMR signed 09-12-1865 by
            Jos. T. Fudge, Clk. Mins. Ret. says
            mar. on 09-12-1865 at home of bride
            by Geo. G. Brooke, Mins.

09-13-1865 (on bk)   09-20-1865 Wednesday (on
43   CTOLMR 09-19-1865 (on Mins. Ret.)
            G. Callaghan (on bk) [George Callag-
            han (on CTOLMR)], Age: ___, Single,
            Occup: farmer, s/o: J. and R. Callag-

- 165 -

han (on bk) [John and Rachel Callaghan (on CTOLMR)]; and R. J. Craft (on bk) [Rebecca Jane Craft (on CTOLMR)], 24, single, dau/o: J. and E. Craft (on bk) [John and Elizabeth Craft (on CTOLMR)]. Both born and lived in Alleg. Co., VA. PL: Alleg. Co., VA "John Craft's res." Mar. by G. G. Brooke. CTOLMR signed 09-13-1865 by Jos. T. Fudge, Clk. Mins. Ret. says mar. on 09-19-1865 at bride's home by Geo. G. Brooke.

09-22-1865   Saturday (on bk) 09-23-1865 (on Mins.
  # 44   Ret.)
J. C. Holms (on bk) [John C. Holms (on CTOLMR)], 19, single, B: Botetourt Co., VA, Lived: Alleg. Co., VA, Occup: farmer, s/o: J. H. and M. A. Holms (on bk) [James H. and Martha W. Holms (on CTOLMR)]; and S. E. McCallister (on bk) [Susan E. McCallister (on CTOLMR)], 23, single, Born and Lived: Alleg. Co., VA, dau/o: R. and N. McCallister (on bk) [Rufus and Nancy McCallister (on CTOLMR)]. PL: Alleg. Co., VA "Mrs. Holm's res." Mar. by G. G. Brooke. CTOLMR signed on 09-22-1865 by Jos. T. Fudge, Clk. Mins. Ret. says mar. on 09-23-1865 at Mrs. Holmes by Geo. G. Brooke.

09-25-165   (on bk)   09-27-1865 (on CTOLMR and
  # 45   Mins. Ret.)
Elias Hepler, 25, single, Occup: farmer, s/o: J. and B. Hepler (on bk) [John and Betsy Hepler (on CTOLMR)]; and M. A. Johnston (on bk) [Malinda Ann Johnston (on CTOLMR)], 19, single, dau/o: B. and A. Johnston (on bk) [Barnard and Ann Johnston (on CTOLMR)] Both born and lived in Alleg. Co., VA.

PL: Alleg. Co., VA "Bernard Johnston's res." Mar. by S. S. Ryder. CTOLMR signed on 09-25-1865 by Joseph T. Fudge, Clk. Mins. Ret. says mar. on 09-27-1865 at "Bend of Jackson" by S. S. Ryder. Consent signed 09-25-1865 by Barnard Johnson, Wit. Lee Persinger, John Johnson [Note: names as on consent.] Oath of Johnson acknowledgement by Lee Persinger on back of consent.

10-02-1865
46

(on bk)   10-05-1865 Thursday (on CTOLMR and Mins. Ret.)
W. C. Peters (on bk) [William Cornelius Peters (on CTOLMR)], 21, single, Occup: farmer, Born and Lived: Alleg. Co., VA, s/o: T. J. and M. Peters (on bk) [Thos. J. and Mary Peters (on CTOLMR)]; and Betsy Hepler (on bk) [Betsey Hepler (on CTOLMR)], 24, widow, B: Bath Co., VA, dau/o: J. L. and R. Lone (on bk) [John Lewis and Rebecca Lone (on CTOLMR)], Lived: Alleg. Co., VA. Mar. by A. Buhrman. PL: Alleg. Co., VA "Wilson's Creek." CTOLMR signed on 10-02-1865 by W. M. Scott, D. C. Mins. Ret. says mar. on 10-05-1865 at Wilson's Creek in Alleg. Co., VA.

10-09-1865
47

(on bk)   10-24-1865 (on CTOLMR and Mins. Ret.)
T. J. Cryzer (on bk) [Thomas J. Crizer (on CTOLMR)], 35, single, B: Bath Co., VA, Lived: Bath Co., VA, Occup: Carpenter, s/o: H. and M. Cryzer (on bk) [Henry and Mary Crizer (on CTOLMR)]; and M. E. Masters (on bk) [Mary E. Masters (on CTOLMR)], 36, widow, B: Bath Co., VA, Lived: Bath Co., VA (on bk) [Alleg. Co., VA (on CTOLMR)], dau/

(Mar. Register Book (1) - Continued)

o: W. D. and N. Kincaid (on bk) [Wm.
D. and Nancy Kincaid (on CTOLMR)].
PL: Alleg. Co., VA "Morris Hill."
Mar. by S. S. Ryder. CTOLMR signed
on 10-09-1865 by Joseph T. Fudge, Clk.
Mins. Ret. says mar. on 10-24-1865 at
Morris Hill in Alleg. Co., VA.

10-30-1865 (on bk) 10-31-1865 Tuesday (on CTOLMR
48 and Mins. Ret.)
Lewis Payne, 24, single, B: Bath Co.,
VA, Occup: farmer, s/o: L. and L. S.
Payne (on bk) [Lewis and Louisa S.
Payne (on CTOLMR)]; and E. StC. Bos-
well (on bk) [Eugenia St.Clair Boswell
(on CTOLMR)], 22, single, B: Alleg.
Co., VA, dau/o: J. L. StC. Boswell (on
bk) [John Lee and Louisa St.Clair Bos-
well (on CTOLMR)]. Both lived in Al-
leg. Co., VA. PL: Alleg. Co., VA
"Covington." Mar. by S. S. Ryder.
CTOLMR signed on 10-30-1865 by W. M.
Scott, D. C. Mins. Ret. says mar. on
10-31-1865 at Covington, VA.

11-21-1865 (on bk) 11-29-1865 (on CTOLMR and
49 Mins. Ret.)
E. Nicely (on bk) [Emmanuel Nicely (on
CTOLMR)], 24, single, Born and Lived:
Alleg. Co., VA, Occup: farmer, s/o: G.
and S. Nicely (on bk) [George and Sallie Nicely (on CTOLMR)]; and E. Acres
(on bk) [Esteline Acres (on CTOLMR)],
20, single, Born and Lived: Alleg. Co,
VA, dau/o: Miner and S. Acres (on bk)
[Minor and Sallie Acres (on CTOLMR)].
PL: Alleg. Co., VA "John Armentrout's
res." Mar. by A. Buhrman. CTOLMR
signed on 11-21-1865 by Jos. T. Fudge,
Clk. Mins. Ret. says mar. on 11-29-
1865 at res. of John Armentrout.

- 168 -

11-21-1865 # 50	James Skeen, 41, widower, B: Alleg. Co., VA (on bk) [Rockbridge Co., VA (on CTOLMR)], Lived: Monroe Co., VA (now W. VA.), Occup: farmer, s/o: R. and P. Skeen (on bk) [Robert and Polly Skeen (on CTOLMR)]; and E.. B. Sively (on bk) [Elizabeth B. Sively (on CTOLMR)], 31, single, Born and Lived: Alleg. Co., VA, dau/o: J. and E. Sively (on ck) [Joseph and Elizabeth Sively (on CTOLMR)]. PL: Alleg. Co., VA "near Covington." Mar. by James M. Rice. CTOLMR signed on 11-21-1865 by Joseph T. Fudge, Clk. Mins. Ret. says mar. on 11-21-1865 at house of Joseph Sively.
11-25-1865 # 51	(on bk) 11-27-1865 Sunday (on CTOLMR and Mins. Ret.) W. F. Stone (on bk) [William Francis Stone (on CTOLMR)], 21, single, B: Wilks Co., N. C., Occup: farmer, Lived: Alleg. Co., VA, s/o: J. and B. Stone (on bk) [John and Betsey Stone (on CTOLMR)]; and L. J. Bennett (on bk) [Lucinda Jane Bennett (on CTOLMR)], 23, widow, Born and Lived: Alleg. Co., VA, dau/o: Charllette Persinger (on bk) [Charlott Persinger (only name--on CTOLMR)]. Mar. by John B. Davis. PL: Alleg. Co., VA "John Stone's res. Peter's Mountain." CTOLMR signed on 11-25-1865 by W. M. Scott, D. C. Mins. Ret. says mar. on 11-27-1865 at John Stone's.
12-09-1865 # 52	(on bk) 12-19-1865 Tuesday (on CTOLMR and Mins. Ret.) B. Karnes (on bk) [Benami Karnes (on CTOLMR)], 28, single, Occup: farmer, s/o: C. and M. Karnes (on bk) [Campbell and Martha Karnes (on CTOLMR)];

(Mar. Register Book (1) - Continued)

and <u>S. J. Griffith</u> (on bk) [<u>Sallie
Jane Griffith</u> (on CTOLMR)], 25, single, dau/o: C. and E. J. Griffith (on
bk) [Caleb and Elizabeth Jane Griffith (on CTOLMR)]. Both born and lived
in Alleg. Co., VA. PL: Alleg. Co.,
VA "Caleb Griffith's res. Jackson River." Mar. by S. S. Ryder. CTOLMR
signed on 12-09-1865 by W. M. Scott,
D. C. Mins. Ret. says mar. on 12-19-
1865 at Caleb Griffith's res. Alleg.
Co.

12-11-1865   Monday
   # 53   <u>J. R. Ratliff</u> (on bk) [<u>James Wesley
             Ratliff</u> (on CTOLMR)], 43, single, B:
             Hardy Co., VA (now W.VA.), Occup: far-
             mer, s/o: J. and P. A. Ratliff (on bk)
             [Johnathan and Phebe Ann Ratliff (on
             CTOLMR)]; and <u>R. J. Anderson</u> (on bk)
             [<u>Rebecca Jane Anderson</u> (on CTOLMR)],
             23, single, B: Bath Co., VA, dau/o:
             W. H. and M. A. Anderson (on bk) [Wil-
             liam Henry and Mary Arabelle Anderson
             (on CTOLMR)]. Both lived in Alleg.
             Co., VA. PL: Alleg. Co., VA "Coving-
             ton." Mar. by G. G. Brooke. CTOLMR
             signed on 12-11-1865 by W. M. Scott,
             D. C. Mins. Ret. says mar. on 12-11-
             1865 at Parsonage in Covington, VA.

12-26-1865   (on bk) 12-27-1865 Tuesday (on CTOLMR
   # 54   and Mins. Ret.)
             <u>C. L. Haynes</u> (on bk) [<u>Charles Lewis
             Haynes</u> (on CTOLMR)], 31, single, B:
             Alleg. Co., VA, Occup: farmer, s/o:
             W. H. and M. E. Haynes (on bk) [Will-
             iam Henry and Mary E. Haynes (on CTOL
             MR)]; and <u>M. A. Zeigler</u> (on bk) [<u>Mag-
             gie Ann Zeigler</u> (on CTOLMR)], 20,
             single, B: Orange Co., VA, dau/o: A.
             and M. Zeigler (on bk) [Abraham and

Matilda Zeigler (on CTOLMR)]. Both lived in Alleg. Co., VA. PL: Alleg. Co., VA "Zeigler res. near Clifton Forge." Mar. by S. S. Ryder. CTOLMR signed on 12-26-1865 by W. M. Scott, D. C. Mins. Ret. says mar. on 12-27-1865 at Abraham Zeigler's res. in Alleg. Co., VA.

01-02-1866
55

Tuesday
W. J. Persinger (on bk) [William Jackson Persinger (on CTOLMR)], 40, single, Occup: farmer, s/o: ____ and E. Persinger (on bk) [___ and Elizabeth Persinger (on CTOLMR)]; and Nancy King, 44, widow, dau/o: J. and May Bennett (on bk) [Jacob and Mary Bennett (on CTOLMR)]. Both born and lived in Alleg. Co., VA. PL: Alleg. Co., VA "Rich Patch." Mar. by John B. Davis. CTOLMR signed on 01-02-1866 by W. M. Scott, D. C. Mins. Ret. says mar. on 01-02-1866 at Nancy King's in Rich Patch in Alleg. Co.,VA.

01-03-1866
56

(on bk) 01-04-1866 (on CTOLMR and Mins. Ret.)
J. S. Sawyers (on bk) [John S. Sawyers (on CTOLMR)], 30, single, Occup; farmer, s/o: A. and S. H. Sawyers (on bk) [Alexander and Sarah H. Sawyers (on CTOLMR)]; and E. A. Stone (on bk) [Elizabeth A. Stone (on Mar. Auth.)], 28, single, dau/o: W. and J. Stone (on bk) [William and Jane Stone (on CTOLMR)]. Both born and lived in Alleg. Co., VA. PL: Alleg. Co., VA "res. bride's father." Mar. by Geo. G. Brooke. CTOLMR signed on 01-03-1866 by Joseph T. Fudge, Clk. Mins. Ret. says mar. on 01-04-1866 at Mr. Rusk's in Alleg. Co., VA. Age oath by William M.

Brown, Teste Jos. T. Fudge, Clk., for
<u>Elizabeth S. Stone</u> being over the age
of 20.

01-03-1866   Wednesday
 # 57   J. B. Pitzer (on bk) [<u>John Bernard
              Pitzer</u> (on CTOLMR)], 27, single, B:
              Covington, Alleg. Co., VA, Occup: DSAC
              [Deputy Sheriff of Alleg. Co. (on CTOL
              MR)], s/o: J. L. and H. A. Pitzer (on
              bk) [John Lewis and Harriett Ann Pit-
              zer (on CTOLMR)]; and <u>S. A. Dungan</u>
              (on ck) [<u>Sarah Ann Dungan</u> (on CTOL
              MR)], 26, single, B: Morgan Co., VA
              (now W.VA.), dau/o: H. M. and E. B.
              Dungan (on bk) [Henry M. and Elizabeth
              B. Dungan (on CTOLMR)]. Both lived
              in Covington, Alleg. Co., VA. PL: Al-
              leg. Co., VA "Covington." Mar. by J.
              W. Cornelius. CTOLMR signed on 01-03-
              1866 by W. M. Scott, D. C. Mins. Ret.
              says mar. on 01-03-1866 at res. of H.
              M.Dungan, Covington, VA.

01-08-1866   (on bk) 01-09-1866 (on COTLMR and
 # 58   Mins. Ret.)
              G. W. Tingler (on bk) [<u>George Washing-
              ton Tingler</u> (on CTOLMR)], 21, single,
              Occup: farmer, s/o: J. and L. Tingler
              (on bk) [Jacob and Lucinda Tingler
              (on CTOLMR)]; and <u>E. C. King</u> (on bk)
              [<u>Ellie Catherine King</u> (on CTOLMR)], 18
              single, dau/o: G. and Nancy King (on
              bk) [George and Nancy King (on CTOL
              MR)]. Both born and lived in Alleg.
              Co., VA. PL: Alleg. Co., VA "Jno. B.
              Davis res. Potts Creek." Mar. by John
              B. Davis. CTOLMR signed on 01-08-1866
              by Joseph T. Fudge, Clk. Mins. Ret.
              says mar. on 01-09-1866 at John B.
              Davis res. Potts Creek.
              "Alleghany Co. VA   January 7, 1866

This is to certify that I have
given my full consent unto the marriage of George W. Tingler and my
Daughter, <u>Elezenia C. King</u>. The clerk
will please easue licence fore them
                    Nancy Persinger
Wit. Geoge P. Perge"
Oath of witness, Geo. P. Persinger,
to Joseph T. Fudge, Clk., on 01-08-
1866 said that Nancy Persinger acknowledged consent note "to be her act and
deed."

01-10-1866   (on bk) 01-11-1866 Thursday (on
  # 59   CTOLMR and Mins. Ret.)
              <u>G. W. Cauly</u> (on bk) [<u>George Washington
Cauley</u> (on CTOLMR)], 47, single, Born
and Lived: Bath Co., VA, Occup: farmer,
s/o: J. and C. Cauly (on bk) [John and
Catharine Cauley (on CTOLMR)]; and <u>S.
A. Silvers</u> (on bk) [<u>Sarah Ann Silvers</u>
(on CTOLMR)], 21, single, B: Bath Co.,
VA, Lived: Alleg. co., VA, dau/o: ____
(on bk and CTOLMR). Mar. by S. S. Ryder. PL: Alleg. Co., VA "Falling Springs Valley." CTOLMR signed on 01-10-
1866 by W. M. Scott, D. C. Mins. Ret.
says mar. on 01-11-1866 at Falling
Springs Valley in Alleg. Co., VA.

01-16-1866   (on bk) 01-18-1866 (on CTOLMR and
  #60   Mins. Ret.)
              <u>B. Johnston</u> (on bk) [<u>Barnard Johnston</u>
(on CTOLMR)], 22, single, Occup: far-
mer, s/o: B. and A. Johnston (on bk)
[Barnard and Ann Johnston (on CTOLMR)];
and <u>S. F. Bowyer</u> (on bk) [<u>Salena F.
Bowyer</u> (on CTOLMR)], 19, single, dau/o:
J. and Nancy Bowyer (on bk) [John and
Nancy Bowyer (on CTOLMR)]. Both born
and lived in Alleg. Co., VA. PL: Alleg. Co., VA "John Bowyer's res." Mar.

(Mar. Register Book (1) - Continued)

by John B. Davis. CTOLMR signed on
01-16-1866 by Jos. T. Fudge, Clk.
Mins. Ret. says mar. on 01-18-1866 at
res. of John Bowyer on Potts Creek in
Alleg. Co., VA. Consent of John Bowyer on 01-16-1866, Wit. Lee Persinger
and David Bowyer. Oath of Bowyer acknowledgement on 01-16-1866 by David
Bowyer.

01-18-1866   Thursday
 # 61   S. Snead (on bk) [Samuel Snead (on
              CTOLMR)], 35, single, B: Bath Co., VA,
              Lived: Bath Co., VA, Occup: farmer,
              s/o: R. and J. Snead (on bk) [Richard
              and Jane Snead (on CTOLMR)]; and E. S.
              Evans (on bk) [Elizabeth Sarah Evans
              (on CTOLMR)], 24, single, Born and
              Lived: Alleg. Co., VA, dau/o: W. and
              K. Evans (on bk) [William and Kesiah
              Evans (on CTOLMR)]. PL: Alleg. Co.,
              VA "S. S. Ryder res." Mar. by S. S.
              Ryder. CTOLMR signed on 01-18-1866 by
              W. M. Scott, D. C. Mins. Ret. says
              mar. 01-18-1866 at res. of S. S. Ryder
              in Alleg. Co., VA.

01-23-1866   (on bk)   01-25-1866 (on CTOLMR and
 # 62   Mins. Ret.)
              C. L. Bess (on bk) [Charles L. Bess
              (on CTOLMR)], 27, single, Born and
              Lived: Alleg. Co., VA, Occup: farmer,
              s/o: H. and B. Bess (on bk) [Hamilton
              and Bettie Bess (on CTOLMR)]; and M.
              Whistman (on bk) [Mary Whistman (on
              CTOLMR)], 18, single, B: Rockingham
              Co., VA, Lived: Alleg. Co., VA, dau/o:
              H. H. and H. Whistman (on bk) [Henry
              H. and Hannah Whistman (on CTOLMR)].
              PL: Alleg. Co., VA "res. bride's fa-
              ther." Mar. by J. B. Davis. CTOLMR
              signed on 01-23-1866 by Joseph T. Fud-

ge, Clk. Mins. Ret. says mar. on 01-
25-1866 at res. of George W. Roof
[Note: suspect he meant ?Wolf] on
Potts Creek was signed John B. Davis.

02-13-1866   (on bk)   02-15-1866 (on CTOLMR and
63   Mins. Ret.)
Sampson Humphries, 29, widower, Occup:
farmer, s/o: W. and R. Humphries (on
bk) [William and Ruth Humphries (on
CTOLMR)]; and L. C. Blaker (on bk)
[Louisa C. Blaker (on CTOLMR)], 27 (on
bk) [28 (on CTOLMR)], widow, dau/o:
John and E. Arritt (on bk) [John and
Elizabeth Arritt (on CTOLMR)]. Both
born and lived in Alleg. Co., VA. PL:
Alleg. Co., VA "John Arritt's res."
Mar. by J. B. Davis. CTOLMR signed on
02-13-1866 by Joseph T. Fudge, Clk.
Mins. Ret. says mar. on 02-15-1866 at
John M. Aritt's in Alleg. Co. Potts
Creek was signed John B. Davis. Age
oath on 02-13-1866 for Louisa that
she was over 21 by Sampson Humphries,
Teste Jos. T. Fudge, Clk.

01-23-1866   (on bk)   01-24-1866 (on CTOLMR and
64   Mins. Ret.)
A. S. Snead (on bk) [Anthony M. Snead
(on CTOLMR)], 25, single, B: Bath Co.,
VA, Lived: Alleg. Co., VA (on bk)
[Bath Co., VA (on CTOLMR)], Occup: farmer, s/o: R. and J. Snead (on bk)
[Richard and Jane Snead (on CTOLMR)];
and J. Richardson (on bk) [Julia Richardson (on CTOLMR)], 23, single, Born
and Lived: Alleg. Co., VA, dau/o: T.
and M. Richardson (on bk) [Thomas and
Margarett Richardson (on CTOLMR)].
PL: Alleg. Co., VA "Charles Richardson
res." Mar. by G. G. Brooke. CTOLMR
signed on 01-23-1866 by Joseph T. Fud-

ge, Clk. Mins. Ret. says mar. on 01-
24-1866 at home of bride in Alleg.
Co., VA, was signed George G. Brooke.

09-24-1866   (on bk)   09-25-1866 (on CTOLMR and
  # 65   Mins. Ret.)
              Jno. Wm. Vauter (on bk) [John William
              Vawter (on CTOLMR)], 32, single, Born
              and Lived: Monroe Co., VA (now W.VA.),
              Occup: farmer, s/o: J. H. and C. S.
              Vauter (on bk) [John H. and Clara S.
              Vawter (on CTOLMR)]; and Eliz. D.
              Kean (on bk) [Elizabeth Dew Kean (on
              CTOLMR)], 28, single, Born and Lived:
              Alleg. Co., VA, dau/o: Sam'l. and Re-
              becca Kean (on bk) [Samuel and Rebec-
              ca Kean (on CTOLMR)]. PL: Alleg. Co.,
              VA "Dunlap Creek." Mar. by H. B.
              Rose. CTOLMR signed on 09-24-1866 by
              W. M. Scott, D. C. Mins. Ret. says
              mar. on 09-25-1866 at Mrs. Kean's in
              Alleg. Co., VA.

12-22-1866   (on bk)   12-26-1866 Wednesday (on
  # 66   CTOLMR and Mins. Ret.)
              Chs. Richardson (on bk) [Charles Rich-
              ardson (on CTOLMR)], 39, single, Born
              and Lived: Alleg. Co., VA, Occup: far-
              mer, s/o: Thos. and Margaret Richard-
              son (on bk) [Thomas and Margarett
              Richardson (on CTOLMR)]; and Maria
              Helmintoller, 26, single, dau/o: P.
              and M. Helmintoller (on bk) [Peter and
              Mary Helmintoller (on CTOLMR)], born
              and lived: Alleg. Co., VA. PL: Alleg.
              Co., VA "Peter's Mountain." Mar. by
              A. Q. Flaherty. CTOLMR signed on 12-
              22-1866 by W. M. Scott, D. C. Mins.
              Ret. says mar. on 12-26-1866 at Peter
              Helmintoller res.

12-31-1866 (on bk)   01-01-1867 Tuesday (on
 # 67   CTOLMR and Mins. Ret.)
           A. J. Doherty (on bk) [Andrew J. Do-
           herty (on CTOLMR)], 34, widower, Born
           and Lived: Monroe Co., VA (now W.VA.),
           Occup: farmer, s/o: P. and R. Doherty
           (on bk) [Phillip and Rachel Doherty
           (on CTOLMR)]; and E. F. Bennett (on
           bk) [Eliza F. Bennett (on CTOLMR)],
           26, widow, Born and Lived: Alleg. Co.,
           VA, dau/o: S. and M. Gillaspie (on bk)
           [Samuel and Mary Gillaspie (on CTOL
           MR)]. PL: Alleg. Co., VA "Potts Cre-
           ek." Mar. by J. B. Davis. CTOLMR
           signed on 12-31-1866 by Joseph T. Fud-
           ge, Clk. Mins. Ret. says mar. on 01-
           01-1867 at David G. Givens res. Potts
           Creek in Alleg. Co., VA, was signed
           by John B. Davis.

01-01-1863 (on bk)   01-05-1863 Tuesday (on
 # 1   CTOLMR and Mins. Ret.)
           Samuel B. Lowry, 27, single, Born and
           Lived: Alleg. Co., VA, Occup: farmer,
           s/o: Samuel B. and Rebecca E. Lowry;
           and Almira S. Keyser, 19, single, Born
           and Lived: Alleg. Co., VA, dau/o:
           Fleming and Nancy Keyser. PL: Alleg.
           Co., VA "Fleming Keyser's res." Mar.
           by S. S. Ryder. CTOLMR signed on 01-
           01-1863 by W. M. Scott, Clk. Pro Tem.
           Mins. Ret. says mar. on 01-05-1863 at
           Fleming Keyser's res.

01-20-1863 Tazewell M. Gibson (on bk) [Tazewell
 # 2   M. Gilson (on CTOLMR)], 41, widower,
           B: Albemarle Co., VA, Lived: Bath Co.,
           VA, Occup: Miller, s/o: Nicholas and
           Elizabeth Gibson (on bk) [Nicholas and
           Elizabeth Gilson (on CTOLMR)]; and
           Rachel Jackson, 34, widow, B: Bath Co,
           VA, Lived: Alleg. Co., VA, dau/o:

Thomas and Jane Jackson. PL: Alleg. Co., VA. Mar. by Stuart S. Ryder. CTOLMR signed on 01-20-1863 by W. M. Scott, Clk. Pro Tem. Mins. Ret. says mar. on 01-20-1863 at Mrs. Jackson's was signed by Stuart L. Rider.

01-29-1863   C. V. Carson, 38, single, Born and
 # 3   Lived: Monroe Co., VA (now W.VA.), Occup: farmer, s/o: Joseph and Kitty Carson; and Isabella Frances Givens, 28, single, Born: ____ ___ ___ [as on CTOLMR--believe it means she was also born in Monroe Co., VA (now W.VA.)], Lived: Alleg. Co., VA "Potts Creek", dau/o: David and Catherine Givens (on bk) [David and Chatharin (?Jane) Givens (on CTOLMR)]. PL: Alleg. Co., VA "Potts Creek." Mar. by J. W. F. Graham. CTOLMR signed on 01-25-1863 by W. M. Scott, Clk. Pro Tem. Mins. Ret. says mar. on 01-29-1863 at David Givens res.

06-09-1863   Thursday
 # 4   William E. Byer, 23, single, Born and Lived: Alleg. Co., VA "Rich Patch", Occup: farmer, s/o: Samuel and Harriett Byer; and Lucinda A. Bush, 25, single, Born and Lived: Alleg. Co., VA "Rich Patch", dau/o: Samuel and Polly Bush. PL: Alleg. Co., VA "Rich Patch." Mar. by S. S. Ryder. CTOLMR signed on 06-08-1863 by W. M. Scott, Clk. Pro Tem. Mins. Ret. says mar. on 06-09-1863 at William Sulender's res.

08-06-1863   Thursday
 # 5   Henry Johnson, 23, single, Born and Lived: Alleg. Co., VA "Potts Creek", Occup: farmer, s/o: Barney and Ann Johnson: and Julia A. Carson (on bk)

(Mar. Register Book (1) - Continued)

[Julia Ann Carson (on CTOLMR)], 25,
single, Born and Lived: Alleg. Co.,
VA "Snake Run", dau/o: William and
Sarah Carson. PL: Alleg. Co., VA
"Snake Run." Mar. by S. S. Ryder.
CTOLMR signed on 08-04-1863 by W. M.
Scott, Clk. Pro Tem. Mins. Ret. says
mar. on 08-06-1863 at William Carson's
res.

12-03-1863   Thursday
6   Thomas E. Dickson, 37, single, Born
and Lived: Monroe Co., VA (now W.VA),
Occup: farmer, s/o: John and Nancy
Dickson; and Amanda R. Carson, 28,
single, Born and Lived: Alleg. Co.,
VA, dau/o: William and Sarah Carson.
PL: Alleg. Co., VA "Snake Run." Mar.
by G. W. Carpenter. CTOLMR signed on
12-03-1863 by W. M. Scott, Clk. Pro
Tem. Mins. Ret. says mar. on 12-03-
1863 at res. of William and Sarah Carson.

12-08-1863   Tuesday
7   Michael Cavner (on bk) [Michael Cave-
ner (on CTOLMR)], 28, single, B: Ire-
land, Lived: Botetourt Co., VA, Occup:
laborer, s/o: James and Mary Carpenter
(on bk) [James and Mary Cavener (on
CTOLMR)]; and Catherine Bennett (on
bk) [Catharine Bennett (on CTOLMR)],
33, widow, B: Botetourt Co., VA, Lived: Alleg. Co., VA, dau/o: Andrew and
Rebecca Persinger. PL: Alleg. Co., VA
"Rich Patch." Mar. by James M. Rice.
CTOLMR signed on 12-08-1863 by W. M.
Scott, Clk. Pro Tem. Mins. Ret. says
mar. on 12-08-1863 at Mrs. Bennet's
res. Rich Patch.

(Mar. Register Book (1) - Continued)

12-09-1863   Wednesday
 # 8   Joseph Zeigler, 26, widower, B: Fred-
             ericksburg, VA, Lived: Alleg. Co, VA,
             Occup: Telegraph Operator, s/o: Abra-
             ham and Matilda Zeigler; and Susan L.
             Haynes, 21 (on bk) [20 (on CTOLMR)],
             single, Born and Lived: Alleg. Co.,
             VA, dau/o: William H. and ___ Haynes
             (on bk) [Wm. H. and ____ Haynes (on
             CTOLMR)]. PL: Alleg. Co., VA "Maj.
             Haynes res. Jackson River." Mar. by
             James M. Rice. CTOLMR signed on 12-
             09-1863 by W. M. Scott, Clk. Pro Tem.
             Mins. Ret. says mar. on 12-09-1863 at
             Maj. Haynes's res. on Jackson River.

12-09-1863   Wednesday
 # 9   Owen C. Moss, 26, single, B: Gooch-
             land Co., VA, Lived: _____ (on bk)
             [Braxton Co., VA (now W.VA.) (on CTOL
             MR)], Occup: farmer, s/o: James A. and
             Martha A. Moss; and Elizabeth R. Jack-
             son, 21, single, Born and Lived: Al-
             leg. Co., VA, dau/o: Abel and Eliza-
             beth Jackson. PL: Alleg. Co., VA
             "Mrs. E. Jackson's res." Mar. by
             James M. Rice. CTOLMR signed on 12-
             09-1863 by W. M. Scott, Clk. Pro Tem.
             Mins. Ret. says mar. on 12-09-1863 at
             mother's res. near Cedar Run.

12-31-1863   Thursday
 # 10   Charles Masters, 40, single, B: Eng-
             land, Occup: laborer, Lived: Alleg.
             Co., VA, s/o: Thomas and Ann Masters;
             and Mary Boley, 18, single, Born and
             Lived: Alleg. Co., VA, dau/o: Presley
             and Nancy Boley. PL: Alleg. Co., VA
             "Presley Boley's res." Mar. by S. S.
             Ryder. CTOLMR signed on 12-28-1863
             by W. M. Scott, Clk. Pro Tem. Mins.
             Ret. says mar. on 12-31-1863 at Pres-

(Mar. Register Book (1) - Continued)

ley Boley's res.

Page 9

02-26-1866
1
(on bk)   02-28-1866 (on CTOLMR and
Mins. Ret.)
George W. Dressler (on bk) [George
Washington Dressler (on CTOLMR)], 30,
single, Occup: farmer, s/o: Peter and
Patsy Dressler; and Sarah F. Brown
(on bk) [Sarah Frances Brown (on CTOL
MR)], 24, single, dau/o: Anderson and
Barbary Brown. Both were born and
lived in Alleg. Co., VA. PL: Alleg.
Co., VA "Mrs. Brown's res." Mar. by
S. S. Ryder. CTOLMR signed on 02-26-
1866 by Jos. T. Fudge, Clk. Mins.
Ret. says mar. on 02-28-1866 at Mrs.
Brown's res.

02-26-1866
2
(on bk)   03-01-1866 (on CTOLMR and
Mins. Ret.)
Edward Kniton, 32, single, B: Louisa
Co., VA, Occup: farmer, s/o: William
and Mary Kniton (on bk) [Wm. and Mary
Kniton (on CTOLMR)]; and Julia A. Goff
(on bk) [Julia Ann Goff (on CTOLMR)],
32, single, B: Monroe Co., VA (now W.
VA), dau/o: Jackson and Harriett Goff
(on bk) [Jackson and Harriet Goff (on
CTOLMR)]. Both lived in Alleg. Co.,
VA. Mar. by S. S. Ryder. PL: Alleg.
Co., VA "Jack Goff's res." CTOLMR
signed on 02-26-1866 by Jos. T. Fudge,
Clk. Mins. Ret. says mar. on 03-01-
1866 at Jno. Goff's in Alleg. Co., VA.

02-21-1866
3
(on bk)   02-22-1866 (on CTOLMR and
Mins. Ret.)
Ballard J. Smith, 34, single, B: Alleg.
Co., VA, Lived: Louisa Co., VA, Occup:
farmer, s/o: Wright and Polly Smith;

- 181 -

(Mar. Register Book (1) - Continued)

and <u>Martha F. Robinson</u>, 24, single,
Born and Lived: Alleg. Co., VA, dau/o:
William and Eliz. Robinson (on bk)
[William and Elizabeth Robinson (on
CTOLMR)]. PL: Alleg. Co., VA "Wm.
Robinson's res." Mar. by S. S. Ryder.
CTOLMR signed on 02-21-1866 by Joseph
T. Fudge, Clk. Mins. Ret. says mar.
on 02-22-1866 at Mr. Robinson's res.
Age oath of William M. Robinson that
<u>Martha</u>, daughter of William Robinson,
is over 21 made on 02-21-1866, Teste
Jos. T. Fudge, Clk.

03-19-1866   (on bk)   03-28-1866 (on CTOLMR and
  # 4   Mins. Ret.)
              <u>James P. Carter</u>, 26, single, Occup:
              farmer, s/o: Lemuel and Patsey Carter
              (on bk) [Lemuel and Patsy Carter (on
              CTOLMR)]; and <u>Mary J. Harmon</u> (on bk)
              [<u>Mary J. Harman</u> (on CTOLMR)], 26, sin-
              gle, dau/o: Thos. and Mary Harmon (on
              bk) [Thos. and Mary Harman (on CTOL
              MR)]. Both were born and lived in
              Alleg. Co., VA. PL: Alleg. Co., VA
              "Frances Harmon res."-(on CTOL) ["Tho-
              mas Harman res."--(on CTOLMR)]. Mar.
              by John B. Davis. CTOL signed on 03-
              19-1866 by Thomas Harman (apparently
              this was used for consent or proof of
              age). CTOLMR signed on 03-19-1866 by
              Joseph T. Fudge, Clk. Mins. Ret. says
              mar. on 03-28-1866 at Thomas Harmon's
              res.

04-02-1866   (on bk)   04-22-1866 (on Mins. Ret.)
  # 4½   <u>Newton Mathews</u>, 46, widower, "A Freed-
              man", Occup: ___ (on bk) [Farmer (on
              CTOLMR)], and <u>Jane Bess</u>, 26, single.
              Mar. by ___ (on bk) [A. Q. Flaherty
              (on Mins. Ret.)]. PL: Alleg. Co., VA
              "Callaghan's". CTOLMR signed on 04-

(Mar. Register Book (1) - Continued)

02-1866 by Joseph T. Fudge, Clk.
Mins. Ret. says mar. on 04-22-1866 at
Fletcher's Chapel. (Colored-- He apparently had been a slave who had been
freed thus the notation " Freedman.")
[Note: There was no other information.]

04-14-1866   (on bk) 04-18-1866 (on CTOLMR and
 # 5   Mins. Ret.)
              Jno. N. Mahon, 21, single, B: Monroe
              Co., VA (now W.VA.), Lived: Monroe
              Co., W. VA. (on bk) [Alleg. Co., VA
              (on CTOLMR)], Occup: farmer, s/o: Law-
              son and Elizabeth Mahon; and Elizabeth
              J. Worsham (on bk) [Eliza J. Worsham
              (on CTOLMR)], 25, single, B: Alleg.
              Co., VA (on bk) [Monroe Co., VA (now
              W.VA.) (on CTOLMR)], Lived: Alleg. Co,
              VA, dau/o: Dan'l. and Emeline Worsham
              (on bk) [Daniel and Emaline Worsham
              (on CTOLMR)]. PL: Alleg. Co., VA
              "Mrs. Worsham's res." Mar. by J. W.
              F. Graham. CTOLMR signed on 04-14-
              1866 by Joseph T. Fudge, Clk. Mins.
              Ret. says mar. on 04-18-1866 at Mrs.
              Worsham's res. Age oath given by ___
              on 04-14-1866, Teste Jos. T. Fudge,
              Clk.

04-24-1866   (on bk) 04-26-1866 (on CTOLMR and
 # 6   Mins. Ret.)
              John R. McPherson (on bk) [James R.
              McPherson (on CTOLMR)], 22, single, B:
              Botetourt Co., VA, Occup: farmer (on
              bk) [Blacksmith (on CTOLMR)], s/o:
              John and Elizabeth McPherson; and
              Rupia L. Poor, 19, single, B: Alleg.
              Co., VA (on bk) [Botetourt Co., VA
              (on CTOLMR)], dau/o: Soloman and Eliz-
              abeth Poor. Both lived in Alleg. Co.,
              VA. PL: Alleg. Co., VA "Mrs. E.

(Mar. Register Book (1) - Continued)

Poor's res." Mar. by S. S. Ryder.
CTOLMR signed on 04-24-1866 by Joseph
T. Fudge, Clk. Mins. Ret. says mar.
on 04-26-1866 at Mrs. E. Poor's res.
Consent dated 04-23-1866 signed Eliz-
abeth (her X mark) Poor, Wit. Lee Per-
singer, John Johnson. Oath of John
Johnson that Elizabeth Poor gave con-
sent dated 04-24-1866, Teste Jos. T.
Fudge, Clk.

05-21-1866 (on bk) 06-21-1866 (on Mins. Ret.)
6½ William Cash, "A Freedman", 27, sing-
le, B: Bath Co., VA, s/o: _____.
Occup: Woodchopper; and Sarah Williams, 17, single, B: Alleg. Co., VA,
dau/o: Armstead and Eliza Williams.
Both lived in Alleg. Co., VA. Mar.
by John L. Beale. PL: Alleg. Co., VA
"Griffith's Turnout." CTOLMR signed
05-01-1866 by Joseph T. Fudge, Clk.
Mins. Ret. says mar. on 06-21-1866 at
Griffith's Turnout. (Colored-- apparently William was a slave that was
freed thus the notation "A Freedman.")

05-23-1866 (on bk) 05-24-1866 Thursday (on CTOL
7 MR) 03-24-1866 (on Mins. Ret.)
George W. Rittinger (on bk) [George
Washington Kitinger (on CTOLMR)], 55,
widower, B: Roanoke Co., VA, Occup:
farmer, s/o: Andr. Dame and Polly Rit-
tinger (on bk) [Andy Dame and Polly
Kittinger (on CTOLMR)]; and Eliz. A.
Anderson (on bk) [Elizabeth Arabella
Anderson (on CTOLMR)], 47, widow, B:
Shenandoah Co., VA "New Market", dau/
o: Jas. and Eliz. Conoway (on bk)
[James and Elizabeth Conaway (on CTOL
MR)]. Both lived in Alleg. Co., VA.
PL: Alleg. Co., VA "Covington." Mar.
by S. S. Ryder. CTOLMR signed on 05-

23-1866 by W. M. Scott, D. C. Mins.
Ret. says mar. on 03-24-1866 in Covington, VA. [Author's Note: I believe the minister made an error in
writing down the date since the other
records have May.]

05-23-1866   Wednesday
8   James N. Shanklin (on bk) [James Nel-
son Shanklin (J. ____ Nelson Shanklin)
(on CTOLMR)], 28, single, Born and
Lived: Monroe Co., VA (now W.VA.),
Occup: farmer, s/o: Lewis A. and Sal-
lie Shanklin; and Mary P. Kean (on bk)
[Mary Phebe Kean (on CTOLMR)], 18,
single, Born and Lived: Alleg. Co.,
VA, dau/o: Sam'l. and Rebecca Kean
(on bk) [Samuel and Rebecca Kean (on
CTOLMR)]. PL: Alleg. Co., VA "Mrs.
R. Kean at Dunlap Creek." Mar. by H.
R. Keans. CTOLMR signed on 05-23-1866
by W. M. Scott, D. C. Mins. Ret. says
mar. on 05-23-1866 at Mrs. R. B.
Kean's res.

05-29-1866   Wednesday
9   Jos. Rideout (on bk) [Joseph Rideout
(on CTOLMR)], "A Freedman", 34 (on bk)
["about 33 or 34" (on CTOLMR)], sing-
le, B: Alleg. Co., VA, Occup: farmer
(on bk) [Laborer (on CTOLMR)], s/o:
Edward and Rossetta Rideout (on bk)
[Edward and Rosetta Rideout (on CTOL
MR)]; and Sarah Robinson, (Colored),
22 (on bk) ["about 21 or 22" (on CTOL
MR)], single, B: Bath Co., VA, dau/o:
Jos. and Charlotte Fields (on bk)
[Joseph and Charlotte Fields (on CTOL
MR)]. Both lived in Alleg. Co., VA.
PL: Alleg. Co., VA "Mrs. Nicely's at
Cowpasture River." Mar. by Joseph
Fields. CTOLMR signed 05-29-1866 by

(Mar. Register Book (1) - Continued)

W. M. Scott, D. C. Mins. Ret. says
mar. on 05-29-1866 at Cowpasture
Bridge in Alleg. Co., VA. (Joseph
was apparently a slave who had been
freed thus the notation "A Freedman.")

05-30-1866   Peyton A. Jackson (on bk) [Payton A.
10   Jackson (on CTOLMR)], 31, single,
              Occup: farmer, s/o: Able and Eliz.
              Jackson (on bk) [Able and Elizabeth
              Jackson (on CTOLMR)]; and Virginia E.
              Johnson (on bk) [Virginia E. Johnston
              (on CTOLMR)], 24, single, dau/o: C.
              T. and Elizabeth Johnson [C. T. and
              Eliza Johnston (on CTOLMR)]. Both
              were born and lived in Alleg. Co.,
              VA. PL: Alleg. Co., VA "Covington."
              Mar. by S. S. Ryder. CTOLMR signed
              on 05-30-1866 by Joseph T. Fudge, Clk.
              Mins. Ret. says mar. 05-30-1866 at
              res. of C. T. Johnson, Covington, VA.
              Age oath of John Baker that Virginia
              E. Johnston was over 21 signed on 05-
              30-1866, Teste Joseph T. Fudge, Clk.

06-09-1866   (on bk) 06-14-1866 Thursday (on
11   CTOLMR and Mins. Ret.)
              William A. Arrington (on bk) [William
              Alexander Arington (on CTOLMR)], 22,
              single, Occup: farmer, s/o: Jas. and
              Jane Arrington (on bk) [James and
              Jane Arington (on CTOLMR)]; and E. R.
              Wolf (on bk) [Eliza Reed Wolf (on
              CTOLMR)], 22, single, dau/o: Isaac
              and Martha Wolf. Both were born and
              lived in Alleg. Co., VA. Mar. by
              John B. Davis. PL: Alleg. Co., VA
              "Isaac Wolf's res." CTOLMR signed on
              06-09-1866 by W. M. Scott, D. C.
              Mins. Ret. says mar. on 06-14-1866 at
              Isaac Wolf's res. Rich Patch in Alleg.
              Co., VA.

06-23-1866   (on bk) 06-28-1866 (on CTOLMR and
  # 12   Mins. Ret.)
              John H. Morrison, 22, single, B: Mon-
              roe Co., VA (now W.VA.), Occup: far-
              mer, s/o: John and Sarah Morrison;
              and Barbary F. Hoke (on bk) [Barbary
              Francis Hoke (on CTOLMR)], 18, single,
              B: Alleg. Co., VA (on bk) [Monroe
              Co., VA (now W.VA.) (on CTOLMR)],
              dau/o: William and Catharine Hoke.
              Both lived in Alleg. Co., VA. Mar.
              by James M. Rice. PL: Alleg. Co., VA
              "William Hoke res." CTOLMR signed on
              06-23-1866 by Joseph T. Fudge, Clk.
              Mins. Ret. says mar. on 06-28-1866 at
              Wm. Hoke's res.

07-23-1866   (on bk) 07-24-1866 (on CTOLMR and
  # 13   Mins. Ret.)
              William Rayhill, 27, single, Occup:
              farmer, s/o: Alex. and Eliz. Rayhill
              (on bk) [Alexander and Elizabeth Ray-
              hill (on CTOLMR)]; and Areanna S. Wal-
              ker, 22, single, dau/o: Henry and
              Maria Walker. Both were born and liv-
              ed in Alleg. Co., VA. Mar. by John B.
              Davis. PL: Alleg. Co., VA "H. Walker
              res." CTOLMR signed 07-23-1866 by
              Joseph T. Fudge, Clk. Mins. Ret. says
              mar. on 07-24-1866 at H. Walker res.
              Potts Creek in Alleg. Co., VA.

08-09-1866   Henry Humphries, 29, single, Born and
  # 14   Lived: Alleg. Co., VA, Occup: farmer,
              s/o: Wm. and Ruth Humphries (on bk)
              [William and Ruth Humphries (on CTOL
              MR)]; and Samantha Steers, 23, single,
              B: Centre Co., Pennsylvania, Lived:
              Alleg. Co., VA, dau/o: Evans and Eliz-
              abeth Steers (on bk) [Evans and Eliza-
              beth Steers (on CTOLMR)]. PL: Alleg.
              Co., VA "E. Steers, Esq. res." Mar.

(Mar. Register Book (1) - Continued)

by S. S. Ryder. CTOLMR signed on 08-
09-1866 by Joseph T. Fudge, Clk.
Mins. Ret. says mar. on 08-09-1866 at
res. of E. Steers. Age oath by William Steers for Samantha, daughter of
Evans Steers, on 08-09-1866, Teste
Joseph T. Fudge, Clk.

09-03-1866 (on bk) 09-04-1866 (on CTOLMR and
15   Mins. Ret.)
            Mathew M. Knick (on bk) [Matthew Mar-
            vin Knick (on CTOLMR)], 25, single,
            Born and Lived: Rockbridge Co., VA,
            Occup: farmer, s/o: John and Polly
            Knick; and M. J. Armintrout (on bk)
            [Mary Jane Armintrout (on COTLMR)],
            28, widow, Born and Lived: Alleg. Co.,
            VA, dau/o: Lewis and Anne Nicely (on
            bk) [Lewis and Annie Nicely (on CTOL
            MR)]. PL: Alleg. Co., VA "Cowpasture
            River." Mar. by A. Bagby, Mins. Bapt.
            Ch. CTOLMR signed on 09-03-1866 by
            W. M. Scott, D. C. Mins. Ret. says
            mar. on 09-04-1866 at Mrs. Jane Arman-
            trout's res.

09-30-1866 Charles Wright, 20, single, Occup:
15½   farmer, s/o: Washington and Polly
            Wright; and Frances Allen, 19, single,
            dau/o: Archibald and Martha Allen.
            Both were born and lived in Alleg. Co,
            VA. Mar. by A. Q. Flaherty. PL: Al-
            leg. Co., VA "Fork Run Church." CTOL
            MR signed on 09-22-1866 by W. M. Scott,
            D. C. Mins. Ret. says mar. on 09-30-
            1866 at Fork Run Church.

09-04-1866 (on bk) 09-06-1866 (on CTOLMR and
16   Mins. Ret.)
            W. S. Wills (on bk) [William S. Wills
            (on CTOLMR)], 27, single, B: Fluvanna
            Co., VA, Lived: Fluvanna Co., VA (on

bk) [Alleg. Co., VA (on CTOLMR)],
Occup: Druggist, s/o: Miles and R. M.
Wills (on bk) [Miles C. and Rebecca
M. Wills (on CTOLMR)]; and <u>Annie S.
Scott</u>, 26, single, Born and Lived:
Alleg. Co., VA, dau/o: A. M. and R.
C. Scott (on bk) [Andrew M. and Rach-
el C. Scott (on CTOLMR)]. PL: Alleg.
Co., VA "Covington." Mar. by James
M. Rice. CTOLMR signed on 09-04-1866
by Joseph T. Fudge, Clk. Mins. Ret.
says mar. on 09-06-1866 at Covington,
Alleg. Co., VA.

10-10-1866   (on bk) 10-11-1866 (on CTOLMR and
. # 17   Mins. Ret.)
                <u>Jas. A. Hamlett</u> (on bk) [<u>James (?An-
                drew) Hamlett</u> (on CTOLMR)], (? 27) (on
                bk) [21 (on CTOLMR)], single, B: Char-
                lotte Co., VA, Occup: farmer, s/o:
                Henry and Polly Hamlett; and <u>A. C.
                Bennett</u> (on bk) [<u>Asena Catharine Ben-
                nett</u> (on CTOLMR)], 22, single, B: Al-
                leg. Co., VA, dau/o: Wm. and Catharine
                Bennett (on bk) [William and Catharine
                Bennett (on CTOLMR)]. Both lived in
                Alleg. Co., VA. PL: Alleg. Co., VA
                "Rich Patch." Mar. by John B. Davis.
                CTOLMR signed on 10-10-1866 by Joseph
                T. Fudge, Clk. Mins. Ret. says mar.
                on 10-11-1866 at John B. Davis res.
                on Potts Creek, Alleg. Co., VA. Age
                oath on 10-10-1866 by Allen M. Stull,
                Teste Joseph T. Fudge, Clk.

10-15-1866   (on bk) 10-18-1866 (on CTOLMR and
 # 18   Mins. Ret.)
                <u>Edwin D. Crow</u>, age: ___, single, B:
                Alleg. Co., VA, Occup: farmer, s/o:
                John and Amanda Crow (on bk) [John and
                Amanda F. Crow (on CTOLMR)]; and <u>E. F.
                Hardy</u> (on bk) [<u>Elizabeth Frances Hardy</u>

(Mar. Register Book (1) - Continued)

(on CTOLMR)], 18, single, B: Mercer
Co., VA (now W.VA.), dau/o: Thos. and
Sopha Hardy (on bk) [Thomas and Sophia M. Hardy (on CTOLMR)]. Both lived
in Alleg. Co., VA. Mar. by H. B.
Rose. PL: Alleg. Co., VA "Thos. Hardy res." CTOLMR signed on 10-15-1866
by Joseph T. Fudge, Clk. Mins. Ret.
says mar. on 10-18-1866 at Thomas
Hardy's res. Five cent U. S. Inter.
Revenue Certificate Stamp attached to
Lic. and written on it "J. T. F. Clk
15 Oct 1866" and had George Washington's picture on the stamp. (The
stamp is like today's postage stamps
in the way it is made. The present
Clerk of Court says he has no idea
what thses stamps were for except
that they may have been to show that
some fee had been paid.)

11-19-1866   (on bk)   11-21-1866 (on CTOLMR and
19   Mins. Ret.)   Wednesday
              Chas. M. Stull (on bk) [Charles M.
              Stull (on CTOLMR)], 27, widower, Oc-
cup: farmer, s/o: Jas. and Hannah
Stull (on bk) [James and Hannah Stull
(on CTOLMR)]; and F. E. Riddlesbarger
(on bk) [Francis E. Riddlesbarger (on
CTOLMR)], 24, widow, dau/o: J. D. and
_____ Morrison (on bk) [James D. and
_____ Morrison (on CTOLMR)]. Both
born and lived in Alleg. Co., VA. PL:
Alleg. Co., VA "James D. Morrison
res." Mar. by James M. Rice. CTOLMR
signed on 11-19-1866 by Joseph T. Fudge, Clk. Mins. Ret. says mar. on 11-
21-1866 at J. D. Morrison's res. Five
cent U. S. Inter. Revenue Certificate
Stamp attached to Lic. and written on
it "JT Fudge, Clk. 19th Nov 1866."
Consent on 11-19-1866 by James D. Mor-

(Mar. Register Book (1) - Continued)

          rison. [Note: Spelling on <u>Francis</u> is
          as on consent.]

11-28-1866 (on bk) 12-06-1866 Thursday (on
  # 20   CTOLMR and Mins. Ret.)
          <u>Wm. T. Switzer</u> (on bk) [<u>William Tho-</u>
          <u>mas Switzer</u> (on CTOLMR)], 21, single,
          B: Botetourt Co., VA, Lived: Craig
          Co., VA, Occup: farmer, s/o: Cary A.
          and J. Switzer (on bk) [Cary A. and
          Jane Switzer (on CTOLMR)]; and <u>H. A.</u>
          <u>Bennett</u> (on bk) [<u>Harriett Ann Bennett</u>
          (on CTOLMR)], 21, single, Born and
          Lived: Alleg. Co., VA, dau/o: Sampson
          and M. E. Bennett (on bk) [Sampson
          and Mary E. Bennett (on CTOLMR)]. PL:
          Alleg. Co., VA "John Davis res." Mar.
          by John B. Davis. CTOLMR signed on
          11-28-1866 by W. M. Scott, D. C.
          Mins. Ret. says mar. on 12-06-1866 at
          John B. Davis res. in Alleg. Co., VA.

12-10-1866 (on bk) 12-12-1866 (on CTOLMR and
  # 21   Mins. Ret.)
          <u>Moses G. Wright</u> (on bk) [<u>Moses George</u>
          <u>Wright</u> (on CTOLMR)], 44, widower, B:
          Monroe Co., VA (now W.VA.), Occup:
          farmer, s/o: John and Catharine Wri-
          ght; and <u>Phoebe Aritt</u>, 32, widow, B:
          Alleg. Co., VA, dau/o: Jos. and Mahaly
          Terry (on bk) [Joseph and Mahaly Terry
          (on CTOLMR)]. Both lived in Alleg.
          Co., VA. Mar. by John B. Davis. PL:
          Alleg. Co., VA "Potts Creek." CTOLMR
          signed on 12-10-1866 by Joseph T. Fud-
          ge, Clk. Mins. Ret. says mar. on 12-
          12-1866 at Phoebe Aritt's res. on
          Potts Creek in Alleg. Co., VA. Five
          Cent Inter. Revenue Certificate Stamp
          attached and signed by clk.

- 191 -

12-18-1866   (on bk)   12-19-1866 (on CTOLMR and
  # 22   Mins. Ret.)
              Ro. A. Dickson (on bk) [Robert A.
              Dickson (on CTOLMR)], 23, single, B:
              Greenbrier Co., VA (now W.VA.), Occup:
              Innkeeper, s/o: Sam'l. and M. F. Dick-
              son (on bk) [Samuel and M. F. Dickson
              (on CTOLMR)]; and J. Emma Layne, 23,
              single, B: Alleg. Co., VA, dau/o:
              Douglas B. and ____ Layne. Both liv-
              ed in Alleg. Co., VA. Mar. by James
              M. Rice. PL: Alleg. Co., VA "Alleg-
              hany Valley." CTOLMR signed on 12-
              18-1866 by Joseph T. Fudge, Clk.
              Mins. Ret. says mar. on 12-19-1866 at
              Alleghany Valley, VA.

02-08-1867   (on bk)   02-11-1867 Monday (on CTOLMR
  # 23   Mins. Ret.)
              Sam'l. Redman, 21, single, B: Bote-
              tourt Co., VA, Occup: farmer, s/o: Wm.
              and Mary Redman (on bk) [William and
              Mary Redman (on CTOLMR)]; and Nancy E.
              Byers (on bk) [Nancy E. Byer (on con-
              sent)], 20, single, B: Craig Co., VA,
              dau/o: Sam'l. and Harriet Byers (on
              bk) [Samuel and Harriet Byers (on
              CTOLMR)]. Consent dated 02-08-1867
              and signed Samuel Byer. Both lived in
              Alleg. Co., VA. PL: Alleg. Co., VA
              "S. Byer's res." Mar. by John B.
              Davis. CTOLMR signed on 01-08-1867
              and Mar. Auth. signed on 02-08-1867
              both by Joseph T. Fudge, Clk. Mins.
              Ret. says mar. on 02-11-1867 at Samuel
              Byers in Rich Patch in Alleg. Co., VA.
              Oath to Samuel Byer signing consent
              was given by D. M. Humphries on 02-08-
              1867, Teste Jos. T. Fudge, Clk. (Note
              There are three--two cent Bankcheck
              Stamps attached and signed by clk.
              Each stamp had George Washington's

(Mar. Register Book (1) - Continued)

picture on it. They are apparently a
sign that some fee had been paid, but
no one knows for sure.)

02-16-1867   (on bk) 02-21-1867 Thursday (on
  # 24   CTOLMR and Mins. Ret.)
             Allen Larison, 42, widower, B: Cincin-
             natti, Ohio, Occup: merchant, s/o:
             J. A. and Eliz. Larison (on bk) [James
             A. and Elizabeth Larison (on CTOLMR)];
             and Martha A. Waren (on bk) [Marta Ann
             Waren (on Mar. Auth.) Martha Ann Waren
             (on CTOLMR)], 22, single, B: Craig Co,
             VA (on bk) [Alleg. Co., VA (on CTOL
             MR)], dau/o: Jas. and ___ Waren (on
             bk) [James and ____ Warren (on CTOL
             MR)]. Both lived in Alleg. Co., VA.
             PL: Alleg. Co., VA "Mrs. Mahan's res."
             Mar. by J. W. F. Graham. CTOLMR sign-
             ed on 02-16-1867 by W. M. Scott, D. C.
             Mins. Ret. says mar. on 02-21-1867 at
             Mrs. Mahan's.

02-16-1867   (on bk) 02-21-1867 Thursday (on
  # 25   CTOLMR and Mins. Ret.)
             A. J. Brown (on bk) [Andrew Jackson
             Brown (on CTOLMR)], 21, single, B:
             Botetourt Co., VA, Occup: farmer, s/o:
             Wm. and Hagar Brown (on bk) [William
             and Hagar Brown (on CTOLMR)]; and Lucy
             H. Mahon (on bk) [Lucy Hughes Mahan
             (on CTOLMR)], 17, single, B: Monroe
             Co., VA (now W.VA.), dau/o: Lawson and
             Eliz. Mahon (on bk) [Lawson and Eliza-
             beth Mahan (on CTOLMR)]. Both lived
             in Alleg. Co., VA. PL: Alleg. Co.,
             VA "Mrs. Mahan's near Sweet Springs,
             W. VA." Mar. by J. W. F. Graham.
             CTOLMR signed on 02-16-1867 by W. M.
             Scott, D. C. Mins. Ret. says mar. on
             02-21-1867 at Mrs. Mahan's res.

(Mar. Register Book (1) - Continued)

02-17-1867   Sunday
  # 26   <u>Michael Hagerty</u>, 35, single, B: County
            Cork, Ireland, Occup: laborer, s/o:
            Peter and Mary Hagerty (on bk) [Peter
            and Mary Hegerty (on CTOLMR)]; and
            <u>Mary Doherty</u>, 37, widow, B: County
            Carle, Ireland [Note: I find no Co.
            spelled this way on Irish map. Believe
            could be Carlow since that is the
            spelling nearest it and the nearest in
            sound.], dau/o: Luke and ___ Murphy
            (on bk) [Luke and McMurphy (?M.Murphy)
            Dogherty (on CTOLMR)]. Both lived in
            Alleg. Co., VA. Mar. by J. H. Walters.
            PL: Alleg. Co., VA "Covington." CTOL
            MR signed on 02-17-1867 by W. M. Scott
            D. C. Mins. Ret. says mar. on 02-17-
            1867 in Covington in Alleg. Co., VA.

02-23-1867   (on bk) 02-28-1867 Thursday (on
  # 27   CTOLMR and Mins. Ret.)
            <u>Henry J. Young</u> (on bk) [<u>Henry Jackson
            Young</u> (on CTOLMR)], 35, single, Born
            and Lived: Monroe Co., W. VA, Occup:
            farmer, s/o: Robert and Mary Young (on
            bk) [Robert and Margarett Young (on
            CTOLMR)]; and <u>Mary J. Bostick</u> (on bk)
            [<u>Mary Jane Bostick</u> (on CTOLMR)], 22,
            single, Born and Lived: Alleg. Co.,
            VA, dau/o: Calvin and C. Bostick (on
            bk) [Calvin and Charlotte Bostick (on
            CTOLMR)]. Mar. by W. K. Williams. PL:
            Alleg. Co., VA "near Sweet Springs."
            CTOLMR signed on 02-23-1867 by W. M.
            Scott, D. C. Mins. Ret. says mar. on
            02-28-1867 near Calvin Bostick res.

02-23-1867   (on bk) __-__-____ (on CTOLMR)
  # 28   02-25-1867 (on Mins. Ret.)
            <u>Gaston Howard</u>, 21, single, B: Monroe
            Co., VA (now W.VA.), Occup: farmer,
            s/o: Geo. and Polly Howard (on bk)

[George and Polly Howard (on CTOLMR)];
and <u>Nancy Costic</u>, 23, widow, B: Alleg.
Co., VA (on bk) [Monroe Co., VA (now
W. VA) (on CTOLMR)], dau/o: Henry and
_____ Woolwine. Both lived in Alleg.
Co., VA. PL: Alleg. Co., VA "Wm. Dam-
ron res." Mar. by J. W. F. Graham.
CTOLMR signed on 02-23-1867 by Joseph
T. Fudge, Clk. Mins. Ret. says mar.
on 02-25-1867 at Franklin Master's
res. Oath of <u>Gaston Howard</u> that <u>Nan-
cy</u> was once married to Frank Costic
and he is dead, 1867, Teste Joseph T.
Fudge, Clk. Five cent Inter. Revenue
Certificate Stamp attached and signed
by Clk.

02-27-1867   (on bk) 02-28-1867 (on CTOLMR and
29   Mins. Ret.)
              <u>Lewis Smith</u>, 32, single, Occup: far-
              mer, s/o: Peter and Susan Smith; and
              <u>M. M. Smith</u> (on bk) [<u>Manervia M. Smith</u>
              (on CTOLMR)], age: ___, single, dau/o:
              Wright and Mary Smith. Both born and
              lived in Alleg. Co., VA. PL: Alleg.
              Co., VA "W. Smith res." Mar. by S. S.
              Ryder. CTOLMR signed on 02-27-1867 by
              Joseph T. Fudge, Clk. Mins. Ret. says
              mar. on 02-28-1867 at Mr. Smith's res.
              in Alleg. Co., VA. Consent signed on
              02-25-1867 has name <u>Manervia M. Smith</u>
              and was signed by Wright Smith, Teste
              M. D. Brown. Five cent U. S. Inter.
              Revenue Certificate Stamp was attached
              and signed by Clk.

01-16-1867   <u>Lewis A. Vautis</u> (on bk) [<u>Lewis A.</u>
30   <u>Vawter</u> (on CTOLMR)], 28, widower,
              Born and Lived: Monroe Co., W. VA,
              Occup: farmer, s/o: J. H. and C. S.
              Vautis (on bk) [John H. and Clara S.
              Vawter (on CTOLMR)]; and <u>E. M. Damron</u>

(on bk) [Emma M. Damron (on CTOLMR)],
27, single, Born and Lived: Alleg. Co,
VA, dau/o: Wm. and M. A. Damron (on
bk) [William and Mary A. Damron (on
CTOLMR)]. Mar. by J. M. Rice. PL:
Alleg. Co., VA "John Allen's res."
CTOLMR signed on 01-15-1867 by Joseph
T. Fudge, Clk. Mins. Ret. says mar.
on 01-16-1867 at J. Allan res. by
James M. Rice. Five cent U. S. Inter.
Revenue Certificate Stamp attached
signed by Clk.

01-16-1867   (on bk) 01-17-1867 (on CTOLMR and
 # 30½   Mins. Ret.)
              John Beale, "A Fredman", 27, widower,
              Born and Lived: Botetourt Co., VA,
              Occup: farmer, s/o: Jordan B. and
              Emma Beale; and Rebecca F. Smith, 21,
              single, Born and Lived: Alleg. Co.,
              VA, dau/o: Thomas and Betty Smith.
              Mar. by James M. Rice. PL: Alleg. Co,
              VA "H. G. Haynes's res." CTOLMR sign-
              ed on 01-16-1867 by Joseph T. Fudge,
              Clk. Mins. Ret. says mar. on 01-17-
              1867 at H. G. Haynes res. [Note: John
              apparently was a slave who had been
              freed.]

01-10-1867   Thursday
 # 31   Wm. G. H. Mankspile (on bk) [William
              Grigg Hodmay Manspile (on CTOLMR)],
              22, single, B: Rockbridge Co., VA,
              Occup: farmer, s/o: R. and P. Manks-
              pile (on bk) [Richard and Polly Mans-
              pile (on CTOLMR)]; and E. S. Wolf (on
              bk) [Emeline Susan Wolf (on CTOLMR)],
              16, single, B: Alleg. Co., VA, dau/o:
              I. and P. Wolf (on bk) [Isaac and Peg-
              gei Wolf (on CTOLMR)]. Both lived in
              Alleg. Co., VA. Mar. by John B. Davis.
              PL: Alleg. Co., VA "Isaac Wolf's in

Rich Patch." CTOLMR signed on 01-07-1867 by W. M. Scott, D. C. Mins. Ret. says mar. on 01-10-1867 at Isaac Wolf's res. in Rich Patch in Alleg. Co., VA.

02-27-1867
32

(on bk) 02-28-1867 (on CTOLMR and Mins. Ret.)

Jno. H. Haynes (on bk) [John H. Haynes (on CTOLMR)], 29, single, Occup: farmer, s/o: Wm. H. Jr. and E. Haynes (on bk) [William H., Jr. and Elizabeth Haynes (on CTOLMR)]; and E. E. Zeigler (on bk) [Emily E. Zeigler (on CTOLMR)], 18, single, dau/o: A. and M. Zeigler (on bk) [Abraham and Matilda Zeigler (on CTOLMR)]. Both were born and lived in Alleg. Co., VA. Mar. by A. Q. Flaherty. PL: Alleg. Co., VA "A. Zeigler res." Consent, from Clifton Forge, VA, has name Emly Elisabeth Zeigler and was dated 02-25-1867 and signed A. Zeigler. CTOLMR signed on 02-27-1867 by Joseph T. Fudge, Clk. Mins. Ret. says mar. on 02-28-1867 at A. Zeigler's res. Five cent U. S. Inter. Revenue Certificate Stamp was attached and signed by Clk.

06-07-1866
33

George Clark, "A Freedman", 22, single, Occup: Woodchopper, s/o:_____; and Jane Strange, "A Freedwoman", 20, single, dau/o:__. Both born and lived in Alleg. Co., VA. Mar. by John L. Beale. PL: Alleg. Co., VA. CTOLMR signed on 06-01-1866 by Joseph T. Fudge, Clk. Mins. Ret. says mar. on 06-21-1866 at Griffith's Turnout. [Note: Apparently both George and Jane were slaves who were freed thus the notations "A Freedman" and "A Freedwoman."]

02-17-1867   (on bk)   03-03-1867 Sunday (on Mins.
  # 34   Ret.)
             Willis Wright, 49, widower, B: Bath
             Co., VA, Occup: farmer (on bk) [labor-
             er (on CTOLMR)], s/o: Edwd. and Rose
             Wright; and Ann Jackson, 40, widow,
             B: Bedford Co., VA, dau/o: Ben and
             Rosetta Jackson. Mar. by James M.
             Rice. PL: Alleg. Co., VA "Covington."
             Both lived in Alleg. Co., VA. CTOLMR
             signed 02-17-1867 by W. M. Scott, D.C.
             Mins. Ret. says mar. on 03-03-1867 at
             Presbyterian Church in Covington, VA.
             Five cent U. S. Inter. Revenue Cert-
             ificate Stamp attached and signed by
             Clk.

05-19-1867   Sunday
  # 35   Lewis Beard, 26, single, B: Washing-
             ton Co., VA, Occup: laborer, s/o: Lace
             and Sarah Beard; and Ann Holms, 18,
             single, B: Alleg. Co., VA, dau/o:
             Lewis and Mauldn Holms (on bk) [Lewis
             and Matilda Holms (on CTOLMR)]. Both
             lived in Alleg. Co., VA. Mar. by
             James M. Rice. PL: Alleg. Co., VA
             "Covington." CTOLMR signed on 05-18-
             1867 by W. M. Scott, D. C. Mins. Ret.
             says mar. on 05-19-1867 in Covington,
             VA.

09-12-1867   Thursday
  # 36   Henry Allen, 21, single, B: Alleg. Co,
             VA, Occup: ____ (on bk) [laborer (on
             CTOLMR)], s/o: Archey and Martha Allen
             and Elizabeth Newton, 21, single, B:
             ____ (on bk) [Botetourt Co., VA (on
             CTOLMR)], dau/o: ____. Both lived in
             Alleg. Co., VA. Mar. by ____ (on bk).
             PL: Alleg. Co., VA "C. Shirkey's res."
             CTOLMR signed on 09-11-1867 by W. M.
             Scott, D. C. Mins. Ret. says mar. on

09-12-1867 at C. Shirkey's in Alleg.
Co., VA, and signed James M. Rice.
Note at bottom: "The minister cele-
brating this marriage is (? "author-
ized away from county"). WMS" [Note:
Part is unreadable and I have given
my best guess above as to what it
meant.]

01-07-1867   (on bk) 01-03-1867 (on CTOLMR and
  # 37   Mins. Ret.)
             Richard Johnson, "A Freedman", 27,
             single, Occup: farmer, s/o: Hilery and
             Malinda Johnson: and Rebecca Apple-
             berry, 28 (on bk) [18 or 28 (on CTOL
             MR)--Note: I believe it is 18], sing-
             le, dau/o: Jefferson and Elizabeth
             Bess. Both born and lived in Alleg.
             Co., VA. PL: Alleg. Co., VA "A.
             Mann's res." Mar. by James M. Rice.
             CTOLMR signed on 01-03-1867 by Joseph
             T. Fudge, Clk. Mins. Ret. says mar.
             on 01-03-1867 at res. of A. Mann.
             [Apparently Richard was a slave who
             had been freed.]

Page 10

03-02-1867   (on bk) 03-19-1867 (on CTOLMR and
  # 1   Mins. Ret.)
             Chs. A. Jones (on bk) [Charles A.
             Jones (on CTOLMR)], 49, widower, Occup:
             farmer, s/o: Chs. and M. Jones (on bk)
             [Charles and Mary Jones (on CTOLMR)];
             and L. A. T. J. Jones (on bk) [Lucy A.
             T. J. Jones (on CTOLMR)], 22, single,
             dau/o: J. C. and M. Jones (on bk)
             [Josiah C. and Martha Jones (on CTOL
             MR)]. Both born and lived in Alleg.
             Co., VA. PL: Alleg. Co., VA "Josiah
             Jones res." Mar. by J. W. F. Graham,
             Meth. CTOLMR signed on 03-02-1867 by

Joseph T. Fudge, Clk. Mins. Ret. says
mar. on 03-19-1867 at Josiah Jones
res. Five cent U. S. Inter. Revenue
Certificate Stamp was attached and
signed by Clk. Consent for <u>Lucy</u> dated
03-01-1867 signed by father, Josiah C.
Jones, Wit. George Moss. Oath of acknowledged consent on 03-02-1867 signed Joseph T. Fudge, Clk.

03-02-1867   (on bk) __-__-____ (on CTOLMR)
  # 2   03-07-1867 (on Mins. Ret.)
              <u>Jns. N. Lawhorn</u> (on bk) [<u>James N. Law-</u>
              <u>horn</u> (on CTOLMR)], 22, single, B: Am-
              herst Co., VA, Occup: farmer, s/o: Wm.
              and L. Lawhorn (on bk) [William and
              Lucinda Lawhorn (on CTOLMR)]; and
              <u>Sarah E. Gadd</u>, 26, widow, B: Monroe
              Co., VA (now W. VA.), dau/o: Jacob
              and _____ Bowyer. Both lived in Al-
              leg. Co., VA. PL: Alleg. Co., VA
              "Red Sweet Springs." Mar. by J. W. F.
              Graham. Oath of <u>James N. Lawhorn</u> that
              <u>Sarah</u> was once mar. to Samford Gadd
              who died, dated 03-02-1867, Joseph T.
              Fudge, Clk. CTOLMR signed 03-02-1867
              by Joseph T. Fudge, Clk. Mins. Ret.
              says mar. on 03-07-1867 at Red Sweet
              Springs. Five cent U. S. Inter. Rev-
              enue Certificate Stamp attached and
              signed by Clk.

03-12-1867   (on bk) 03-13-1867 (on CTOLMR and
  # 3   Mins. Ret.)
              <u>Wm. H. Hamlett</u> (on bk) [<u>William H.</u>
              <u>Hamlett</u> (on CTOLMR)], 24, single, B:
              Alleg. Co., VA (on bk) [Charlotte Co.,
              VA (on CTOLMR)], Occup: farmer, s/o:
              H. and M. Hamlett (on bk) [Henry and
              Maryetta Hamlett (on CTOLMR)]; and <u>E.</u>
              <u>F. Stull</u> (on bk) [<u>Elvira F. Stull</u> (on
              CTOLMR)], 22, single, B: Alleg. Co.,

VA, dau/o: Geo. and C. Stull (on bk)
[George and Charlotte Stull (on CTOL
MR)]. Both lived in Alleg. Co., VA.
Mar. by James M. Rice, Presbyterian.
PL: Alleg. Co., VA "Geo. Stull's res."
CTOLMR signed on 03-12-1867 by Joseph
T. Fudge, Clk. Mins. Ret. says mar.
on 03-13-1867 at Geo. Stull res. Age
oath by Franklin P. Tinsley for <u>Elvi-</u>
<u>ra</u> on 03-12-1867, Teste Joseph T.
Fudge, Clk. Five cent U. S. Inter.
Revenue Certificate Stamp attached
and signed by Clk.

03-20-1867   (on bk)   03-21-1867 (on CTOLMR and
  # 4   Mins. Ret.)
  W. A. Matheny (on bk) [<u>William A. Ma-</u>
<u>theny</u> (on CTOLMR)], 22, single, Occup:
farmer, s/o: S. and J. R. Matheny (on
bk) [Sam'l. and Jane R. Matheny (on
CTOLMR)]; and <u>P. Callaghan</u> (on bk)
[<u>Palina Callaghan</u> (on CTOLMR)], 25,
single, dau/o: J. and R. Callaghan
(on bk) [John and Rachel Callaghan (on
CTOLMR)]. Both born and lived in Alleg. Co., VA. PL: Alleg. Co., VA
"Jno. Callaghan res." Mar. by A. Q.
Flaherty, Meth. CTOLMR signed 03-20-
1867 by Jos. T. Fudge, Clk. Mins.
Ret. says mar. on 03-21-1867 at John
Callaghan res. Age oath for <u>Palina</u>
by Dennis Callaghan on 03-20-1867,
Teste Jos. T. Fudge, Clk. Three--two
cent Bankcheck stamps attached. [Note:
No one knows what these stamps mean
except that the Clerk of Court says
he believes they are for some fee and
the stamps show it was collected.]

04-02-1867   Tuesday
  # 5   J. W. Gillaspie (on bk) [<u>James William</u>
<u>Gillaspie</u> (on CTOLMR)], 25, single,

Born and Lived: Greenbrier Co., W.VA.,
Occup: farmer, s/o: J. H. and M. Gillaspie (on bk) [James H. and Margarett
Gillaspie (on CTOLMR)]; and C. A. Hilliany (on bk) [Catharine Adalade Hilliany (on CTOLMR) -Note: last name
could be Hilliary, difficult to tell
which], 23, single, B: State of Ohio,
Lived: Greenbrier Co., W. VA., dau/o:
J. B. and S. Hilliany (on bk) [J. B.
and Susan Hilliary (on CTOLMR)]. Mar.
by James M. Rice, Presb. PL: Alleg.
Co., VA "Covington." CTOLMR signed on
04-02-1867 by W. M. Scott, D.C. Mins.
Ret. says mar. on 04-02-1867 at Mc-
Curdy's in Covington, VA. Five cent
U.S. Inter. Revenue Certificate Stamp
attached and signed by Clk.

04-08-1867   (on bk) 04-10-1867 Wednesday (on
  # 6   CTOLMR and Mins. Ret.)
               Alex. Bess (on bk) [Alexander Bess (on
               CTOLMR)], 24 (on bk) [? 29 (on CTOL
               MR)], Occup: farmer, s/o: H. and N.
               Bess (on bk) [Henry and Nelly Bess (on
               CTOLMR)]; and F. Bennett (on bk) [Fran-
               ces Bennett (on CTOLMR)], 22, single,
               dau/o: S. and P. Bennett (on bk) [Sam-
               pson and Phebe Bennett (on CTOLMR)].
               Both born and lived in Alleg. Co., VA.
               PL: Alleg. Co., VA "John B. Davis res."
               Mar. by John B. Davis, Dunkard. CTOLMR
               signed on 04-08-1867 by W. M. Scott,
               D. C. Mins. Ret. says mar. on 04-10-
               1867 at John B. Davis's res. Potts
               Creek in Alleg. Co., VA. Five cent U.
               S. Inter. Revenue Certificate Stamp
               signed by Clk.

04-08-1867   (on bk) 04-11-1867 (on CTOLMR and
  # 7   Mins. Ret.)
               J. S. Deisher (on bk) [Jacob S. Deisher

(on CTOLMR)], 44, single, Born and
Lived: Botetourt Co., VA, Occup: far-
mer, s/o: P. and M. Deisher (on bk)
[Peter and Mary Deisher (on CTOLMR)];
and M. A. J. Scott (on bk) [Mary A.
J. Scott (on CTOLMR)], 18, single,
Born and Lived: Alleg. Co., VA, dau/o:
L. D. and H. Scott (on bk) [Lorenzo
D. and Harriet Scott (on CTOLMR)].
Mar. by John B. Davis, Dunkard. PL:
Alleg. Co., VA "John B. Davis res."
Three--two cent Bankcheck Stamps at-
tached and signed by Clk. CTOLMR
signed on 04-08-1867 by Jos. T. Fudge,
Clk. Mins. Ret. says mar. on 04-11-
1867 at John B. Davis's res. on Potts
Creek in Alleg. Co., VA. Consent of
Harriet Scott for Josafine Scott was
dated 04-08-1867.

04-09-1867   Abraham Wolf, 40, widower, Born and
 # 8   Lived: Alleg. Co., VA, Occup: farmer,
             s/o: I. and M. Wolf (on bk) [Isaac and
             Martha Wolf (on CTOLMR)]; and M. A.
             Arrington (on bk) [Mary Ann Arrington
             (on CTOLMR)], 35, single, B: Botetourt
             Co., VA, Lived: Alleg. Co., VA, dau/o:
             J. and J. Arrington (on bk) [James and
             Jane Arrington (on CTOLMR)]. Mar. by
             John B. Davis, Dunkard. PL: Alleg.
             Co., VA "Rich Patch." Three-two cent
             Bankcheck Stamps attached and signed
             by Clk. CTOLMR signed on 04-09-1867
             by Jos. T. Fudge, Clk. Mins. Ret.
             says mar. on 04-09-1867 at James Arrig-
             ton's res. in Rich Patch in Alleg. Co,
             VA.

04-12-1867   (on bk) 04-16-1867 (on CTOLMR and
 # 9   Mins. Ret.)
             J. R. P. Deeds (on bk) [Joseph R. P.
             Deeds (on CTOLMR)], 22, single, Occup:

farmer, s/o: Wm. and R. Deeds (on bk)
[William and Rachel Deeds (on CTOL
MR)]; and C. J. Stull (on bk) [Char-
lotte June (? Jane) Stull (on CTOL
MR)], 24, single, dau/o: Jno. and A.
Stull (on bk) [John and Ann Stull (on
CTOLMR)]. Mar. by James M. Rice,
Presb. PL: Alleg. Co., VA "Mrs. Ann
Stull's res." Three--two cent Bank-
check Stamps attached and signed by
Clk. CTOLMR signed on 04-12-1867 by
Jos. T. Fudge, Clk. Mins. Ret. says
mar. on 04-16-1867 at Mrs. Ann Stull's
res. Both were born and lived in Al-
leg. Co., Va.

04-07-1867   Jno. H. Stone (on bk) [John H. Stone
  # 10   (on CTOLMR)], 52, single, B: Bote-
              tourt Co., VA, Lived: Alleg. Co., VA,
              Occup: farmer, s/o: J. and M. Stone
              (on bk) [John and Mary Stone (on CTOL
              MR)]; and M. A. Armstrong (on bk)
              [Mary Ann Armstrong (on CTOLMR)],30,
              widow, Born and Lived: Alleg. Co., VA,
              dau/o: S. and P. Bennett (on bk)
              [Sampson and Phoebe Bennett (on CTOL
              MR)]. CTOLMR signed 12-21-1866 by
              Joseph T. Fudge, Clk. Mins. Ret. says
              mar. on 04-07-1867 at John H. Stone's
              house on Potts Creek. PL: Alleg. Co.,
              VA "John H. Stone's res. on Potts
              Creek" (on CTOLMR). Mar. by John B.
              Davis, Dunkard.

05-06-1867   (on bk)   05-07-1867 (on CTOLMR and
  # 11   Mins. Ret.)
              Jackson Nicely, 21, single, B: Alleg.
              Co., VA, Occup: farmer, s/o: J. and M.
              Nicely (on bk) [Jake and Margaret Nice
              ly (on CTOLMR)], Lived: Botetourt Co.,
              VA (on bk) [Alleg. Co., VA (on CTOL
              MR)]; and Ellen N. Nicely (on bk)

(Mar. Register Book (1) - Continued)

[Ellen Ann Nicely (on CTOLMR)], 14,
single, B: Botetourt Co., VA, Lived:
Alleg. Co., VA, dau/o: J. and E. Nicely (on bk) [John and Elizabeth Nicely
(on CTOLMR)]. Mar. by Davis M. Woods,
Presb. PL: Alleg. Co.,VA "Clifton
Forge." Five cent U. S. Inter Revenue
Certificate Stamp attached and signed
by Clk. CTOLMR signed on 05-06-1867
by Jos. T. Fudge, Clk. Mins. Ret.
says mar. on 05-07-1867 at John Nicely's res. was signed by Davis M. Wood,
L. D. [Note: L. D.--Local Deacon.]

05-15-1867   (on bk) _____ (on CTOLMR) 05-16-1867
12   (on Mins. Ret.)
              Cornelius Shea (on bk) [Cornelias
              Shea (on CTOLMR)], 45, widower, B:
              County, Cork, Ireland, Occup: laborer,
              s/o: J. and M. Shea (on bk) [M. John
              and Margaret Shea (on CTOLMR)]; and
              M. McNamarra (on bk) [Mary McNamara
              (on CTOLMR)], 24, single, B: County
              Clair, Ireland [Note: Clare Co.], dau/
              o: ___ and ___ McNamarra (on bk) [___
              McNamara (on CTOLMR)]. Both lived in
              Alleg. Co., VA. PL: Alleg. Co., VA
              "Sweet Springs." Mar. by J. H. Walt-
              ers, R. Catholic. CTOLMR signed on
              05-15-1867 by Jos. T. Fudge, Clk.
              Five cent U. S. Inter. Revenue Certi-
              ficate Stamp attached and signed by
              Clk. Mins. Ret. says mar. on 05-16-
              1867 at Sweet Springs.

05-22-1867   (on bk) 05-23-1867 Thursday (on
13   CTOLMR and Mins. Ret.)
              T. J. Smith (on bk) [Thomas Jefferson
              Smith (on CTOLMR)], 33, single, Occup:
              farmer, s/o: T. E. and E. Smith (on
              bk) [Thomas E. and Elizabeth Smith
              (on CTOLMR)]; and A. H. Damron (on bk)

- 205 -

[Ann Henrietta Damron (on CTOLMR)], 28, single, dau/o: Jos. and L. Damron (on bk) [Joseph and Lucy Damron (on CTOLMR)]. Mar. by A. Q. Flaherty, Meth. PL: Alleg. Co., VA "Jos. Damron's res." on Dunlap Creek." Both born and lived in Alleg. Co., VA. CTOLMR signed on 05-22-1867 by W. M. Scott, D. C. Mins. Ret. says mar. on 05-23-1867 at res. of bride's mother.

05-29-1867   J. L. Boswell (on bk) [John L. Boswell
14   (on CTOLMR)], 28, single, Occup: farmer, s/o: A. and S. McCallister (on bk) [Archibald and Susan McCallister (on CTOLMR--backwards--should be James H. and Maria A. Boswell)]; and E. A. McCallister (on bk) [Elizabeth A. McCallister (on CTOLMR)], 22, single, dau/o: J. H. and M. A. Boswell (on bk) [James H. and Maria A. Boswell (on CTOLMR)-backwards--should be Archibald and Susan McCallister]. Both born and lived in Alleg. Co., VA. PL: Alleg. Co., VA "Archd. McCallister res." Mar. by A. Q. Flaherty, Meth. Five cent U. S. Inter Revenue Certificate Stamp attached and signed by Clk. CTOLMR signed on 05-27-1867 by Jos. T. Fudge, Clk. Mins. Ret. says mar. on 05-29-1867 at res. of bride's father. Consent of A. M. McCallister on 05-26-1867, Alleg. Co., VA.

05-31-1867   (on bk) 06-04-1867 Tuesday (on CTOL
15   MR and Mins. Ret.)
              Wm. T. Falls (on bk) [William Thomas Falls (on CTOLMR)], 21, single, B: Botetourt Co., VA (on bk) [? Maulries Co., VA -- written over this on CTOLMR] [Note: I can't find a town or county with this spelling or any spell-

ing similar. ?Raleigh Co., W. Va. is
the closest in sound I can find. I
have no way of knowing which of the
counties is correct.], s/o: I. and S.
Falls (on bk) [Isaeh and Susan A.
Falls (on CTOLMR)], Lived: Botetourt
Co., VA, Occup: farmer; and H. A.
Hall (on bk) [Harriett Ann Hall (on
CTOLMR)], 18, single, Born and Lived:
Alleg. Co., VA, dau/o: J. H. and S.
P. Hall (on bk) [Joseph H. and Sarah
(P or T ?) Hall (on CTOLMR)]. Mar.
by John B. Davis, Dunkard. PL: Alleg.
Co., VA "Jos. H. Hall's res. on Potts
Creek." Five cent U. S. Inter Revenue
Certificate Stamp attached and signed.
CTOLMR signed 05-31-1867 by W. M.
Scott, D. C. Mins. Ret. says mar. on
06-04-1867 at Joseph H. Hall's on
Potts Creek in Alleg. Co., VA.

06-15-1867   (on bk) 06-17-1867 (on CTOLMR and
 # 16   Mins. Ret.)
             Chs. H. Bess (on bk) [Charles H. Bess
             (on CTOLMR)], 22, single, Occup: far-
             mer, s/o: H. and E. Bess (on bk)
             [Henry and Ellen Bess (on CTOLMR)];
             E. J. Tingler (on bk) [Eliza Jane
             Tingler (on CTOLMR)], 22, single, dau/
             o: J. and L. Tingler (on bk) [Jacob
             and Lucinda Tingler (on CTOLMR)].
             Both born and lived in Alleg. Co., VA.
             PL: Alleg. Co., VA "Jacob Tingler's
             res." Mar. by A. Q. Flaherty, Meth.
             CTOLMR signed on 06-15-1867 by Jos.
             T. Fudge, Clk. Mins. Ret. says mar.
             on 06-17-1867 at bride's father's res.

06-18-1867   Peter Nicely, 23, single, B: Alleg.
 # 17   Co., VA, Occup: farmer, s/o: J. M. and
             Mary Nicely (on CTOLMR)]; and Eliz.

Acres (on bk) [Elizabeth Acres (on
CTOLMR)], 18, single, B: Rockbridge
Co., VA, dau/o: M. and E. Acres (on
bk) [Minor and Edaline Acres (on
CTOLMR)]. Both lived in Alleg. Co.,
VA. Mar. by James M. Rice, Presb.
PL: Alleg. Co., VA "Minor Acres's
res." CTOLMR signed on 06-15-1867 by
Jos. T. Fudge, Clk. Mins. Ret. says
mar. on 06-18-1867 at M. Acres's res.

08-10-1867   (on bk)   07-10-1867 (on CTOLMR and
  # 18   Mins. Ret.)
              Wm. Oiler (on bk) [William Oiler (on
              CTOLMR)], 21, single, Born and Lived:
              Alleg. Co., VA, Occup: farmer, s/o:
              J. and R. Oiler (on bk) [John and
              Rebecca Oiler (on CTOLMR)]; and N. W.
              Knighton (on bk) [Nancy Wyatt Nighton
              (on CTOLMR)], 19, single, B: Alleg.
              Co., VA (on bk) [____ (on CTOLMR)],
              Lived: Alleg. Co., VA (on bk) [Green-
              brier Co., W.VA. (on CTOLMR)], dau/o:
              Wm. and S. F. Knighton (on bk) [Will-
              iam and Sarah Frances Nighton (on
              CTOLMR)]. Mar. by A. Q. Flaherty.
              PL: Alleg. Co., VA "Covington." CTOL
              MR signed on 07-10-1867 by Jos. T.
              Fudge, Clk. Mins. Ret. says mar. on
              07-10-1867 at parsonage in Covington.
              Consent has Salt Sulphur Springs writ-
              ten on back with other writing torn
              off.
              "July 9, 1867
                  I this day give my son William
              Oiler the Privelage to get married to
              whom he Pleases this 9th Day of July
              1867.
                              R. B. Oiler
                              William H. Oiler"
              "To the Clerk of Alleghany County,
              Virginia

(Mar. Register Book (1) - Continued)

      We the undersigned, the father
and Mother of <u>Nancy Wyatt and Martha
Susan Nighton</u>, our daughters, do hereby give our consent, that <u>Sampson
Craft</u> and <u>William Oiler</u> marry the
said daughters, that is to say <u>Samp-
son Craft</u> to marry <u>Martha Susan</u> and
<u>William Oiler</u> to marry <u>Nancy Wyatt
Nighten</u>.
      Given under our hands this 6th
day of July 1867.
        William (his X mark) Nighten
  Sarah Frances (her X mark) Nighten"
"State of West Virginia/
      Greenbrier County_/ --ss
      Township of the White Sulphur
      Springs in said County
      I do hereby certify that William
Nighten and Sarah Frances Nighten
personally appeared before me a Justice for the county, State of West
Virginia, and acknowledged that the
writing hereto annexed is their sig-
natures and that the above certificate is their act.
      Given under my hand this 6th day
of July 1867.
        John Bowyer [? Calwik]
        Justice Pc."
[Note: On back of previous statements
is statements below.]
"July the 10th 1867
      I John Craft do this day give
consent for my son <u>Sampson Craft</u> to
Join in mariage to <u>Martha Susin Nigh-
ton</u>.
      Given under my hand this 10th day
of July 1867.
        John (his X mark) Craft
      Elizabeth (her X mark) Craft."
"Alleghany County Court Clerk's Office
        10th July 1867

- 209 -

This day personally appeared before me Geo. W. (? Horace) and made
oath that the above certificate was
signed & acknowledged by John Craft
and Elizabeth his wife as their act
and in his presents.
Teste, Joseph T. Fudge, Clk."
[Author's Note: See also # 20 for
07-10-1867 Sampson Craft and M. S.
Knighton.
I suspect this was a double wedding since all this paperwork was
together. Both CTOLMR's were side by
side and the paper was not separated
between them.]

08-17-1867   (on bk) 07-17-1867 (on CTOLMR and
19   Mins. Ret.)
G. W. Huddleston (on bk) [George W.
Huddleston (on CTOLMR)], 24, single,
B: Alleg. Co., VA, Occup: farmer, s/o:
A. J. and L. Huddleston (on bk) [Abra-
ham J. and Leamah Huddleston (on CTOL
MR)]; and H. A. Ham (on bk) [Hester
Ann Ham (on CTOLMR)], 26, single, B:
Rockbridge Co., VA (on bk) [Rocking-
ham Co., VA (on CTOLMR)], dau/o: Wm.
and E. Ham (on bk) [William and Elizabeth Ham (on CTOLMR)]. Both lived in
Alleg. Co., VA. PL: Alleg. Co., VA
"Wilson's Creek." Mar. by A. Q. Flaherty, Meth. Ten cent U. S. Inter.
Revenue Power Of Atty. Stamp attached
and signed by "JTF, Clk 12th July
1867" and has picture of George Washington on it. [Author's Note: I
have no idea what this means except
the Clerk of Court thinks it means
that some fee was paid and this shows
it was collected.] CTOLMR signed on
07-12-1867 by Jos. T. Fudge, Clk.
Mins. Ret. says mar. on 07-17-1867 at

res. of bride's mother. Consent and
age oath given by Elisabeth Ham on
07-13-1867 with Wit. note of A. Q.
Flaherty that told Clk. it was O.K.
to grant Lic. to couple.

07-10-1867   Sampson Craft, 18, single, B: Alleg.
20   Co., VA, Lived: Alleg. Co., VA, Occup:
              farmer, s/o: J. and E. Craft (on bk)
              [John and Elizabeth Craft (on CTOL
              MR)]; and M. S. Knighton (on bk) [Mar-
              tha Ann Knighten (on CTOLMR)], 18,
              single, B: Alleg. Co., VA (on bk) [___
              (on CTOLMR)], Lived: Alleg. Co., VA
              (on bk) [Greenbrier Co., W.VA. (on
              CTOLMR)], dau/o: W. and S. Knighton
              (on bk) [William and Sarah Frances
              Nighten (on CTOLMR)]. Mar. by A. Q.
              Flaherty, Meth. PL: Alleg. Co., VA
              "Covington." CTOLMR signed on 07-10-
              1867 by Jos. T. Fudge, Clk. Mins.
              Ret. says mar. on 07-10-1867 at par-
              sonage in Covington. [Author's Note:
              I suspect this is a double wedding.
              SEE ALSO # 18 07-10-1867 Wm. Oiler and
              Nancy Wyatt Nighton for consent and
              oaths for Sampson and Martha. Paper-
              work for both these marriages was to-
              gether and attached.]

08-05-1867   (on bk)   __-__-____   (on CTOLMR)
21   08-15-1867 (on Mins. Ret.)
              Wm. Shumaker (on bk) [William Shumaker
              (on CTOLMR)], 48, widower, B: Rock-
              bridge Co., VA, Lived: Alleg. Co., VA,
              Occup: farmer, s/o: D. and J. Shumaker
              (on bk) [David and Jemima Shumaker (on
              CTOLMR)]; and M. A. Grubbs (on bk)
              [Mary A. Grubbs (on CTOLMR)], 25, sin-
              gle, B: Appomattox Co., VA, Lived: Al-
              leg. Co., VA, dau/o: ___ Grubbs. PL:
              Alleg. Co., VA (on bk) [_____ (on

CTOLMR)]. Mar. by A. Q. Flaherty,
Meth. CTOLMR signed on 08-05-1867 by
Jos. T. Fudge, Clk. Mins. Ret. says
mar. on 08-15-1867 at parsonage in
Covington, VA. Age oath for <u>Mary</u> by
Martin W. Holmes on 08-05-1867, Teste
Joseph T. Fudge, Clk.

09-05-1867 Thursday
22 <u>L. G. Wolf</u> (on bk) [<u>Liberty Greene
Wolf</u> (on CTOLMR)], 20, single, Occup:
farmer, s/o: J. R. and M. A. E. Wolf
(on bk) [Jacob R. and Maria A. E.
Wolf (on CTOLMR)]; and <u>V. A. Dew</u> (on
bk) [<u>Victoria Almira Dew</u> (on CTOLMR)],
19, single, dau/o: A. and S. Dew (on
bk) [Absolem and Sarah Dew (on CTOL
MR)]. Both born and lived in Alleg.
Co., VA. PL: Alleg. Co., VA "A. Dew
res." Mar. by John B. Davis, Dunkard.
Five cent U. S. Inter. Revenue Certificate Stamp attached and signed by
Mins. CTOLMR signed on 09-03-1867 by
W. M. Scott, D. C. Mins. Ret. says
mar. on 09-05-1867 at Absolem Dew's
res. Potts Creek in Alleg. Co. "I
authorize the minister who celebrates
this marriage to affix this (?micis-
sary) 5 ¢ stamp. W. M. Scott, Dept.
Clk."

09-05-1867 (on bk) 10-01-1867 Tuesday (on
23 CTOLMR and Mins. Ret.)
<u>Jos. Craft</u> (on bk) [<u>Joseph Craft</u> (on
CTOLMR)], 22, single, Occup: farmer,
s/o: J. and B. Craft (on bk) [John
and Betsey Craft (on CTOLMR)]; and <u>R.
E. Bennett</u> (on bk) [<u>Rebecca E. Bennett</u>
(on CTOLMR)], 17, single, dau/o: Wm.
and C. Bennett (on bk) [William and
Catharine Bennett (on CTOLMR)]. Both
born and lived in Alleg. Co., VA. PL:

Alleg. Co., VA "Rich Patch." Mar. by
John B. Davis, Dunkard. CTOLMR sign-
ed on 09-03-1867 by W. M. Scott, D. C.
Mins. Ret. says mar. on 10-01-1867 at
John B. Davis's res. on Potts Creek.

09-05-1867   Thursday
  # 24   L. H. Williams (on bk) [Lewis Hazel
              Williams (on CTOLMR)], 34, single, B:
              Bath Co., VA, Lived: Bath Co., VA,
              Occup: farmer, s/o: L. and N. Williams
              (on bk) [Lewis and Nancy Williams (on
              CTOLMR)]; and Alice Mann, 18, single,
              Born and Lived: Alleg. Co., VA, dau/o:
              A. G. and C. Mann (on bk) [Archibald
              G. and Clemantine Mann (on CTOLMR)].
              Mar. by James M. Rice, Presb. PL: Al-
              leg. Co., VA "A. Mann's res. Jackson
              River." CTOLMR signed on 09-05-1867
              by W. M. Scott, D. C. Mins. Ret. says
              mar. on 09-05-1867 at A. Mann's res.

09-14-1867   (on bk) 09-23-1867 Monday (on
  # 25   CTOLMR and Mins. Ret.)
              Jacob Tingler, 84, widower, B: Alleg.
              Co., VA (on bk) [Hudleston VA (on
              CTOLMR) (Note: Huddleston is in Bed-
              ford Co., VA)], Lived: Alleg. Co., VA,
              Occup: farmer, s/o: M. and R. Tingler
              (on bk) [Michael and (?Ruthy) Tingler
              (on CTOLMR)]; and B. Fogle (on bk)
              [Barbara Fogle (on CTOLMR)], 65, widow,
              Born and Lived: Alleg. Co., VA, dau/o:
              A. and M. Fogle (on bk) [Adam and Mary
              Fogle (on CTOLMR)]. Mar. by John B.
              Davis, Dunkard. PL: Alleg. Co., VA
              "Rich Patch." CTOLMR signed on 09-14-
              1867 by W. M. Scott, D. C. Mins. Ret.
              says mar. on 09-23-1867 at Jacob Ting-
              ler's in Rich Patch in Alleg. Co., VA.

(Mar. Register Book (1) - Continued)

09-19-1867   R. R. Ailstock (on bk) [Robert R.
26   Ailstock (on CTOLMR)], 21, single, B:
              Rockbridge Co., VA, Lived: Alleg. Co.,
              VA, Occup: farmer, s/o: J. and P. Ail-
              stock (on bk) [John and Peggy Ailstock
              (on CTOLMR)]; and S. E. Cave (on bk)
              [Sarah Elizabeth Cave (? Case) (?Car)
              (on CTOLMR)], 29, widow, dau/o: L. and
              S. A. Brown (on bk) [Lemuel and Sarah
              Ann Brown (on CTOLMR)], B: Rockbridge
              Co., VA, Lived: Alleg. Co., VA. PL:
              Alleg. Co., VA "Covington." Mar. by
              James M. Rice, Presb. Mins. Ret. says
              mar. on 09-19-1867 at Old Crawford
              house near C. Shirkey's. CTOLMR sign-
              ed on 09-19-1867 by Jos. T. Fudge, Clk.
              Note: "The minister will place stamp
              when this ____ I have mine." [Author's
              Note: I believe this refers to Five
              Cent U. S. Inter. Revenue Certificate
              Stamp that was attached on forms dur-
              ing this period and believes is to
              show that some fee had been paid.]

09-24-1867   (on bk) 09-26-1867 (on CTOLMR and
27   Mins. Ret.)
              T. F. Kimberlin (on bk) [Thadeus F.
              Kimberlin (on CTOLMR)], 24, single, B:
              Smith Co., Tennessee, Occup: farmer,
              s/o: Wm. and E. Kimberlin (on bk)
              [William and Elizabeth Kimberlin (on
              CTOLMR)]; and N. E. Helmintoller (on
              bk) [Nancy E. Helmintoller (on CTOL
              MR)], 23, single, B: Alleg. Co., VA,
              dau/o: P. and P. Helmantoller (on bk)
              [Peter and Polly Helmintoller (on
              CTOLMR)]. Both lived in Alleg. Co.,
              VA. PL: Alleg. Co., VA "Peter Helmin-
              toller's res." CTOLMR signed on 09-
              24-1867 by Jos. T. Fudge, Clk. Mins.
              Ret. says mar. on 09-26-1867 at Peter
              Helmintoller's res. in Alleg. Co., VA

(Mar. Register Book (1) - Continued)

and was signed John B. Davis, Dunkard.
Age oath for <u>Nancy</u> by <u>Thadeus F. Kim-
berlin</u> on 09-24-1867 Teste Jos. T.
Fudge, Clk.

09-26-1867 Thursday
 # 28   P. H. <u>Sharp</u> (on bk) [<u>Patrick Henry
           Sharp</u> (on CTOLMR)], 27, single, B:
           Louisa Co., VA, Lived: Alleg. Co., VA
           (on bk) [Albemarle Co., VA (on CTOL
           MR)], Occup: carpenter, s/o: D. and
           L. Sharp (on bk) [David and Louisa
           Sharp (on CTOLMR)]; and <u>S. M. Nichols</u>
           (on bk) [<u>Sarah Mildred Nichol</u> (on
           CTOLMR)], 21, single, B: Rockbridge
           Co., VA, Lived: Alleg. Co., VA, dau/o:
           D. and M. A. Nichols (on bk) [David
           and Mary A. Nichol (on CTOLMR)]. PL:
           Alleg. Co., VA "Jackson's River."
           Mar. by James M. Rice, Presb. CTOLMR
           signed on 09-26-1867 by W. M. Scott,
           D. C. Mins. Ret. says mar. on 09-26-
           1867 at Mrs. Nichols res. Five cent
           U. S. Inter. Revenue Certificate Stamp
           attached.

10-01-1867 (on bk) 10-02-1867 (on CTOLMR)
 # 29   10-03-1867 (on Mins. Ret.)
           <u>Jesse Carter</u>, 24, single, Occup: far-
           mer, s/o: L. and M. Carter (on bk)
           [Lemuel and Martha Carter (on CTOLMR)];
           and <u>A. P. Harmon</u> (on bk) [<u>Arrena P.
           Harman</u> (on CTOLMR)], 20, single, dau/o:
           Thos. and P. Harmon (on bk) [Thomas
           and Polly Harman (on CTOLMR)]. PL:
           Alleg. Co., VA "Thos. Harman's." Mar.
           by John B. Davis, Dunkard. Both born
           and lived in Alleg. Co., VA. CTOLMR
           signed on 10-01-1867 by Jos. T. Fudge,
           Clk. Mins. Ret. says mar. on 10-03-
           1867 at Thomas Harmon's on Snake Run
           in Alleg. Co., VA. Consent of Thomas

- 215 -

(Mar. Register Book (1) - Continued)

Harman for <u>Arreny P. Harman</u> on 10-01-
1867, Wit. Geo. W. Wilkerson. Oath
of <u>Jesse Carter</u> of Thomas Harman's
acknowledgement on 10-01-1867, Teste
Jos. T. Fudge, Clk.

10-21-1867   (on bk) ___-___-____ (on CTOLMR)
  # 30   11-05-1867 (on Mins. Ret.)
             M. J. Arritt (on bk) [<u>Michael J. Aritt</u>
             (on CTOLMR)], 24, single, Occup: far-
             mer, s/o: J. and E. Arritt (on bk)
             [John and Elizabeth Aritt (on CTOL
             MR)]; and <u>M. E. Arritt</u> (on bk) [<u>Mary</u>
             <u>E. Arritt</u> (on CTOLMR)], 21, single,
             dau/o: M. and E. B. Arritt (on bk)
             [Michael and Ellen B. Arritt (on CTOL
             MR)]. Both born and lived in Alleg.
             Co., VA. PL: Alleg. Co., VA (on bk)
             [____ (on CTOLMR)]. Mar. by John B.
             Davis, Dunkard. CTOLMR signed on 10-
             21-1867 by Jos. T. Fudge, Clk. Mins.
             Ret. says mar. on 11-05-1867 at Mich-
             ael Aritt's on Potts Creek in Alleg.
             Co., VA. Five cent U. S. Inter. Rev-
             enue Certificate Stamp attached.

10-21-1867   (on bk) ___-___-____ (on CTOLMR)
  # 31   11-05-1867 (on Mins. Ret.)
             J. H. McDivet (on bk) [<u>John H. (McC-</u>
             <u>devitt ?) (? McCderitt)</u> (on CTOLMR)],
             24, single, B: Monroe Co., VA (now
             W. VA), Occup: farmer, s/o: N. and L.
             McDivet (on bk) [Neal and Lucinda
             (McCdevitt?) (?McCderitt) (on CTOL
             MR)]; and <u>M. A. Rayhill</u> (on bk) [<u>Mary</u>
             <u>J. Rayhill</u> (on CTOLMR)], 24, single,
             B: Alleg. Co., VA, dau/o: A. and E.
             Rayhill (on bk) [Alexander and Eliza-
             beth Rayhill (on CTOLMR)]. Both liv-
             ed in Alleg. Co., VA. PL: Alleg. Co.,
             VA (on bk) [____(on CTOLMR)]. Mar.

by John B. Davis, Dunkard. Five cent
U. S. Inter Revenue Certificate Stamp
attached. CTOLMR signed on 10-21-
1867 by Jos. T. Fudge, Clk. Mins.
Ret. says mar. on 11-05-1867 at Harriett Pinnell's on Potts Creek in Alleg. Co., VA.

10-23-1867 H. P. Mason (on bk) [Horatio P. Mason
 # 32   (on CTOLMR)], 27, single, B: Louisa
           Co., VA, Lived: Orange Co., VA, Occup:
           farmer, s/o: C. R. and D. W. Mason;
           and S. B. Anthony (on bk) [Samuella
           B. Anthony (on CTOLMR)], 22, single,
           B: Orange Co., VA (on bk) [Botetourt
           Co., VA (on CTOLMR)], Lived: Alleg.
           Co., VA, dau/o: S. B. and C. P. Antho-
           ny (on bk) [Sam'l. B. and Chare. P.
           Anthony (? Charlotte P.) (on CTOLMR)].
           PL: Alleg. Co., VA "res. of late
           Robert Irvine." Mar. by James M.
           Rice, Presb. Five cent U. S. Inter.
           Revenue Certificate Stamp attached
           signed by J. M. R. CTOLMR signed on
           10-23-1867 by Jos. T. Fudge, Clk.
           Mins. Ret. says mar. on 10-23-1867 at
           res. of late R. Irvine.

11-02-1867 (on bk) 11-07-1867 Thursday (on
 # 33   CTOLMR) 11-06-1867 (on Mins. Ret.)
           J. L. A. Bush (on bk) [John Lee Allen
           Bush (on CTOLMR)], 21, single, Born
           and Lived: Alleg. Co., VA, Occup: far-
           mer, s/o: A. and P. Bush (on bk) [Adam
           and Peggy Bush (on CTOLMR)]; and N. C.
           Kimberlin (on bk) [Nancy Caroline Kim-
           berlin (on CTOLMR)], 26, single, B:
           Smith Co., Tennessee, dau/o: Wm. and
           E. Kimberlin (on bk) [William and Bet-
           sey Jane Kimberlin (on CTOLMR)], Liv-
           ed: Alleg. Co., VA. Mar. by John B.

(Mar. Register Book (1) - Continued)

Davis, Dunkard. PL: Alleg. Co., VA
"Washington Wolf's res." CTOLMR sign-
ed 11-02-1867 by W. M. Scott, Clk.
Mins. Ret. says mar. on 11-06-1867 at
George W. Wolf's on Potts Creek in
Alleg. Co.

12-12-1867   J. T. Plymale (on bk) [John Taylor
34   Plymale (on CTOLMR)], 21, single,
             Occup: farmer, s/o: W. B. and E. F.
             Plymale (on bk) [William B. and Eliz-
             abeth Frances Plymale (on CTOLMR)];
             and E. F. Byer (on bk) [Emma Francis
             Byer (on CTOLMR)], 20, single, dau/o:
             P. and P. Byer (on bk) [Peter and
             (?Patsey) Byer (on CTOLMR)]. Both
             born and lived in Alleg. Co., VA. PL:
             Alleg. Co., VA "Peter Byer's res. on
             Potts Creek." Mar. by James M. Rice,
             Presb. CTOLMR signed on 12-02-1867
             by W. M. Scott, D. C. Mins. Ret. says
             mar. on 12-12-1867 at bride's father's
             house. Five cent U. S. Inter. Revenue
             Certificate Stamp attached and signed
             J. M. R.

**** Found in with the above Lic. but apparently
      having nothing to do with the above***

             "The Clerk of the County Court of Al-
             leghany is authorised to Grant Marri-
             age Licens to my daughter Mary Ann
             Sidney and Geo. W. Plymale. December
             January 23rd 1868
                               Pet. Byer
             Attest Charles P. Byer"
             "Alleghany County Court Clerk's Office
                        23rd Jany 1868
                This day personally appeared Chs. D.
             Byer & made oath that Peter Byer sign-
             ed & Acknowledged the within certifi-
             cate in his presence.

- 218 -

(Mar. Register Book (1) - Continued)

> Joseph T. Fudge, Clk."
> [Author's Note: No one knows if there
> was a marriage Lic. for this or not.
> One was not found in the files and
> there is no other records.]

12-24-1867 (on bk) 12-26-1867 (on CTOLMR and
35 Mins. Ret.)
Wm. Craft (on bk) [William Craft (on
CTOLMR)], 21, single, Born and Lived:
Alleg. Co., VA, Occup: farmer, s/o:
A. J. and H. Nicely (on book--was put
backwards and was done same on CTOLMR)
[Wm. S. Craft (on bk) William and
Sarah Craft (on CTOLMR)]; and S. E.
Nicely (on bk) [Sarah Elizabeth Nicely
(on CTOLMR)], 17, single, Born and
Lived: Alleg. Co., VA, dau/o: Wm. and
S. Craft (on book--was put backwards
and was done same on CTOLMR)) [A. J.
and H. Nicely (on bk) (Andrew Jackson
and Helcy Nicely (on CTOLMR)]. PL:
Alleg. Co., VA "Andr. J. Nicely's res."
Mar. by Davis M. Wood, Meth. CTOLMR
signed on 12-24-1867 by W. M. Scott,
D. C. Mins. Ret. says mar. on 12-26-
1867 at Andrew J. Nicely res. and was
signed Davis M. Wood, L. D. M. E. C.
S. [L.D.--Local Deacon].

01-15-1868 (on bk) 01-28-1868 Tuesday (on
36 CTOLMR and Mins. Ret.)
Eli Persinger, 46, widower, Born and
Lived: Alleg. Co., VA, Occup: farmer,
s/o: ___ and Sah Persinger (on bk) [__
and Sarah Persinger (on CTOLMR)]; and
S. A. Hamlett (on bk) [Sarah (? L. or
S.) Hamlett (on CTOLMR)], 34, single,
B: Rockbridge Co., VA, Lived: Alleg.
Co., VA, dau/o: H. and M. Hamlett (on
bk) [Henry and Mary Hamlett (on CTOL
MR)]. PL: Alleg. Co., VA "William

Sulender's res. in Rich Patch." Mar. by John B. Davis, Dunkard. CTOLMR signed on 01-15-1868 by Jos. T. Fudge, Clk. Mins. Ret. says mar. on 01-28-1868 at William Sulender's in Rich Patch in Alleg. Co., VA.

01-29-1868 # 37   G. W. Paxton (on bk) [George W. Paxton (on CTOMLR)], 25, single, B: Botetourt Co., VA, Lived: Alleg. Co., VA, Occup: farmer, s/o: J. and M. Paxton (on bk) [James and Mary Paxton (on CTOLMR)]; and J. C. Plymale (on bk) [Jennetta C. Plymale (on CTOLMR)], 18, single, B: Alleg. Co., VA, Lived: Alleg. Co., VA, dau/o: Wm. B. and E. Plymale (on bk) [Wm. B. and Elizabeth Plymale (on CTOLMR)]. PL: Alleg. Co., VA "Eliz. Plymale res." Mar. by John B. Davis, Dunkard. CTOLMR signed on 01-25-1868 by Jos. T. Fudge, Clk. Mins. Ret. says mar. on 01-29-1868 at Elizabeth Plymale's on Potts Creek in Alleg. Co, VA. Oath of Plymale acknowledgement by (?), Teste Jos. T. Fudge, Clk. Consent of Elizabeth (her X mark) Plymale, Wit. William Helmintoller. [Note: Oath was probably made by Helmintoller since he was the Wit.]

03-07-1868 # 37 ½   (on bk) 02-07-1868 (on CTOLMR) 03-07-1868 (on Mins. Ret.) John Roper, 22, single, Occup: _____ (on bk and CTOLMR), s/o: ____ (on bk) [____ and Milly Moely? (?Mosely) (on CTOLMR)]; and Ann Davis, 22, single, dau/o: ____ (on bk and CTOLMR). PL: Alleg. Co., VA "Covington." Both were born and lived in Alleg. Co., VA. Mar. by James M. Rice, Presb. Five cent U. S. Inter. Revenue Certificate Stamp

(Mar. Register Book (1) - Continued)

attached and signed JMR Mar/68. CTOL
MR signed on 02-06-1868 by Jos. T.
Fudge, Clk. Mins. Ret. says mar. on
03-07-1868 in Covington, VA.

03-24-1868   (on bk) 03-26-1868 Thursday (on
38   CTOLMR and Mins. Ret.)
              H. A. Hoke (on bk) [Henry Alexander
              Hoke (on CTOLMR)], 21, single, Born
              and Lived: Monroe Co., VA (now W.VA.),
              Occup: farmer, s/o: C. and M. Hoke (on
              bk) [Christopher and Malinda Hoke (on
              CTOLMR)]; and M. C. Hoke (on bk) [Mary
              Catharine Hoke (on CTOLMR)], 18, sin-
              gle, B: Monroe Co., VA (now W.VA.),
              Lived: Alleg. Co., VA, dau/o: Wm. and
              C. Hoke (on bk) [William and Catharine
              Hoke (on CTOLMR)]. PL: Alleg. Co.,
              VA "William Hoke's, Ogley's Creek."
              Mar. by A. Q. Flaherty, Meth. CTOLMR
              signed on 03-24-1868 by W. M. Scott,
              D. C. Mins. Ret. says mar. on 03-26-
              1868 at Wm. Hoke res.

03-31-1868   P. M. Pence (on bk) [Peter M. Pence
39   (on CTOLMR)], 27, single, Occup: Sad-
              dler (on bk) [CTOLMR also says he was
              a shoemaker], s/o: P. and N. Pence (on
              bk) [Peter and Nelly Pence (on CTOL
              MR)]; and M. C. Myers (on bk) [Margar-
              et C. Myers (on CTOLMR)], 17, single,
              dau/o: G. and J. Myers (on bk) [George
              and Julia Myers (on CTOLMR)]. PL: Al-
              leg. Co., VA "Geo. Myer's res." Mar.
              by A. Q. Flaherty, Meth. CTOLMR sign-
              ed on 03-31-1868 by Jos. T. Fudge, Clk.
              Mins. Ret. says mar. on 03-31-1868 at
              Geo. Myer's res. both born and lived
              in Alleg. Co., VA.

04-27-1868   (on bk) 04-28-1868 (on CTOLMR and
40   Mins. Ret.)

(Mar. Register Book (1) - Continued)

I. Paxton (on bk) [Isaac Paxton (on
CTOLMR)], 21, single, B: Craig Co.,
VA, Lived: Alleg. Co., VA, Occup: far-
mer, s/o: J. and M. Paxton (on bk)
[James and Mary Paxton (on CTOLMR)];
and Sarah Bowyer, 24, widow, B: Alleg.
Co., VA, Lived: Alleg. Co., VA, dau/o:
L. W. and M. Haynes (on bk) [Lemuel
W. and May (? Mary) Haynes (on CTOL
MR)]. PL: Alleg. Co., VA "John Bow-
yer, Esq. res." Mar. by John B. Davis,
Dunkard. CTOLMR signed on 04-27-1868
by Jos. T. Fudge, Clk. Mins. Ret.
says mar. on 04-28-1868 at John Bow-
yer's on Potts Creek in Alleg. Co.,
VA.

04-30-1868   (on bk)   __-__-____ (on CTOLMR)
40 ½   04-30-1868 (on Mins. Ret.)
William H. Talliferro (on bk) [Willis
H. Talliaferro (on CTOLMR)], 23, sin-
gle; and Catherine Jordan (on bk)
[Catharine Jordan (on CTOLMR)], 21,
single. Both lived in Alleg. Co., VA.
PL: Alleg. Co., VA (on bk) [_____
(on CTOLMR)]. Mar. by James M. Rice,
Presb. CTOLMR signed on 04-30-1868
by Jos. T. Fudge, Clk. Mins. Ret.
says mar. on 04-30-1868 in Covington,
VA. Five cent U. S. Inter. Revenue
Certificate Stamp attached and signed
JMR Apr.30/86. [Note: There was no
other information on the records.]

05-04-1868   (on bk)   05-05-1868 (on CTOLMR and
42   Mins. Ret.)
A. J. Sively (on bk) [Andrew J. Sively
(on CTOLMR)], 51, widower, B: Greenbrier Co., VA (now W.VA.), Lived: Alleg. Co., VA, Occup: farmer, s/o: G.
and M. Sively (on bk) [George and Mary

- 222 -

Sively (on CTOLMR)]; and <u>C. E. Wolf</u>
(on book) [Charlotte E. Wolf (on CTOL
MR)], 40, single, Born and Lived: Alleg. Co., VA, dau/o: J. and S. Wolf
(on book) [John and Sarah Wolf (on
CTOLMR)]. PL: Alleg. Co., VA "res.
of John Wolf, deceased." Mar. by John
B. Davis, Dunkard. Five cent U. S.
Inter. Revenue Certificate Stamp attached signed JBD. CTOLMR signed on
05-04-1868 by Jos. T. Fudge, Clk.
Mins. Ret. says mar. on 05-05-1868 at
the former res. of Jno. Wolf, deceased, on Potts Creek. Age oath for
<u>Charlotte</u> given by Capt. A. Given,
Teste Jos. T. Fudge, Clk. on 05-04-
1868.

05-04-1868   (on bk) __-__-____ (on CTOLMR)
  # 42   05-07-1868 (on Mins. Ret.)
<u>J. A. Andrews</u> (on book) [<u>John A. An-
drews</u> (on CTOLMR)], 44, single (on bk)
[widower (on CTOLMR)], Born and Lived:
Alleg. Co., VA, Occup: farmer, s/o:
J. and J. Andrews (on book) [John and
Jane Andrews (on CTOLMR)]; and <u>Va.
Thomas</u> (on book) [<u>Virginia Thomas</u> (on
CTOLMR)], 25, single, B: Botetourt
Co., VA, Lived: Alleg. Co., VA, dau/o:
____ & ____ Thomas (on book & CTOLMR).
PL: Alleg. Co., VA (on book) [____
(on CTOLMR)]. Mar. by John B. Davis,
Dunkard. Five cent U. S. Inter. Rev-
enue Certificate Stamp attached sign-
ed by JBD. CTOLMR signed on 05-04-
1868 by Jos. T. Fudge, Clk. Mins. Ret.
says mar. on 05-07-1868 at <u>John A.
Andrew's</u> on Potts Creek in Alleg. Co.,
VA. Age oath for <u>Virginia</u> by Jacob
Arritt on 05-04-1868, Teste Jos. T.
Fudge, Clk.

(Mar. Register Book (1) - Continued)

05-24-1868   (on bk)   05-26-1868 (on CTOLMR and
  # 43   Mins. Ret.)
              S. Fridley (on bk) [Sampson Fridly
              (on CTOLMR)],21, single, Occup: far-
              mer, s/o: J. and J. A. Fridley (on bk)
              [Jesse and Julia A. Fridly (on CTOL
              MR)]; and C. A. Humphries (on bk)
              [Charlotte A. Humphries (on CTOLMR)],
              20, single, dau/o: O. and C. Humphries
              (on bk) [Oliver and Caroline Humphries
              (on CTOLMR)].   Both born and lived in
              Alleg. Co., VA. PL: Alleg. Co., VA
              "George W. Tingler res.." Mar. by
              Aaron Boon, Meth. Mar. Lic. signed by
              the step-father of the bride on 05-25-
              1868 signed George W. Tingler. CTOLMR
              signed on 05-24-1868 by Jos. T. Fudge,
              Clk. Mins. Ret. says mar. on 05-26-
              1868 at res. of Geo. W. Tingler in Al-
              leg. Co. Five cent U. S. inter. Rev-
              enue Certificate Stamp attached and
              signed by A. Boon on May 26, 1868.
              [Author's Note: Mar. Lic. form seems
              to have been used for consent. There
              were two forms: Mar. Lic. and CTOLMR.]

05-26-1868   (on bk)   05-27-1868 (on CTOLMR and
  # 44   Mins.Ret.)
              Beale Hook, 36, single, B: Albemarle
              Co., VA (on bk) [Alleg. Co., VA (on
              CTOLMR)], Lived: Alleg. Co., VA, Occup:
              farmer, s/o: S. and E. Hook (on bk)
              [Stephen and Elizabeth Hook (on CTOL
              MR)]; and S. R. Eagon (on bk) [Sallie
              R. Eagon (on CTOLMR)], 31, single, B:
              Alleg. Co., VA (on bk) [Albemarle Co.,
              VA (on CTOLMR)], dau/o: J. and M. Eagon
              (on bk) [John and Mildred Eagon (on
              CTOLMR)], Lived: Alleg. Co., VA.   PL:
              Alleg. Co., VA "Mrs. W. W. Paxton's
              res." Mar. by James M. Rice, Presb.
              CTOLMR signed on 05-26-1868 by Jos. T.

Fudge, Clk. Five cent U. S. Inter.
Revenue Certificate Stamp attached
and signed JMR. Mins. Ret. says mar.
on 05-27-1868 at res. of Mrs. W. W.
Paxton.

06-04-1868   J. Donovan (on bk) [James Donovan (on
45   CTOLMR)], 28, single, B: County Cork,
              Ireland, Lived: Alleg. Co., VA, Occup:
              farmer, s/o: Wm. and A. Donovan (on
              bk) [William and Ann Donovan (on CTOL
              MR)]; and Rebecca Goff, 34, single,
              B: Monroe Co., VA (now W.VA.), Lived:
              Alleg. Co., VA, dau/o: J. and H. Goff
              (on bk) [John and Harriet Goff (on
              CTOLMR)]. PL: Alleg. Co., VA "Cov-
              ington." Mar. by S. B. Dolly, Meth.
              Handwritten CTOLMR by D. C. CTOLMR
              signed on 06-04-1868 by W. M. Scott,
              D. C. Mins. Ret. says mar. on 06-04-
              1868 in Covington in Alleg. Co., VA.
              Five cent U. S. Inter. Revenue Certifi-
              cate Stamp attached and signed by SBD.

06-26-1868   (on bk) 06-23-1868 (on CTOLMR and
46   Mins. Ret.)
              W. K. Chapman (on bk) [William K, Chap-
              man (on CTOLMR)], 28, single, B: Staun-
              ton, Augusta Co., VA, Lived: Alleg.
              Co., VA, Occup: farmer (on bk) [School
              Teacher (on CTOLMR)], s/o: A. and M.
              E. Chapman (on bk) [Alfred and May
              (? Mary) E. Chapman (on CTOLMR)]; and
              M. S. Haynes (on bk) [M. J. S. Haynes
              (on CTOLMR)], 21, single, B: Alleg.
              Co., VA, Lived: Alleg. Co., VA, dau/o:
              J. P. and E. S. Haynes (on bk) [John
              P. and Elizabeth S. Haynes (on CTOLMR)].
              PL: Alleg. Co., VA "John P. Haynes res."
              Mar. by James M. Rice, Presb. CTOLMR
              signed on 06-22-1868 by Jos. T. Fudge,
              Clk. Mins. Ret. says mar. on 06-23-

1868 at J. P. Haynes res. Five cent
U. S. Inter. Revenue Certificate Stamp
attached and signed JMR. Consent has
Mary Jane Sarah Haynes and was dated
on 06-22-1868 and signed John P. Haynes, Attest W. A. Haynes. Age oath
for Mary by W. A. Haynes was signed
Jos. T. Fudge, Clk. on 06-22-1868.

07-01-1868   (on bk)   07-08-1868 (on CTOLMR and
47   Mins. Ret.)
              F. P. Sizer (on bk) [Fielding P. Sizer
              (on CTOLMR)], 62, widower, B: Rock-
              bridge Co., VA, Lived: Alleg. Co., VA,
              Occup: farmer, s/o: J. and C. Sizer
              (on bk) [John and Catharine Sizer (on
              CTOLMR)]; and M. C. Cummings (on bk)
              [May K. C. Cummings (on CTOLMR)], 38,
              single, Born and Lived: Alleg. Co., VA,
              dau/o: A. and R. Cummings (on bk) [Ab-
              solam and Rebecca Cummings (on CTOL
              MR)]. PL: Alleg. Co., VA "Castle Run.'
              Mar. by John B. Davis, Dunkard. CTOL
              MR signed on 07-01-1868 by Jos. T.
              Fudge, Clk. Mins. Ret. says mar. on
              07-08-1868 at John B. Davis res. on
              Potts Creek in Alleg. Co., VA.

07-03-1868   (on bk)   07-08-1868 (on CTOLMR and
48   Mins. Ret.)
              A. M. Stull (on bk) [Allen M. Stull
              (on CTOLMR)], 21, single, Born and Liv-
              ed: Alleg. Co., VA, Occup: farmer, s/o:
              G. and C. Stull (on bk) [Geo. and Char-
              lotte Stull (on CTOLMR)]; and M. D.
              Lemon (on bk) [Mary D. Lemon (on CTOL
              MR)], 17, single, B: Botetourt Co., VA,
              Lived: Alleg. Co., VA, dau/o: E. and M.
              R. Lemon (on bk) [Ellis and Mildred R.
              Lemon (on CTOLMR)]. PL: Alleg. Co.,
              VA "Maj. Haynes's res." Mar. by James
              M. Rice, Presb. CTOLMR signed on 07-

(Mar. Register Book (1) - Continued)

> 03-1868 by Jos. T. Fudge, Clk. Mins.
> Ret. says mar. on 07-08-1868 at Maj.
> Haynes's res. Consent of step-father
> M. L. Pendell, guardian for Mary D.
> Lemmon signed on 06-29-1868, Wit.
> James A. Hamilton. Oath acknowledge-
> ment of Pendell by James A. Hamilton
> on 07-03-1868, Teste Jos. T. Fudge,
> Clk.

Page 11

07-25-1868   (on bk) __-__-____ (on CTOLMR)
  # 49   08-20-1868 (on Mins. Ret.
              H. Humphries (on bk) [Harvey Humphries
              (on CTOLMR)], 38, widower, Occup: far-
              mer, s/o: Wm. and R. Humphries (on bk)
              [Wm. and Ruth Humphries (on CTOLMR)];
              and E. Bowen (on bk) [Elizabeth Bowen
              (on CTOLMR)], 25, single, dau/o: J.
              and N. Bowen (on bk) [Johnson and
              Nancy Bowen (on CTOLMR)]. Both born
              and lived in Alleg. Co., VA. PL: Al-
              leg. Co., VA "Wm. Sullender's res."
              Mar. by Aaron Boon, Meth. CTOLMR
              signed on 07-25-1868 by Jos. T. Fudge,
              Clk. Mins. Ret. says mar. on 08-20-
              1868 at Johnson Bowen res. in Alleg.
              Co., VA. Age oath for Elizabeth by
              William Sullender on 07-25-1868.

08-03-1868   Ellwood Byers, 28, single, B: Nelson
  # 50   Co., VA, Lived: Philadelphia, Pennsyl-
              vania, Occup: Druggist, s/o: J. and J.
              Byers (on bk) [Joseph and Jane Byers
              (on CTOLMR)]; and A. V. Dickson (on
              bk) [Agnes V. Dickson (on CTOLMR)],
              17, single, B: Alleg. Co., VA (on bk)
              [Greenbrier Co., VA (now W.VA.) (on
              CTOLMR)], Lived: Alleg. Co., VA, dau/
              o: R. and V. Dickson (on bk) [Robert
              and Virginia Dickson (on CTOLMR)].

- 227 -

PL: Alleg. Co., VA "Robert Dickson res." Mar. by S. B. Dolly, Dunkard. CTOL signed on 08-03-1868 by Robt. Dickson [apparently used for consent]. CTOLMR signed on 08-03-1868 by Jos. T. Fudge, Clk. Mins. Ret. says mar. on 08-03-1868 at Robert Dickson res.

08-10-1868 # 51

(on bk)   08-13-1868 (on CTOLMR and Mins. Ret.)
B. F. Manning (on bk) [Benjamin F. Maning (on CTOLMR)], 21, single, B: Watanger, N. C. (on bk) [Watauger Co., N. C. (on CTOLMR)] [Author Note: Spelling should be Watauga per N. C. map.], Lived: Alleg. Co., VA, Occup: farmer (on bk) [Tanner (on CTOLMR)], s/o: A. J. and S. Manning (on bk) [Andr. J. and Sarah Maning (on CTOLMR)]; and M. E. Smith (on bk) [May (? Mary) E. Smith (on CTOLMR)], 20, single, Born and Lived: Alleg. Co., VA, dau/o: J. C. and S. Smith (on bk) [Jno. C. and Susannah Smith (on CTOLMR)]. PL: Alleg. Co., VA "J. C. Smith res." Mar. by John B. Davis, Dunkard. Handwritten CTOLMR Five cent U. S. Inter. Revenue Certificate Stamp attached with "X" on it for signature. CTOLMR signed on 08-10-1868 by Jos. T. Fudge, Clk. Mins. Ret. says mar. on 08-13-1868 at John C. Smith's res. on Blue Spring in Alleg. Co., VA. Consent has Mary Emeline Smith and was signed John C. Smith, Wit. G. M. Smith on 08-10-1868. Oath of acknowledgement by G. M. Smith on 08-10-1868.

09-01-1868 # 52

D. J. Wolf (on bk) [Daniel J. Wolfe (on CTOLMR)], 19, single, Occup: farmer, s/o: J. R. and M. A. E. Wolf (on bk) [Jacob R. and Maria A. E. Wolfe

(Mar. Register Book (1) - Continued)

(on CTOLMR)]; and E. T. Dew (on bk)
[Elizabeth T. (? or J.) Dew (on CTOL
MR)], 23, single, dau/o: A. and S.
Dew (on bk) [Absalom and Sarah Dew (on
CTOLMR)]. Both born and lived in Al-
leg. Co., VA. PL: Alleg. Co., VA
"Absolom Dew's res." Mar. by John B.
Davis, Dunkard. Five cent U. S. Inter.
Revenue Certificate Stamp attached and
signed JBD. CTOLMR signed on 09-01-
1868 by Jos. T. Fudge, Clk. Mins. Ret.
says mar. on 09-01-1868 at Absalom
Dew's on Potts Creek in Alleg. Co.
Consent for Daniel J. Wolfe by Jacob
R. Wolfe on 08-31-1868, Wit. S. A. J.
Wolfe and J. O. Terry. Oath of acknow-
ledgement of Jacob R. Wolfe and age
oath for Elizabeth by Jacob O. Terry
on 09-01-1868, signed Jos. T. Fudge,
Clk.

09-19-1868   (on bk) 09-21-1868 (on CTOLMR and
  # 53   Mins. Ret.)
             A. Donnally (on bk and CTOLMR) [Allen
             Donnelly (on CTOL)], 37, single, B:
             Greenbrier Co., VA (now W.VA.), Lived:
             Alleg. Co., VA, Occup: Glovemaker, s/o:
             C. and S. Donnally (on bk) [Chs. and
             Synthia Donnally (on CTOL)] [Charles
             and Synthia Donnally (on CTOLMR)]; and
             M. E. Dickson (on bk) [Bettie Dickson
             (on CTOL)] [M. Bessie Dickson (on CTOL
             MR)], 20, single, B: Greenbrier Co.,
             VA (now W.VA.), Lived: Alleg. Co., VA,
             dau/o: R. and V. Dickson (on bk) [Rob-
             ert and Virginia Dickson (on CTOLMR)].
             PL: Alleg. Co., VA "Callaghan's."
             Mar. by James M. Rice, Presb. CTOL
             signed on 09-19-1868 by Robt. Dickson.
             CTOLMR signed on 09-19-1868 by Jos. T.
             Fudge, Clk. Mins. Ret. says mar. on
             09-21-1868 at house of bridge's father.

10-10-1868   (on bk) 10-15-1868 (on CTOLMR and
  # 54   Mins. Ret.)
              Benton Bowyer, 27, single, Occup: far-
              mer, s/o: J. and N. Bowyer (on bk)
              [John and Nancy Bowyer (on CTOLMR)];
              and E. Hepler (on bk) [Emmarillia
              Hepler (on CTOLMR)], 22, single, dau/
              o: J. and S. Hepler (on bk) [John and
              Sarah Hepler (on CTOLMR)]. Both born
              and lived in Alleg. Co., VA. PL: Al-
              leg. Co., VA "A. W. Bush res." Mar.
              by John B. Davis, Dunkard. [Author's
              Note: Because of a stain on the form,
              some type of fee stamp was apparently
              attached but is now missing.] CTOLMR
              signed on 10-10-1868 by Jos. T. Fudge,
              Clk. Mins. Ret. says mar. on 10-15-
              1868 at A. W. Bush's on Potts Creek.
              Age oath of Emmarillia by John Hepler
              on 10-10-1868, Teste Jos. T. Fudge,
              Clk.

10-12-1868   (on bk) 10-14-1868 (on CTOLMR and
  # 55   Mins. Ret.)
              J. L. Deeds (on bk) [John L. Deeds (on
              CTOLMR)], 27, single, Born and Lived:
              Alleg. Co., VA, Occup: Plasterer, s/o:
              Wm. and R. Deeds (on bk) [William and
              Rachel Deeds (on CTOLMR)]; and S. E.
              Zeigler (on bk) [Sarah E. Zeigler (on
              CTOLMR)], 21, single, B: Orange Co.,
              VA, Lived: Alleg. Co., VA, dau/o: A.
              and M. Zeigler (on bk) [Abraham and
              Matilda Zeigler (on CTOLMR)]. PL: Al-
              leg. Co., VA "A. Zeigler res." Mar.
              by James M. Rice. CTOLMR was signed
              on 10-12-1868 by Jos. T. Fudge, Clk.
              Mins. Ret. says mar. on 10-14-1868 at
              A. Zeigler res. Age oath of Sarah was
              given by Paul Gleason on 10-12-1868
              Teste Jos. T. Fudge, Clk.

(Mar. Register Book (1) - Continued)

10-12-1868   (on book)   10-13-1868 (on CTOLMR and
 # 56   Mins. Ret.)
              W. J. Dickson (on book) [William J.
              Dickson (on CTOLMR)], 27, single, Born
              and Lived: Alleg. Co., VA, Occup: Inn-
              keeper, s/o: S. and M. F. Dickson (on
              book) [Sam'l. and Margaret F. Dickson
              (on CTOLMR)]; and R. C. Karnes (on
              book) [Rebecca C. Karnes (on CTOLMR)],
              23, single, Born and Lived: Alleg. Co.,
              VA dau/o: S. and C. H. Karnes (on
              book) [Sampson and Clarissa H. Karnes
              (on CTOLMR)]. PL: Alleg. Co., VA
              "Mrs. C. H. Karnes's res." Mar. by
              James M. Rice. CTOLMR was signed on
              10-12-1868 by Jos. T. Fudge, Clk.
              Mins. Ret. says mar. on 10-13-1868 at
              Mrs. Karnes's res. Age oath of Rebecca
              daughter of Clarissa, was given by John
              D. Sadler on 10-12-1868, Teste Jos. T.
              Fudge, Clk.

10-12-1868   (on book)   10-13-1868 (on CTOLMR and
 # 57   Mins. Ret.)
              N. W. Bishop (on book) [Norval W.
              Bishop (on CTOLMR)], 27, single, B:
              Botetourt Co., VA, Lived: Alleg. Co.,
              VA, Occup: Miller, s/o: J. S. and M.
              A. Bishop (on book) [James S. and Mar-
              tha A. Bishop (on CTOLMR)]; and L. L.
              Dickson (on book) [Lillie L. Dickson
              (on CTOLMR)], 16, single, B: Greenbrier
              Co., VA (now W.VA.), Lived: Alleg. Co.,
              VA, dau/o: S. and M. F. Dickson (on
              book) [Samuel and Margaret F. Dickson
              (on CTOLMR)]. PL: Alleg. Co., VA
              "Callaghan's." Mar. by Saul B. Dolly.
              CTOLMR signed on 10-12-1868 by Jos. T.
              Fudge, Clk. Mins. Ret. says mar. on
              10-13-1868 at Callaghan's in Alleg.
              Co., VA.

(Mar. Register Book (1) - Continued)

10-22-1868 Giles M. Smith, 23, single, Born and
57 ½   Lived: Alleg. Co., VA, Occup: farmer,
            s/o: John and Susanna Smith; and
            Louisa J. Humphries (on book) [Louisa
            Jane Humphries (on CTOLMR)], 18, sin-
            gle, B: Nicholas Co., VA (now W.VA.),
            Lived: Alleg. Co., VA, dau/o: Wm. A.
            and H. Maria Humphries. Handwritten
            CTOLMR. Mins. Ret. says mar. on 10-
            22-1868 at W. A. Humphries in Alleg.
            Co., VA, was signed Aaron Boon, Min-
            ister. CTOLMR signed on 10-15-1868
            by W. M. Scott, D. C. PL: Alleg. Co.,
            VA "Wm. A. Humphries res. in Rich
            Patch."

10-22-1868 W. H. Leighton (on book) [William H.
58   Leighton (on CTOLMR)], 23, single, B:
            Botetourt Co., VA, Lived: Alleg. Co.,
            VA, Occup: blacksmith, s/o: D. B. and
            L. Leighton (on book) [Daniel B. and
            Louisa Leighton (on CTOLMR)]; and J.
            S. Brown (on book) [Jennie S. Brown
            (on CTOLMR)], 17, single, Born and
            Lived: Alleg. Co., VA, dau/o: M. D.
            and _____ Brown (on book) [Mathews D.
            and _____ Brown (on CTOLMR)]. PL:
            Alleg. Co., VA "M. D. Brown res." Mar.
            by Saul B. Dolly. CTOLMR signed on
            10-22-1868 by Jos. T. Fudge, Clk. Min-
            ister's Ret. says mar. on 10-22-1868
            at bride's res. in Alleg. Co. Consent
            of Mathew D. Brown on 10-14-1868, Wit.
            Wm. H. Leighton. Oath acknowledgement
            of Mathew D. Brown on 10-22-1868,
            Teste Jos. T. Fudge, Clk.

11-03-1868 (on book) 11-05-1868 (on CTOLMR and
59   Mins. Ret.)
            W. J. Hanes (on book) [William J. Hanes
            (on CTOLMR)], 20, single, Occup: farmer,

s/o: L. W. and M. A. Hanes (on book)
[Lemuel W. and Mary A. Hanes (on CTOL
MR)]; and S. V. Bowyer (on book)
[Sarah V. Bowyer (on CTOLMR)], 24,
single, dau/o: J. and N. Bowyer (on
book) [John and Nancy Bowyer (on CTOL
MR)]. Both were born and lived in
Alleg. Co., VA. PL: Alleg. Co., VA
"John Bowyer res." Mar. by John B.
Davis. Oath acknowledgement of L. W.
Hanes by Benton Bowyer on 11-03-1868
Teste Jos. T. Fudge, Clk. CTOLMR
signed on 11-03-1868 by Jos. T. Fudge,
Clk. Mins. Ret. says mar. on 11-05-
1868 at John Bowyer's on Potts Creek
in Alleg. Co., VA. Consent of Lemuel
W. Hanes was signed on 11-02-1868.
Age oath of Benton Bowyer for Sarah
was given on 11-03-1868, Teste Jos.
T. Fudge, Clk.

11-05-1868   Thursday
59 ½   James Hoke (on book) [James Horam
              Hoke (on CTOLMR)], 24, single, B:
              Monroe Co., VA (now W.VA.), Lived:
              Alleg. Co., VA, Occup: Lawyer, s/o:
              William and Catherine Hoke (on book)
              [William and Catharine Hoke (on CTOL
              MR)]; and Elizabeth Jane Lockhart, 24,
              single, Born and Lived: Alleg. Co.,
              VA, dau/o: David B. and Nancy Lock-
              hart. CTOLMR signed on 11-05-1868 by
              W. M. Scott, D. C. Mins. Ret. says
              mar. on 11-05-1868 at father's res.
              was signed by James M. Rice. PL: Al-
              leg. Co., VA "D. B. Lockhart's res."

11-05-1868   (on book) 11-05-1867 (on CTOLMR and
60   Mins. Ret.)
              W. N. Loudermilk (on book) [William N.
              Loudermilk (on CTOLMR)], 24, single,

(Mar. Register Book (1) - Continued)

Born and Lived: Greenbrier Co., VA
(now W.VA.), Occup: farmer, s/o: D.
and S. Loudermilk (on book) [David
and Susanah Loudermilk (on CTOLMR)];
and M. E. Loudermilk (on book) [Mar-
garet E. Loudermilk (on CTOLMR)], 21,
single, Born and Lived: Greenbrier
Co., VA (now W.VA.), dau/o: J. and R.
Loudermilk (on book) [Joseph and Rachel Loudermilk (on CTOLMR)]. Mar. by
A. Q. Flaherty. PL: Alleg. Co., VA
"Covington." CTOLMR was signed on
11-05-1867 by Jos. T. Fudge, Clk.
Mins. Ret. says mar. on 11-05-1867 at
parsonage in Covington, VA.

11-12-1868   Thursday
 # 61   H. Gilliland (on book) [Hazle Gilleland (on CTOLMR)], 33, single, Occup:
farmer, s/o: J. and M. Gilliland (on
book) [Joseph and Mahala Gilleland
(on CTOLMR)]; and M. A. Haynes (on
book) [Margarette A. Haynes (on CTOL
MR)], 20, single, dau/o: W. H. and J.
Haynes (on book) [William H. and Jen-
netta Haynes (on CTOLMR)]. Both were
born and lived in Alleg. Co., VA.
Handwritten CTOLMR was signed on 11-12-
1868 by W. M. Scott, D. C. Mins. Ret.
says mar. on 11-12-1868 at Wm. Haynes's
res. Mar. by James M. Rice. PL: Alleg. Co., VA "Wm. Haynes's res."

11-17-1868   (on book)   _-_-____ (on CTOLMR)
 # 62   11-18-1868 (on Mins. Ret.)
S. B. Lowry (on book) [Samuel B. Lowry
(on CTOLMR)], 32, widower, B: Alleg.
Co., VA, Lived: Pocahontas Co., W. VA.,
Occup: farmer, s/o: S. B. and R. Lowry
(on book) [Sam'l. B. and Rebecca Lowry
(on CTOLMR)]; and F. A. Williams (on

- 234 -

book) [Fannie A. Williams (on CTOL
MR)], 17, single, B: Bath Co., VA,
Lived: Alleg. Co., VA, dau/o: E. I.
and L. Williams (on book) [Erasmus T.
and Leah Williams (on CTOLMR)]. Mar.
by S. S. Ryder, Meth. PL: Alleg. Co,
VA "E. T. Williams's res." CTOLMR
signed on 11-17-1868 by Jos. T. Fudge,
Clk. Mins. Ret. says mar. on 11-18-
1868 at E. T. Williams's res. Consent was signed by Erasimus T. Williams, Teste S. B. Lowry, "Jr." Oath
acknowledgement of Erasmus was given
by S. B. Lowry, Jr., on 11-17-1868,
Teste Jos. T. Fudge, Clk.

11-24-1868   (on book) 11-26-1868 Thursday (on
 # 63   CTOLMR and Mins. Ret.)
               J. L. Fridley (on book) [Jacob Lewis
               Fridley (on CTOLMR)], 24, single,
               Occup: farmer, s/o: J. and R. Fridley
               (on book) [John and Ruth Fridley (on
               CTOLMR)]; and J. C. Humphries (on
               book) [Jennetta Catharine Humphries
               (on CTOLMR)], 21, single, dau/o: J.
               and E. Humphries (on book) [Jessee
               and Eunice Humphries (on CTOLMR)].
               Both were born and lived in Alleg. Co,
               VA. Handwritten CTOLMR was signed on
               11-24-1868 by W. M. Scott, D. C. Min-
               ister's Ret. says mar. on 11-26-1868
               at Jessee Humphries's res. in Alleg.
               Co., VA, and was signed Aaron Boon,
               Mins. PL: Alleg. Co., VA "Jessee
               Humphries res."

12-03-1868   (on book) 12-06-1868 (on CTOLMR and
 # 64   Mins. Ret.)
               N. L. Bess (on book) [Nash L. Bess (on
               CTOLMR)], 22, single, Born and Lived:
               Alleg. Co., VA, Occup: farmer, s/o:
               H. and N. Bess (on book) [Henry and

Nelly Bess (on CTOLMR)] [Author's
Note: names for parents are backwards
on CTOLMR.]; and N. L. Hoke (on book)
[Nancy L. Hoke (on CTOLMR)], 22,
single, B: Monroe Co., VA (now W.VA),
Lived: Alleg. Co., VA, dau/o: Wm. and
C. Hoke (on book) [Wm. and Catharine
Hoke (on CTOLMR)] [Author's Note:
names for parents are backwards on
CTOLMR.] PL: Alleg. Co., VA "Wm.
Hoke, Jr. res." Mar. by James M.
Rice. CTOLMR signed on 12-03-1868
by Jos. T. Fudge, Clk. Mins. Ret.
says mar. on 12-06-1868 at res. of
bride's father. Age oath for Nancy
L. Hoke, daughter of Wm. Hoke, Jr.,
was given by David L. Gilbert on 12-
03-1868, Teste Jos. T. Fudge, Clk.

12-13-1868   (on book)   12-16-1868 Wednesday (on
 # 65   CTOLMR and Mins. Ret.)
             Thos. Ross (on book) [Thomas O. Ross
             (on CTOLMR)], 50, widower, B: Alleg.
             Co., VA, Lived: Bath Co., VA, Occup:
             farmer, s/o: T. and E. Ross (on book)
             [Thos. and Eunice Ross (on CTOLMR)];
             and N. Hoilman (on book) [Nancy Hoil-
             man (on Mar. Auth.)] [Nancy Hoylman
             (on CTOLMR)], 49, widow, B: Bath Co.,
             VA, Lived: Alleg. Co., VA, dau/o: I.
             and M. Mayse (on book) [Isaac and
             Martha Mayse (on CTOLMR)]. PL: Alleg.
             Co., VA "Nancy Hoilman's res." Mar.
             by Davis M. Wood, L. D., M. E. C. S.
             Handwritten CTOLMR was signed on 12-
             13-1868 by W. M. Scott, D. C. Mins.
             Ret. says mar. on 12-16-1868 at res.
             of Nancy Hoilman. "Hoilman" was writ-
             ten on the back of the Lic.

12-17-1868   J. G. Lockhart (on book) [John G.
 # 66   Lockhart (on CTOLMR)], 21, single,

Born and Lived: Alleg. Co., VA, Occup: farmer, s/o: D. B. and N. Lockhart (on book) [David B. and Nancy Lockhart (on CTOLMR)]; and Ellen Hoke, 20, single, B: Monroe Co., VA (now W. VA.), Lived: Alleg. Co., VA, dau/o: Wm. and C. Hoke (on book) [William and Catharine Hoke (on CTOLMR)]. [Author's Note: Parents names were backwards on CTOLMR, but listed in their correct places here.] PL: Alleg. Co., VA "Wm. Hoke, Jr., res." Mar. by S. B. Dolly. CTOLMR was signed on 12-17-1868 by Jos. T. Fudge, Clk. Mins. Ret. says mar. on 12-17-1868 at res. of bride's father in Alleg. Co. Consent of Wm. Hoke was signed on 12-07-1868, Wit. D. L. Gilbert. Oath acknowledgement of Wm. Hoke was given by David L. Gilbert on 12-17-1868, Teste Jos. T. Fudge, Clk.

12-19-1868 (on book)   12-24-1868 (on CTOLMR and
67   Mins. Ret.)
J. N. Lemon (on book) [John N. Lemon (on CTOLMR)], 33 (on book) [33 or 34 on CTOLMR--unreadable], Born and Lived: Botetourt Co., VA, Occup: farmer, s/o: J. and H. Lemon (on book) [John and Harriet Lemon (on CTOLMR)]; and E. Johnson (on book) [Elizabeth Johnson (on CTOLMR)], 29, single, Born and Lived: Alleg. Co., VA, dau/o: J. and M. Johnson (on book) [Jabez and Maria Johnson (on CTOLMR)]. PL: Alleg. Co., VA "J. Johnson, Senr., res." Mar. by George T. Lyle. CTOLMR signed on 12-19-1868 by Jos. T. Fudge, Clk. Mins. Ret. says mar. on 12-24-1868 at res. of J. Johnson, Sr., in Alleg. Co., VA. Consent of Jabez Johnson for Elizabeth, daughter of Jabez

Johnson, Senr., was signed on 12-19-1868, Teste Jos. T. Fudge, Clk.

12-19-1868   (on book)   12-23-1868 (on CTOLMR and
68   Mins. Ret.)
              J. C. Simmons (on book) [James C.Sim-
              mons (on CTOLMR)], 22, single, B:
              Giles Co., VA, Lived: Alleg. Co., VA,
              Occup: farmer, s/o: W. M. and E. Sim-
              mons (on book) [Wm. M. and Elizabeth
              Simmons (on CTOLMR)]; and E. M. Ting-
              ler (on book) [Eliza M. Tingler (on
              CTOLMR)], 19, single, Born and Lived:
              Alleg. Co., VA, dau/o: J. and D.
              Tingler (on book) [John and Didama
              Tingler (on CTOLMR)]. PL: Alleg. Co.,
              VA "James S. Nida's res." Mar. by
              John B. Davis. Consent of Vidama
              Tingler was signed on 12-17-1868 by
              Vidama Tingler, Wit. Henry Myers and
              Charles L. Bess. CTOLMR was signed
              on 12-19-1868 by Jos. T. Fudge, Clk.
              Mins. Ret. says mar. on 12-23-1868 at
              James S. Nida's res. on Potts Creek
              in Alleg. Co., VA. Oath acknowledge-
              ment for Vidama's consent was given
              by Chs. L. Bess on 12-19-1868, Teste
              Jos. T. Fudge, Clk.

12-21-1868   (on book)   12-24-1868 (on CTOLMR and
69   Mins. Ret.)
              J. C. Gilbert (on book) [James Claring-
              ton Gilbert (on CTOLMR)], 24, single,
              B: Botetourt Co., VA, Lived: Alleg.
              Co., VA, Occup: farmer, s/o: A. H. and
              S. Gilbert (on book) [A. H. and Susan
              Gilbert (on CTOLMR)]; and M. A. Mathe-
              ny (on book) [Mary A. Matheny (on CTOL
              MR)], 20, single, Born and Lived: Al-
              leg. Co., VA, dau/o: Wm. and M. Mathe-
              ny (on book) [Wm. and Mary Matheny (on

(Mar. Register Book (1) - Continued)

CTOLMR)]. PL: Alleg. Co., VA "James
Skeen's res." Mar. by James M. Rice.
CTOL signed on 12-21-1868 by James
Skeen, Guardian of M. A. Matheney
[Author's Note: This was apparently
used for consent.] CTOLMR was signed
on 12-21-1868 by Jos. T. Fudge, Clk.
Mins. Ret. says mar. on 12-24-1868 at
J. Skeen's res.

12-21-1868   (on book) ___-__-____ (on CTOLMR)
  # 70   12-24-1868 (on Mins. Ret.)
             J. O. Paxton (on book) [James O. Pax-
             ton (on CTOLMR)], 20, single, B: Craig
             Co., VA, Lived: Alleg. Co., VA, Occup:
             farmer, s/o: J. and M. Paxton (on bk)
             [James and Mary Paxton (on CTOLMR)];
             and S. E. Hepler (on book) [Sarah E.
             Hepler (on CTOLMR)], 25, single, Born
             and Lived: Alleg. Co., VA, dau/o: D.
             and A. Hepler (on book) [David and
             Abeshaby Hepler (on CTOLMR)]. PL: Al-
             leg. Co., VA "David Hepler res." Mar.
             by John B. Davis. CTOLMR signed on
             12-21-1868 by Jos. T. Fudge, Clk.
             Mins. Ret. says mar. on 12-24-1868 at
             David Hepler's on Cast Steel Run in
             Alleg. Co., VA. Consent of James Pax-
             ton was given on 12-21-1868, Wit. Lee
             Persinger. Oath of Paxton's acknow-
             ledgement was given by Lee Persinger
             on 12-21-1868, Teste Jos. T. Fudge,
             Clk.

12-22-1868   (on book) 12-23-1868 (on CTOLMR and
  # 71   Mins. Ret.)
             W. C. Fudge (on book) [William C.
             Fudge (on CTOLMR)], 30, single, Born
             and Lived: Alleg. Co., VA, Occup: far-
             mer, s/o: A. and H. K. Fudge (on book)
             [Andrew and Harriet K. Fudge (on CTOL
             MR)]; and M. E. A. Boswell (on book)

- 239 -

[Mollie E. A. Boswell (on CTOLMR)], 27, single, Born and Lived: Alleg. Co., VA, dau/o: H. and M. Boswell (on book) [Jas. H. and Maria Boswell (on CTOLMR)]. PL: Alleg. Co., VA "Jas. H. Boswell res." Mar. by S. B. Dolly. CTOLMR was signed on 12-22-1868 by Jos. T. Fudge, Clk. Mins. Ret. says mar. on 12-23-1868 at res. of bride's father in Alleg. Co.

11-26-1868   Thursday
71 ½   William Oliver Anders, 25, single,
              Born and Lived: Alleg. Co., VA, Occup:
              farmer, s/o: William and Elizabeth
              Anders; and Matilda Va. Guy (on book)
              [Matilda Virginia Guy (on CTOLMR)],
              21, single, B: Alleg. Co., VA (on bk)
              [_____ (on CTOLMR)], Lived: Alleg. Co,
              VA, dau/o: William and Mary Guy. PL:
              Alleg. Co., VA "William Guy's res."
              Mar. by J. M. Rice. Handwritten CTOL
              MR was signed on 11-25-1868 by W. M.
              Scott, D. C. Mins. Ret. says mar. on
              11-26-1868 at house of bride's father.

12-29-1868   (on book)   12-30-1868 (on CTOLMR and
72   Mins. Ret.)
              Wm. Acres (on book) [William Acres (on
              CTOLMR)], 24, single, B: Rockbridge
              Co., VA (on book) [Rockingham Co., VA
              (on CTOLMR)], Lived: Alleg. Co., VA,
              Occup: farmer, s/o: M. and A. Acres
              (on book) [Minor and Adaline Acres (on
              CTOLMR)]; and D. James (on book) [Due-
              silla James (on CTOLMR)], 20, single,
              B: Rockbridge Co., VA, Lived: Alleg.
              Co., VA, dau/o: M. and E. James (on
              book) [Madison and Elizabeth James (on
              CTOLMR)]. PL: Alleg. Co., VA "Minor
              Acres's res." Mar. by Saul B. Dolly.
              CTOLMR signed on 12-29-1868 by Jos. T.

Fudge, Clk. Mins. Ret. says mar. on 12-30-1868 at Miner Acres res. in Alleg. Co.

12-30-1868
73

(on book) 12-31-1868 (on CTOLMR and Mins. Ret.)
J. H. Tucker (on book) [John H. Tucker (on CTOLMR)], 24, single, B: Botetourt Co., VA, Lived: Alleg. Co., VA, Occup: farmer, s/o: B. S. and B. Tucker (on book) [Beverally S. and Bevaline Tucker (on CTOLMR)]; and R. S. Sawyers (on book) [Rebecca S. Sawyers (on CTOLMR)], 23, single, Born and Lived: Alleg. Co., VA, dau/o: A. and S. Sawyers (on book) [Archer and Susan Sawyers (on CTOLMR)]. PL: Alleg. Co., VA. Mar. by Saul B. Dolly. CTOLMR was signed on 12-30-1868 by Jos. T. Fudge, Clk. Mins. Ret. says mar. on 12-31-1868 at Christopher Damron's in Alleg. Co. Age oath for Rebecca was given by Leadford Sawyers on 12-30-1868, Teste Jos. T. Fudge, Clk.

01-01-1869
74

(on book) 01-04-1869 (on CTOLMR and Mins. Ret.)
Jno. Fox (on book) [John Fox (on CTOLMR)], 25, single, B: County Latrem, Ireland (on book & CTOLMR) [Author's Note: I believe spelling should be Leitrim from looking at a map of Ireland.], Lived: Alleg. Co., VA, Occup: laborer, s/o: C. and E. Fox (on book) [Chs. and Eliza Fox (on CTOLMR)]; and Mary Holland, 26, single, B: County Galway, Ireland, Lived: Alleg. Co., VA, dau/o: P. and C. Holland (on book) [Patrick and Catherine Holland (on CTOLMR)]. PL: Alleg. Co., VA "Alleghany Tunnel." Mar. by Hugh P. McMenamin. CTOLMR was signed on 01-01-1869

by Jos. T. Fudge, Clk. Mins. Ret. says mar. on 01-04-1869 at Alleg. Tunnel. Age oath was given by Patrick Fox for <u>Mary</u> on 01-01-1869, Teste Jos. T. Fudge, Clk.

01-07-1869
75

(on book) ___-__-____ (on CTOLMR) 01-10-1869 (on Mins. Ret.) <u>Alex. Tucker</u> (on book) [<u>Alexander Tucker</u> (on CTOLMR)], 32, single, B: Craig Co., VA, Lived: Alleg. Co., VA, Occup: farmer, s/o: J. and M. Tucker (on book) [John and Margaret Tucker (on CTOLMR)]; and <u>M. J. Bennett</u> (on book) [<u>Mary J. Bennett</u> (on CTOLMR)], 21, widow, B: Washington Co., Tennessee, Lived: Alleg. Co., VA, dau/o: J. and E. Jones (on book) [James and Elizabeth Jones (on CTOLMR)]. PL: Alleg. Co., VA. Mar. by John B. Davis. CTOLMR was signed on 01-07-1869 by Jos. T. Fudge, Clk. Mins. Ret. says mar. on 01-10-1869 at Margaret Tucker's res. in Alleg. Co., VA.

01-07-1869
75 ½

<u>Charles B. Thompson</u>, 20, single, B: Bath Co., VA, Lived: Alleg. Co., VA, Occup: farmer, s/o: J. C. and Sarah E. Thompson; and <u>Martha C. Byrd</u> (on book) [<u>Martha E. Byrd</u> (on CTOLMR)], 27, single, Born and Lived: Alleg. Co., VA, dau/o: William and Nancy Byrd (on book) [Wm. and Nancy Byrd (on CTOLMR)]. Age oath for <u>Martha</u> was given by Minor Acres on 01-06-1869, Teste Jos. T. Fudge, Clk. Mins. Ret. says mar. on 01-07-1869 at J. C. Thompson's res. in Alleg. Co., VA, was signed Saul B. Dolly. CTOLMR was signed on 01-06-1869 by Jos. T. Fudge, Clk. PL: Alleg. Co., VA "John C. Thom-

pson's res." Consent for <u>Charles</u> has
bride's name as <u>Marthy E. Byrd</u> and
was signed J. C. Thompson, Wit. Minor
Acres and George (his X mark) Mieley,
Teste J. T. Fudge. Oath of Thompson
acknowledgement by Minor Acres on 01-
06-1869 was signed Jos. T. Fudge, Clk.
[Author's Note: This oath was on the
back of the consent.]

01-18-1869   (on book)   01-28-1869   (on CTOLMR)
76   01-27-1869   (on Mins. Ret.)
<u>Wm. B. Sively</u> (on book) [<u>William B.
Sively</u> (on CTOLMR)], 21, single, Occup:
farmer, s/o: A. J. and M. Sively (on
book) [Andrew J. and Mary Sively (on
CTOLMR)]; and <u>O. S. Stone</u> (on book)
[<u>Olivia T. Stone</u> (on CTOLMR)], 20,
single, dau/o: Jos. P. and _____ Stone.
Both were born and lived in Alleg. Co.,
VA. CTOLMR was signed on 01-18-1869
by Jos. T. Fudge, Clk. Mins. Ret.
says mar. on 01-27-1869 at Joseph P.
Stone's res. on Snake Run in Alleg.
Co., VA, was signed by John B. Davis.
PL: Alleg. Co., VA "Jos. P. Stone's
res." Consent of Jos. P. Stone was
given on 01-18-1869, Attest James P.
Gillaspie. Oath of Stone acknowledgement was given by James P. Gillaspie
on 01-18-1869, Teste Jos. T. Fudge,
Clk.

01-29-1869   (on book)   ~~Sunday/31/Jany/1869~~ (as on
77   CTOLMR)   02-01-1869 (on Mins. Ret.)
<u>Edward Roper</u>, 21, single, B: Richmond,
VA, Lived: Alleg. Co., VA, Occup: mil-
ler, s/o: C. and L. Roper (on book)
[Charles and Lucinda Roper (on CTOL
MR)]; and <u>Rebecca Bess</u>, 20, single,
Born and Lived: Alleg. Co., VA, dau/o:
H. and N. Bess (on book) [Henry and

Nelly Bess (on CTOLMR)]. PL: Alleg.
Co., VA "H. Bess res." Mar. by James
M. Rice. Handwritten CTOLMR was si-
gned on 01-29-1869 by W. M. Scott, D.
C. Mins. Ret. says mar. on 02-01-
1869 at H. Bess res.

02-14-1869   (on book and Mins. Ret.) __-__-____
77 ½   (on CTOLMR)
             James Holland, 27, single, B: Franklin
             Co., VA, Lived: Alleg. Co., VA, Occup:
             laborer, s/o: Daniel and Sarah Hol-
             land; and Susan Jackson, 26, single,
             B: Augusta Co., VA, dau/o: ___ & ___
             Jackson, Lived: Alleg. Co., VA. PL:
             Alleg. Co., VA (on book) [_____ (on
             CTOLMR)]. CTOLMR was signed on 02-
             06-1869 by Jos. T. Fudge, Clk. Mins.
             Ret. says mar. on 02-14-1869 in Cov-
             ington in Alleg. Co., VA, by Saul B.
             Dolly.

02-15-1869   (on book) 02-07-1869 (on CTOLMR and
78   Mins. Ret.)
             Jos. Engram (on book) [Joseph Engram
             (on CTOLMR)], 27, single, B: Rock-
             bridge Co., VA, Lived: Alleg. Co., VA,
             Occup: laborer, s/o: W. and D. Engram
             (on book) [William and Delina Engram
             (on CTOLMR)]; and R. Bennington (on
             book) [Rebecca Bennington (on CTOLMR)],
             16, single, B: Rockbridge Co., VA,
             Lived: Alleg. Co., VA, dau/o: J. and
             C. Bennington (on book) [James and
             Caroline Bennington (on CTOLMR)]. PL:
             Alleg. Co., VA "James Bennington's
             res." CTOL was signed on 02-06-1869
             by James (his X mark) Bennington,
             Attest Jos. T. Fudge [Author's Note:
             This was apparently used for consent.].
             CTOLMR was signed on 02-06-1869 by
             Jos. T. Fudge, Clk. Mins. Ret. says

mar. on 02-07-1869 at J. Bennington's
res. and was signed by James M. Rice.

02-15-1869   (on book) 02-18-1869 (on CTOLMR and
  # 79   Mins. Ret.)
              Z. Womack (on book) [Zacariah Womack
              (on CTOLMR)], 24, single, B: Halifax
              Co., VA, Lived: Alleg. Co., VA, Oc-
              cup: laborer, s/o: Jos. P. and C. A.
              Womack; and S. Anderson (on book)
              [Susan Anderson (on CTOLMR)], 18,
              single, B: Alleg. Co., VA, Lived: Al-
              leg. Co., VA, dau/o: _____ and
              Arabella Kitinger. PL: Alleg. Co.,
              VA "James Ratliff res." Mar. by S.
              B. Dolly. CTOL was signed on 02-15-
              1869 by Arabella (her X mark) Kiting-
              er. CTOLMR was signed on 02-15-1869
              by Jos. T. Fudge, Clk. Mins. Ret.
              says mar. on 02-18-1869 at Mud Tunnel
              in Alleg. Co., VA. [Author's Note:
              CTOL apparently was used for consent.]

03-03-1869   (on book) 03-04-1869 (on CTOLMR and
  # 80   Mins. Ret.)
              A. Kittinger (on book) [Abraham Kitin-
              ger (on CTOLMR)], 20, single, Born and
              Lived: Alleg. Co., VA, Occup: laborer,
              s/o: G. W. and _____ Kittinger (on
              book) [Geo. W. and _____ Kitinger
              (on CTOLMR)]; and S. M. Anderson (on
              book) [Sarah M. Anderson (on CTOLMR)],
              21, single, Born and Lived: Alleg. Co,
              VA, dau/o: _____ & "Same" [Note: This
              is what was on the book where the
              names of the parents are written. The
              name "Arabella Kitinger" is listed
              above it on the previous entry.] [___
              and Arabella Anderson (on CTOLMR)].
              PL: Alleg. Co., VA "Jas. Ratliff res."
              Mar. by James M. Rice. CTOLMR signed
              on 03-03-1869 by Jos. T. Fudge, Clk.

(Mar. Register Book (1) - Continued)

Mins. Ret. says mar. on 03-04-1869 at
res. of Jas. Ratcliff. Consent for
Abraham Kittinger to marry Sarah M.
Anderson given by George W. Kitinger
on 03-03-1869, Attest, Mr. Womack.
Oath of Kitinger acknowledgement given
on 03-03-1869 by [(?Mr.) (?L.) (?Z.)]
Womack, Teste Jos. T. Fudge, Clk.
Age oath for Sarah M. Anderson, dau-
ghter of Lizzie Anderson, that she
was over 21 years old was given by
James Ratliff on 03-03-1869, Teste
Jos. T. Fudge, Clk.

03-16-1869   (on book) 03-18-1869 (on CTOLMR and
81   Mins. Ret.)
Alex. Freeman (on book) [Alexander
Freeman (on CTOLMR)], 26, single, B:
Southampton Co., VA, Lived: Alleg.
Co., VA, Occup: laborer, s/o: P. and
P. Freeman (on book) [Peter and Patsey
Freeman (on CTOLMR)]; and Juda Tyler,
20, single, B: Fluvanna Co., VA, Liv-
ed: Alleg. Co., VA, dau/o: _____ and
M. Tyler (on book) [_____ and Merica
Tyler (on CTOLMR)]. PL: Alleg. Co.,
VA "A. Mann's res." CTOLMR signed on
03-16-1869 by Jos. T. Fudge, Clk.
Mins. Ret. says mar. on 03-18-1869 at
A. Mann's res. was signed James M.
Rice. Consent has Elexander Fremon
and was signed America (her X mark)
Tyler on 10-20-1868, Teste Sarah D.
Mann.

03-16-1869   (on book) 03-18-1869 (on CTOLMR and
82   Mins. Ret.)
J. V. Bess (on book) [Jesse V. Bess
(on CTOLMR)], 39, single, Born and
Lived: Alleg. Co., VA, Occup: merchant,
s/o: H. and R. Bess (on book) [Hamil-
ton and Rebecca Bess (on CTOLMR)]; and

- 246 -

A. J. Byer (on book) [Alwilda J. Byer (on CTOLMR)], 21, single, Born and Lived: Alleg. Co., VA, dau/o: D. and E. Byer (on book) [David and Elizabeth Byers (on CTOLMR)]. PL: Alleg. Co., VA "D. Byer's res." Oath of Byer acknowledgement by J. V. Bess on 03-16-1869, Teste Jos. T. Fudge, Clk. CTOLMR was signed on 03-16-1869 by Jos. T. Fudge, Clk. Mins. Ret. says mar. on 03-18-1869 at David Byers on Potts Creek in Alleg. Co., VA, was signed John B. Davis. Consent to the "intermarriage" of Aldwilda Jane Byer with Jesse V. Bess was signed David Byer on 03-15-1869, Wit. J. V. Bess.

03-17-1869
83

(on book)   03-24-1869 (on CTOLMR and Mins. Ret.)

J. Johnson, Jr. (on book) [Jabez Johnson, Jr. (on CTOLMR)], 21, single, B: Alleg. Co., VA, Lived: Alleg. Co., VA (on book) [Greenbrier Co., W. VA (on CTOLMR)], Occup: farmer, s/o: J. and M. Johnson (on book) [Jabez and Maria Johnson (on CTOLMR)]; and N. J. Lemon (on book) [Nancy J. Lemon (on CTOLMR)], 17, single, B: Alleg. Co., VA, Lived: Greenbrier Co., W. VA (on book) [Alleg. Co., VA (on CTOLMR)], dau/o: J. Y. and M. Lemon (on book) [James Y. and Margaret Lemon (on COTLMR)]. PL: Alleg. Co., VA "Jas. Y. Lemon's res." CTOLMR signed on 03-17-1869 by Jos. T. Fudge, Clk. Mins. Ret. says mar. on 03-24-1869 at Jas. Y. Lemon's res. was signed James M. Rice. Consent of father, James Y. Lemon, on 03-17-1869, Wit. Francis Lemon. Oath of Lemon acknowledgement was given by Francis Lemon on 03-17-1869, Teste Jos. T. Fudge, Clk.

03-17-1869   (on book)   _-__-____ (on CTOLMR)
  # 84   05-20-1869 (on Mins. Ret.)
             H. C. Wolf (on book) [Hugh C. Wolf
             (on CTOLMR)], 40, widower, Born and
             Lived: Alleg. Co., VA, Occup: farmer,
             s/o: A. and M. Wolf (on book) [Abra-
             ham and Margaret Wolf (on CTOLMR)];
             and E. J. Tucker (on book) [Eliza
             Jane Tucker (on CTOLMR)], 21, single,
             B: Craig Co., VA, Lived: Alleg. Co.,
             VA, dau/o: J. and M. Tucker (on book)
             [John and Margaret Tucker (on CTOL
             MR)]. PL: Alleg. Co., VA "Hugh C.
             Wolf's res." CTOLMR signed on 05-14-
             1869 by Henry C. Vaughan, Clk. Mins.
             Ret. says mar. on 05-20-1869 at Hugh
             C. Wolf's on Potts Creek in Alleg.
             Co., VA, was signed John B. Davis.
             Age oath of Eliza was given by Dan-
             berry Tucker on 05-14-1869, Teste H.
             C. Vaughan, Clk.

03-17-1869   (on book) 05-19-1869 (on CTOLMR and
  # 85   Mins. Ret.)
             Wm. T. Clark (on book) [William T.
             Clark (on CTOLMR)], 27, single, Born
             and Lived: Alleg. Co., VA, Occup:
             blacksmith, s/o: J. B. and C. Clark
             (on book) [Jos. B. and Christina Clark
             (on CTOLMR)]; and Mattie Farmer (on
             book and Mar. Auth.) [M. A. H. Farmer
             (on CTOLMR)], 23, single, B: Campbell
             Co., VA, Lived: Alleg. Co., VA, dau/o:
             Chs. E. and ____ Farmer. PL: Alleg.
             Co., VA "A. D. Clark's res." CTOLMR
             was signed on 05-17-1869 by H. C.
             Vaughan, Clk. Mins. Ret. says mar. on
             05-19-1869 in Covington in Alleg. Co.,
             VA, was signed S. B. Dolly.

06-16-1869   J. T. Jones (on book) [Jas. T. Jones
  # 86   (on CTOLMR)], 22, single, B: Hanover

Co., VA, Lived: Alleg. Co., VA, Occup:
farmer, s/o: G. W. and M. N. Jones (on
book) [Geo. W. and Malvina N. Jones
(on CTOLMR)]; and E. E. Haynes (on bk)
[Elizabeth E. Haynes (on CTOLMR)]
[Bettie Haynes (on Mar. Auth.)], 23,
single, Born and Lived: Alleg. Co.,
VA, dau/o: J. P. and E. Haynes (on bk)
[John P. and Elizabeth Haynes (on
CTOLMR)]. PL: Alleg. Co., VA "J. P.
Haynes's res." CTOLMR signed on 06-
16-1869 by H. C. Vaughan, Clk. Mins.
Ret. says mar. on 06-16-1869 at J. P.
Haynes's res. was signed James M.
Rice. Age oath was given by father on
06-16-1869 and signed John P. Haynes.

06-21-1869   (on book) 06-24-1869 (on CTOLMR and
87   Mins. Ret.)
              J. R. Fury (on book) [James R. Fury
              (on CTOLMR)], 21, single, B: Monroe
              Co., VA (now W.VA.), Lived: Alleg.
              Co., VA, Occup: farmer, s/o: T. and R.
              J. Fury (on book) [Thomas and Ruth
              Jane Fury (on CTOLMR)]; and M. S.
              Vance (on book) [Martha S. Vance (on
              CTOLMR)], 19, single, B: Greenbrier
              Co., VA (now W.VA.), Lived: Alleg. Co.,
              VA, dau/o: Wm. and V. Vance (on book)
              [Wm. and Virginia Vance (on CTOLMR)].
              PL: Alleg. Co., VA "Wm. Vance's res."
              CTOLMR signed on 06-21-1869 by H. C.
              Vaughan, Clk. Mins. Ret. says mar. on
              06-24-1869 at Wm. Vance's res. was
              signed James M. Rice. Consent was
              signed 06-21-1869 by William Vance,
              Attest James H. Vance. Oath of Vance
              acknowledgement by James H. Vance on
              06-21-1869, Teste H. C. Vaughan, Clk.

06-23-1869   Wm. A. Gilliam, 31, single, B: Bote-
88   tourt Co., VA, Lived: Alleg. Co., VA

(on book) [Botetourt Co., VA (on CTOLMR)], Occup: farmer, s/o: Wm. A. and E. D. Gilliam (on book) [Wm. A. and Eliza D. Gilliam (on CTOLMR)]; and M. E. Fudge (on book) [Martha E. Fudge (on CTOLMR)] [Bettie Fudge (on Mar. Auth.)], 20, single, Born and Lived: Alleg. Co., VA, dau/o: A. and H. K. Fudge. PL: Alleg. Co., VA "A. Fudge's res." CTOLMR was signed on 06-23-1869 by Jos. T. Fudge, D. C. Mins. Ret. says mar. on 06-23-1869 at A. Fudge's res. and was signed James M. Rice.

06-24-1869   Charles Smith, 22, single, Occup: la-
88 ½   borer, s/o: Thomas and Bettie Smith (on book) [Thos. and Bettie Smith (on CTOLMR)]; and Polly Davis, 22, single, dau/o: George and Caroline Davis (on book) [Geo. and Caroline Davis (on CTOLMR)]. Both were born and lived in Alleg. Co., VA. PL: Alleg. Co., VA "W. A. McCleary's res." CTOLMR was signed on 06-19-1869 by Henry C. Vaughan, Clk. Mins. Ret. says mar. on 06-24-1869 at Mr. McCrary's in Al-leg. Co., VA, was signed S. B. Dolly. Age oath for Polly by Wm. A. McCray, Teste H. C. Vaughan, Clk.

07-01-1869   Wm. Rucker (on book) [William Rucker
89   (on CTOLMR)], 56, widower, B: Green-brier Co., VA (now W.VA.), Lived: Al-leg. Co., VA, Occup: farmer, s/o: E. and F. Rucker (on book) [Elzy and Frances Rucker (on CTOLMR)]; and E. A. Minor (on book) [Eliza Ann Minor (on CTOLMR)], 28, single (on book) [widow (on CTOLMR)], B: Union Co., Inda. [Indiana[, Lived: Alleg. Co., VA (on book) [Botetourt Co., VA (on CTOLMR)],

- 250 -

dau/o: M. P. and S. V. Myers (on bk)
[Michael P. and Sarah V. Myers (on
CTOLMR)]. PL: Alleg. Co., VA "Cov-
ington." CTOLMR was signed on 07-01-
1869 by H. C. Vaughan, Clk. Mins.
Ret. says mar. on 07-01-1869 in Cov-
ington in Alleg. Co., VA, was signed
S. B. Dolly.

07-01-1869 (on book) ___-___-_____ (on CTOLMR)
90 07-16-1869 (on Mins. Ret.)
Wm. Leighton (on book) [William Leigh-
ton (on CTOLMR)], 54, widower, B:
Rockbridge Co., VA, Lived: Alleg. Co.,
VA (on book) [Rockbridge Co., VA (on
CTOLMR)], Occup: farmer, s/o: W. and
N. Leighton (on book) [Wm. and Nancy
Leighton (on CTOLMR)]; and S. J.
Miller (on book) [Sarah J. Miller (on
CTOLMR)], 33, widow, B: Rockbridge
Co., VA, Lived: Alleg. Co., VA (on
book) [Rockbridge Co., VA (on CTOLMR)],
dau/o: E. and N. Hayslett (on book)
[Ezekiel and Nancy Hayslett (on CTOL
MR)]. PL: Alleg. Co., VA "Wm. Leigh-
ton's res."["R̶e̶s̶i̶d̶e̶n̶c̶e̶ ̶o̶f̶ ̶S̶.̶ ̶J̶.̶ ̶M̶i̶l̶l̶-̶
e̶r̶" (as on CTOLMR)]. CTOLMR was
signed on 06-21-1869 by H. C. Vaughan,
Clk. Mins. Ret. says mar. on 07-16-
1869 at Wm. Leighton's res. and was
signed Davis M. Wood.

07-01-1869 (on book) 06-30-1869 (on CTOLMR and
91 Mins. Ret.)
R. B. McCaleb (on book) [Robert B. Mc-
Caleb (on CTOLMR)], 41, single, B:
Campbell Co., VA, Lived: Alleg. Co.,
VA, Occup: farmer (on book) [Mechanic
(on CTOLMR)], s/o: T. and S. McCaleb
(on book) [Thos. and Sarah McCaleb (on
CTOLMR)]; and S. T. Walker (on book)
[Sallie T. Walker (on CTOLMR)], 22,

(Mar. Register Book (1) - Continued)

single, Born and Lived: Alleg. Co.,
VA, dau/o: H. and M. R. Walker (on
book) [Henry and Maria R. Walker (on
CTOLMR)]. PL: Alleg. Co., VA "Henry
Walker's res." CTOLMR signed on 06-
29-1869 by H. C. Vaughan, Clk. Mins.
Ret. says mar. on 06-30-1869 at Henry
Walker's res. on Potts Creek in Alleg.
Co., VA, was signed John B. Davis.
Age oath for Sallie was given by Rob-
ert B. McCaleb on 06-29-1869, Teste
H. C. Vaughan, Clk. Consent for Sal-
lie by H. Walker and Marie R. Walker
on 06-28-1869.

07-19-1869   (on book) 07-20-1869 (on CTOLMR and
92   Mins. Ret.)
              G. W. Surber (on book) [George W. Sur-
              ber (on CTOLMR)], 22, single, B: Bath
              Co., VA, Lived: Alleg. Co., VA, Occup:
              farmer, s/o: L. and S. Surber (on bk)
              [Levi and Sallie Surber (on CTOLMR)];
              and Sallie McCallister, 19, single,
              Born and Lived: Alleg. Co., VA, dau/o:
              R. and N. McCallister (on book) [Rufus
              and Nancy McCallister (on CTOLMR)].
              PL: Alleg. Co., VA "Rufus McCallister
              res." CTOLMR signed on 07-19-1869 by
              H. C. Vaughan, Clk. Mins. Ret. says
              mar. on 07-20-1869 at "my residence"
              and was signed James M. Rice. Consent
              of Rufus McAllister 07-19-1869, Attest
              William Surber and Peter McAlister.
              Oath of McAllister acknowledgement on
              07-19-1869 by G. W. Surber, Teste H.
              C. Vaughan, Clk.

08-13-1869   (on book) 08-12-1869 (on CTOLMR)
92 ½   08-13-1869 (on Mins. Ret.)
              Wyatt Hill, "Colored", 28, single,
              Born and Lived: Alleg. Co., VA, Occup:
              laborer, s/o: Gabrael Hill and Nancy

- 252 -

Hill; and <u>Harriet Womack</u> (on book)
[<u>Harriet Worrack</u> (on CTOLMR)] [<u>Harriet
Worrick</u> (on Mar. Auth.)], "Colored",
19, single, Born and Lived: Alleg. Co,
VA, dau/o: Burl and Mary Womack (on
book) [Burl and Mary Worrack (on CTOL
MR)]. PL: Alleg. Co., VA, "Miss Liz-
zie Hansbarger's res." CTOLMR signed
on 08-11-1869 by H. C. Vaughan, Clk.
Mins. Ret. says mar. on 08-13-1869 at
Miss Hansbarger's res. and was signed
by John L. Beale. Consent has <u>Harriet
Worrick</u>, born March 1850, Mary is 56
years old and Burl is 40 years old;
and it was dated 08-10-1869 at Wilson
Creek and was signed Burl (his X mark)
Worrick and Mary (her X mark) Worrick,
Wit. Lizzie Hansbarger.

09-20-1869   (on book)   09-22-1869 (on CTOLMR and
  # 93   Mins. Ret.)
             <u>Jas. Lawler</u> (on book) [<u>James Lawler</u>
             (on CTOLMR)], 40, single, B: County
             Cork, Ireland, Lived: Alleg. Co., VA,
             Occup: farmer (on book) [laborer (on
             CTOLMR)], s/o: D. and H. Lawler (on
             book) [Daniel and Hannorah Lawler (on
             CTOLMR)]; and <u>E. H. Franklin</u> (on book)
             [<u>Elizabeth H. Franklin</u> (on CTOLMR)],
             28, single, Born and Lived: Alleg. Co,
             VA, dau/o: B. and A. Franklin (on bk)
             [(Note: Has either "Jesse" or "B"-- is
             written over) and Annie Franklin (on
             CTOLMR)]. PL: Alleg. Co., VA "Jas.
             Lawler's res." CTOLMR was signed on
             09-20-1869 by H. C. Vaughan, Clk.
             Mins. Ret. says mar. on 09-22-1869 in
             Clifton Forge, VA in Alleg. Co. and
             was signed by Hugh P. McMenanim. Age
             oath for <u>Elizabeth</u> was given by Jos.
             Zeigler on 09-20-1869, Teste H. C.
             Vaughan, Clk.

07-25-1869   (on book)   09-25-1869 (on Mins. Ret.)
94   Perry Jackson, 30, "Colored", single,
              B: St. Mary Co., MD, Lived: Alleg. Co,
              VA, Occup: laborer, s/o: Perry and
              Minnie Jackson; and Patsey Barber, 31,
              "Colored", widow, Born and Lived: Al-
              leg. Co., VA, dau/o: _____ & _____
              Barber (on book and CTOLMR).   PL: Al-
              leg. Co., VA "Callaghan's."   CTOLMR
              signed on 07-22-1869 by H. C. Vaughan,
              Clk. Mins. Ret. says mar. on 09-25-
              1869 at Callaghan's in Alleg. Co., VA,
              and was signed S. B. Dolly.

Page 12

08-28-1869   F. M. Humphries (on book) [Ferdinand
1   M. Humphries (on CTOLMR)], 25, single,
              Born and Lived: Alleg. Co., VA, Occup:
              farmer, s/o: A. and ____ Humphries (on
              book) [Anderson Humphries and Martha
              Persinger (on CTOLMR)]; and Margaret
              Damron, 30, widow, Born and Lived: Al-
              leg. Co., VA, dau/o: S. and P. Bennett
              (on book) [Sampson and Phoebe Bennett
              (on CTOLMR)].   PL: Alleg. Co., VA,
              "Bride's res."   CTOLMR was signed on
              08-28-1869 by H. C. Vaughan, Clk.
              Mins. Ret. says mar. on 08-28-1869 at
              bride's res. in Alleg. Co., VA, was
              signed S. B. Dolly.

08-29-1869   (on book)   09-29-1869 (on CTOLMR and
2   Mins. Ret.)
              G. W. Nicely (on book) [George W. Nice-
              ly (on CTOLMR)], 21, single, Born and
              Lived: Alleg. Co., VA, Occup: farmer,
              s/o: J. and A. Nicely (on book) [Jacob
              and Ann Nicely (on CTOMR)]; and H. Rod-
              enizer (on book) [Harriet Rodenizer
              (on CTOLMR)], 23, single, B: Rock-
              bridge Co., VA, Lived: Alleg. Co., VA,

dau/o: H. and R. Rodenizer (on book)
[Henry and Rachel Rodenizer (on CTOL
MR)]. PL: Alleg. Co., VA "Geo. Nicely's res." CTOLMR was signed on 09-
29-1869 by H. C. Vaughan, Clk. Mins.
Ret. says mar. on 09-29-1869 in Clifton Forge in Alleg. Co., VA, was signed by S. B. Dolly, Meth. Age oath for
Harriet was given by Minor Acres on
09-29-1869, Teste H. C. Vaughan, Clk.

08-30-1869   J. Hurley (on book) [John Hurley (on
  # 3   CTOLMR)], 28, single, B: County Cork,
              Ireland, Lived: Alleg. Co., VA, Occup:
              laborer, s/o: J. and M. Hurley (on bk)
              [James and Mary Hurley (on CTOLMR)];
              and H. Hurley (on book) [Hannora Hur-
              ley (on CTOLMR)], 20, single, B: Vt.
              (Vermont), Lived: Alleg. Co., VA, dau/
              o: T. and C. Hurley (on book) [Thomas
              and Catharine Hurley (on CTOLMR)].
              PL: Alleg. Co., VA "Mud Tunnel" (on
              CTOL) ["Thos. Hurley res." (on CTOL
              MR)]. CTOL was signed on 08-30-1869
              by Thomas Hurley [Note: apparently
              used for consent]. CTOLMR was signed
              on 08-30-1869 by H. C. Vaughan, Clk.
              Mins. Ret. says mar. on 08-30-1869 at
              Red Hill Tunnel and was signed Hugh P.
              McMenanim, Roman Catholic.

10-04-1869   Thomas Luke, 44, "Colored", widower,
  # 3 ½   B: Nancemond Co., VA, Lived: Alleg.
              Co., VA, Occup: laborer, s/o: Hasker
              Luke and Betsy Luke (on book) [?Hasher
              and Betsey Luke (on CTOLMR)]; and
              Maria Prian, 45, "Colored", widow,
              Born and Lived: Alleg. Co., VA, dau/o:
              _____ and _____ Prian (on book and
              CTOLMR). PL: Alleg. Co., VA "Coving-
              ton." CTOLMR signed on 10-04-1869 by
              H. C. Vaughan, Clk. Mins. Ret. says

(Mar. Register Book (1) - Continued)

mar. on 10-04-1869 in Covington in
Alleg. Co., VA, and was signed S. B.
Dolly.

10-06-1869   (on book)   _-_-____ (on CTOLMR)
4   11-09-1869 (on Mins. Ret.)
              Abra. Wolfe (on book) [Abraham Wolf
              (on CTOLMR)], 40, widower, Born and
              Lived: Alleg. Co., VA, Occup: farmer,
              s/o: I. and M. Wolf (on book) [Isaac
              and Martha Wolf (on CTOLMR--parents
              names listed backwards on CTOLMR)];
              and J. Arrington (on book) [Janetta
              Arington (on CTOLMR)], 27, single,
              (on book) [widow (on CTOLMR)], Born
              and Lived: Alleg. Co., VA, dau/o: Jas.
              and J. Arrington (on book) [Jas. and
              Jane Arington (on CTOLMR--parents
              names were listed backwards, but in
              their correct places here)]. PL: Al-
              leg. Co., VA (on book) [_____ (on
              CTOLMR)]. CTOLMR signed on 11-06-
              1869 by H. C. Vaughan, Clk. Mins.
              Ret. says mar. on 11-09-1869 at grooms
              res. was signed by Aaron Boon, Meth.

10-12-1869   W. F. Gillespie (on book) [William F.
5   Gillespie (on CTOLMR)], 30, single,
              Born and Lived: Greenbrier Co., VA
              (now W.VA.), Occup: stage driver, s/o:
              J. K. and J. Gillespie (on book) [John
              K. and Jane Gillespie (on CTOLMR)];
              and B. J.Shriggs (on book) [Barbara J.
              Shriggs (on Mar. Auth.)] [Barbara J.
              Shiggs (?Shriggs) (on CTOLMR), 21,
              single, B: Greenbrier Co., VA (now W.
              VA), Lived: Alleg. Co., VA, dau/o: H.
              and M. Shriggs (on book) [Henry and
              Margaret Shriggs (on CTOLMR)]. PL:
              Alleg. Co., VA, "Geo. Lynch's res. at
              Alleghany Station." CTOLMR signed on
              10-11-1869 by H. C. Vaughan, Clk.

- 256 -

Mins. Ret. says mar. on 10-12-1869 at
Alleghany Station in Alleg. Co., VA,
and was signed S. B. Dolly, Meth. Age
oath was made by Wm. N. Tyree on 10-
11-1869 for Barbara, Teste H. C. Vaughan, Clk.

10-14-1869   G. F. Fridley (on book) [George F.
  # 6   Fridley (on CTOLMR)], 21, single, Born
             and Lived: Alleg. Co., VA, Occup: far-
             mer, s/o: N. and E. Fridley (on book)
             [Nelson and Elizabeth Fridley (on CTOL
             MR)]; and J. E. Armintrout (on book)
             [Joanah E. Armintrout (on CTOLMR)],
             21, single, Born and Lived: Alleg. Co,
             VA, dau/o: J. and M. E. Armintrout (on
             book) [Jos. and Mary E. Armintrout (on
             CTOLMR)]. PL: Alleg. Co., VA, "Jos.
             Armintrout's res." CTOLMR was signed
             on 10-13-1869 by H. C. Vaughan, Clk.
             Mins. Ret. says mar. on 10-14-1869 at
             Mary E. Armontrout's on Potts Creek in
             Alleg. Co., VA, and was signed by John
             B. Davis, Dunkard. Age oath was given
             by M. G. Wright on 10-13-1869, Teste
             H. C. Vaughan, Clk.

10-14-1869   J. O. Coleman (on book) [John O. Cole-
  # 7   man (on CTOLMR)], 26, single, Born and
             Lived: Fayette Co., VA (now W.VA.),
             Occup: farmer, s/o: J. P. and E. Cole-
             man (on book) [J. P. and Elizabeth
             Coleman (on CTOLMR)]; and E. B. Atkin-
             son (on book) [Evaline B. Atkinson (on
             CTOLMR)], 27, single, Born and Lived:
             Fayette Co., VA (now W.VA.), dau/o: A.
             and A. Atkinson (on book) [Anderson
             and Ann Atkinson (on CTOLMR)]. PL: Al-
             leg. Co., VA, "Covington." CTOLMR was
             signed on 10-14-1869 by H. C. Vaughan,
             Clk. Mins. Ret. says mar. on 10-14-
             1869 in Covington in Alleg. Co., VA,

and was signed S. B. Dolly. Age oath
was given by John O. Coleman, who
said Anderson Atkinson lived in "La-
Fayette Co., W. VA," on 10-14-1869,
Teste H. C. Vaughan, Clk. [Author's
Note: I can find only the spelling
Fayette County on present day West
Virginia maps.]

10-14-1869   J. M. Hall (on book) [James M. Hall
8   (on CTOLMR)], 23, single, Born and
             Lived: Greenbrier Co., VA (now W.VA.),
             Occup: farmer, s/o: R. A. and J. Hall
             (on book) [Reuben A. and Jane Hall (on
             CTOLMR)]; and L. T. R. Hoke, 15, sing-
             le, B: Monroe Co., VA (now W.VA.), Liv-
             ed: Alleg. Co., VA, dau/o: W. and C.
             Hoke (on book) [Wm. and Catharine Hoke
             (on CTOLMR)]. PL: Alleg. Co., VA,
             "Wm. Hoke's res." CTOLMR was signed
             on 10-14-1869 by H. C. Vaughan, Clk.
             Mins. Ret. says mar. on 10-14-1869 at
             Wm. Hoke's res. was signed James M.
             Rice, Presb. Consent on 10-14-1869
             by William Hoke, Wit. Nash L. (his X
             mark) Bess. Oath of Hoke acknowledge-
             ment by Nash L. Bess on 10-14-1869,
             Teste H. C. Vaughan, Clk.

10-20-1869   D. E. Driscoll (on book) [Dennis E.
9   Driscoll (on CTOLMR)], 26, single, B:
             Bedford Co., VA, Lived: Botetourt Co.,
             VA, Occup: farmer, s/o: T. and M. Dris-
             coll (on book) [Thimothy and Mary Dris-
             coll (on CTOLMR)]; and E. V. Richardson
             (on book) [Eliza Va. Richardson (on
             CTOLMR)], 18, single, Born and Lived:
             Alleg. Co., VA, dau/o: W. and A. T.
             (? or F.) Richardson (on book) [Will-
             iam and A. T. Richardson (on CTOLMR)].
             PL: Alleg. Co., VA, "Wm. Richardson's
             res." CTOL was signed on 10-15-1869

by Wm. Richardson [Note: apparently
used as consent]. CTOLMR was signed
on 10-15-1869 by H. C. Vaughan, Clk.
Mins. Ret. says mar. on 10-20-1869 at
Callaghan's in Alleg. Co., VA, was
signed S. B. Dolly.

10-20-1869   R. H. Hurbard (on book and CTOLMR)
  # 10   [Robert H. Hubard (on Mar. Auth.)],
             37, widower, B: Botetourt Co., VA,
             Lived: Alleg. Co., VA, Occup: farmer
             (on book) [carpenter (on CTOLMR)],
             s/o: S. W. and E. Hurbard (on book)
             [Sam'l. W. and Elizabeth Hurbard (on
             CTOLMR)]; and E. Armintrout (on book)
             [Elizabeth Armintrout (on CTOLMR)],
             32, widow, Born and Lived: Alleg. Co.,
             VA, dau/o: I. and ____ Wolf (on book)
             [Isaac and ____ Wolf (on CTOLMR)].
             PL: Alleg. Co., VA. CTOLMR signed on
             10-20-1869 by H. C. Vaughan, Clk.
             Mins. Ret. says mar. on 10-20-1869 at
             Elizabeth An Armontrout's on Potts
             Creek in Alleg. Co. was signed by John
             B. Davis.

10-27-1869   Wm. W. Womack (on book) [William W.
  # 11   Womack (on CTOLMR)], 29, single, Born
             and Lived: Botetourt Co., VA, Occup:
             farmer, s/o: W. E. and M. Walkup (on
             book) [William E. and Marietta (Walker
             ?) (?Walkup), Jr.--can't read (on CTOL
             MR)]; and H. N. Ryals (on book) [Hat-
             tie N. Ryals (on Mar. Auth.)] [Harriet
             N. Ryals (on CTOLMR)], 24, single, B:
             Cumberland [Note: nothing else was
             listed--There is a town and a county
             in VA by this name, also there is Cum-
             berland, Maryland and perhaps other
             places, so it is hard to tell what is
             meant here.], Lived: Alleg. Co., VA,
             dau/o: V. C. and H. C. Ryals. PL: Al--

(Mar. Register Book (1) - Continued)

leg. Co., VA, "Clifton Forge." Mar.
by Wm. E. Hill. CTOLMR signed on 10-
21-1869 by H. C. Vaughan, Clk. Mins.
Ret. says mar. on 10-27-1869 in Clifton
Forge in Alleg. Co., VA, was signed W.
E. Hill. Age oath for Harriet was
given by James D. Ryals on 10-21-1869,
Teste H. C. Vaughan, Clk.

10-28-1869   J. W. Givens (on book) [James W. Givens
12   (on CTOLMR)], 23, single, Born and Liv-
             ed: Craig Co., VA, Occup: farmer, s/o:
             A. F. and P. A. Givens (on book) [A. F.
             and Parnelia A. Givens (on CTOLMR)];
             and S. C. King (on book) [Sallie C.
             King (on CTOLMR)], 19, single, Born
             and Lived: Alleg. Co., VA, dau/o: W.
             F. and E. King (on book) [Wm. F. and
             Eliza King (on CTOLMR)]. PL: Alleg.
             Co., VA, "Mrs. Eliza King's res."
             CTOLMR signed on 10-25-1869 by H. C.
             Vaughan, Clk. Mins. Ret. says mar. on
             10-28-1869 at Mrs. King's res. was
             signed by James M. Rice. Consent of
             Eliza King on 10-25-1869, Wit. William
             D. King and S. H. King. Oath of King's
             acknowledgement by Wm. D. King on 10-
             25-1869, Teste H. C. Vaughan, Clk.

10-28-1869   Wm. E. Hill (on book) [William E. Hill
13   (on CTOLMR)], 33, single, B: Roanoke
             Co., VA, Lived: Richmond, VA, Occup:
             Minister, s/o: C. G. and M. R. Hill (on
             book) [Clifton G. and Mary R. Hill (on
             CTOLMR)]; and J. K. Pitzer (on book)
             [Jane Kyle Pitzer (on CTOLMR)], 23,
             single, Born and Lived: Alleg. Co., VA,
             dau/o: J. L. and H. A. Pitzer (on book)
             [Jno. L. and Harriet Ann Pitzer (on
             CTOLMR)]. PL: Alleg. Co., VA, "Coving-
             ton." CTOL signed on 10-26-1869 by
             John L. Pitzer [Note: apparently used

- 260 -

for consent]. CTOLMR was signed on
10-26-1869 by H. C. Vaughan, Clk.
Mins. Ret. says mar. on 10-28-1869 in
Covington in Alleg. Co., VA, was signed S. B. Dolly.

10-29-1869   Charles L. Bess, 32, widower, Born and
13 ½   Lived: Alleg. Co., VA, Occup: farmer,
             s/o: Hamilton and Rebecca Bess; and
             Lucinda Kimberlin, 35, single, B:
             Tennessee, Lived: Alleg. Co., VA, dau/
             o: William and Elizabeth Kimberlin.
             PL: Alleg. Co., VA. CTOLMR signed
             on 10-28-1869 by H. C. Vaughan, Clk.
             Mins. Ret. says mar. 10-29-1869 at
             John B. Davis's res. on Potts Creek
             in Alleg. Co., VA, was signed John B.
             Davis. Age oath was given by Charles
             Bess for Lucinda on 10-28-1869, Teste
             H. C. Vaughan, Clk.

11-18-1869   J. W. Thompson (on book) [John W.
14   Thompson (on CTOLMR)], 25, single, B:
             Rockbridge Co., VA, Lived: Alleg. Co.,
             VA, Occup: farmer, s/o: W. H. and M.
             Thompson (on book) [Wm. H. and Maria
             Thompson (on CTOLMR)]; and F. C. Boley
             (on book) [Fannie C. Boley (on Mar.
             Auth.)] [Francis C. Boley (on CTOLMR)],
             20, single, B: Monroe Co., VA (now W.
             VA), Lived: Alleg. Co., VA, dau/o: P.
             and S. Boley (on book) [Pitman and
             Sarah Boley (on CTOLMR)]. PL: Alleg.
             Co., VA, "Pitman Boley's res." CTOLMR
             was signed on 11-18-1869 by H. C. Vaug-
             han, Clk. Mins. Ret. says mar. on 11-
             18-1869 at bride's father's res. in
             Alleg. Co., VA, was signed S. B. Dolly.

11-04-1869   (on book) 11-05-1869 (on CTOLMR)
14 ½   11-04-1869 (on Mins. Ret.)
             Parson Blake, 23, "Colored," single,

B: Sussex Co., VA, Lived: Alleg. Co., VA, Occup: laborer, s/o: William and Peggy Blake (on book) [Wm. and Peggy Blake (on CTOLMR)]; and Rachel Byrd, 22, "Colored," single, B: Botetourt Co., VA, Lived: Alleg. Co., VA, dau/o: Albert and Lucy Byrd. PL: Alleg. Co., VA, "Miss Lucie Irvine's res." CTOL MR was signed on 10-05-1869 and Mar. Auth. was signed on 11-05-1869 by H. C. Vaughan, Clk. [Note: believe clk. made date error since everything else is November] Mins. Ret. says mar. on 11-04-1869 at Jackson River Depot and was signed by John G. Beal [John L. Beale (on book)].

11-18-1869
15

W. Fisher (on book) [Warrick Fisher (on CTOLMR)], 25, single, Born and Lived: Greenbrier Co., VA (now W.VA.), Occup: farmer, s/o: J. and H. Fisher (on book) [John and Hettie Fisher (on CTOLMR)]; and M. S. Brackman (on book) [Margaret S. Brackman (on CTOLMR)], 21, single, Born and Lived: Greenbrier Co., VA (now W.VA.), dau/o: W. and L. Brackman (on book) [William and Luticia Brackman (on CTOLMR)]. PL: Alleg. Co., VA, "Covington." CTOLMR was signed on 11-18-1869 by H. C. Vaughan, Clk. Mins. Ret. says mar. on 11-18-1869 in Covington in Alleg. Co., VA, was signed S. B. Dolly. Age oath for Margaret was given by Warrick Fisher on 11-18-1869, Teste H. C. Vaughan, Clk.

11-23-1869
16

H. J. Clinebell (on book) [Henry J. Clinebell (on CTOLMR)], 39, widower, B: Rockbridge Co., VA, Lived: Craig Co., VA, Occup: farmer, s/o: G. and S. Clinebell (on book) [Geo. and Sarah

Clinebell (on CTOLMR)]; and <u>N. J. Ply-male</u> (on book) [<u>Nancy J. Plymale</u> (on CTOLMR)], 26, single, Born and Lived: Alleg. Co., VA, dau/o: W. B. and E. Plymale (on book) [Wm. B. and Elizabeth Plymale (on CTOLMR)]. PL: Alleg. Co., VA, "Wm. Craft's res." CTOLMR signed on 11-22-1869 by H. C. Vaughan, Clk. Mins. Ret. says mar. on 11-25-1869 at William Craft's on Potts Creek in Alleg. Co., VA, was signed John B. Davis. Age oath for <u>Nancy</u> was given by Wm. Craft on 11-22-1869, Teste H. C. Vaughan, Clk.

11-28-1869 H. D. Ketton (on book) [<u>Henry D. Ketton</u>
17 <u>(? Kelton</u> --can't determine) (on CTOL MR)], 38, single, Born and Lived: Chesterfield Co., VA, Occup: miner, s/o: H. and E. Ketton (on book) [Henry and Elizabeth Ketton (?Kelton) (on CTOL MR)]; and <u>M. E. Robinson</u> (on book) [<u>Mary Elizabeth Robinson</u> (on CTOLMR)], 28, single, Born and Lived: Alleg. Co., VA, dau/o: Jas. T. and A. Robinson (on book) [James T. and Ann Robinson (on CTOLMR)]. PL: Alleg. Co., VA, "John Richardson's res." CTOLMR was signed on 11-27-1869 by H. C. Vaughan, Clk. Mins. Ret. says mar. on 11-28-1869 at "10 in the morning" was signed Wm. Richardson.

12-02-1869 <u>Preston Davis</u>, 21, "Colored," single,
17 ½ B: Alleg. Co., VA, Lived: ___ (on bk) [Alleg. Co., VA (on CTOLMR)], Occup: ___ (on book) [farmer (on CTOLMR)], s/o: ___ (on book) [Spencer and Harriet Davis (on CTOLMR)]; and <u>C. Gibson</u> (on book) [<u>Charlotte Gibson</u> (on CTOLMR)], 21, "Colored," single, B: Alleg. Co., VA, Lived: ___ (on book) [Alleg. Co.,

VA (on CTOLMR)], dau/o: ___ (on book)
[_____ Gibson (on CTOLMR)]. CTOLMR
signed on 12-01-1869 by H. C. Vaughan,
Clk. Mins. Ret. says mar. on 12-02-
1869 at Fork Run was signed Rev. John
L. Beale. PL: Alleg. Co., VA, "Peter
Jordan's res." Age oath for <u>Charlotte</u>
was given by Peter Jordan on 12-01-
1869, Teste H. C. Vaughan, Clk.

12-15-1869   Wednesday
18   <u>S. H. Sims</u> (on book) [<u>Samuel Henry</u>
<u>Sims</u> (on CTOLMR)], 25, single, B: Han-
over Co., VA, Lived: Alleg. Co., VA,
Occup: laborer, s/o: G. and P. Sims
(on book) [Garland and Pelina Sims (on
CTOLMR)]; and <u>R. E. Ham</u> (on book) [<u>Ra-
chel E. Ham</u> (on CTOLMR)], 19, single,
Born and Lived: Alleg. Co., VA, dau/o:
W. and E. Ham (on book) [William and
Elizabeth Ham (on CTOLMR)]. PL: Alleg.
Co., VA, "Mrs. Hanes in Clifton Forge,
VA." CTOLMR signed on 12-13-1869 by H.
C. Vaughan, Clk. Mins. Ret. says mar.
on 12-15-1869 in Clifton Forge in Al-
leg. Co., VA, was signed S. B. Dolly.

02-20-1870   <u>Edward Davis</u>, "Colored"; and <u>Mary S.</u>
18 ½   <u>Lovins</u> (? Lovens), "Colored." PL: Al-
leg. Co., VA. [Author's Note: Above
was all that was on book--below are the
only documents found in the files.]
"The Clerk of Alleghany County
    Will please grant and Issue Lic-
ense for me to marry <u>Mary S. Lovins</u>
collered, my age is over 21 years, I
am a collered man. You will please
hand them to Mr. Damron the bearer of
this & he will bring them to me.
    <u>Edward (his X mark) Davis</u>, Col."
"This man & woman has been living in
Alleghany County on my place over 12

months. You will see the mother of
the girl has given consent. She has
no Father living.

Wm. Damron"

"This is to authorise the Clerk of
Alleghany County to grant & issue
License for my Daughter <u>Mary S. Lov-
ens</u>, age 17 years collered, to marry
<u>Edward Davis</u> collered, Given under
my hand this 18th day of February
1871.

Ellen (her X mark) Lovens
Wit. C. A. Damron"

"C. A. Damron this day appeared before
me in my office and made oath that the
signature to the within certificate
was acknowledged in his presence.

Given under my hand as Clk. of
the County Ct. of Alleghany Co. this
10th Feby 1870.

J. R. Pharr, Clk. Alleghany Co.
Court"

[Note: There was no other information
found on the records or in the files.]

12-22-1869   J. B. Hoylman (on book) [<u>John Brenard
19   (?Breward) Hoylman</u> (on CTOLMR)], 25,
              single, Born and Lived: Botetourt Co.,
              VA, Occup: farmer, s/o: A. and M. Hoyl-
              man (on book) [Addison and Malinda
              Hoylman (on CTOLMR)]; and <u>M. A. Lemon</u>
              (on book) [<u>Martha Ann Lemon</u> (on CTOL
              MR)], 20, single, Born and Lived: Al-
              leg. Co., VA, dau/o: J. G. and B. Lem-
              on (on book) [Joseph G. and Betsey
              Lemon (on CTOLMR)]. PL: Alleg. Co.,
              VA "Jos. Lemon's res." CTOLMR was
              signed on 12-17-1869 by H. C. Vaughan,
              Clk. Mins. Ret. says mar. on 12-22-
              1869 at Joseph Lemon's and was signed
              Geo. T. Lyle.

(Mar. Register Book (1) - Continued)

___-___-1869   (page tore on book) 12-22-1869 (on
  # 20   CTOLMR and Mins. Ret.)
                S. L. Biggs (on book) [Samuel Lucian
                Biggs (on CTOLMR)], 24, single, B:
                Botetourt Co., VA, Lived: Alleg. Co.,
                VA, Occup: farmer, s/o: W. and S. J.
                Biggs (on book) [Wmsson (?Williamsson)
                and Susan J. Biggs (on CTOLMR)]; and
                M. C. Griffith (on book) [Martha C.
                Griffith (on CTOLMR)], 19, single,
                Born and Lived: Alleg. Co., VA, dau/o:
                C. and E. Griffith (on book) [Caleb
                and Elizabeth Griffith (on CTOLMR)].
                PL: Alleg. Co., VA, "C. Griffith's
                res." CTOLMR was signed on 12-20-1869
                by H. C. Vaughan, Clk. Mins. Ret. says
                mar. on 12-22-1869 at Caleb Griffith's
                res. was signed S. S. Ryder.

___-28-1869   (page tore on book) 12-28-1869 (on
  # 21   CTOLMR and Mins. Ret.)
                J. M. Bennett (on book) [Jacob M. Ben-
                nett (on CTOLMR)], 20, single, Born
                and Lived: Alleg. Co., VA, Occup: far-
                mer, s/o: S. and M. E. Bennett (on
                book) [Sampson and Mary E. Bennett (on
                CTOLMR)]; and R. Wolf (on book) [Rebec-
                ca Wolf (on CTOLMR)], 21, single, Born
                and Lived: Alleg. Co., VA, dau/o: J.
                A. and S. Wolf (on book) [Jacob A. and
                Sarah Wolf (on CTOLMR)]. PL: Alleg.
                Co., VA, "Sampson Bennett res." CTOL
                MR signed on 10-26-1869 by H. C. Vaug-
                han, Clk. Mins. Ret. says mar. on 12-
                28-1869 at Sampson Bennet's on Potts
                Creek in Alleg. Co., VA, was signed by
                John B. Davis. Age oath was given by
                Sampson Bennett for Rebecca on 10-26-
                1869, Teste H. C. Vaughan, Clk.

___-28-1869   (page tore on book) 12-28-1869 Tuesday
  # 22   (on CTOLMR - planned date of Mar.) (?

as to actual date)
Jos. A. Kayser (on book) [Joseph A.
Kayser (on CTOLMR)], 22, single, B:
Alleg. Co., VA, Lived: Rockbridge Co.,
VA, Occup: cabinetmaker, s/o: A. and
E. A. Kayser (on book) [Addison and
Eliza A. Kayser (on CTOLMR)]; and M.
E. Leighton (on book) [Margarette
(? Margaret) E. Leighton (on CTOLMR)],
17, single, B: Alleg. Co., VA, Lived:
Alleg. Co., VA, dau/o: W. and E. G.
Leighton (on book) [William and Emily
G. Leighton (on CTOLMR)]. PL: Alleg.
Co., VA (on book) [Note: There was no
section written in for "place" on
CTOLMR]. Handwritten CTOLMR was sign-
ed on 12-27-1869 by H. C. Vaughan,
Clk. Note to Clk. on back of CTOLMR
was dated 01-01-1870 and says T. E.
Reynolds married parties named within
--date of mar. was not stated nor
where it took place. [Author's Note:
The minister's part on the regular
CTOLMR form that is printed was not
written in on the handwritten one so
the minister could fill it out, just
as "Place of Marriage" was also omitted
on the handwritten one.]

___-30-1869   (page tore on book) 12-30-1869 (on
23   CTOLMR and Mins. Ret.)
               H. C. Herbert (on book) [Henry C. Her-
               bert (on CTOLMR)], 30, single, Born
               and Lived: Monroe Co., VA (now W.VA.),
               Occup: laborer, s/o: W. and L. Herbert
               (on book) [Wm. and Luvenia Herbert (on
               CTOLMR)]; and M. A. Brown (on book)
               [Amanda A. Brown (on CTOLMR)], 19,
               single, Born and Lived: Alleg. Co., VA,
               dau/o: L. and ___ Brown (on book) [Lem-
               uel and ____ Brown (on CTOLMR)].   PL:

(Mar. Register Book (1) - Continued)

Alleg. Co., VA, "Wm. Damron's res."
CTOLMR was signed on 12-20-1869 by H.
C. Vaughan, Clk. Mins. Ret. says mar.
on 12-30-1869 at Wm. Damron's on Dunlap Creek in Alleg. Co., VA, was signed John B. Davis. Note to Clk. from
H. C. Herbert requesting he issue and
give the license to Wm. Damron who
would bring it to him was dated on 12-
10-1869.

12-30-1869   John Grasty, 26, "Colored", single, B:
23 ½   Henrico Co., VA, Lived: Alleg. Co.,
             VA, Occup: stone mason, s/o: George
             and Malinda Grasty; and Salia Ann
             Brown (on book) [Jalia Ann Brown (on
             CTOLMR)], 30, "Colored", widow, Born
             and Lived: Alleg. Co., VA, dau/o: Ar-
             thur and Ann Lee. PL: ___ (on book)
             [Arthur Lee's res. in Alleg. Co., VA.
             (on CTOLMR)]. CTOLMR signed on 12-27-
             1869 by H. C. Vaughan, Clk. Mins.
             Ret. says mar. on 12-30-1869 at Calla-
             ghan's in Alleg. Co., VA, was signed
             S. B. Dolly.

01-13-1870   L. D. Bowers (on book) [Lorenzo W.
24   Bowers (on CTOLMR)], 25, single, B:
             Davison Co., N. C., Lived: Alleg. Co.,
             VA, Occup: photographer, s/o: S. L.
             and S. Bowers (on book) [Sam'l. L. and
             Sarah Bowers (on CTOLMR)]; and M. F.
             Smith (on book) [Merinda F. (?Mirenda
             F.) Smith (on CTOLMR)], 19, single,
             Born and Lived: Alleg. Co., VA, dau/o:
             W. J. and M. E. Smith (on book) [Wm.
             J. and Malinda E. Smith (on CTOLMR)].
             PL: Alleg. Co., VA "Wm. J. Smith's
             res." CTOL signed on 01-03-1870 by
             John A. Smith [Note: apparently used
             for consent]. CTOLMR signed on 01-03-
             1870 by H. C. Vaughan, Clk. Mins. Ret.

says mar. on 01-13-1870 at Mr. J.
Smith's res. and was signed S. S. Ryder.

01-03-1870   Robert Hughes, 21, "Colored", single,
24 ½   B: Greenbrier Co., VA (now W.VA.),
            Lived: Alleg. Co., VA, Occup: laborer,
            s/o: _____ and Ellen Hughes; and Re-
            becca Burks, 17, "Colored", single, B:
            Botetourt Co., VA, Lived: Alleg. Co.,
            VA, dau/o: Wm. and Charlotte Burks.
            PL: Alleg. Co., VA, "Sam'l. Coleman's
            res." CTOLMR signed on 01-01-1870 by
            H. C. Vaughan, Clk. Mar. by H. C.
            Vaughan (on book). Mins. Ret. says
            mar. on 01-03-1870 at Mr. Coleman's
            was signed Rev. John L. Beale. Con-
            sent has "Robbert Hughes and my dau-
            ghter Elizabeth" and was signed Will-
            iam (his X mark) Burks and dated 01-
            01-1870 at Simpson's Creek, Teste M.
            W. King and J. W. Sifford.

01-13-1870   J. M. Sizer (on book) [James M. Sizer
25   (on CTOLMR)], 20, single, Born and
            Lived: Alleg. Co., VA, Occup: farmer,
            s/o: F. P. and M. Sizer (on book) [F.
            P. and Mary Sizer (on CTOLMR)]; and
            M. M. Walker (on book) [Mollie M. Wal-
            ker (on CTOLMR)], 18, single, Born and
            Lived: Alleg. Co., VA, dau/o: H. and
            M. Walker (on bk) [Henry and Maria Wal-
            ker (on CTOLMR)]. PL: Alleg. Co., VA,
            "Henry Walker's res." CTOLMR signed
            on 01-07-1870 by H. C. Vaughan, Clk.
            Mins. Ret. says mar. on 01-13-1870 at
            Henry Walker's on Potts Creek in Alleg.
            Co., VA, was signed John B. Davis.
            Consent for Mollie given by Henry Wal-
            ker on 01-06-1870, Wit. W. Rayhill.
            Wm. Rayhill gave oath acknowledgement
            for Walker and Sizer on 01-07-1870,
            Teste H. C. Vaughan, Clk. Consent for

James by F. P. Sizer on 01-06-1870,
Wit. W. Rayhill.

01-12-1870   J. R. Smith (on book) [John R. Smith
  # 26   (on CTOLMR)], 24, single, Born and
             Lived: Alleg. Co., VA, Occup: farmer,
             s/o: W. J. and M. E. Smith (on book)
             [Wm. J. and Malinda E. Smith (on CTOL
             MR)]; and S. B. Robinson (on book)
             [Sallie B. Robinson (on CTOLMR)], 21,
             single, Born and Lived: Alleg. Co.,
             VA, dau/o: W. and E. Robinson (on bk)
             [William and Elizabeth Robinson (on
             CTOLMR)]. PL: Alleg. Co., VA, "Wm.
             Robinson's res." CTOLMR signed on 01-
             11-1870 by H. C. Vaughan, Clk. Mins.
             Ret. says mar. on 01-12-1870 at Wm.
             Robinson's res. was signed S. S. Ry-
             der. Age oath given by Sallie's fa-
             ther, William Robinson, on 01-10-1870.

01-28-1870   (on book)   _ - _   (on CTOLMR)
  # 27   01-31-1870 (on Mins. Ret.)
             E. Bowen (on book) [Erastus Bowen (on
             CTOLMR)], 23, single, Born and Lived:
             Alleg. Co., VA, Occup: wheelright,
             s/o: J. and N. Bowen (on bk) [Johnson
             and Nancy Bowen (on CTOLMR)]; and Car.
             Wolf (on bk) [Caroline Wolf (on CTOL
             MR)], 22, single, Born and Lived: Al-
             leg. Co., VA, dau/o: A. and H. Wolf
             (on bk) [Abraham and Harriet Wolf (on
             CTOLMR)]. PL: Alleg. Co., VA "John
             B. Davis's res." CTOLMR signed on 01-
             28-1870 by H. C. Vaughan, Clk. Mins.
             Ret. says mar. on 01-31-1870 at Har-
             riet Wolf's on Potts Creek in Alleg.
             Co., VA, was signed John B. Davis.
             Age oath for Caroline given by Erastus
             Bowen, Teste H. C. Vaughan, Clk. on
             01-28-1870.

(Mar. Register Book (1) - Continued)

***** Found in with the above file was the following document. No other records have
been found concerning this document.**
"Alleghany County Court Clerk's Office
2nd March 1868
    This day appeared before me Benj.
F. Hepler & made oath that Catharine
Fridly, the daughter Delilah Fridly
was over the age of twenty-one years.
T̶h̶i̶s̶ o̶f̶ a̶g̶e̶. This day above written.
          Joseph T. Fudge, Clk."

02-08-1870   J. M. C. Sullender (on book) [James
28   M. C. Sullender (on CTOLMR)], 21 (on
book and CTOLMR) [27 (on CTOL], single, B: Alleg. Co., VA, Lived: Alleg.
Co., VA (on book) [Botetourt Co., VA
(on CTOLMR)], Occup: farmer, s/o: W.
and S. F. Sullender (on bk) [William
and (? Sasshona or ? Saphrina-- on
CTOL) (? Sasshrond or ? Saphrona -- on
CTOLMR) F. Sullender]; and S. F. Helmintoller (on bk) [Susannah F. Helmintoller (on CTOLMR)], 23, single, Born
and Lived: Alleg. Co.,VA, dau/o: P.
and M. Helmintoller (on bk) [Peter and
Mary Helmintoller (on CTOLMR)]. PL:
Alleg. Co., VA, "Lee Persinger's res."
CTOL signed on 02-04-1870 by P. Helmintoller [Note: apparently used for con-
sent]. CTOLMR signed on 02-04-1870 by
H. C. Vaughan, Clk. Mins. Ret. says
mar. on 02-08-1870 at Lee Persinger's
in Alleg. Co., VA, was signed by Aaron
Boon.

02-19-1870   George H. Adams (on book) [George Hen-
28 ½   ry Adams (on CTOLMR)], 23, "Colored",
single, B: St. Mary County, Maryland,
Lived: Alleg. Co., VA, Occup: farmhand,
s/o: John Lewis and Eliza Chisley; and
Lucy Barbour, 20, "Colored", single,

- 271 -

B: Covington in Alleg. Co., VA, Lived:
Alleg. Co., VA, dau/o: Dock (? Dick)
and Lucy Richards. PL: Alleg. Co.,
VA, "Covington." CTOLMR signed on
02-19-1870 by Henry C. Vaughan, Clk.
Mins. Ret. says mar. on 02-19-1870 at
T. McAllister's near Covington, VA,
was signed by James M. Rice.

03-02-1870   Wednesday
 # 29   Thos. Bush (on book) [Thomas Bush (on
               CTOLMR)], 20, single, Born and Lived:
               Alleg. Co., VA, Occup: farmer, s/o:
               F. and N. Bush (on bk) [Franklin and
               Nancy Bush (on CTOLMR)]; and R. J.
               Brown (on bk) [Rebecca Jane Brown (on
               CTOLMR)], 23, single, Born and Lived:
               Alleg. Co., VA, dau/o: Lem and ____
               Brown (on bk) [____ Brown (on CTOL
               MR)]. PL: Alleg. Co., VA, "Levi Sur-
               ber's res." CTOLMR signed on 03-01-
               1870 by Henry C. Vaughan, Clk. Mins.
               Ret. says mar. on 03-02-1870 at Levi
               Surber's res. in Alleg. Co., VA, was
               signed by James M. Rice.

03-03-1870   William Bethel, 21, single, "Colored",
 # 29 ½   B: Pittsylvania Co., VA, Lived: Alleg.
               Co., VA, Occup: laborer, s/o: Robert
               and Charity Bethel; and Sarah Carter,
               25, "Colored", single, Born and Lived:
               Alleg. Co., VA, dau/o: ____ and Har-
               riet Taliaforo. PL: Alleg. Co., VA,
               "T. McAllister's res." CTOLMR signed
               on 03-03-1870 by H. C. Vaughan, Clk.
               Mins. Ret. says mar. on 03-03-1870 at
               T. McAllister's near Covington, VA,
               was signed James M. Rice.

03-11-1870   Zac. Hamilton (on book) [Zaceriah Ham-
 # 30   ilton (on CTOLMR)], 22, single, Born
               and Lived: Rockbridge Co., VA, Occup:

laborer, s/o: R. and M. Hamilton (on bk) [Robert and Margaret Hamilton (on CTOLMR)]; and <u>Dora Pring</u>, 21, single, Born and Lived: Rockbridge Co., VA, dau/o: W. W. and S. Pring (on book) [William W. and Sarah Pring (on CTOL MR)]. PL: Alleg. Co., VA, "Jas. M. Rice's res., Covington, VA." CTOLMR signed on 03-11-1870 by H. C . Vaughan, Clk. Mins. Ret. says mar. on 03-11-1870 at my res. and was signed James M. Rice. Age oath by <u>Dora Pring</u> on 03-11-1870, Teste H. C. Vaughan, Clk.

03-16-1870
31

<u>Ro. Hamilton</u> (on book) [<u>Robert Hamilton</u> (on CTOLMR)], 22, single, Born and Lived: Rockbridge Co., VA, Occup: farmer, s/o: R. and M. Hamilton (on bk) [Robert and Margaret Hamilton (on CTOLMR)]; and <u>N. Bartley</u> (on book) [<u>Novella Bartley</u> (on CTOLMR)], 21, single, Born and Lived: Rockbridge Co., VA, dau/o: J. and E. J. Bartley (on bk) [John and Elizabeth J. Bartley (on CTOLMR)]. PL: Alleg. Co., VA, "Covington." CTOLMR signed on 03-16-1870 by H. C. Vaughan, Clk. Mins. Ret. says mar. on 03-16-1870 in Covington in Alleg. Co., VA, was signed James M. Rice. Age oath by <u>Miss Novella Bartley</u> on 03-16-1870, Teste H. C. Vaughan, Clk.

04-02-1870
32

<u>Hey George</u> (on book) [<u>Henry George</u> (on CTOLMR)], 22, single, Born and Lived: Greenbrier Co., VA (now W.VA.), Occup: farmer, s/o: W. and R. George (on bk) [William and Ruth George (on CTOLMR)]; and <u>V. Jarrett</u> (on bk) [<u>Victoria Jarrett</u> (on CTOLMR)], single, 21, Born and Lived: Greenbrier Co., VA (now W. VA.), dau/o: Jas. and E. Jarrett (on

(Mar. Register Book (1) - Continued)

bk) [James and Elizabeth Jarrett (on CTOLMR)]. PL: Alleg. Co., VA, "Mc-Curdy's Hotel." CTOLMR signed on 04-02-1870 by H. C. Vaughan, Clk. Mins. Ret. says mar. on 04-02-1870 at Mc-Curdy's Hotel in Covington, VA, was signed James M. Rice. Age oath given by <u>Victoria Jarrett</u>, Teste H. C. Vaughan, Clk.

04-14-1870
33

J. D. Hippert (on book) [John D. Hippert (on CTOLMR)], 21, single, B: Nelson Co., VA, Lived: Alleg. Co., VA, Occup: bricklayer, s/o: G. W. and S. A. Hippert (on bk) [Geo. W. and Sarah Ann Hippert (on CTOLMR)]; and <u>Bettie L. Richardson</u>, 15, single, Born and Lived: Alleg. Co., VA, dau/o: J. F. and M. J. Richardson (on bk) [John F. and Margaret J. Richardson (on CTOLMR)]. PL: Alleg. Co., VA, "John F. Richardson's res." CTOLMR signed on 04-09-1870 by H. C. Vaughan, Clk. Mins. Ret. says mar. on 04-14-1870 at Jno. F. Richardson house was signed James M. Rice.

04-29-1870
34

<u>Wm. Hill</u> (on book) [<u>William Hill</u> (on CTOLMR)], 28, single, B: Monroe Co., VA (now W.VA.), Lived: Alleg. Co., VA, Occup: farmer, s/o: F. and E. Hill (on bk) [Fran and Emaline Hill (on CTOLMR)]; and <u>Rebecca J. James</u> (on book) [<u>Rebecca Jane James</u> (on CTOLMR)], 15, single, Born and Lived: Alleg. Co., VA, dau/o: M. and E. James (on bk) [Madison and Elizabeth James (on CTOLMR)]. PL: Alleg. Co., VA "W. T. Acres's res." CTOLMR signed on 04-26-1870 by Joseph T. Fudge, Clk. Mins. Ret. says mar. on 04-29-1870 at W. T. Acres's res. was signed A. Buhrman. Consent

of Elizabeth (her X mark) James, Attest A. J. Turner and W. T. Acres.
Oath acknowledgement of James consent
by W. T. Acres, Teste Jos. T. Fudge,
Clk.

04-27-1870 (on book) 04-2̶0̶ 27-1870 (on CTOLMR)
  # 35   04-27-1870 (on Mins. Ret.)
Geo. (H.) Surber (on book) [George
Surber (on CTOLMR)], 28, single, Born
and Lived: Greenbrier Co., VA (now W.
VA), Occup: farmer, s/o: D(avid) and
(Jane) Surber (on book) [Author's
Note: The "(H)", "D(avid)" and "(Jane)"
add-in on book was done in pencil as
though put in later, () used to show
where was put in] [David and _____
Surber (on CTOLMR)]; and Rose Hilliary,
18, single, B: Miami, Ohio, Lived:
Greenbrier Co., VA (now W.VA), dau/o:
J. B. and M. S. Hilliary (on bk) [J.
B. and Mary S. Hilliary (on CTOLMR)].
PL: Alleg. Co., VA, "Covington." CTOL
MR signed on 04-26-1870 by Jos. T.
Fudge, Clk. Mins. Ret. says mar. on
04-27-1870 at McCurdy's Hotel was
signed A. Weller. Oath of Hilliary
acknowledgement on 04-26-1870 by Wm.
H. Hilliary, Teste Jos. T. Fudge, Clk.
Consent has George H. Surber and Rose
Hilliary and was signed on 04-27-1870
by J. B. Hilliary, M.D., and Wm. H.
Hilliary, Wit.

05-26-1870 (on book) 05-19-1870 (on CTOLMR)
  # 36   05-26-1870 (on Mins. Ret.)
Michael Rairdon, 19, single, B: Bedford Co., VA, Lived: Alleg. Co., VA,
Occup: wagoneer, s/o: J. and S. Rairdon (on book) [John and Sarah Rairdon
(on CTOLMR)]; and Mary Hogan, 17, B:
_____, single, Lived: Alleg. Co., VA,

(Mar. Register Book (1) - Continued)

dau/o: J. and J. Hogan (on bk) [Joseph
and Joannah Hogan (on CTOLMR)]. [Note:
There was no birthplace on any record
for Mary.] PL: Alleg. Co., VA (on bk)
[_____ (on CTOLMR)]. CTOLMR signed
on 05-12-1870 by Jos. T. Fudge, Clk.
Mins. Ret. says mar. on 05-26-1870 at
Sweet Springs in Monroe Co., W.VA.
was signed Hugh P. Menamin. Consent
of Mrs. Sarah Rairdon who says her
husband is deceased, Wit. Michael
Rairdon on 05-10-1870. Oath of Rairdon and Hogan acknowledgements on 05-
12-1870, Teste Jos. T. Fudge, Clk.
Consent of Mrs. (her X mark) Hogan,
Wit. Michael Rairdon on 05-09-1870.

05-31-1870   Tuesday
37   Js. Wm. Hepler (on book) [James Will-
iam Hepler (on CTOLMR)], 24, single,
Born and Lived: Alleg. Co., VA, Occup:
farmer, s/o: D. and B. Hepler (on bk)
[David and Bashaba Hepler (on CTOLMR)];
and W. C. Carson (on bk) [Wilsonia
Caroline Carson (on CTOLMR)], 22,
single, Born and Lived: Alleg. Co.,
VA, dau/o: J. and C. Carson (on book)
[James and Caroline Carson (on CTOL
MR)]. PL: Alleg. Co., VA, "Mrs. Car-
oline Carson's res." CTOLMR signed
on 05-24-1870 by W. M. Scott, D. C.
Mins. Ret. says mar. on 05-31-1870 at
Caroline Carson's on Snake Run in Al-
leg. Co., VA, was signed John B. Davis.

05-10-1870   Jos. T. Ayers (on book) [Joseph T.
38   Ayres (on CTOLMR)], 24, single, B:
Bedford Co., VA, Lived: Alleg. Co.,
VA, Occup: farmer, s/o: Jno. W. and H.
Ayers (on bk) [John W. and Henrietta
Ayres (on CTOLMR)]; and R. J. Hoke (on
bk) [Rebecca J. Hoke (on CTOLMR)], 17,

- 276 -

(Mar. Register Book (1) - Continued)

single, Born and Lived: Alleg. Co.,
VA, dau/o: Wm. and C. Hoke (on book)
[William and Catharine Hoke (on CTOL
MR)]. PL: Alleg. Co., VA, "Wm. Hoke's
res." CTOLMR signed on 05-09-1870 by
Jos. T. Fudge, Clk. Mins. Ret. says
mar. on 05-10-1870 at Wm. Hoke's res.
was signed James M. Rice. Consent
has Joseph Ayers and Rebebba J. Hok
and was signed on 05-09-1870 by Wm.
Hoke. Oath of Hoke acknowledgement
on 05-09-1870 by John H. Morris, Teste
Jos. T. Fudge, Clk.

05-31-1870
39

Chs. Fleshman (on book) [Charles Fleshman (on CTOLMR)], 33, widower, Born
and Lived: Greenbrier Co., VA (now W.
VA.), Occup: farmer, s/o: H. and P.
Fleshman (on bk) [Harrison and Pal-
mira Fleshman (on CTOLMR)]; and E. J.
Fleshman (on bk) [Elizabeth J. Flesh-
man (on CTOLMR)], 38, widow, B: Mon-
roe Co., VA (now W.VA.), Lived: Green-
brier Co., W. Va. dau/o: C. and N.
Hoke (on bk) [Christopher and Nancy
Hoke (on CTOLMR)]. PL: Alleg. Co., VA
"Covington." CTOLMR signed on 05-31-
1870 by Jos. T. Fudge, Clk. Mins. Ret.
says mar. on 05-31-1870 at McCurdy's
Hotel in Covington, VA, was signed A.
Weller. Age oath given by Charles
Fleshman on 05-31-1870, Teste Jos. T.
Fudge, Clk.

06-16-1870
40

Thursday
Jno. L. Bess (on book) [John Lee Bess
(on CTOLMR)], 32, single, Born and
Lived: Alleg. Co., VA, Occup: school
teacher, s/o: H. and R. Bess (on bk)
[Hamilton and Rebecca Bess (on CTOL
MR)]; and Mary F. Lynch (on bk) [Mary
Fletcher Lynch (on CTOLMR)], 21, sing-

- 277 -

le, Born and Lived: Alleg. Co., VA,
dau/o: J. B. and H. E. Lynch (on bk)
[John B. and Harriett Elizabeth Lynch
(on CTOLMR)]. PL: Alleg. Co., VA,
"Mrs. Harriett Pernell's res." CTOL
MR signed on 06-09-1870 by W. M.
Scott, Clk. Mins. Ret. says mar. on
06-16-1870 at Mrs. Harriett Pernell's
in Alleg. Co., VA, was signed Aaron
Boon.

06-25-1870   Saturday
 # 41   Jno. Vernon (on book) [John Vernon
              (on CTOLMR)], 34 single, B: Goochland
              Co., VA, Lived: Alleg. Co., VA, (on
              bk) [Covington, VA (on CTOLMR)], Oc-
              cup: telegraph operator, s/o: L. B.
              and M. E. Vernon (on bk) [Littleberry
              B. and Mary Vernon (on CTOLMR)]; and
              M. J. Lewis (on bk) [Margaret Jose-
              phine Lewis (on CTOLMR)], 20, single,
              B: Monroe Co., VA (now W.VA.), Lived:
              Alleg. Co., VA (on bk) [Covington, VA
              (on CTOLMR)], dau/o: P. E. and E. Lew-
              is (on bk) [Peter Ervine and Eliza
              Lewis (on CTOLMR)]. PL: Alleg. Co.,
              VA, "Covington." CTOLMR signed on 06-
              25-1870 by W. M. Scott, D. C. Mins.
              Ret. says mar. on 06-25-1870 in Coving-
              ton, VA, was signed James M. Rice.
              Consent of P. E. Lewis has names Mar-
              gret Josephen Lewse and John Burnin
              and was dated 05-07-1870. Oath of
              Lewis acknowledgement by Margarette
              Josephine Lewis to receiving consent
              certificate and Mr. Burning having
              seen him give her the certificate,
              Teste W. M. Scott, D. C. on 07-25-
              1870.

**** Found in with the above document was the fol-
     lowing document--No other records have

been found concerning this document.**
"Alleghany County Court Clerk's Office
John Vernon this day made oath
before me that <u>Miss Elizabeth Lewis,</u>
the daughter of W. L. Lewis of Alleghany County, is over the age of twenty-one years.
Given under my hand this 5th day
May 1870.

Jos. T. Fudge, Clk."

07-11-1870 (on book)   07-13-1870 (on CTOLMR and
42   Mins. Ret.)
             <u>J. A. McClung</u> (on book) [<u>James A. Mc-</u>
             <u>Clung</u> (on CTOLMR)], 36, single, B:
             Augusta Co., VA, Lived: Alleg. Co.,
             VA, Occup: merchant, s/o: Jas. and S.
             R. McClung (on bk) [James and Sarah
             R. McClung (on CTOLMR)]; and <u>Lizzie</u>
             <u>F. Kyle</u> (on bk and Mar. Auth.) [<u>Eliz-</u>
             <u>abeth F. Kyle</u> (on CTOLMR)], 19, sing-
             le, B: Augusta Co., VA, Lived: Alleg.
             Co., VA, dau/o: Wm. and F. G. Kyle
             (on bk) [William and Felicia G. Kyle
             (on CTOLMR)]. PL: Alleg. Co., VA,
             "Covington." CTOLMR signed on 07-11-
             1870 by Jos. T. Fudge, Clk. Mins.
             Ret. says mar. on 07-13-1870 in Cov-
             ington, VA, was signed W. E. Hill,
             Minister.

09-02-1870 (on book)   09-03-1870 Saturday (on
42 ½   CTOLMR and Mins. Ret.)
             <u>George H. Davenport</u> (on book) [<u>George</u>
             <u>Henry Davenport</u> (on CTOLMR)], 21, Born
             and Lived: Greenbrier Co., VA (now W.
             VA), single, Occup: hotel servant,
             s/o: Henry and Lucinda Davenport; and
             <u>Sally Fountaine</u>, 21, single, Born and
             Lived: Greenbrier Co., VA (now W.VA.),
             dau/o: Alexander and ___ Fountaine.
             Mar. by ___ (on book). PL: Alleg. Co.,
             "Covington." CTOLMR signed on 09-02-

(Mar. Register Book (1) - Continued)

1870 by W. M. Scott, D. C. Mins. Ret.
says mar. on 09-03-1870 in Covington,
VA, was signed William Richardson.

09-11-1870 Mat Jones, 22, "Colored", single, B:
43   Albermarle Co., VA (on book) [Char-
            lottesville (on CTOLMR)], Lived: Al-
            leg. Co., VA, Occup: hotel servant,
            s/o: ___ and ___ Jones (on book and
            CTOLMR)]; and Mary Kimberlin, 19,
            "Colored", single, Born and Lived: Al-
            leg. Co., VA, dau/o: ___ and _____
            Kimberlin (on book and CTOLMR)]. PL:
            Alleg. Co., VA, "Covington." CTOLMR
            signed on 08-31-1870 by Jos. T. Fudge,
            Clk. Mins. Ret. says mar. on 09-11-
            1870 at "The Old M. E. Church In Town
            of Covington" was signed A. Weller.

10-07-1870 Jno. L. Taylor (on book) [John L.
44   Taylor (on CTOLMR)], 24, single, B:
            Albermarle Co., VA, Lived: Alleg. Co.,
            VA, Occup: school teacher, s/o: B. and
            M. P. Taylor (on bk) [Benjamin and
            Mary P. Taylor (on CTOLMR)]; and M. L.
            Paxton (on bk) [Mary L. Paxton (on
            CTOLMR)], 26, widow, B: Alleg. Co.,
            VA (on bk) [___ (on CTOLMR)], Lived:
            Alleg. Co., VA, dau/o: ___ and _____
            Eagon (on book and CTOLMR). PL: Alleg.
            Co., VA, "M. L. Paxton res." CTOLMR
            signed on 10-05-1870 by Jos. T. Fudge,
            Clk. Mins. Ret. says mar. on 10-07-
            1870 at bride's res. was signed A.
            Weller.

10-27-1870 Wm. H. Tinsley (on book) [William H.
45   Tinsley (on CTOLMR)], 27, single, Born
            and Lived: Alleg. Co., VA, Occup: far-
            mer, s/o: R. M. and M. A. Tisley (on
            bk) [Roderick M. and Mary A. Tisley
            (on CTOLMR)]; and M. F. Hamilton (on

bk) [Mary F. Hamilton (on CTOLMR)],
19, single, B: Rockbridge Co., VA,
Lived: Alleg. Co., VA, dau/o: W. H.
and L. J. Hamilton (on bk) [Wm. H.
and L. J. Hamilton (on CTOLMR)]. PL:
Alleg. Co., VA, "Wm. H. Hamilton's
res." CTOLMR signed on 10-17-1870 by
Jos. T. Fudge, Clk. Mins. Ret. says
mar. on 10-27-1870 at Wm. H. Hamilton
res. was signed S. S. Ryder.

11-02-1870   Wm. M. Robinson (on book) [William M.
46   Robinson (on CTOLMR)], 34, single,
Born and Lived: Alleg. Co., VA, Occup:
farmer, s/o: Wm. and E. Robinson (on
bk) [William and Elizabeth Robinson
(on CTOLMR)]; and A. C. Given (on bk)
[Araminta C. Given (on CTOLMR)], 21,
single, Born and Lived: Alleg. Co.,
VA, dau/o: D. G. and C. Given (on bk)
[David G. and Catharine Given (on
CTOLMR)]. PL: Alleg. Co., VA, "Capt.
A. Given's res." CTOLMR signed on 10-
28-1870 by Jos. T. Fudge, Clk. Mins.
Ret. says mar. on 11-02-1870 at Capt.
Given's res. was signed S. S.Ryder.

11-22-1870   Wm. Skeen (on book) [William Skeen (on
47   CTOLMR)], 52, widower, B: Rockbridge
Co., VA, Lived: Alleg. Co., VA (on bk)
[Covington, VA (on CTOLMR)], Occup:
lawyer, s/o: Ro. and Polly Skeen (on
bk) [Robert and Polly Skeen (on CTOL
MR)]; and G. A. Payne (on bk) [George
Anna Payne (on CTOLMR)], 27, single,
B: Alleg. Co., VA, Lived: Alleg. Co.,
VA (on bk) ["near Covington, VA, at
Edge Hill" (on CTOLMR)], dau/o: G. H.
and S. A. Payne (on bk) [George H. and
Sarah Ann Payne (on CTOLMR)]. PL: Al-
leg. Co., VA, "Edge Hill." CTOLMR
signed on 11-21-1870 by A. B. Persing-

(Mar. Register Book (1) - Continued)

er, J. P. Mins. Ret. says mar. on
11-22-1870 at Edge Hill in Alleg. Co.,
VA, was signed James M. Rice.

Page 13

12-07-1870   G. W. Dickson (on book) [George Wash-
48   ington Dickson (on CTOLMR)], 26, sing-
             le, Born and Lived: Alleg. Co., VA,
             Occup: farmer, s/o: W. M. and E. Dick-
             son (on bk) [Wm. M. and Elizabeth
             Dickson (on CTOLMR)]; and S. E. Boley
             (on bk) [Sarah Elizabeth Boley (on
             CTOLMR)], 29, widow, B: Campbell Co.,
             VA, Lived: Alleg. Co., VA, dau/o: P.
             and A. Boley (on bk) [Presley and Ann
             Boley (on CTOLMR)]. PL: Alleg. Co.,
             VA, "Callaghan's." Handwritten CTOLMR
             signed on 12-06-1870 by Jno. R. Pharr,
             Clk. Mins. Ret. says mar. on 12-07-
             1870 at res. bride's father near Cal-
             laghan's was signed A. Weller, Meth.

12-13-1870   P. N. Snow, 26, single, B: Louisa Co.,
49   VA, Lived: Alleg. Co., VA, Occup: la-
             borer, s/o: R. E. and M. Snow (on bk)
             [Richard E. and Marietta Snow (on CTOL
             MR)]; and Joana Shea, 17, single, B:
             Augusta Co., VA, Lived: Alleg. Co.,
             VA, dau/o: C. and J. Shea (on book)
             [Cornelias and Joanna Shea (on CTOL
             MR)]. PL: Alleg. Co., VA, "Office of
             C & O RR, Covington, VA." CTOLMR
             signed on 11-12-1870 by Jos. T. Fudge,
             Clk. Mins. Ret. says mar. on 12-13-
             1870 at office of C & O RR in Coving-
             ton, VA, was signed James M. Rice,
             Presb. Minister.

12-22-1870   Geo. H. Newcomer (on book) [George
50   Hilth Newcomer (on CTOLMR)], 34, sing-
             le, B: Augusta Co., VA, Lived: Staun-

- 282 -

ton, VA, Occup: butcher, s/o: Jno. W.
and M. Newcomer (on bk) [John W. and
Mary Newcomer (on CTOLMR)]; and Ella
R. Peters (on bk) [Ella Rebecca Peters
(on CTOLMR)], 18, single, B: Campbell
Co., VA, Lived: Alleg. Co., VA, dau/o:
Wm. and N. J. Peters (on bk) [Wm. and
Nancy J. Peters (on CTOLMR)]. PL: Al-
leg. Co., VA, "McCurdy's Hotel, Cov-
ington." Handwritten CTOLMR signed
on 12-22-1870 by Jno. R. Pharr, Clk.
Mins. Ret. says mar. on 12-22-1870 at
McCurdy's Hotel in Covington, VA, was
signed James M. Rice, Presb. Mins.

12-22-1870   D. B. Lockhart (on book) [David Brit-
51   tan Lockhart (on CTOLMR)], 53, widower,
             B: Page Co., VA, Lived: Alleg. Co.,
             VA, Occup: farmer, s/o: J. D. and E.
             Lockhart (on bk) [Jas. L. and Eliza-
             beth Lockhart (on CTOLMR)]; and E. A.
             Huddleston (on bk) [Elizabeth Ann Hud-
             dleston (on CTOLMR)], 25, single, Born
             and Lived: Alleg. Co., VA, dau/o: A.
             I. (? or J.) and L. Huddleston (on bk)
             [A. J. and Leah Huddleston (on CTOL
             MR)]. PL: Alleg. Co., VA, "A. J. Hud-
             dleston's res." CTOLMR signed on 12-
             21-1870 by Jno. R. Pharr, Clk. Mins.
             Ret. says mar. on 12-22-1870 at A. J.
             Huddleston res. was signed A. Weller,
             Meth. Mins. Consent with age of Eliz-
             abeth mentioned given by A. J. Huddles-
             ton dated 12-19-1870 Peter's Mountain.
             [Author's Note: Consent was on station-
             ery with "H" on it made of tree trunks
             and branches and made of thick paper
             indicating it may have been expensive]

12-27-1870   Geo. Wilkinson (on bk) [George Wilkin-
52   son (on CTOLMR)], 24, "Colored", sing-
             le, B: Albermarle Co., VA, Lived: Al-

(Mar. Register Book (1) - Continued)

leg. Co., VA, Occup: laborer, s/o: G.
and A. Wilkinson (on bk) [George and
Julia Wilkinson (on CTOLMR)]; and
Eliza Smith, 22, "Colored", single,
B: Alleg. Co., VA, Lived: Alleg. Co.,
VA, dau/o: Thos. and Betsey Smith.
PL: Alleg. Co., VA, "near Callag-
han's." Handwritten CTOLMR signed on
12-27-1870 by Jno. R. Pharr, Clk.
Mins. Ret. says mar. on 12-27-1870 at
house of Lewis Beard, Col'd., was
signed James M. Rice, Presb. Mins.

12-29-1870   C. L. Pence (on book) [Charles Lewis
53   Pence (on CTOLMR)], 22, single, B:
             Alleg. Co., VA (on bk) [Covington, VA
             (on CTOLMR)], Lived: Alleg. Co., VA,
             Occup: farmer, s/o: Peter and Ellen
             Pence; and S. C. Haston (on book)
             [Susan Catharine Haston (on CTOLMR)],
             19, single, B: Botetourt Co., VA, Liv-
             ed: Alleg. Co., VA, dau/o: W. M. and
             M. Haston (on bk) [Wm. M. and Margaret
             Haston (on CTOLMR)]. PL: Alleg. Co.,
             VA, "W. M. Haston res." Handwritten
             CTOLMR signed on 12-27-1870 by Jno. R.
             Pharr, Clk. Mins. Ret. says mar. on
             12-29-1870 at W. M. Haston's res. was
             signed by James M. Rice, Presb. Mins.

01-11-1871   (on book) 01-10-1871 (on CTOLMR)
1   01-11-1871 (on Mins. Ret.)
             F. N. Burrass (on bk) [Frederick Na-
             polean Burrass (on CTOLMR)], 30, B:
             Campbell Co., VA (on bk) [Lynchburg,
             VA (on CTOLMR)], "White", single, Liv-
             ed: Appomattox Co., VA (on bk) [Pamp-
             lin's Depot (on CTOLMR)], Occup: mer-
             chant, s/o: J. P. and S. M. Burrass;
             and Katie Pitzer (on bk) [Eliza Cath-
             arine McKinney Pitzer (on CTOLMR)],
             21, "White", single, B: Alleg. Co.,

VA (on bk) [Covington (on CTOLMR)],
Lived: Alleg. Co., VA. "Covington,"
dau/o: J. L. and H. A. Pitzer (on bk)
[Jno. L. and H. A. Pitzer (on CTOL
MR)]. PL: Alleg. Co., VA "Covington."
CTOLMR signed on 01-09-1871 by Jno.
R. Pharr, Clk. Mins. Ret. says mar.
on 01-11-1871 in Covington, VA, was
signed Wm. E. Hill, Presb. Mins.

08-11-1870 Thursday
54 Jacob Bowyer, 71, widower, Born and
Lived: Monroe Co., VA (now W.VA.),
Occup: farmer, s/o: Adam and Christina Bowyer; and Rebecca Z. Hepler,
34, widow, Born and Lived: Alleg. Co.,
VA, dau/o: A. J. and Mary Sively (on
book) [Andrew Jackson and Mary Sively
(on CTOLMR)]. PL: Alleg. Co., VA "J.
B. Davis's res." CTOLMR signed on 08-
11-1870 by W. M. Scott, D. C. Mins.
Ret. says mar. on 08-11-1870 at my
res. on Potts Creek in Alleg. Co., VA,
and was signed John B. Davis, Dunkard.

10-20-1870 Wm. D. Wilcher (on book) [William D.
55 Wilcher (on CTOLMR)], 21, single, Born
and Lived: Alleg. Co., VA, Occup: farmer, s/o: Wm: and M. A. Hastings (on
bk--listed parents backwards on CTOL
MR so was listed backwards in book)
[John and Amanda Wilcher (on CTOLMR--
listed correctly here)]; and Martha C.
Hastings, 17, single, B: Bedford Co.,
VA, Lived: Alleg. Co., VA, dau/o: John
and Amanda Wilcher (on book--listed
parents backwards on CTOLMR so was
listed backwards in book) [William
and M. A. Hastings (on CTOLMR--listed
correctly here)]. PL: Alleg. Co., VA,
"res. of bride's father." CTOLMR
signed on 10-08-1870 by Jos. T. Fudge,

Clk. Mins. Ret. says mar. on 10-20-
1870 at Mrs. C. Harne's res. and was
signed James M. Rice, Presb.

11-15-1870   (on book)   11-17-1870 (on CTOLMR)
 # 55 ½   11-17-1869   (on Mins. Ret.)
W. M. Reynolds, 23, single, B: Rock-
bridge Co., VA, Lived: Alleg. Co., VA,
Occup: farmer, s/o: Geo. and Malinda
Reynolds (on book) [George and Malinda
Reynolds (on CTOLMR)]; and Miss Jane
H. Gilliland, 24, single, Born and
Lived: Alleg. Co., VA, dau/o: Henry G.
and Maria Gilliland.   PL: Alleg. Co.,
VA, "Shepherd Gilliland's res."   CTOL
MR signed on 11-15-1870 by Jos. T.
Fudge, Clk. Mins. Ret. says mar. on
11-17-1869 at res. of Shepard Gilli-
llands and was signed Rev. A. Wilson
(or ? Wm. A. Wilson). [Author's Note:
There may have been an error made by
the minister on year of marriage, all
other dates are 1870.]

01-11-1871   A. D. Byer (on book) [Achilles Dew
 # 2   Byers (on CTOLMR)], 21, single, Born
and Lived: Alleg. Co., VA, Occup: farmer, s/o: D. and E. Byer (on book)
[David and Elizabeth Byer (on CTOLMR)];
and Julia H. Walker (on bk) [Julia
Hamilton Walker (on CTOLMR)], 21,
single, Born and Lived: Alleg. Co., VA,
dau/o: H. and M. Walker (on bk) [Henry
and Maria Walker (on CTOLMR)].   PL: Alleg. Co., VA, "Henry Walker's res."
Handwritten CTOLMR signed on 01-02-
1871 by Jno. R. Pharr, Clk. Mins. Ret.
says mar. on 01-11-1871 at Henry Walker's res. in Alleg. Co., VA, was signed Aaron Boon, Meth.

01-11-1871   Henry Givens, 22, "White", widower, B:
 # 3   Kanawha Co., VA (now W.VA.), Lived: Al-

leg. Co., VA, Occup: farmer, s/o: A.
and M. Givens (on book) [Adam and Mary
Givens (on CTOLMR)]; and Mary Ann
Johnson, 19, single, Born and Lived:
Alleg. Co., VA, "White", dau/o: A.
and J. A. Johnson (on bk) [Allen and
July Ann Johnson (on CTOLMR)]. PL:
Alleg. Co., VA, "Philip Johnson's
res." CTOLMR signed on 01-10-1871 by
Jno. R. Pharr, Clk. Mins. Ret. says
mar. on 01-11-1871 at Philip Johnson's
res. in Alleg. Co., VA, was signed
Aaron Boon, Meth.

01-11-1871   Wm. H. Morrison (on book) [Wm. Henry
 # 4   Morrison (on CTOLMR)], 21, "White",
             single, Born and Lived: Alleg. Co.,
             VA, Occup: farmer, s/o: Jas. and M. J.
             Morrison (on bk) [Jas. and Mary J.
             Morrison (on CTOLMR)]; and Sarah A.
             Harwood (on bk) [Sarah Ann Harwood (on
             CTOLMR)], 30, "White", B: Rockbridge
             Co., VA, Lived: Alleg. Co., VA, dau/o:
             _____ (on bk and CTOLMR). PL: Alleg.
             Co., VA, "Wm. Harwood's res." CTOLMR
             signed on 01-11-1871 by Jno. R. Pharr,
             Clk. Mins. Ret. says mar. on 01-11-
             1871 at Mrs. Harwood's res. in Alleg.
             Co., VA, was signed James M. Rice.

01-12-1871   (on book and Mins. Ret.)   01-13-1871
 # 5   (on CTOLMR)
             Andr. J. Nicely (on book) [Andrew Jack-
             son Nicely (on CTOLMR)], 22, "White",
             single, Born and Lived: Alleg. Co.,
             VA, Occup: miner, s/o: A. J. and H.
             Nicely (on bk) [A. J. and Hattie Nice-
             ly (on CTOLMR)]; and Catharine Nicely,
             16, "White", single, Born and Lived:
             Alleg. Co., VA, dau/o: Jacob and M.
             Nicely (on bk) [Jacob and Margaret
             Nicely (on CTOLMR)]. PL: Alleg. Co.,

VA "Cowpasture Bridge." CTOLMR signed on 01-10-1871 by Jno. R. Pharr,
Clk. Mins. Ret. says mar. on 01-12-
1871 at bride's father's res. and was
signed M. A. Wilson. Consent dated
01-11-1871 was signed Jacob Nicely
and wife Margaret Nicely. Oath of
Nicely acknowledgement given by A. J.
Nicely and G. W. Mayse on 01-10-1871,
Teste Jno. R. Pharr, Clk.

01-19-1871
6

Wm. H. Arthur (on book) [Wm. Henry
Arthur (on CTOLMR)], 22, "White",
single, B: Illinois, Lived: Alleg. Co,
VA, Occup: farmer, s/o: Jno. and S.
E. Arthur (on bk) [Jno. and Sarah E.
Arthur (on CTOLMR)]; and Mary J.
Leighton (on bk) [Mary Jane Leighton
(on CTOLMR)], 21, single, "White",
Born and Lived: Alleg. Co., VA, dau/o:
Isaac and S. Leighton (on bk) [Isaac
and Sallie Leighton (on CTOLMR)]. PL:
Alleg. Co., VA, "Isaac Leighton's
res." CTOLMR signed on 01-09-1871 by
Jno. R. Pharr, Clk. Mins. Ret. says
mar. on 01-19-1871 at bride's father's
res. and was signed A. Weller, Meth.
Age oath for Mary given by James E.
Leighton.

01-25-1871
7

Isaac M. Scaggs (on book) [Isaac Mari-
on Scaggs (on CTOLMR)], 21, "White",
single, B: Monroe Co., VA (now W.VA.),
Lived: Nicholas Co., W.VA., Occup:
cabinetmaker (on bk) [cabinet workman
(on CTOLMR)], s/o: Jno. and M. A.
Scaggs (on bk) [John and Mary Ann
Scaggs (on CTOLMR)]; and A. A. Wills
(on bk) [Araminta A. Wills (on CTOL
MR)], 20, "White", single, B: Monroe
Co., VA (now W.VA.), Lived: Nicholas
Co., W. VA., dau/o: M. H. and L. J.
Wills. PL: Alleg. Co., VA. CTOLMR

signed on 01-25-1871 by Jno. R. Pharr,
Clk. Mins. Ret. says mar. on 01-25-
1871 at McCurdy's Hotel in Covington,
VA, and was signed A. Weller, Meth.
Consent was to Clk. of Nicholas Co.--
Mr. James S. Craig--for Araminta on
12-26-1870 and was signed Malon H.
Wills, Teste Robbert T. (his X mark)
Shawver, Isaac M. Skaggs, and James A.
Copenhaver. Oath of Wills acknow-
ledgement given by Isaac M. Scaggs on
01-25-1871, Teste Jno. R. Pharr, Clk.

02-01-1871   H. W. Massie (on book) [Hezekiah Wm.
 # 8   Massie (on CTOLMR)], 35, "White",
single, Born and Lived: Alleg. Co.,
VA, Occup: farmer, s/o: Henry and E.
R. Massie (on bk) [Henry and Eliza-
beth R. Massie (on CTOLMR)]; and Emma
J. Ryals (on bk) [Emma Judson Ryals
(on CTOLMR)], 24, "White", single, B:
Cumberland Co., VA, Lived: Alleg. Co.,
VA, dau/o: V. C. and H. C. Ryals. PL:
Alleg. Co., VA, "Clifton Forge."
CTOLMR signed on 01-25-1871 by Jno. R.
Pharr, Clk. Mins. Ret. says mar. on
02-01-1871 at bride's father's res.
was signed L. A. Cutler, Christian.
Consent given by V. C. Ryal dated on
01-18-1871 at Clifton Forge, VA.

02-09-1871   Jacob M. Stone (on book) [Jacob Mathew
 # 9   Stone (on CTOLMR)], 21, "White", sing-
le, Born and Lived: Alleg. Co., VA,
Occup: farmer, s/o: Wm. M. and Jane
Stone; and M. C. Brown (on book) [Mar-
garet Catharine Brown (on CTOLMR)],
25, single, "White", Born and Lived:
Alleg. Co., VA, dau/o: Sam'l. and S.
W. Brown (on bk) [Samuel and Sarah W.
Brown (on CTOLMR)]. PL: Alleg. Co.,
VA, "near Callaghan's." CTOLMR signed
on 02-06-1871 by Jno. R. Pharr, Clk.

Mins. Ret. says mar. on 02-09-1871 at
bride's mother's near Callaghan's was
signed A. Weller, Meth. Age oath
given by Millard F. Brown for <u>Margaret</u>
on 02-06-1871, Teste Jno. R. Pharr,
Clk.

02-16-1871 Thursday
10   <u>Geo. L. Baker</u> (on book) [<u>George Alex-
            ander Baker</u> (on CTOLMR)] [<u>George L.
            Baker</u> (on Mar. Auth.)], 24, single,
            "White", Born and Lived: Monroe Co.,
            VA (now W.VA.), Occup: farmer, s/o: G.
            M. and S. J. Baker (on bk) [George M.
            and Sarah J. Baker (on CTOLMR)]; and
            <u>Mary Booth</u>, 20, "White", single, Born
            and Lived: Alleg. Co., VA, dau/o: Wm.
            and ___ Booth (on bk) [William and __
            Booth (on CTOLMR)]. PL: Alleg. Co.,
            VA, "Red Sweet Springs." CTOLMR sign-
            ed on 02-13-1871 by Jno. R. Pharr, Clk.
            Mins. Ret. says mar. on 02-16-1871 at
            Mr. Humphries's res. at Sweet Springs
            [Note: now in W.VA.] and was signed
            A. Weller, Meth. Consent signed on
            02-13-1871 by W. Booth, Wit. Jos.
            Baker. Oath of Booth acknowledgement
            given by Joseph Baker and <u>Geo. L.
            Baker</u>, Teste Jno. R. Pharr, Clk.

02-26-1871 (on book) 01-27-1871 (on CTOLMR)
11   01-26-1871 (on Mins. Ret.)
            <u>Thos. R. Campbell</u> (on book) [<u>Thomas
            Robert Campbell</u> (on CTOLMR)], 21,
            single, "White", B: Nelson Co., VA,
            Lived: Alleg. Co., VA, Occup: miner,
            s/o: S. S. and C. Campbell (on book)
            [S. S. and Catharine Campbell (on
            CTOLMR)]; and <u>Ellen J. Kelly</u> (on book)
            [<u>Ellen Jane Kelley</u> (on CTOLMR)], 21,
            "White", single, Born and Lived: Al-
            leg. Co., VA, dau/o: Jas. A. and N. E.
            Kelley (on bk) [Jas. A. and Nancy E.

(Mar. Register Book (1) - Continued)

Kelley (on CTOLMR)]. PL: Alleg. Co.,
VA, "near Lucy Selina Furnace." CTOL
MR signed on 01-21-1871 by Jno. R.
Pharr, Clk. Mins. Ret. says mar. on
01-26-1871 at bride's father's at
Lucy Selina Furnace and was signed M.
A. Wilson. Consent 01-20-1871 at L.
S. Furnace has name Ellen Jane Kelly,
says both parties are of legal age,
both fathers consent, and there are
no objections to the marriage Lic.
being granted and was signed J. E.
Johnson. Age oath for Ellen given by
Thos. R. Campbell on 01-21-1872,Teste
Jno. R. Pharr, Clk.

06-28-1870   Jas. B. Andrews (on book) [James B.
 # 12   Andrews (on CTOLMR)], 18, single,
             Born and Lived: Alleg. Co., VA,Occup:
             farmer, s/o: Wm. and Betsey Andrews
             (on bk) [William and Betsey Andrews
             (on CTOLMR)]; and Mary Gay (on book
             and CTOLMR) [May Gay (on Mar. Auth.)],
             26, single, B: Bath Co., VA, Lived:
             Alleg. Co., VA, dau/o: Mustoe and
             Mary (? May) Gay. PL: Alleg. Co., VA,
             "res. Crawford Jackson." CTOLMR sign-
             ed on 06-28-1870 by Jos. T. Fudge,
             Clk. Mins. Ret. says mar. on 06-28-
             1870 at Crawford Jackson's res. was
             signed S. S. Ryder, Meth. Age oath
             given by (?) on 05-28-1870, Teste
             Jos. T. Fudge, Clk.

11-22-1870   Thos. M. Kincaid (on book) [Thomas
 # 13   Moses Kincaid (on CTOLMR)], 48, wid-
 Tuesday   ower, B: Alleg. Co., VA, Lived: Bath
             Co., VA, Occup: farmer, s/o: Andrew
             and Ann Kincaid; and Elisabeth Hans-
             barger (on book) [Elizabeth Hansbar-
             ger (on CTOLMR)], 26, single, Born
             and Lived: Alleg. Co., VA, dau/o:

- 291 -

Sebastian and ___ Hansbarger (on bk and CTOLMR). PL: Alleg. Co., VA, "Elizabeth Hansbarger's res." CTOL MR signed on 11-19-1870 by A. B. Persinger, J. P. Mins. Ret. says mar. on 11-22-1870 at Elizabeth Hansberger res. was signed S. S. Ryder, Meth.

02-15-1871
14

Wm. Paxton Burks, 21, single, "white", Born and Lived: Botetourt Co., VA, Occup: farmer, s/o: Wm. and Mary Burks; and Maggie E. Griffith (on bk and Mar. Auth.) [Margaret Elizabeth Griffith (on CTOLMR)], 21, single, "White", Born and Lived: Alleg. Co., VA, dau/o: Caleb and Elizabeth Griffith. PL: Alleg. Co., VA, "bride's father's res." CTOLMR signed on 02-14-1871 by Jno. R. Pharr, Clk. Mins. Ret. says mar. on 02-15-1871 at bride's father's was signed by S. S. Ryder, Meth. Consent for Maggie on 02-14-1871 by Wm. P. Burks, Teste Jno. R. Pharr, Clk.

03-20-1871
15

William Stark, 31, single, "White", B: Ireland, Lived: Greenbrier Co., W. VA., Occup: wagoneer, s/o: Wm. and Nancy Stark; and Sarah Gladwell, 36, "White", widow, B: Augusta Co., VA, Lived: Greenbrier Co., W.VA., dau/o: Braxton and Delila Davis. PL: Alleg. Co., VA. CTOLMR signed on 03-16-1871 by Jno. R. Pharr, Clk. Mins. Ret. says mar. on 03-20-1871 at Mr. Rese's res. was signed A. Weller, Meth.

03-30-1871
16

Edward Jones, 32, single, "Colored", B: Albemarle Co., VA, Lived: Alleg. Co., VA, Occup: laborer, s/o:"Colored" (on book) [___ (on CTOLMR)]; and Julia French, 21, single, "Colored",

- 292 -

B: Albemarle Co., VA, Lived: Alleg. Co., VA, dau/o: "Colored" (on book) [_____ (on CTOLMR)]. PL: Alleg. Co., VA, "Lewis Tunnel." CTOLMR signed on 03-30-1871 by Jno. R. Pharr, Clk. Mins. Ret. says mar. on 03-30-1871 at Lewis Tunnel was signed W. H. Wiley. Baptist.

03-02-1871
16 ½

James Arrington, 24, single, "White", Born and Lived: Alleg. Co., VA, Occup: farmer, s/o: James and Jane Arrington; and Emeline S. Manspile (on book) [Emeline Susan Manspile (on CTOLMR)], 21, widow, "White", Born and Lived: Alleg. Co., VA, dau/o: Isaac and Margaret Wolf. PL: Alleg. Co., VA, "Rich Patch." CTOLMR signed on 03-02-1871 by Jno. R. Pharr, Clk. Mins. Ret. says mar. on 03-02-1871 at Isaac Wolf's res. in Alleg. Co., VA, was signed Aaron Boon. [Author's Note: See also 03-11-1871 # 28 Mar. Book Page 14. Listed twice.]

05-02-1871
17

Jas. T. Johnson (on book) [James Taylor Johnson (on CTOLMR)], 33, "White", single, B: Hanover Co., VA, Lived: Alleg. Co., VA, Occup: RR hand (on book) [night watcher C & O RR (on CTOLMR)], s/o: Geo. and Nancy Johnson (on book) [George and Nancy Johnson (on CTOLMR)]; and Mary E. Armstrong (on book) [Mary Elizabeth Armstrong (on CTOLMR)], 21, "White", single, B: Gordonsville, VA [Note: Orange Co., VA on border of Louisa Co.], Lived: Alleg. Co., VA, dau/o: Jno. and ____ Armstrong (on book) [John and ____ Armstrong (on CTOLMR)]. PL: Alleg. Co., VA, "McCurdy's Hotel, Covington." CTOLMR signed on 05-02-1871 by Jno. R.

(Mar. Register Book (1) - Continued)

Pharr, Clk. Mins. Ret. says mar. on
05-02-1871 at McCurdy's Hotel in Covington, VA, was signed A. Weller.
Age oath given by <u>Jas. T. Johnson</u> for
<u>Mary</u> on 05-02-1871, Teste John R.
Pharr, Clk.

05-18-1871   (on book and Mins. Ret.) 05-1̸Ø18-1871
18   (on CTOLMR)
              <u>Wm. P. Scott</u> (on book) [<u>William Page
              Scott</u> (on CTOLMR)], 24, "White", sing-
              le, Born and Lived: Greenbrier Co.,
              VA (now W.VA.), Occup: farmer, s/o:
              W. H. and E. J. Scott (on bk) [Wm. H.
              and Elizabeth J. Scott (on CTOLMR)];
              and <u>Laura B. Beard</u> (on book) [<u>Laura
              Belle Beard</u> (on CTOLMR)], 21, "White",
              single, Born and Lived: Greenbrier
              Co., VA (now W.VA.), dau/o: Andr. and
              Eliza Beard. PL: Alleg. Co., VA, "Mc-
              Curdy's Hotel" [A̸l̸l̸e̸g̸/ S̸t̸a̸t̸i̸o̸n̸ C̸h̸e̸s̸/
              &̸ Ø̸h̸i̸ø̸ R̸R̸ --as on CTOLMR]. CTOLMR
              signed on 05-06-1871 by Jno. R. Pharr,
              Clk. Mins. Ret. says mar. on 05-18-
              1871 at McCurdy's Hotel in Covington,
              VA, was signed A. Weller. Age oath
              for <u>Laura</u> given by Wm. Tyree on 05-
              06-1871, Teste Jno. R. Pharr, Clk.

05-24-1871   <u>Anderson Boggs</u>, 35, single, "White",
19   Born and Lived: Greenbrier Co., VA
              (now W.VA.), Occup: carpenter, s/o:
              Stephen and Jane Boggs; and <u>M. P. A.
              E. Winfree</u> (on bk) [<u>Martha Phoebe Ann
              Elizabeth Winfree</u> (on CTOLMR)], 21,
              single, "White", B: Cumberland Co.,
              VA, Lived: Alleg. Co., VA, dau/o: W.
              H. and A. C. Winfree (on bk) [W. H.
              and Ann C. Winfree (on CTOLMR)]. PL:
              Alleg. Co., VA. CTOLMR signed on 05-
              22-1871 by Jno. R. Pharr, Clk. Mins.
              Ret. says mar. on 05-24-1871 at bri-
              de's father's res. was signed A. Wel-

- 294 -

ler.

05-25-1871   Augustus E. White (on bk) [Augustus
 # 20   Ervin White (on CTOLMR)], 21, single,
              "White", B: Augusta Co., VA, Lived:
              Staunton in Augusta Co., VA, Occup:
              clerk, s/o: J. D. and E. A. White
              (on book) [John D. and Eliza A.White
              (on CTOLMR)]; and Mollie M. White,
              21, single, "White", Born and Lived:
              Greenbrier Co., VA (now W.VA.), dau/
              o: M. B. and S. E. White (on book)
              [Moorman B. and Sarah E. White (on
              CTOLMR)]. PL: Alleg. Co., VA, "Mc-
              Curdy's Hotel, Covington." CTOLMR
              signed on 05-25-1871 by Jno. R.
              Pharr, Clk. Mins. Ret. says mar. on
              05-25-1871 at McCurdy's Hotel in Cov-
              ington, VA, was signed A. Weller.
              Age oath for Mollie given by A. E.
              White on 05-25-1871, Teste J. J.
              Hobbs, D. C.

05-26-1871   Friday
 # 21   Henry Douglas, 22, single, "Colored",
              B: Albemarle Co., VA, Lived: Alleg.
              Co., VA, Occup: blacksmith, s/o: Jas.
              and Eliza Douglas (on bk) [James and
              Eliza Douglas (on CTOLMR)]; and Ellen
              Jackson, 17, single, "Colored", B:
              Culpepper Co., VA, Lived: Alleg. Co.,
              VA, dau/o: Thos. and Sarah Jackson
              (on book) [Thomas and Sarah Jackson
              (on CTOLMR)]. PL: Alleg. Co. VA,
              "Covington." CTOLMR signed on 05-26-
              1871 by Jno. R. Pharr, Clk. Mins.
              Ret. says mar. on 05-26-1871 in Cov-
              ington was signed W. H. Wiley.
              Ellen's father came to the courthouse
              with them per note on CTOLMR.

05-27-1871   Levi Read, 40, single, "Colored", B:

22   Southampton Co., VA, Lived: Alleg. Co., VA, Occup: laborer, s/o: "Colored" (on book) [____ (on CTOLMR)]; and Rosetta Robinson, 30, "Colored", B: Bath Co., VA, single, Lived: Alleg. Co., VA, dau/o: "Colored" (on book) [_____ (on CTOLMR)]. PL: Alleg. Co., VA, "Covington." CTOLMR signed on 05-27-1871 by Jno. R. Pharr, Clk. Mins. Ret. says mar. on 05-27-1871 in Covington was signed W. H. Wiley.

06-15-1871 David J. Wise (on book) [David Joshua
23   Wise (on CTOLMR)], 40, "White", widower, B: Augusta Co., VA, Lived: Alleg. Co., VA, Occup: farmer, s/o: Jno. and Ellen Wise (on book) [John and Ellen Wise (on CTOLMR)]; and Catharine A. Boley (on book) [Catharine Agnes Boley (on CTOLMR)], 22, single, Born and Lived: Alleg. Co., VA, "White", dau/o: Presley and Nancy Boley. PL: Alleg. Co., VA, "res. bride's father." CTOLMR signed on 06-14-1871 by Jno. R. Pharr, Clk. Mins. Ret. says mar. on 06-15-1871 at bride's father's res. in Alleg. Co., VA, was signed A. Weller. Consent of Presley Boley (seal) on 06-11-1871 says Catharine is of age. Oath of Boley acknowledgement by David J. Wise on 06-14-1871, Teste Jno. R. Pharr, Clk.

06-29-1871 Henry Minor, 27, single, "Colored",
24   B: Madison Co., VA, Lived: Bath Co., VA, Occup: laborer, s/o: "Colored" (on book) [___ (on CTOLMR)]; and Violet Wright, 21, single, "Colored", Born and Lived: Alleg. Co., VA, dau/o: "Colored" (on book) [___ (on CTOLMR)]. PL: Alleg. Co., VA. CTOLMR signed on 06-29-1871 by Jno. R. Pharr, Clk. Mins. Ret. says mar. on 06-29-1871 at

Mrs. Mallow's res. in Alleg. Co. was
signed W. H. Wiley.
"Mr. Hobbs
     Give marrage Licens to Henry
Minor col to mary Vilett Wright col.
All parties are now ready and want
the matter over as soon as possible.
                    Resptl.
                    W. A. McCray
June 29th 1871"

06-29-1871   Adison Hamilton Vance (on book)
  # 25   [Addison Hamilton Vance (on CTOLMR)],
             "white", 24, single, B: Monroe Co.,
             VA (now W.VA.), Lived: Alleg. Co.,
             VA, Occup: farmer, s/o: Wm. and Vir-
             ginia Vance; and E. C. Sams (on bk)
             [Elizabeth C. Sams (on CTOLMR)], 23,
             single, "white", B: Greenbrier Co.,
             VA (now W.VA.), Lived: Alleg. Co.,
             VA, dau/o: Jos. H. and Lucinda Sams
             (on bk) [Joseph H. and Lucinda Sams
             (on CTOLMR)]. PL: Alleg. Co., VA.
             CTOLMR signed on 06-21-1871 by Jno.
             R. Pharr, Clk. Mins. Ret. says mar.
             on 06-29-1871 at groom's mother's in
             Alleg. Co., VA, was signed A. Weller.
             Consent dated on 02-27-1871 at Green-
             brier Co., W. VA., gives names as
             Elizabeth Catharine Sams and Addison
             Hamilton Vance and says Elizabeth is
             23 years old was signed Joseph H.
             (his X mark) Sams, Wit. Addison H.
             (his X mark) Vance. Oath of Sam's
             acknowledgement given by Addison H.
             Vance on 06-21-1871, Teste Jno. R.
             Pharr, Clk.

07-18-1871   Jno. R. Spangler (on book) John Read
  # 26   Spangler (on CTOLMR)], 24, "White",
             single, Born and Lived: Botetourt Co.,
             VA, Occup: farmer, s/o: Adam and Mary.

(Mar. Register Book (1) - Continued)

Spangler; and <u>Charlotte E. Stull</u> (on
book and Mar. Auth.) [~~Ellen~~ Elizabeth
<u>Charlotte Stull</u> (on CTOLMR)], 24,
"White", single, Born and Lived: Alleg. Co., VA, dau/o: James and Hannah
Stull. PL: Alleg. Co., VA, "bride's
mother's res." CTOLMR signed on 07-
15-1871 by Jno. R. Pharr, Clk. Mins.
Ret. says mar. on 07-18-1871 at
bride's mother's res. in Alleg. Co.,
VA, was signed A. Buhrman.

07-19-1871   <u>Shelton R. Harman</u> (on book) [<u>Shelton</u>
27   <u>Raglan Harman</u> (on CTOLMR)], 43, widow-
             er, "White", Born and Lived: Alleg.
             Co., VA, Occup: farmer, s/o: Peter
             and Mary Harman; and <u>Mary A. E. Fan-
             nin</u> (on bk) [<u>Mary A. Elizabeth Fannin</u>
             (on CTOLMR)], 32, widow, "White",
             Born and Lived: Alleg. Co., VA, dau/
             o: Jno. and Sarah Dodd. PL: Alleg.
             Co., VA. CTOLMR signed on 07-17-1871
             by Jno. R. Pharr, Clk. Mins. Ret.
             says mar. on 07-19-1871 at bride's
             res. in Alleg. Co., VA, was signed by
             A. Weller.

08-03-1871   Thursday
28   <u>Geo. H. Bowyer</u> (on book) [<u>George Ham-
             mond Bowyer</u> (on CTOLMR)], 20, single,
             "White", Born and Lived: Alleg. Co.,
             VA, Occup: farmer, s/o: Jno. and Nan-
             cy Bowyer (on CTOLMR)]; and <u>Naomi B.
             Myers</u> (on bk) [<u>Naomy Bevaline Myers</u>
             (on CTOLMR)] [~~Nancy~~ <u>Naomy Bevaline
             Myers</u> (Mar. Auth. was marked thru and
             changed to this but not on CTOLMR)],
             19, single, "white", Born and Lived:
             Alleg. Co., VA, dau/o: Henry and Char-
             lotte Myers. PL: Alleg. Co., VA,
             "bride's father's res." CTOLMR sign-
             ed on 07-31-1871 by Jno. R. Pharr,

Clk. Mins. Ret. says mar. on 08-03-1871 at Henry Myers res. was signed D. H. Plaine. Consent for <u>Naomy B. Myers</u> given by Henry Myers on 07-31-1871, Wit. John M. Simmons. Consent for <u>George H. Bowyer</u> given by John Bowyer on 07-31-1871, Wit. John M. Simmons. Oath of Myers acknowledgement given by John M. Simmons on 07-31-1871, Teste Jno. R. Pharr, Clk.

08-09-1871
29

<u>Allen T. Loudermilk</u> (on book) [<u>Allen Taylor Loudermilk</u> (on CTOLMR)], 21, single, "White", Born and Lived: Greenbrier Co., VA (now W.VA.), Occup: farmer, s/o: M. and H. Loudermilk (on book) [Michael and Hannah Loudermilk (on CTOLMR)]; and <u>Hannah F. Loudermilk</u> (on book) [<u>Hannah Francis Loudermilk</u> (on CTOLMR)], 23, single, Born and Lived: Greenbrier Co., VA (now W. VA), "white", dau/o: Geo. and S. E. Loudermilk (on bk) [George and Susan E. Loudermilk (on CTOLMR)]. PL: Alleg. Co., VA "Covington." CTOLMR signed on 08-09-1871 by Jno. R. Pharr, Clk. Mins. Ret. says mar. on 08-09-1871 at Meth. Parsonage in Covington, VA, was signed A. Weller. Note on CTOLMR: "Parties made oath to age."

08-23-1871
30

<u>Wm. Lee Kimberlin</u>, 22, "White", single, Born and Lived: Alleg. Co., VA, Occup: farmer, s/o: Wm. and E. Kimberlin (on book) [Wm. and Elizabeth Kimberlin (on CTOLMR)]; and <u>Mary I. Hepler</u> (on bk) [<u>Mary Isabella Hepler</u> (on CTOLMR)], 17, single, "White", Born and Lived: Alleg. Co., VA, dau/o: Jno. and Margaret Hepler (on bk) [John and Margaret Hepler (on CTOLMR)]. PL: Alleg. Co., VA, "Lorenzo Kimberlin's

(Mar. Register Book (1) - Continued)

res." CTOLMR signed on 08-23-1871
by Jno. R. Pharr, Clk. Mins. Ret.
says mar. on 08-23-1871 at Lorenzo
Kimberlin's res. on Potts Creek in
Alleg. Co., VA, was signed John B.
Davis. Consent of John Hepler on 08-
23-1871, Wit. David Persinger and
John B. Davis. Oath of Hepler acknowledgement given by David Hepler
on 08-23-1871, Teste Jno. R. Pharr,
Clk.

08-31-1871 Thursday
31 Edmund Brown, 22, single, "Colored",
B: West Tennessee, Lived: Alleg. Co.,
VA, Occup: miner, s/o: A. and C.
Brown (on book) [Armistead and Cherry
Brown (on CTOLMR)]; and Emily Johnson,
20, "Colored", single, B: Albemarle
Co., VA, Lived: Alleg. Co., VA, dau/o:
T. and E. Johnson (on bk) [Thos. and
Ede Johnson (on CTOLMR)]. PL: Alleg.
Co., VA, "Lewis Tunnel C & O RR."
CTOLMR signed on 08-29-1871 by Jno.
R. Pharr, Clk. Note on CTOLMR: "Em-
ily's father present." Mins. Ret.
says mar. on 08-31-1871 at Lewis Tun-
nel in Alleg. Co., VA, was signed Wm.
H. Wiley.

09-28-1871 Caleb Persinger, 23, single, "White",
32 Born and Lived: Alleg. Co., VA, Occup:
cabinetmaker, s/o: E. and L. Persinger (on bk) [Eli. and Lydia Persinger
(on CTOLMR)]; and Melissa B. Dew, 19,
single, "White", Born and Lived: Alleg. Co., VA, dau/o: ___ Sarah Dew
(on book and CTOLMR). CTOLMR signed
on 09-25-1871 by Jno. R. Pharr, Clk.
Mins. Ret. says mar. on 09-28-1871 at
Sarah Dew's on Potts Creek in Alleg.
Co., VA, was signed John B. Davis.

Consent has name as <u>Malissa B. Dew</u>
and dated 09-25-1871 and signed Sarah
Dew, Wit. Joseph Persinger. PL: Alleg. Co., VA, "bride's mother's res."

10-17-1871   <u>Thos. Jackson</u> (on book) [<u>Thomas Jack-</u>
 # 32   <u>son</u> (on CTOLMR)], 30, single, "White",
             B: Georgia, Lived: Alleg. Co., VA,
             Occup: farmer, s/o: Wm. and E. Jack-
             son (on book) [Wm. and Elizabeth
             Jackson (on CTOLMR)]; and <u>Deborah</u>
             <u>Steers</u>, 18, single, "White", B: Penn-
             sylvania, Lived: Alleg. Co., VA, dau/
             o: Evan and E. Steers (on bk) [Evan
             and Elizabeth Steers (on CTOLMR)].
             PL: Alleg. Co., VA, "Jackson River."
             CTOLMR signed on 10-13-1871 by Jno.
             R. Pharr, Clk. Mins. Ret. says mar.
             on 10-17-1871 at Evan Steers res.
             was signed James M. Rice.
             "The Western Union Telegraph Co.
             Dated: Goshen, VA. 10-13-1871
             TO: <u>Thos. Jackson</u>, Covington, VA.
             I gave my consent that <u>Thomas Jackson</u>
             shall marry my daughter <u>Debora</u>.
                                     E. Steers
                                     12 Collect"

10-21-1871   (on book) 10-22-1871 (on CTOLMR and
 # 34   Mins. Ret.)
             <u>Ro. Richardson</u> (on book) [<u>Robert Rich-</u>
             <u>ardson</u> (on CTOLMR)], 33, "Colored",
             single, B: Roanoke Co., VA, Lived:
             Alleg. Co., VA, Occup: laborer, s/o:
             D. and K. Richardson (on bk) [David
             and Keziah Richardson (on CTOLMR)];
             and <u>Emma Shields</u>, 16, single, "Color-
             ed", Born and Lived: Alleg. Co., VA,
             dau/o: ___ and Mahala Shields (on bk
             and CTOLMR). PL: Alleg. Co., VA,
             "Lewis Tunnel C & O RR." CTOLMR was
             signed on 10-21-1871 by Jno. R. Pharr,

Clk. Mins. Ret. says mar. on 10-22-1871 at Lewis Tunnel on C & O RR was signed W. H. Wiley. Consent has Amy Shields and was dated 10-21-1871 and signed Mahala (her X mark) Shields, Wit. Ro. (his X mark) Richardson. Oath of Shield's acknowledgement on 10-21-1871, Teste Jno. R. Pharr, Clk.

10-26-1871
35

Thursday
Chas. F. Putnam (on book) [Charles F. Putnam (on CTOLMR)], 21, "White", single, Born and Lived: Alleg. Co., VA, Occup: farmer, s/o: Jno. and Sarah Putnam; and M. V. Griffith (on bk) [Mahaleth V. Griffith (on CTOLMR)], 19, single, "White", B: Bath Co., VA, Lived: Alleg. Co., VA, dau/o: Ches. and Lucy Griffith (on book) [Chls. and Lucy Griffith (on CTOLMR)]. PL: Alleg. Co., VA, "bride's mother's res." CTOLMR signed on 10-23-1871 by Jno. R. Pharr, Clk. Mins. Ret. says mar. on 10-26-1871 at Mrs. Lucy Griffith's res. was signed Davis M. Wood, L. D., M. E. C. S. Consent on 10-23-1871 has Mahalaeth Va. Griffith and was signed Mrs. Lucy Griffith, Wit. Andrew S. Turner and Jas. E. Ross.

11-01-1871
36

Hez. P. Robinson (on bk) [Hezekiah P. Robinson (on CTOLMR)], 24, "White", single, Born and Lived: Alleg. Co., VA, Occup: farmer, s/o: Wm. and E. Robinson (on bk) [Wm. and Elizabeth Robinson (on CTOLMR)]; and Julia F. Hamilton, 23, single, "White", Born and Lived: Alleg. Co., VA, dau/o: Jno. and Sarah Hamilton (on bk) [John and Sarah Hamilton (on CTOLMR)]. PL: Alleg. Co., VA, "bride's father's res." CTOLMR signed on 10-27-1871 by Jno. R.

Pharr, Clk. Mins. Ret. says mar. on 11-01-1871 at bride's father's res. was signed A. Weller. Consent for Julie F. Hamilton on 10-11-1871 signed John Hamilton, Wit. A.P.Hamilton.

11-02-1871
37

Jas. H. Huges (on book) [James H. Hughes (on CTOLMR)], 30, "White", B: Fluvanna Co., VA, single, Lived: Alleg. Co., VA, Occup: carpenter, s/o: Ro. and M. Hughes (on bk) [Robert and Martha Hughes (on CTOLMR)]; and Melissa L. Bryant, 19, single, "White", B: Lynchburg, VA [Author's Note: This city is part in Bedford Co. and part in Campbell Co., VA.], Lived: Alleg. Co., VA, dau/o: S. M. and M. J. Bryant (on bk) [Shelton M. and Mary J. Bryant (on CTOLMR)]. PL: Alleg. Co., VA, "bride's father's res." CTOLMR signed on 10-30-1871 by Jno. R. Pharr, Clk. Mins. Ret. says mar. on 11-02-1871 at Lewis Tunnel at father's res. was signed James M. Rice. Consent has Melissa L. Brient dated on 10-30-1871 was signed Shelton M. Brient and Mary J. Brient. Oath of Brient acknowledgement by Jas. H. Hughes on 10-30-1871.

11-08-1871
38

Ro. A. M. Skeen (on bk) [Robert A. M. Skeen (on CTOLMR)], 22, single, Born and Lived: Alleg. Co., VA, "White", Occup: ___ (on bk and CTOLMR), s/o: Wm. and C. J. Skeen (on bk) [Wm. and Catharine J. Skeen (on CTOLMR)]; and Lucie E. Montague, 21, single, "White", Born and Lived: Alleg. Co., VA, dau/o: Jas. M. and C. Montague (on bk) [Jas. M. and Catharine Montague (on CTOL MR)]. PL: Alleg. Co., VA, "J. M. Montague, Esq. res." CTOLMR signed

on 11-03-1871 by Jno. R. Pharr, Clk.
Mins. ret. says mar. on 11-08-1871
at J. M. Montague res. was signed
James M. Rice.

11-20-1871   (on book)   11-30-1871 (on Mins. Ret.)
39   Wm. M. Hughes, 21, single, "White",
              B: Fluvanna Co., VA, Lived: Alleg.
              Co., VA, Occup: Engineer, s/o: Jno.
              G. and E. W. Hughes (on bk) [Jno. G.
              and Emily W. Hughes (on CTOLMR)]; and
              Wylie E. Turner (on book) [Willie
              Turner (on CTOLMR)], 17, single, B:
              Buckingham Co., VA, "White", Lived:
              Alleg. Co., VA, dau/o: Jas. and Bar-
              bary Turner (on bk) [Jas. and Barbara
              G. Turner (on CTOLMR)]. PL: Alleg.
              Co., VA, "McCurdy's Hotel, Covington."
              CTOLMR signed on 11-20-1871 by Jno.
              R. Pharr, Clk. Mins. Ret. says mar.
              on 11-30-1871 at McCurdy's Hotel in
              Covington, VA, was signed A. Weller.
              Note on CTOLMR: "Guardian present"
              when License gotten.

11-25-1871   Saturday
40   Wells (page tore on book)
              [James Wells (on CTOLMR)], 22, sing-
              le, "Colored", B: Fluvanna Co., VA,
              Lived: Alleg. Co., VA, Occup: laborer,
              s/o: Henry and Mary Wells; and Sallie
              Johnson, 17, single, "Colored", Born
              and Lived: Alleg. Co., VA, dau/o: Pe-
              ter and A. Johnson (on bk) [Peter and
              Amanda Johnson (on CTOLMR)]. PL: Al-
              leg. Co., VA, "Alleghany Station."
              CTOLMR signed on 11-24-1871 by Jno.
              R. Pharr, Clk. Mins. Ret. says mar.
              on 11-25-1871 at Alleg. Station was
              signed Wm. H. Wiley.

(Mar. Register Book (1) - Continued)

Page 14

12-05-1871   (on book)   12-06-1871 (on CTOLMR and
  # 1   Mins. Ret.)
             Wm. A. Smith, 20, single, "White",
             Born and Lived: Alleg. Co., VA, Oc-
             cup: farmer, s/o: Wm. and Ann Smith;
             and Nancy E. Huddleston, 22, single,
             "White", Born and Lived: Alleg. Co.,
             VA, dau/o: A. J. and Joana Huddleston.
             PL: Alleg. Co., VA, "bride's res."
             CTOLMR signed on 12-04-1871 by Jno.
             R. Pharr, Clk. Mins. Ret. says mar.
             on 12-06-1871 at bride's res. was
             signed William Richardson. Consent
             dated 12-04-1871 says Nancy was born
             on May 30, 1849, and was signed A. J.
             Huddleston, Wit. Sarah J. Brown.

12-05-1871   Jno. W. McKenney (on bk) [John W. Mc-
  # 2   Kenney (on CTOLMR)], 33, single, Born
             and Lived: Alleg. Co., VA, "White",
             Occup: farmer, s/o: Nathaniel and S.
             McKenney (on bk) [Nathaniel and Sarah
             McKenney (on CTOLMR)]; and Minerva A.
             Mann, 25, single, "White", Born and
             Lived: Alleg. Co., VA, dau/o: A. G.
             and Clementina Mann. PL: Alleg. Co.,
             VA, "bride's father's res." CTOLMR
             signed on 12-05-1871 by Jno. R. Pharr,
             Clk. Mins. Ret. says mar. on 12-05-
             1871 at bride's father's res. was
             signed A. Weller.

02-29-1872   (on book)   11-28-1871 (on CTOL)
  # 3   02-29-1872 (on Mins. Ret.)
             Jno. Longacre (on bk) [John Longacre
             (on CTOLMR)], 63, single, "White",
             Born and Lived: Alleg. Co., VA, Occup:
             boatbuilder, s/o: Sam'l. and Nancy
             Longacre (on bk) [Samuel and Nancy
             Longacre (on CTOLMR)]; and Nancy Jane

Miller, 20, single, "White", Born:
Rockbridge Co., VA, Lived: Alleg.
Co., VA, dau/o: Jno. H. and Sarah J.
Miller. PL: "Alleg. Co." (on CTOL
MR). CTOLMR signed on 11-20-1871 by
Jno. R. Pharr, Clk. CTOL signed on
11-28-1871. Mins. Ret. says mar. on
02-29-1872 at groom's res. was sign-
ed M. A. Wilson.

12-13-1871   Jas. Stull (on book) [James Stull
4   (on CTOLMR)], 24, "White", single,
              Born and Lived: Alleg. Co., VA, Oc-
              cup: farmer, s/o: Jas. and Hannah
              Stull (on bk) [James and Hannah
              Stull (on CTOLMR)]; and Sarah E.
              Leighton (on bk) [Sarah Ellen Leigh-
              ton (on CTOLMR)], 20, single,"White",
              B: Botetourt Co., VA, Lived: Alleg.
              Co., VA, dau/o: Dan'l. B. and Louisa
              Leighton. PL: Alleg. Co., VA, "Mrs.
              King's res." CTOLMR signed on 12-11-
              1871 by Jno. R. Pharr, Clk. Mins.
              Ret. says mar. on 12-13-1871 at Mrs.
              King's res. was signed A. Buhrman.

01-02-1872   James Grimes, 23, single, "Colored",
1   B: Louisa Co., VA, Lived: Bath Co.,
              VA, Occup: farmer, s/o: ___ (on book
              and CTOLMR); and Ann Pollard, 20, B:
              Louisa Co., VA, single, "Colored",
              Lived: Alleg. Co., VA, dau/o: John
              Pollard and ___ (on book) [John and
              ____ Pollard (on CTOLMR)]. PL: Cov-
              ington, VA, in Alleg. Co. CTOLMR
              signed 01-02-1872 by Jno. R. Pharr,
              Clk. Mins. Ret. says mar. on 01-02-
              1872 in Covington, VA, was signed
              Wm. H. Wiley.

01-09-1872   John J. Bogart, 20, single, "White",
2   Born and Lived: Botetourt Co., VA,

Occup: farmer, s/o: Garrett and Ann
Bogart; and <u>Nancy J. Leslie</u> (on book)
[<u>Nany Jane Leslie</u> (on CTOLMR)], 18,
single, "White", B: Botetourt Co.,VA,
Lived: Alleg. Co., VA, dau/o: Wm. W.
and Mary Leslie. PL: Alleg. Co., VA,
"Rich Patch." CTOLMR signed on 01-
02-1872 by Jno. R. Pharr, Clk. Mins.
Ret. says mar. on 01-09-1872 at house
of Wm. Leslie was signed M. A. Wilson.
Consent dated 01-01-1872 for <u>Nancy
Jane Leslie</u> was signed Wm. W. Leslie,
Wit. J. T. Whitten and L. B. Whitten.
L. B. Whitten made oath to signature
on 01-02-1872. Consent dated 01-01-
1872 for <u>John J. Bogart</u> was signed
Garrett (his X mark) Bogart, Wit. D.
Reese Staley. <u>John J. Bogart</u> made
oath to signature on 01-02-1872.

01-09-1872   <u>Jos. C. Lowman</u>, 47, widower, "White",
  # 3   Born and Lived: Rockbridge Co., VA,
              Occup: Minister of Gospel [Note:
              written in after Occup. "mistake
              nothing" (on CTOLMR)], s/o: Wm. and
              Margaret Lowman; and <u>Carrie H. Evans</u>,
              21, single, "White", Born and Lived:
              Alleg. Co., VA, dau/o: Wm. and Kesiah
              Evans. PL: Alleg. Co., VA, "Anthony
              Harman's res." CTOLMR signed by Jno.
              R. Pharr, Clk. on 01-08-1872. Mins.
              Ret. says mar. on 01-09-1872 at
              Anthony Harman's res. was signed by
              M. A. Wilson. "Jno. R. Harman made
              oath to age of <u>Miss E.</u>"--Note on
              CTOLMR.

01-11-1872   <u>Littleton T. Dickey</u>, 36, "White", B:
  # 4   Botetourt Co., VA, single, Lived:
              Monroe Co., VA (now W.VA.), Occup:
              merchant, s/o: Jas. and Catharine
              Bowles (on bk) [Ro. S. and Margaret

Dickey (on CTOLMR) (parents names backwards on book)]; and B. E. Bowles, 26, single, "White", B: Ireland, Lived: Alleg. Co., VA, dau/o: Ro. S. and Margaret Dickey (on bk) [James Bowles and Catherine McCarthy (on CTOLMR) (parents names backwards on book)]. PL: Alleg. Co., VA, "Covington." CTOLMR signed on 01-11-1872 by Jno. R. Pharr, Clk. Mins. Ret. says mar. on 01-11-1872 in Covington, VA, was signed Hugh P. McMenamin.

01-18-1872 Cornelius T. Stull, 25, single, Born
5   and Lived: Alleg. Co., VA, "White", Occup: farmer, s/o: Sam'l. and E. A. Stull (on bk) [Samuel and E. A. Stull (on CTOLMR)]; and Nancy A. McCoy, 19, "White", single, B: Botetourt Co., VA, Lived: Alleg. Co., VA, dau/o: Wm. E. and Mary J. McCoy (on bk) [Wm. E. and Mary Jane McCoy (on CTOLMR)]. PL: Alleg. Co., VA, "bride's father's res." Father was present when Lic. gotten per note on CTOLMR. CTOLMR signed on 01-15-1872 by Jno. R. Pharr, Clk. Mins. Ret. says mar. on 01-18-1872 at bride's father's res. was signed M. A. Wilson.

01-17-1872 Michael Armentrout, 36, "White" Born
6   and Lived: Alleg. Co., VA, widower, Occup; farmer, s/o: Jacob and Catharine Armentrout; and Sallie Gunter, 27, single, "White", B: Kanawha Co., VA (now W.VA), Lived: Alleg. Co., VA, dau/o: John and __ Gunter (on bk and CTOLMR). PL: Alleg. Co., VA, "Jacob Armentrout's res." CTOLMR signed on 01-17-1872 by Jno. R. Pharr, Clk. Mins. Ret. says mar. on 01-17-1872 at Jacob Armontrout's res. on Potts

Creek in Alleg. Co., VA, was signed
John B. Davis.

01-18-1872   Geo. A. Arritt (on bk) [George Alex-
  # 7   ander Aritt (on CTOLMR)], 22, single,
             "White", Born and Lived: Alleg. Co.,
             VA, Occup: farmer, s/o: Michael and
             Ellen Arritt (on bk) [Michael and
             Ellen Aritt (on CTOLMR)]; and Catha-
             rine E. Armentrout (on bk) [Catharine
             Elizabeth Armentrout (on CTOLMR)],
             26, single, "White", Born and Lived:
             Alleg. Co., VA, dau/o: Geo. and Mary
             A. Armentrout (on bk) [George and
             Mary Ann Armentrout (on CTOLMR)].
             PL: Alleg. Co., VA, "bride's mother's
             res." CTOLMR signed on 01-18-1872 by
             Jno. R. Pharr, Clk. Mins. Ret. says
             mar. on 01-18-1872 at Mary A. Armon-
             trout's res. on Potts Creek in Alleg.
             Co. was signed John B. Davis.

01-25-1872   Samuel Green, 55, "white", widower,
  # 8   Born and Lived: Rockbridge Co., VA,
             Occup; farmer, s/o: Sam'l. and Eliza-
             beth Green; and Maria L. Hornbarger,
             40, widow, "White", Born and Lived:
             Alleg. Co., VA, dau/o: Anthony and
             Sarah Harman (on bk) [Anthony and
             Sarah Harmon (on CTOLMR)]. PL: Alleg.
             Co., VA, "bride's father's res."
             CTOLMR signed on 01-25-1872 by Jno.
             R. Pharr, Clk. Mins. Ret. says mar.
             on 01-25-1872 at Anthony Harman's res.
             was signed E. G. Jameson, Minister.

01-25-1872   (on book) 01-25-1871 (on CTOLMR)
  # 9   01-25-1872 (on Mins. Ret.)
             Elisha F. Callison, 27, single, Born
             and Lived: Greenbrier Co., VA (now W.
             VA), "White", Occup: farmer, s/o: J.
             S. B. and M. A. Callison (on book)

[James S. B. and Mary A. Callison
(on CTOLMR)]; and Mary E. Callison,
17, single, "White", Born and Lived:
Greenbrier Co., VA (now W.VA), dau/o:
E. F. and S. F. Callison (on book)
[Elisha F. and Sallie F. Callison
(on CTOLMR)]. PL: Alleg. Co., VA,
"Covington." CTOLMR signed on 01-25-
1872 by Jno. R. Pharr, Clk. Mins.
Ret. says mar. on 01-25-1872 at Mc-
Curdy's Hotel, Covington, VA, was
signed James M. Rice. Consent dated
01-23-1872 has name Mary Elizabeth
Callison and was signed by mother,
Sallie F. Merritte, Wit. C. B. Renick
and Thomas Perry and Elisha F. Calli-
son.

01-31-1872 James Craft, 21, single, "White", B:
10   Botetourt Co., VA, Lived: Alleg. Co.,
            VA, Occup: farmer, s/o: Wm. and Sarah
            Craft; and Eliz. A. Helmintoller (on
            bk) [Elizabeth A. Helmintoller (on
            CTOLMR)], 20, single, "White", Born
            and Lived: Alleg. Co., VA, dau/o: W.
            and R. Helmentoller (on bk) [Wm. and
            Rebecca Helmentoller (on CTOLMR)].
            PL: Alleg. Co., VA, "Peter Helmintol-
            ler's res." CTOLMR signed on 01-30-
            1872 by Jno. R. Pharr, Clk. Mins.
            Ret. says mar. on 01-31-1872 at res.
            of Peter Helmentoller was signed
            William Richardson.
            "Alleghany County, VA January 27th
            1872
            Mr. John C. Poor or his Deputy will
            give James Craft marriage license.
                            Wm. Helmintoller"

02-07-1872 Edwin W. Jordan, 39, single, "White",
11   Born and Lived: Alleg. Co., VA, Oc-
            cup: RR Contractor (on bk) [Contrac-
            tor (on CTOLMR)],   s/o: Edwin   and

(Mar. Register Book (1) - Continued)

Mary Jordan; and Mattie J. Montague,
26, single, "White", B: Alleg. Co.,
VA (on bk) [___ (on CTOLMR)], Lived:
Alleg. Co., VA, dau/o: J. M. and
Jane Montague (on bk) [James M. and
Jane Montague (on CTOLMR)]. PL: Alleg. Co., VA "J. M. Montague, Esq.,
res." CTOLMR signed on 02-07-1872
by Jno. R. Pharr, Clk. Mins. Ret.
says mar. on 02-07-1872 at J. M. Montague house was signed James M. Rice.

03-02-1872 (on book) 02-11-1872 (on CTOLMR)
12   03-02-1872 (on Mins. Ret.)
Allen E. Bowers, 33, "White", single,
B: Carroll Co., VA, Lived: Bath Co.,
VA, Occup: miner, s/o: Wm. and Reeca
Bowers (on bk) [Wm. and Recca Bowers
(on CTOLMR)]; and Maggie E. Creeden,
25, single, "White", B: Ireland, Liv-
ed: Alleg. Co., VA, dau/o: John and
Mary Creeden. PL: Staunton, VA (on
bk) [Lewis Tunnel C & O RR (on CTOL
MR--was planned place but not where
took place)]. CTOLMR signed on 02-
07-1872 by Jno. R. Pharr, Clk. Mins.
Ret. says mar. on 03-02-1872 at
Staunton in Augusta Co., VA, was
signed John McVerry (on Mins. Ret.)
[John McVeriss (on book)].

02-22-1872 George Fraser, 21, "White", single,
13   B: Scotland, Lived: Alleg. Co., VA,
Occup: Engineer, s/o: A. and J. Fra-
ser (on bk) [Alexander and Jennett
Fraser (on CTOLMR)]; and Mary Duwese,
21, single, "White", B: Philadelphia,
PA, Lived: Alleg. Co., VA, dau/o:
Chs. and Martha Duwese. PL: Alleg.
Co., VA "Covington." CTOLMR signed
on 02-22-1872 by Jno. R. Pharr, Clk.
Mins. Ret. says mar. on 02-22-1872
in Covington in Alleg. Co., VA, was

(Mar. Register Book (1) - Continued)

signed James M. Rice. Note on CTOL MR: "<u>Miss Duwese</u> made oath to her age."

02-28-1872
14

(on book) 02-29-1872 (on CTOLMR and Mins. Ret.)
<u>Elijah Powers</u>, 32, single, "Black", B: Southampton Co., VA, Lived: Alleg. Co., VA, Occup: laborer, s/o: ___ (on bk and CTOLMR); and <u>Nancy Cooper</u>, 19, single, "Black", B: Botetourt Co., VA, Lived: Alleg. Co., VA, dau/o: Aldridge Cooper (on bk and CTOLMR). PL: Alleg. Co., VA, "Jordan's Furnace." CTOLMR signed on 02-28-1872 by Jno. R. Pharr, Clk. Mins. Ret. says mar. on 02-29-1872 at Aldridge Cooper's res. was signed M. A. Wilson.

03-15-1872
15

<u>Alfred Tucker</u> (on bk) [A̶l̶t̶h̶u̶r̶ Alfred Tucker (as on Mar. Auth. and CTOLMR)], 22, single, "White", B: Craig Co., VA, Lived: Alleg. Co., VA, Occup: farmer, s/o: Jas. A. and Eliz. Tucker (on bk) [Jas. A. and Elizabeth Tucker (on CTOLMR)]; and <u>Phoebe H. Wolf</u>, 21, single, "White", Born and Lived: Alleg. Co., VA, dau/o: Abram and Hettie Wolf. PL: Alleg. Co., VA, "J. A. Arritt's res." CTOLMR signed on 02-29-1872 by Jno. R. Pharr, Clk. Mins. Ret. says mar. on 03-15-1872 at Jacob A. Aritt res. on Potts Creek in Alleg. Co., VA, was signed John B. Davis. Note on CTOLMR: "J. A. Arritt makes oath as to age of bride."

03-20-1872
16

<u>Andrew McGibbeny</u>, 26, single, "Colored", B: Roan Co., N. C., Lived: Alleg. Co., VA, Occup: laborer, s/o: ___ (on bk and CTOLMR); and <u>Biddy Bagby</u>, 18, single, "Colored", B: Rockbridge Co., VA, Lived: Alleg. Co., VA, dau/o: ___

- 312 -

(on bk and CTOLMR). PL: Alleg. Co.,
VA, "Lewis Tunnel." CTOLMR signed on
03-20-1872 by Jno. R. Pharr, Clk.
Mins. Ret. says mar. on 03-20-1872 at
Lewis Tunnel was signed Wm. H. Wiley.
"We do consent to the marridge of our
Daugher to A. McGibbenny.
                          Wyat Bagby
                          Mary A. Bagby
Wit. Charly (his X mark) Brown
I solemnly swear in the presence of
Almighty God that Wyat and Mary A.
Bagby signed and acknowledged the
above certificate in my presence.
          Charles (his X mark) Brown
Attest: John L. Boswell"

03-21-1872 Robert Nicely, 18, single, "White",
  # 17   Born and Lived: Alleg. Co., VA, Occup:
            farmer, s/o: Andr. J. and Hester Nice-
            ly; and Margaret Nicely, 17, single,
            "White", Born and Lived: Alleg. Co.,
            VA, dau/o: Jacob and Margaret Nicely.
            PL: Alleg. Co., VA "bride's mother's
            res." CTOLMR signed on 03-21-1872 by
            Jno. R. Pharr, Clk. Mins. Ret. says
            mar. on 03-21-1872 at bride's mother's
            res. was signed M. A. Wilson. Consent
            dated 03-__-1872 has Margaret L. Nice-
            ly and Andre. J. Nicely as parents who
            signed in Clk's. presence   so   Lic.
            could be obtained.

03-21-1872 Garrett G. Gooch, 35, single, "White",
  # 18   B: Orange Co., VA, Lived: West Virgin-
            ia (on bk) [Sweet Springs, W.VA. (on
            CTOLMR)], Occup: merchant, s/o: Thom-
            son and Eliz. Gooch (on bk) [Thomson
            and Elizabeth M. Gooch (on CTOLMR)];
            and Mary Watson Payne, 26, single,
            "White", Born and Lived: Alleg. Co.,
            VA, dau/o: Geo. H. and S. A. Payne (on
            bk) [Geo. H. and Sarah A. Payne (on

(Mar. Register Book (1) - Continued)

CTOLMR)]. PL: Alleg. Co., VA "bride's
mother's res." CTOLMR signed on 03-
21-1872 by Jno. R. Pharr, Clk. Mins.
Ret. says mar. on 03-21-1872 at "Edge
Hill", res. of bride's mother, was
signed James M. Rice.

03-27-1872   Wm. A. Oliver, 24, single, "White",
19   Born and Lived: Alleg. Co., VA, Occup:
             farmer, s/o: Jas. and Charlotte Oliver
             (on bk) [James and Charlotte Oliver
             (on CTOLMR)]; and Jane E. Keyser, 17,
             single, "White", Born and Lived: Al-
             leg. Co., VA, dau/o: Wm. H. and Nancy
             Keyser (on bk) [Wm. H. and Nancy N.
             Keyser (on CTOLMR)]. PL: Alleg. Co.,
             VA, "Wm. H. Keyser, Esq., res." CTOL
             MR signed on 03-25-1872 by Jno. R.
             Pharr, Clk. Mins. Ret. says mar. on
             03-27-1872 at bride's father's res.
             in Alleg. Co., VA, was signed A. Wel-
             ler.

03-28-1872   Geo. W. Craft (on bk) [George W. Craft
20   (on CTOLMR)], 23, single, "White", B:
             Botetourt Co., VA, Lived: Craig Co.,
             VA, Occup: farmer, s/o: Geo. M. and E.
             Craft; and Mary C. Persinger, 23, sing-
             le, "White", Born and Lived: Alleg.
             Co., VA, dau/o: Cs. A. and Mary Per-
             singer. PL: Alleg. Co., VA "Rich
             Patch." CTOLMR signed on 03-25-1872
             by Jno. R. Pharr, Clk. Mins. Ret.
             says mar. on 03-28-1872 at Andrew J.
             Arington's in Rich Patch in Alleg. Co.
             was signed John B. Davis.

04-04-1872   (on Book) 04-03-1872 (on Mins. Ret.)
#21   Galvanni McKenney, 23, single, "White",
             B: Monroe Co., VA (now W.VA.), Lived:
             Alleg. Co., VA, Occup: school teacher,
             s/o: Jno. Y. and Lucy McKenney (on bk)

[John Y. and Lucy McKenney (on CTOL
MR)]; and <u>Cornelia Helmentoller</u>, 19,
single, "White", Born and Lived: Alleg. Co., VA, dau/o: Jordan and R.
Helmentoller (on bk) [Jordan and Rebecca Helmentoller (on CTOLMR)]. PL:
Alleg. Co., VA "bride's father's res."
CTOLMR signed on 04-01-1872 by Jno. R.
Pharr, Clk. Mins. Ret. says mar. on
04-03-1872 at Jordan Helmentoller's
on Potts Creek in Alleg. Co. was signed John B. Davis. Note on CTOLMR:
"Bride's father present" --meaning he
was with the couple when they came to
get the Lic.

04-08-1872 <u>Ambrose Swann</u>, 37, widower, "Colored",
  # 22   B: Richmond, VA, Lived: Alleg. Co.,
           VA (on bk) [Covington, VA (on CTOLMR)],
           Occup: laborer (on bk) [factory hand
           (on CTOLMR)], s/o: Osborn and Rose
           Swann (on bk) [Osborn and Rosetta
           Swann (on CTOLMR)]; and <u>Harriet Smith</u>
           (on bk) [<u>Harriet Ann Smith</u> (on CTOL
           MR)], 28, "Colored", widow, B: Suffolk
           Co., VA, Lived: Alleg. Co., VA (on bk)
           [Covington, VA (on CTOLMR)], dau/o:
           _____ (on bk) [unknown (on CTOLMR)].
           CTOLMR signed on 04-08-1872 by Jno. R.
           Pharr, Clk. Mins. Ret. says mar. on
           04-08-1872 in Covington in Alleg. Co.
           was signed Wm. H. Wiley. PL: Alleg.
           Co., VA.

04-16-1872 (on book) 04-18-1872 (on CTOLMR and
  # 23   Mins. Ret.)
           <u>James Jackson</u>, 22, single, "Colored",
           B: Amherst Co., VA, Lived: Alleg. Co.,
           VA, Occup: laborer, s/o: Geo. and Eme-
           line Jackson (on bk) [George and Emi-
           line Jackson (on CTOLMR)]; and <u>Ginnie</u>
           <u>Walker</u>, 22, single, "Colored", B:

- 315 -

Craig Co., VA, Lived: Alleg. Co., VA, dau/o: Anderson and T. Walker (on bk) [Anderson and Tabitha Walker (on CTOL MR)]. PL: Alleg. Co., VA "Lucy Selina Furnace." CTOLMR signed on 04-16-1872 by Jno. R. Pharr, Clk. Mins. Ret. says mar. on 04-18-1872 at Lucy Furnace was signed John L. Beale.

05-30-1872 Charles J. Potter, 25, single, "White",
24   B: New York, Lived: Greenbrier Co., W. VA, Occup: carpenter, s/o: Horace and Julia Potter; and Mollie C. Mann, 28, single, "White", B: West Virginia, Lived: Greenbrier Co., W. VA, dau/o: Wm. W. and H. D. Mann. PL: Alleg. Co., VA "Covington." CTOLMR signed on 05-30-1872 by Jno. R. Pharr, Clk. Mins. Ret. says mar. on 05-30-1872 at McCurdy's Hotel in Covington, VA, was signed A. Weller. Age oath for Mollie given by W. H. Mann on 05-30-1872, Teste Jno. R. Pharr, Clk.

06-13-1872 John C. Jones, 21, single, "White", B.
25   Kanawha Co., VA (now W.VA), Lived: Alleg. Co., VA, Occup: farmer, s/o: Chs. A. and Mary J. Jones (on bk) [Chs. A. and Mary Jane Jones (on CTOLMR)]; and Eliza J. Reid, 24, "White", single, Born and Lived: Alleg. Co., VA, dau/o: Jno. C. and Mary A. Reid (on bk) [Jno. C. and Mary Ann Reid (on CTOLMR)]. PL: Alleg. Co., VA "bride's res." CTOLMR signed on 06-08-1872 by Jno. R. Pharr, Clk. Mins. Ret. says mar. on 06-13-1872 at John C. Reid's on Cove Creek in Alleg. Co., VA, was signed John B. Davis. Consent dated 06-08-1872 has John Charles Jones and Elisa Jane Reed, age 24, and was signed John C. Reed and Maryann A. Reed, Wit. C. A. Jones.

(Mar. Register Book (1) - Continued)

06-12-1872   David B. Hepler, 22, single, "White",
 # 26   Born and Lived: Alleg. Co., VA, Occup:
             farmer, s/o: Jno. and Peggy Hepler (on
             bk) [John and Peggy Hepler (on CTOL
             MR)]; and Elizabeth Kimberlin, 21,
             single, "White", Born and Lived: Al-
             leg. Co., VA, dau/o: Wm. and E. Kim-
             berlin (on bk) [Wm. and Elizabeth Kim-
             berlin (on CTOLMR)]. PL: Alleg. Co.,
             VA, "bridegroom's res." CTOLMR sign-
             ed on 06-10-1872 by Jno. R. Pharr,
             Clk. Mins. Ret. says mar. on 06-12-
             1872 at John Hepler's on Potts Creek
             in Alleg Co., VA, was signed John B.
             Davis. Age oath given by John L. A.
             Bush for Elizabeth on 06-10-1872,
             Teste Jno. R. Pharr, Clk.

06-27-1872   Chs. C. Chapman (on bk) [Charles C.
 # 27   Chapman (on CTOLMR)], 22, single, Born
             and Lived: Petersburg, VA, "White",
             Occup: butcher, s/o: W. B. and M. J.
             Chapman (on bk) [W. B. and Margaret J.
             Chapman (on CTOLMR)]; and Martha
             Brooks, 22, widow, "White", B: Eng-
             land, Lived: Greenbrier Co., W.VA.,
             dau/o: Sam'l. and M. Aldress (on bk)
             [Samuel and Martha Aldress (on CTOL
             MR)]. PL: Alleg. Co., VA "Covington."
             CTOLMR signed on 06-27-1872 by Jno. R.
             Pharr, Clk. Mins. Ret. says mar. on
             06-27-1872 at Cogbill's Hotel in Cov-
             ington was signed A. Weller.

03-11-1871   (on book) 03-02-1871 (on CTOLMR and
 # 28   Mins. Ret.)
             [Author's Note: See also # 16 ½ Mar.
             Book page 13, 03-02-1871--listed twice]
             James Arrington, 24, single, Occup:
             farmer, s/o: Jas. and Jane Arrington;
             and Emelina S. Manspile, 21, widow,
             dau/o: Isaac and __ Wolf. PL: Alleg.
             Co., VA. Mar. by A. Boon. Clerk's

note on book: "not returned at proper time. [More information listed
on other listing.]B.&L. Alleg. Co.,VA.

11-24-1870 Thursday
  # 29   Jas. P. Gillaspie (on bk) [James Polk
           Gillespie (on CTOLMR)], 24, single,
           B: Bath Co., VA, Lived: Alleg. Co.,VA,
           Occup: farmer, s/o: Sam'l. and Mary
           Gillespie; and Mary C. McCaleb, 21,
           single, Born and Lived: Alleg. Co.,
           VA, dau/o: Jos. T. and Nancy McCaleb.
           PL: Alleg. Co., VA "Potts Creek."
           Consent dated 11-21-1870 for Mary by
           Joseph T. McCaleb, Wit. A. T. Hamil-
           ton. CTOLMR signed on 11-23-1870 by
           W̷. C̷. V̷a̷u̷g̷h̷a̷n̷, Clk. Jno. R. Pharr.
           Mins. Ret. says mar. on 11-24-1870 at
           Joseph T. McCaleb's res. in Alleg. Co,
           VA, was signed Aaron Boon. Clerk's
           note on book: "not returned at proper
           time." [Author's Note: Lic. was filed
           in 1872 because of Clerk's # and time
           received.]

11-24-1870 Thursday
  # 30   Nathan L. Bush (on bk) [Nathan Lewis
           Bush (on CTOLMR)], 20, single, Occup:
           farmer, s/o: A. A. and P. A. Bush (on
           bk) [Andrew A. and Patsey Ann Bush (on
           CTOLMR)]; and A. J. Helmentoller (on
           bk) [Alwilda Jane Helmentoller (on CT
           OLMR)], 22, single, dau/o: P. and M.
           Helmentoller (on bk) [Peter and Mary
           Helmentoller (on CTOLMR)]. PL: Alleg.
           Co., VA "Peter Helmentoller's res."
           CTOLMR signed on 11-21-1870 by Jno. R.
           Pharr, Clk. Mins. Ret. says mar. on
           11-24-1870 at Peter Helmentoller's
           res. in Alleg. Co. was signed Aaron
           Boon. Both were born and lived in Al-
           leg. Co., VA. Clerk's note on book:

"not returned at proper time."

07-25-1872   George W. Masters, 21, single,"White",
  # 31   B: Monroe Co., VA (now W.VA), Lived:
              Alleg. Co., VA, Occup: laborer, s/o:
              Frank and Rhoda Masters; and Eliza J.
              Howard (on bk) [Eliza Jane Howard (on
              CTOLMR)], 22, single, "White", B: Mon-
              roe Co., VA (now W.VA), Lived: Alleg.
              Co., VA, dau/o: Geo. and Polly Howard
              (on bk) [George and Polly Howard (on
              CTOLMR)].   PL: Alleg. Co., VA.   CTOL
              MR signed on 07-23-1872 by Jno. R.
              Pharr, Clk. Mins. Ret. says mar. on
              07-25-1872 at Shelton Harman's res.
              was signed James M. Rice. Age oath
              for himself and Eliza on 07-23-1872
              given by George W. Masters, Teste Jno.
              R. Pharr, Clk.

08-07-1872   Lewis C. Nicely, 23, single, "White",
  # 32   Occup: farmer, s/o: Mathias and M. J.
              Nicely (on bk) [Mathias and Mary Jane
              Nicely (on CTOLMR)]; and Estaline
              Nicely, 19, single, "White", dau/o:
              Jacob and M. Nicely (on bk) [Jacob and
              Margaret Nicely (on CTOLMR)].   Both
              were born and lived in Alleg. Co.,VA.
              PL: Alleg. Co., VA.   CTOLMR signed on
              08-06-1872 by Jno. R. Pharr, Clk.
              Mins. Ret. says mar. on 08-07-1872 at
              bride's father's res. was signed M. A.
              Wilson. Consent dated 08-06-1872 by
              Jaceb (his X mark) Nisely for Estyline
              Nisely and also has name Lewis Nisely
              "in presence of Willie A. King", Wit.
              M. W. King. Oath acknowledgement of
              Jacob Nicely by William A. King on 08-
              06-1872, Teste Jno. R. Pharr, Clk.

08-13-1872   Jas. J. Lockhart (on bk) [James J.
  # 33   Lockhart (on CTOLMR)], 22, single,

"White", Occup: farmer, s/o: D. B.
and N. Lockhart (on bk) [David B. and
Nancy Lockhart (on CTOLMR)]; and
Nancy E. Fridley, 22, single, "White",
dau/o: Jno. and Ruth Fridley. CTOLMR
signed on 08-12-1872 by Jno. R. Pharr,
Clk. Both were born and lived in Alleg. Co., VA. PL: Alleg. Co., VA "D.
Rose, Esq., res." Mins. Ret. says mar.
on 08-13-1872 at D. Rose's res. in
Alleg. Co. was signed James M. Rice.

08-17-1872 Ferdinand Green, 25, single, "Color-
34   ed", Occup: laborer, s/o: ___ (on bk
            and CTOL); and Caroline Dawson, 26,
            "Colored", single, dau/o: ___ (on bk
            and CTOLMR). Both were born and liv-
            ed in Alleg. Co., VA. PL: Alleg. Co,
            VA. CTOLMR signed on 08-17-1872 by
            Jno. R. Pharr, Clk. Mins. Ret. says
            mar. on 08-17-1872 at Mrs. S. A.
            Payne's near Covington, VA, was sign-
            ed W. H. Wiley. Consent of mother,
            Fanny (her X mark) Dawson, was dated
            08-17-1872, Wit. S. A. Payne.

09-05-1872 Moses Strange, 23, "Colored", single,
35   B: Albermarle Co., VA, Lived: Alleg.
            Co., VA, Occup: laborer, s/o: ___ (on
            bk and CTOLMR); and Tilda Jordan, 24,
            "Colored", single, B: Norfolk, VA,
            Lived: Alleg. Co., VA, dau/o: ___ (on
            bk and CTOLMR). PL: Alleg. Co., VA.
            CTOLMR signed on 09-05-1872 by Jno. R.
            Pharr, Clk. Mins. Ret. says mar. on
            09-05-1872 at Holloway Farm in Alleg.
            Co., VA, was signed by W. H. Wiley.
            Age oath for Tilda given by Arch Allen
            on 09-05-1872, Teste J. J. Hobbs, D.C.

09-05-1872 John L. Morris, 21, single, "White",
36   B: Kanawha Co., VA (now W.VA), Lived:
            Alleg. Co., VA, Occup: Wagoneer, s/o:

W. F. and E. Morris (on bk) [W. F.
and Elizabeth Morris (on CTOLMR)];
and Martha E. Bryant, 21, "White", B:
Rockbridge Co., VA, single, Lived:
Alleg. Co., VA, dau/o: Wm. and _____
Bryant (on bk and CTOLMR). PL: Alleg.
Co., VA "Jackson River." CTOLMR signed on 09-05-1872 by Jno. R. Pharr,
Clk. Mins. Ret. says mar. on 09-05-
1872 at N. W. King's res. was signed
by M. A. Wilson. Consent dated 09-04-
1872 by father, Wm. Bryant, Wit. John
Pulse who made oath before clk. to
witnessing Bryant signature.

09-18-1872   (on book and Mins. Ret.) 09-17-1872
  # 37   (on CTOLMR)
             Wm. Anderson, 22, single, "Colored",
             B: Bedford Co., VA, Lived: Alleg. Co.,
             VA, Occup: laborer, s/o: ___ (on bk
             and CTOLMR); and Paulina Burrell, 20,
             "Colored", single, Born and Lived: Al-
             leg. Co., VA, dau/o: ___ (on bk and
             CTOLMR). PL: Alleg. Co., VA. CTOLMR
             signed on 09-16-1872 by Jno. R. Pharr,
             Clk. Mins. Ret. says mar. on 09-18-
             1872 at Lick Run Bridge was signed
             John L. Beale. Consent of mother,
             Silvie (her X mark) Rideout, says
             Paulina lived in Alleg. Co. for the
             "last 10 months", Wit. Robt. Jones who
             made oath to clk. that he witnessed
             Silvie sign consent.

Page 15

09-26-1872   (on book) 10-01-1872 (on CTOLMR and
  # 1   Mins. Ret.)
             Albert Hackney, 28, single, "Colored",
             B: Louisa Co., VA, Lived: Alleg. Co.,
             VA, Occup: laborer, s/o: Fleming and
             M. Hackney (on bk) [Fleming and Mary

Hackney (on CTOLMR)]; and Melinda Moore, 27, "Colored", widow, Born and Lived: Alleg. Co., VA, dau/o: Arthur and Ann Lee (on bk) [Arthur and Annie Lee (on CTOLMR)]. PL: Alleg. Co., VA "near Callaghan's." CTOLMR signed on 09-26-1872 by Jno. R. Pharr, Clk. Mins. Ret. says mar. on 10-01-1872 near Callaghan's was signed W.H.Wiley.

09-29-1872   Charles Lee, 21, single, "White", B:
2   Montgomery Co., VA, Lived: Alleg. Co., VA, Occup: laborer, s/o: Jas. and Jane Lee (on bk) [James and Jane Lee (on CTOLMR)]; and Jennie McNulty (on bk) [Jinnie McNulty (on CTOLMR)], 23, single, "White", Born and Lived: Alleg. Co., VA, dau/o: Pat and Susan McNulty (on bk) [Patrick and Susan McNulty (on CTOLMR)]. PL: Alleg. Co., VA "bride's res." CTOLMR signed on 09-26-1872 by Jno. R. Pharr, Clk. Mins. Ret. says mar. on 09-29-1872 at Deisher's Schoolhouse on Craigs Creek was signed A. Buhrman. Consent of father, Patrick McNulty, on 09-25-1872 has name Jinnie. Jinnie McNulty made oath as to signature of father on consent on 09-25-1872, Teste J. R. Pharr, Clk. Age oaths were given by Jinnie McNulty and Charles Lee on 09-26-1872, Teste Jno. R. Pharr, Clk.

10-02-1872   Thos. B. Robinson (on bk) [Thomas B.
3   Robinson (on CTOLMR)], 25, "White", single, B: Warren, N.C. [Author's Note: I assume this is a county since there is a county by this name. I can find no town or city on present day maps.], Lived: Alleg. Co., VA, Occup: wagon maker, s/o: Thos. B. and E. Robinson (on bk) [Thos. B. and Emily M. Robinson (on CTOLMR)]; and

(Mar. Register Book (1) - Continued)

Jestinah A. Lemon, 22, "White", Born
and Lived: Alleg. Co., VA, single,
dau/o: J. Y. and M. M. Lemon (on bk)
[James Y. and Margaret M. Lemon (on
CTOLMR)]. PL: Alleg. Co., VA "bride's
father's res." CTOLMR signed on 09-
26-1872 by Jno. R. Pharr, Clk. Mins.
Ret. says mar. on 10-02-1872 at bride's father's res. was signed by M.
A. Wilson.

10-02-1872   H. H. Robertson (on bk) [Henry H. Rob-
4   ertson (on CTOLMR)], 47, "White", B:
Augusta Co., VA, widower, Lived: Al-
leg. Co., VA, Occup: lawyer, s/o: Geo.
C. and A. C. Robertson (on bk) [Geo.
C. and Annie C. Robertson (on CTOL
MR)]; and Drucilla W. Mason, 26, B:
Hanover Co., VA, single, "White", Liv-
ed: Alleg. Co., VA, dau/o: C. R. and
D. W. Mason. PL: Alleg. Co., VA.
CTOLMR signed on 09-27-1872 by Jno. R.
Pharr, Clk. Mins. Ret. says mar. on
10-02-1872 at Jerry's Run near Coving-
ton, VA, was signed Geo. B. Taylor.

10-09-1872   Wm. E. Clark, 25, single, "White", B:
5   Prince Edward Co., VA, Lived: Alleg.
Co., VA, Occup: farmer, s/o: Jas. and
Mary Clark (on bk) [James and Mary
Clark (on CTOLMR)]; and Hester Nicely,
27, single, "White", Born and Lived:
Alleg. Co., VA, dau/o: J. and M. Nice-
ly (on bk) [Jacob and Margaret Nicely
(on CTOLMR)]. PL: Alleg. Co., VA.
CTOLMR signed on 10-08-1872 by Jno. R.
Pharr, Clk. Mins. Ret. says mar. on
10-09-1872 at Bogarth's res. in Bote-
tourt Co., VA, was signed C. L. Damron
[C. L. Dameron (on book)]. Consent,
dated Lucy Selina Furnace, Alleg. Co.,
VA, on 10-07-1872, given by father,
Jacob (his X mark) Nicely, Sr., Wit.

(Mar. Register Book (1) - Continued)

S̶a̶m̶u̶e̶l̶ Daniel S. Nicely [as on con-
sent]. Jackson Nicely, brother of
bride, made age oath.

10-17-1872   H. H. C. Ayers (on bk and CTOLMR), 25,
6   single, "White", B: Georgia, Lived:
             Greenbrier Co., W.VA., Occup: ___ (on
             bk and CTOLMR), s/o: Jno. T. and H.
             Ayres (on bk) [John T. and Henrietta
             Ayres (on CTOLMR)]; and Angenetta Eddy,
             21, single, "White", B: Monroe Co., VA
             (now W.VA), Lived: Alleg. Co., VA,
             dau/o: W. and L. Eddy (on bk) [Wash-
             ington and Lucinda Eddy (on CTOLMR)].
             PL: Alleg. Co., VA. CTOLMR signed on
             10-16-1872 by Jno. R. Pharr, Clk.
             Mins. Ret. says mar. on 10-17-1872 at
             Wm. Cunningham's was signed A. Weller.

10-22-1872   Chs. Ross, 23, single, "Colored", B:
7   Pena (on bk) [Pennsylvania (on CTOL
             MR)], Lived: Bath Co., VA, Occup: la-
             borer, s/o: ___ Ellen Ross (on bk and
             CTOLMR); and Maria Kelley, 17, single,
             "Colored", B: Bath Co., VA, Lived: Al-
             leg. Co., VA, dau/o: Charles and ___
             Kelley (on bk and CTOLMR). PL: Alleg.
             Co., VA. CTOLMR signed on 10-21-1872
             by Jno. R. Pharr, Clk. Mins. Ret.
             says mar. on 10-22-1872 at Mrs. L. S.
             Payne's res. in Bath Co., VA, was
             signed J. M. Pilcher.

10-24-1872   Jacob L. Bush, 20, single, "White",
8   Born and Lived: Alleg. Co., VA, Occup:
             farmer, s/o: Ambrose and P. A. Bush
             (on bk) [Ambrose and Patsey Ann Bush
             (on CTOLMR)]; and Harriet M. Smith, 21,
             single, "White", Born and Lived: Alleg.
             Co., VA, dau/o: Jno. C. and S. Smith
             (on bk) [John C. and Susan Smith (on
             CTOLMR)]. PL: Alleg. Co., VA "bride's

(Mar. Register Book (1) - Continued)

father's res." CTOLMR signed on 10-
23-1872 by Jno. R. Pharr, Clk. Mins.
Ret. says mar. on 10-24-1872 at John
C. Smith's res. was signed E. C. Lee.
Consent for <u>Jacob</u> given 10-23-1872
was signed "Anoboso Bush." James R.
Wilson made oath that Ambrose Bush
signed consent and made age oath for
<u>Harriet</u> on 10-23-1872, Teste Jno. R.
Pharr, Clk.

10-24-1872   <u>Johnathan A. Robinson</u>, 28, single,
   # 9   "White", Born and Lived: Alleg. Co.,
            VA, Occup: farmer, s/o: Wm. and E.
            Robinson (on bk) [Wm. and Elisabeth
            Robinson (on CTOLMR)]; and <u>Lizzie C.
            Minnick</u>, 27, single, "White", B: Rock-
            ingham Co., VA, Lived: Alleg. Co., VA,
            dau/o: John and ___ Minnick (on bk and
            CTOLMR). PL: Alleg. Co., VA "Coving-
            ton." CTOLMR signed on 10-23-1872 by
            Jno. R. Pharr, Clk. Mins. Ret. says
            mar. on 10-24-1872 at Mr. Bell's res.
            in Covington was signed A. Weller.
            Age oath given by <u>J. A. Robinson.</u>

10-31-1872   <u>Chs. Brown</u> (on bk) [<u>Charles Brown</u> (on
   # 10   CTOLMR)], 24, single, "Colored", B:
            Botetourt Co., VA, Lived: Alleg. Co.,
            VA, Occup: laborer, s/o: N. and M.
            Brown (on bk) [Nelson and Martha Brown
            (on CTOLMR)]; and <u>Maria Hunter</u>, 21,
            single, "Colored", Born and Lived: Al-
            leg. Co., VA, dau/o: Jno. and S. Hunter
            (on bk) [John and Sarah Hunter (on CTO
            LMR)]. PL: Alleg. Co., VA. CTOLMR
            signed on 10-31-1872 by Jno. R. Pharr,
            Clk. Mins. Ret. says mar. on 10-31-
            1872 in Covington was signed Wm. H.
            Wiley.

11-02-1872   <u>Patrick Lawrence</u>, 26, single, "White",

11   B: Ireland, Lived: Alleg. Co., VA, Occup: R. R. Employee, s/o: Jno. and Mary Lawrence (on bk) [John and Mary Lawrence (on CTOLMR)]; and <u>Margaret Griffin</u>, 20, single, "White", Born: Staunton, VA, Lived: Alleg. Co., VA, dau/o: Thos. and M. Griffin (on bk) [Thomas and Mary Griffin (on CTOLMR)]. PL: Alleg. Co., VA "Lewis Tunnel." CTOLMR signed on 10-30-1872 by Jno. R. Pharr, Clk. Mins. Ret. says mar. on 11-02-1872 at Lewis Tunnel and <u>Mgrt. Griffin</u> was signed Rev. D. L. Walsh and <u>Patrick Lawrence.</u>

11-06-1872   <u>J. N. Switzer</u> (on bk) [<u>James N. Switzer</u> (on CTOLMR)], 27, single, "White",
12   B: Botetourt Co., VA, Lived: Alleg. Co., VA, Occup: blacksmith, s/o: B. and E. Switzer (on bk) [Benoni and Elsie Switzer (on CTOLMR)]; and <u>Nancy V. Lemon</u>, 21, single, "White", Born and Lived: Alleg. Co., VA, dau/o: Jos. G. and E. Lemon (on bk) [Jos. G. and Elizabeth Lemon (on CTOLMR)]. PL: Alleg. Co., VA "bride's father's res." CTOLMR signed on 11-04-1872 by Jno. R. Pharr, Clk. Mins. Ret. says mar. on 11-06-1872 at bride's father's res. was signed M. A. Wilson. Age oath given by brother, L. T. Lemon.

11-07-1872   <u>Achillis Wolfe</u>, 23, single, "White",
13   Born and Lived: Alleg. Co., VA, Occup: farmer, s/o: J. A. and S. A. Wolfe (on bk) [Jacob A. and Sarah S. Wolfe (on CTOLMR)]; and <u>S. A. J. Wolfe</u> (on book) [<u>Sarah A. J. Wolfe</u> (on CTOLMR)], 19, single, "White", Born and Lived: Alleg. Co., VA, dau/o: J. R. and M. Wolfe (on bk) [Jacob R. and Maria Wolfe (on CTOLMR)]. PL: Alleg. Co., VA "J. R. Wolfe, Esq. res." CTOLMR signed on 11-04-

(Mar. Register Book (1) - Continued)

1872 by Jno. R. Pharr, Clk. Mins. Ret. says mar. on 11-07-1872 at Jacob R. Wolf's res. on Potts Creek in Alleg. Co. was signed John B. Davis. Consent dated 11-01-1872 given by Jacob R. Wolfe, Teste Michael Aritt and Oceana S. S. Dew. Oath of Wolfe acknowledgement given by Michael Aritt, Teste Jno. R. Pharr, Clk. on 11-04-1872.

11-19-1872
14

Chs. Oliver (on bk) [Charles Oliver (on CTOLMR)], 25, single, "White", Born and Lived: Alleg. Co., VA, Occup: farmer, s/o: Jas. and S. Oliver (on bk) [James and Sharloty Oliver (on CTOLMR)]; and Henrietta D. Mann, 23, single, "White", Born and Lived: Alleg. Co., VA, dau/o: J. McD. and J. Mann (on bk) [John McD. and Julia Mann (on CTOLMR)]. PL: Alleg. Co., VA "John McD. Mann's res." CTOLMR signed on 11-18-1872 by Jno. R. Pharr, Clk. Mins. Ret. says mar. on 11-19-1872 at John McDowell Mann's res. was signed James M. Rice.

11-27-1872
15

Hugh C. Byers, 19, single, "White", Born and Lived: Alleg. Co., VA, Occup: farmer, s/o: Sam'l. and H. Byer (on bk) [Samuel and Harriet Byer (on CTOLMR)]; and Lizzie Wright (on bk) [Mary Elizabeth Wright (on CTOLMR)], 20, single, "White", Born and Lived: Alleg. Co., VA, dau/o: G. W. and E. Wright (on bk) [George W. and Elizabeth Wright (on CTOLMR)]. PL: Alleg. Co., VA, "bride's father's res." CTOLMR signed on 11-25-1872 by Jno. R. Pharr, Clk. Mins. Ret. says mar. on 11-27-1872 at G. W. Wright's on Potts Creek in Alleg. Co. was signed John B. Davis. "Nov. 22d, 1872 Mr. John R. Pharr

(Mar. Register Book (1) - Continued)

Sir you will please give <u>Hugh C.
Byers</u> marriage licence for him and my
daughter <u>E. Martha E. Wright</u> and
obige.
Age 20 years

G. W. Wright
Wit.: Charles Redman"
"I have no objection of you giving my
son <u>Hugh C. Byer</u> the license his age
is 19 years

Yours truley Samuel Byer
Wit: Charles Redman"
Oath of both acknowledgements given
by Charles Redman.

12-19-1872   <u>Jas. Harington</u> (on bk) [<u>James Haring-</u>
16   <u>ton</u> (on CTOLMR)], 24, single, "Color-
             ed", B: Louisa Co., VA, Lived: Alleg.
             Co., VA, Occup: RR Hand, s/o: M. and
             S. Harrington (on bk) [Minor and Susan
             Harington (on CTOLMR)]; and <u>Virginia
             Battles</u>, 21, single, "Colored", B:
             Buckingham Co., VA, Lived: Alleg. Co.,
             VA, dau/o: Jno. and N. Battles (on bk)
             [John and Nancy Battles (on CTOLMR)].
             PL: Alleg. Co., VA. CTOLMR signed on
             11-29-1872 by Jno. R. Pharr, Clk.
             Mins. Ret. says mar. on 12-19-1872 in
             Alleg. Co. was signed Wm. H. Wiley.
             Note on CTOLMR: "Bride's father pre-
             sent"(meaning he was there when Lic.
             was gotten).

12-04-1872   <u>Wm. T. Bowling</u>, 26, single, "White",
17   B: Nelson Co., VA, Lived: Alleg. Co.,
             VA, Occup: wagon maker, s/o: Jno. J.
             and L. J. Bowling (on bk) [John J. and
             Lucy J. Bowling (on CTOLMR)]; and <u>Car-
             oline Lemon</u>, 18, single, "White", Born
             and Lived: Alleg. Co., VA, dau/o: G.
             W. and D. Lemon (on bk) [G. W. and Di-
             anna Lemon (on CTOLMR)]. PL: Alleg.

Co., VA. CTOLMR signed on 12-03-1872
by Jno. R. Pharr, Clk. Mins. Ret.
says mar. on 12-04-1872 at bridge's
father's res. was signed M. A. Wilson.
Note on CTOLMR: "G. W. Lemon present"
(when Lic. gotten).

12-12-1872 Thos. McFarland (on bk) Thomas McFar-
18 land (on CTOLMR)], 27, "White", sing-
le, B: Botetourt Co., VA, Lived: Alleg. Co., VA, Occup: hotel keeper,
s/o: M. and E. McFarland (on bk) [Mar-
tin and Elizabeth McFarland (on CTOL
MR)]; and Kate G. Stack, 21, "White",
single, B: Monroe Co., VA (now W.VA),
Lived: Alleg. Co., VA, dau/o: J. J.
and M. A. Stack (on bk) [John J. and
Mary A. Stack (on CTOLMR)]. PL: Alleg. Co., VA. CTOLMR signed on 12-
10-1872 by Jno. R. Pharr, Clk. Mins.
Ret. says mar. on 12-12-1872 at bride's res. in Alleg. Co. was signed
Rev. D. T. Walsh (on bk) [D. P. Walsh
(on CTOLMR)]. Note on CTOLMR: "Bride's father present" (when Lic.gotten).

12-17-1872 (on book) 12-18-1872 (on Mins. Ret.)
19 Alex Johnson, 24, single, "Colored",
B: Rockbridge Co., VA, Lived: Alleg.
Co., VA, Occup: laborer, s/o: ___ (on
bk and CTOLMR); and Emma Osborne, 21,
"Colored", single, Born and Lived:
Alleg. Co., VA, dau/o: ___ (on bk and
CTOLMR). PL: Alleg. Co., VA. CTOLMR
signed on 12-17-1872 by Jno. R. Pharr,
Clk. Mins. Ret. says mar. on 12-18-
1872 at Frank Duglis's res. was sign-
ed John L. Beale. Age oath for Emma
Osburn, "whose parents are both dead"
was given by neighbors, Charles R.
Mathews and A. S. Kayser and was dated
12-16-1872 near Clifton Forge, VA.

(Mar. Register Book (1) - Continued)

12-19-1872   <u>Michael Aritt</u>, 40, widower, "White",
 # 20   Born and Lived: Alleg. Co., VA, Occup:
             farmer, s/o: Geo. and Mary Aritt (on
             bk) [George and Mary Aritt (on CTOL
             MR)]; and <u>O. S. S. Dew</u> (on bk) [<u>Oce-
             anna S. S. Dew</u> (on CTOLMR)], 20, sing-
             le, "White", Born and Lived: Alleg.
             Co., VA, dau/o: Abs. and Sarah Dew (on
             bk) [Absalom and Sarah Dew (on CTOL
             MR)]. PL: Alleg. Co., VA. Mins. Ret.
             says mar. on 12-19-1872 at Sarah Dew
             res. on Potts Creek in Alleg. Co. was
             signed John B. Davis. CTOLMR signed
             on 12-19-1872 by Jno. R. Pharr, Clk.
             Consent dated 12-18-1872 given by
             Sarah Dew, Teste S. Sophia W. Terry
             and <u>Michael Aritt</u>. Oath acknowledge-
             ment given by <u>M. Aritt</u> on 12-19-1872,
             Teste Jno. R. Pharr, Clk.

12-24-1872   <u>Wm. T. McClure</u>, 29, single, "White",
 # 21   B: Lancaster Co., Pennsylvania, Lived:
             Alleg. Co., VA, Occup: miner (on bk)
             [Mining Engineer (on CTOLMR)], s/o:
             Jno. and E. R. McClure (on bk) [John
             and Elizabeth R. McClure (on CTOLMR)];
             and <u>Susan J. Potter</u> (on bk) [<u>Susan
             Jane Peters</u> (on CTOLMR)], 22, single,
             "White", Born and Lived: Alleg. Co.,
             VA, dau/o: T. J. and M. J. Peters (on
             bk) [Thomas J. and Mary J. Peters (on
             CTOLMR)]. PL: Alleg. Co., VA. CTOLMR
             signed on 12-17-1872 by Jno. R. Pharr,
             Clk. Mins. Ret. says mar. on 12-24-
             1872 in Covington in Alleg. Co. was
             signed James M. Rice.

12-25-1872   <u>James Rogers</u>, 35, widower, "Colored",
 # 22   B: Botetourt Co., VA, Lived: Alleg.
             Co., VA, Occup: laborer, s/o: J. and
             B. Rogers (on bk) [Jupiter and Betsey
             Rogers (on CTOLMR)]; and <u>Francis Bar-</u>

ber (on bk) [Frances Barber (on CTOL
MR)], 21, single, "Colored", Born and
Lived: Alleg. Co., VA, dau/o: Jordan
and ___ Barber (on bk and CTOLMR).
PL: Alleg. Co., VA. CTOLMR signed on
12-24-1872 by Jno. R. Pharr, Clk.
Mins. Ret. says mar. on 12-25-1872 at
Lucy Selina Furnace was signed M. A.
Wilson. Consent of Jordan (his X
mark) Barber has name as Francis Bar-
ber and was dated 12-23-1872. Oath
acknowledgement was given by James
Rogers and James Deed.

12-26-1872   James Freeman, 23, single, "Colored",
23   B: Caroline Co., VA, Lived: Alleg. Co,
              VA, Occup: laborer, s/o: W. and M.
              Freeman (on bk) [Winka and Mincy Free-
              man (on CTOLMR)]; and Kate Wright, 18,
              single, "Colored", Born and Lived: Al-
              leg. Co., VA, dau/o: W. and P. Wright
              (on bk) [Washington and Polly Wright
              (on CTOLMR)]. PL: Alleg. Co., VA.
              Note on CTOLMR: "Bride's father pre-
              sent" (when Lic. gotten). CTOLMR
              signed on 12-25-1872 by Jno. R. Pharr,
              Clk. Mins. Ret. says mar. on 12-26-
              1872 in Alleg. Co. was signed Wm. H.
              Wiley.

12-26-1872   Phil Herbert, 25, single, "Colored",
24   B: Cumberland Co., VA, Lived: Alleg.
              Co., VA, Occup: laborer, s/o: D. and
              E. Herbert (on bk) [Daniel and Eliza
              Herbert (on CTOLMR)]; and Maglin Ed-
              wards, 28, single, "Colored", Born and
              Lived: Alleg. Co., VA, dau/o: Hy and
              M. Edwards (on bk) [Henry and Mary Ed-
              wards (on CTOLMR)]. PL: Alleg. Co.,
              VA. CTOLMR signed on 12-23-1872 by
              Jno. R. Pharr, Clk. Note on CTOLMR:
              "Bride's brother made oath of age."
              [Author's Note: Brother's name was

not mentioned.] Mins. Ret. says mar.
on 12-26-1872 at Henry Edwards res.
was signed John L. Beale.

12-30-1872 Wm. Lee (on bk) [William Lee (on CTOL
25   MR)], 21, single, "Colored", Born and
            Lived: Alleg. Co., VA, Occup: laborer,
            s/o: ___ Rachel Lee (on bk and CTOL
            MR); and Dicie Scott, 19, single, B:
            Louisa Co., VA, "Colored", Lived: Al-
            leg. Co., VA, dau/o: N. and M. Scott
            (on bk) [Nicholas and Marinda Scott
            (on CTOLMR)]. PL: Alleg. Co., VA,
            "Covington." CTOLMR signed on 12-28-
            1872 by Jno. R. Pharr, Clk. Mins.
            Ret. says mar. on 12-30-1872 in Cov-
            ington in Alleg. Co. was signed Wm. H.
            Wiley.

12-31-1872 Jno. W. Fridley (on bk) [John W. Frid-
26   ley (on CTOLMR)], 22, "White", single,
            Born and Lived: Alleg. Co., VA, Occup:
            farmer, s/o: N. and E. Fridley (on bk)
            [Nelson and Elizabeth Fridley (on
            CTOLMR)]; adn F. V. (? Jcenhower) (on
            bk) [Frances V. (? Janhower) (on CTOL
            MR)], 25, single, "White", B: Bote-
            tourt Co., VA, Lived: Alleg. Co., VA,
            dau/o: G. and J. (? Jcenhower) (on bk)
            [George and Julia (? Janhower) (on
            CTOLMR)]. PL: Alleg. Co., VA. CTOLMR
            signed on 12-28-1872 by Jno. R. Pharr,
            Clk. Mins. Ret. says mar. on 12-31-
            1872 at Wm. Folk's res. on Dunlap
            Creek in Alleg. Co. was signed John B.
            Davis. Age oath given by W. T. Falls.
                          "Dec the 27th 1872
            To the Clerk of Alleghany County
            Pleas isue Lisons to John W. Fridly
            to marry Mis Francis Virginia Jaen-
            hower
                    age twenty-five years
              Francis V. (my X mark) Janhower"

PART (3)
List of Ministers
For Part (1)
1822 - 1855

Best, Hezekiah   p. 6
Bishop, William P.   p. 16
Bland, H. J.   p. 31
Boteler, J. W. (John Wesley)
    [Sweet Springs (VA--now W.VA.) Circuit Rider
    for Meth. E. Church]   p. 33, 34, 35
Carper, Jacob   p. 21
Cochran, Jno. M.   p. 26
Corron, J. T. (?J. P.)
    [Baptist of White Sulphur Springs, VA (now
    W.VA.)]   p. 24, 25, 26, 27, 29, 30, 31
Douss, Jacob   p. 8
Elmore, A. J.   p. 22, 23, 25, 26, 28, 33
Enos, William H.   p. 7, 8
Eskridge, Alfred A.   p. 8, 9
Freeman, Alexander   p. 9
Gilbert, John L.   p. 21, 22, 40
Hank, J.   p. 24
Hogshead, A. S.   p. 29, 30, 31, 32, 35, 37, 38,
    39, 40
Jordan, Zach^h   p. 16
Kelley, J. W. (John W.)
    [Methodist Episcopal Church]   p. 29, 30, 31,
    32, 33, 34,
Kinninson, Davis   p. 8, 40
Knox, Elisha   p. 1, 2, 3, 4, 5
Leffel, Charles B.   p. 8
Meniken, Joseph   p. 10, 11, 12
Morgan, Tillotson A.   p. 23, 24
Murgrave, W. G.   p. 20, 22
Paine, Henry H.   p. 21, 22
Paine, James   p. 10
Pennell, Joseph   p. 1, 2, 3, 4, 5, 6, 7, 8, 9,
    10, 11, 12, 13, 14, 15, 16, 19, 20, 21, 22,
    23, 24
Pharr, D. C. (Dion C.)   p. 16, 17, 18, 19, 25,
    26, 27, 28, 31, 32, 35, 36, 37, 38
Phelps, J. T. (James T.)   p. 24, 25, 26
Reese, Philip B.   p. 20

Remley, James   p. 16
Renick, William H.   p. 20
Richardson, Jno. W. (John W.)   p. 13, 14
Scott, J.   p. 21, 25, 26, 27
Shoaff (Shoff) (Shraff), D.
    [Methodist Episcopal Church]   p. 28, 29
Shumaker, William   p. 6, 7, 8, 9, 13, 14, 20, 21
Smith, Amos   p. 2
Snow, Dexter A.   p. 22
Tackitt, J____ H. [Jgnalius (? Jonatin) H.] p.5
Taylor, William   p. 22
Trout, David   p. 19
Vanlear, John A.   p. 2, 3, 5, 8, 9, 11, 12, 14
Waring, Edward W.   p. 36
Watts, James   p. 4, 5, 8, 9, 11
Wilson, Wm. H.   p. 23
Wood, Davis M.
    [Local Deacon with Lic. to Marry; Of
    "Pleasant Hill" in Botetourt County, VA.;
    Methodist Episcopal Church]   p. 34

Total Number Of Ministers This Part: 45

List of Ministers
For Part (2)
1854 - 1872

Bagby, A.
    [Baptist Church] p. 188
Beale, John L. (John G.) p. 184, 197, 253, 262,
    264, 269, 316, 321, 329, 332
Behrman, A.
    [Methodist Episcopal Church - North] p. 86,
    87, 88, 90, 92, 93
Boon, Aaron (A.)
    [Methodist Church] p. 224, 227, 232, 235,
    256, 271, 278, 286, 287, 293, 317, 318, 319
Boteler, J. Wesley (John Wesley)
    [Sweet Springs (VA--now W.VA.) Circuit Rider
    for Methodist Episcopal Church] p. 42, 56,
    58, 64
Brillhart, Jacob
    [Methodist Episcopal Church - South] p. 68
Brooke, George G. (Geo. G.) (G. G.)
    [Covington, VA -- Methodist Episcopal Church]
    p. 137, 139, 161, 162, 163, 164, 165, 166,
    170, 171, 175, 176
Buhrman, Abraham (A.) p. 47, 59, 66, 71, 77, 80,
    128, 129, 147, 158, 159, 167, 168, (? 274),
    (? 298), (? 306), (? 322)
Buhrman, Alfred (A.) p. 67, 69, 70, 71, 74, 77,
    p. 83, (? 274), (? 298), (? 306), (? 322)
Carpenter, G. W. p. 179
Cornelius, J. W. p. 172
Corron, J. P.
    [White Sulphur Springs, W. VA. -- Baptist
    Church] p. 76
Cronin, C. C.
    [Methodist Episcopal Church] p. 45, 46, 48,
    53, 54, 55, 56, 57, 58, 62, 63, 64, 65, 66
Cutler, L. A.
    [Christian Church] p. 289
Damron (Dameron), C. L. p. 323
Davidson, M. A.
    [P. (? probably Presbyterian)] p. 130
Davis, John B.
    [Potts Creek in Alleghany County, VA. --

      Dunkard (Brethren Church)] p. 146, 148, 152,
156, 157, 158, 159, 160, 169, 171, 172, 173,
174, 175, 177, 182, 186, 187, 189, 191, 192,
196, 203, 204, 207, 212, 213, 215, 216, 217,
218, 220, 222, 223, 226, 228, 229, 230, 233,
238, 239, 242, 243, 247, 248, 252, 257, 259,
261, 263, 266, 268, 269, 270, 276, 285, 300,
309, 312, 314, 315, 316, 317, 327, 330, 332
Dolly, S. B. (Saul B.)
      [Methodist Church] p. 225, 228, 231, 232,
237, 240, 241, 242, 244, 245, 248, 250, 251,
254, 255, 256, 257, 258, 259, 261, 262, 263,
264, 268
Ewan (Evan), J. W. p. 122, 124, 125, 126, 129,
130
Field(s), Staunton
      [Methodist Episcoapl Church -- South] p. 72,
118, 119
Fields, Joseph p. 185
Flaherty, A. Q.
      [Covington, VA -- Methodist Church] p. 176,
182, 188, 197, 201, 206, 207, 208, 210, 211,
212, 221, 234
Gaver, H. A. (Hamilton A.)
      [Methodist Episcopal Church -- North (and
later, South) or B. R.] p. 96, 101, 102, 103,
104, 105, 106, 108, 110, 112, 115, 119, 121
Graham, J. W. F.
      [Methodist Church] p. 178, 183, 193, 195,
199, 200, 201, 202
Goble, Genham p. 132
Hargiss, S. p. 78
Hill, Wm. E. (W. E.)
      [Presbyterian Church] p. 260, 279, 285
Hogshead, A. S.
      [Minister of the Gospel] p. 42, 43, 48, 49,
50, 51, 52, 53, 59, 60, 61
Huff, S. P. (? S. T.)
      [Baptist Church] p. 45, 68, 77
Jameson, E. G. p. 309
Keans, H. R. p. 185
Kennedy, W. p. 141

Smyth, James L.
    [O. M. (? Orthodox Methodist)]   p. 116
Stringer, William R.   p. 80
Tabler, J. T. (John T.)   p. 79
Taylor, Geo. B.   p. 323
Tinsley, J. C. (Joshua C.)
    [Southern Methodist Church]   p. 110, 111,
    112, 113, 114, 116
Wade, T. S.   p. 155
Walsh, D. L.   p. 326
Walsh, D. T. (? D. P.)   p. 329
    [Author's Note: It is possible that both of
    the two previous ministers are the same per-
    son.]
Walters, J. H.
    [Roman Catholic Priest]   p. 45, 85, 91, 94,
    95, 97, 98, 99, 104, 106, 107, 109, 111, 113,
    115, 117, 119, 123, 126, 131, 133, 136, 143,
    144, 154, 194, 205
Walters, J. W. (? J. H.)
    [Roman Catholic Priest]   p. 41
Waters, J. H. [See J. H. Walters]
    [Catholic Church]   p. 72, 75, 76, 80, 98, 99
Waters, J. W.   p. 70
    [Author's Note: It is possible that the four
    previous ministers (Walters, Walters, Waters,
    & Waters) are the same person.]
Weller, A.
    [Covington, VA -- Methodist Church]   p. 275,
    277, 280, 282, 283, 288, 289, 290, 292, 294,
    295, 296, 297, 298, 299, 303, 304, 305, 314,
    316, 317, 324, 325
Wiley, W. H. (Wm. H.)
    [Baptist Church]   p. 293, 295, 296, 297, 300,
    302, 304, 306, 313, 315, 320, 322, 325, 328,
    331, 332
Williams, H. S.
    [Methodist Episcopal Church]   p. 66
Williams, W. K.   p. 194
Wilson, [Rev.] A. (? Wm. A.)   p. 286
Wilson, M. A.   p. 288, 291, 306, 307, 308, 312,
    313, 319, 321, 323, 326, 329, 331

[List of Ministers: Part (2) - (Continued)]

    [Author's Note: The two previous persons
    may be the same person.]
Wood(s), Davis M.
    [Local Deacon with License to Marry; of
    "Pleasant Hill" in Botetourt County, VA --
    Methodist Episcopal Church - South] p. 41,
    47, 81, 143, 205, 219, 236, 251, 302

Total Number Of Ministers This Part: 68

f - father		m - mother
g - guardian		w - witness
c - consenter to marriage		s - step-father
cc - Clerk of Court		d - Deputy Clerk
BK - book,	LT - List	LD - Lic. Date

Name	Date	Page
Acre, Lewis	09-13-1822	1
Alexander, Catharine	11-25-1840	18
Allen, Charles	02-17-1824	2
" , Franklin	12-07-1830	6
Anders, Catharine	08-05-1840	18
" , Elizabeth	04-18-1850	25
" , Jane	09-03-1829	5
" , Moses	01-17-1826	3
" , Ruth	09-07-1849	24
Anderson, Mary E.	12-18-1851	28
Andrews, John A.	10-17-1848	24
Armentrout, Julia A.	10-17-1850	26
Armontrout, Abraham	12-15-1831	8
" , Abraham [f]	12-16-1853	35
" ,Amanda C.	no mar. date	35
(Mandy Catharine)	12-16-1853	35
" , Delila	11-27-1834	12
" , Elizabeth	10-16-1841	19
" , George	01-18-1831	7
" , Jacob	10-24-1822	1
" , Joannah		
(Joanna)	08-08-1850	25
" , John	12-01-1825	3
" , John	10-17-1833	10
" , Jonathan	11-04-1852	30
" , Joseph	12-30-1834	12
" , Joseph [w]	12-16-1853	35
" , Malinda	11-27-1834	12
" , Milton	09-07-1843	20
" , Patsey	01-13-1842	19
" , Sarah	02-14-1839	15
Armstrong, Henry	04-26-1832	9
" , John	12-30-1834	12

Name	Date	Page
Armstrong, Malinda	06-04-1834	13
Aritt, Catharine	10-24-1822	1
" , Elizabeth	03-25-1834	10
" , Elizabeth	08-29-1850	25
" , Elizabeth [m]	08-04-1853	33
" , George [f]	08-04-1853	33
" , Jacob A.		
(Jacob Anderson)	08-04-1853	33
" , John [g]	08-04-1853	33
	05-11-1854	38
" , John S.		
(Arritt, John S.)	10-01-1851	28
" , John S. [w]	08-04-1853	33
" , Michael [w]	08-04-1853	33
	12-16-1853	35
" , Sarah	10-20-1846	23
Arrington, Sarah C.	09-22-1847	23
Arritt, John	01-28-1830	6
" , John S.		
(Aritt, John S.)	10-01-1851	28
" , Mary M. [w]	08-04-1853	33
Ballard, William	03-23-1854	37
Beckner, John A.		
(Becknor, John A.)	10-31-1848	24
Becknor, John A.		
(Beckner, John A.)	10-31-1848	24
Belcher, Jonathan	03-01-1840	16
Bennet, Elizabeth	05-11-1837	15
" , Elizabeth	01-18-1854	36
" , Henry	10-29-1835	13
" , Jane	1831	6
" , John	03-24-1845	21
" , John O.	11-26-1850 LD	26
" , Mary Ann	06-10-1845	21
" , Miriah T.	04-02-1851	27
" , Nancy	11-09-1837	15
" , Sampson	1831	7
" , William	01-15-1834	10
Bennett, John	07-03-1823	2

Name	Date	Page
Bennett, Margaret	10-06-1825	3
Bess, Hamilton	01-28-1823	1
" , Rebecca	08-18-1833	9
Birn, Patrick	10-15-1853	34
Bishop, Abraham	10-12-1828	4
" , Jacob	03-15-1827	4
" , Mary E.		
(Mary C.)	12-04-1851	28
" , Sarah E.	10-31-1848	24
Black, John A.	07-23-1839	17
" , Sarah A.		
(Sarah Ann)	05-05-1853	32
Blair, Martha	04-08-1834	11
" , Nancy	04-12-1827	4
" , Rachael	08-05-1830	8
Blakee, Virginia	12-30-1845	22
Blaker, Lucy	01-27-1853	31
Boley, Cornelia A.	03-20-1851	27
" , Manson L.		
(Manson D.)	05-31-1854	38
" , Rebecca	05-31-1854	38
Booth, William	09-22-1847	23
Boswell, Elizabeth Y.	(?01)-27-1836	13
" , James H.	01-26-1836	13
" , Mary G.	11-30-1842	20
Boteler, Eliza [m]	02-14-1854	36
" , John D. [f]	02-14-1854	36
" , J. W.		
[(Rev.) J. Wesley]		
[(Rev.) John W.]	02-14-1854	36
Bowen, Leah	01-24-1832	9
Bowyer, Elizabeth	01-28-1830	6
" , John	12-18-1839	15
" , Polly	02-05-1834	12
Bowyers, Mary A.	02-15-1853	31
Boyed, Porterfield		
(Boyod, Porterfield)	10-31-1830	6
Boyod, Porterfield		
(Boyed, Porterfield)	10-31-1830	6
Bradford, Synthia A.	01-23-1850	26

Name	Date	Page
Bratten, Jane E.	10-05-1849	24
Bratton, Evaline	10-24-1841	19
Brennemer, Charlott	10-30-1828	4
Bright, Jesse	05-28-1835	13
Bromwell, Jacob L.	10-30-1828	4
Brown, Anderson	07-12-1838	17
" , Frances Ann	11-04-1852	30
" , George [w]	03-21-1854 LD	37
" , Jane	03-16-1836	17
" , John	04-26-1836	17
" , John	11-04-1841	19
" , John	12-27-1832	9
" , Lemuel	10-03-1853 LD	33
" , Matthews D.	10-31-1850	26
" , Samuel	11-04-1852	30
" , Samuel	02-03-1831	8
" , Sophia M.	11-12-1840	18
" , William	12-15-1825	3
Broyhill, Alexander (Rayhill, Alexander)	02-01-1827	3
Brunnemer, Amanga Jane (?Amanda Jane)	03-11-1834	11
" , Catharine	05-04-1826	3
" , Elizabeth	09-09-1830	8
" , Joanna	12-03-1835	17
" , Mary	10-12-1828	4
" , Mary C.	03-28-1822	1
" , William	02-23-1825	2
Bryan, Hugh	09-13-1822	1
Burk, Emely Almira Jane	02-03-1846	22
" , Mary	06-18-1835	13
Bush, Adam	07-16-1840	16
" , Andrew	01-09-1840	15
" , Barbara	10-17-1833	10
" , Charles	10-06-1831	7
" , John A.	04-07-1853	32
" , Malinda	12-02-1835	17
" , Margaret	02-19-1834	12
" , Mary	08-19-1830	6
" , Nimrode	02-13-1830	6

[Name and Date Index: Part (1) - (Continued)]

Name	Date	Page
Bush, Nimrod	09-12-1851	27
" , Samuel	08-24-1830	6
" , Susan	02-09-1837	14
Byer, David	07-04-1844	20
" , George		
(Byers, George)	08-15-1844	20, 21
" , John	06-22-1831	8
" , Mary A. E.	10-21-1847	24
Byrd, Thomas	12-10-1822	1
Caldwell, Mary	11-22-1830	6
Callaghan, Ellen	05-26-1826	3
" , John P.	10-31-1848	24
" , Julia	08-15-1824	2
" , Julia E.	11-26-1850	26
" , Margarett	11-21-1834	11
" , Maria	01-26-1836	13
" , Mary	10-20-1831	7
" , Sarah Jane	10-28-1847	23
Campbell, Rachael	1831	7
Carpenter, Martha	06-02-1825	2
" , Rebecca	07-03-1832	9
" , Sally	02-23-1825	2
Carr, Hannarah	no mar. date	
(Margaret)	03-21-1854 LD	37
" , John [f]	03-21-1854 LD	37
" , Margaret	no mar. date	
(Hannarah)	03-21-1854 LD	37
Carson, James	05-19-1831	8
" , James [f]	09-08-1853	33
" , John	05-07-1834	13
" , Nancy E.	04-21-1853	32
" , Rachel	12-08-1829	5
" , Sarah	10-06-1831	7
" , Sarah G.		
(Sarah Green)	09-08-1853	33
" , William	11-29-1832	9
Carter, Juda B.	11-17-1852	31
Childs, Mary Ann	01-06-1854 BK	
	01-04-1854 LT	35

[Name and Date Index: Part (1) - (Continued)]

Name	Date	Page
Childs, Robert	12-16-1851	28
" , Samuel W.	01-06-1854 BK	
	01-04-1854 LT	35
Clark, Jane K.	04-07-1853	32
" , John		
(Cleak, John)	07-31-1842	20
" , Joseph B.	12-03-?1828	
	?1827	4
" , William	02-16-1829	4
Clarkson, Henry	11-12-1834	13
Clarkston, Mary Ann	01-10-1832	9
" , Nelson	11-03-1832	9
" , William	02-12-1835	12
Claughton, Richard A.	08-25-1825	3
Cleak, John		
(Clark, John)	07-31-1842	20
Cleek, Polly	09-13-1822	1
Clement, Benjamin	06-04-1834	13
Cook, James	08-11-1849	24
Cosby, Martin E.	07-12-1853	32
Cotton, Benjamine	03-03-1831	8
" , Michael G.	12-25-1839	16
" , Sally	02-16-1829	5
Counts, Felander		
(Frelander)	07-23-1840	16
" , Frelander		
(Felander)	07-23-1840	16
Cox, Harriet	10-26-1834	11
", Lucy	09-24-1840	18
", Mary Ann	11-15-1832	9
Craft, John	05-18-1834	10
" , Nancy	12-18-1839	15
" , William	11-18-1852	30
Crawford, Marietta	07-07-1851	27
Crider, Margaret P.	10-10-1822	1
Crow, Joseph	05-10-1822	1
Crowder, James A.	no mar. date	35
	12-16-1853	35
Crowly, John	12-(?)-1854 LD	39
(See Part II)	no mar. date	

- 345 -

Name	Date	Page
Cunningham, William	10-17-1849	24
Damron, Andrew	02-28-1832	8
" , Christopher	07-01-1832	8
" , Elizabeth	08-23-1822	1
" , William	09-23-1841	19
Davidson, Salina	01-29-1852	29
Davies, John B.		
(Davis, Jno. B.)	08-08-1850	25
Davis, Edna J.		
[Edney (?T)]	no mar. date	
[See Part II]	12-(?)-1854 LD	39
Davis, Edney (?T.)		
[Edna J.]	no mar. date	
[See Part II]	12-(?)-1854 LD	39
" , Jno. B.		
(Davies, John B.)	08-08-1850	25
" , Sabina	02-01-1831	6
Deacon, John	02-14-1839	17
Dean, W. H. (Wm. H.)	11-25-1852	31
Deaton, John T.	no mar. date	28
Deeds, Cornelius B.	09-08-1853	33
" , Elizabeth Ann	(?03)-27-1834	10
" , John	01-13-1842	19
" , Joseph	07-28-1836	14
" , Mary Jane	12-21-1853	35
" , Phoebe	09-29-1836	14
" , William	03-25-1834	11
" , Wm. [f]	12-21-1853	35
Dew, Absolem	02-09-1837	14
", Ann	08-15-1844	20, 21
", Betsy	12-27-1832	9
", Betty L.	10-15-1846	23
", Catharine	01-14-1839	15
", Julius	06-16-1831	7
", Lucy	06-14-1838	15
", Malinda	02-17-1842	19
", Parnelia	12-10-1835	14
", Rebecca	03-01-1842	20
", Sarah M.	04-15-1847	40

Name	Date	Page
Dew, Sarah P.	11-17-1841	19
", Savenia	03-10-1836	14
Dickson, John A.	no mar. date	
(See Part II)	07-(?)-1854 LD	39
" , Joseph	08-02-1851 BK	
	08-28-1851 LT	27
" , Robert	10-28-1847	23
" , Samuel	11-21-1834	11
" , William	08-21-1851	27
" , Wm.	02-23-1843	20
Dobey, Elizabeth	1831	7
Dorolly, Thomas	1831	6
Doss, John	04-02-1846	22
Douglas, Benjamin	07-08-1830	5
" , Gilson	11-05-1832	9
" , Narcissa		
(Alias) (See Mary		
Sanders)	06-04-1835	12
Downey, Margaret	02-19-1839	17
Dressler, Barbara	07-12-1838	17
" , Charles H.	10-19-1852	30
" , Christena	12-03-?1828	
	?1827	4
" , George	08-13-1827	4
" , Henry	10-14-1852	30
" , Julia A.	10-09-1832	9
" , Malinda	08-13-1827	4
" , Martha	06-01-1834	11
" , Peter	01-10-1826	2
" , Wm. H.		
(William H.)	05-21-1853	32
Dudly, George F.	10-23-1823	2
Duke, George	03-28-1822	1
" , Hugh	02-05-1829	5
" , John	03-26-1829	5
" , William	03-12-1829	4
Dunsmore, William (Wm.)	10-20-1846	23
Early, Noraden D.	06-04-1835	12
Eddy, George W.	03-08-1853	31

Name	Date	Page
Edgar, Francis	12-13-1822	1
" , Wm.	09-29-1836	14
Ellis, Elizabeth N.	01-06-1854 BK	
	01-04-1854 LT	35
" , Parmelia	03-23-1854	37
" , Richard G.	01-06-1854 BK	
	01-04-1854 LT	35
Evans, William	(?09)-19-1833	10
Ervin, Elisha		
(Erwin, Elisha)	12-02-1835	14
" , Joseph [w]	10-13-1853	34
" , Sarah	02-15-1831	7
Erwin, Elisha		
(Ervin, Elisha)	12-02-1835	14
Farmer, Charles E.	12-04-1851	28
Faudree, W. M.		
(See Faudree,		
William A.)	01-27-1853	31
" , William A.		
(See Faudree, W. M.)	01-27-1853	31
Flarherty, James	12-24-1840	16
Fleet, Agnes	09-01-1832	8
" , Patsy	01-10-1826	2
" , Rebecca	02-12-1840	16
Flint, John C.	07-12-1831	7
Forbass, Quincy		
(See Forbess,		
Quincy)	10-08-1840	18
Forbes, George		
(See Forbess,		
George)	1831	7
Forbess, George		
(See Forges,		
George)	1831	7
" , Quincy		
(See Forbass,		
Quincy)	10-08-1840	18
Foster, Sarah	11-09-1831	40
Frazier, Henry	01-20-1825	2

Name	Date	Page
Freeland, George	no mar. date	29
Fridley, Febe	1831	7
" , Gideon	12-13-1837	15
" , Isacc	09-05-1830	6
" , Lewis	08-15-1839	15
" , Lydia	03-05-1844	20
" , Nelson	10-26-1841	19
" , Polly	10-29-1835	13
" , Polly	12-14-1837	15
" , Richard	01-18-1854	36
" , Thomas	01-24-1839	15
Fridly, Charles	09-02-1841	19
" , Jesse	10-25-1843	20
" , Lydia	11-12-1840	16
Fry, Elizabeth	10-14-1852	30
" , Henry	12-18-1851	28
Fudge, Andrew [cc]		22, 25, 27
		33, 36, 37
		38, 40
" , Catherine	08-01-1833	10
" , Maria Louisa	12-18-1834	11
" , Mary Ann	12-24-1840	18
" , Nancy	06-17-1830	5
Fuory, Elizabeth	09-11-1851	28
Gardner, Francis	01-29-1835	12
Gilbert, Austin	03-26-1840	17
" , Eliza Ann d.	12-24-1840	16
" , Thomas	11-10-1853	34
Gillaspie, Alexander	12-22-1825	3
" , Elizabeth A.	09-18-1850	25
" , Margaret C.	08-24-1852	30
" , Maria S.		
(See Gilliland,		
Maria S.)	07-02-1850	25
" , Samuel	04-16-1835	12
" , William	08-30-1822	1
" , William		
(William W.)	11-19-1850	26
" , William H.	09-18-1850	25

Name	Date	Page
Gillaspy, Henry	12-01-1829	5
Gilliland, H. D. [w]	09-08-1853	33
" , Henry	04-24-1851	27
" , Julia G.	02-14-1850	25
" , Maria S. (See Gillaspie, Maria S.)	07-02-1850	25
" , William H. [w]	no mar. date	37
" , Wm. S. (William S.)	12-21-1853	35
Givens, William J.	11-08-1849	24
Glasburn, Nancy	03-12-1829	4
Goheen, Wm.	05-19-1831	8
Goode, Francis	12-02-1835	17
Goodwin, George W.	08-13-1840	18
" , Robert	1831	7
Gordan, Samuel (See Gordon, Samuel)	11-22-1830	6
Gordon, Samuel (See Gordan, Samuel)	11-22-1830	6
Grady, Hamilton C.	06-17-1830	5
Gray, John (See Gross, John)	03-12-1827	4
" , Oliver P.	08-07-1850	25
Griffey, Jefferson	02-19-1834	12
Griffith, Aurena (Arveney)	10-15-1853	34
" , Benjamin [w]	11-10-1853	34
" , Caleb	07-25-1839	16
" , Elizabeth	12-02-1835	14
" , Hannah	10-31-1833	11
" , Harriet	no mar. date	29
" , Joshua [w]	no mar. date	37
" , Louisa	12-28-1853	35
" , Nancy	no mar. date	36
" , Orlando [f]	no mar. date	37
" , Sarah	11-10-1853	34

Name	Date	Page
Griffith, Wesley [f]	10-15-1853	34
[f]	11-09-1853	34
Gross, John		
(See, Gray,		
John)	03-12-1827	4
" , Samuel	(?01)-28-1836	13
Guy, Elizabeth	02-17-1853	31
Hall, Joseph	11-17-1841	19
Hammer, Mary Ann	02-14-1839	17
Hammond, George W.		
[(Dr.) George W.]	04-12-1853	32
Hamner, ____hn E.		
(?John E.)	05-20-1839	17
Hancock, Malcijah	01-23-1850	26
Hann, Michael	06-26-1845	22
Hansbarger, Caroline	03-18-1830	5
" , Nancy	02-21-1823	2
" , Rachael	07-23-1839	17
Hardy, Elizabeth	12-25-1839	16
" , Mary Ann	02-15-1845 BK	
	01-15-1846 LT	21
" , Thomas	11-12-1840	18
Harmon, Anthony [w]	12-21-1853	35
" , Barbara	09-02-1841	19
" , George	12-10-1835	14
" , Henry B.	12-24-1840	18
" , Kisiah	(?09)-19-1833	10
" , Louisa	02-13-1846	22
" , Nancy	06-04-1835	13
" , Sarah E.	12-16-1851	28
" , Shelton R.	09-11-1851	28
" , Thomas	02-05-1834	12
(?Harras), Geo. F.	no mar. date	29
Hart, Mary A. K.		
(Mary E. K.)	05-21-1853 BK	
	05-24-1853 LT	32
" , Moses	12-22-1825	3
Haynes, C. L. [w]	12-21-1853	35
" , Grandvill D.	no mar. date	28

Name	Date	Page
Haynes, John N.	04-05-1853	32
" , Mary Jane	04-28-1841	21, 22
" , Rachael	03-25-1834	11
" , William, Jr.	04-26-1834	11
" , Wm. H., Jr.[w]	12-21-1853	35
Hayse, Ann Eliza	11-24-1844	20
" , Elizabeth J.	08-21-1851	27
Heivley, Mildred		
(See Hevrley,		
Mildred)	12-01-1829	5
Hellmantoller, Jordan		
(See Helmantoller,		
Jordan)	12-04-1851	28
Helmantoller, Jordan		
(See Hellmantoller,		
Jordan)	12-04-1851	28
" , Wm.	10-16-1850	26
Helmintoller, Peter		
(See Holmintoller,		
Peter)	06-23-1825	3
Helms, Eliza		
(See Holms, Eliza)	06-25-1835	12
Henderson, William		
(See Henduson,		
William)	09-05-1839	16
Henduson, William		
(See Henderson,		
William)	09-05-1839	16
Hepler, Elizabeth	02-03(13)-1845	21
" , Harriet P.	08-15-1839	15
" , John	07-17-1834	11
" , John		
(John, Jr.)	05-04-1854	38
" , Sally	11-29-1832	9
Hevrley, Mildred		
(See Heivley,		
Mildred)	12-01-1829	5
Hickman, Andrew	11-27-1834	12
Hines, G. W. [w]	04-12-1853	32
Hinton, Julia	04-26-1832	9

Name	Date	Page
Hinton, Peter	07-07-1851	27
" , Sarah	07-31-1842	20
Hobbs, James O.	(?01)-27-1836	13
Hoileman, Rebecca	01-21-1836	14
Hoilman, Addison	11-27-1834	12
" , Henry	01-29-1852	29
Holley, Wm.	02-17-1842	19
Holloway, Mary I.	06-18-1832	9
Holmintoller, Peter		
(See Helmintoller,		
Peter)	06-23-1825	3
Holms, Eliza		
(See Helms, Eliza)	06-25-1835	12
Hook, Eli	11-15-1832	9
" , Elias	02-21-1823	2
" , Elizabeth Mary	07-28-1836	14
" , John	06-25-1835	12
" , Kisiah	(?02)-24-1831	7
" , Madison	09-01-1833	10
" , Mary J.	04-24-1851	27
" , Rebecca		
(Rebecca L.)	12-04-1851	28
Hoover, Harry	10-01-1840	18
" , Mary	(?01)-28-1836	13
" , Phobe (Phebe)	09-04-1851	27
Hoy, Charles F.	no mar. date	
(See Part II)	05-29-1854 LD	38
Hoylman, Simon	03-17-1853	31
Huddleston, Abrahrum		
J.	01-24-1832	9
Huet, Elizabeth		
(See Hurt,		
Elizabeth)	1831	6
Hughes, J. F. [w/c]	12-19-1849	
	?1847	40
" , Jane M.		
(Jane R.)	05-23-1854	38
Humphries, Anderson	06-10-1845	21
" , Caroline	03-09-1854	37
" , Charles L.	07-27-1852	29

Name	Date	Page
Humphries, Harvey	10-13-1853	34
" , Hugh	10-20-1834	13
" , John [w]	10-13-1853	34
[w]	05-11-1854	38
" , Judith	03-26-1829	5
" , Matilda	10-17-1822	1
Hurt, Elizabeth		
(See Huet,		
Elizabeth)	1831	6
Jackson, Alice H.		
(Allice H.)	07-12-1853	32
" , Jesse J.	02-02-1851	26
James, Israel	10-20-1831	7
" , Virginia M.		
(See Jones,		
Virginia M.)	12-22-1847	23
Jameson. Geprge		
(See Jamison,		
George	05-11-1854	38
Jamison, Benjamin P.	02-12-1833	8
" , George		
(See Jameson,		
George)	05-11-1854	38
" , Margaret L.	08-11-1841	19
Jarvis, Fielding	02-15-1831	7
Johnson, Allen	10-17-1850	26
" , Elizabeth	02-01-1827	3
" , Jabez	05-18-1837	15
" , Margaret J. B.		
(Margaret J. P.)	11-10-1852	30
" , Philip	no mar. date	
(See Part II)	10-(?)-1854 LD	39
" , Polly	06-23-1825	3
Johnston, Sarah	07-17-1834	11
Jones, Eliza C.		
(Elisa C.)	03-08-1853	31
" , Francis M.	10-24-1841	19
" , Henry	05-12-1852	29
" , John A.	11-17-1852	31

Name	Date	Page
Jones, Jonathan	04-18-1850	25
" , Leah C.	01-16-1851	26
" , Oliver	07-04-1836	14
" , Virginia M.		
(See James,		
Virginia M.)	12-22-1847	23
Jordan, Ira F.	05-05-1840	18
Karnes, Campbell	04-08-1834	11
" , Harriet	02-12-1835	12
" , Harry	02-12-1840	16
" , James	11-24-1844	20
" , Manda Jane		
(Amanda J.)	01-09-1854 BK	
	01-03-1854 LT	35
" , Maria	08-13-1840	18
" , Mary Ann	09-02-1841	19
Kayser, Margaret E.		
(See Keyser,		
Margaret)	05-17-1842	21, 22
Kean, Catharine	no mar. date	
(See Part II)	07-17-1854 LD	39
Keeble, James		
(See Ruble, James)	11-27-1827	4
" , Rachel	06-11-1833	10
Keefe, Richard		
(See Kiefe, Richard)		
(See Reefe, Richard)	no mar. date	37
(See Ruffe, Richard)		
Kieme, William P.		
(See Kierne, William		
P.)	06-18-1835	13
Kierne, William P.		
(See Kieme, William		
P.)	06-18-1835	13
Kilingsworth, Malinda	11-25-1852	31
Kimberlin, Diannah	12-10-1822	1
" , Eliza A.	01-14-1834	11
" , Henry	06-09-1836	14
" , Jacob	04-12-1827	4

Name	Date	Page
Kimberlin, Joseph	10-31-1833	11
" , Mary	09-01-1833	10
" , Nancy	12-29-1840	18
Kincaid, Archibald M.	08-01-1833	10
" , Liza	01-29-1835	12
" , Sarah	03-13-1823	2
Kindell, Frances (See Kendell, Frances)	03-17-1853	31
" , Mary A. (See Kendell, Mary A.)	09-01-1852	30
Kindle, Catharine	10-04-1845	22
" , Lucinda	10-17-1849	24
" , Sarah J.	11-08-1849	24
Kiney, William H.	09-27-1849	24
King, Charles	1831	6
" , George P.	11-09-1837	15
" , Hanna	11-05-1833	10
" , Rebecca	01-18-1823	1
" , Rebecca A.	04-10-1851	27
" , Ruth R.	12-13-1837	15
Kittinger, Samuel	06-26-1844	21
Knox, Charlotte	03-03-1831	8
" , Isaac	05-04-1826	3
" , John	09-24-1829	5
Kyle, Edwin	11-30-1852	31
" , Galbraith	06-15-1837	17
" , William	10-10-1826	3
Landers, Elizabeth	03-05-1846	22
" , John	12-04-1834	12
" , Peter	12-08-1829	5
Lange, David	04-17-1827	4
Lantz, Ellen (See Lantz, Ellonor H.)	09-05-1850	25
" , Ellonor H. (See Lantz, Ellen)	09-05-1850	25
" , Joseph H.	08-05-1840	18
" , Martha J.	10-31-1848	24

Name	Date	Page
Lark, Susannah	04-12-1832	9
Layne, Eliza J.	06-22-1852	29
Leighton, Daniel	03-07-1839	17
" , Malinda N.		
(Malinda T.)	04-05-1853	32
" , Margaret	06-29-1854	39
" , William	06-02-1841	19
Lemmon, Caroline	06-22-1831	8
" , Elizabeth	12-15-1825	3
Lemon, George W.	07-08-1841	19
" , James	01-21-1841	18
" , James Y.	12-30-1847	24
" , Martin		
(See Lemon, Morton)	11-17-1851	28
" , Morton		
(See Lemon, Martin)	11-17-1851	28
" , William	12-01-1825	3
Lewis, William J.	04-21-1853	32
Linton, Eujama N.	05-07-1834	13
" , Wm.	03-01-1842	20
Littlepage, Patsey E.	04-26-1836	17
Lockhart, Sarah	12-13-1822	1
Lockheart, David B.	12-29-1840	18
Low, James	05-05-1853	32
Lynxwiler, Elizabeth	10-08-1840	18
McCallister, Barbara	10-01-1840	18
" , Julia	07-20-1827	4
" , Synthia	09-24-1829	5
" , William	08-27-1845 BK	
	08-27-1846 LT	21
McDaniel, Frances J.A.	04-25-1852	29
" , Nancy	12-30-1834	12
McKenney, John G.	06-14-1838	15
" , Nathaniel	11-24-1836	14
McNabb, George	08-24-1852	30
McReynolds, Augustus		
(See McRinolds,		
Augustus)	09-07-1849	24
McRinolds, Augustus	09-07-1849	
(See McReynolds, Augustus)		24

Name	Date	Page
Neel, Elizabeth B.	07-04-1844	20
Nida, Chapman J.	10-11-1853	33
" , David J. [w]	10-11-1853	34
Nicely, Anna	07-18-1833	9
" , Circle	11-30-1843	21, 22
" , Frances	05-19-1831	8
" , Jacob	02-19-1839	17
" , Jacob M.	06-29-1854	39
" , Lewis	07-18-1833	9
" , Magdaline	06-26-1845	22
" , Margaret	12-22-1825	3
" , Mary M.	11-19-1850	26
" , Samuel	10-07-1834	12
" , Sarah A.	no mar. date	37
Nichol, Rachel		
(See Nickol,		
Rachel)	10-31-1830	6
Nickol, Rachel		
(See Nichol,		
Rachel)	10-31-1830	6
Oiler, Delila	no mar. date	29
" , John	08-18-1833	9
" , Mary A.	no mar. date	
(See Part II)	01-09-1855 LD	40
" , Nancy	04-26-1854	37
" , Sarah	no mar. date	29
" , Susan	03-26-1840	17
Oliver, Agness	11-27-1827	4
Ownsby, Joby	04-16-1835	12
Paris, Avelinah	05-20-1839	17
Paul, Ferdinand H.	05-23-1854	38
Paxton, James	04-26-1854	37
" , John J.	06-22-1852	29
" , Nancy	04-02-1846	22
" , Sarah	11-20-1827	4
Payne, Charles C.	02-15-1838	19
" , Robert	08-19-1830	8

Name	Date	Page
Pitzer, Frances	02-15-1838	19
" , Harriet	12-01-1825	3
" , Racheal	12-01-1825	3
" , Sarah	11-24-1836	14
Pleasants, John H.	12-15-1829	5
" , Thomas W.	05-19-1842	20
Plymale, James G.	07-28-1847	23
" , Rebecca B.	10-16-1850	26
" , Sarah Ann	11-18-1852	30
Prinz, Martha		
(See Printz, Martha)	09-08-1847	23
Printz, Cornelius [f]	02-14-1854	36
" , Heaster A. [m]	02-14-1854	36
" , Martha		
(See Prinz,		
Martha)	09-08-1847	23
" , Susan	08-25-1825	3
" , Susan H.	02-14-1854	36
Pullium, Sophina H.	11-11-1841	16
Putnam, Eli	no mar. date	36
Quickel, Henry	04-08-1834	10
" , J. Peggy [m]	10-13-1853	34
" , Mandy C. [w]	10-13-1853	34
" , Mary	02-17-1839	15
" , Mary J.	10-13-1853	34
" , William H.	11-09-1837	15
" , William H.[c]	05-11-1854	38
" , Wm. H.	08-11-1841	19
Quickle, Catharine	07-03-1823	2
" , Elizabeth	02-14-1826	3
Rader, Daniel		
(Danl. K.)	11-04-1852	30
Ragland, Martha Jane	11-19-1840	16
Rayhill, Alexander		
(See Broyhill,		
Alexander)	02-01-1827	3
" , Catharine E.	no mar. date	
(See Part II)	10-(?)_1854 LD	39

- 362 -

Name	Date	Page
Rayhill, Jacob	04-10-1851	27
" , Susan E.	11-04-1852	30
Reefe, Richard		
(See Keefe, Richard)		
(See Kiefe, Richard)		
(See Ruffe, Richard)	no mar. date	
	03-21-1854 LD	37
Reynolds, Frances		
(? Francis)	11-17-1851	28
" , Judith	05-30-1841	19
" , Lililian	1831	7
" , Louisa	03-07-1839	17
" , Nancy W.	no mar. date	
(See Part II)	05-29-1854 LD	38
" , Thomas	07-07-1833	10
Richardson, John F.	11-10-1852	30
Rigney, Louisa	11-04-1841	19
Roadcap, Christian	no mar. date	
(See Part II)	08-08-1855 LD	39
Roberts, Purthina	11-17-1846	22, 23
Robinson, Elizabeth	10-07-1834	12
" , Eliza H.	10-19-1852	30
" , Samuel		
(See Robison,		
Samuel)	1831	7
Robison, Samuel		
(See Robinson,		
Samuel)	1831	7
Rodgers, James	06-04-1835	13
Root, Mary Jane	05-12-1852	29
Rose, Dennison	01-14-1834	11
" , Jackson	02-09-1837	14
" , William W.	06-04-1846	22
Rosendale, Lambert	03-13-1823	2
Ross, Ankey	11-05-1832	9
" , Griffith		
(Griffeth)	10-26-1834	11
" , Harriet	11-30-1843	21, 22
" , Kesiah	04-22-1825	2
" , William	09-24-1840	18

[Name and Date Index: Part (1) - (Continued)]

Name	Date	Page
Shields, Margaret	07-12-1831	7
Shirkey, George		
(See Shirky,		
George)	05-26-1826	3
Shirky, George		
(See Shirkey,		
George)	05-26-1826	3
Short, William	04-16-1840	16
Shumaker, Charles P.	09-05-1850	25
" , John K. E.	01-23-1834	11
" , Nicholas	09-04-1851	27
" , Thomas		
(Thomas T.)	03-04-1852	29
Silvers, Margaret	12-19-1839	16
Simmon, Maria		
(See Semmon, Maria)	02-15-1834	11
Simmons, Ephraim	05-30-1841	19
" , Ephraine, Jr.	02-09-1837	14
" , Harriet	12-08-1836	14
" , James A.		
(See Simmons,		
Jarvis A.)	02-15-1853	31
" , Jarvis A.		
(See Simmons,		
James A.)	02-15-1853	31
" , Peggy	04-08-1834	10
" , Roling	08-19-1830	6
" , Ruthy	06-26-1844	21
Simpson, Alexander	11-09-1831	40
" , Preston	06-11-1833	10
Sites, Caleb	10-04-1845	22
Siveley, Margaret		
(See Sively,		
Margaret)	02-12-1833	8
Sively (Sivey),		
Abigale	03-23-1826	2
Sively, George		
(George L.)	09-30-1854	40
" , Joseph		
(See Joseph Sevely)	09-09-1830	8

[Name and Date Index: Part (1) - (Continued)]

Name	Date	Page
Sively, Louisa	02-18-1834	11
" , Margaret (See Siveley, Margaret)	02-12-1833	8
" , Mary	04-16-1835	12
" , Mary C.	09-30-1854	40
" , Sarah A.	11-29-1849	25
Sivey (Sively), Abigale	03-23-1826	2
Sizer, Diannah J. (Diannah Jane)	08-04-1853	33
" , Fielding P.	10-12-1848	24
" , Fielding P. [f]	08-04-1853	33
" , Martha A.	09-25-1851	28
Skeen, Polly	05-05-1840	18
" , Joseph	02-01-1831	6
Smith, Andrew J.	12-22-1847	23
" , John H.	02-13-1846	22
" , Mary	10-31-1850	26
" , Moses	09-01-1832	8
" , Moses	04-15-1847	40
" , Sarah	12-27-1849	25
" , Thomas	08-23-1822	1
" , William	03-20-1851	27
" , William W.	02-15-1845 BK 01-15-1846 LT	21
Snead, Amanda (Amanda M.)	08-27-1845 BK 08-27-1846 LT	21
" , Ann J.	no mar. date 02-03-1852 LD	29
" , Austin	10-05-1849	24
Sorrel, Frances Ann (See Part II)	no mar. date 05-29-1854 LD	38
" , William (See Part II)	no mar. date 05-29-1854	38
Spencer, Sarah	02-13-1830	6
Standly, Francis	10-18-1827	4
Steele, Isaac	08-15-1824	2
Stinesheet, Rachel (See Stonestreet, Rachel)	02-02-1851	26

Name	Date	Page
Stone, John	03-05-1846	22
" , Sarah	06-19-1828	5
" , William	03-16-1836	17
Stonestreet, Rachel (See Stinesheet, Rachel)	02-02-1851	26
Stull, Catharine	01-15-1834	10
" , Charlotte	06-09-1836	14
" , Elizabeth	09-05-1830	6
" , Elizabeth	01-09-1840	15
" , George	07-04-1844	20, 21
" , Jacob	10-06-1825	3
" , James	11-05-1833	10
" , Jane	06-16-1831	7
" , Maria Elvira E. [Maria (?Elvina) E.]	03-01-1842	20
" , Rebecca	03-25-1824	2
" , Rebecca	09-07-1843	20
" , Rebecca B.	07-27-1852	29, 30
" , Samuel	(?03)-27-1834	10
" , Sarah	02-09-1837	14
Sullivan, John [w]	10-15-1853	34
(?Sumpter, Janice) (See Semter, Sanis)	07-04-1836	14
Sumpter, Sarah	12-04-1834	12
Surber, Andrew	03-18-1830	5
" , Levi [f]	05-23-1854	38
" , Martha M.	05-23-1854	38
Tackitt, Isaac W.	03-11-1834	11
Tate, James	06-01-1834	11
" , Thos.	08-05-1830	8
" , William P. (Wm.) (William)	05-17-1852	21, 22
Taylor, Frederick A.	02-17-1853	31
" , John C.	11-13-1840	18
" , Julia Ann	03-12-1827	4
" , Margaret	07-07-1833	10
" , William W.	11-30-1842	20
Terry, Hetty	02-17-1848	24

Name	Date	Page
Terry, James	05-20-1830	6
" , John W.	12-28-1853	35
" , Joseph	1831	7
" , Joseph	08-29-1850	25
" , Mary	03-22-1847	23
" , Phobe (?Phebe)	10-01-1851	28
Thacker, Mary C.	08-11-1849	24
Thomas, Sarah Ann	07-23-1840	16
" , William	12-27-1832	9
Thompson, Frances	05-28-1835	13
Tingler, Michael	12-14-1837	15
" , George W. [w]	10-11-1853	34
" , George W.	03-09-1854	37
" , Mary J.	03-06-1851	27
Tinsley, Roderick M.	09-02-1841	19
Trussler, George W.	03-10-1836	14
Tyree, Cornelius	11-11-1841	16
" , Francis	05-23-1854	38
Vaughan, Sarah J.	09-27-1849	27
Walker, Alfred	10-15-1846	23
Walton, Ganthe Ann		
(?Garethe Ann)	04-17-1827	4
" , Moses	12-27-1849	25
Watson, Bob [c]	12-19-1849	
	(?1847)	40
Watts, Mary	02-28-1832	8
Weekline, William (Wm.)	12-30-1845	22
Welcher, Alexander	no mar. date	
	03-03-1852 LD	29
White, Daniel G.	06-18-1832	9
" , Paulina L.	02-05-1829	5
Whiten, Joseph C.	09-25-1851	28
Whiteside, Hays F.	11-19-1840	16
Wiford, Elizabeth	08-13-1835	13
Wilcher, Margaret J.	no mar. date	
	10-03-1853 LD	33
" , Richard H.	no mar. date	
(See Part II)	01-09-1855 LD	40

Name	Date	Page
Wiley, Robert M.	09-09-1845 BK	
	09-09-1846 LT	21
" , Robert M. [w]	04-12-1853	32
Williams, Erasmus T.		
(Eruzmus T.)	01-16-1851	26
" , John	03-23-1826	3
Williamson, Elizabeth	no mar. date	
(See Part II)	08-08-1855 LD	39
Wills, Fielding	10-10-1822	1
Wilson, Andrew	06-09-1834	13
" , James	02-03(13)-1845	21
" , Samuel	09-22-1847	23
Wise, David J.	11-26-1850	26
Withey, Polly		
(See Withors, Polly)	02-17-1824	2
Withors, Polly		
(See Withey, Polly)	02-17-1824	2
Wolf, Abraham	02-17-1848	24
" , Bethsaida	12-15-1831	8
" , Caroline	05-19-1831	8
" , Catharine	01-17-1826	3
" , Delila	01-24-1839	15
" , Eliza N.	10-17-1848	24
" , George	11-20-1827	4
" , George W.	02-19-1851	26
" , Gilla	08-04-1846	23
" , Hugh	03-05-1844	20
" , Jacob	02-14-1839	15
" , Jacob	03-01-1842	20
" , Jacob	08-04-1846	23
" , Jacob	12-05-1850	26
" , Mahala	1831	7
" , Margaret	07-16-1840	16
" , Margaret	05-04-1854	38
" , Mary	04-30-1834	13
" , Mary (Mary E.)	12-05-1850	26
" , Mary E.	no mar. date	
	08-16-1852 LD	30
" , Mary E.	05-11-1854	38
" , Mary Magdaline	08-15-1833	10

Name	Date	Page
Wolf, Mary P.	10-12-1848	24
" , Palina (Polina)	02-19-1851	26
" , Ruth	02-09-1837	14
" , Sampson	02-14-1826	3
Wood, John C.	07-02-1850	25
Woody, Richard	04-25-1852	29
Wright, Elizabeth	01-20-1825	2
" , George	05-11-1837	15
" , Jane	03-01-1840	16
" , John	09-03-1829	5
" , John [f]	12-19-1849	
	?1847	40
" , Mariah	12-27-1832	9
" , Moses G. [s]	08-04-1853	33
" , Patsy (Polly)	12-22-1825	3
" , Sophia [c]	12-19-1849	
	?1847	40
" , Stephen	11-25-1840	18
" , Vincent	10-17-1822	1
Wyat, John W.		
(See Wyatt, John W.)	09-01-1852	30
Wyatt, John W.		
(See Wyat, John W.)	09-01-1852	30

Total Number of Names This Part: 941

b - brother   h - husband
bil - brother-in-law   jp - Justice of Peace
BK - book   m - mother
c - consenter to marriage   mes - messenger
cc - Clerk of Court   MR - Minister's Return
CL - CTOL   p - printer
CLM - CTOLMR   pet - petitioner
cpt - Clerk Pro Tem   PL - place
csin - cousin   s - son
dc - Deputy Clerk   sf - step-father
f - father   sis - sister
fd - deceased father   u - uncle
g - guardian   w - witness
gf - grandfather

Name	Date	Page
Ailstock, R. R.		
(Robert R.)	09-19-1867	214
Aldress, M. (Martha)		
[m]	06-27-1872	317
" (Brooks), Martha	06-27-1872	317
" , Sam'l.		
(Samuel) [f]	06-27-1872	317
Allen, Arch	09-05-1872	320
" , Archey [f]	09-12-1867	198
" , Archibald [f]	09-30-1866	188
" , Frances	09-30-1866	188
" , Henry	09-12-1867	198
" , Jane [m]	01-05-1858	92
" , John [f]	01-05-1858	92
" , Martha [m]	09-12-1867	198
" , Martha [m]	09-30-1866	188
" , Rebeca J.	01-05-1868	92
Allen's (Allan's),		
John [PL]	01-16-1867	196
Amick, Jacob	09-12-1856	57
" , Jacob [f]	09-12-1856	57
" , Rachael [m]	09-12-1856	57
Anders, Elizabeth [m]	11-26-1868	240
" , William [f]	11-26-1868	240
" , William Oliver	11-26-1868	240
" , Wm. [w]	02-25-1858	80
Anderson, Ann E.	07-05-1857	68
" , Arabella [m]	02-08-1855	45
" (Kitinger),		
Arabella (Lizzie)	03-03(04)-1869	245
[m]	02-15(18)-1869	246
Anderson, C. S.		
(Charles Snyder)	05-30-1865	163, 164
" (Conoway) (Conaway),	05-23(24)-1866	
Eliz. A. (Elizabeth	[BK] [CLM]	
Arabella)	03-24-1866 [MR]	184
" (Tyree), Esabel		
(Isabella) [m]	07-05-1857	68
" , H. (Harry)[f]	05-30-1865	164
" (Tyree), Hy (Henry)		
[f]	07-05-1857	68, 69

Name	Date	Page
Arington's, Andrew J.		
[PL]	03-28-1872	314
Aritt, Eliz.		
(Elizabeth) [m]	07-12-1855	51
[m]	12-20-1855	52
" , Geo. (George)[f]	12-19-1872	330
" , Grandville E.		
(Granville E.)	07-12-1855	51
" , Jno. (John) [f]	07-12-1855	51
[f]	12-20-1855	52
" , Mary [m]	12-19-1872	330
" , Mary M.	12-20-1855	52
" , Michael (M.)	12-19-1872	330
[w]	04-19-1855	46
[w]	07-02-1856	55
[w]	11-07-1872	327
" (Terry), Phoebe	12-10(12)-1866	191
Armentrout, Catharine		
[m]	01-17-1872	308
" , Catharine E.		
(Catharine Elizabeth)	01-18-1872	309
" , [Mr.] Elvira		
E. [w]	09-12-1861	131
" , Geo. (George)		
[f]	01-18-1872	309
" (Armontrout),		
Jacob [f]	01-17-1872	308
" (Armontrout), Mary		
A. (Mary Ann) [m]	01-18-1872	309
" , Michael	07-02-1856	55
	01-17-1872	308
Armentrout's, John [PL]	11-21(29)-1865	168
Armintrout (Armontrout)		
(Wolf), E. (Elizabeth)		
(Elizabeth An)	10-20-1869	259
" , J. (Jos.)[f]	10-14-1869	256
" , J. E.		
(Joanah E.)	10-14-1869	256
" (Armontrout),		
Jacob [f]	08-16-1860	117

Name	Date	Page
Armintrout (Armontrout),		
M.E. (Mary E.) [m]	10-14-1869	256
" (Armantrout)		
(Nicely), M. J.		
(Mary Jane)	09-03(04)-1866	188
" (Armontrout),		
Nancy [m]	08-16-1860	117
Armontrout, Cath.		
(Catharane) [m]	11-15-1855	51, 52
" , Cath.		
(Catharine) [m]	07-02-1856	55
" (Fridley), Delila		
[m]	06-08-1858	82
" , Geo. [f]	11-15-1855	51, 52
" , Jacob [f]	07-02-1856	55
" , James [f]	06-08-1858	82
" , John W.	08-16-1860	117
" , Martha J.	11-15-1855	51
Armontrout's, Smith [PL]	11-15-1855	52
Armstrong, Elizabeth		
(Elisabeth) [m]	09(08)-28-1857	69
" , I. (Israel) [f]	09(08)-18-1857	69
" , Jno. (John) [f]	05-02-1871	293
" (Bennett), M. A.		
(Mary Ann)	04-07-1867	204
" , Mary E.		
(Mary Elizabeth)	05-02-1871	293, 294
" , Wm. R.		
(William R.)	09(08)-18-1857	69
Arrington, J. (James)[f]	04-09-1867	203
" (Arington), Jas.		
(James) [f]	06-09(14)-1866	186
[f]	10-06-1869 [BK]	
	11-09-1869 [MR]	256
(Listed [f]	03-02-1871	293
Twice) [f]	03-11(02)-1871	317
Arrington, James	03-02-1871	293
(Listed Twice)	03-11(02)-1871	317
" (Arington), J.		
(Jane) [m]	04-09-1867	203

Name	Date	Page
Arrington (Arington),		
J. (Jane) [m]	10-06-1869 [BK]	
	11-09-1869 [MR]	256
[m]	06-09(14)-1866	186
[m]	03-02-1871	293
(Listed Twice) [m]	03-11(02)-1872	317
" (Arington), J.	10-06-1869 [BK]	
(Janetta)	11-09-1869 [MR]	256
" , M. A. (Mary Ann)	04-09-1867	203
" , Thomas M. [w]	12-31-1855	59
" (Arington), William		
A. (William Alexander)	06-09(14)-1866	186
Arritt (Aritt), E.		
(Elizabeth) [m]	08-29(31)-1865	157
[m]	02-13(15)-1866	175
	10-21-1867 [BK]	
[m]	11-05-1867 [MR]	216
" (Aritt), Ellen [m]	01-18-1872	309
" , E. B. (Ellen B.)	10-21-1867 [BK]	
[m]	11-05-1867 [MR]	216
" (Aritt), Geo. A.		
(George Alexander)	01-18-1872	309
" , Hary H. [w]	07-12-1855	51
" , Jacob [w]	05-04(07)-1868	223
" , J. A. (Jacob A.)		
[w/PL]	03-15-1872	312
" (Aritt), J. (John)		
[f]	08-29(31)-1865	157
	10-21-1867 [BK]	
[f]	11-05-1867 [MR]	216
" , J. H. (John		
Marion)	08-29(31)-1865	156, 157
" , John [f]	02-13(15)-1866	175
" (Blaker), L. C.		
(Louisa C.)	02-13(15)-1866	175
" (Aritt), M.	10-21-1867 [BK]	
(Michael) [f]	11-05-1867 [MR]	216
[f]	01-18-1872	309
Arritt, M. E. (Mary E.)	10-21-1867 [BK]	
	11-05-1867 [MR]	216

Name	Date	Page
Arritt (Aritt), M. J.	10-21-1867 [BK]	
(Michael J.)	11-05-1867 [MR]	216
Arritt's, John M. [PL]	02-13(15)-1866	175
Arthur, Jno. [f]	01-19-1871	288
" , S. E.		
(Sarah E.) [m]	01-19-1871	288
" , Wm. H.		
(Wm. Henry)	01-19-1871	288
Atkinson, A. (Anderson)		
[f]	10-14-1869	257, 258
" , A. (Ann) [m]	10-14-1869	257
" , E. B.		
(Evaline B.)	10-14-1869	257
Ayers (Ayres), H. H. C.	10-17-1872	324
" (Ayres), H.		
(Henrietta) [m]	05-10-1870	276
" (Ayres), Jno. W.		
(John W.) [f]	05-10-1870	276
" (Ayres), Jos. T.		
(Joseph T.)(Joseph)	05-10-1870	276, 277
Ayres (Ayers), H.		
(Henrietta) [m]	10-17-1872	324
" (Ayers), Jno. T.		
(John T.) [f]	10-17-1872	324
Bachlet (Bachtel),		
(Lenford)(Linford)	11-15-1855	51
Bachtel, Eliz. [m]	11-15-1855	51
" , Sam'l. [f]	11-15-1855	51
Bacon, Cath.		
(Catharine) [m]	09-23-1856	58
" , Jane (Mary Jane)	05-26(25)-1861	132
" , Mary Jane [m]	05-26(25)-1861	132
" , Sam'l. [f]	09-23-1856	58
" , Sam'l. (Samuel)		
[f]	05-26(25)-1861	132, 133
" , Sarah A. V.	09-23-1856	58
Bagby, Biddy	03-20-1872	312
" , Mary A. [m]	03-20-1872	313
" , Wyat [f]	03-20-1872	313

Name	Date	Page
Beale, Emma [m]	01-16(17)-1867	196
" , John	01-16(17)-1867	196
" , Jordan B. [f]	01-16(17)-1867	196
Beard, Amelia [m]	08-15-1861	121
" , Andr. [f]	05-(Χ∅)18-1871	294
" , Eliza [m]	05-(Χ∅)18-1871	294
" , John [f]	08-15-1861	121
" , John A.	08-15-1861	121
" , Lace [f]	05-19-1867	198
" , Laura B.		
(Laura Belle)	05-(Χ∅)18-1871	294
" , Lewis	05-19-1867	198
" , Sarah [m]	05-19-1867	198
Beard's, Lewis [PL]	12-27-1870	284
Beckner, Allen	01-11-1859	92
" , Daniel [f]	06-20-1859 [BK]	
	07-14-1859 [MR]	100
" , David [f]	01-11-1859	92
" , Elizabeth		
(Bitcy) [m]	01-11-1859	92
" , Margaret	06-20-1859 [BK]	
(Margaret R.) [m]	07-14-1859 [MR]	100
" , Sophia E.	06-20-1859 [BK]	
	07-14-1859 [MR]	100
Bell's, [Mr.] [PL]	10-24-1872	325
Bennet (Bennit),		
Andrew J.	08-23-1855	47
Bennet,Elizabeth		
(Phebe) [m]	09(08)-28-1857	69
" (Bennett), John J.	03-18-1858	80
" (Damron),		
Margaret	08-14-1862	138
" , Margaret	04-19-1855	45
" (Bennett),		
Margaret A.		
(Margaret Ann)	12-24(23)-1858	89
" , Mary A. (Mary		
Ann)	09(08)-28-1857	69
" (Bennett), Mary A.	03-18-1858	80
" (Fridley) (King),	04-19-1855	45
Phebe [m]		

Name	Date	Page
Bennet (Bennett),		
Perry	01-17-1860	109, 110
" (Bennett) (Tingler),		
Peggy [m]	03-18-1858	80
" , Sampson [f]	04-19-1855	45
[f]	09(08)-28-1857	69
" (Bennit), Sarah		
(Sarah C.) [m]	08-23-1855	47
" (Bennett), Solomon		
(Solman) [f]	03-18-1858	80
[f]	12-24(23)-1858	89
[f]	04-18-1861	121
" (Bennett), Susan		
[m]	12-24(23)-1858	89
[m]	03-18-1858	80
[m]	04-18-1861	121
" (Bennett), Tenpy		
(Tempy) (?Temssy)		
[m]	01-17-1860	109, 110
" (Bennett), Thos.		
(Thomas) [f]	01-17-1860	109, 110
" (Bennit), William		
[f]	08-23-1855	47
Bennet, William A.	04-18-1861	121
Bennett, A. C.		
(Asena Catharine)	10-10(11)-1866	189
" , C. (Catharine)	09-05-1867 [BK]	
[m]	10-01-1867 [MR]	212
" , Catharine [m]	12-29-1864	144
[m]	10-10(11)-1866	189
" (Persinger),		
Catherine (Catharine)		
[m]	12-08-1863	179
" (Gillaspie), E. F.	12-31-1866 [BK]	
(Eliza F.)	01-01-1867 [MR]	177
" , F. (Frnaces)	04-08(10)-1867	202
" , H. A.	11-28-1866 [BK]	
(Harriett Ann)	12-06-1866 [MR]	191
" , J. (Jacob) [f]	01-02-1866	171
" , J. M. (Jacob M.)	___-28-1869 [BK]	
	12-28-1869 [MR]	266

Name	Date	Page
Bennett, John J. [w]	12-24(23)-1858	89
" , John L.	12-29-1864	144
" (Persinger), L. J.		
(Lucinda Jane)	11-25(27)-1865	169
" (Damron), Margaret	08-28-1869	254
" (Armstrong), M. A.		
(Mary Ann)	04-07-1867	204
" (Bennet), M̶a̶r̶y̶ [m]	08-14-1862	138
" , May (Mary) [m]	01-02-1866	171
" , M. E.	11-28-1866 [BK]	
(Mary E.) [m]	12-06-1866 [MR]	191
	__-28-1869 [BK]	
[m]	12-28-1869 [MR]	266
" (Jones), M. J.		
(Mary J.)	01-07(10)-1869	242
" (King), Nancy	01-02-1866	171
" , P. (Phebe) [m]	04-08(10)-1867	202
" , P. (Phoebe)[m]	04-07-1867	204
[m]	08-28-1869	254
" , R. E.	09-05-1867 [BK]	
(Rebecca E.)	10-01-1867 [MR]	212
" , S. (Sampson)[f]	04-08(10)-1867	202
[f]	04-07-1867	204
[f]	08-28-1869	254
	__-28-1869 [BK]	
[f]	12-28-1869 [MR]	266
" (Bennet), Sampson		
[f]	08-14-1862	138
" , Sampson [f]	11-28-1866 [BK]	
	12-06-1866 [MR]	191
" , William [f]	12-29-1864	144
" , Wm. (William)[f]	10-10(11)-1866	189
[f]	09-05-1867 [BK]	
	10-01-1867 [MR]	212
Bennington, C.		
(Caroline) [m]	02-15(07)-1869	244
" , J. (James) [f]	02-15(07)-1869	244, 245
" , R. (Rebecca)	02-15(07)-1869	244
Bennit (Bennet),		
Andrew J.	08-23-1855	47

Name	Date	Page
Bennit (Bennet), Sarah		
(Sarah C.) [m]	08-23-1855	47
" (Bennet), William		
[f]	08-23-1855	47
Bess, Alex. (Alexander)	04-08(10)-1867	202
" , B. (Bettie) [m]	01-23(25)-1866	174
" , Charles L.	10-29-1869	261
" , Charles L.		
(Chs. L.) [w]	12-19(23)-1868	238
" , Chs. H.		
(Charles H.)	06-15(17)-1867	207
" , C. L.		
(Charles L.)	01-23(25)-1866	174
" , E. (Ellen) [m]	06-15(17)-1867	207
" (Appleberry),		
Elizabeth [m]	01-07(03)-1867	199
" , H. (Henry) [f]	09-21-1865	149, 150
" , H. (Hamilton)[f]	01-23(25)-1866	174
" , H. (Henry) [f]	04-08(10)-1867	202
[f]	06-15(17)-1867	207
[f]	12-03(06)-1868	235, 236
	01-29-1869 [BK]	
[f]	02-01-1869 [MR]	243, 244
" , H. (Hamilton)[f]	03-16(18)-1869	246
[f]	06-16-1870	277
" , Hamilton [f]	09-26-1865	146, 147
[f]	10-29-1869	261
" , Henry [f]	03-06-1856	60
[f]	02-16-1857	64
" , Jane [m]	10-19-1857	71
" , Jane	04-02(22)-1866	182
" , Jefferson [f]	01-07(03)-1867	199
" , Jno. L.		
(John Lee)	06-16-1870	277
" , J. C. (John C.)	09-21-1865	149
" , John F. [w]	03-06-1856	60
" , John L. [w]	09-26-1865	146
" , Joseph [f]	10-19-1857	71
" , J. V. (Jesse V.)	03-16(18)-1869	246, 247
" , Lewallen (Luallen)		
(Lewallen H.)	03-06-1856	60

Name	Date	Page
Bess, Martha	02-16-1857	64
" , Mary	03-06-1856	60
" , N. (Nellie) [m]	09-21-1865	149
" , N. (Nelly) [m]	04-08(10)-1867	202
[m]	12-03(06)-1868	235, 236
[m]	01-29-1869 [BK]	
	02-01-1869 [MR]	243, 244
" , Nash L. [w]	10-14-1869	258
" , Nelly (Nellie)[m]	02-16-1857	64
" , N. L. (Nash L.)	12-03(06)-1868	235
" , R. (Rebecca) [m]	03-16(18)-1869	246
[m]	06-16-1870	277
" , Rebecca [m]	03-06-1856	60
" , Rebecca	10-19-1857	71
" , Rebecca [m]	09-26-1865	146
" (Appleberry),		
Rebecca	01-07(03)-1867	199
" , Rebecca	01-29-1869 [BK]	
	02-01-1869 [MR]	243
" , Rebecca [m]	10-29-1869	261
" , Rebecca B.		
(Rebecca Beviline)	09-26-1865	146, 147
Bethel, Charity [m]	03-03-1870	272
" , Robert [f]	03-03-1870	272
" , William	03-03-1870	272
Biggs, S. J.	-__-1869 [BK]	
(Susan J.) [m]	12-22-1869 [MR]	266
" , S. L.	-__-1869 [BK]	
(Samuel Lucian)	12-22-1869 [MR]	266
" , W. (Wmsson)	-__-1869 [BK]	
(? Williamsson)[f]	12-22-1869 [MR]	266
Billey (Pittser),		
Margaret E.	03-04-1858	78
Bishop, J. S.		
(James S.) [f]	10-12(13)-1868	231
" , M. A.		
(Martha A.) [m]	10-12(13)-1868	231
" , N. W.		
(Norval W.)	10-12(13)-1868	231
Black, Jno. (John) [f]	01-26-1856	54

Name	Date	Page
Black, Rebecca [m]	01-26-1856	54
" , Wm. B.		
(William B.)	01-26-1856	54
Blake, Parson	11-04(05)-1869	261
" , Peggy [m]	11-04(05)-1869	262
" , William (Wm.)[f]	11-04(05)-1869	262
Blaker, Ailcy [m]	04-01-1856	56
" , Eley [m]	10-03-1861	122
" , James [f]	04-01-1856	56
[f]	10-03-1861	122
" (Arritt), L. C.		
(Louisa C.)	02-13(15)-1866	175
" , Mary J.		
(Mary Jane)	04-01-1856	56
" , William F.		
(Wm. F.)	10-03-1861	122
Bliss, Catharine [m]	03-31-1859	95
" , Henry	03-31-1859	95
" , Nicholas [f]	03-31-1859	95
Bogart, Ann [m]	01-09-1872	307
" , Garrett [f]	01-09-1872	307
" , John J.	01-09-1872	306, 307
Bogarth's house [PL]	10-09-1872	323
Boggs, Anderson	05-24-1871	294
" , Jane [m]	05-24-1871	294
" , Stephen [f]	05-24-1871	294
Boley, A. (Ann) [m]	12-07-1870	282
" , Betsada		
(Rosoltha)	12-04-1856	61
" , Bluford [f]	09-12-1856	57
[f]	12-04-1856	61
" , Catharine A.		
(Catharine Agnes)	06-15-1871	296
" , Ellen [m]	01-25-1859	92
" , F. C. (Fannie C.)		
(Francis C.)	11-18-1869	261
" , Henrietta	09-12-1856	57
" , J. Newton [w]	01-25-1859	93
" , John (John W.)	01-25-1859	92
" , Mary [m]	09-12-1856	57

Name	Date	Page
Boley, Mary	12-31-1863	180
" , Nancy [m]	01-25-1859	92
[m]	12-31-1863	180
[m]	06-15-1871	296
" , P. (Pitman) [f]	11-18-1869	261
" , P. (Presley)[f]	12-07-1870	282
" , Pitman [f]	01-25-1859	92
" , Presley [f]	01-25-1859	92
[f]	12-31-1863	180, 181
[f]	06-15-1871	296
" , R. (Rosoltha)[m]	12-04-1856	61
" , S. (Sarah) [m]	11-18-1869	261
" , Sarah	01-25-1859	92
" (Boley), S. E.		
(Sarah Elizabeth)	12-07-1870	282
" , V. (Virginia)	02-16-1863	161
Boly (Boley), Pitman		
(Pittman) [f]	02-16-1863	161
Boly (Boley), M. (Mary)		
[m]	02-16-1863	161
Booth, Mary	02-16-1871	290
" , Wm. (William)		
(W.) [f]	02-16-1871	290
Bostic (Costic) (Crostic),		
Francis	07-07-1859	102
" (Crostic), Josiah		
[f]	07-07-1859	102
" (Crostic), Martha		
Ann (Marthan Ann)		
[m]	07-07-1859	102
Bostick, C. (Charlotte)		
[m]	02-23(28)-1867	194
" , Calvin [f]	02-23(28)-1867	194
" , Caroline	07-11-1861	133
" , Mary J.		
(Mary Jane)	02-23(28)-1867	194
" , Polly [m]	07-11-1861	133
" , Wm. (William)[f]	07-11-1861	133
Boswell, Catharine	08-22-1855	56

[Name and Date Index: Part (2) - (Continued)]

Name	Date	Page

Boswell, E. StC.
   (Eugenia StClair) 10-30(31)-1865   168
  " , H. (Jas. H.) [f] 12-22(23)-1868   240
  " , J. H.
   (James H.) [f]   05-29-1867   206
  " , J. L.
   (John Lee) [f]   09-05-1865   149
  " , J. L.
   (John L.)   05-29-1867   206
  " , J. L. StC.
   (John Lee) [f]   10-30(31)-1865   168
  " , J. M. (Joseph
   Merriken) (Joseph
   M.)   09-05-1865   149
  " , Jno. (John) [f] 09-02-1856   57
  " , John L.
   (John Lee) [f] 08-22-1855   56
  " , John L. [w] 03-20-1872   313
  " [Junr.], John S.
       [JP]   64, 73
  " , Joseph   09-02-1856   57
  " , Louisa St.Clair
      [m]   10-30(31)-1865   168
  " , M. (Maria) [m] 12-22(23)-1868   240
  " , M. A.
   (Martha Ann) [m] 09-05-1865   149
  " , M. A.
   (Maria A.) [m] 05-29-1867   206
  " , Martha
   (Martha H.) [m] 08-22-1855   56
  " , Martha [m] 09-02-1856   57
  " , M. E. A.
   (Mollie E. A.) 12-22(23)-1868 239, 240
Bowan (Rowan), Boston[f] 04-01-1858   79
  " (Rowan), Chas. L.
   (Charles L.)   04-01-1858   79
  " (Rowan), Frances[m] 04-01-1858   79
Bowen, E. (Elizabeth) 07-25-1868 [BK]
                08-20-1868 [MR] 227
  " , E. (Erastus) 01-28(31)-1870 270

Name	Date	Page
Bowen, J. (Johnson)[f]	08-20-1868 [MR]	227
" [f]	01-28(31)-1870	270
" , Johner (Johnson)		
[f]	06-21(23)-1864	141
" , N. (Nancy) [m]	08-20-1868 [MR]	227
[m]	01-28(31)-1870	270
" , Nancy [m]	06-21(23)-1864	141
" , William	06-21(23)-1864	141
Bowers, Allen E.	03-02-1872 [MR]	311
" , L. D.(Lorenzo W.)	01-13-1870	268
" , Reeca (Recca)[m]	03-02-1872 [MR]	311
" , S. (Sarah) [m]	01-13-1870	268
" , Wm. [f]	03-02-1872 [MR]	311
Bowles, B. E.	01-11-1872	308
" (McCarthy), Catharine		
(Catherine) [m]	01-11-1872	307, 308
" , Jas. (James)[f]	01-11-1872	307, 308
" , John H. [f]	03-01-1864	144
" , Nancy C. [m]	03-01-1864	144
" , Thomas P.	03-01-1864	144
Bowling, Jno. J.		
(John J.) [f]	12-04-1872	328
" , L. J. (Lucy J.)		
[m]	12-04-1872	328
" , Wm. T.	12-04-1872	328
Bowyer, Adam [f]	08-14-1862	138
[f]	08-11-1870	285
" , Benton	10-10(15)-1868	230
" , Benton [w]	11-03(05)-1868	233
" , Christina		
(Christianna) [m]	08-14-1862	138
" , Christina [m]	08-11-1870	285
" , David [w]	01-16(18)-1866	174
" , Elizabeth [m]	04-01-1856	56
" , Geo. H.		
(George Hammond)	08-03-1871	298
" , J. (John) [f]	10-10(15)-1868	230
[f]	11-03(05)-1868	233
[f]	01-16(18)-1866	173, 174
" , Jacob	08-14-1862	137, 138
" , Jacob [f]	03-02(07)-1867	200

- 387 -

Name	Date	Page
Bowyer, Jacob	08-11-1870	285
" , Jno. (John) [f]	04-01-1856	56
[f]	08-03-1871	298, 299
" , N. (Nancy) [m]	10-10(15)-1868	230
[m]	11-03(05)-1868	233
" , Nancy [m]	01-16(18)-1866	173
[m]	08-03-1871	298
" (Gadd), Sarah E.	03-02(07)-1867	200
" (Haynes), Sarah	04-27(28)-1868	221, 222
" , S. F.(Salena F.)	01-16(18)-1866	173
" , S. V.(Sarah V.)	11-03(05)-1868	233
" , Wm. P. (William Patton)	04-01-1856	55
Bowyer's, John [Esq.] [PL]	04-27(28)-1868	221, 222
Boyer, D. (David)	09-04(07)-1865	157
" , J. (John) [f]	09-04(07)-1865	157
" , Nancy [m]	09-04(07)-1865	157
Brackman, L. (Luticia) [m]	11-18-1869	262
" , M. S. (Margaret S.)	11-18-1869	262
" , W. (William)[f]	11-18-1869	262
Bradshaw, F. (Franklin)	06-01-1865 [MR]	164
" , I. (Isabella)[m]	06-01-1865 [MR]	164
" , J. (James) [f]	06-01-1865 [MR]	164
Bratton (Otey), Hannah [m]	04-02-1857	64
" , Hannah [m]	12-20-1860	118, 119
" , Mary A.	12-20-1860	118
" , Robert (Robt.) [f]	04-02-1857	64
[f]	12-20-1860	118, 119
" , Tilford J.	04-02-1857	64
Bridgeet, Geo. (George) [f]	12-19-1855	53
" , Phebe [m]	12-19-1855	53
Bridget (Bridgeet), Ann E.	12-19-1855	53
Bridgett, Geo. W. (George W.) [f]	02-27-1861	120

Name	Date	Page
Bridgett, Jacob H.		
(J. H.)	02-27-1861	120
" , Phebe [m]	02-27-1861	120
Brooks, Cath.		
(Catharine) [m]	07-03-1856	55
" , James	07-03-1856	55
" , Lawson [f]	07-03-1856	55
" (Aldress), Martha	06-27-1872	317
Broughman, Andrew J.[w]	09-06-1865	159
" , E. (Elizabeth)	09-06-1865	159
" , J. (James) [f]	09-06-1865	159
" , M. E. (Mary E.)		
[m]	09-06-1865	159
Brown, A. (Armistead)[f]	08-31-1871	300
" , Anderson [f]	02-26(28)-1866	181
" , A. J.		
(Andrew Jackson)	02-16(21)-1867	193
" , Barbary [m]	02-26(28)-1866	181
" , C. (Cherry) [m]	08-31-1871	300
" , Catharine J.		
(Catharine)	08-26-1856	59
" , Charles (Chesley)		
[f]	10-31-1854	42
" , Charly (Charles)		
[w]	03-20-1872	313
" , Chs. (Charles)	10-31-1872	325
" , E. (Elizabeth)[m]	09-04(07)-1865	158
" , Edmund	08-31-1871	300
" , Elizabeth [m]	08-26-1856	59
" , Emma V.	06-20-1859	99
" , Francis (Frances)		
[m]	06-20-1859	99
" , George C.	10-31-1854	43
" , Hagar [m]	02-16(21)-1867	193
" , James M. [f]	06-20-1859	100
" , J. S. (Jennie S.)	10-22-1868	232
" , L. (Lemuel) [f]	09-19-1867	214
[f]	12-30-1869 [MR]	267
" , Lem [f]	03-02-1870	272
" , Lemuel [f]	05-10-1862	137
[Listed Twice]		

Name	Date	Page
Brown, Lemuel [f]	05-09-1862	161
[Listed Twice]		
" , Lucinda [m]	08-19-1856	57
" , M. (Martha) [m]	10-31-1872	325
" , M. A. (Amanda A.)	12-30-1869 [MR]	267
" , Madison [w]	08-26-1856	59
" , Marshal B.	08-19-1856	57
" , Mary [m]	10-31-1854	43
" , Mary	09-04(07)-1865	157, 158
" , M. C. (Margaret		
Catharine)	02-09-1871	289, 290
" , M. D. [w]	02-27(28)-1867	195
" , M. D. (Mathews D.)		
(Mathew D.) [f]	10-22-1868	232
" , Millard F. [w]	02-09-1871	290
" , N. (Nelson) [f]	10-31-1872	325
" , Nancy [m]	06-20-1859	100
" , R. J. (Rebecca		
Jane)	03-02-1870	272
" , S. [m]		
[Listed Twice]	05-09-1862	161
" , S. A. (Sarah		
Ann) [m]	09-19-1867	214
" (Lee), Salia Ann		
(Jalia Ann)	12-30-1869	268
" , Sam'l. (Samuel)		
[f]	02-09-1871	289
" , Samuel (Sam'l.)		
[f]	06-20-1859	99
[f]	06-20-1859	99
" , Sarah [m]	06-20-1859	99
" , Sarah	06-20-1859	100
" , Sarah [m]		
[Listed Twice]	05-10-1862	137
" , Sarah E.		
[Listed Twice]	05-10-1862	137
" , Sarah F. (Sarah		
Frances)	02-26(28)-1866	181
" , Sarah J. [w]	12-05(06)-1871	305
" , S. E. [Listed	05-09-1862	161
Twice]		

Name	Date	Page
Brown [(Cave)(?Case) (?Car)], S. E. (Sarah Elizabeth)	09-19-1867	214
" , S. W. (Sarah W.) [m]	02-09-1871	289
" , W. B. (Wm. B.) (William B.) [f]	09-04(07)-1865	158
" , William M. (Wm. M.)	06-20-1859	99
" , William M.[w]	01-03(04)-1866	171, 172
" , Wm. [f]	08-19-1856	57
" , Wm. (William)[f]	02-16(21)-1867	193
" , Wm. B. (W. B.) (William B.) [f]	08-26-1856	59
Brown's, Mathias [PL]	11-13-1862	139
Bryant, Martha E.	09-05-1872	321
" (Brient), Melissa L.	11-02-1871	303
" (Brient), M. J. (Mary J.) [m]	11-02-1871	303
" (Brient), S. M. (Shelton M.) [f]	11-02-1871	303
" , Wm. [f]	09-05-1872	321
Burden (Crow), Ann (Anne)	08-21-1856	58, 59
Burke (Burk), Jeremiah [f]	01-29-1864	143
" (Burk), Julia [m]	01-29-1864	143
" (Burk), Margarette	01-29-1864	143
Burks, Charlotte [m]	01-03-1870	269
" , Mary [m]	02-15-1871	292
" , Rebecca (Elizabeth)	01-03-1870	269
" , Wm. [f]	02-15-1871	292
" , Wm. (William)[f]	01-03-1870	269
" , Wm. P. [c]	02-15-1871	292
" , Wm. Paxton	02-15-1871	292
Burnin (Vernon), Jno. (John)	06-25-1870	278
Burrass, F. N.(Frederick Napolean)	01-11(10)-1871	284

Name	Date	Page
Burrass, J. P. [f]	01-11(10)-1871	284
" , S. M. [m]	01-11(10)-1871	284
Burrell, Paulina	09-18(17)-1872	321
" (Rideout), Silvie		
[m]	09-18(17)-1872	321
Bush, A. (Adam) [f]	11-02(07)(06)-1867	217
" , A. A. (Andrew A.)		
[f]	11-24-1870	318
" , Adam [f]	09-26-1865	148
" , Alchany		
(Alchany W.)	04-30-1857	66
" , Ambrose		
(Anoboso) [f]	10-24-1872	324, 325
" , E. A.		
(Elizabeth A.)	09-26-1865	147, 148
" , F. (Franklin)[f]	03-02-1870	272
" , Jacob L.	10-24-1872	324, 325
" , James S.	02-14-1856	54
" , J. L. A. (John		
Lee Allen)	11-02(07)(06)-1867	217
[w]	06-12-1872	317
" , Lucinda A.	06-09-1863	178
" , Mary [m]	04-30-1857	66
" , N. (Nancy) [m]	03-02-1870	272
" , Nathan L.		
(Nathan Lewis)	11-24-1870	318
" , Nimrod [f]	02-14-1856	54
" , P. (Peggy) [m]	09-26-1865	148
[m]	11-02(07)(06)-1867	217
" , P. A. (Patsey		
Ann) [m]	11-24-1870	318
[m]	10-24-1872	324
" , Polly [m]	06-09-1863	178
" , Polly (Poly) [m]	06-04-1857	68
" , Sam'l. [f]	04-30-1857	66
" , Sam'l. (Samuel)[f]	06-04-1857	68
" , Samuel [f]	06-09-1863	178
" , Sarah [m]	02-14-1856	54
" , Sarah J. (Sarah		
J. S.)	06-04-1857	68
" , Thos. (Thomas)	03-02-1870	272

Name	Date	Page
Bush's, A. W. [PL]	10-10(15)-1868	230
Byer (Byers), A. D.		
(Achilles Dew)	01-11-1871	286
" , A. J. (Alwilda		
J.)(Aldwilda Jane)	03-16(18)-1869	247
" , Charles P.		
(Chs. D.) [w]	01-23-1868	218
" (Byers), D. (David)		
[f]	03-16(18)-1869	247
" , D. (David) [f]	01-11-1871	286
" , David [w]	07-02-1856	55
" (Byers), E.		
(Elizabeth) [m]	03-16(18)-1869	247
" , E.		
(Elizabeth) [m]	01-11-1871	286
" , E. F.		
(Emma Francis)	12-12-1867	218
" , H. (Harriet)[m]	11-27-1872	327
" , Harriet [m]	08-08-1861	125
" , Harriett [m]	06-09-1863	178
" , Henrietta		
(Harriette) [m]	04-19-1864	145
" , Martha S.	04-19-1864	145
" , Mary Ann Sidney	01-23-1868	218
" , P. (Peter) [f]	12-12-1867	218
" , P. (?Patsey)[m]	12-12-1867	218
" , Pet. (Peter)[f]	01-23-1868	218
" , Ruthy Ann	08-08-1861	125
" , Sam'l. (Samuel)		
[f]	08-08-1861	125
[f]	11-27-1872	327, 328
" , Samuel [f]	04-19-1864	145
[f]	06-09-1863	178
" , William E.	06-09-1863	178
" , Wm. E.[s/b/w]	08-08-1861	125
Byers, Ellwood	08-03-1868	227
" (Byer), Harriet [m]	02-08(11)-1867	192
" (Byer), Hugh C.	11-27-1872	327, 328
" , J. (Jane) [m]	08-03-1868	227
" , J. (Joseph) [f]	08-03-1868	227

Name	Date	Page
Byers (Byer), Nancy E.	02-08(11)-1867	192
" (Byer), Sam'l. (Samuel) [f]	02-08(11)-1867	192
Byer's, David [PL]	04-19-1855	46
Byrd, Albert [f]	11-04(05)-1869	262
" , Allen M. [f]	10-31-1854	43
" , Lucy [m]	11-04(05)-1869	262
" , Margaret B. [m]	10-31-1854	43
" , Martha C. (Martha E.) (Marthy E.)	01-07-1869	242, 243
" , Mary A.	10-31-1854	43
" , Nancy [m]	01-07-1869	242
" , Rachel	11-04(05)-1869	262
" , William (Wm.)[f]	01-07-1869	242
Cahoon (Carson), Mary C.	03-31-1859	95, 96
Calaghan (Callahan), D.(Dennis) [f]	02-18-1858	77
" (Callahan), Mary (Margaret) [m]	02-18-1858	77
" (Callahan) (Jones), Mary	02-18-1858	77
Caldwell, Arthur L.	11-11-1858	88
" , Bartlet (Bartlett) [f]	11-11-1858	88
" , Margaret [m]	11-11-1858	88
Callaghan (Callighan), Chas.(Charles)[f]	12-17-1856	63
" , Dennis	04-22(21)-1858	81
[w]	03-20(21)-1867	201
" , G. (George)	09-13(19)(20)-1865	165
" , J. (John)(Jno.) [f]	09-13(19)(20)-1865	166
[f]	03-20(21)-1867	201
" , John [f]	04-22(21)-1858	81
" (Callighan), Manama (Manamme)(Mariamne)	12-17-1856	63, 64
" (Callighan), Nancy [m]	12-17-1856	63

Name	Date	Page

Carpenter, M.A.
    (Mareh A.) [m]   03-20(30)-1865   152
   " (Cavener), Mary[m] 12-08-1863   179
   " (Cavener)(Cavner),
    Michael   12-08-1863   179
   " , M. C. (Mary C.) 01-10-1864(1865) 150
   " , S. (Samuel) [f] 01-10-1864(1865) 150
             [f] 03-20(30)-1865   152
   " , S. S.
    (Samuel S.)   03-20(30)-1865   152
Carson, Amanda R.   12-03-1863   179
   " , C. (Caroline)[m]05-31-1870   276
             [m] 09-07-1865 [MR] 156
   " , Caroline [m] 03-31-1859   96
   " , C. V.   01-29-1863   178
   " , George   06-14-1855   46
   " , J. (James) [f] 05-31-1870   276
             [f] 09-07-1865   156
   " , James   [f] 03-31-1859   96
   " , James M. [w] 02-27-1857   65
             [w] 03-31-1859   96
   " , Jno. (John) [f] 06-14-1855   46
   " , Joseph [f]   01-29-1863   178
   " , Julia A.
    (Julia Ann)   08-06-1863   178, 179
   " , Kitty [m]   01-29-1863   178
   " (Cahoon), Mary C. 03-31-1859   95, 96
   " , Nancy [m]   06-14-1855   46
   " , Sarah [m]   08-06-1863   179
             [m] 12-03-1863   179
   " , V. C.
    (Virginia Catherine) 09-07-1865 [MR]156
   " , W. C. (Wilsonia
    Caroline)   05-31-1870   276
   " , William [f] 08-06-1863   179
             [f] 12-03-1863   179
Carter, Bradley   11-17-1858   89
   " , E. W.(Elvira W.)10-07(11)-1864 142
   " , Gerard [w] 07-12-1855   51
   " , Grandville [w] 12-20-1855   52
   " , Henry J.   01-08-1856   53

Name	Date	Page
Carter, James P.	03-19(28)-1866	182
" , Jesse	10-01(02)(03)-1867	215,216
" , John (Jarred)	12-20-1855	52
" , John [f]	05-24(23)-1858	82
" , Jno. (John L.)[f]	12-19-1855	53
" , Jno. L.		
(John L.) [f]	10-13-1857	71
" , Jno. M. (John		
M.)	10-13-1857	71
" , L. (Lemuel)[f]	10-07(11)-1864	142
[f]	10-01(02)(03)-1867	215
" , Lemuel [f]	12-20-1855	52
[f]	11-17-1858	89
[f]	03-19(28)-1866	182
[f]	07-12-1855	51
" , Lucy [m]	12-19-1855	53
" (Eubank), Lucy [m]	10-13-1857	71
" , M. (Martha)[m]	10-07(11)-1864	142
[m]	10-01(02)(03)-1867	215
" , Martha [m]	12-20-1855	52
" , Mary	05-24(23)-1858	82
" , Nancy [m]	05-24(23)-1858	82
" , Patsey (Patsy)[m]	03-19(28)-1866	182
" , Patsy [m]	11-17-1858	89
" (Taliaforo), Sarah	03-03-1870	272
" , Thomas	07-12-1855	51
[w]	12-20-1855	52
" , William A.	12-19-1855	53
Cary (McCary), Maria[m]	09-12-1861	130
" (McCary), Philip		
(Phillip) [f]	09-12-1861	130
" (McCary), Sam'l. M.		
(Samuel M.)	09-12-1861	130
Cash, William	06-21-1866 [MR]	184
Cassada (Cassedy), C.		
(Conn) [f]	02-18-1858	77
" (Cassedy), Jane[m]	02-18-1858	77
" (Cassedy), William	02-18-1858	76
Cauly (Cauley), C.		
(Catharine) [m]	01-10(11)-1866	173

Name	Date	Page
Cauly (Cauley), G. W.		
(George Washington)	01-10(11)-1866	173
" (Cauley), J. (John)		
[f]	01-10(11)-1866	173
Cave, E. [m]	05-09-1862	160
[Listed Twice]		
" , Elizabeth [m]	05-10-1862	137
[Listed Twice]		
" , James R.	05-10-1862	137
[Listed Twice]		
" , J. R.	05-09-1862	160
[Listed Twice]		
" , T. [f]	05-09-1862	160
[Listed Twice]		
" , Thomas [f]	05-10-1862	137
[Listed Twice]		
" [(?Case)(?Car)]		
(Brown), S. E.		
Sarah Elizabeth	09-19-1867	214
Cavener (Carpenter),		
James [f]	12-08-1863	179
" (Carpenter), Mary		
[m]	12-08-1863	179
Cavner (Cavener)		
(Carpenter), Michael	12-08-1863	179
Chapman, A. (Alfred)[f]	06-26(23)-1868	225
" , Chs. C.		
(Charles C.)	06-27-1872	317
" , M. E. (May E.)		
(? Mary E.) [m]	06-26(23)-1868	225
" , M. J.		
(Margaret J.) [m]	06-27-1872	317
" , W. B. [f]	06-27-1872	317
" , W. K.		
(William K.)	06-26(23)-1868	225
Charry (Chary), Bridgett		
[m]	07-17-1861	122
" (Chary), Mathias		
(Matthias) [f]	07-17-1861	122
" , Thomas	07-17-1861	122

Name	Date	Page
Chewing, Jos. [f]	12-04-1856	61
" , Lucinda [m]	12-04-1856	61
" (Chewning), Sam'l.		
(Samuel)	12-04-1856	61
Chisley (Adams), Eliza		
[m]	02-19-1870	271
" , John Lewis [f]	02-19-1870	271
Circle, Daniel (Dan'l.)	09-14-1858	86
" , John (John L.)		
[f]	09-14-1858	86
" , Martha L.		
(Martha Lee) [m]	09-14-1858	86
Clark, Aaron D.	11-08-1859	106
" (Clarke), Aron		
(Aaron)	08-07-1856	56
" , C. (Christina)[m]	05-19-1869 [MR]	248
" , Christ.		
(Christina) [m]	11-08-1859	106
" (Clarke),		
Christeana [m]	08-07-1856	56
" , Christina		
(Christena) [m]	10-07-1858	87
" , George	06-07-1866	197
" , Jas. (James) [f]	10-09-1872	323
" , J. B. (Jos. B.)[f]	05-19-1869 [MR]	248
" , Jos. [f]	11-08-1859	106
" , Jos. B.		
(Joseph B.) [f]	10-07-1858	87
" (Clarke), Joseph[f]	08-07-1856	56
" , Lucinda L.	10-07-1858	87
" , Mary [m]	10-09-1872	323
" , Wm. E.	10-09-1872	323
" , Wm. T.(William T.)	05-19-1869 [MR]	248
Clark's, A. D. [PL]	05-19-1869 [MR]	248
Clinebell, G. (Geo.)[f]	11-23-1869	262, 263
" , H. J.(Henry J.)	11-23-1869	262
" , S. (Sarah) [m]	11-23-1869	262, 263
Coady, Edward [f]	04-24-1859	97
" , Mary [m]	04-24-1859	97
" (Coody), Patrick	04-24-1859	97

Name	Date	Page
Cole, H. W. [w]	05-26(25)-1861	133
Coleman, Bridgett	07-17-1861	122
" , Bridgett [m]	07-17-1861	123
" , E. (Elizabeth) [m]	10-14-1869	257
" , J. O. (John O.)	10-14-1869	257, 258
" , J. P. [f]	10-14-1869	257
" , Mary (Mary D.)[m]	06-23-1857	75
" , Pat. (Patrick)[f]	07-17-1861	123
" , Sam'l.	06-23-1857	75, 76
" , Sam'l. [f]	06-23-1857	75
Coleman's, Sam'l. [PL]	01-03-1870	269
Connel (Fitzgerald), Grace [m]	01-16-1860	111
" , Jeffery	02-(?)-1859	97
[w]	02-10(20)-1859	97
" , Jno. (John)	08-13-1857	70
" (O'Connel), Jno. (John) [f]	08-13-1857	70
" (Harrigan), Joanna	02-(?)-1859	97
" (O'Connel) (Foley), Mary (May) [m]	08-13-1857	70
" , Mary	02-10(20)-1859	96
" , Patrick [f]	02-10(20)-1859	96
Conner (Harington), Joana (Johana)	12-29-1860	119
" (O'Conner), Matthew O.	11-17-1857	72
" (Connor) (Kennelly), M. (Mary) [m]	02-01-1858	76
Conner(s), Hanorah [m]	08-20-1860	117
" , Jeremiah (Jeremah)	08-20-1860	117
" , Jeremiah [f]	08-20-1860	117
Conoway (Conaway) (Anderson), Eliz. (Elizabeth) [m]	05-23-1866 [BK] 05-24-1866 [CL] 03-24-1866 [MR]	184
" (Conaway) (Anderson), Eliz. A. (Elizabeth Arabella)	05-23-1866 [BK] 05-24-1866 [CL] 03-24-1866 [MR]	184

Name	Date	Page
Conoway (Conaway),	05-23-1866 [BK]	
Jas. (James) [f]	05-24-1866 [CL]	
	03-24-1866 [MR]	184
Conway (Fenton)(Farton),		
Catherine [m]	11-17-1857	72
", James (John)[f]	11-17-1857	72
", Jonna (Joanna)	11-17-1857	72
Coody (Coady), Patrick	04-24-1859	97
Cook, Benjn. S. (B. S.)		
(Benjamin S.)	10-27-1859	105
", Cath. (Catharine)		
[m]	10-27-1859	105
", Thos. N.		
(Thomas N.) [f]	10-27-1859	105
Cooper, Aldridge [f]	02-28(29)-1872	312
", Nancy	02-28(29)-1872	312
Copenhaver, James A.[w]	01-25-1871	289
Cosby, W. J. [w]	07-16(07)-1858	83
Costic (Crostic)(Bostic),		
Francis	07-07-1859	102
", Frank [h]	02-23(25)-1867	195
" (Woolwine), Nancy	02-23(25)-1867	195
Cotton, Elizabeth A.		
(E. A.) (Elisabeth		
A.)	08-24-1858	85, 86
", Michael [f]	08-24-1858	85
Courtney, Michael	07-06-1857	67
", Nancy (Ann)[m]	07-06-1857	67
", Tim [f]	07-06-1857	67
Craft, B. (Betsey)[m]	10-01-1867 [MR]	212
", E. (Elizabeth)		
[m]	09-13(19)(20)-1865	165
[m]	07-10-1867 [MR]	209, 210, 211
", Elizabeth		
(Elisabeth) [m]	09-04(03)-1857	70
", Elizabeth [m]	06-05-____ [CL]	
	05-27-1860 [BK]	114
", E. [m]	03-28-1872	314
", Geo. M. [f]	03-28-1872	314
", Geo. W.(George W.)	09-04(03)-1857	70

Name	Date	Page
Craft, Geo. W.		
(George W.)	03-28-1872	314
" , J. (John) [f]	07-10-1867 [MR]	209, 210, 211
[f]	10-01-1867 [MR]	212
[f]	09-13(19)(20)-1865	165
" , James [f]	01-25-1855	50
" , James	01-31-1872	310
" , Jno. (John)[f]	09-04(03)-1857	70
" , Jos. (Joseph)	10-01-1867 [MR]	212
" , Martha	01-25-1855	50
" , R. J.		
(Rebecca Jane)	09-13(19)(20)-1865	166
" , Sampson	07-10-1867	209, 210, 211
" , Sarah	06-05-_____ [CL]	
	05-27-1860 [BK]	114
" , Sarah [m]	12-24(26)-1867	219
[m]	01-31-1872	310
" , Sofa [m]	01-25-1855	50
" , Wm. (William)	12-24(26)-1867	219
[w]	11-23-1869	263
" , Wm. S.		
(William S.) [f]	12-24(26)-1867	219
Cragham (Croghan),		
Hennera (Hanora)[m]	02-17-1859	94
" (Croghan), Michael		
[f]	02-17-1859	94
Craig, James S. [CC]	01-25-1871	289
Crane & Wheeler [p]	09-20-1855	49
Crawford, Coatney [m]	02-06-1861	122
" , Margaret		
(Margaret M.)	06-30-1859	103
" (Crofford), Owen		
(Oen) [f]	06-30-1859	103
" , Owen [f]	02-06-1861	122
" , Wm. T. (William)	02-06-1861	122
Crawford's house [PL]	09-19-1867	214
Creeden, John [f]	02-11-1872 [CLM]	
	03-02-1872 [MR]	311

Name	Date	Page
Creeden, Maggie E.	02-11-1872 [CLM]	
	03-02-1872 [MR]	311
" , Mary [m]	02-11-1872 [CLM]	
	03-02-1872 [MR]	311
Crizer (Cryzer), H.		
(Henry) [f]	10-09(24)-1865	167
" (Cryzer), M. (Mary)		
[m]	10-09(24)-1865	167
" (Cryzer), T. J.		
(Thomas J.)	10-09(24)-1865	167
Crogham (Croghan),		
Thomas	02-17-1859	94
Croghan, Daniel [w]	10-21-1859	107
Crookshanks, Alexander		
[f]	05-13-1863	140, 141
" , James	05-13-1863	140
" , Margaritta		
(Margaretta) [m]	05-13-1863	140, 141
Crostic (Costic)(Bostic),		
Francis	07-07-1859	102
" (Bostic), Josiah[f]	07-07-1859	102
" (Bostic), Marthan		
Ann (Martha Ann)[m]	07-07-1859	102
Crow, Amanda (Amanda		
F.) [m]	10-15(18)-1866	189
" (Burden), Ann		
(Anne)	08-21-1856	58
" , Edwin D.	10-15(18)-1866	189
" , John [f]	10-15(18)-1866	189
" , Mary [m]	08-21-1856	58
" , Thos. (Thomas)		
[f]	08-21-1856	58
Crowley (Crowly),		
Ellen [m]	12-30-1855(1854)	52
" (Crowly), John	12-30-1855(1854)	52
"[(Discel) (Driscol)		
(Dischel)], Mary[m]	08-15-1858	85
" (Crowly), Wm.		
(William) [f]	12-30-1855(1854)	52
Crowly, Dan'l.(Daniel)		
[f]	01-16-1860	111

Name	Date	Page
Crowly (Crowley), Ellen		
[m]	12-30-1855(1854)	52
" (Crowley), John	12-30-1855(1854)	52
" (Crouly), Mary	01-16-1860	111
" (Canten), Mary [m]	01-16-1860	111
" (Crowley), Wm.		
(William) [f]	12-30-1855(1854)	52
Crow's, [Col.] John [PL]	08-21-1856	58
Crutchfield, Cath.		
(Catharine) [m]	12-24-1857	73
" , Jno. M.(John M.)	12-24-1857	73, 74
" , Jno. M.		
(John M.) [f]	12-24-1857	73
Cryzer (Crizer), H.		
(Henry) [f]	10-09(24)-1865	167
" (Crizer), M. (Mary)		
[m]	10-09(24)-1865	167
" (Crizer), T. J.		
(Thomas J.)	10-09(24)-1865	167
Cumings (Cummings), A.		
(Abraham) [f]	12-21-1857	73
" (Cumnings), Isaiah		
S. (Isaiah Stanley)	12-21-1857	73
" (Cumnings), Rebecca		
(Rebeca) [m]	12-21-1857	73
Cummings, A.(Absolam)		
[f]	07-01(08)-1868	226
" , M. C. (May		
K. C.)	07-01(08)-1868	226
" , R. (Rebecca)[m]	07-01(08)-1868	226
Cunningham's, Wm. [PL]	10-17-1872	324
Daily (Dailey), John	01-12-1860	109
" , Nora [m]	01-12-1860	109
" , Thos. (Thomas)[f]	01-12-1860	109
Daley, Catherine [m]	05-24-1864	143
" (O'Conner), Mary	05-24-1864	143
" , Eugene [f]	05-24-1864	143
Damron, A. H. (Ann		
Henrietta)	05-22(23)-1867	205, 206

Name	Date	Page
Damron, Andr.		
(Andrew) [f/w]	10-10-1861	132
" , Bev. E. [m]	09-28-1858	87
" , C. (Christopher)		
[f]	05-05(09)-1865	163
" , C. A. [w]	02-20-1870	265
" , E. M. (Emma M.)	01-16-1867	195, 196
" , Isaac P.	04-19-1855	45
" , J. A. C.		
(Julia Ann C.)[m]	05-05(09)-1865	163
" , Jos.(Joseph)[f]	05-22(23)-1867	206
" , Joseph [f]	04-19-1855	45
[f]	07-16(07)-1858	82
" , L. (Lucy) [m]	05-22(23)-1867	206
" , Louisa		
(Louisa Allen)	09-28-1858	87
" , Lucy [m]	07-16(07)-1858	82
" , M. A. (Mary A.)		
[m]	01-16-1867	196
" (Bennett), Margaret	08-14-1862	138
	08-28-1869	254
" , Mary J.	10-10-1861	132
" , Mary W. [m]	10-10-1861	132
" , [Mr.]		
[C. A. Damron][mes]	02-20-1870	264, 265
" (Neel), Rebecca[m]	04-19-1855	45
" , S. L.		
(Stanard Littleton)	05-05(09)-1865	163
" , Wm. [f]	09-28-1858	87
" , Wm. (William)[f]	01-16-1867	196
" , Wm. [w]	02-20-1870	265
[mes]	12-30-1869 [MR]	268
" , [Dr.] Wm. L.		
(William L.)	07-16(07)-1858	82
Damron's, Christopher		
[PL]	12-30(31)-1868	241
" , Wm. [PL]	02-23(25)-1867	195
Davenport, George H.		
(George Henry)	09-02(03)-1870	279

Name	Date	Page
Davenport, Henry [f]	09-02(03)-1870	279
" , Lucinda [m]	09-02(03)-1870	279
Davidson, F. [w]	09-12-1861	130
" , Martha A. [w]	09-12-1861	130
Davis, Ann	03(02)-07-1868	220
" , Braxton [f]	03-20-1871	292
" , Caroline [m]	06-24-1869	250
" , Delila [m]	03-20-1871	292
" , Edney (Edna J.)	12-30-1855(1854)	52, 53
" , Edward	02-20-1870	264, 265
" , George (Geo.)[f]	06-24-1869	250
" , Harriet [m]	12-02-1869	263
" , Jas. (James)[f]	12-30-1855(1854)	53
" , John B. [w]	08-23-1871	300
" , Nancy [m]	12-30-1855(1854)	53
" , Polly	06-24-1869	250
" , Preston	12-02-1869	263
" (Gladwell), Sarah	03-20-1871	292
" , Spencer [f]	12-02-1869	263
" , Virginia M.	10-21-1858	88
Davis's, John B. [PL]	01-08(09)-1866	172
[PL]	12-06-1866 [MR]	191
[PL]	04-08(10)-1867	202
[PL]	04-08(11)-1867	203
[PL]	09-05-1867	213
[PL]	07-01(08)-1868	226
Dawson, Caroline	08-17-1872	320
" , Fanny [m]	08-17-1872	320
Deed, James [w]	12-25-1872	331
Deeds, Eliz.		
(Elizabeth) [m]	09-31(30)-1862	140
" , Elizabeth	09-31(30)-1862	140
" , J. L.(John L.)	10-12(14)-1868	230
" , Joseph R. P.[w]	06-10(13)-1865	156
" , J. R. P.		
(Joseph R. P.)	04-12(16)-1867	203
" , M. A. (Martha A.)	06-10(13)-1865	156
" , R. (Rachel) [m]	06-10(13)-1865	156
[m]	04-12(16)-1867	204
[m]	10-12(14)-1868	230

Name	Date	Page
Deeds, W. (Wm.)		
(William) [f]	06-10(13)-1865	156
" , Wm.		
(William) [f]	09-31(30)-1862	140
[f]	04-12(16)-1867	204
[f]	10-12(14)-1868	230
Deisher, J. S.		
(Jacob S.)	04-08(11)-1867	202
" , M. (Mary) [m]	04-08(11)-1867	203
" , P. (Peter) [f]	04-08(11)-1867	203
Dew, A. (Absolem) [f]	09-05-1867	212
", A. (Absalom) [f]	09-01-1868	229
", Abs. (Absalom)[f]	12-19-1872	330
", Absalom [f]	07-24(25)-1860	116
" , Archilles	04-01-1862	137
" , E. T. [Elizabeth		
T. (or ? J)]	09-01-1868	229
" , Mary [m]	04-01-1862	137
" , Melissa B.		
(Malissa B.)	09-28-1871	300, 301
" , O. S. S.		
(Oceanna S. S.)	12-19-1872	330
" , Oceanna S. S.[w]	11-07-1872	327
" , S. (Sarah) [m]	09-05-1867	212
[m]	09-01-1868	229
" , Sarah [m]	07-24(25)-1860	116
[m]	09-28-1871	300, 301
[m]	12-19-1872	330
" , Sophia W.	07-24(25)-1860	116
" , V. A.		
(Victoria Almira)	09-05-1867	212
" , Wm. [f]	04-01-1862	137
Dickey, Littleton T.	01-11-1872	307
" , Margaret [m]	01-11-1872	307, 308
" , Ro. S. [f]	01-11-1872	307, 308
Dickson, A. V.		
(Agnes V.)	08-03-1868	227
" , E. (Elizabeth)[m]	12-07-1870	282
" , G. W.		
(George Washington)	12-07-1870	282
" , Geo. W.(George W.)	10-29-1857	71

Name	Date	Page
Dickson, James H.	10-23-1856	62
" , Jno. (John) [f]	10-29-1857	71
" (Dixon ?), Jno. A.		
(John A.)	08-16-1854	43
" , John [f]	12-03-1863	179
" , Jos. (? Jones)		
(? James) [f]	10-23-1856	62
" , L. L. (Lillie L.)	10-12(13)-1868	231
" , M. E. (Bettie)		
(M. Bessie)	09-19(31)-1868	229
" , M. F.		
(Margaret F.) [m]	10-12(13)-1868	231
[m]	10-12(13)-1868	231
" , M. F. [m]	12-18(19)-1866	192
" , Nancy [m]	10-23-1856	62
[m]	10-29-1857	71
[m]	12-03-1863	179
" , R. (Robert) [f]	08-03-1868	227, 228
" , R. (Robert)		
(Robt.) [f]	09-19(21)-1868	229
" , Ro. A.		
(Robert A.)	12-18(19)-1866	192
" , Robt. [w]	12-17-1856	64
" , S. (Sam'l.) [f]	10-12(13)-1868	231
" , S. (Samuel) [f]	10-12(13)-1868	231
" (Dixon), Sally [m]	08-16-1854	43
" , Sam'l. (Samuel)[f]	12-18(19)-1866	192
" , Thomas E.	12-03-1863	179
" (Dixon), Thos. [f]	08-16-1854	43
" , V. (Virginia)[m]	08-03-1868	227
[m]	09-19(21)-1868	229
" , W. J.(William J.)	10-12(13)-1868	231
" , W. M. (Wm. M.)[f]	12-07-1870	282
Discel [Driscol,Dischel]		
(Crowley), Mary [m]	08-15-1858	85
" (Driscol), Patrick		
[f]	08-15-1858	85
Dnycol (Sulivan)		
(O'Sullivan),		
Catherine [m]	08-13-1857	70

Name	Date	Page
Dobbin(s) (Dolbins),		
Dan'l.(Daniel)	02-10(20)-1859	96
Dobbins (Dolbin),		
Catharine [m]	02-10(20)-1859	96
Dobbins (Dolbin),		
Dan'l. [w]	02-(?)-1859	97
" (Dolbin), Michael[f]	02-10(20)-1859	96
Dodd, Jno. [f]	07-19-1871	298
" (Fannin), Mary A.E.		
(Mary A.Elizabeth)	07-19-1871	298
" , Sarah [m]	07-19-1871	298
Dogherty (?Doherty)		
(?Murphy), Luke [f]	02-17-1867	194
" (Doherty?),		
McMurphy (M.Murphy?)		
[m]	02-17-1867	194
Doherty, A. J.		
(Andrew J.)	01-01-1867 [MR]	177
" (?Murphy), Mary	02-17-1867	194
" , P. (Phillip) [f]	01-01-1867 [MR]	177
" , R. (Rachel) [m]	01-01-1867 [MR]	177
Donnally (Donnelly),		
A. (Allen)	09-19(21)-1868	229
" , C. (Chs.)		
(Charles) [f]	09-19(21)-1868	229
" , S. (Synthia) [m]	09-19(21)-1868	229
Donovan, A. (Ann) [m]	06-04-1868	225
" , J. (James)	06-04-1868	225
" , Wm. (William)[f]	06-04-1868	225
Dore, Catherine [m]	01-08-1861	123
" (Doore), Robert		
(Robt.)	01-08-1861	123
" , Robt. [f]	01-08-1861	123
Douglas, Alcinda	12-24-1857	73
" , B. (Benjamin)[f]	12-24-1857	73
" , Eliza [m]	05-26-1871	295
" , Harriet [m]	12-24-1857	73
" , Henry	05-26-1871	295
" , Jas.(James) [f]	05-26-1871	295

[Name and Date Index: Part (2) - (Continued)]

Name	Date	Page
Downey, Archibald (Archobold) [f]	01-25-1855	50
" , Eliz.(Elizabeth) [m]	01-25-1855	50
" , Michael	01-25-1855	50
" , Robert [w]	01-25-1855	50
Dressler, George W. (George Washington)	02-26(28)-1866	181
" , Patsy [m]	02-26(28)-1866	181
" , Peter [m]	02-26(28)-1866	181
Driscol, Hennora	09-15-1861	133
" , Margaret	08-15-1858	85
" (Discel) (Dischel) (Crowley), Mary[m]	08-15-1858	85
" , Mary [m]	09-15-1861	133
" (Discel), Patrick[f]	08-15-1858	85
" , Patrick [f]	09-15-1861	133
Driscoll, D. E. (Dennis E.)	10-20-1869	258
" , M. (Mary) [m]	10-20-1869	258
" , T. (Thimothy)[f]	10-20-1869	258
Dugan (Quinlen), Ellen	06-17(19)-1859	99
Duglis's, Frank [PL]	12-17(18)-1872	329
Duncan, Elizabeth	08-04-1859	104
" , Frances [m]	08-04-1859	104
" , Geo. (George)[f]	08-04-1859	104
Dunford, Margarett (Margaret)	08-20-1860	117
" (Dunnivant), Hannah [m]	08-20-1860	117
Dungan, E. B. (Elizabeth B.)[m]	01-03-1866	172
" , H. M. (Henry M.) [f]	01-03-1866	172
" , S. A. (Sarah Ann)	01-03-1866	172
Dunnahoo (Forely), Ellen [m]	12-17-1859	107
" , John [f]	12-17-1859	107
" , John	12-17-1859	107
Dunnivant (Dunford), Hannah [m]	08-20-1860	117

- 410 -

Name	Date	Page
Dunnivant, James [f]	08-20-1860	117
Duran, John [w]	05-09(14)-1859	98
Duwese, Chs. [f]	02-22-1872	311
" , Martha [m]	02-22-1872	311
" , Mary	02-22-1872	311, 312
Eagon, _____ (Parents)	10-07-1870	280
" , J. (John) [f]	05-26(27)-1868	224
" , M. (Mildred)[m]	05-26(27)-1868	224
" (Paxton), M. L.		
(Mary L.)	10-07-1870	280
" , S. R.(Sallie R.)	05-26(27)-1868	224
East, William C.(W.C.)[w]	10-23-1856	62
Eavans, Edward [w]	04-30-1857	67
Eddy, Angenetta	10-17-1872	324
" , L.(Lucinda) [m]	10-17-1872	324
" , W.(Washington)[f]	10-17-1872	324
Edwards, Hy (Henry)[f]	12-26-1872	331, 332
" , M.(Mary) [m]	12-26-1872	331
" , Maglin	12-26-1872	331
Eggars, Caroline [m]	03-19-1861	123
" , Daniel (Dan'l.)[f]	03-19-1861	123
" (Egger), William	03-19-1861	123
Engram, D.(Delina)[m]	02-15(07)-1869	244
" , Jos.(Joseph)	02-15(07)-1869	244
" , W.(William) [f]	02-15(07)-1869	244
Ervine (Irvin) (Wall),		
Ann [m]	10-21-1859	106
" (Irvine), Ellen	10-21-1859	106
" (Irvin), Maurice[f]	10-21-1859	106
Eubank (Carter), Lucy[m]	10-13-1857	71
Evans, Abraham [f]	12-20-1860	118
" , Carrie H.	01-09-1872	307
" , Deliah [m]	03-11-1861	125
" , Edward R.	01-02-1862	135
" , Elisha [f]	09-21(20)-1860	117
[f]	01-02-1862	135
" , E.S.(Elizabeth		
Sarah)	01-18-1866	174
" , K.(Kessiah) [m]	02-09-1865	150
" , K. (Kesiah) [m]	01-18-1866	174

Name	Date	Page
Evans, Kesiah [m]	01-09-1872	307
" , Mary (?May) [m]	09-21(20)-1860	117
" , Mary	03-11-1861	125
" , Mary [m]	01-02-1862	135
" , Patterson	12-20-1860	118, 119
" , R. J.(Rebecca Jane)	02-09-1865	150
" , S.A.(Sarah A.)[m]	12-20-1860	118
" , W.(William) [f]	02-09-1865	150
[f]	01-18-1866	174
" , William [f]	03-11-1861	125
" , Wm. [f]	01-09-1872	307
" , Wm. L.	09-21(20)-1860	117, 118
Falls, I. (Isaeh) [f]	06-04-1867 [MR]	207
" , S.(Susan A.) [m]	06-04-1867 [MR]	207
" , W. T. [w]	12-31-1872	332
" , Wm.T.(William Thomas)	06-04-1867 [MR]	206
Fannin (Dodd), Mary A.E. (Mary A.Elizabeth)	07-19-1871	298
Farmer, Chs. E. [f]	05-19-1869 [MR]	248
" , Harriet	11-08-1859	106
" , Martha [m]	11-08-1859	106
" , Mattie (M.A.H.)	05-19-1869 [MR]	248
" , M. B. [f]	11-08-1859	106
Farton (Fenton)(Conway), C.(Catherine) [m]	11-17-1857	72
Feamster, P.J.(Patsey Jane)	05-30-1865	164
" , P.J.(Patsey Jane) [m]	05-30-1865	164
" , W. (William)[f]	05-30-1865	164
Feannelly (Nolin), Mary [m]	04-04(09)-1857	75
F̶e̶a̶n̶t̶(Hollerin or Hollorin), Mary [m]	08-15-1858	85
Fenton(Farton)(Conway), C.(Catherine) [m]	11-17-1857	72
Fields (Robinson), Charlotte [m]	05-29-1866	185

Name	Date	Page
Fields, Jos.(Joseph)[f]	05-29-1866	185
" (Robinson),Sarah	05-29-1866	185
Fisher, H.(Hettie) [m]	11-18-1869	262
" , J.(John) [f]	11-18-1869	262
" , W.(Warrick)	11-18-1869	262
Fitzgerald (Stack),		
Catherine [m]	02-16-1858	76
" (Francis), E.(Ellen)		
[m]	02-16-1858	76
" (Connel), Grace[m]	01-16-1860	111
" , James	01-16-1860	111
" , Jno. (John)	02-16-1858	76
" , John	10-16-1859	104
" , John [f]	10-16-1859	104
" , Margaret [m]	10-16-1859	104
" , Mary	02-16-1858	76
" , Phil [f]	01-16-1860	111
" , T. (Thos.) [f]	02-16-1858	76
" , Thos. [f]	02-16-1858	76
Flaherty, James	01-03-1859	91
" , James [f]	01-03-1859	91
" , Joanna [m]	01-03-1859	91
Flanagan, Barbara [m]	02-17-1859	94
" , Mary[Joanna Mary]	02-17-1859	94
" , Mike (Michael)[f]	02-17-1859	94
Fleshman, Chs.(Charles)	05-31-1870	277
" (Hoke),E.J.		
(Elizabeth J.)	05-31-1870	277
" , H.(Harrison)[f]	05-31-1870	277
" , John A.	07-26-1860	116
" , P.(Palmira) [m]	05-31-1870	277
" , Sarah [m]	07-26-1860	116
" , Simon [f]	07-26-1860	116
Flinn, Mary [m]	10-21-1859	106
" , Michael	10-21-1859	106
" , Michael [f]	10-21-1859	106
Fogel(Nagle),George(Geo.)	02-14-1856	60
Fogle, A.(Adam) [f]	09-14(23)-1867	213
" , B.(Barbara)	09-14(23)-1867	213
" , M. (Mary) [m]	09-14(23)-1867	213

Name	Date	Page
Foley (Connel,O'Connel),		
May (Mary)	08-13-1857	70
Folk's, Wm. [PL]	12-31-1872	332
Ford (Levisay), [Mrs.]		
Mary	05-13-1863	141
Forely (Dunnahoo),		
Ellen [m]	12-17-1859	107
Fouly, Catharine	01-03-1859	91
" , Ellen [m]	01-03-1859	91
" , Martin [b/g]	01-03-1859	91
" , Patrick [f]	01-03-1859	91
Fountaine, Alexander[f]	09-02(03)-1870	279
" , Sally	09-02(03)-1870	279
Fox, C. (Chs.) [f]	01-01(04)-1869	241
" , E. (Eliza) [m]	01-01(04)-1869	241
" , Jno. (John)	01-01(04)-1869	241
" , Patrick [w]	01-01(04)-1869	242
Francis (Fitzgerald),		
E. (Ellen) [m]	02-16-1858	76
Franklin, A.(Annie)[m]	09-20(22)-1869	253
" , B. (? Jesse) [f]	09-20(22)-1869	253
" , E.H.(Elizabeth H.)	09-20(22)-1869	253
Fraser, A.(Alexander)[f]	02-22-1872	311
" , George	02-22-1872	311
" , J. (Jennett)[m]	02-22-1872	311
Freeman (Fremon), Alex.		
(Alexander)(Elexander)	03-16(18)-1869	246
" , James	12-26-1872	331
" , M. (Mincy) [m]	12-26-1872	331
" , P. (Patsey) [m]	03-16(18)-1869	246
" , P. (Peter) [f]	03-16(18)-1869	256
" , W. (Winka) [f]	12-26-1872	331
Fremon(Freeman),Alex.		
(Alexander)(Elexander)	03-16(18)-1869	246
French, Julia	03-30-1871	292
Fridley (Fridly),Chas.		
(Charles)	08-02-1859	101
" (Armontrout),Delila[m]	06-08-1858	82
" , E.(Elizabeth) [m]	05-13-1858	80
" (Fridly),E.(Elizabeth)		
[m]	08-02-1859	101

Name	Date	Page
Fridley, E.(Elizabeth)		
[m]	10-14-1869	256
[m]	12-31-1872	332
" , G.F.(George F.)	10-14-1869	257
" (Fridly), Gideon[f]	08-23-1855	47
" , Hanna L.(Hannah)[m]	02-16-1857	64
" , Isaac [f]	05-13-1858	80
" (Fridly), Isaac [f]	08-02-1859	101
" (Fridly),J.(Jesse)	05-24(26)-1868	224
" , J. (John) [f]	11-24(26)-1868	235
" (Fridly), J.A. (Julia A.)	05-24(26)-1868	224
" , James	02-16-1857	64
" , J.L.(Jacob Lewis)	11-24(26)-1868	235
" , Jno.(John) [f]	02-16-1857	64
" , Jno. [f]	08-13-1872	320
" (Fridly), Jno.W. (John W.)	12-31-1872	332
" , John [f]	06-21(23)-1864	141
" (Fridly), Margaret	08-23-1855	47
" , Maria F.(Mariah F.)	05-13-1858	80
" , Mary J.(Mary Jane)	06-21(23)-1864	141
" , N. (Nelson) [f]	10-14-1869	256
[f]	12-31-1872	332
" , Nancy E.	08-13-1872	320
" , Nelson [w]	04-19-1855	46
" (Bennet) (King), Phebe [m]	04-19-1855	45
" , R. (Ruth) [m]	11-24(26)-1868	235
" (Fridly), Ruth [m]	08-23-1855	47
" , Ruth (Rutha)[m]	06-21(23)-1864	141
" , Ruth [m]	08-13-1872	320
" (Fridly), S.(Sampson)	05-24(26)-1868	224
" , Wm. H.	06-08-1858	82
Fridly (Fridley),Chas. (Charles)	08-02-1859	101
" , Catharine	03-02-1868	271
" , Delilah [m]	03-02-1868	271
" , Gideon [w]	10-17-1855	47
Fry, Christopher	11-13-1862	139

Name	Date	Page

Name	Date	Page
Garibaldia,Therissa[m]	09-11-1862	138, 139
Gaugh, Catharine [m]	08-07-1860	116
" , James	08-07-1860	116
" , John [f]	08-07-1860	116
Gay, Mary (May)	06-28-1870	291
" , Mary (?May) [m]	06-28-1870	291
" , Mustoe [f]	06-28-1870	291
George, Hey (Henry)	04-02-1870	273
" , R. (Ruth) [m]	04-02-1870	273
" , W. (William) [f]	04-02-1870	273
Gibbon (Gibbons)(Kendall)		
(Kindle),Sarah	11-11-1858	88
Gibson, C. (Charlotte)	12-02-1869	263, 264
" (Gilson),Elizabeth[m]	01-20 1863	177
" (Gilson),Nicholas[f]	01-20-1863	177
" (Gilson),Tazewell M.	01-20-1863	177
Gilbert, A.(Alcy) [m]	06-04(07)-1865	155
" , A. H. [f]	12-21(24)-1868	238
" , Alice [m]	09-20-1855	48
" , Andrew J.(Nelson J.)	09-20-1855	48, 49
" , D. (David) [f]	06-04(07)-1865	155
" , David [f]	09-20-1855	48
" , David L. [w]	12-03(06)-1868	236
[w]	12-17-1868	237
" , G.H. (George H.)	06-04(07)-1865	155
" , James C. [w]	06-04(07)-1865	155
" , J.C.(James		
Clarington)	12-21(24)-1868	238
" , Nelson J.(Andrew J.)	09-20-1855	48
" , S. (Susan) [m]	12-21(24)-1868	238
Gillaspie (Bennett),E.F.		
(Eliza F.)	01-01-1867 [MR]	177
" , James P. [w]	01-18(28)(27)-1869	243
" (Gillespie),Jas.P.		
(James Polk)	11-24-1870	318
" , J. H. (James H.)[f]	04-02-1867	202
" , J.W. (James William)	04-02-1867	201
" , M. (Mary) [m]	01-01-1867	177
" , M. (Margarett)[m]	04-02-1867	202
" , Polly [m]	01-17-1860	110
" , S. (Samuel) [f]	01-01-1867 [MR]	177

Name	Date	Page
Gillaspie, Samuel [f]	01-17-1860	110
Gillespie (Gillaspie),		
Eliza F.(M̶a̶r̶t̶h̶a̶)		
(Eliza Francis)	01-17-1860	110
" , J. (Jane) [m]	10-12-1869	256
" , J.K. (John K.)[f]	10-12-1869	256
" , Mary [m]	11-24-1872	318
" , Sam'l. [f]	11-24-1872	318
" , W.F.(William F.)	10-12-1869	256
Gillham, Elizabeth		
Patterson [Eliz		
Hubbard] [m]	12-17-1857	74
Gilliam, E.D.(Eliza D.)[m]	06-23-1869	250
" , Wm. A.	06-23-1869	249
" , Wm. A. [f]	06-23-1869	250
Gilliland, Agness(Egness)	12-20-1855	52
" (Gilleland), H.(Hazle)	11-12-1868	234
" , Henry G. [f]	11-15(17)-1870	286
" (Gilleland),J.		
(Joseph) [f]	11-12-1868	234
" , Jane H.	11-15(17)-1870	286
" , Jos.(Joseph) [f]	08-03-1858 [CL]	84
" , Lucy J.	08-03-1858 [CL]	84
" (Gilleland),M.		
(Mahala) [m]	11-12-1868	234
" , Mahaletts (Mahala)		
(?Matilda) [m]	08-03-1858 [CL]	84
" , Maria [m]	11-15(17)-1870	286
" , Selina (Selena E.)	12-20-1855	52
Gilliland's (Gillilland's),		
Shepherd [PL]	11-15(17)-1870	286
" , Wm. [PL]	06-10(13)-1865	156
Gilson(Gibson),Elizabeth[m]	01-20-1863	177
" (Gibson),Nicholas[f]	01-20-1863	177
" (Gibson),Tazewell M.	01-20-1863	177
Given, A. (Adam)	09-11(12)-1865	159
" ,[Capt.] A. [w]	05-04(05)-1868	223
" , A.C.(Araminta C.)	11-02-1870	281
" , C.(Catherine)	09-11(12)-1865	160
" , C. (Catharine)[m]	11-02-1870	281

Name	Date	Page
Given, Catharine		
[Catharine Bowyer][m]07-26-1860		116
" , David G.(D.G.)[f] 07-26-1860		116
" , D. G.(David G.) 09-11(12)-1865		160
" , D. G.(David G.)[f] 11-02-1870		281
" , Mary (Mary Ann) 07-26-1860		116
Given's, [Capt.] A.[PL] 11-02-1870		281
" , David G. [PL]	01-01-1867 [MR]	177
Givens, A.(Adam) [f]	01-11-1871	287
" , A. F. [f]	10-28-1869	260
" , Catharine [m]	01-29-1863	178
[Chatharin (?Jane)]		
" , David [f]	01-29-1863	178
" , Henry	01-11-1871	286
" , Isabella Frances	01-29-1863	178
" , J.W.(James W.)	10-28-1869	260
" , M. (Mary) [m]	01-11-1871	287
" , P.A.(Parnelia A.)[m]	10-28-1869	260
Gladwell, Lucy Ann	05-19-1863	141
" , Sarah [m]	05-19-1863	141
" (Davis), Sarah	03-20-1871	292
" , Valentine [f]	05-19-1863	141
Gleason, Michael [f]	12-20-1855	52
" , Nancy [m]	12-20-1855	52
" , Paul	12-20-1855	52
[w]	10-12(14)-1868	230
Goff, H.(Harriet) [m]	06-04-1868	225
" , Harriett (Harriet)[m]03-01-1866[MR]		181
" (Groff), John [f]	06-15-1858 [CL]	83
" , Julia A.(Julia Ann) 03-01-1866 [MR]		181
" (Groff),Manerva A.		
(Minerva A.)	06-15-1858 [CL]	83
" , Rebecca	06-04-1868	225
Goff's, Jno. [PL]	03-01-1866 [MR]	181
Gofney, Thos. [w]	12-17-1859	107
Gooch, Eliz.(Elizabeth		
M.) [m]	03-21-1872	313
" , Garrett G.	03-21-1872	313
" , Thomson [f]	03-21-1872	313
Gorman, Ann (Ame)	01-09-1862	135
" , Bernard [f]	01-09-1862	135

Name	Date	Page
Griffith, Maggie E.		
(Margaret Elizabeth)	02-15-1871	292
" , Mary A.	03-20(30)-1865	152
" , M.C.(Martha C.)	12-22-1869 [MR]	266
" , M.V.(Mahaleth V.)		
(Mahalaeth Va.)	10-26-1871	302
" , Nicy [m]	02-20-1862	136
" , Orlando [f]	09-31(30)-1862	140
" , R. (Robert) [f]	05-10(17)-1865	153
" , S. (Sarah) [m]	05-10(17)-1865	153
" , S.J.(Sallie Jane)	12-09(19)-1865	170
" , Wesley [f]	02-20-1862	136
Grimes, James	01-02-1872	306
Groff (Goff),Harriet[m]	06-15-1858 [CL]	83
" (Goff), John [f]	06-15-1858 [CL]	83
" (Goff),Minerva A.		
(Manerva A.)	06-15-1858 [CL]	83
Grose, Chris(Christeana)[m]	01-03-1856	53
" , Elizabeth		
(Elisabeth) [m]	12-17-1857	74
" , Hy (Henry) [f]	12-17-1857	74
" , Jacob	01-03-1856	53
" , Jacob [f]	01-03-1856	53
" , Jacob, [Jr.'s][PL]	01-03-1856	53
" , Wm.A. (William)	12-17-1857	74
Grubbs, M.A.(Mary A.)	08-05(15)-1867	211, 212
Gunter, John [f]	01-17-1872	308
" , Sallie	01-17-1872	308
Guy, Eliza	09-10-1862	138
" , Mary [m]	11-26-1868	240
[m]	09-10-1862	138
" , Matilda Va.		
(Matilda Virginia)	11-26-1868	240
" , William [f]	11-26-1868	240
" , Wm.(William) [f]	09-10-1862	138
Hackney, Albert	10-01-1872 [MR]	321
" , Fleming [f]	10-01-1872 [MR]	321, 322
" , M.(Mary) [m]	10-01-1872 [MR]	321, 322
Hagerty(Hegerty),Mary[m]	02-17-1867	194

Name	Date	Page
Hagerty, Michael	02-17-1867	194
" (Hegerty), Peter[f]	02-17-1867	194
Hall, H.A.(Harriett		
Ann)	06-04-1867 [MR]	207
" , H.L.(Henry Lewis)	09-26-1865	146, 147
" , J. (Jane) [m]	10-14-1869	258
" , J.H.(Joseph H.)[f]	09-26-1865	146
" , J.H.(Jos. H.)		
(Joseph H.)[f]	06-04-1867 [MR]	207
" , J.M.(James M.)	10-14-1869	258
" , Joseph H. [w]	12-17-1857	74
" , R.A.(Reuben A.)[f]	10-14-1869	258
" , S.P.(Sarah P.)[m]	09-26-1865	146
" , S.P.[Sarah (?P or		
T.)] [m]	06-04-1867 [MR]	207
Ham, E.(Elizabeth)		
(Elisabeth) [m]	07-17-1867 [MR]	210, 211
" , E.(Elizabeth)[m]	12-15-1869	264
" , H.A.(Hester Ann)	07-17-1867 ¼MR]	210
" , Hester [m]	08-07-1860	116
" , Martin [f]	08-07-1860	116
" , Nancy	08-07-1860	116
" (Hamilton),R.		
(Rachel) [m]	02-16-1860	110
" , R.E.(Rachel E.)	12-15-1869	264
" , W.(William) [f]	12-15-1869	264
" , Wm.(William)[f]	07-17-1867 [MR]	210
(?Hamer)(?Hamun)(?Hanna)		
(?Harmon),Mary [m]	11-17-1858	89
" (?Hamun)(?Hanna)		
(?Harmon),Thos.[f]	11-17-1858	89
Hamilton, A. P. [w]	11-01-1871	303
" , A. T. [w]	11-24-1870	318
" , James [f]	02-16-1860	110
" , James A. [w]	07-03(08)-1868	227
" , Jno. (John) [f]	11-01-1871	302, 303
" , Julia F.(Julie F.)	11-01-1871	302, 303
" , L. J. [m]	10-27-1870	281
" , M.(Margaret) [m]	03-11-1870	273
[m]	03-16-1870	273
" , M.F. (Mary F.)	10-27-1870	280, 281

Name	Date	Page
Hamilton (Ham), R.		
(Rachel) [m]	02-16-1860	110
" , R. (Robert)[f]	03-11-1870	273
[f]	03-16-1870	273
" , Ro.(Robert)	03-16-1870	273
" , Sarah [m]	11-01-1871	302
" , W.H.(Wm.H.)[f]	10-27-1870	281
" , Zac. (Zaceriah)	03-11-1870	272
Hamler (Hamlet),Henry[f]	06-08-1858	82
" (Hamlet),Martha		
(Marthay)	06-08-1858	82
" (Hamlet), Mary [m]	06-08-1858	82
Hamlett, H.(Henry)[f]	03-12(13)-1867	200
[f]	01-15(28)-1868	219
" , Henry [f]	10-10(11)-1866	189
" , Jas.A. [James		
(?Andrew)]	10-10(11)-1866	189
" , M.(Maryetta)[m]	03-12(13)-1867	200
" , M. (Mary) [m]	01-15(28)-1868	219
" , Polly [m]	10-10(11)-1866	189
" , S.A.[Sarah (? L.		
or ? S.]	01-15(28)-1868	219
" , Wm.H.(William H.)	03-12(13)-1867	200
Handley, Amanda [w]	05-30-1865	164
" , Mary F.	02-08-1855	45
" (Mason), Mary F.	02-08-1855	45
" , Robert W.[bil]	06-10-1857	67
Handly (Hanoly)(Shanklin),		
Elizabeth [m]	04-25-1855	46
Hanes, L.W.(Lemuel W.)[f]	11-03(05)-1868	233
" , M.A.(Mary A.)[m]	11-03(05)-1868	233
" , W.J.(William J.)	11-03(05)-1868	232
Hanes's, [Mrs.] [PL]	12-15-1869	264
Hanger (Surber),Sally[m]	02-25-1858	79
(?Hanna)(?Harmon)(?Hamer)		
(?Hamun),Rosanna	11-17-1858	89
Hannassy,Catharine	06-17-1860	114, 115
" , Mary [m]	06-17-1860	115
" , Patrick [f]	06-17-1860	115
Hannon (Honnon),Elizabeth		
[m]	04-05-1855	51

Name	Date	Page
Hannon (Honnon),James A.	04-05-1855	51
Hanoly (Handly)(Shanklin),		
Elizabeth [m]	04-25-1855	46
" (Handly),Harrison	04-25-1855	46
" (Handly), John [f]	04-25-1855	46
Hansbarger(Hansberger),		
Elisabeth(Elizabeth)	11-22-1870	291
" , Lizzie [w]	08-13(12)-1869	253
" , Sebastian [f]	11-22-1870	292
Hardy, E.F.(Elizabeth		
Frances)	10-15(18)-1866	189
" , Jno. (John) [gf]	08-24-1858	86
" , Sopha(Sophia M.)[m]	10-15(18)-1866	189
Hargan(Hogan)(Barrett)		
(Barritt),Mary [m]	02-01-1858	76
" , Thos.(Thomas)[f]	10-15(18)-1866	189
Harington, Jas.(James)	12-19-1872	328
Harlan(Hollerin),		
John (Jno.)	08-15-1858	85
Harlow, Lucy [m]	07-06-1857	67
" , Lucy M.	07-06-1857	67
" , Thos.(Thomas)[f]	07-06-1857	67
Harman(Harmon),Andr.		
(Andrew) [f]	03-12(28)-1860	112
" (Harmon), Anthony[f]	01-25-1872	309
" , Jno. R. [w]	01-09-1872	307
" (Harmon)(Hornbarger),		
Maria L.	01-25-1872	309
" , Maria L. C. S.		
(Maria Louisa		
Catharine Sarah)	03-12(28)-1860	112
" , Mary [m]	07-19-1871	298
" , Peter [f]	07-19-1871	298
" , Sarah [m]	03-12(28)-1860	112
" (Harmon), Sarah [m]	01-25-1872	309
" , Shelton R.		
(Shelton Raglan)	07-19-1871	298
Harmon's, A. [PL]	02-09-1865	151
Harman's, Anthony [PL]	01-09-1872	307
" , Shelton [PL]	07-25-1872	319

[Name and Date Index: Part (2) - (Continued)]

Name	Date	Page
Harmon(Harman), Andr. (Andrew) [f]	03-12(28)-1860	112
" (Harman), A.P.(Arrena P.)(Arreny P.)	10-01(02)(03)-1867	215,216
" , Jas. A.(James A.)	10-19-1857	71
" , Mary [m]	10-19-1857	71
" ?Hanna)(?Hamun)(?Hamer), Mary [m]	11-17-1858	89
" (Harman), Mary [m]	03-19(28)-1866	182
" (Harman), Mary J.	03-19(28)-1866	182
" (Harman),P.(Polly)[m]	10-01(02)(03)-1867	215
" , Peter [f]	10-19-1857	71
" (?Hanna)(?Hamer) (?Hamun),Rosanna	11-17-1858	89
" , Shelton [w]	05-24-1861	124
" (?Hanna)(?Hamer) (?Hamun), Thos.[f]	11-17-1858	89
" (Harman),Thos. (Thomas) [f]	03-19(28)-1866	182
[f]	10-01(02)(03)-1867	215,216
Harmon's, Frances [PL]	03-19(28)-1866	182
Harnes's, [Mrs.] C.[PL]	10-20-1870	286
Harrigan (Horrigan) (Connel),Joanna	02-(?)-1859	97
" (Horrigan), Peter[f]	02-(?)_1859	97
Harington (Conner), Joana (Johana)	12-29-1860	119
Harrington (Harington), David [f]	12-29-1860	119
" , Dennis	06-23-1859	98, 99
" , Jeremiah [f]	06-23-1859	98
" , Joana	06-23-1859	98
" (Harington),Johana[m]	12-29-1860	119
" (Harington),M.(Minor) [f]	12-19-1872	328
" , Margarit(Margaret) [m]	06-23-1859	98
" (Harington), S. (Susan) [m]	12-19-1872	328
Harris (Sullivan),Betsey (Betsy) [m]	04-25-1858	80

[Name and Date Index: Part (2) - (Continued)]

Name	Date	Page
Haynes, M.(Mary) [m]	09-04(07)-1865	157
[m]	09-04(07)-1865	158
" , M.(May)(?Mary)[m]	04-27(28)-1868	221, 222
" , M.A.(Margarette A.)	11-12-1868	234
" , Mary E.	03-12-1861 [CL]	134
" , M.E.(Mary E.)[m]	12-26(27)-1865	170
" (Lemon),Millerd R. (Mildred R.)	09-02-1855	49
" , M.S.(M.J.S.)(Mary Jane Sarah)	06-26(23)-1868	225, 226
" , S.A.(Sarah Ann)	09-04(07)-1865	157
" (Bowyer), Sarah	04-27(28)-1868	221, 222
" , Susan L.	12-09-1863	180
" , W. A. [w]	06-26(23)-1868	226
" , W.H.(William Henry) [f]	12-26(27)-1865	170
" , W.H.(William H.) (Wm.) [f]	11-12-1868	234
" , William H.(Wm.H.) [Maj.] [f]	12-09-1863	180
" , Wm. H.(William H.) [f]	03-12-1861 [CL]	134
" , Wm. H. [f]	09(08)-02-1855	49
" , Wm.H.(William H.) [Jr.] [f]	02-27(28)-1867	197
Haynes's, H.G. [PL]	01-16(17)-1867	196
" , [Maj.] [PL]	07-03(08)-1868	226, 227
Hayse, Dephia(Delphia)[m]	10-07-1859	108
" , James [f]	10-07-1859	108
" , John J.	10-07-1859	108
Hayslett, E.(Ezekiel)[f]	07-01(16)-1869	251
" , N. (Nancy) [m]	07-01(16)-1869	251
" (Miller), S. J. (Sarah J.)	07-01(16)-1869	251
Hederman (Hedeman), Ellen	01-08-1861	123
" , Nancy [m]	01-08-1861	123
" , Thomas [f]	01-08-1861	123
Helmantoler's, Gordon[PL]	03-22-1855	51
Helmantoller(Helmentoller), D.M.(Delolah M.)	08-27-1865[MR]	148

Name	Date	Page
Hepler, A.(Abeshaby)[m]	12-21(24)-1868	239
" , Absha (Abasha)[m]	02-14-1856	54
" , B. (Betsy) [m]	09-25(27)-1865	166
" , B.(Bashaba)[m]	05-31-1870	276
" , Basha [m]	01-31-1861	124
" , Benj. F. [w]	03-02-1868	271
" , Bersheba [m]	03-31-1859	95
" , Betshe (Bathsheba)		
[m]	02-(ØZ)21-1856	54
" (Lone), Betsy		
(Betsey)	10-02(05)-1865	167
" , D. (David) [f]	12-21(24)-1868	239
[f]	05-31-1870	276
" , David [f]	02-(ØZ)21-1856	54
[f]	02-14-1856	54
[f]	03-31-1859	95
[f]	01-31-1861	124
" , David [w]	08-23-1871	300
" , David B.	06-12-1872	317
" , E.(Emmarillia)	10-10(15)-1868	230
" , Elias	09-25(27)-1865	166
" , Harriet S.	06-19-1856	55
" , J. (John) [f]	09-25(27)-1865	166
[f]	10-10(15)-1868	230
" , Jabes M.(Iabes M.)	02-27-1857	64, 65
" , Jno. (John) [f]	06-19-1856	55 •
[f]	04-30-1857	66, 67
[f]	08-23-1871	299, 300
[f]	06-12-1872	317
" , John [f]	01-31-1861	124
" , John A.	03-31-1859	95, 96
[w]	02-14-1856	54
" , Js. Wm.(James		
William)	05-31-1870	276
" , Julia A. H.		
(Julia A. R.)		
(Julia Anna Rebecca)	04-30-1857	66, 67
" , Margaret [m]	08-23-1871	299
" , Mary I.(Mary		
Isabella)	08-23-1871	299
" , Mary Jane	01-31-1861	124

[Name and Date Index: Part (2) - (Continued)]

Name	Date	Page
Hepler, Peggy [m]	06-12-1872	317
" , Rebecca A. (Rebecca Ann)	02-(Ø2)21-1856	54
" (Sively),Rebecca Z.	08-11-1870	285
" , Robert	01-31-1861	124
" , S.(Sarah) [m]	10-10(15)-1868	230
" , Sallie [m]	01-31-1861	124
" , S.E.(Sarah E.)	12-21(24)-1868	239
" , Sarah [m]	06-19-1856	55
[m]	04-30-1857	66
" , Susan	02-14-1856	54
Herbert,D.(Daniel)[f]	12-26-1872	331
" , E. (Eliza) [m]	12-26-1872	331
" , H.C.(Henry C.)	12-30-1869 [MR]	267, 168
" , L.(Luvenia) [m]	12-30-1869 [MR]	267
" ,Levina(Lavina)[m]	11-06-1856	63
" ,Lureua(Luvena)[m]	02-20-1862	136
" , Margaret S.	02-20-1862	136
" , Phil	12-26-1872	331
" , Sarah A.	11-06-1856	62
" , W. (Wm.) [f]	12-30-1869 [MR]	267
" ,Wm.(William)[f]	11-06-1856	63
" , Wm. [JP]	....	78
" , Wm. [f]	02-20-1862	136, 137
Hickman, Fred A.(F.A.) (Frederick A.)	08-04-1859	104
" , Pleasant [f]	08-04-1859	104
" , R.(Rebecca)[f]	08-04-1859	104
Hill,C.G.(Clifton G.)[f]	10-28-1869	260
" , E.(Emaline)[m]	04-29-1870	274
" , F. (Fran) [f]	04-29-1870	274
" , Gabrael [f]	08-13(12)-1869	252
" ,M.R.(Mary R.)[m]	10-28-1869	260
" , Nancy [m]	08-13(12)-1869	252
" ,Wm.(William)	04-29-1870	274
" , Wm.E.(William E.)	10-28-1869	260
" , Wyatt	08-13(12)-1869	252
Hilliany(Hilliary),C.A. (Catharine Adalade)	04-02-1867	202
" (?Hillary),J.B.[f]	04-02-1867	202

Name	Date	Page
Hilliany(?Hillary), S.		
(Susan) [m]	04-02-1867	202
Hillary, J.B.,[M.D.][f]	04-27-1870	275
" , M.S.(Mary S.)[m]	04-27-1870	275
" , Rose	04-27-1870	275
" , Wm. H. [w]	04-27-1870	275
Hinton, Peter [w]	06-30-1859	103
Hippert, G.W.(Geo.W.)[f]	04-14-1870	274
" , J.D.(John D.)	04-14-1870	274
" , S.A.(Sarah Ann)[m]	04-14-1870	274
Hix, Arch(Archibald)[f]	06-30-1859	103
" ,Jane [m]	06-30-1859	103
" , Wm.(William)	06-30-1859	103
Hobbs, J. J. [DC]	05-25-1871	295
[DC]	06-29-1871	297
[DC]	09-05-1872	320
Hogan, J.(Joannah)[m]	05-26(19)-1870	276
" ,J.(Joseph) [f]	05-26(19)-1870	276
" , Mary	05-26(19)-1870	275
" (Hargan)(Barrett?)		
(?Barritt),Mary[m]	02-01-1858	76
Hoilman (Hoylman)(Mayse),		
N. (Nancy)	12-13(16)-1868	236
" , Simon [w]	06-18-1861	129
Hoke, Barbary F.		
(Barbary Francis)	06-23(28)-1866	187
" , C.(Christopher)[f]	03-24(26)-1868	221
[f]	05-31-1870	277
" , C.(Catharine)[m]	03-24(26)-1868	221
[m]	12-03(06)-1868	236
[m]	12-17-1868	237
[m]	10-14-1869	258
[m]	05-10-1870	277
" , Catharine [m]	06-23(28)-1866	187
" , Catherine		
(Catharine) [m]	11-05-1868	233
" (Fleshman), E. J.		
(Elizabeth J.)	05-31-1870	277
" , Ellen	12-17-1868	237
" , H.A.(Henry Alexander)	03-24(26)-1868	221

Name	Date	Page
Hoke, James(James Horam)	11-05-1868	233
" , Josiah [f]	10-27-1859	105
" , L. T. R.	10-14-1869	258
" , M. (Malinda)[m]	03-24(26)-1868	221
" , Marg.(Margaret)[m]	10-27-1859	105
" , M.C.(Mary Catharine)	03-24(26)-1868	221
" , N. (Nancy)[m]	05-31-1870	277
" , N.L. (Nancy L.)	12-03(06)-1868	236
" (Hok), R.J.(Rebecca J.)(Rebebba J.)	05-10-1870	276, 277
" , Sarah E.	10-27-1859	105
" , W.(Wm.)(William)[f]	10-14-1869	258
" , William [f]	06-23(28)-1866	187
[f]	11-05-1868	233
" , Wm.(William)[f]	03-24(26)-1868	221
" , Wm. [Jr.] [f]	12-03(06)-1868	236
" , Wm.(William)[Jr.] [f]	12-17-1868	237
" , Wm.(William) [f]	05-10-1870	277
Hoke's, Wm. [PL]	07-11-1861	134
Holland,C.(Catherine)[m]	01-01(04)-1869	241
" , Daniel [f]	02-14-1869	244
" , James	02-14-1869	244
" , Mary	01-01(04)-1869	241
" , P. (Patrick)[f]	01-01(04)-1869	241
" , Sarah [m]	02-14-1869	244
Hollerin (Harlan),Jno.	08-15-1858	85
" (Hollorin),Jno.[f]	08-15-1858	85
" (Hollorin)(F~~eary~~), Mary [m]	08-15-1858	85
Holloway (Holoway),Lewis P.(L.)(L.P.) [CC]	· · · · · · · · · · · · · · ·	83,84,86, 90,91,93, 98,102, 108, 115, 121, 124
Holloway, Wm. G. [DC]	· · · · · · · · · · · · · · · · · ·	121, 122, 123, 124,
125,126,127,128,129,130,131,132,133,134,135 136, 137, 138		

- 432 -

Name	Date	Page
Holmes, James [f]	01-11-1859	92
" ,Martha A.(Martha Ann) [m]	01-11-1859	92
" , Martha J. [Martha (?Jane)]	01-11-1859	92
" , Martin W. [w]	08-05(15)-1867	212
Holms, Ann	05-19-1867	198
" , J.C.(John C.)	09-22(23)-1865	166
" , J.H.(James H.)[f]	09-22(23)-1865	166
" , M.A.(Martha W.)[m]	09-22(23)-1865	166
" , Mauldn(Matilda)[m]	05-19-1867	198
" , Lewis [f]	05-19-1867	198
Honnon(Hannon),Elizabeth [m]	04-05-1865	51
" (Hannon),James A.	04-05-1855	51
Hook, Agness	03-22-1855	51
" , Beale	05-26(27)-1868	224
" , E.(Elizabeth)[m]	05-26(27)-1868	224
" , Elias [f]	03-22-1855	51
" , Madison [w]	02-01(26)-1855	44
" , Nancy [m]	03-22-1855	51
" , S. (Stephen)[f]	05-26(27)-1868	224
(?Horace), Geo. W.[w]	07-10-1867 [MR]	210
Hornbarger, Daniel [f]	03-12(28)-1860	112
" , Daniel L.	03-12(28)-1860	112
" (Harman)(Harmon), Maria L.	01-25-1872	309
" , Nancy [m]	03-12(28)-1860	112
" (Hornberger)(Hernberger), William P.	03-11-1861	125
Hornberger(Hornbarger), Daniel [f]	03-11-1861	125
" (Hornbarger),Nancy[m]	03-11-1861	125
Howard, Eliz.(Elizabeth) [m]	01-29-1857	66
" , Eliza J.(Eliza Jane)	07-25-1872	319
" , Gaston	02-23(25)-1867	194, 195
" ,Geo.(George) [f]	02-23(25)-1867	194, 195
[f]	07-25-1872	319

- 433 -

Name	Date	Page
Howard, Polly [m]	02-23(25)-1867	194, 195
" [m]	07-25-1872	319
" , John [f]	01-29-1857	66
" , John C.	01-29-1857	66
Hoy, Charles F.	05-30-1854	41
" , Elizabeth [m]	05-30-1854	41
" , Zachariah [f]	05-30-1854	41
Hoylman, A.(Addison)[f]	12-22-1869	265
" , J.B.(John Brenard)		
(John Breward?)	12-22-1869	265
" , M. (Malinda) [m]	12-22-1869	265
" , Mary [m]	04-13-1859	96
" , Simon (Limon)[f]	04-13-1859	96
" , Wm.(William T.)		
(Wm.T.)(Wm.F)	04-13-1859	96
Hubbard, Eliz.(Elizabeth		
Patterson Gillham)[m]	12-17-1857	74
" , Maria L.[Maria		
Luemily(LuEmily)]	12-17-1857	74
" , Sam'l.(Samuel W.)		
(Sam'l.W.)(S.W.)[f]	12-17-1857	74, 75
" , Samuel E. [s]	12-17-1857	74
Huddleston,[A.(?I.?J.)]		
(A.J.) [f]	12-22-1870	283
" (Huddleson),Abraham[f]	07-31-1856	57
" , Abraham J. [f]	03-22-1855	50, 51
" , A.J.(Abraham J.)[f]	07-17-1867 [MR]	210
" , A. J. [f]	12-05(06)-1871	305
" , David	03-22-1855	50
" , E.A.(Elizabeth Ann)	12-22-1870	283
" , G.W.(George W.)	07-17-1867 [MR]	210
" , Joana [m]	12-05(06)-1871	305
" , L. (Leamah) [m]	07-17-1867 [MR]	210
" , L. Leah [m]	12-22-1870	283
" , Leah [m]	03-22-1855	50, 51
" (Huddleson),Leah [m]	07-31-1856	57
" , Nancy E.	12-05(06)-1871	305
" (Huddleson),Sarah	07-31-1856	57
Huff, L. M. [w]	02-25-1858	80
Huffman, Alfred	09-23-1859	106

Name	Date	Page
Huffman, Andr.(Andrew)[f]	09-23-1859	106
" , Betsy (Betsey)[m]	09-23-1859	106
" , Geo.	11-14-1856	62
" , James	11-06-1856	62, 63
" , Soloman [f]	11-14-1856	62
[f]	11-06-1856	62
" , Susan [m]	11-14-1856	62
[m]	11-06-1856	62
Hughes, Ellen [m]	01-03-1870	269
" , E.W.(Emily W.)[m]	11-20(30)-1871	304
" , Jas. H.(James H.)	11-02-1871	303
" , Jno. G. [f]	11-20(30)-1871	304
" , M. (Martha) [m]	11-02-1871	303
" , Ro. (Robert) [f]	11-02-1871	303
" , Robert (Robbert)	01-03-1870	269
" , Wm. M.	11-20(30)-1871	304
Humphries, A.(Anderson)[f]	08-28-1869	254
" , Almyra V.(A.V.)	12-31-1855	59
" , C.(Caroline)[m]	05-24(26)-1858	224
" , C.A.(Charlotte A.)	05-24(26)-1868	224
" , Chas. K.(Charles K.)	08-02-1859	101
" , Davis M.(David M.)	04-19-1864	145
" , D. M. [w]	02-08(11)-1867	192
" , E. (Eunice)	11-24(26)-1868	235
" , Eunice [m]	02-01(26)-1855	44
" , F.M.(Ferdinand M.)	08-28-1869	254
" , Granville	08-02-1859	101
" , H. (Harvey)	08-20-1868 [MR]	227
" , Harvey [w]	08-02-1859	101
" , H. Maria [m]	10-22-1868	232
" , Henry	09-16-1858	86
	08-09-1866	187
" , J. (Jessee)	11-24(26)-1868	235
" , J.C.(Jennetta Catharine)	11-24(26)-1868	235
" , Jesse [f]	02-01(26)-1855	44
" , Jessee [f]	12-31-1855	59
" , Logan S.	02-01(26)-1855	44
" , Louisa J.(Louisa Jane)	10-22-1868	232

Name	Date	Page
Humphries (Persinger),		
Martha [m]	08-28-1869	254
" , O. (Oliver) [f]	05-24(26)-1868	224
" , R.(Ruth) [m]	02-13(15)-1866	175
[m]	08-20-1868 [MR]	227
" , Ruth (Ruthy)[m]	09-16-1858	86
[m]	08-02-1859	101
" , Ruth (Rutha) [m]	08-02-1859	101
" , Ruth [m]	08-08-1861	125
[m]	08-09-1866	187
" , Rutha [m]	04-19-1864	145
" , Ruthy [m]	05-18-1858	81
" , Sampson	05-18-1858	81
	08-08-1861	125
	02-13(15)-1866	175
[w]	02-13(15)-1866	175
" , Unice [m]	12-31-1855	59
" , W.(William) [f]	02-13(15)-1866	175
" , William [f]	04-19-1864	145
" , Wm. (William)[f]	05-18-1858	81
[f]	09-16-1858	86
[f]	08-02-1859	101
[f]	08-02-1859	101
" , Wm. [f]	08-08-1861	125
" , Wm. (William)	08-09-1866	187
" , Wm. [f]	08-20-1868 [MR]	227
" , Wm.A. (W.A.) [f]	10-22-1868	232
Humphries's, [Mr.] [PL]	02-16-1871	290
Hunter, E.(Elizabeth)[m]	06-14-1855	46
" , Jno. (John) [f]	10-31-1872	325
" , Margaret	06-14-1855	46
" , Maria	10-31-1872	325
" , Matthew [f]	06-14-1855	46
" , S.(Sarah) [m]	10-31-1872	325
Hurbard, E.(Elizabeth)[m]	10-20-1869	259
" (Hubard), R.H.		
(Robert H.)	10-20-1869	259
' , S.W. (Sam'l.W.)[f]	10-20-1869	259
Hurley, C.(Catharine)[m]	08-30-1869	254
" , H. (Hannora)	08-30-1869	255
" , J. (James [f]	08-30-1869	255

Name	Date	Page
Hurley, J.(John)	08-30-1869	255
" , M. (Mary) [m]	08-30-1869	255
" , T. (Thomas) [f]	08-30-1869	255
Hynes, Bridgett(Bridget)		
[m]	10-07-1861	131
" , Mary	10-07-1861	131
" , Michael [f]	10-07-1861	131
" , Patrick [w]	10-07-1861	131
Irvin (Ervine)(Wall),		
Ann [m]	10-21-1859	106
" (Ervine), Maurice[f]	10-21-1859	106
Irvine, Ann [m]	01-28-1860	120
" (Ervine), Ellen	10-21-1859	106
" , James [f]	01-28-1860	120
" , Margarett	01-28-1860	120
Irvine's, Lucie [PL]	11-04(05)-1869	262
" , Robert (R.) [PL]	10-23-1867	217
Irwin (Irwine),Morris		
(Maurice)	02-07-1861	125, 126
Irwine, Anne (Ane)[m]	02-07-1861	125
" , Jas. (Jammes) [f]	02-07-1861	125
" (Irwin), Maurice		
(Morris)	02-07-1861	125, 126
Jackson, Abel [f]	12-09-1863	180
" , Able (Abel) [f]	05-30-1866	186
" , Ann	03-03-1867 [MR]	198
" , Ben [f]	03-03-1867 [MR]	198
" , E.(Elizabeth)[m]	10-17-1871	301
" , Eliz.(Elizabeth)[m]	05-30-1866	186
" , Elizabeth R.	12-09-1863	180
" , Elizabeth [m]	12-09-1863	180
" , Ellen	05-26-1871	295
" , Emeline(Emiline)[m]	04-16(18)-1872	315
" , Geo.(George)[f]	04-16(18)-1872	315
" , James	04-16(18)-1872	315
" , Jane [m]	01-20-1863	178
" , Minnie [m]	07-25-1869	254
" , Perry	07-25-1869	254
" , Perry [f]	07-25-1869	254

Name	Date	Page
Jackson, Peyton A.		
(Payton A.)	05-30-1866	186
" , Rachel	01-20-1863	177
" , Rosetta [m]	03-03-1867 [MR]	198
" , Sarah [m]	05-26-1871	295
" , Susan	02-14-1869	244
" , Thomas [f]	01-20-1863	178
" , Thos.(Thomas)[f]	05-26-1871	295
" , Thos. (Thomas)	10-17-1871	301
" , Wm. [f]	10-17-1871	301
Jackson's, Crawford [PL]	06-28-1870	291
James, D.(Duesilla)	12-29(30)-1868	240
" , E.(Elizabeth)[m]	12-29(30)-1868	240
[m]	04-29-1870	274, 275
" , M.(Madison) [f]	12-29(30)-1868	240
[f]	04-29-1870	274
" , Rebecca J.		
(Rebecca Jane)	04-29-1870	274
Jarrett,E.(Elizabeth)[m]	04-02-1870	273, 274
" , Jas.(James) [f]	04-02-1870	273, 274
" , V.(Victoria)	04-02-1870	273, 274
(?Jcenhower)(?Janhower)		
(?Jaenhower),F.V.(Francis V.)		
(Frances V.)		
(Francis Virginia)	12-31-1872	332
" (?Janhower), G.		
(George) [f]	12-31-1872	332
" (?Janhower), J.		
(Julia) [m]	12-31-1872	332
Johnson, A.(Allen)[f]	01-11-1871	287
" , A. (Amanda)[m]	11-25-1871	304
" , Alex	12-17(18)-1872	329
" , Ann [m]	10-12-1854	42
[m]	06-04-1857	68
[m]	08-06-1863	178
" , Barney [f]	08-06-1863	178
" , Bernard [f]	06-04-1857	68
[f]	10-12-1854	42
" (Johnston),C. T.[f]	05-30-1866	186
" (Johnston),David	08-03-1858	85
(Dave) [f]		

Name	Date	Page
Johnson, E.(Elizabeth)	12-19(24)-1868	237
" , E. (Ede) [m]	08-31-1871	300
" (Johnston),Eliza[m]	10-17-1858	87
" (Johnston),Elizabeth[m]	08-03-1858	85
" (Johnston),Elizabeth (Eliza) [m]	05-30-1866	186
" (Johnston), Eliza S. (Elisa S.)	08-03-1858	84, 85
" , Geo.(George)[f]	05-02-1871	293
" , Henry	08-06-1863	178
" , Hilery [f]	01-07(03)-1867	199
" , J.(Jabez), [Sr.][f]	12-19(24)-1868	237, 238
" , J.(Jabez),[Jr.]	03-17(24)-1869	247
" , J.(Jabez) [f]	03-17(24)-1869	247
" , J.A.(July Ann)[m]	01-11-1871	287
" , Jabes [f]	05-22(23)-1861	126
" , Jas. T.(James Taylor)	05-02-1871	293, 294
" , J.E. [w/c]	01-27(26)-1871[CLM]	291
" , John [w]	04-30-1857	66, 67
[w]	09-25(27)-1865	167
[w]	04-24(26)-1866	184
" , Jno. (John)	06-04-1857	68
" (Johnston),John S. (Jno. S.) [f]	10-17-1858	87
" , Lewis	05-22(23)-1861	126
" , M. (Maria) [m]	12-19(24)-1868	237
[m]	03-17(24)-1869	247
" , Malinda [m]	01-07(03)-1867	199
" , Maria W. [m]	05-22(23)-1861	126
" , Mary Ann	01-11-1871	287
" , Nancy [m]	05-02-1871	293
" , Peter [f]	11-25-1871	304
" , Philip (Phillip)	10-12-1854	42
" , Richard	01-07(03)-1867	199
" , Sallie	11-25-1871	304
" (Johnston), Solomon	10-17-1858	87
" , T. (Thos.) [f]	08-31-1871	300
" (Johnston), Virginia E.	05-30-1866	186
Johnson's, Philip [PL]	01-11-1871	287

Name	Date	Page

Johnston (Johnson), A.
   (Ann) [m]   09-25(27)-1865   166
" , A. (Ann) [m]   01-16(18)-1866   173
" (Johnson), B.(Barnard)
   (Bernard) [f]   09-25(27)-1865   166, 167
" , B.(Barnard)   01-16(18)-1866   173
" , B.(Barnard) [f]   01-16(18)-1866   173
" , Charlotte(Charlott) 09(08)-30-1865 145
" (Johson), C.T. [f] 05-30-1866   186
" (Johnson), Dave
   (David) [f]   08-03-1858   84, 85
" (Johnson),Eliza [m] 10-17-1858   87
" (Johnson),Elizabeth[m] 08-03-1858   84
" (Johnson),Elizabeth
   (Eliza) [m]   05-30-1866   186
" , Jabez (Jabz) [f] 09-30-1865   145
" (Johnson),Jno. S.
   (John S.) [f]   10-17-1858   87
" (Johnson), M.A.
   (Malinda Ann)   09-25(27)-1865   166
" , Maria [m]   09(08)-30-1865   145
" (Johnson),Solomon 10-17-1858   87
" (Johnson), Virginia E. 05-30-1866   186
Jones, Abel [f]   09-10-1861   126
" , Abraham   09-10-1861   126, 127
" , Chs. (Charles)[f] 03-02(19)-1867 199
" , Chs.A. (Charles A.) 03-02(19)-1867 199
" , Chs.A. (C.A.)[f] 06-13-1872   316
" , E.(Elizabeth) [m] 01-07(10)-1869 242
" , Edward   03-30-1871   292
" , Eliz. (Elisabeth) 10-29-1857   71
" , Elizabeth R.   01-08-1856   53
" , G.W.(Geo. W.)[f] 06-16-1869   249
" , Henry [w]   01-08-1856   53
" , J. (James) [f]   01-07(10)-1869 242
" , J.C.(Josiah C.)[f] 03-02(19)-1867 199, 200
" , John A. [w]   10-03-1861   122
" , John C.(John Charles) 06-13-1872 316
" , Josiah [f]   10-29-1857   71
" , Josiah C. [f]   01-08-1856   53

Name	Date	Page

Name	Date	Page
Karnes, M.(Martha)[m]	12-09(19)-1865	169
" , R.C.(Rebecca C.)	10-12(13)-1868	231
" , S.(Sampson) [f]	10-12(13)-1868	231
" , Sarah [m]	03-22-1855	45
[m]	11-20-1856	62
Karnes's(Carnes's),		
Campbell [PL]	12-04-1862	139, 140
" , C. H. [PL]	09-06-1865	159
Kayser, A.(Addison)[f]	12-28-1869[CLM]	267
" , A.S. [c]	12-17(18)-1872	329
" , E.A.(Eliza A.)[m]	12-28-1869[CLM]	267
" , Jos.A.(Joseph A.)	12-28-1869[CLM]	266, 267
Kean,Cath.A.(Catharine A.) No Mar.Date		
	?02-26-1854[MR]	44
" ,Eliz.D.(Elizabeth		
Dew)	09-24(25)-1866	176
" , Mary P.(Mary Phebe)	05-23-1866	185
" , Rebecca [m]	09-24(25)-1866	176
" , Rebecca (R.B.)[m]	05-23-1866	185
" , Rebecca [m]	No Mar. Date	
	?02-26-1854 [MR]	44
" ,Sam'l.(Samuel)[f]	09-24(25)-1866	176
[f]	05-23-1866	185
[f]	No Mar. Date	
	?02-26-1854 [MR]	44
Keef (Riordan),Eliza		
(Elizabeth)	05-09(14)-1859	98
Kellen(Keller)(Baldwin),		
Eveaeen[(Eveaeen Eveaun)		
(Evance) Ann] Ann[m]	04-04(09)-1857	75
Keller(Kellen)(Baldwin),		
Ann [(Eveaeen Eveaun)		
(Evance)(Eveaeen Ann)]		
[m]	04-04(09)-1857	75
Kelley(KellY),Catharine		
(Cinthia) [m]	03-19-1861	124
" ,Charles [f]	10-22-1872	324
" (Kelly),Henry [f]	03-19-1861	124
" , Jas. A. [f]	01-27(26)-1871[CLM]	290,291
" (Kelly),Lucy Ann	03-19-1861	123, 124
" (Kelly),Madison	10-17-1855	47

Name	Date	Page
Kelley, Maria	10-22-1872	324
" ,N.E.(Nancy E.)[m]	01-27(26)-1871[CLM]	290,291
Kelly, Catharine [m]	10-17-1855	47
" (Kelley),Ellen J.		
(Ellen Jane)	01-27(26)-1871[CLM]	290,291
" , John [f]	10-17-1855	47
"(Kelley), James [f]	12-18-1856	63
Kelly(Kelley),Joshua	12-18-1856	63
" ,(Myers)(Oliver),		
Patsey [m]	09-10(15)-1863	162
" (Kelley),Rebecca[m]	12-18-1856	63
Kemper, Clementine	08-07-1856	56
" , Eliza [m]	08-07-1856	57
" , Geo. [f]	08-07-1856	56
Kenady, Robert [w]	11-17-1857	72
Kendall(Kindle),James[f]	11-11-1858	88
" (Kindle)(Gibbon)		
(Gibbons), Sarah	11-11-1858	88
Kenedy, Pat [w]	11-17-1857	72
Kennedy, James [w]	10-30-1859	107
Kennelly, Honora	02-01-1858	76
" , Jno.(John) [f]	02-01-1858	76
" (Conner ? Connor),		
M. (Mary) [m]	02-01-1858	76
Kesterson, F. M. [w]	12-27(30)-1858	91
" , John M.(Jno.M.)	12-27(30)-1858	91
" , Mary [m]	12-27(30)-1858	91
" , Wm.(William)[f]	12-27(30)-1858	91
Ketton(?Kelton), E.		
(Elizabeth) [m]	11-28-1869	263
" (?Kelton),H.(Henry)[f]	11-28-1869	263
" (?Kelton),H.D.		
(Henry D.)	11-28-1869	263
Keyser, Almira S.	01-01(05)-1863	177
" , Andr.J.(Andrew T.) No Mar.Date		
	?02-26-1854 [MR]	44
" , E.V.(Estaline V.)	06-01-1865 [MR]	164
" , F.(Fleming)[f]	06-01-1865 [MR]	164
[f]	08-23(24)-1865	165
" , Fleming [f]	08-16-1854	43
[f] NO MAR.Date	02-26-1854?[MR]	44

Name	Date	Page
Keyser (Kiser),Fleming[f]	03-31-1859	94
" , Fleming [f]	01-01(05)-1863	177
" , James [f]	10-04-1855	48
" , James A.	10-04-1855	48
" , Jane E.	03-27-1872	314
" (Keeser), Jas.(James)[f]	02-01-1857	65
" , Lucinda [m]	10-04-1855	48
" (Keeser),Lucinda [m]	02-01-1857	65
" , Margaret	08-16-1854	43
" (Simpson),Martha A.		
(Martha Ann)(M.A.)	03-31-1859	94
" , N.(Nancy) [m]	08-16-1854	43
[m]	06-01-1865[MR]	164
[m]	08-23(24)-1865	165
" , Nancy [m] No Mar.Date	02-26-1854?[MR]	44
[m]	03-31-1859	94
[m]	01-01(05)-1863	177
" , Nancy(Nancy N.)[m]	03-27-1872	314
" , S.C.(Sarah Catherine)	08-23(24)-1865	165
" (Keeser),Sidney A.	02-01-1857	65
" , Wm.H., [Esq.][f]	03-27-1872	314
Kimberlin, Arminda	01-21-1861 [CL]	134
" , E.(Elizabeth)[m]	09-24(26)-1867	214
" , E.(Betsey Jane)[m]	11-02(07)(06)-1867	217
" , E.(Elizabeth) [m]	08-23-1871	299
[m]	06-12-1872	317
" , Elizabeth		
(Eizabeth) [m]	11-15-1860	119
" , Elizabeth [m]	01-21-1861 [CL]	134
[m]	10-29-1869	261
" , Elizabeth	06-12-1872	317
" , Lorenzo	11-15-1860	119
" , Lucinda	10-29-1869	261
" , Mary	09-11-1870	280
" , N.C.(Nancy Caroline)	11-02(07)(06)-1867	217
" , T.F.(Thadeus F.)	09-24(26)-1867	214,215
" , William [f]	10-29-1869	261
" , Wm. [f]	11-15-1860	119
" , Wm.(William)[f]	01-21-1861[CL]	134
[f]	09-24(26)-1867	214
[f]	11-02(07)(06)-1867	217

Name	Date	Page
Kimberlin, Wm. [f]	08-23-1871	299, 300
" [f]	06-12-1872	317
" , Wm. Lee	08-23-1871	299
Kimberlin's,Lorenzo [PL]	08-23-1871	299
Kincaid, Andrew [f]	11-22-1870	291
" , Ann [m]	11-22-1870	291
" , [Miss] Elisabitt J.C.	03-03-1859	93
" (Masters), M. E.		
(Mary E.)	10-09(24)-1865	167
" , N. (Nancy) [m]	10-09(24)-1865	168
" ,Thos.M.(Thomas Moses)	11-22-1870	291
" , W.D.(Wm.D.)[f]	10-09(24)-1865	168
Kindell, Joel [u]	08-15-1861	129, 130
Kindle (Kindell), Delela		
(Delia) [m]	07-22-1857	69
" (Kindell),Evaline J.		
(Eveline J.)	07-22-1857	69
" (Kindell), Joel[f]	07-22-1857	69
King, C.I.(Charlotte		
Isabella)	02-06(09)-1865	151
" ,E.(Eliza) [m]	10-28-1869	260
" ,E.C.(Ellie Catherine)		
(Elezenia C.)	01-08(09)-1866	172, 173
" , Eliza [m]	12-11-1860	118
" , G.(George) [f]	09-05(06)-1865	159
" , G.(George) [f]	01-08(09)-1866	172
" , G.P.(George P.)[f]	02-06(09)-1865	151
" ,Hannabell C.[Hannah		
M. Catharine(Katharine)]	10-17-1855	47
" (O'Connor),Honora[m]	11-17-1857	72
" , J.A.(James Alfred)	09-05(06)-1865	158
" , Lucy J. (L.J.)	12-11-1860	118
" (O'Connor),M.(Mathew)[f]	11-17-1857	72
" , M. W. [w]	01-03-1870	269
" [f]	08-07-1872	319
" , Nancy [m]	02-06(09)-1865	151
" [m]	09-05(06)-1865	159
" (Bennett), Nancy	01-02-1866	171
" (Persinger), Nancy[m]	01-08(09)-1866	172
" (Bennet)(Fridley),		
Phebe [m]	04-19-1855	45

Name	Date	Page
King, Ruth(Rutha)		
(Ruthy) [m]	10-17-1855	47
" ,S.C.(Sallie C.)	10-28-1869	260
" , S.H. [w]	10-28-1869	260
" ,W.F.(Wm.F.) [f]	10-28-1869	260
" , William D.(Wm.D.)[w]	10-28-1869	260
" , Willie A.(William		
A.) [w]	08-07-1872	319
" , Wm. [f]	12-11-1860	118
King's, John [PL]	08-23-1855	47
[PL]	10-17-1855	47
King's, [Mrs.] [Pl]	12-13-1871	306
" , N. W. [PL]	09-05-1872	321
Kitinger(Anderson),	02-15(18)-1869	245
Arabella(Lizzie)[m]	03-03(04)-1869	246
" (Rittinger),George		
Washington(George W.)	03-24-1866[MR]	184
Kittinger(Kitinger), A.		
(Abraham)	03-03(04)-1869	245, 246
" (Rittinger), Andy.		
Dame(Andr.Dame)	03-24-1866 [MR]	184
" (Kitinger),G.W.(Geo.		
W.)(George W.) [f]	03-03(04)-1869	245, 246
" (Rittinger), Polly	03-24-1866 [MR]	184
Knick, John [f]	09-03(04)-1866	188
" , Mathew M.(Matthew		
Marvin)	09-03(04)-1866	188
" , Polly [m]	09-03(04)-1866	188
Knight, Lovast [c]	03-31-1859	95
" (Night), Mary Susan		
(Mary S.)	03-31-1859	95
Knighton(Knighten)(Nighten),		
Martha Susan(Martha		209, 210,
Susin)(Martha Ann)	07-10-1867 [MR]	211
" (Nighton)(Nighten),		
S.F.(Sarah Frances)		208, 209,
(S.) [m]	07-10-1867 [MR]	211
" (Nighton)(Nighten),		208, 209,
Wm.(William)(W.)[f]	07-10-1867 [MR]	211
Kniton, Edward	03-01-1866[MR]	181
" , Mary [m]	03-01-1866[MR]	181

Name	Date	Page
Kniton, William(Wm)[f]	03-01-1866 [MR]	181
Kyle, E.A.(Elizabeth Ann)	09-11(12)-1865	160
" , Eliza [m]	08-15-1861	121
" , F.G.(Felicia G.)[m]	07-11(13)-1870	279
" , G.(Galbraith)[f]	09-11(12)-1865	160
" , Harriet A. T.		
(Harret A. T.)	08-15-1861	121
" , Julia [m]	09-11(12)-1865	160
" , Lizzie F.(Elizabeth F.)	07-11(13)-1870	279
" , Wm. [f]	08-15-1861	121
" , Wm.(William) [f]	07-11(13)-1870	279
Larison, Allen	02-16(21)-1867	193
" , Eliz.(Elizabeth)[m]	02-08(11)-1867	193
" ,J.A.(James A.)[f]	02-08(11)-1867	193
Law, Aaron [f]	09-06-1855	56
" ,Elizabeth [m]	09-06-1855	56
" , James	09-06-1855	56
Lawhorn,Jns.N.(James N.)	03-02(07)-1867	200
" , L.(Lucinda)[m]	03-02(07)-1867	200
" ,Wm.(William)[f]	03-02(07)-1867	200
Lawler,D.(Daniel) [f]	09-20(22)-1869	253
" , H.(Hannorah)[m]	09-20(22)-1869	253
" , Jas. (James)	09-20(22)-1869	253
Lawrence, Jno.(John)[f]	11-02-1872	326
" , Mary [m]	11-02-1872	326
" , Patrick	11-02-1872	325, 326
Lawson, M.[Listed Twice]	12-01-1862	161
" , Margarette[Listed Twice]	12-04-1862	139
Layne, Douglas B.[f]	12-18(19)-1866	192
" , J. Emma	12-18(19)-1866	192
Leary, John	01-29-1864	143
" , Mary [m]	01-29-1864	143
" , Sylva [f]	01-29-1864	143
Lee,Ann(Annie) [m]	12-30-1869	268
[m]	10-01-1872[MR]	322
" , Arthur [f]	12-30-1869	268
[f]	10-01-1872 [MR]	322
" , Charles	09-29-1872	322
" , Jane [m]	09-29-1872	322
" , Jas.(James) [f]	09-29-1872	322

Name	Date	Page
Lee (Moore),Melinda	10-01-1872 [MR]	322
" , Rachel [m]	12-30-1872	332
" (Brown),Salia Ann		
(Jalia Ann)	12-30-1869	268
" , Wm.(William)	12-30-1872	332
Leighton,D.B.(Daniel B.)[f]	10-22-1868	232
" , Dan'l. B. [f]	12-13-1871	306
" , E.G.(Emily G.)[m]	12-28-1869 [CLM]	267
" , Eliza [m]	01-29-1857	66
" (Leyton), Eliza A.		
(Elizan)	02-22(25)-1858	77
" , Frances(Francis M.)	10-13-1859	103
" , Harriet A.	01-29-1857	66
" , Isaac [f]	04-02-1857	64
" , Isaac (Issac N.)[f]	10-13-1859	103
" , Isaac [f]	01-19-1871	288
" , James E. [w]	01-19-1871	288
" , Jno. [f]	01-29-1857	66
" , L. (Louisa) [m]	10-22-1868	232
" , Louisa [m]	12-13-1871	306
" , Martha	04-02-1857	64
" , Mary J.(Mary Jane)	01-19-1871	288
" , M.E.(Margarette E.)		
(?Margaret E.)	12-28-1869 [CLM]	267
" , N.(Nancy) [m]	07-01(16)-1869	251
" (Leyton), Nancy[m]	02-22(25)-1858	77
" , S.(Sallie) [m]	01-19-1871	288
" (Adams), Sarah [m]	04-02-1857	64
" , Sarah [m]	10-13-1859	103
" , Sarah E.(Sarah Ellen)	12-13-1871	306
" , W.(William) [f]	12-28-1869 [CLM]	267
" , W.(Wm.) [f]	07-01(16)-1869	251
" , Wm.(William)	07-01(16)-1869	251
" , W.H.(William H.)		
(Wm.H.)	10-22-1868	232
" (Leyton), Wm.	02-22(25)-1858	77
Lemon, B.(Betsey) [m]	12-22-1869	265
" , C.(?Koonrad,?Koonror)		
[f]	09-10-1856	66
" , Caroline	12-04-1872	328

Name	Date	Page
Lemon (Rose),Cath. S.		
(Catharine S.)	09-10-1856	66
" , D.(Dianna) [m]	12-04-1872	328
" , E. (Ellis) [f]	07-03(08)-1868	226
" , E.(Elizabeth)[m]	11-06-1872	326
" , Francis [w]	03-17(24)-1869	247
" , G. W. [f]	12-04-1872	328, 329
" , H.(Harriet) [m]	12-19(29)-1868	237
" , J. (John) [f]	12-19(24)-1868	237
" , Jestinah A.	10-02-1872	323
" , J.G.(Joseph G.)		
(Jos.)(Joseph)[f]	12-22-1869	265
" , J.N.(John N.)	12-19(24)-1868	237
" , Jos. G. [f]	11-06-1872	326
" , J.Y.(James Y.)		
(Jas. Y.) [f]	03-17(24)-1869	247
" , J.Y.(James Y.) [f]	10-02-1872	323
" , L. T. [b]	11-06-1872	326
" , M.(Margaret) [m]	03-17(24)-1869	247
" , M. A.(Martha Ann)	12-22-1869	265
" (Lemmon), M.D.(Mary D.)	07-03(08)-1868	226,227
" (Haynes), Millerd R.		
(Mildred R.)	09(08)-02-1855	49
" , M.M.(Margaret M.)[m]	10-02-1872	323
" , Morton [w]	09-10-1856	66
" (Pendell),M.R.		
(Mildred R.) [m]	07-03(08)-1868	226
" , Nancy [m]	09-10-1856	66
" , Nancy V.	11-06-1872	326
" , N.J.(Nancy J.)	03-17(24)-1869	247
" , William H. [w]	06-18-1861	129
Lenz, A.(Abraham)[f]	08-23(24)-1865	165
" , L. (Leopold)	08-23(24)-1865	165
" , R. (Rose) [m]	08-23(24)-1865	165
Leslie, Mary [m]	01-09-1872	307
" , Nancy J.(Nany Jane)		
(Nancy Jane)	01-09-1872	307
" , Wm.W.(Wm.)[f]	01-09-1872	307
Levisay (Ford),[Mrs.]Mary	05-13-1863	141
" , Peter [f]	05-13-1863	141

Name	Date	Page
Lewis, Barbara	05-24-1861	124
" , Catharine	11-14-1856	62
" , E.(Eliza)[m]	06-25-1870	278
" , Elizabeth	04-05-1855	51
" , Elizabeth [m]	04-05-1855	51
[m]	01-03-1856	61
[m]	11-14-1856	62
" , Elizabeth (Elisabeth) [m]	06-15-1858 [CL]	83
" , Elizabeth [m]	05-24-1861	124
" , Elizabeth	05-05-1870	279
" , John [f]	04-05-1855	51
[f]	05-24-1861	124
" , John W. [w]	01-03-1856	61
" , Jno. (John) [f]	01-03-1856	61
[f]	11-14-1856	62
" , M.J.(Margaret Josephine)(Margret Josephen)(Margarette Josephine)	06-25-1870	278
" , P.E.(Peter Ervine)[f]	06-25-1870	278
" , Susan	01-03-1856	61
" , W. L. [f]	05-05-1870	278
" , Wm. E.(William E.)	06-15-1858 [CL]	83
" , Zebada B. (Zebadee B.)[f]	06-15-1858 [CL]	83
Linkenhoger (Linkenhoker), Adam [f]	06-20-1859	100
" (Linkenhoker),Isaac N.(Isaac W.)(Isaac Wistley)	06-20-1859	100
" (Linkenhoker), Mary (May) [m]	06-20-1859	100
Lockhart, David B.(D.B.)[f]	11-05-1868	233
" , D.B.(David B.) [f]	06-04(07)-1865	155
[f]	12-17-1868	237
[f]	08-13-1872	320
" , D.B.(David Brittan)	12-22-1870	283
" , E.(Elizabeth)[m]	12-22-1870	283
" , Elizabeth Jane	11-05-1868	233
" , G.L.(Georgeanna L.)	06-04(07)-1865	155

Name	Date	Page
Lockhart, Jas. J.		
(James J.)	08-13-1872	319
" , J.D.(Jas. L.)[f]	12-22-1870	283
" , J.G. (John G.)	12-17-1868	236
" , N. (Nancy) [m]	06-04(07)-1865	155
[m]	12-17-1868	237
[m]	08-13-1872	320
" , Nancy [m]	11-05-1868	233
Lockhart's, [Mrs.]		
Elizabeth [PL]	08-15-1861	129, 130
Lockheart's, [Mr.][PL]	02-18-1858	77
Lone (Hepler), Betsy		
(Betsey)	10-02(05)-1865	167
" , J.L.(John Lewis)[f]	10-02(05)-1865	167
" , R.(Rebecca)[m]	10-02(05)-1865	167
Long, Geo.(George)[f]	10-11-1859	104
" , Jacob B.	10-11-1859	104
" , Martha [m]	10-11-1859	104
Longacre, Jno.(John)	02-29-1872 [MR]	305
" , Nancy [m]	02-29-1872 [MR]	305
" , Sam'l.(Samuel)[f]	02-29-1872 [MR]	305
Loudermilk, Allen T.		
(Allen Taylor)	08-09-1871	299
" , D.(David) [f]	11-05-1868(1867)	234
" , Geo.(George)[f]	08-09-1871	299
" , H.(Hannah) [m]	08-09-1871	299
" , Hannah F.(Hannah		
Francis)	08-09-1871	299
" , J.(Joseph) [f]	11-05-1868(1867)	234
" , M.(Michael)[f]	08-09-1871	299
" , M.E.(Margaret E.)	11-05-1868(1867)	234
" , R.(Rachel) [m]	11-05-1868(1867)	234
" , S.(Susanah) [m]	11-05-1868(1867)	234
" , S.E.(Susan E.)[m]	08-09-1871	299
" , W.N.(William N.)	11-05-1868(1867)	233
Lovens, Ellen [m]	02-20-1870	265
Lovins (Lovens?), Mary S.	02-20-1870	264, 265
Lowman,Elizabeth C.	08-19-1856	57
" , Jos. C.	01-09-1872	307
" , Lydia [m]	08-19-1856	57
" , Margaret [m]	01-09-1872	307

Name	Date	Page
Lowman, Sam'l. [f]	08-19-1856	57
" , Wm. [f]	01-09-1872	307
Lowry, R.(Rebecca)[m]	11-17(18)-1868	234
" , Rebecca E. [m]	01-01(05)-1863	177
" , Samuel B.	01-01(05)-1863	177
" , Samuel B. [f]	01-01(05)-1863	177
" , S.B.(Samuel B.),		
[Jr.]	11-17(18)-1868	234, 235
" , S.B.(Sam'l.B.)[f]	11-17(18)-1868	234
Lowther, Lorenzo D.(L.D.)	08-24-1858	85, 86
" , Melipa(Mellipi)		
(?Melissa)(Mellissi)[m]	08-24-1858	85
" , Wm.W.(William W.)[f]	08-24-1858	85
Luke, Betsy(Betsey)[m]	10-04-1869	255
" , Hasker (?Hasher)[f]	10-04-1869	255
" , Thomas	10-04-1869	255
Lynch (?Pernell), H.E.		
(Harriett Elizabeth)[m]	06-16-1870	278
" , J.B. (John B.)[f]	06-16-1870	278
" , Mary F. (Mary		
Fletcher)	06-16-1870	277
Lynch's, Geo. [PL]	10-12-1869	256
McAlister,Peter [w]	07-19(20)-1869	252
McAllister, A.A.(Abram		
Adam)(A.Adam)	05-09(10)-1865	153
" (McCallister),Clara	09-29-1859	105
" , L. (Lydia)[m]	05-09(10)-1865	153
" (McCallister),Lydia[m]	09-29-1859	105
" (McCallister),Maria F.	10-07-1859	108
" (McCallister),Nancy[m]	10-07-1859	108
" (McCallister),Rufus[f]	10-07-1859	108
[f]	07-19(20)-1869	252
" , T.(Thompson) [f]	05-09(10)-1865	153
" (McCallister),		
Thompson [f]	09-29-1859	105
McAllister's, T. [PL]	02-19-1870	272
[PL]	03-03-1870	272
McArdle, Ellen [m]	01-09-1862	135
" , Henry [f]	01-09-1862	135
" , Peter	01-09-1862	135

Name	Date	Page
McCaleb, Jos. T.		
(Joseph T.)[f]	11-24-1870	318
" , Mary C.	11-24-1870	318
" , Nancy [m]	11-24-1870	318
" , R.B.(Robert B.)	06-30-1869 [MR]	251, 252
" , S.(Sarah) [m]	06-30-1869 [MR]	251
" , T.(Thos.) [f]	06-30-1869 [MR]	251
McCalfin(McCalpin ?),		
Catharine [m]	02-21-1855	50
" (?McCalpin), Jos.		
(Joseph) [f]	02-21-1855	50
" (?McCalpin), Wm.	02-21-1855	50
McCallister(McCalister),		
A.(Archibald)		
(Archabald) [f]	09-13-1865	149
" , A.(Archibald)		
(A.M.)(Archd.)[f]	05-29-1867	206
" (McAloster),Arch.		
(Archabald) [f]	02-05-1857	65
" (McAllister),Clara[m]	09-29-1859	105
" , E.A. (Elizabeth A.)	05-29-1867	206
" (McAllister),Lydia		
(Lydia M.) [m]	09-29-1859	105
" (McAllister),Maria F.	10-07-1859	108
" (McAloster), M.[m]	02-05-1857	65
" (McAloster), Mary F.	02-05-1857	65
" , M.S.(Margaret		
Susan) [m]	09-13-1865	143
" , N.(Nancy) [m]	09-22(23)-1865	166
[m]	07-19(20)-1869	252
" (McAllister),Nancy[m]	10-07-1859	108
" , P.A.(Phebe Agnes)	09-13-1865	149
" ,R.(Rufus) [f]	09-22(23)-1865	166
" (McAllister), R.		
(Rufus) [f]	07-19(20)-1869	252
[f]	10-07-1859	108
" , S.(Susan) [m]	05-29-1867	206
" , Sallie	07-19(20)-1869	252
" , S.E.(Susan E.)	09-22(23)-1865	166
" (McAllister),Thompson[f]	09-29-1859	105
McCarthey(Sulivan),Mary[m]	04-25-1858	80

Name	Date	Page
McCarthy (Bowles),		
Catharine(Catherine)[m] 01-11-1872		307,308
" , Jno.(John) [f]	02-07-1861	125,126
" , Mary	02-07-1861	125,126
" , Mary [m]	02-07-1861	126
McCary(Cary),Maria [m]	09-12-1861	130
" (Cary),Philip		
(Phillip) [f]	09-12-1861	130
" (Cary),Sam'l. M.		
(Samuel M.)	09-12-1861	130
McCleary's(McCrary's)		
(McCray's), W.A.[PL]	06-24-1869	250
McClintic (Mann),Alice[m]	04-25-1855	46
McClung,J.A.(James A.)	07-11(13)-1870	279
" , Jas.(James) [f]	07-11(13)-1870	279
" ,S.R.(Sarah R.) [m]	07-11(13)-1870	279
McClure,E.R.(Elizabeth		
R.) [m]	12-24-1872	330
" , Jno.(John) [f]	12-24-1872	330
" , Wm. T.	12-24-1872	330
McCormack(McOrmack),		
John [f]	03-14-1861	128
" (McOrmack),Jubel W.		
(J.W.)	03-14-1861	128
" (McOrmack),Susan[m]	03-14-1861	128
McCoy, James [f]	09-21(20)-1860	117
[f]	08-15-1861	129
[f]	01-02-1862	135
" , Mary J.(Mary Jane)[m]	01-18-1872	308
" , Nancy [m]	09-21(20)-1860	117
[m]	08-15-1861	129
[m]	01-02-1862	135
" , Nancy A.	01-18-1872	308
" , Rebecca B.(Rebecca V.)	01-02-1862	135
" , Sam'l. B.(Samuel B.)	08-15-1861	129,130
" , Sarah M.	09-21(20)-1860	117
" , William E. [w]	01-02-1862	135
" , Wm. E. [f]	01-18-1872	308
McCray,A.(Alexander)[f]	09-06-1865	146
" , M.J.(Mary Jane)[m]	09-06-1865	146

Name	Date	Page
McCray, W.A.(Wm.A.)		
(Wm.Alexander)	09-06-1865	146
" , W. A. [pet]	06-29-1871	297
" , Wm. A. [w]	06-24-1869	250
McDaniel, Jno.S.(John S.)[f]	09-04(03)-1857	70
" , M. R. E.		
(Mary R. E.)	09-04(03)-1857	70
" , Phebe(Rebecca N.)[m]	09-04(03)-1857	70
McDaniel's, [Mr.] [PL]	02-21-1855	50
McDivet(?McCdevitt)		
(?McCderitt), J.H.		
(John H.)	11-05-1867 [MR]	216
" (?McCdevitt)(?McCderitt),		
L.(Lucinda) [m]	11-05-1867 [MR]	216
" (?McCdevitt)(?McCderitt),		
N. (Neal) [f]	11-05-1867 [MR]	216
McDonald, [Dr.] G.		
(Gabriel)	09-29-1859	105
" , Jas.(James)[f]	09-29-1859	105
" , M.E.(Mary G.)[m]	09-29-1859	105
McDonel(McDonnell),		
Duncan B.	02-20-1856	60
McDonnell(McDonel),		
Donald [f]	02-20-1856	60
" (McDonel),Flora[m]	02-20-1856	60
McElwee, Chas. M.	01-05-1858	91
" , John [f]	01-05-1858	91
McFarland, E.(Elizabeth)[m]	12-12-1872	329
" , M.(Martin) [f]	12-12-1872	329
" , Thos.(Thomas)	12-12-1872	329
McGibbeny, Andrew	03-20-1872	312,313
McGrath, John	06-17-1860	114,115
" (McGath),John [f]	06-17-1860	114
" (McGath),Margarett		
(Margaret) [m]	06-17-1860	114
McKenney, Galvanni	04-04(03)-1872	314
" , Jno.W.(John W.)	12-05-1871	305
" , Jno. Y.(John Y.)[f]	04-04(03)-1872	314,315
" ,Lucy [m]	04-04(03)-1872	314,315
" , Nathaniel [f]	12-05-1871	305

Name	Date	Page
McKenney,S.(Sarah) [m]	12-05-1871	305
McNamarra(McNamara),		
M. (Mary)	05-15(16)-1867	205
McNulty,Jennie(Jinnie)	09-29-1870	322
" , Pat (Patrick) [f]	09-29-1870	322
" ,Susan [m]	09-29-1870	322
McOrmack(McCormack),		
John [f]	03-14-1861	128
" (McCormack),Jubel W.		
(J. W.)	03-14-1861	128
" (McCormack), Susan[m]	03-14-1861	128
McPherson, Elizabeth[m]	04-24(26)-1866	183
" ,J. (John) [f]	02-19(22)-1865	151
" , John [f]	04-24(26)-1866	183
" , John R.(James R.)	04-24(26)-1866	183
" , M. (Mary) [m]	02-19(22)-1865	151
" ;W.H.(William		
Harrison)	02-19(22)-1865	151
McReynolds (Reynolds),		
A. (A.M.) [w]	04-24-1860	113
Mahan's, [Mrs.] [PL]	02-16(21)-1867	193
Mahon(Mahan),Eliz.		
(Elizabeth)[m]	02-16(21)-1867	193
" ,Elizabeth [m]	04-14(18)-1866	183
" , Jno. N.	04-14(18)-1866	183
" , Lawson [f]	04-14(18)-1866	183
" (Mahan),Lawson [f]	02-16(21)-1867	193
" (Mahan),Lucy H.		
(Lucy Hughes)	02-16(21)-1867	193
Mallow,Charlotte A.	02-27-1861	120
" , John [f]	09-06-1865	146
" , Jno. (John)[f]	03-24-1858	78
[f]	02-27-1861	120
" , Martha [m]	03-24-1858	78
[m]	02-27-1861	120
" , Martha (Mattie)[m]	09-06-1865	146
" , Martha A.(Mattie		
Arabella)(Mattie A.)	09-06-1865	146
" , Mary C.	03-24-1858	78
Mallow's, [Mrs.] [PL]	06-29-1871	297

Name	Date	Page
Mallow's, Wm.M. [PL]	09-06-1865	146
Malory(Molonay),Thomas	12-05-1858	89, 90
Manahan(Minahan)(Moynahan),		
Patrick	01-18-1861	128
Mankspile(Manspile),		
P. (Polly) [m]	01-10-1867	196
" (Manspile), R.		
(Richard) [f]	01-10-1867	196
" (Manspile),Wm.G.H.		
(William Grigg Hodmay)	01-10-1867	196
Mann, A.G.(Archibald G.)[f]	09-13-1865	149
[f]	09-05-1867	213
" , A.G. [f]	12-05-1871	305
" (McClintic),Alice[m]	04-25-1855	46
" , Alice	09-05-1867	213
" , Ar.G.(Archabald G.)[f]	12-17-1857	74
" ,Augustus A. [w]	09-11(12)-1865	160
" ,C.(Clemantine)[m]	09-05-1867	213
" ,Clementina [m]	12-05-1871	305
" ,Clementine(Clementine		
C.) [m]	12-17-1857	74
" , Clementine [m]	09-13-1865	149
" , Eliz. J.(Elisabeth J.)	12-17-1857	74
" , H. D. [m]	05-30-1872	316
" , Henrietta D.	11-19-1872	327
" , J. (Julia) [m]	05-10(17)-1865	153
[m]	11-19-1872	327
" , James [w]	06-10-1857	68
" , J.McD.(John McD.)		
(John McDowell)[f]	11-19-1872	327
" ,J.M.D.(John McDowell)		
[f]	05-10(17)-1865	153,154
" , Jno. M.D.(John		
McD.) [f]	03-14-1861	132
" , Julia [m]	03-14-1861	132
" , Lewis T. [f]	04-22(21)-1858	81
" , M.(Margarette)	05-10(17)-1865	153
" , Minerva A.	12-05-1871	305
" , Mollie C.	05-30-1872	316
" , Moses H. [f]	04-25-1855	46
" (Man),Moses M.,[Esq.][f]	06-10-1857	67, 68

Name	Date	Page
Mann, Rebecca S.	04-22(21)-1858	81
" , Sarah [m]	04-22-1858	81
" (Man), Sarah Ann	06-10-1857	67
" , Sarah D. [w]	03-16(18)-1869	246
" , Sarah E.	03-14-1861	132
" , Susan M.	04-25-1855	46
" , W. H. [w]	05-30-1872	316
" , Wm.C.(William Clask)	09-13-1865	148
" , Wm. W. [f]	05-30-1872	316
Manning (Maning), A.J.		
(Andr.J.) [f]	08-10(13)-1868	228
" (Maning),B.F.		
(Benjamin F.)	08-10(13)-1868	228
" (Maning),S.(Sarah)[m]	08-10(13)-1868	228
Mann's, A. [PL]	01-07(03)-1867	199
[PL]	03-16(18)-1869	246
[PL]	09-05-1867	213
" , John [PL]	09-11(12)-1865	160
Manspile (Wolf),Emeline		
S. [Listed Twice]	03-11(02)-1871	317
" (Wolf),Emeline S.		
(Emeline Susan)		
[Listed Twice]	03-02-1871	293
Mason, D.R. [f]	10-23-1867	217
[f]	10-02-1872	323
" , Drucilla W.	10-02-1872	323
" , D.W. [m]	10-02-1872	323
[m]	10-23-1867	217
" , H.P.(Horatio P.)	10-23-1867	217
" (Handley), Mary [m]	02-08-1855	45
Massie, E.R.(Elizabeth		
R.) [m]	02-01-1871	289
" , Henry [f]	02-01-1871	289
" , H.W.(Hezekiah Wm.)	02-01-1871	289
Masters, Ann [m]	12-31-1863	180
" , Charles	12-31-1863	180
" , Frank [f]	07-25-1872	319
" , George W.	07-25-1872	319
" (Kincaid),M.E.(Mary E.)	10-09(24)-1865	167
" , Rhoda [m]	07-25-1872	319
" , Thomas [f]	12-31-1863	180

Name	Date	Page
Master's, Franklin [PL]	02-23(25)-1867	195
Matheney, Ann [m]	02-01(26)-1855	44
" , Lorenzo D. [w]	02-26-1855	48
" (Matheny),Martha	02-26-1855	48
" , Nancy [m]	02-26-1855	48
" , Sam'l.(Samuel)[f]	02-26-1855	48
" , Samuel	02-01(26)-1855	44
" , Sarah E.	02-01(26)-1855	44
Matheny(Matheney), A. (Asberry) [f]	04-22(23)-1863	162
" , J.R.(Jane R.)[m]	03-20(21)-1867	201
" (Matheney),J.W. (John W.) [Listed Twice]	04-22(23)-1863	161, 162
" (Matheney), M. (Malinda) [m]	04-22(23)-1863	162
" , M. (Mary) [m]	12-21(24)-1868	238
" , M.A.(Mary A.)	12-21(24)-1868	238, 239
" , Mary [m]	10-07-1858	87
" , S. (Sam'l.) [f]	03-20(21)-1867	201
" , Sam'l. [f]	10-07-1858	87
" , W. A.(William A.)	03-20(21)-1867	201
" , Wm. (William)	10-07-1858	87
" , Wm. [f]	12-21(24)-1868	238
Mathews, Charles R.[c]	12-17(18)-1872	329
" , Newton	04-02(22)-1866	182
Mays, Jos. M.(Joseph M.)	09-29-1857	70
" , Nancy [m]	09-29-1857	70
Mayse, G.W. [w]	01-12(13)-1871	288
" , I. (Isaac) [f]	12-13(16)-1868	236
" , James	06-18-1861	128, 129
" , Joseph [w]	06-18-1861	129
" , M.(Martha) [m]	12-13(16)-1868	236
" (Hoilman)(Hoylman), N. (Nancy)	12-13(16)-1868	236
" , Nancy [m]	06-18-1861	128, 129
Menefee (Menifee), Benjamin K.[f]	03-12-1861	127
" (Menifee),Emily [m]	03-12-1861	127
Menfee(Menefee),Thomas K. (T.K.)	03-12-1861	127

Name	Date	Page

Merritte (Callison),
    S.F.(Sallie F.)[m] 01-25-1872(1871) 310
Metheney, Nancy [m]   08-26-1856   59
  " (Matheney),Oliver 08-26-1856   59
  " , Sam'l. (Samuel) [f] 08-26-1856   59
Michael, Catharine   01-18-1861   128
  " (Milchael),Johanna[m] 01-18-1861   128
  " (Milchael),Patrick[f] 01-18-1861   128
Mieley, George [w]   01-07-1869   243
Miller, Jno.H. [f]   02-29-1872 [MR] 306
  " , Nancy Jane   02-29-1872 [MR] 305,306
  " , Sarah J. [m]   02-29-1872   306
  " (Hayslett),S.J.
      (Sarah J.)   07-01(16)-1869   251
Minahan, Mary L. [m] 01-18-1861   128
  " , Thos. [f]   01-18-1861   128
Minnick, John [f]   10-24-1872   325
  " , Lizzie C.   10-24-1872   325
Minor (Myers), E.A.
    (Eliza Ann)   07-01-1869   250
  " , Henry   06-29-1871   296, 297
Molonay (Malory), Thomas 12-05-1858   90
Montague, C.(Catharine)[m] 11-08-1871   303
  " , Jane [m]   02-07-1872   311
  " , Jas. M.(J.M.),
    [Esq.] [f]   11-08-1871   303,304
  " , J.M.(James M.),
    [Esq.] [f]   02-07-1872   311
  " , Lucie E.   11-08-1872   303
  " , Mattie J.   02-07-1872   311
Moore (Lee), Melinda 10-01-1872 [MR] 322
Morris, E.(Elizabeth)[m] 09-05-1872   321
  " , John H. [w]   05-10-1870   277
  " , John L.   09-05-1872   320
  " , W. F. [f]   09-05-1872   321
Morrison (Riddlesbarger),
    F.E.(Francis E.) 11-19(21)-1866   190
  " , Frances E.   08-04-1859   102
  " , J.(James) [f] 04-22(23)-1863   162
  " , J. (Jane) [m] 04-22(23)-1863   163
  " , James[Listed Twice] 12-01-1862   161

Name	Date	Page
Morrison, James		
[Listed Twice]	12-04-1862	139
" , James (James D.)[f]	08-04-1859	102
" , Jane [m]	08-04-1859	102
" , Jas. [f]	01-11-1871	287
" , J.D.(James D.)[f]	11-19(21)-1866	190,191
" , J.G.(Juliet		
Granville)	04-22(23)-1863	162
" , John [f]	06-23(28)-1866	187
" , John H.	06-23(28)-1866	187
" , M.J.(Mary J.)[m]	01-11-1871	287
" , Sarah [m]	06-23(28)-1866	187
" , Wm.H.(Wm.Henry)	01-11-1871	287
Morton, J.M.(Jane Maria)	09-12-1865	165
" , M.L.(Maria L.)[m]	09-12-1865	165
" , W.F.(Wm.F.) [f]	09-12-1865	165
(?Mosely)(?Moely)(Roper),		
Milly [m]	03(02)-07-1868	220
Moss, George [w]	03-02(19)-1867	200
" , James A. [f]	12-09-1863	180
" , Martha A. [m]	12-09-1863	180
" , Owen C.	12-09-1863	180
Moyer(s), Elizabeth	08-15-1861	129,130
Moyers,Augustus(Augusta)[f]	08-15-1861	129
" , Catharine	09-10-1861	126
" , Geo.(George)[f]	09-10-1861	126
" ,Julia Ann(July Ann)[m]	09-10-1861	126
" , Margarett [m]	08-15-1861	129
" (Oliver), Patsey	12-18-1856	63
" (Myers),P.A.(Polly Anne)	09-10(15)-1863	162
Murfey, Michael [w]	04-04(09)-1857	75
Murphy, Daniel [f]	12-29-1860	119
" , Jas.(James) [f]	10-16-1859	104
" (Rearidan),Joanna		
(Johanan) [m]	12-29-1860	119
" (Dogherty),Luke [f]	12-17-1867	194
" , Margaret	10-16-1859	104
" (Murry), Mary	10-30-1859	107
Murry, Cate(Catharine) [m]	05-09(14)-1859	98
" , Jeremiah [f]	05-09(14)-1859	98
" (Murphy), Mary	10-30-1859	107

Name	Date	Page
Nealson (Nealon),		
Martin [f]	10-07-1861	131
" (Nealon), Mary[m]	10-07-1861	131
Neel (Damron),Rebecca[m]	04-19-1855	45
Neligham(Nelligan),		
James [f]	04-28-1859	95
" (Nelligan),Mary	04-28-1859	95
Newcomb, Betsy [m]	05-03-1860	113
" , John [f]	05-03-1860	113
" , Mary (Nancy)	05-03-1860	113
Newcomer,Geo.H.(George		
Hilth)	12-22-1870	282
" , Jno.W.(John W.)[f]	12-22-1870	283
" , M.(Mary) [m]	12-22-1870	283
Newton, Elizabeth	09-12-1867	198
Nicely, A.(Annie) [m]	12-01-1864[CLM]	143
" , A.(Ann) [m]	08(09)-29-1869	254
" ,A.J.(A.S.) [f]	12-01-1864[CLM]	143
" , A. J. [f]	09-26-1865	147
" , A.J.(Andrew J.)		
(Andrew Jackson)		
(Andr.J.) [f]	12-24(26)-1867	219
" , A. J. [f]	01-12(13)-1871	287, 288
" ,Andr.J.(Andrew		
Jackson)	01-12(13)-1871	287
" , Andr.J.(Andre.J.)[f]	03-21-1872	313
" , Ann (Anna) [m]	08-16-1860	117
" , Anne (Annie)[m]	09-03(04)-1866	188
" ,Catharine	01-12(13)-1871	287
" , Daniel S. [w]	10-09-1872	324
" , E.(Elizabeth)[m]	09-26-1865	147
" , E.(Emmanuel)	11-21(29)-1865	168
" ,E.(Elizabeth)[m]	05-06(07)-1867	205
" , Ellen N.(Ellen Ann)	05-06(07)-1867	204, 205
" (Nisely),Estaline		
(Estyline)	08-07-1872	319
" , G.(George) [f]	11-21(29)-1865	168
" , George [f]	01-08-1861[CL]	120
" ,G.W.(George W.)	08(09)-29-1869	254
" , H.(Helcy) [m]	12-24(26)-1867	219
" , H.(Hattie) [m]	01-12(13)-1871	287

Name	Date	Page
Nicely, Hester [m]	09-26-1865	147
[m]	03-21-1872	313
" , Hester	10-09-1872	323
" , J.(John) [f]	09--6-1865	159
" , J.(Jake) [f]	05-06(07)-1867	204
" ,J (John) [f]	05-06(07)-1867	205
" , J.(Jacob) [f]	08(09)-29-1869	254
" , J.(Jacob),[Sr.][f]	10-09-1872	323
" , Jacob [f]	09-29-1857	71
" (Niceley), Jacob [f]	02-20-1860	110
" , Jacob [f]	06-18-1861	128, 129
" , Jacob	09-26-1865	147
" , Jacob [f]	01-12(13)-1871	287, 288
[f]	03-21-1872	313
" (Nisely), Jacob		
(Jaceb) [f]	08-07-1872	319
" , Jackson	05-06(07)-1867	204
" , Jackson [b]	10-09-1872	324
" , James [w]	09-04(07)-1865	158
" , James	09-06-1865	159
" , J.M. [f]	06-18-1867	207
" , John [f]	09-26-1865	147
" , L. (Lewis) [f]	12-01-1864[CLM]	143
" , Lewis [f]	08-16-1860	117
[f]	09-03(04)-1866	188
" (Nisely), Lewis C.	08-07-1872	319
" , M.(Margaret) [m]	05-06(07)-1867	204
" , M. (on book)	06-18-1867	207
[Mary (on CTOLMR)][m]		
" , M.(Margaret) [m]	01-12(13)-1871	287, 288
[m]	08-07-1872	319
[m]	10-09-1872	323
" , Margaret [m]	09-29-1857	71
" , Margaret	03-21-1872	313
" ,Margaret(Margaret		
L.) [m]	03-21-1872	313
" , Margarett [m]	06-18-1861	128
" , Margaretta	02-20-1860	110
" (Niceley),Margaretta		
(Margaret) [m]	02-20-1860	110
" , Mary	06-18-1861	128, 129

Name	Date	Page
Nicely, Mary J.(Mary		
Jane)	08-16-1860	117
" , Mathias [f]	08-07-1872	319
" , Matthias [w]	02-22(25)-1858	77
" (Armintrout)(Armantrout),		
M.J.(Mary Jane)	09-03(04)-1866	188
" , M.J.(Mary Jane)[m]	08-07-1872	319
" , N.(Nellie) [m]	12-01-1864[CLM]	143
" , N.(Nancy) [m]	09-06-1865	159
" , Nannie E.	09-26-1865	147
" , Peter	06-18-1867	207
" , Robert	03-21-1872	313
" , S.(Sallie) [m]	11-21(29)-1865	168
" ,Sarah [m]	01-08-1861 [CL]	120
" ,Sarah Ama(Sarah Ann)	01-08-1861[CL]	120
" , Sarah E.	09-29-1857	71
" , S.E.(Sarah Elizabeth)	12-24(26)-1867	219
" , S.M.(Sarah M.)	12-01-1864[CL]	143
" , S.S.(Samuel S.)	12-01-1864[CL]	143
Nicely's,J.A.(John A.)[PL]	09-26-1865	147
" , [Mrs.] [PL]	05-29-1866	185
Nichols(Nichol), D.		
(David) [f]	09-26-1867	215
" (Nichol),M.A.		
(Mary A.) [m]	09-26-1867	215
" (Nichol),S.M.(Sarah		
Mildred)	09-26-1867	215
Nida, Chapman I. [w]	04-24-1860	113
" , Cherpman J. [w]	10-12-1854	42
" , D.(David) [f]	03-30(31)-1865	152
" ,David [f]	04-24-1860	113
[f]	03-11-1861	127
" , Deliah	03-11-1861	127
" , James S.[James		
(S. ? T.)]	04-24-1860	113
" , J.S.(James S.)	03-30(31)-1865	152
. " , M. (Mary) [m]	03-30(31)-1865	152
" , Mary [m]	04-24-1860	113
[m]	03-11-1861	127
Nida's, James S. [PL]	12-19(23)-1868	238

Name	Date	Page

Night(Knight), Mary S.
    (Mary Susan)   03-31-1859   95
Nighton(Knighton)
    (Nighten),Martha
    Susan(Martha Susin)   211
    (Martha Ann)   07-10-1867[MR]   209, 210
  " (Knighton)(Nighten),   208, 209
    N.W.(Nancy Wyatt) 07-10-1867[MR] 211
  " (Knighton)(Nighten),
    S.F.(Sarah Frances)   208,209
    (S.) [m]   08(07)-10-1867 211
  " (Knighton)(Nighten),   208,209,
    Wm.(William)(W.)[f] 08(07)-10-1867 211
Nixon, C.(Charlotte)[m] 02-16-1863   161
  " , F.R.(Frederick
    R.) [f]   02-16-1863   161
  " , T.W.(Theopholus
    Walker)   02-16-1863   161
Noel, Annie C.   07-16(07)-1858 82
  " , Louisa (Lewisa)[m] 07-16(07)-1858 82
  " , Robt. C.(Robert
    C.) (R.C.) [f]   07-16(07)-1858 82, 83
Nolin (Feannelly), Mary[m] 04-04(09)-1857 75
  " (Nalin), Patrick 04-04(09)-1857   75
  " , Patrick [f]   04-04(09)-1857   75

O'Connel(Connel),John[f] 08-13-1857   70
  " (Connel)(Foley),
    Mary(May) [m]   08-13-1857   70
O'Conner (Relihan), ___ 03-13-1855   45
O'Conner (King),Honora[m] 11-17-1857 72
  " (Relihan), Margaret[m] 03-13-1855 45
  " (Griffin), Margaret[m] 03-13-1855 45
  " (Dalcy),Mary   05-24-1864   143
  " (King), Mathew (M.)[f] 11-17-1857 72
  " (Conner), Matthew 11-17-1857   72
O'Donnel(Rochford),Ann 12-17-1859   107
  " (White),Mary [m] 12-17-1859   107
  " , Thos. [f]   12-17-1859   107
Ogdon, Agness G.   02-21-1855   50
  " , Allen [f]   02-21-1855   50

Name	Date	Page
Ogdon, Lucinda [m]	02-21-1855	50
Oiler, B.(Beckie) [m]	09-21-1865	150
" , E.(Elizabeth)	09-21-1865	149, 150
" , Elizabeth [m]	01-09-1855	49
" , J.(John) [f]	09-21-1865	150
[f]	07-10-1867 [MR]	208
" , Mary A.	01-09-1855	49
" , R.(Rebecca)(R.B.)[m]	07-10-1867[MR]	208
" , William H. [w]	07-10-1867 [MR]	208
" , Wm. (William)[f]	01-09-1855	49
" , Wm.(William)		211
(William H.)	07-10-1867 [MR]	208,209
Oliver, Charlotte [m]	03-27-1872	314
" , Chs. (Charles)	11-19-1872	327
" , James	02-01-1857	65
" , Jas. (James) [f]	11-19-1872	327
[f]	03-27-1872	314
" , Lucy [m]	02-01-1857	65
" , Nancy (Lucy) [m]	12-18-1856	63
" (Myers)(Kelly),		
Patsey [m]	)9-10(15)-1863	162
" (Moyers), Patsey	12-18-1856	63
" , S.(Sharloty) [m]	11-19-1872	327
" , Wm. (William) [f]	12-18-1856	63
" , Wm. [f]	02-01-1857	65
" , Wm. A.	03-27-1872	314
Orn.(Orndorff), Israel [f]	12-29-1859	107,108
" (Orndorff), Rebecca[m]	12-29-1859	107,108
Orndorf(Orndorff), John		
E. (John C.)	12-29-1859	107
Osborne(Osburn),Emma	12-17(18)-1872	329
O'Sulivan (O'Sullivan),		
Ellen	08-13-1857	70
O'Sullivan(Sulivan)		
(Dnycol), Catherine[m]	08-13-1857	70
" (Sulivan), John[f]	08-13-1857	70
Otey (Bratton),Hannah[m]	04-02-1857	64
Owen, Nancy	07-07-1859	102
Owen(s), John [f]	07-07-1859	102
Owen(s), Rhoda [m]	07-07-1859	102

Name	Date	Page
Patterson (Gillham)		
(Hubbard),Elizabeth		
(Eliz.) [m]	12-17-1857	74
" , Francis [f]	03-31-1859	94
" , Helen [m]	03-31-1859	94
" , Hezekiah [w]	12-05-1858	90
" , John	03-31-1859	94
Paxton, A.M.(Ann Maria)	09-28-1865	160
" , G.W.(George W.)	01-29-1868	220
" , I.(Isaac)	04-27(28)-1868	221, 222
" , J.(James) [f]	01-29-1868	220
[f]	04-27(28)-1868	221, 222
[f]	12-21(24)-1868	239
" , J.O.(James O.)	12-21(24)-1868	239
" , M. (Mary) [m]	01-29-1869	220
[m]	04-27(28)-1868	221, 222
[m]	12-21(24)-1868	239
" (Eagon),M.L.(Mary L.)	10-07-1870	280
" , S.A.(Sarah Ann)[m]	09-28-1865	160
" , W.B.(William B.)[f]	09-28-1865	160
Paxton's, [Mrs.]W.W.[PL]	05-26(27)-1868	224, 225
Payne,G.A.(George Anna)	11-22-1870	281
" , Geo. H. [f]	03-12-1872	313
" , G.H.(George H.)[f]	11-22-1870	281
" , J.P.(James P.)	01-10-1864(1865)	150
" , L.(Lewis) [f]	01-10-1864(1865)	150
" , L.(Louisa)[m]	01-10-1864(1865)	150
" , L.(Lewis) [f]	10-30(31)-1865	168
" , Lewis	10-30(31)-1865	168
" , L.S.(Louisa S.)[m]	10-30(31)-1865	168
" , Mary Watson	03-21-1872	313
" , S.A.(Sarah Ann)[m]	11-22-1870	281
[m]	03-12-1872	313
" , S.A. [w]	08-17-1872	320
Payne's, L. S. [PL]	10-22-1872	324
Pence, C.L.(Charles Lewis)	12-29-1870	284
" , Ellen [m]	12-29-1870	284
" , N. (Nelly) [m]	03-31-1868	221
" , P.(Peter) [f]	03-31-1868	221
" , Peter [f]	12-29-1870	284
" , P.M.(Peter M.)	03-31-1868	221

Name	Date	Page
Pendell (Purdell),		
Mary A. [m]	09(08)-02-1855	49
" (Purdell),Matthew		
L.(Mathew L.)	09(08)-02-1855	49
" ,M.L. [Lemmon-step-		
father]	07-03(08)-1868	227
" (Lemon),M.R.		
(Mildred R.)	07-03(08)-1868	226
Perge, Geoge P.[George		
P.Persinger][w]	01-08(09)-1866	173
Perkins, A. A.	03-03-1859	93
" , Alexd.A. (A.A.)		
(Alexander A.)	03-14-1861	131
" , Jane V. [m]	03-14-1861	131, 132
" , Tyree[Tynis H.		
(?A. ?G.)] [f]	03-14-1861	131, 132
Pernell's (Lynch),		
Harriett [PL/?m]	06-16-1870	278
Perry, Thomas [w]	01-25-1872(1871)	310
Persinger, A.(Andrew)[f]	09-05-1865	149
" , A.(Ann)(Anna) [m]	08-29(31)-1865	157
" , A.(Ann) [m]	09-04(07)-1865	158
" , A.B. [JP]	11-22-1870	281, 282
[JP]	11-22-1870	292
" , Anderson [w]	05-18-1858	82
[w]	03-29-1860	112, 113
" , Andr.(Andrew)[f]	03-12-1861	127
" , Andrew [f]	12-08-1863	179
" , Annie [m]	03-29-1860	112
" , Betsey [m]	12-29-1864	144
" , Caleb	09-28-1871	300
" (Bennett),Catherine		
(Catharine)	12-08-1863	179
" , Charllette(Charlott)		
[m]	11-25(27)-1865	169
" , Charlotte [m]	08-02-1859	102
" (Myers), Charlotte [m]	04-01-1862	137
" , Charlotte	04-18-1861	121
" , Chas. A.(Charles A.)	03-29-1860	112
" , Choltt(Charlotte)[m]	08-27-1865[MR]	148

Name	Date	Page
Persinger, Christ		
(Charlotte) [m]	03-30(31)-1865	152
" , Cs. A. [f]	03-28-1872	314
" , David [w]	08-23-1871	300
" , E.(Elizabeth)[m]	09-05-1865	149
[m]	01-02-1866	171
" , E.(Eli.) [f]	09-28-1871	300
" , E.F.(Eliza F.)	03-30(31)-1865	152
" , Eli	01-15(28)-1868	219
" , Elizabeth [m]	03-12-1861	127
" , Elizabeth F.	10-13-1859	103
" , Geo. P.	01-08(09)-1866	173
" , George P.[Geoge		
P.Perge] [w]	01-08(09)-1866	173
" , G.P.(George Payne)	02-06(09)-1865	151
" , H.(Henry) [f]	08-29(31)-1865	157
" , Henry [f]	03-29-1860	112
[f]	09-04(07)-1865	158
" , J. (John)	09-04(07)-1865	158
" , Jane	04-18-1861	121
" , Jennetta F.	03-12-1861	127
" , J.H.(Joseph H.)[f]	02-06(09)-1865	151
[f]	05-22(25)-1865	154
" , John S. [w]	07-24(25)-1860	116
" , Joseph [f]	08-02-1859	102
" , Joseph [w]	09-28-1871	301
" , Jos. H. [w]	03-06-1856	60
[f]	10-13-1859	103
" , Jos. W.(Joseph W.H.)	08-02-1859	102
" , L.(Lydia) [m]	09-28-1871	300
" , Lee	08-27-1865[MR]	148
[w]	09-25(27)-1865	167
[w]	01-16(18)-1866	174
[w]	04-24(26)-1866	184
[w]	12-21(24)-1868	239
" (Bennett),L.J.		
(Lucinda Jane)	11-25(27)-1865	169
" , M.(Mary) [m]	02-06(09)-1865	151
" , M. (Mary P.)[m]	05-22(25)-1865	154
" (Humphries),Martha [m]	08-28-1869	254
" , Mary [m]	10-13-1859	103

Name	Date	Page

Name	Date	Page
Plymale (Plymal),Virgil S.[Virgile A. (?Sotouqre ?Sotougro)]	05-27-1860[BK]	114
" , W.B.(William B.)[f]	12-12-1867	218
" , W.B.(Wm.B.)[f]	11-23-1869	263
" , Wm.B. [f]	07-31-1856	57
[f]	05-27-1860 [BK]	114
[f]	01-29-1868	220
Pollard, Ann	01-02-1872	306
" , John [f]	01-02-1872	306
Poor, Elizabeth [m]	04-24(26)-1866	183, 184
" (Poe),Elizabeth (Elizabeth A.) [m]	06-14-1860	115
" (Poe),George A. (Geo.A.)(G.A.)	06-14-1860	115
" , James Isaiah [w]	06-14-1860	115
" , John C. [CC]	01-31-1872	310
" , Mary [m]	09-11-1862	139
" , Rupia L.	04-24(26)-1866	183
" , Sarah A. V.	09-11-1862	139
" , Soloman [f]	09-11-1862	139
[f]	04-24(26)-1866	183
" (Poe), Solomon [f]	06-14-1860	115
Porter, E.G.(Ezekial G.)[f]	04-13-1859	96
" , Ezekial [w]	01-26-1856	54
[f]	12-17-1856	63
" , John L.	12-17-1856	63, 64
" , Mary [m]	01-26-1856	54
" , Matilda [m]	12-17-1856	63
[m]	04-13-1859	96
" , Minerva G. (Minerva G. J.)	04-13-1859	96
" , Nancy	01-26-1856	54
" , Wm.(William) [f]	01-26-1856	54
Potter, Charles J.	05-30-1872	316
" , Horace [f]	05-30-1872	316
" , Julia [m]	05-30-1872	316
" (Peters),Susan J. (Susan Jane)	12-24-1872	330
Powers, Elijah	02-28(29)-1872	312

Name	Date	Page
Prian, Maria	10-04-1869	255
Pring, Dora	03-11-1870	273
" , S. (Sarah) [m]	03-11-1870	273
" , W.W.(William W.)[f]	03-11-1870	273
Pritchard, Mary [m]	02-05-1857	65
" , Stephen [f]	02-05-1857	65
" , Stephen A. (Stephen C.)	02-05-1857	65
Pulse, John [w]	09-05-1872	321
Purdell(Pendell),Mary A. [m]	09(08)-02-1855	49
" (Pendell), Matthew L.(Mathew L.)	09(08)-02-1855	49
Putnam, Chas. F.(Charles F.)	10-26-1871	302
" , Jno. [f]	10-26-1871	302
" , Sarah [m]	10-26-1871	302
Quickel, Adam [f]	02-14-1856	60
" , Barbara	02-14-1856	60
" , Mary [m]	02-14-1856	60
Quickell, William H. [Jr.] [w]	08-02-1859	102
Quickel's, Harrison [PL]	02-14-1856	60
Quickle, H. [g]	01-17-1860	110
" (Quicle), Henry[f]	05-18-1860	81
" (Quicle), Peggy (Margaret) [m]	05-18-1860	81, 82
" (Quicle)(Quickel), Ruthy M.	05-18-1858	81
Quinlan (Quinlin), Darby [f]	06-17(19)-1859	99
" (Quinlin),Margaret[m]	06-17(19)-1859	99
" (Quinlen),Martin	06-17(19)-1859	99
Quinlen (Dugan), Ellen	06-17(19)-1859	99
" , Patrick [csin]	06-17(19)-1859	99
Ragland,James T.(James P.) [f]	07-14-1859[CL]	100. 101
" , John D. D.	07-14-1859 [CL]	100
" , Polly [m]	07-14-1859 [CL]	100
Rairdon,J.(John) [f]	05-26(19)-1870	275

Name	Date	Page
Rairdon, Michael	05-26(19)-1870	275, 276
" ,S.(Sarah) [m]	05-26(19)-1870	275, 276
Ratliff,J.(Johnathan)[f]	12-11-1865	170
" , J.R.(James Wesley)	12-11-1865	170
" , P.A.(Phebe Ann)[m]	12-11-1865	170
Ratliff's, James [PL]	02-15(18)-1869	245
[PL/w]	03-03(04)-1869	246
Rayhill, A.(Alexander)[f]	11-05-1867 [MR]	216
" , Alex.(Alexander)[f]	07-23(24)-1866	187
" , Alexander (A.)[f]	10-12-1854	42
" , Alexander (Alexandre) [f]	03-17-1857	78
" , Catharine E.	10-12-1854	42
" , Charlotte (Charlotte M.)	03-17-1857	78
" , E. [m]	10-12-1854	42
" , E.(Elizabeth) [m]	11-05-1867 [MR]	216
" , Eliz.(Elizabeth)[m]	07-23(24)-1866	187
" , Elizabeth(Elisabeth)[m]	03-17-1857	78
" , M.A.(Mary J.)	11-05-1867 [MR]	216
" (Wolfe)(Wolf),Sarah[m]	02-10-1857	65
" , W. (Wm.) [w]	01-13-1870	269, 270
" , William	07-23(24)-1866	187
Read, Levi	05-27-1871	295
Rearidan (Murphy),Joanna (Johanan) [m]	12-29-1860	119
" , William	12-29-1860	119
Redinger, Louisa [m]	04-24(14)-1860	113
" , Mary A.(Mary Ann)	04-24(14)-1860	113
" , Nicholas [f]	04-24(14)-1860	113
Redman, Charles [w]	11-27-1872	328
" , Mary [m]	02-08(11)-1867	192
" , Sam'l.	02-08(11)-1867	192
" , Wm.(William) [f]	02-08(11)-1867	192
Reece's, [Mrs.] [PL]	05-19-1863	141
Reed, Martha	12-05-1858	90
" , Rebecca [m]	12-05-1858	90
" , Robert [f]	12-05-1858	90
Reid (Reed),Eliza J. (Elisa Jane)	06-13-1872	316

Name	Date	Page
Reid (Reed), Jno. C.		
(John C.) [f]	06-13-1872	316
" (Reed), Mary A.		
(Mary Ann)		
(Maryann A.) [m]	06-13-1872	316
Relihan (O'Conner), ___	03-13-1855	45
Relihan(O'Conner),		
Margaret [m]	03-13-1855	45
" , Morris [f]	03-13-1855	45
Renick, C. B. [w]	01-25-1872(1871)	310
Rese's, [Mr.] [PL]	03-20-1871	292
Reynolds, A. M. [w]	02-27-1857	65
" (McReynolds),		
A. M. (A.) [w]	04-24-1860	113
" ,Dioclesian [f]	05-30-1854	41
" , Geo (George) [f]	11-15(17)-1870	286
" , James [w]	05-30-1854	41
" , Malinda [m]	11-15(17)-1870	286
" , Nancy W.	05-30-1854	41
" , Polly [m]	05-30-1854	41
" , W. M.	11-15(17)-1870	286
Rhine, Catharine [m]	04-28-1859	94
" , Dennis [f]	04-28-1859	94
" , John	04-28-1859	94, 95
Rice, James M.	10-10-1861	132
" , Sam'l. D. [f]	10-10-1861	132
" , Sarah D. [m]	10-10-1861	132
Richards, Dock (?Dick)[f]	02-19-1870	272
" (Barbour),Lucy [m]	02-19-1870	272
Richardson, A.T.(?A.F.)[m]	10-20-1869	258
" , Bettie L.	04-14-1870	274
" , Chs.(Charles)	12-22(26)-1866	176
" , D.(David) [f]	10-21(22)-1871	301
" , E.V.(Eliza Va.)	10-20-1869	258
" , J. (Julia)	01-23(24)- 1866	175
" , J.F.(John F.)		
(Jno. F.) [f]	04-14-1870	274
" , K. (Keziah) [m]	10-21(22)-1871	301
" , M.(Margarett) [m]	01-23(24)-1866	175
" , Margaret [m]	08-03-1858	84
" , Margaret(Margarett)[m]	12-22(26)-1866	176

Name	Date	Page

Richardson,M.J.
  (Margaret J.)[m]   04-14-1870   274
  " , Ro.(Robert)   10-21(22)-1871   301, 302
  " , T. (Thomas) [f] 01-23(24)-1866   175
  " ,Thomas W.(Thos.W.) 08-03-1858   84, 85
  " , Thos. [f]   08-03-1858   84
  " , Thos.(Thomas)[f] 12-22(26)-1866   176
  " , W.(William)(Wm.)[f] 10-20-1869   258, 259
Richardson's,Charles [PL] 01-23(24)-1866 175
  " , John   [PL]   11-28-1869   263
Riddlebarger(Riddlesbarger),
    Elizabeth [m]   08-04-1859   102
Riddlesbarger(Ridlesbarger),
    Dingud   12-31-1857   72
Riddlesbarger(Morrison),
    F.E.(Francis E.)   11-19(21)-1866   190
Riddlebarger(Riddlesbarger),
    Frederic(Frederick) 08-04-1859   102, 103
Riddlesbarger(Ridlesbarger),
    Sam'l.(Samuel [f] 12-31-1857   72
Riddlebarger(Riddlesbarger),
    Sam'l. [f]   08-04-1859   102
Riddlesbarger(Ridlesbarger),
    Susan(Suasan) [m] 12-31-1857   72
Rideout, Edward [f]   05-29-1866   185
  " , Jos.(Joseph)   05-29-1866   185
  " , Rossetta (Rosetta)[m] 05-29-1866   185
  " (Burrell), Silvie[m] 09-18(17)-1872 321
Rittinger(Kittinger),   [f]
    Andr.Dame(Andy Dame) 03-24-1866 [MR] 184
  " (Kitinger),George W.
    (George Washington) 03-24-1866 [MR] 184
  " (Kittinger),Polly [m] 03-24-1866[MR] 184
Roach (Murry), Mary[m] 10-30-1859   107
Roadcap, Christian   01-19(18)-1855   49
  " , Christian [f]   01-19(18)-1855   50
            [f]   02-25-1858   77
  " , David L.   02-25-1858   77
  " , E.(Elizabeth)[m] 02-25-1858   77
  " , Elizabeth [m]   01-19(18)-1855   50

Name	Date	Page
Robertson,A.C.(Annie C.)[m]	10-02-1872	323
" , Geo. C. [f]	10-02-1872	323
" , H.H.(Henry H.)	10-02-1872	323
Robinson,A. (Ann) [m]	11-28-1869	263
" (Fields),Charlotte	05-29-1866	185
" , E. [m]	02-28-1860	111
" , E.(Elizabeth)[m]	01-12-1870	270
[m]	11-02-1870	281
[m]	11-01-1871	302
" , E.(Emily M.)[m]	10-02-1872	322
" , E.(Elisabeth)[m]	10-24-1872	325
" , Eliz.(Elizabeth)[m]	02-21(22)-1866	182
" , Hez.P.(Hezekiah P.)	11-01-1871	302
" , Jas.T.(James T.)[f]	11-28-1869	263
" , Johnathan A.(J.A.)	10-24-1872	325
" , Margaret L.	02-28-1860	111
" , Martha F.	02-21(22)-1866	182
" , M.E.(Mary Elizabeth)	11-28-1869	263
" , Rosetta	05-27-1871	296
" (Fields), Sarah	05-29-1866	185
" , S.B.(Sallie B.)	01-12-1870	270
" , Thos.B.(Thomas B.)	10-02-1872	322
" , Thos. B. [f]	10-02-1872	322
" , W.(William)(Wm.)[f]	01-12-1870	270
" , William(Wm.)[f]	02-21(22)-1866	182
" , William M. [w]	02-21(22)-1866	182
" , Wm. [f]	02-28-1860	111
" , Wm. (William)[f]	11-02-1870	281
" , Wm. [f]	11-01-1871	302
[f]	10-24-1872	325
" , Wm. M.(William M.)	11-02-1870	281
Rochford(O'Donnel),[Mrs.]		
Ann	12-17-1859	107
Rock's, [Mrs.] [PL]	05-09(10)-1865	153
Rodenizer, H.(Harriet)	08(09)-29-1869	254
" , H.(Henry) [f]	08(09)-29-1869	254
" , R.(Rachel) [m]	08(09)-29-1869	254
Rogers,B.(Betsey) [m]	12-25-1872	330
" , J.(Jupiter) [f]	12-25-1872	330
" , James	12-25- 1872	330, 331
" (Walker),M.E.(Margaret E.)	10-01(11)-1864	142

Name	Date	Page
Roof's(?wolf's),		
George W. [PL]	01-23(25)-1866	175
Roper, C.(Charles)[f]	02-01-1869 [MR]	243
" ,Edward	02-01-1869 [MR]	243
" , John	03(02)-07-1868	220
" , L.(Lucinda) [m]	02-01-1869 [MR]	243
" (?Mosely)(?Moely),		
Milly [m]	03(02)-07-1868	220
Roradin(Rusradan)(Roradon)		
(Riordan), Bridgett		
(Bridget)	05-09(14)-1859	98
" (Keef),Elizabeth		
(Eliza) [m]	05-09(14)-1859	98
" (Riordan),John [f]	05-09(14)-1859	98
Rose (Lemon),Cath.S.		
(Catharine S.)	09-10-1856	66
" , Eliza [m]	05-22(23)-1861	126
" , Denison [f]	05-22(23)-1861	126
" , Milissa(?Melissa)		
(?Milipa)(?Melipa)		
Phelps	05-22(23)-1861	126
Rose's, D.,[Esq.] [PL]	08-13-1872	320
Ross, Absolom F.		
(Absalom F.)	11-15-1860	118
" , Chs.	10-22-1872	324
Ross, E.(Eunice) [m]	12-13(16)-1868	236
" , Ellen [m]	10-22-1872	324
" , Jas. E. [w]	10-26-1871	302
" , Jos. D. [f]	11-15-1860	118
" , T.(Thos.) [f]	12-13(16)-1868	236
" , Thos.(Thomas O.)	12-13(16)-1868	236
" , Winney (Wincy)[m]	11-15-1860	118
Rowan(Bowan), Boston[f]	04-01-1858	79
" (ronaw),Bridgett[m]	04-24-1859	97
" (Ronaw),Catharine		
(Catherine)	04-24-1859	97
" (Bowan), Chas. L.		
(Charles L.)	04-01-1858	79
" (Bowan),Frances[m]	04-01-1858	79
" (Ronaw),Jas.(James)[f]	04-24-1859	97
Rucker,E.(Elzy) [f]	07-01-1869	250

Name	Date	Page
Rucker, F.(Frances)[m]	07-01-1869	250
" , Wm. (William)	07-01-1869	250
Rusk, Hugh B. [w]	10-07-1859	108
Rusk's, [Mr.] [PL]	01-03-1866	171
Ryals,Emma J.(Emma Judson)	02-01-1871	289
" , H. C. [m]	02-01-1871	289
[m]	10-27-1869	259
" , H.N.(Hattie N.) (Harriet N.)	10-27-1869	259, 260
" , James D. [w]	10-27-1869	260
" , V. C. [f]	10-27-1869	259
" (Ryal), V. C.	02-01-1871	289
Sadler, John D. [w]	10-12(13)-1868	231
Sams, E.C.(Elizabeth C.) (Elizabeth Catharine)	06-29-1871	297
" , Jos.H.(Joseph H.)[f]	06-29-1871	297
" , Lucinda [m]	06-29-1871	297
Sarver,Jno.(John) [f]	04-01-1858	79
" , Martha [m]	04-01-1858	79
" , Nancy (Nancy H.)	04-01-1858	79
Sawyers,A.(Alexander)[f]	01-03(04)-1866	171
" , A.(Arch)(Arch.)[f]	06-01-1865[MR]	163
" , A.(Archer) [f]	12-30(31)-1868	241
" , Archer	01-03-1856	60
" , H.(Henryetta)	06-01-1865 [MR]	163
" , J.S.(John S.)	01-03(04)-1866	171
" , Leadford [w]	12-30(31)-1868	241
" , Nancy (Mary)[m]	01-03-1856	60, 61
" , R.S.(Rebecca S.)	12-30(31)-1868	241
" , S.(Susan) [m]	06-01-1865 [MR]	163
[m]	12-30(31)-1868	241
" , Sampson [f]	01-03-1856	60
" , S.H.(Sarah H.)[m]	01-03(04)-1866	171
Sawyers, William [DC]		41, 42
Scaggs (Skaggs),Isaac M. (Isaac Marion)	01-25-1871	288, 289
" , Jno. (John) [f]	01-25-1871	288
" , M.A.(Mary Ann)[m]	01-25-1871	288
Scott,A.M.(Andrew M.)[f]	09-04(06)-1866	190
" , Annie S.	09-04(06)-1866	190

Name	Date	Page
Shea, J.(Joanna)[m]	12-13-1870	282
" , Joana	12-13-1870	282
" , M.(Margaret)[m]	05-15(16)-1867	205
" (Sullivan)(Sulivan),		
Margaret [m]	12-15-1854	41
" (Sulivan), Mary [m]	12-15-1854	41
" (Sulivan), Mary	12-15-1854	41
Shields, Emma (Amy)	10-21(22)-1871	301, 302
" , Mahala [m]	10-21(22)-1871	301, 302
Shipner, Elizabeth [m]	04-24(14)-1860	113
" , Henry [f]	04-24(14)-1860	113
" (Shepner), Peter	04-24(14)-1860	113,114
Shirkey's, C. [PL]	09-12-1867 [PL]	198, 199
[PL]	09-19-1867	214
Shriggs(Shiggs),B.J.		
(Barbara J.)	10-12-1869	256,257
" , H.(Henry) [f]	10-12-1869	256
" , M.(Margaret) [m]	10-12-1869	256
Shumaker,D.(David) [f]	08-05(15)-1867	211
" , Eliza [m]	02-06-1861	122
Skaggs(Scaggs),Isaac M.		
(Isaac Marion)	01-25-1871	288, 289
Shumaker,Elizabeth		
(Eliza) [m]	02-04(08)-1859	93
" , J.(Jemina) [m]	08-04(15)-1867	211
" , Mary Jane	02-06-1861	122
" , Jno.K.E.(John K.E.)		
(John K.) [f]	02-04(08)-1859	93
[f]	02-06-1861	122
" , Thomas (Thos.)	02-04(08)-1859	93
" , Wm. (William)	08-05(15)-1867	211
Siders, Conrad [f]	01-08-1861 [CL]	120
" , Hugh L.	01-08-1861 [CL]	119, 120
" , Margaret [m]	01-08-1861 [CL]	120
Sifford, J.W.	01-03-1870	269
Silvers, S.A.(Sarah Ann)	01-10(11)-1866	173
Simmons,E.(Elizabeth)[m]	12-19(23)-1868	238
" , Ephraim(Epraim)[f]	09-16-1858	86
" , Ephraim [f]	08-02-1859	101
" , James A. [w]	12-31-1855	59
" , J.C.(James C.)	12-19(23)-1868	238

Name	Date	Page
Simmons,John M. [w]	08-03-1871	299
" , Mary Ann	09-16-1858	86
" , Nancy M.	08-02-1859	101
" , Ruth [m]	09-16-1858	86
" , Ruth (Ruthy)[m]	08-02-1859	101
" , W.M.(Wm.M.) [f]	12-19(23)-1868	238
Simpson, Alex.(Alexander)[f]	10-11-1859	104
" , Annie E.	10-11-1859	104
" (Keyser), Martha A.		
(Martha Ann)(M.A.)	03-31-1859	94
" , Sarah [m]	10-11-1859	104
Sims, G.(Garland) [f]	12-15-1869	264
" , P.(Pelina) [m]	12-15-1869	264
" , S.H.(Samuel Henry)	12-15-1869	264
Sittington, Thomas [JP]	09-12-1861	131
Sively,A.J.(Andrew		
Jackson) [f]	08-11-1870	285
" , A.J.(Andrew J.)[f]	01-18(28)(27)-1869	243
" , A.J.(Andrew J.)	05-04(05)-1868	222
" , Andrew(Andrew J.)[f]	02-27-1857	64, 65
" , E.(Elizabeth)[m]	11-21-1865	169
" , E.B.(Elizabeth B.)	11-21-1865	169
" , G.(George) [f]	05-04(05)-1868	222, 223
" , J.(Joseph)[f]	11-21-1865	169
" , M.(Mary) [m]	01-18(28)(27)-1869	243
[m]	05-04(05)-1868	222,223
" , Mary [m]	08-11-1870	285
" (Seively),Rebecca Jane	02-27-1857	64, 65
" (Hepler), Rebecca Z.	08-11-1870	285
" , Wm. B.(William B.)	01-18(28)(27)-1869	243
Sizer,C.(Catharine)[m]	07-01(08)-1868	226
" , F.P. [f]	01-13-1870	269,270
" , F.P.(Fielding P.)	07-01(08)-1868	226
" , F.P.(Fielding P.)[f]	09-18-1862	140
" , J. (John) [f]	07-01(08)-1868	226
" , J.M.(James M.)	01-13-1870	269, 270
" , Lucinda C.	09-18-1862	140
" , M. (Mary) [m]	01-13-1870	269
Skeen, C.J.(Catharine J.)[m]	11-08-1871	303
" , Isaac [DC]		54,54,59

Name	Date	Page
Skeen, James (J.)		
[g]	12-21(24)-1868	239
" , James	11-21-1865	169
" , P.(Polly)[m]	11-21-1865	169
" , Polly [m]	11-22-1870	281
" , R. (Robert) [f]	11-21-1865	169
" , Ro. (Robert)[f]	11-22-1870	281
" , Ro.A.M.(Robert A.M.)	11-08-1871	303
" , Wm. [f]	11-08-1871	303
" , Wm. (William)	11-22-1870	281
Smails, Mary F.	12-29-1859	108
" , Mary (Mary F.)[m]	12-29-1859	108
" , Thos.(Thomas)[f]	12-29-1859	108
Smales, Mary [m]	05-24(23)-1858	82
" (Snales),Mary A.		
(Mary Ann) [m]	10-13-1857	72
" , Mathew [f]	05-24(23)-1858	82
" (Snales), Matthias[f]	10-13-1857	72
" (Snales), Susan	10-13-1857	71, 72
" , Thomas	05-24(23)-1858	82
Smith, Ann [m]	12-05(06)-1871	305
" , Archibald H.	02-(02)(21)-1856	54
" , Ballard J.	02-21(22)-1866	181
" , Betsey [m]	12-27-1870	284
" , Bettie [m]	06-24-1869	250
" , Betty [m]	01-16(17)-1867	196
" , Charles	06-24-1869	250
" , E.(Elizabeth)[m]	05-22(23)-1867	205
" , E.J.(Eliza Jane)	09-05(06)-1865	159
" , Eliza	12-27-1870	284
" , Elizabeth [m]	02-(02)21- 1856	54
" , Giles M.	10-22-1868	232
" , G. M. [w]	08-10(13)-1868	228
" , Harriet (Harriet Ann)	04-08-1872	315
" , Harriet M.	10-24-1872	324,325
" , J.C.(Jno.C.)[f]	08-10(13)-1868	228
" , J.C.(John Crocket)[f]	09-05(06)-1865	159
" , J.J.(John J.)[f]	10-01(11)-1864	142
" , Jno.A.(John A.)[f]	02-04(08)-1859	93
" , Jno.C.(John C.)[f]	10-24-1872	324,325
" , John [f]	10-22-1868	232

Name	Date	Page
Smith, John A.(? Wm.		
John A.) [f]	01-13-1870	268,269
" , Josiah (Josh)	02-28(25)-1860(?1862)	108,
		109
" , J.R.(John R.)	01-12-1870	270
" , Lewis	02-27(28)-1867	195
" , Lucy [m]	10-01(11)-1864	142
" , M. A.(Mark A.)	10-01(11)-1864	142
" , Mary [m]	02-27(28)-1867	195
" , Mary A.	02-04(08)-1859	93
" , M.E.(Malinda E.)[m]	01-13-1870	268
[m]	01-12-1870	270
" , M.E.(May E.)		
(?Mary E.)(Mary		
Emeline)	08-10(13)-1868	228
" , M.F.(Merinda F.)		
(?Mirenda F.)	01-13-1870	268
" , M.M.(Manervia M.)	02-27(28)-1867	195
" , Peter [f]	02-27(28)-1867	195
[f]	02-28(25)-1860(?1862)	109
" , Polly [m]	02-21(22)-1866	181
" , Rebeca J.(Rebecca		
J.) [m]	02-04(08)-1859	93
" , Rebecca F.	01-16(17)-1867	196
" , S.(Susan) [m]	10-24-1872	324
" , S.(Susanah) [m]	08-10(13)-1868	228
" , S.(Susan) [m]	09-05(06)-1865	159
" , Susan [m]	02-27(28)-1867	195
" , Susanna [m]	10-22-1868	232
" , Susanah [m]	02-28(25)-1860(?1862)	109
" , T.E.(Thomas E.)[f]	05-22(23)-1867	205
" , Thomas [f]	01-16(17)-1867	196
" , Thomas (Thos.) [f]	06-24-1869	250
" , Thos. [f]	12-27-1870	284
" , Thos.(Thomas)[f]	02-(02)21-1856	54
" , T.J.(Thomas Jefferson)	05-22(23)-1867	205
" , W.J.(Wm.J.)		
(?Wm.John A.)[f]	01-13-1870	268, 269
" , W.J.(Wm.J.) [f]	01-12-1870	270
" , Wm. [f]	12-05(06)-1871	305
" , Wm. A.	12-05(06)-1871	305

Name	Date	Page
Smith, Wright [f]	02-21(22)-1866	181
" [f]	02-27(28)-1867	195
Snead, A.S.(Anthony M.)	01-23(24)-1866	175
" , J.(Jane) [m]	01-18-1866	174
[m]	01-23(24)-1866	175
Snead, R.(Richard)[f]	01-18-1866	174
[f]	01-23(24)-1866	175
" , S.(Samuel)	01-18-1866	174
Snow,M.(Marietta)[m]	12-13-1870	282
" , P.N.	12-13-1870	282
" , R.E.(Richard E.)[f]	12-13-1870	282
Sorrel, Frances A.		
(Frances Ann)	06-01-1854	43
" , Mary [m]	06-01-1854	43
" , Thomas [f]	06-01-1854	43
" , William	06-01-1854	43
Sorrell(Sourel),Isaac		
(Isaack)	02-22(25)-1858	77
" (Sourel),Mary [m]	02-22(25)-1858	77
" (Sourel),Thos.(Thomas)		
[f]	02-22(25)-1858	77
Spangler, Adam [f]	07-18-1871	297,298
" , Jno. R.(John Read)	07-18-1871	297
" , Mary [m]	07-18-1871	297,298
Sprouse,Jeff(Jefferson)[f]	09-10(15)-1863	162
" (Spouce),Jefferson[f]	09-06-1855	56
" , Lewis	09-10(15)-1863	162
" (Spouce), Mary	09-06-1855	56
" (Spouce), Susan[m]	09-06-1855	56
Sprowl's Tavern,Wm.B.[PL]	09(08)-02-1855	49
Stack (Fitzgerald), C.		
(Catherine) [m]	02-16-1858	76
" , J.J.(John J.)[f]	12-12-1872	329
" , Kate G.	12-12-1872	329
" , M.A.(Mary A.)[m]	12-12-1872	329
Staley, D. Reese [w]	01-09-1872	307
Stark, Nancy [m]	03-20-1871	292
" , William	03-20-1871	292
" , Wm. [f]	03-20-1871	292
Steele, Agness M.	10-29-1856	61

[Name and Date Index: Part (2) - (Continued)]

Name	Date	Page
Steele, Dewitt C.	03-24-1858	78
" , Isaac [f]	10-29-1856	61
[f]	03-24-1858	78
" , Julia [m]	10-29-1856	61
[m]	03-24-1858	78
Steers,Deborah(Debora)	10-17-1871	301
" , E.(Elizabeth)[m]	05-18-1865	154
[m]	10-17-1871	301
" , Eliz.(Elizabeth)[m]	08-09-1866	187
" , Erwin (Evans)[f]	05-18-1865	154
" , Evan [f]	10-17-1871	301
" , Evans,[Esq.]		
(E.) [f]	08-09-1866	187,188
" , M.(Margarette)	05-18-1865	154
" , Samantha	08-09-1866	187, 188
" , William [w]	08-09-1866	188
Steveson(Stevenson),		
James H.(James)	06-10-1857	67, 68
Stewart(Stuart),Emma	07-03-1856	55
" (Stuart),Fielding[f]	07-03-1856	55
" (Stuart),Fielding		
[f]	09-02-1856	58
" (Stuart),Jennette	09-02-1856	57
(Jenett)		
" (Stuart),Leah [m]	07-03-1856	55
[m]	09-02-1856	58
Stiles (Steiles),Geo.W.		
(George W.) [f]	10-23-1856	62
" , Lucinda(Loncinda)	10-23-1856	62
" , Mary (Mary M.)[m]	10-23-1856	62
Stone, B.(Betsey) [m]	11-25(27)-1865	169
" (Slone), Caleb	05-03-1860	113
" , E.A.(Elizabeth A.)	01-03(04)-1866	171,172
" , J.(John) [f]	04-07-1867	204
" , J. (Jane) [m]	01-03(04)-1866	171
" , J. (John) [f]	11-25(27)-1865	169
" , Jacob M.(Jacob		
Mathew)	02-09-1871	289
" , Jane [m]	04-22-1860	114
[m]	02-09-1871	289
" , Jno.H.(John H.)	04-07-1867	204

Name	Date	Page
Stone, John [f]	09-18-1862	140
" (Slone), John [f]	05-03-1860	113
" , John H. [w]	09(08)-28-1857	69
" , Jos.P.(Joseph P.) [f]	01-18(28)(27)-1869	243
" , Jos.P.(Joseph P.)	09-18-1862	140
" , M. (Mary) [m]	04-07-1867	204
" , Mary [m]	09-18-1862	140
" , Mary F.	04-22-1860	114
" , O.S. (Olivia T.)	01-18(28)(27)-1869	243
" (Slone), Sally [m]	05-03-1860	113
" , W.(William)[f]	01-03(04)-1866	171
" , W.F.(William Francis)	11-25(27)-1865	169
" , William [f]	04-22-1860	114
" , Wm. M. [f]	02-09-1871	289
Strange, Jane	06-07-1866	197
" , Moses	09-05-1872	320
Stratton, J.D.(Joseph D.) [f]	05-09(10)-1865	153
" , J.E.(Julia Ellen) (J. Ellen)	05-09(10)-1865	153
" , M. A.(Mary A.)[m]	05-09(10)-1865	153
Strickler,Dan'l.(Daniel M.)[f]	02-28-1860	111
" , John J.(Jno.J.)	02-28-1860	111
" , Mary J.(Mary Jane)[m]	02-28-1860	111
Strong, Dianna	11-13-1862	139
" , Dianna(Dianah)[m]	11-13-1862	139
" , William [f]	11-13-1862	
Stuart(Stewart), Emma	07-03-1856	55
" (Stewart),Fielding [f]	07-03-1856	55
[f]	09-02-1856	58
" (Stewart),Jennette (Jenett)	09-02-1856	57
" (Stewart),Leah [m]	07-03-1856	55
[m]	09-02-1856	58
Stull, A. (Ann) [m]	04-12(16)-1867	204
" , Allen M. [w]	10-10(11)-1866	189
" , A.M.(Allen M.)	07-03(08)-1868	226

Name	Date	Page

Name	Date	Page
Sullivan, Jane	02-12-1862	136
" , John [f]	09-15-1861	133
[f]	05-24-1864	143
" , Lelia (Julia)[m]	05-24-1864	143
" , Mary [m]	02-12-1862	136
" , Mary	04-25-1858	80
" , Mich'l.(Micheal)[f]	04-25-1858	80
" , Patrick	04-25-1858	80
	05-24-1864	143
" , Timothy	09-15-1861	133
Summers, Ann [m]	05-26(25)-1861	132
" , Castlereigh	05-26(25)-1861	132, 133
" , Sam'l. (Samuel)[f]05-26(25)-1861		132
Surber, Adam [f]	12-11-1860	118
" , Andr. (Adrew)[f]	12-17-1857	74
" , Andr.J.(Andrew Jackson)	12-17-1857	74
" , [D(avid)] (David) [f]	04-27-1870	275
" , David [JP]	06-14-1855	46
" , Eliza J.(Eliza Jane)	11-16-1854	43
" , [Geo.(H.)](George) (George H.)	04-27-1870	275
" , G. W. (George W.)	07-19(20)-1869	252
" , Jane [m]	12-11-1860	118
" , (Jane) [m]	04-27-1870	275
" , L. (Levi) [f]	07-19(20)-1869	252
" , Larissa(?Lurana)[m]	12-17-1857	74
" , Levi [f]	11-16-1854	43
[f]	02-25-1858	79, 80
" , Mary F.(Mary Frances)	02-25-1858	79
" , Mathew P.(Mathew T.) [M. (?P, ?T.]	12-11-1860	118
" , S. (Sallie) [m]	07-19(20)-1869	252
" , Sally [m]	11-16-1854	43
" (Hanger), Sally [m]	02-25-1858	79
" , William [w]	07-19(20)-1869	252
Surber's, Levi [PL]	03-02-1870	272

Name	Date	Page
Swann, Ambrose	04-08-1872	315
" , Osborn [f]	04-08-1872	315
" , Rose (Rosetta)[m]	04-08-1872	315
Switzer, B.(Benoni)[f]	11-06-1872	326
" , Cary A. [f]	12-06-1866 [MR]	191
" , E. (Elsie) [m]	11-06-1872	326
" , Jane [m]	12-06-1866 [MR]	191
" , J. N. (James N.)	11-06-1872	326
" , Wm. T.(William Thomas)	12-06-1866 [MR]	191
Taliaforo(Carter), Harriet [m]	03-03-1870	272
Talliferro(Talliaferro), William H.(Willis H.)	04-30-1868	222
Taverin(Toverin), Bridgett [m]	10-30-1859	107
" (Toverin), Thomas	10-30-1859	107
" (Toverin), Wm. [f]	10-30-1859	107
Taylor, B.(Benjamin)[f]	10-07-1870	280
" , Jno. L.(John L.)	10-07-1870	280
" , M.P. (Mary P.)[m]	10-07-1870	280
Terrill, James	11-15-1860	118
" , Jane [m]	02-16-1860	110
" , Julia(Julia An)	11-15-1860	118
" , Margarette A. (Margarett An)	11-15-1860	118
" , Wm.(William) [f]	02-16-1860	110
" (Terril), Wm.H. (William H.)	02-16-1860	110
Terry, Eliz.(Elizabeth)[m]	09-23-1859	106
" (Tery), Eliza [m]	06-19-1856	55
" , Elizabeth [m]	08-02-1859	102
" , Harriet	09-23-1859	106
" , Jacob O.	07-24(25)-1860	115,116
" , J.O.(Jacob O.)[w]	09-01-1868	229
" , Jos.(Joseph)[f]	12-10(12)-1866	191
" (Tery),Joseph	06-19-1856	55
" , Joseph [f]	07-24(25)-1860	115
[f]	08-02-1859	102

Name	Date	Page
Terry, Mahala [m]	07-24(25)-1860	115
" , Mahaly [m]	12-10(12)-1866	191
" (Aritt), Phoebe	12-10(12)-1866	191
" , Sarah M.	08-02-1859	102
" , S. Sophia W. [w]	12-19-1872	330
" , William [f]	09-23-1859	106
" (Tery), Wm. (William) [f]	06-19-1856	55
Thomas, Charles (Charles William)	02-10-1857	65
" , Elizabeth [m]	12-23(29)-1858	90
" , John R.	12-23(29)-1858	90
" , Jos. A. (Joseph Arthur)(Joseph A.)	08-21-1856	58
" , Mary [m]	02-10-1857	65
" , Peter [f]	12-23(29)-1858	90
" , Thusar A.(Thursa Ann) [m]	08-21-1856	58
" , Va. (Virginia)	05-04(07)-1868	223
" , Valentine [f]	08-21-1856	58
" , W.B.(Wright B.)[f]	02-10-1857	65
Thompson, Abner [f]	10-04-1855	48
" [f]	11-20-1856	62
" [f]	02-25-1858	79
" , Charles B.	01-07-1869	242, 243
" , Elizabeth P.	11-20-1856	62
" , J. C.(John C.)[f]	01-07-1869	242, 243
" , J.W.(John W.)	11-18-1869	261
" , Lucy	10-04-1855	48
" , M. (Maria) [m]	11-18-1869	261
" (Tompson), Oliver (Olliver)	02-25-1858	79
" , Sarah [m]	10-04-1855	48
" [m]	11-20-1856	62
" [m]	02-25-1858	79
" , Sarah E. [m]	01-07-1869	242
" , W.H.(Wm.H.) [f]	11-18-1869	261
Tingler, D.(Didama) (Vidama) [m]	12-19(23)-1868	238
" , E.J.(Eliza Jane)	06-15(17)-1867	207
" , E.M.(Eliza M.)	12-19(23)-1868	238

Name	Date	Page
Tingler, George W.		
(Geo. W.) [sf]	05-24(26)-1868	224
" , G.W.(George		
(Washington)		
(George W.)	01-08(09)-1866	173, 173
" , J. (John) [f]	12-19(23)-1868	238
" , J. (Jacob) [f]	01-08(09)-1866	172
[f]	06-15(17)-1867	207
" , Jacob [f]	03-18-1858	80
" , Jacob	09-14(23)-1867	213
" , L.(Lucinda) [m]	01-08(09)-1866	172
[m]	06-15(17)-1867	207
" , M.(Michael) [f]	09-14(23)-1867	213
" (Bennet)(Bennett),		
Peggy [m]	03-18-1858	80
" , R. (?Ruthy) [m]	09-14(23)-1867	213
Tinsley, Bennet [f]	05-13-1858	80
" , E. P. (E. O.)	05-13-1858	80
" , Franklin P. [w]	09-05(06)-1865	159
[w]	03-12(13)-1867	201
" , Permelia [m]	05-13-1858	80
" (Tisley), Wm. H.		
(William H.)	10-27-1870	280
Tisley (?Tinsley), M.A.		
(Mary A.) [m]	10-27-1870	280
" (?Tinsley), R. M.		
(Roderick M.)[f]	10-27-1870	280
Tompson (Thompson),		
Olliver (Oliver)	02-25-1858	79
Tucker, Alex.(Alexander)	01-07(10)-1869	242
" , Alfred (A̶r̶t̶h̶u̶r̶		
Alfred)	03-15-1872	312
" , B.(Bevaline)[m]	12-30(31)-1868	241
" , B.S.(Beverally		
S.) [f]	12-30(31)-1868	241
" , Danberry [w]	05-20-1869 [MR]	248
" , E.J.(Eliza Jane)	05-20-1869 [MR]	248
" , Eliz.(Elizabeth)[m]	03-15-1872	312
" , J. (John) [f]	01-07(10)-1869	242
[f]	05-20-1869 [MR]	248
" , Jas. A. [f]	03-15-1872	312

Name	Date	Page
Vance, James H. [w]	06-21(24)-1869	249
" , J.D. [w]	07-11-1861	134
" , J.D. (John D.)	06-01-1865 [MR]	155
" , Lucinda	06-01-1865 [MR]	155
" , M.S.(Martha S.)	06-21(24)-1869	249
" , V.(Virginia) [m]	06-01-1865 [MR]	155
[m]	07-11-1861	133
[m]	06-21(24)-1869	249
[m]	06-29-1871	297
" , Wm.(William) (W.)[f]	07-11-1861	133
[f]	06-01-1865 [MR]	155
[f]	06-21(24)-1869	249
[f]	06-29-1871	297
" , William	07-11-1861	133
Vaughan, Eliza(Elisa)[m]	07-22-1857	69
" , Henry C.	07-22-1857	69
" , Henry C. [CC]...................		248,249, 250, 251, 252,253,254,255, 256,257,258,259,260,261,262, 263,264,265,266,267,268,269,270,271,272,273, 274
" , Wm. (William)[f]	07-22-1857	69
Vauter (Vawter),C.S. (Clara S.) [m]	09-24(25)-1866	176
" (Vawter), J.H. (John H.) [f]	09-24(25)-1866	176
" (Vawter),Jno. Wm. (John William)	09-24(25)-1866	176
Walker, Anderson [f]	04-16(18)-1872	316
" , Areanna S.	07-23(24)-1866	187
" , Ginnie	04-16(18)-1872	315
" , H.(Henry) [f]	09-07-1865 [MR]	156
[f]	01-13-1870	269
[f]	06-30-1869 [MR]	252
[f]	01-11-1871	286
" , Henry [f]	07-23(24)-1866	187
" , Henry [w]	12-17-1857	74
" , Julia H. (Julia Hamilton)	01-11-1871	286
" , M.(Maria) [m]	09-07-1865 [MR]	156

Name	Date	Page
Walker, M.(Maria)[m]	01-13-1870	269
[m]	10-01(11)-1864	142
[m]	01-11-1871	286
" , Maria [m]	07-23(24)-1866	187
" (Rogers), M.E.		
(Margaret E.)	10-01(11)-1864	142
" , M.M. (Mollie M.)	01-13-1870	269
" , M. R. (Maria R.)[m]	06-30-1869[MR]	252
" , (? S.)(Henry)[f]	10-01(11)-1864	142
" , S. T.(Sallie T.)	06-30-1869 [MR]	251,252
" , T.(Tabitha) [m]	04-16(18)-1872	316
" , W.H.(Wade Hampton)	09-07-1865[MR]	156
Walkup (?Walker)(Womack),		
M. (Marietta)[m]	10-27-1869	259
" (?Walker), W. E.		
(William E.)[Jr.][f]	10-27-1869	259
Wall(Ervine)(Irvin),		
Ann [m]	10-21-1859	106
" , Hannah [m]	02-12-1862	136
Wall, John	02-12-1862	136
" , John [f]	02-12-1862	136
Walton, Jas. M.		
(James M.)[f]	12-23(29)-1858	90
" , Maria [m]	12-23(29)-1858	90
" , Susan E.(Susan		
Elizabeth)	12-23(29)-1858	90
" , William [b/w]	12-23(29)-1858	90
" , William A.	02-20-1860	110
Waren (Warren), Jas.		
(James) [f]	02-16(21)-1867	193
" , Martha A.(Marta		
Ann)(Martha Ann)	02-16(21)-1867	193
" (Weaver), Sarah J.	03-14-1861	128
Warren, Isabela W.		
(Isabell W.)	10-17-1858	87
" (Weaver), James [f]	03-14-1861	128
" , James (Jas.) [f]	10-17-1858	87
Weaver (Warren), James[f]	03-14-1861	128
" (Waren), Sarah J.	03-14-1861	128
Wells, Henry [f]	11-25-1871	304
" , James	11-25-1871	304

Name	Date	Page
Wells, Mary [m]	11-25-1871	304
Whistman, H.(Hannah)[m]	01-23(25)-1866	174
" , H.H. (Henry H.)[f]	01-23(25)-1866	174
" , M. (Mary)	01-23(25)-1866	174
White, Augustus E.		
(Augustus Ervin)		
(A. E.)	05-25-1871	295
" , E. A.(Eliza A.)[m]	05-25-1871	295
" , George [w]	06-14-1855	46
" (O'Donnel),Mary [m]	12-17-1859	107
" , J.D. (John D.)[f]	05-25-1871	295
" , M. B.(Moorman B.)[f]	05-25-1871	295
" , Mollie M.	05-25-1871	295
" , S. E.(Sarah E.)[m]	05-25-1871	295
Whitten, J. T.[w]	01-09-1872	307
" , L. B. [w]	01-09-1872	307
Wilcher, Amanda [m]	10-20-1870	285
" , Jane [m]	01-09-1855	49
" , John [f]	10-20-1870	285
" , Richard [f]	01-09-1855	49
" , Richard H.	01-09-1855	49
" , Wm. D.(William D.)	10-20-1870	285
Wiley, Benton	04-11-1860	111,112
" , Lucy [m]	04-11-1860	111
" , Robert [f]	04-11-1860	111
Wilkerson, Geo. W.[w]	10-01(02)(03)-1867	216
Wilkinson, A. (Julia)[m]	12-27-1870	284
" , G. (George) [f]	12-27-1870	284
" , Geo. (George)	12-27-1870	283
Wilkson(Wilkerson), E.		
(Elijah) [f]	10-07(11)-1864	142
" (Wilkerson), G.W.		
(George W.)	10-07(11)-1864	142
" (Wilkerson), M.		
(Mary) [m]	10-07(11)-1864	142
Willard, Sam'l. (Samuel)	12-31-1855	59
Williams, Armstead [f]	06-21-1866 [MR]	184
" , E.I.(Erasmus T.)		
(Erasimus T.)		
(E. T.) [f]	1-17(18)-1868	235
" , Eliza [m]	06-21-1866 [MR]	184

Name	Date	Page
Winfree, W. H. [f]	05-24-1871	294
Wise, David J.(David		
Joshua)	06-15-1871	296
" , Ellen [m]	06-15-1871	296
" , Jno. (John)[f]	06-15-1871	296
Wolf, A.(Abraham)[f]	05-20-1869 [MR]	248
[f]	01-28(31)-1870	270
" , Abraham [f]	01-21-1861 [CL]	134
" , Abraham	04-09-1867	203
" , Abram [f]	03-15-1872	312
" , Car. (Caroline)	01-28(31)-1870	270
" , C.E.(Charlotte E.)	05-04(05)-1868	223
" (Wolfe),D.J.(Daniel		
J.)	09-01-1868	228,229
" , E. (Elizabeth)[m]	06-01-1865 [MR]	163
" (Armontrout)(Armintrout),		
E. (Elizabeth)		
(Elizabeth An)	10-20-1869	259
" , Elizabeth	07-02-1856	55
" (Manspile), Emelina		
S.[Listed Twice]	03-11(02)-1871	317
" (Manspile), Emeline		
S. (Emeline Susan)		
[Listed Twice]	03-02-1871	293
" , E. R. (Eliza Reed)	06-09(14)-1866	186
" , E. S.(Emeline Susan)	01-10-1867	196
" (Wolfe), G. W.		
(George W.)	11-15-1860	119
" (Woolf), H. (Hugh)[f]	09-28-1865	160
" , H. (Harriet)[m]	01-28(31)-1870	270
" , Harriet [m]	01-21-1861 [CL]	134
" , H.C.(Hugh C.)	05-20-1869 [MR]	248
" , Hettie [m]	03-15-1872	312
" , Hugh [w]	09-28-1865	160
" , I. (Isaac) [f]	01-10-1867	196, 197
[f]	04-09-1867	203
[f]	11-09-1869 [MR]	256
[f]	10-20-1869	259
" , Isaac [f]	06-09(14)-1866	186
[Listed Twice]	[f]03-02-1871	293

Name	Date	Page
Wolf, Isaac [f]		
[Listed Twice]	03-11(02)-1871	317
" , Isaac [f]	07-02-1856	55
" , J.(Jonathan)	06-01-1865 [MR]	163
" , J. (John)(Jno.)[f]	05-04(05)-1868	223
" , J.A.(Jacob A.)[f]	12-28-1869 [MR]	266
" , Jacob H. [w]	05-18-1858	82
" (Wolfe), John [f]	02-10-1857	65
" (Wolfe), J.R.		
(Jacob R.) [f]	09-05-1867	212
[f]	09-01-1868	228,229
" , King A.	01-21-1861[CL]	134
" (Woolf), L. (Lidia)[m]	09-28-1865	160
" , L.G.(Liberty Greene)	09-05-1867	212
" , M. (Martin) [f]	06-01-1865 [MR]	163
" , M. (Martha) [m]	04-09-1867	203
" , M.(Margaret) [m]	05-20-1869 [MR]	248
" , M. (Martha) [m]	11-09-1869[MR]	256
" , M. A. E. (Maria		
A. E.) [m]	09-05-1867	212
[m]	09-01-1868	228
[Listed Twice]		
" , Margaret [m]	03-02-1871	293
" , Martha [m]	07-02-1856	55
[m]	06-09(14)-1866	186
" (Wolfe), M. E. M.		
(Mary E. M.)	11-15-1860	119
" , P. (Peggei) [m]	01-10-1867	196
" (Wolfe), Paulin		
(Paulina) [m]	11-15-1860	119
" , Phoebe H.	03-15-1872	312
" , R. (Rebecca)	12-28-1869 [MR]	266
" (Woolf), S.(?Seevi)		
(?Seeri)(?Suvi)	09-28-1865	160
" , S. (Sarah) [m]	05-04(05)-1868	223
[m]	12-28-1869 [MR]	266
" (Wolfe)(Rayhill),		
Sarah [m]	02-10-1857	65
" (Wolfe), Sarah M.		
(Margaret)	02-10-1857	65

Name	Date	Page
Wolfe, Abra.(Abraham)	11-09-1869 [MR]	256
" , Achillis	11-07-1872	326
" , J. A. (Jacob A.)[f]	11-07-1872	326
" (Wolf), J. R.(Jacob R.),[Esq.][f]	11-07-1872	326,327
" , M. (Maria) [m]	11-07-1872	326
" , S.A.(Sarah S.)[m]	11-07-1872	326
" , S. A. J. [w]	09-01-1868	229
" , S. A. J.(Sarah A.J.)	11-07-1872	326
(?Wolf's) (?Roof's), George W. [PL]	01-23(25)-1866	175
Wolf's, George W.[PL]	11-02(07)(06)-1867	218
" , Sarah [PL]	02-10-1857	66
" , Washington [PL]	11-02(07)(06)-1867	218
Womack (Worrack)(Worrick), Burl [f]	08-13(12)-1869	253
" ; C. A. [m]	02-15(18)-1869	245
" (Worrick)(Worrack), Harriet	08-13(12)-1869	253
" , Jos. P. [f]	02-15(18)-1869	245
" (?Walkup)(?Walker), M. (Marietta)	10-27-1869	259
" (Worrack)(Worrick), Mary [m]	08-13(12)-1869	253
" , Wm. W. (William W.)	10-27-1869	259
" , Z. (Zacariah)	02-15(18)-1869	245
" , [?Mr.] (?Z.)(?L.) [w]	03-03(04)-1869	246
Wood, Augustus [f]	09-12-1861	130
" , David [f]	06-14-1860	115
" , Harriet S. (Harriett S.)	09-12-1861	130, 131
" , Jane [m]	06-14-1860	115
" , Mary [m]	09-12-1861	130
" (Woods), [Mrs.] Mary F.	06-14-1860	115
" , Sarah I. C.[w]	09-12-1861	131
Woods, M.(Moses) [f]	05-05(09)=1865	163
" , M.J.(Mary Jane)	05-05(09)-1865	163
Woolwine, Henry [f]	02-23(25)-1867	195

Name	Date	Page
Woolwine (Costic),		
Nancy	02-23(25)-1867	195
Worsham, Cath. M.		
(Cathrine Matilda)		
(Catharine)	12-(24)26-1854	42
" , Daniel [f]	12-(24)26-1854	42
" , Dan'l. (Daniel)[f]	04-14(18)-1866	183
" , E.(Emmaline)[m]	12-(24)26-1854	42
" , Elizabeth J.		
(Eliza J.)	04-14(18)-1866	183
" , Emeline (Emaline)[m]	04-14(18)-1866	183
Wright, Catharine [m]	12-10(12)-1866	191
[m]	03-17-1857	78
" , Charles	09-30-1866	188
" , E.(Elizabeth) [m]	11-27-1872	327
[m]	09-26-1865	147
" , Edwd. [f]	03-03-1867 [MR]	198
" , Eliz.(Elizabeth)[m]	09(08)-30-1865	145
" , Francis B.[Francis		
(? R.)]	03-17-1857	78
" , Geo.W.(G.L.)		
(George Lee)	09(08)-30-1865	145
" , Geo. W.(George W.)		
[f]	09(08)-30-1865	145
" , G.W.(George W.)[f]	11-27-1872	327,328
" , G.W.(Gitanio W.)	09-26-1865	147,148
" , G.W.(Geo. W.)		
(George W.) [f]	09-26-1865	147,148
" , Jno. (John) [f]	03-17-1857	78
" , John [f]	12-10(12)-1866	191
" , John	01-28-1860	120
" , John [f]	01-28-1860	120
" , Julia [m]	01-28-1860	120
" , Kate	12-26-1872	331
" , Lizzie (Mary		
Elizabeth)(E.Martha		
E.)	11-27-1872	327,328
" , M. G. [w]	10-14-1869	256
" , Moses G.(Moses		
George)	12-10(12)-1866	191

Name	Date	Page
Wright, P.(Polly) [m]	12-26-1872	331
" ,Polly [m]	09-30-1866	188
" , Rose [m]	03-03-1867 [MR]	198
" , Violet(Vilett)	06-29-1871	296,297
" , W. (Washington)[f]	12-26-1872	331
" , Washington [f]	09-30-1866	188
" , Willis	03-03-1867 [MR]	198
Wright's, Moses [PL]	04-18-1861	121
Wyatt, J. W.		
(Jno. W.) [w]	07-22-1857	69
Young, Henry J.(Henry		
Jackson)	02-23(28)-1867	194
" , Mary (Margarett)[m]	02-23(28)-1867	194
" , Robert [f]	02-23(28)-1867	194
Zeigler, A.(Abraham)[f]	03-12-1861 [CL]	134
[f]	12-26(27)-1865	170,171
[f]	12-09-1863	180
[f]	02-27(28)-1867	197
[f]	10-12(14)-1868	230
" , E.E.(Emily E.)		
(Emly Elisabeth)	02-27(28)-1867	197
" , J.(Joseph)(Jos.)	03-12-1861	134
	12-09-1863	180
[w]	09-20(22)-1869	253
" , M.(Matilda)[m]	12-26(27)-1865	170,171
[m]	12-09-1863	180
[m]	02-27(28)-1867	197
[m]	10-12(14)-1868	230
" , M.A.(Maggie Ann)	12-26(27)-1865	170
" , Mary (Marth) [m]	03-12-1861 [CL]	134
" , S. E. (Sarah E.)	10-12(14)-1868	230

Total Number of Names This Part: 4,595

REFERENCES

Bostic Family Of Monroe County, West Virginia:
  With Information on Reynolds, Rose, Wolf,
  Jarvis and Other Related Families
  By David S. Turk [Charles Pickney Jones
  Memorial Library, Riverside St.,Covington,VA.
  [Note: Used page III for counties Monroe Co.
  was formed from and date W.VA. became state.]

The Official Military Atlas Of The Civil War
  by Major George B. Davis, U.S.Army, Leslie
  J. Perry, Civilian Expert, Joseph W. Kirkley,
  Civilian Expert, Compiled by Capt. Calvin
  D. Cowles, 23d U.S.Infantry. The Fairfax
  Press, New York, Copyright MCMLXXVIII by
  Arno Press, Inc. and Crown Publishers, Inc.
  All rights reserved. 1983. ISBN:0-517-415666
  [Dabney S. Lancaster Community College
  Library, Dabney Drive Rt. 60W, Clifton
  Forge, VA 24422]
  Series 1 Vol. XLVII   Plate LXXXIV No. 9
  No. 37 Map showing positions of the camps
  and pickets of the army of the Valley Dis-
  trict. Jan. 31st 1865 by Jed.Hotckiss, Top.
  Eng. Val. Dist.
  Plate XCIV No. 1 General Map Apr. 25, 1864
  A map of a Line of Defenses in the Alleg-
  hanies Compiled from Whitcomb's Railroad Map
  and Original Surveys by Lieut. Koerner's
  Topographical Party under direction of Capt.
  C.R. Howard, C.S.E.; H.J. Miller, Asst. and
  Draftsm.
  Plate CXXXV-C No. 1
  Map of a Part of VA. exhibiting the Routes
  of Genl. W.W.Averell in August, November, &
  December 1863. Drawn under the Direction of
  Lieut.J.R. Meigs Corps of Engrs. Chief Engr.
  Dept. W.VA. (Series 1, Vol. XXIX)
  Plate CXXXVII - General Topographical Map,
  Sheet II, Sections C1,2; D1,2,E1,2,F1 & 2
  Plate CXLI General Topographical Map Sheet
  VI Sections D13,14; # 13,14
  [Note: Used page X to try to determine loca-
  tion of Jordan's Forge and Jackson River
  Depot.]

[References - Continued]

"Virginia's Western Highlands: Alleghany Highlands
    Bath and Highland Counties" [Tourism Bro-
    chure] Published in July 1989, 1992 by Alleg-
    hany Highlands Chamber of Commerce with off-
    ices located at 403 E. Ridgeway St., Clifton
    Forge, VA 24422, (703) 862-4969, FAX: (703)
    862-4969; and 241 W. Main St., Covington, VA
    24426, (703) 962-2178, FAX: (703) 962-2179.
    [Note: Used page III Sweet Chalybeate Springs
    was antebellum resort,which is common know-
    ledge in this area of the state.]

1988 - 1989 Official W. VA. Highway Map issued by
    W. VA. Dept. of Highways Planning Division

1990 Official VA Dept. of Transportation Highway
    Map, Copyright 1990

January 1, 1975 Commonwealth of VA General High-
    way Map of Alleghany County prepared by VA
    Dept. of Highways & Transportation, 1221
    East Broad St., Richmond, VA 23219

1983 Maps of The Alleghany Highlands--Alleghany
    County, Clifton Forge, & Covington, Virginia
    Prepared and printed for Greater Alleghany
    Highlands Chamber of Commerce, Executive
    Office, 241 W. Main Street, Covington, VA
    24426 and Clifton Forge Office, 403 E. Ridge-
    way St., Clifton Forge, VA 24422, Copyright
    1983 Alleghany Publishers, Inc., Covington,
    VA

[Note: The (4) maps above used pages 206,207,213,
    258, 116,259,293,303,(and page XVI for veri-
    fication of my own knowledge of 45 years liv-
    ing in this area) for spelling and location
    of towns and counties in the text.]

Peopling of Virginia by R. Bennett Bean. [Charles
    P. Jones Memorial Library, Riverside St.,
    Covington, VA 24426]
    [Note: Used page III for nationality of area

[References - Continued]

people who settled here.]

Historical Sketches by Gay Arritt. Edited by
     Horton P. Beirne. Published by The Alleg-
     hany Historical Society, Covington, VA. 1982
     Copyright. All rights reserved. Pages 100-
     103. [Dabney S. Lancaster Community College
     Library, Dabney Drive Rt. 60W, Clifton Forge,
     VA 24422]
  ** [Note: Most interesting reading for geneal-
     ogists.]
     [Note: Used page IX, X, location of Cogbill
     Hotel and McCurdy's Hotel (location, dates
     of building, sold, and burning).]

Alleghany County Clerk of Court Office, Alleghany
     County Courthouse, Main St., Covington, VA
     24426   Telephone: (703) 965-1730
     [Note: Used records from original documents
     for direct quotes in body of text and all
     marriage records.]

Alleghany Highlands Genealogical Society, River-
     mont School, Rockbridge St., Covington, VA
     24426
     [Note: Contributed help with spelling of
     people's names in part of Part I.]
     [Note: They have a room for genealogical
     research with microfilm, books, and many
     other collections made by their members and
     are expanding their collections. They will
     also help with research for people who con-
     tact them.]

Official Highway Map of North Carolina: 1974-75.
     Edited For the Department of Transportation
     by H. Boyce Midgette, Raleigh, N. C.
     [Note: Used pages 228, 322 for spelling and
     location of towns and counties.]

Heraldic Scroll & Map of Family Names & Origins
     of Ireland, Copyright. Mullins of Dublin, 36
     Upper O'Connell St., Dublin, Ireland.

[References - Continued]

[Note: Used page 98, 194, 241 for spelling.]

Source of Map on Page XVI: This map was drawn by
    the compiler of this book.   It is not to
    scale.   The compiler has lived in Alleghany
    County for 45 years and has driven over
    every road listed on the map and drew the
    map from her personal knowledge of the areas.
    The map was drawn only to clarify the written
    directions in the Geographic Locations
    section of this book.

Note: There are no direct verbatim quotes from
    any reference listed here except those
    records pertaining to Alleghany County mar-
    riage records that were located in the
    Clerk's Office in the Alleghany County Court-
    house and are open to the public.

www.ingramcontent.com/pod-product-compliance
Lightning Source LLC
Chambersburg PA
CBHW071352290326
41932CB00045B/1430